SEVENTH EDITION

FAMILY THERAPY
An Overview

HERBERT GOLDENBERG
California State University, Los Angeles

IRENE GOLDENBERG
University of California, Los Angeles

THOMSON
BROOKS/COLE

AUSTRALIA • BRAZIL • CANADA • MEXICO • SINGAPORE • SPAIN • UNITED KINGDOM • UNITED STATES

THOMSON
★ ™
BROOKS/COLE

Family Therapy: An Overview, **Seventh Edition**

Herbert Goldenberg, Irene Goldenberg

Senior Acquisitions Editor: *Marquita Flemming*
Assistant Editor: *Samantha Shook*
Editorial Assistant: *Meaghan Banks*
Technology Project Manager: *Julie Aguilar*
Marketing Manager: *Meghan McCullough*
Marketing Communications Manager: *Shemika Britt*
Project Manager, Editorial Production: *Rita Jaramillo*
Creative Director: *Rob Hugel*
Art Director: *Vernon Boes*

Print Buyer: *Linda Hsu*
Permissions Editor: *Roberta Broyer*
Production Service: *Aaron Downey, Matrix Productions Inc.*
Text and Cover Designer: *Lisa Henry*
Copy Editor: *Jane Tilden*
Cover image: © *Diana Ong/SuperStock*
Cover and Text Printer: *West Group*
Compositor: *International Typesetting and Composition*

Printed in the United States of America
2 3 4 5 6 7 11 10 09 08

Thomson Higher Education
10 Davis Drive
Belmont, CA 94002-3098
USA

For more information about our products, contact us at:

Thomson Learning Academic Resource Center
1-800-423-0563

For permission to use material from this text or product, submit a request online at
http://www.thomsonrights.com.
Any additional questions about permissions can be submitted by e-mail to
thomsonrights@thomson.com.

Library of Congress Control Number: 2006935749

ISBN-13: 978-0-495-09759-4
ISBN-10: 0-495-09759-4

To our generative family
Children, grandchildren, students, and
readers of this book

C O N T E N T S

3   GENDER, CULTURE, AND ETHNICITY FACTORS IN FAMILY FUNCTIONING   54

4   INTERLOCKING SYSTEMS: THE INDIVIDUAL, THE FAMILY, AND THE COMMUNITY   77

PART II The Development and Practice of Family Therapy

PART IV New Directions in Family Therapy

The publication of this text represents an achievement of extraordinary scope in which Irene and Herbert Goldenberg bring together more than five decades of developments in the ideas and practices of family therapy. Extraordinary scope, because in doing this these authors have not been content to incorporate just the principal developments in this field. In the space of this one text, Irene and Herbert Goldenberg also trace many of the tributaries that have branched out of those developments in ideas and practice that have been accorded mainstream status in the field of family therapy.

Before reading this text, I had made some assumptions about it. To cover the history of developments in a field like family therapy, one in which there has been little orthodoxy and great diversity, would surely require considerable economy of writing. *Overview*, a word from the book's title, seemed to my mind to imply a very limited perspective. I was expecting the sort of academic writing that would provide a reasoned gloss of developments through the history of family therapy. I had forecast the sort of dry account of these developments that is intended to provide the reader with a passing knowledge of this broad subject matter. I had assumed that the authors of such a text would have little option but to rein in their ambitions for the reader's engagement with this material and to keep modest their hopes for the reader's experience of its reading—perhaps simply to hope to kindle the reader's interest in specific ideas that might be pursued through consulting more dedicated sources.

Not so! Upon reading this book I discovered that Herbert and Irene Goldenberg had not been content to offer their readers a summary account of developments that simply conveys a passing knowledge of this material. Despite the limitations associated with an economy in writing imposed by the circumstances, these authors have produced a highly engaging text that introduces the reader to the profundity of the principal ideas and practices of family therapy, while at the same time rendering the complexities associated with these ideas and practices readily available to the comprehension of the reader. Rather than acquainting the reader with a passing knowledge, this text takes him or her to a vantage point that allows a vital, close-up view of the terrain.

How is this achieved? This text does not constitute the expected "armchair exposition." Instead, it is alive with the adventures initiated and the journeys traveled through the history of family therapy. The reader gains a strong sense of the authors' significant personal experiences of these adventures and journeys, of their intimate familiarity with many expeditions into new territories of ideas and practices. In the reading of this text, one is left with no doubt that Herbert and Irene Goldenberg have been at the scene, actively joining with others over many years in explorations of new forms of human inquiry. In this recounting, these authors succeed in evoking the original spirit of these developments in human inquiry and the inspiration that was an outcome of numerous efforts to think beyond what has been routinely thought about people's lives and their relationships. These authors also succeed in conveying to the reader the excitement of these adventures and journeys—the sense of actually undertaking these expedtions.

The authors also engage readers vitally through user-friendly writing devices that provide a scaffold for comprehension of the text. The text is organized with functional headings and subheadings, with topics divided into six parts: "Fundamentals of Family Psychology," "The Development and Practice of Family Therapy," "The Established Schools of Family Therapy," "New Directions in Family Therapy," "Clinical Research: The Synergy of Science and Practice," and "Family Theories and Family Therapies: An Overview." Each chapter is thoughtfully structured and replete with helpful and concise summaries and recommended readings. The judicious use of tables, illustrations, and quotes contributes to this easy-to-use composition. Particularly important is the even-handed and respectful way in which Irene and Herbert Goldenberg present the various developments in the history of family therapy and the available critiques of these developments. This fair-mindedness encourages the reader's fuller involvement with the text—it recruits the reader's contemplation and rouses his or her fascination.

I believe there is something for everybody to be found in this book. For those new to the field of family therapy, this book provides a gripping account of the history of developments in the family therapy field, of the continuities and discontinuities in these developments, and of many context- and era-specific influences that have contributed to the shape of these developments. For other readers, this book offers a ready reference to, and will instigate further explorations of, those developments that have most captured their imaginations and exercised their minds. For yet other readers, this text provides a source of renewed reflection on the history of their own family therapy practice and will encourage a richer appreciation of the traditions of thought that have shaped their work. And, of course, this text gives many readers an opportunity to become more fully acquainted with traditions in thought and practice that they might not otherwise be familiar with.

Apart from these comments about what is in store for you as you open the pages of this book, I will include here a few comments about the authors. Although there is much that can be said about their own contributions to the family therapy field over a considerable period of its development, my desire here is to say something about the personae of Irene and Herbert Goldenberg, for I would like you to get to know them just a little as I have known them.

Although I had been expecting this book to represent a relatively limited summary of the history of developments in the field of family therapy, I was nonetheless not surprised to find these expectations so contradicted in my reading of this text. I had met Herbert and Irene Goldenberg on various occasions over the years, principally in the context of workshops that I have given in the Los Angeles area. I first became aware of their presence in these workshops some years ago. I recall, toward the end of one of these events, being asked some particularly thought-provoking, searching, and persistent questions about some of the ideas and practices I had been discussing. In this workshop context, the questions—coming in particular from two people in the room—provided a foundation for conversations that contributed to significant clarification of certain similarities and distinctions in a range of ideas and practices.

At the end of the workshop, I approached these two figures for personal introductions. Through this and my subsequent contacts with Herbert and Irene Goldenberg, I have come to admire the breadth of their experience, the scope of their knowledge, and their capacity for thoughtfulness. All of these qualities are so evident in this book. But they have contributed much more than this to the family therapy field. I have also come to admire the part that their strong social consciousness and their generosity of spirit play in their personal and professional worlds. Herbert and Irene Goldenberg are always quick to recognize transgressions of the principles of fairness, equality and justice, and they are never tardy in naming these transgressions. They are also quick to offer support to those who have experienced unfairness, inequality, and injustice. And, in their efforts to challenge these wrongs, Herbert and Irene Goldenberg manage to stay true to their principles of understanding and to their appreciation of difference and diversity. In this way they make it possible for people to find new places in which to stand in the territories of their lives and work. When I am in the presence of Irene and Herbert Goldenberg, I know that I am in good company.

Michael White

Co-director of Dulwich Centre
Adelaide, South Australia

For us, each new edition of our text represents a transition point, an opportunity to try once again to tell family therapy's updated story in a clear and coherent fashion. Looking back on the previous edition, written five years ago, we needed to consider which developments that were emerging then have continued to gain prominence, and which, for a brief period, showed promise but faded over time. What new issues have taken center stage, and what is the likelihood of their continued eminence? How well will we be able to represent the contemporary ideas and principal players that together define today's evolving theories and practices of family therapy?

Family therapy, with its revolutionary emphasis on systems thinking and the search for identifiable and recurrent family patterns, first emerged in the mid-1950s, half a century ago. By the 1970s, having been inspired by the active demonstrations of trailblazers Virginia Satir, Salvador Minuchin, Jay Haley, and Carl Whitaker, the two of us, accustomed to working with individuals, had "caught the bug"—become convinced of the therapeutic power of understanding individual behavior in the context of the family system. The more we learned, the more we came to grasp the influence of larger systems—race, social class, gender, ethnicity, sexual orientation—on the functioning of the family and its separate members. Postmodern thinking introduced us to the further importance of language and belief systems in understanding how people construct their views of reality.

As we first shared our growing enthusiasm for this up-and-coming field with our students, we recognized that a comprehensive textbook offering an overview of the field—not merely a biased description of any one of the specific models then vying for the clinician's attention—might be needed, and if done even-handedly, could prove a useful guide to others interested in entering the field of family therapy. As we stated in our first edition, published in 1980, we set ourselves the challenge of offering readers a balanced presentation of the major theoretical underpinnings and clinical practices in the field. We promised not only to provide an overview of the evolving viewpoints, perspectives, values, intervention techniques, and goals of family therapy but also to attempt to keep pace with the field's clinical and research developments. That promise continues to be our goal in this latest edition.

We have been chronicling the field of family therapy for more than half its lifetime, trying to keep pace with its broadening conceptualizations, expanded populations served, new treatment and consultation settings, internal challenges (from women, minorities, researchers within the field), as well as external challenges (competition from other newly minted medical and psychological approaches). The field has come to value diversity, to realize that there are multiple ways of defining what constitutes a functional family, and that no one therapeutic technique fits all. During that period, family therapy has gone mainstream—no longer so revolutionary and anti-therapeutic an establishment, but now one of several approaches for helping people in distress. Its systems view, however, has influenced all forms of therapy, and remains vibrant. We love the idea of keeping alive, in this current edition, the excitement we have felt for family therapy for 30 years.

In order to do so, we have revised every chapter in this edition to include up-to-date references and contemporary thinking about its central issues. We have added numerous, detailed case studies throughout the text, and boxes or sidebars filled with themes that we think the reader will find informative and stimulating. When appropriate, we've added Clinical Notes, brief personal reflections based on our clinical experiences, of what is being discussed in the text. Certain topics have been expanded—types of family forms present today, family violence, school-family issues, gender and multicultural issues, home-based services, and an ecological view of the interlocking systems of the individual, the family, and the community. The established schools of family therapy are described, but emphasis is placed on their evolving developments, and cases are added to illustrate the application of a particular set of techniques for each theory. Newer models, such as the social constructionist views, have gained prominence in recent years and are elaborated more fully than in previous editions, and an effort has been made to emphasize the growing integrative nature of the current practice of family therapy. Criteria for developing core competencies in family therapy are spelled out in detail.

We have shifted the order of some chapters and, most important, have followed the advice of professors who wished their students to grasp the ethical issues involved in family therapy practice and research before studying the prevalent theories. Chapter 6 now deals with professional and ethical issues, and Appendix A offers the Code of Ethics of the American Association for Marriage and Family Therapy as representative of such codes maintained by other professional groups, such as the National Association of Social Workers or the American Psychological Association.

Research on family assessment and therapeutic outcomes has gained prominence in the field, and we have attempted to reflect that change, especially regarding evidence-based psychotherapy. We have carefully presented an up-to-date discussion of this controversial issue. Each chapter in the text is accompanied by a list of recommended readings, handpicked by us to best give readers a taste (hopefully whetting the appetite) of the best presentations of the topic. Several new photos have been added to recognize emerging leaders in the field. An earlier chapter on training has been moved to the Appendix, with charts describing what training and supervision programs currently are available and where to receive such instruction in various parts of the United States and Canada.

A book of this size requires help in the form of suggestions from numerous professors on how best to improve it. In this regard, we wish to thank our reviewers: Joan Atwood, Hofstra University; Ronald Bramlett, University of Central Arkansas; Robin Dock, Georgia State University; Valerie Dripchak, Southern Connecticut State University; Steven Harris, Texas Tech University; Matthew Leary, Immaculata College;

Savador Lopez-Arias, Grand Valley State University; Wendy Smith, University of Southern California; and William Kent Youngman, Wright State University.

Once again, Michael White has graciously consented to write the foreword, and we thank him for his generosity as well as his friendship. Marquita Flemming at Thomson has always believed in us, and her editorial help and organization have made the task easier.

Finally, after 40 years together, we continue to learn how to collaborate professionally and continue to develop as separate human beings.

Herbert Goldenberg
Irene Goldenberg

ADOPTING A FAMILY RELATIONSHIP FRAMEWORK

A family is far more than a collection of individuals sharing a specific physical and psychological space. While families occur in a diversity of forms and complexities in today's rapidly changing society, and represent a multiplicity of cultural heritages, each may be considered a natural, sustained social **system**[1] with properties all its own—one that has evolved a set of rules, is replete with assigned and ascribed roles for its members, has an organized power structure, has developed intricate overt and covert forms of communication, and has elaborated ways of negotiating and problem solving that permit various tasks to be performed effectively. The relationship between members of this microculture is deep and multilayered, and is based largely on a shared history, shared internalized perceptions and assumptions about the world, and a shared sense of purpose. Within such a system, individuals are tied to one another by powerful, durable, reciprocal, multigenerational emotional attachments and loyalties that may fluctuate in intensity and psychological distances between members over time, but nevertheless persist over the lifetime of the family.

Each family system is itself embedded in a community and society at large, is molded by its existence at a particular place and time in history, and is shaped further by a multitude of interlocking phenomena such as:

race

ethnicity

social class membership

family life cycle stage

number of generations in this country

sexual orientation

religious affiliation

the physical and mental health of its members

---

[1]Terms in **boldface** are defined in the Glossary at the back of the book.

level of educational attainment

financial security

family values and belief systems

All of these factors, and many others, as we shall see, influence the system's development, beliefs, standards for acceptable behavior, degree of flexibility in meeting both normal developmental challenges and unanticipated crises, and in general its adaptability and stability over time.

TODAY'S FAMILIES: A PLURALISTIC VIEW

While entrance into such an organized system traditionally has been considered to occur only through *birth, adoption,* or *marriage,* today's outlook must make room for other *committed* family households beyond legally married heterosexual couples and their children (Carter & McGoldrick, 1999). Clearly, any definition of contemporary family life must include the following major family forms, but at the same time must not lose sight of further divisions and complexities within each type of family structure, brought about by such unique situations as early or later marriages, interracial coupling, foster parenting, informal kinship adoptions, social class position, and so forth. In general, an inclusive twenty-first-century definition of family must go beyond traditional thinking to include people who choose to spend their lives together in a kinship relationship despite the lack of legal sanctions or blood lines.

It no longer is realistic to speak of a typical American family, since contemporary life is filled with families with different living arrangements, styles of living, and organizational patterns. As Goldenberg and Goldenberg (2002) observe:

> The idealized, nostalgic portrait of the American nuclear family depicts a carefree, white family with a suburban residence, sole-provider father in a 9-5 job, and a full-time, stay-at-home mother always available when the children return from school. Both parents are dedicated to child-rearing and remain together for life; children are educated in a neighborhood school and attend church with their parents on Sunday; plenty of money and supportive grandparents are available. (p. 10)

Not only is such a romanticized depiction of intact (middle-class) family life alien to the vast majority of people today, but there is doubt about whether it ever existed (Coontz, 1992). Although divorce was less common in the past, families were often disrupted by the early death of a parent, or by abandonment by a breadwinner; changes such as remarriage, child placement with relatives, foster care, and orphanages often followed. Thus, despite the idealized picture of family life, the risk of not growing up in an intact family has been a part of American life for some time (Walsh, 2003a).

Marriage and intact family life, as Coontz (2005) observes, may be viewed as a social invention that in its earliest form emerged from the division of labor between men and women in early societies, and thus served to ensure family survival and efficiency, as men and women were assigned different, but collaborative, complementary roles. Today's occupational opportunities, the evolution of women's rights, a more flexible commitment to marriage as a permanent union, and the expectation of greater love and intimacy in marriage, have changed expectations that only an enduring marriage provides what partners seek. What has broadened our view of family life is the visible impact of working mothers, single-parent households, dual-earner families, long-term unmarried cohabiting couples, the high divorce rate, never-married couples with children, stepfamilies, adoptive families, and same-sex couples living together with or without children.

SOME FURTHER FAMILY CONSIDERATIONS

Regardless of type, all families create and indoctrinate new members, and although most ultimately give these members autonomy and no longer expect them to live under the same roof into adulthood, family membership remains intact for life. The power of the family is such that despite the possible separation of members by vast distances, sometimes even by death, the family's influence remains (Kaye, 1985). Even when a member experiences a temporary or permanent sense of alienation from the family, he or she can never truly relinquish family membership. Should divorce occur, co-parenting continues, and the former marriage continues to be recognized with the designation of "ex-spouse" (McGoldrick & Carter, 2003). For most of us, relationships with siblings are likely to represent our longest continuous commitments (Cicirelli, 1995).

As Carter and McGoldrick (1999) point out, families are subject to unique constraints. A business organization may fire an employee viewed as dysfunctional, or conversely, members may resign and permanently sever their relationships with the group if the structure or values of the company are not to their liking. The pressures of retaining family membership allow few such exits, even for those who attempt to gain great geographic distance from their family of origin. Further, unlike members of non-family systems, who can generally be replaced if they leave, family members are irreplaceable, primarily because the main value in a family is in the network of relationships developed by its members. Should a parent leave or die, for example, and another person be brought in to fill a parenting role, the substitute, regardless of successful effort, can never truly replace the lost parent's personal and emotional ties to the remaining members.

ENABLING AND DISABLING FAMILY SYSTEMS

Growth and change in families and the individual members who compose them occur concurrently, and understanding their interactions, as we shall see, is essential in carrying out any reparative or preventive work (Nichols & Pace-Nichols, 2000). In the process of growing up, family members develop individual identities but nevertheless remain attached to the family group, which in turn maintains an evolving identity or collective image of its own. These family members do not live in isolation, but rather are dependent on one another—not merely for money, food, clothing, and shelter but also for love, affection, mutual commitment, companionship, socialization, the expectation of long-lasting relationships, and fulfillment of other nontangible needs. They maintain a history by telling and retelling their family "story" from one generation to the next, thus ensuring a sense of family continuity and shaping the expectations of members regarding the future. To function successfully, members need to adapt to the changing needs and demands of fellow family members as well as the changing expectations of the larger kinship network, the community, and society in general (Rice, 1993).

Apart from its survival as a system, a well-functioning family encourages the realization of the individual potential of its members—allowing them freedom for exploration and self-discovery along with protection and the instillation of a sense of security.

Constantine (1986) distinguishes between what he calls "enabled" and "disabled" family systems. The former succeeds at balancing system needs as a family unit while simultaneously operating on behalf of the interests of all its members as individuals. Enabled family regimes inevitably invent procedures that attempt to satisfy the sometimes conflicting interests of their members. Constantine maintains that to do less, or to prevail but only at the expense of certain members, reflects family disablement, often manifested in unstable, rigid, or chaotic family patterns.

Some families, unfortunately, are themselves so depleted as a result of excess external or internal stress (poverty, migration to a country where they lack language skills or understanding of unfamiliar customs, serious health problems, legal issues, unforeseen accidents) that they may need long-term community support if they are ever to feel self-sufficient. Low-income families receiving social assistance and working poor families in particular may increase their chances for success and self-sufficiency when they receive such social support. Pigott and Monaco (2004), Canadian community workers in a multiservice center in Toronto, describe the debilitating, disenabling effects of poverty and living in inadequate housing in unsafe neighborhoods. Often led by a lone parent, with few siblings, limited contact with grandparents, parents who work or otherwise are unavailable for long periods, such families feel isolated and defeated, and in need of social networks (healthcare facilities, after-school programs, recreation centers, libraries, community agencies). Being a part of such a social system often represents a step toward reducing isolation and increasing the possibilities of more effective self-care and improved quality of life.

Family Structure

Families are organizationally complex emotional systems that may comprise at least three—and increasingly today, as a result of longer life expectancies—four generations.

Whether traditional or innovative, adaptive or maladaptive, efficiently or chaotically organized, married or committed life partners with or without children, a family inevitably attempts, with varying degrees of success, to arrange itself into as functional or enabling a group as possible so that it can meet its collective or jointly defined needs and goals without consistently or systematically preventing particular members from meeting their individual needs and goals (Kantor & Lehr, 1975). To facilitate the cohesive process, a family typically develops rules that outline and allocate the roles and functions of its members. Those who live together for any length of time develop repeatable, preferred patterns for negotiating and arranging their lives to maximize harmony and predictability.

Affection, loyalty, and a continuity or durability of membership characterize all families. Even when these qualities are challenged, as in a family crisis situation or where there is severe conflict between members, families are typically resistant to change, and are likely to engage in corrective maneuvers to reestablish familiar interactive patterns. Regardless of format (for example, **nuclear family** or **stepfamily**) or ultimate success, all families must work at promoting positive relationships among members, attend to the personal needs of their constituents, and prepare to cope with developmental or maturational changes (such as children leaving home) as well as unplanned or unexpected crises (job dislocation or loss, divorce, death of a key member, a sudden acute illness). In general, all must organize (or reorganize) themselves in order to get on with the day-to-day problems of living. More specifically, all must develop their own special styles or strategies for coping with stresses imposed from outside or from within the family itself.

GENDER ROLES AND GENDER IDEOLOGY

Males and females typically are indoctrinated from early in life into different socially based gender role behavior in the family. While biology undoubtedly plays a determining role in gender differences, most of the differences (value systems, personality characteristics, roles, problem-solving techniques, attitudes toward sexuality, etc.) result from learning that is reinforced by society and passed down across generations (Philpot, 2000). As a result of their differing socialization experiences, supported by general societal (and specific cultural) stereotypes, members of each sex for the most part develop distinct behavioral expectations and are granted disparate opportunities and privileges. Male and females typically grow up with different senses of entitlement, exercise differing degrees of power, and have differing life experiences.

Gender shapes our individual identity and expectations, our role and status within our family, and the real and perceived life choices open to us (Haddock, Zimmerman, & Lyness, 2003). Men traditionally have played the more powerful role in most heterosexual families: a man's career moves and personal interests were apt to be prioritized; less was expected of him in carrying out household chores; he was likely to be granted the major (or final) influence in family decisions; his leisure time and discretionary spending were given primary attention; and he was expected to have less emotional investment in family relationships.

However, as society's awareness of the crucial role of gender—as a determinant of personal identity, sociocultural privilege, or oppression—has grown in recent decades, largely because of women's increased employment and the feminist movement, so has recognition of the need to overcome gender inequalities and stereotypes that limit psychological functioning for both sexes (see Chapter 3) and for men and women to co-construct new interactive patterns (Avis, 1996). As a consequence, gender-role changes in recent decades have had a powerful impact on family structure and functioning. As the percentage of women in paid employment has risen, at-home responsibilities of men and women have had to be redefined by each couple, and overall, the pattern of gender-linked behaviors, expectations, and attitudes regarding a family's sex-defined roles has begun to change. Male and female role differences have become less clearly defined today as many families, especially those led by the younger generations, struggle to find more flexible if not yet fully worked out patterns for living together harmoniously in a dual working household. Time pressures, how best to juggle work and family obligations, who takes time off from work to care for a sick child—these are some of the day-to-day issues two-income families typically face. In the case of working-class dual-earners, a sick child may become a family crisis if their jobs do not permit time off for either parent.

CULTURAL DIVERSITY AND THE FAMILY

Cultural factors, largely overlooked by family psychologists in the past, have come to play an increasingly central role in our understanding of family life. Increased immigration, particularly over the last 20 years—the largest two-decade influx in American

BOX 1.1   RESEARCH REPORT

Two-Income Families and Gender Ideology

Today's average American family is apt to have two working adults and to rely on the income of both partners for economic survival. Typically, they face a major challenge in determining how best to balance work and nonwork tasks (Barnett & Hyde, 2001). Employed married women now spend less time in child care and household tasks than they did 30 years ago, and correspondingly, their employed husbands spend more time on those home-based activities. Inevitably, such shifts have caused striking changes in the relationships between men and women; in many cases, they have resulted in family instability, temporarily or more permanently, as couples work out differences in their gender-role ideologies (the extent to which they hold traditional or nontraditional views of the proper social roles of men and women). Fraenkel (2003) has examined the challenges of navigating work and family responsibilities in two-parent, two-income heterosexual families, recognizing that race, ethnicity, and social class play a decisive role in how such families manage best to cope. In single-parent households, the sole parent is almost certain to be working outside the home (Galinsky, 1999).

Barnett and Hyde (2001) suggest that the father who spends long hours caring for his children while his wife works a different shift may resent child caregiving because he perceives it as a "woman's job" and thus may get little benefit from his new father role. Similarly, if a wife works outside the home but prefers to be at home because she believes it is a woman's duty to be a full-time mother, she may not benefit from her new work role. Men usually believe they are carrying out their role within the family by working, while working women sometimes worry that they are being bad mothers (Coltrane, 1998). In general, those who adopt a more egalitarian attitude benefit more from combining work and family roles than do those with more traditional gender-role ideologies.

history—has added substantially to our appreciation of the primacy of *cultural diversity* in our society. Values, rituals, common transactional patterns, ways of communicating—even the very definition of "family" in different cultures—all require examination if an accurate, unbiased, and comprehensive family assessment and effective counseling are to be carried out (Aponte & Wohl, 2000). The importance of kinship networks, the roles of extended family members, expectations regarding male and female behavioral patterns, levels of acculturation and ethnic identification, and socioeconomic power or lack thereof differ for different groups; all these factors, as well as others, have an impact on how (and how well) families function.

For example, while the dominant American (Anglo) definition typically focuses on the intact nuclear family, Italians tend to refer to family as the entire network of aunts, uncles, cousins, and grandparents, all of whom are likely to be involved in family decision making. African Americans are apt to think of family as a wide network of kin plus longtime friends and other community members. For the Chinese, family includes all their ancestors and descendants (Hines, Garcia-Preto, McGoldrick, Almeida, & Weltman, 1999). In their landmark text, *Ethnicity and Family Therapy*, McGoldrick, Giordano, and Pearce (2005) present descriptions of common structural patterns between families from over 40 different ethnic groups, underscoring that family therapy clients from each group may make different assumptions about the therapeutic process, emphasize different family issues of importance to them, and may bring different problem-solving tools and resources in dealing with those issues. Boyd-Franklin (2003a) has elaborated on African American life experiences, as has Hayden (2001) in describing Irish American life, and Falicov (1998) in offering guidance in considering the cultural context while working with Latino families.

McGoldrick (2003) emphasizes the need for clinicians to examine the various facets of their own identity, their own **ethnicity** and cultural heritage—and to become aware of their own cultural biases and prejudices—in order to increase their flexibility and competence to work with clients they are likely to encounter in our multicultural society. As she notes:

> Cultural competence requires not a cookbook approach to cultural differences but an appreciation for the often hidden cultural aspects of our psychological, spiritual, and physical selves, a profound respect for the limitations of our own cultural perspective and the ability to deal respectfully with those whose values differ from our own. (p. 239)

Social class differences also add to diversity between families, shaping the resources, expectations, opportunities, privileges, and options of their members (Kliman & Madsen, 1999). Depending to a large extent on social class membership, work may be fulfilling or demoralizing; a means to achieving upward mobility or a dead end; filled with satisfactions or boredom; or, in the case of the underclass, frequently nonexistent (Wilson, 1996).

Kliman and Madsen (1999) emphasize that more than family income is involved in class definitions; the interplay of ethnicity, religion, and education also influences perceived social status. As they illustrate:

> A professor is seen as being in a higher class than a contractor who has equal income—unless the professor is a Latina single mother and the contractor is an Anglo-American man from "an old family." Women's and children's class standing plummets after divorce. A Black executive has less effective class standing than White subordinates when trying to hail a cab, join a country club, buy an elegant house, or insure his children's class stability. In restaurants and hotels, Whites may ask him to serve them. (p. 89)

Boyd-Franklin (2003b) draws attention to the complex interplay of race and social class. Beyond the simplistic equation of Whites as middle class and Blacks as poor, considerable variety occurs within each group. She notes, for example, that a Black family classified as poor because of low income may have middle-class values, aspirations, and expectations for their children.

Families living in poverty represent approximately 12 percent of the general American population and 28 percent of households headed by single women (U.S. Census Bureau, 2000). Those most vulnerable to poverty are nonwhite minorities, single mothers, children under 18, and the elderly (Lott & Bullock, 2001). As we describe family behavior patterns throughout this text, it is important to bear in mind how client lives are constrained by the larger forces of racial, cultural, sexual, and class-based inequalities (McGoldrick, 1998).

FAMILY INTERACTIVE PATTERNS

Families typically display stable, collaborative, purposeful, and recurring patterns of interactive sequences. These largely go unnoticed by outsiders, frequently are unstated, and are not always understood by the participants themselves. Nonverbal exchange patterns between family members, in particular, represent subtle, coded transactions that transmit family rules and functions governing the range of acceptable behaviors tolerated by the family (for instance, that a son does not speak before his mother speaks, and she herself can take her turn only after her husband has spoken). Such patterned interactions are jointly engaged-in, highly predictable transactional patterns generated by all family members on cue, as though each participant feels compelled to play a well-rehearsed part, like it or not.

Minuchin, Lee, and Simon (1996) illustrate this point with the following easily recognizable examples:

> The complementary construction of family members requires long periods of negotiating, compromising, rearranging, and competing. These transactions are usually invisible, not only because context and subject constantly change but also because they are generally the essence of minutiae. Who passes the sugar? Who checks the map for directions, chooses the movie, changes the channel? Who responds to whom, when, and in what manner? This is the cement by which families solidify their relationships. (p. 30)

Shared family rituals—holiday celebrations, christenings, confirmations, bar mitzvahs, graduations, weddings, funerals, wakes—are part of ongoing family interaction patterns that help ensure family identity and continuity. Rituals are symbolic actions that help families adapt to change rather than struggle against it, at the same time that they reaffirm their group unity in dealing with a life transition. They anchor family members to the past, providing a sense of family history and rootedness, while at the same time implying future family interactions. Participating in rituals links the members not only to the family system but also to the wider community and culture (Imber-Black, 1999).

FAMILY NARRATIVES AND ASSUMPTIONS

A family is a maker of meaning (Constantine, 1986), and our individual judgment about what constitutes reality is a function of the beliefs and stories that the family (as well as the culture) imparts about their experiences (Becvar, 2000). Throughout the course of its development, a family fashions and helps instill fundamental and enduring assumptions about the world in which it lives. As a result, the meanings and understandings we attribute to events and situations we encounter are embedded in our family's social, cultural, and historical experiences (Anderson, Burney, & Levin, 1999).

The narratives or stories a family recounts help explain, and in some cases help justify, their interactive patterns. Despite any differences or disagreements between members, the core of family membership is based on acceptance of, and belief in, a set of abiding suppositions or shared constructs about the family itself and its relationship to its social environment. These in turn are often limited by social class expectations and restraints, influencing what members of that class consider to be possible, acceptable, conceivable, or ever attainable in their lifetimes. Language and dialogue thus play crucial roles in how human beings come to know the world and how they interpret or make sense of their subsequent experiences.

Some families generally view the world as trustworthy, orderly, predictable, masterable; they are likely to view themselves as competent, to encourage individual input by their members, and to feel comfortable, perhaps enjoyably challenged, as a group coping with life. Other families perceive their environment as mostly menacing, unstable, and thus unpredictable and potentially dangerous; in their view, the outside world appears confusing and at times chaotic, so they band together, insist on agreement from all members on all issues, and in that way protect themselves against intrusion and threat. Thus, the narrative a family develops about itself, which is derived largely from its history, passed on from one generation to the next, and influenced by social class expectations, has a powerful impact on its functioning.

The ways in which individuals and their families characteristically deal with their lives are not based on some objective or "true" view of reality, but rather on family social constructions—unchallenged views of reality created and perpetuated in conversation with one another, possibly carried on over generations. Such views may act as blinders or restraints—limitations a family places upon itself by its beliefs and values—that prevent its members from noticing other aspects of their lives or seeing other behavioral options. Members of these families typically construct a rationale for why undesirable behavior continues and how they have no alternative but to live their lives in spite of it (Atwood, 1997).

In the **postmodern** outlook there is no "true" reality, only the family's collectively agreed-upon set of constructions, created through language and knowledge that is relational and generatively based, that the family calls reality. As we will illustrate throughout the book, the postmodern view has had a powerful influence on how many family therapists view family life—the social basis for acquiring knowledge—and how these therapists work collaboratively with families to generate new possibilities and co-construct alternative narratives (Gergen, 1996; White, 1995).

FAMILY RESILIENCY

All families face challenges and upheavals during their life cycle; some are expectable strains (brought on by such potential crises as retirement or divorce or remarriage), while others are sudden and untimely (an unforeseen job loss, the unexpected death of a key family member or family friend, a holdup or rape or other violent and life-threatening experience, an earthquake or flood). However, not all families react to these potentially disturbing and disruptive events in the same way. Some may experience prolonged distress from which they seem never to recover; others suffer less intensely and for shorter periods. For some families, recovery may come quickly, but they later begin to experience unexpected health problems or somehow never again enjoy life the way they once did. Nevertheless, there are large numbers who manage to cope with the temporary upheaval or loss, rebound, and move on to the next challenge. This ability to thrive and maintain relatively stable psychological and physical functioning after extremely aversive experiences, often showing only minor, transient disruption, reveals a great deal about a family's **resilience** (Bonanno, 2004). Box 1.2 presents such a case.

Few if any families can expect to avoid exposure to stress, loss, or potentially traumatic events at some points in their life cycle. At the same time, as illustrated in Box 1.2, families have the potential for growth and repair in response to distress, threat, trauma, or crisis, emerging stronger and more resourceful than before (Walsh, 2003b). A family as a whole, or one or more of its members, may manifest dysfunctional behavior during periods of persistent stress, but family processes may mediate the person's recovery,

BOX 1.2   CASE STUDY

A TRAUMATIZED FAMILY REBOUNDS FROM A SUDDEN CRISIS

When Hurricane Katrina hit New Orleans in 2005, thousands of lives were disrupted as people lost their homes and possessions, their jobs, and sometimes loved ones who were caught up in the subsequent floods. Paul and Margaret, both in their early thirties and near the beginning of their careers, had come to New Orleans three years earlier, he as an architect, she as a real estate broker. When they were forced to leave their newly purchased home, which had been devastated by the hurricane, they were unable to recover any articles or possessions. With their one-year-old daughter, Christine, they fled in their car to the West Coast to move in with his parents for an indefinite period as they planned their suddenly disrupted future.

Although their marriage had been a relatively stable one, it now faced several crises simultaneously: addressing questions of how to earn a living, where to live, how to arrange child care, how to resume a social life, etc. Living with Paul's parents was difficult, since the house was crowded, his mother was ill, his father was upset by the intrusion of the baby, and Paul and Margaret felt too old to now be living with, and be largely supported by, his parents. Arguments broke out between family members, and in general the home was filled with tensions between the couples.

Despite the strain on their relationship, Paul and Margaret, each with a history of personal as well as

professional achievement, ultimately retained their belief that together they would meet the challenge. After a short period in which both felt downcast and despondent, Paul looked up old high school friends, finally landing a job at a construction company where his architectural skills made him a desired employee. Margaret, no longer able to afford child care, and struggling with the responsibilities of being a full-time mom, began to recognize some of the satisfactions that came with being a stay-at-home mother, something she had not contemplated in the past. With no choice but to make decisions regarding where and how they would live, they reassessed their priorities, recognized how much being together as a family meant to them, and acknowledged that they were young people with resources who would learn to adapt.

Initially confused and despairing, feeling desperate at times during their first months in a new environment, they gradually realized that they needed to reorganize their lives to face the new challenges. The new situation was hardly to their liking, but they had each other, their child, and faith in their relationship. Forming new friendships, retaining a sense of humor, recasting the crisis they faced as a challenge rather than a defeat, all helped. As they moved into their new small apartment, they retained the dream of returning to New Orleans soon, better prepared as a family to deal with future adversity.

allowing the family system to rally, buffer stress, reduce the chances of dysfunction, and support optimal adaptation.

Rather than view resiliency as a rare or special set of qualities a family may or may not possess, Masten (2001) contends that such recuperative skills are common phenomena arising from ordinary adaptive processes successfully mastered by most children in the process of development. She maintains that a relatively small set of global factors support resilience in children: connection to competent and caring adults in the family and community, cognitive and self-regulating skills, a positive view of oneself, and motivation to be effective in the environment. Moving away from a search for deficits or pathology in families in favor of seeking its strengths and potentials—family resiliencies—is part of the evolving movement of *positive psychology* (Seligman & Csikszentmihalyi, 2000; Sheldon & King, 2001). Here, researchers and therapists have

BOX 1.3   CLINICAL NOTE

Spirituality and the Family Belief System

Spiritual beliefs and practices represent powerful human experiences that have largely been neglected in clinical training and practice as being unscientific, too private, or perhaps best left to clergy or pastoral counselors. Some family therapists, concerned that they might impose their own religious values (or lack of them) on vulnerable clients, have avoided the topic. Yet for many people, religion and spirituality represent a central set of organizing beliefs that give their lives meaning and guidance. Many families turn to a supreme being, engaging in meditation or faith-healing rituals, in times of severe distress or adversity, and, as Walsh and Pryce (2003) point out, may recover from loss, trauma, or suffering as a result. For these families, spiritual practices are essential to recovery and resilience, particularly at a time of upheaval and disruption.

Increased interest in examining cultural factors in working therapeutically with families has led to a growing awareness of the importance of spirituality in family life. As Hodge (2005) observes, spiritual beliefs and practices often animate every aspect of family life, and frequently represent a source of family strength. As he illustrates, for many Muslim families Islamic beliefs and practices are basic to family functioning, and family therapists need to understand the role these factors play in the lives of Muslim families if they are to enhance their level of cultural competency. Walsh (1999b) has edited a volume of writings that examine spiritual resources (religious beliefs, faith, values, prayer, meditation, rites, and rituals) among a variety of culturally diverse families, all emphasizing the role of spirituality in family functioning.

begun to study the nature of effective functioning and adaptation, paying close attention to human capabilities and adaptive systems in individuals and families.

Undoubtedly, some families—regardless of type, number of problems, ethnic or racial makeup, religion and spirituality, socioeconomic status, sexual orientation, or degree of education—are happier and more stable than others. They are more flexible in seeking solutions to problems, more purposeful in pursuing satisfactions, more adaptive to changing conditions, and better able to recover from misfortune or adversity than other families. Walsh (2003b) identifies some key family processes in family resilience: (a) a consistent and positive *belief system* that provides shared values and assumptions so as to offer guidelines for meaning and future action (e.g., viewing disruptions as milestones on their shared life passages, without assigning blame, and recasting a crisis as a manageable challenge); (b) the family's *organizational processes* (how effectively it organizes its resources) that provide the "shock absorbers" when confronted with stress (e.g., remaining flexible, open to change, connected to each other); and (c) a set of family *communication/problem-solving processes* that are clear, consistent, and congruent and that establish a climate of mutual trust and open expression among its members (maintaining a shared range of feeling, shared decisions, creative brainstorming).

While some families may be (temporarily) shattered by crises, others emerge strengthened and more resourceful. Rather than view a symptomatic family member as a vulnerable victim (how did the family damage that individual?), thus pathologizing the family, the emerging viewpoint is that while problems may certainly exist within the family, family competencies nevertheless can be harnessed to promote self-corrective changes.

Resilience should not be thought of as a static set of strengths or qualities, but as a developmental process unique to each family that enables families to create adaptive responses to stress and, in some cases, to thrive and grow in their response to the stressors (Hawley & DeHaan, 1996). Adopting a resiliency-based approach in working with families calls for identifying and fortifying those key interactional processes that enable families to withstand and rebound from disruptive challenges. That is, it does not suggest that families are problem-free or that they are not engaging in damaging behavior, but rather that survival, regeneration, and empowerment can occur through collaborative efforts even in the midst of severe personal and family stress and adversity.

How the family organizes itself, how it retains its cohesion, how openly it communicates and problem-solves together to cope with the threat largely forecasts its ability to recover. An affirming belief system aids the process. The support of a network of friends, extended family, clergy, neighbors, employers, and fellow employees and the availability of community resources often contribute to family recovery.

As Karpel (1986) emphasizes, even chaotic, disorganized, abusive, and multi-problem families have resources. Here he is referring to the rootedness, intimacy, support, and meaning a family can provide. In poor families, especially, the members need to feel their self-worth, dignity, and purpose; resilience is facilitated for them if they experience a sense of control over their lives rather than viewing themselves as helpless victims of an uncaring society (Aponte, 1994; 1999).

In general, what factors increase the likelihood of greater family resiliency? Goldenberg and Goldenberg (2002) suggest the following:

> All families possess the resources, and thus the potential, for resilience. In traditional families, usually organized according to some form of generational hierarchy, those with greater resilience are able to balance intergenerational continuity and change and to maintain ties among the past, the present, and the future without getting stuck in the past or cut off from it. Clarity and ease of communication also characterize such families; a clear set of expectations about roles and relationships within the family is provided. In whatever type of family form—whether led by never-married mothers, stepfathers, two working parents, or grandparents—resilient families respect individual differences and the separate needs of family members. These families have mastered successful problem-solving strategies by developing reparative, resiliency-enabling processes that promote endurance and survival. (p. 12)

The resiliency construct challenges the family therapist to attend to the family's resources that can be mobilized to deal with a present crisis or adversity (as opposed to a deficit-focusing model directed at detecting what's wrong with the family). It is intended to have an empowering or enabling effect as it encourages the family to search for resiliencies, including previously untapped resources, within its network of relationships. Successfully managing a crisis together deepens the family bond and strengthens its confidence in its capacity to prevent or manage future adversities.

THE PERSPECTIVE OF FAMILY THERAPY

Scientific models help shape the boundaries of a discipline and set the agenda regarding the subject matter and methodology to be followed in seeking answers. If the individual is the unit of study, clinical theories regarding human behavior, such as **psychoanalysis,** are likely to emphasize internal events, psychic organization, and **intrapsychic** conflict. Methodology in such a situation tends to be retrospective, revisiting the past; explanations of current problems tend to have a historical basis and to search out root causes in early childhood experiences. Symptom formation in an adult individual, for example, is considered a result of unresolved conflict carried over from that person's early formative years. Uncovering significant traumatic childhood events becomes essential if the client is to be helped in alleviating current emotional conflict. Typically, clinicians with this intrapsychic orientation seek answers to the question of *why* symptoms of **psychopathology** have occurred.

Primarily influenced by Freud's psychoanalytic formulations, clinicians traditionally have maintained an intrapsychic outlook, focusing their attention on uncovering and reconstructing the patient's past, including memories previously locked up in the unconscious. They assumed such knowledge or awareness would produce the necessary insights that would lead to behavioral changes and the amelioration of symptoms.

While Freud acknowledged in theory the sometimes powerful impact of family conflict and alliances (such as the Oedipus complex in boys) on the development of neurotic behavior in the individual, he assumed that the person internalized the problem; thus, Freud chose to direct his treatment toward helping that person resolve intrapsychic conflicts rather than attempting to change or modify the properties of the family system directly.[2]

By helping bring about changes in the patient's psychic organization, Freud hoped to evoke behavioral changes, including changes in response to others, that would presumably lead others to ultimately change their response patterns to the patient. Thus later therapists, following the lead of Freud and others, would treat a distressed individual in private but refuse to see that person's spouse or other family members, believing that as the patient resolved handicapping internal problems, a corresponding positive change would occur in his or her relationships with family members. Unfortunately, this was frequently not the case.

Without negating the significance of individual internal processes and intrapsychic dynamics, today's broader view of human problems focuses on the family context in which individual behavior currently occurs (rather than as recalled from the past). While bearing in mind the often complex ways in which individual behavior contributes to that interaction, such an **interpersonal** perspective—as opposed to an intrapsychic one—regards all behavior as part of a sequence of ongoing, interactional, recursive, or recurring events with no obvious beginning or end. Rather than attempt to discover the single answer to why something occurred by searching the past of each of the players, the family relational view directs the clinician's attention externally, to *transaction patterns* currently taking place within the family.

People and events are assumed to exist in a context of mutual influence and mutual interaction, as participants share in each other's destiny. Within such a framework, all family members are embedded in a network of relationships, and helping families change their structure, typical interactive patterns, or belief systems alters each member's behavior. Clinicians with a systems outlook concern themselves with

---

[2]Karpel (1986) notes that Freud, by limiting himself to uncovering the experiences, fantasies, and mental perceptions of his individual clients, in effect denied the relevance of the family itself as anything other than a source of trauma for that person. In such an essentially negative and psychopathology-focused view, centered on the past, the potentially positive and enhancing properties of current family relationships are likely to be minimized or overlooked entirely.

understanding *what* is occurring (say, conflict between a troubled marital pair), *how* it occurs (observing its repetitive patterns), and *when* it occurs (whenever issues over power and control arise), rather than searching for *why* it is occurring. That is, systems-oriented clinicians are more interested in the *process* of what they are observing in the couple's interactions than in the *content* of those transactions. For example, a therapist working with a couple quarreling over spending money is likely to draw their attention to the trouble they are having making decisions together, rather than focusing specifically on finances. How power and control in the family is distributed, who does or does not feel listened to, what gender roles influence their outlooks, where these differences transfer to other areas of their relationship, what past resentments poison their ability to work in partnership to resolve problems—answers to these questions reveal how they relate to one another more than the specific problems around spending money. Box 1.4 illustrates such a situation.

Recasting the individual as a unit of a larger system, such as the family,[3] enables us to search for recurring patterns of interaction in which that person might engage. Our conceptualization of what that person does, what his or her motives are for doing so, and how that behavior can be changed therapeutically, takes on new dimensions as we shift our attention to the broader context in which that person functions. From this new wide-angle perspective, psychopathology or dysfunctional behavior can be redefined as more the product of a struggle between persons than simply the result of opposing forces within each of the participants.

Various therapeutic consequences follow from such a shift of perspective. When the locus of pathology is defined as internal, the property of a single individual or **monad,** the therapist focuses on individual processes and behavior patterns. If the dysfunctional behavior is viewed as a reflection of a flawed relationship between members of a **dyad** or **triad,** then it is the relationship that becomes the center of therapeutic attention and the target of intervention strategies. The therapist collaborating with couples or entire families as they alter their transactional patterns replaces the therapist as psychological sleuth seeking to uncover and decipher what goes on within the mind of the individual.

If successful, family therapy alters the system, helping families replace their previously limiting and self-defeating repetitive interactive patterns, or opening up the style and manner of communicating with one another across generations through a consideration of new options or beliefs. Within this changed family context, enriched relationship skills, improved communication skills, and enhanced problem-solving skills may lead to more rewarding interpersonal experiences, in most cases extending beyond the family.

Paradigm Shift

So long as one set of attitudes, philosophy, viewpoint, procedure, or methodology dominates scientific thinking (known as a **paradigm**), solutions to problems are

---

[3]The family, in turn, is itself part of a larger system, and its experiences are often profoundly influenced by involvements with the workplace, the school system, the healthcare system, the legal system, and so forth, in addition to reflecting aspects of the particular family's cultural background, ethnicity, race, and social class. An **ecosystemic approach** (McDaniel, Lusterman, & Philpot, 2001) in assessment and treatment takes into account the multiple systems in which the family is embedded. We'll elaborate on some of these systems-within-systems issues in Chapter 4.

BOX 1.4   CASE STUDY

A COUPLE IN CONFLICT SEEK HELP OVER MONEY ISSUES

Bob and Tess had been married for 10 years and had two children, an 8-year-old boy and a 6-year-old girl, when they contacted a family therapist. They were immediately hostile to one another in the first session, calling each other names, threatening divorce. She said she could no longer deal with her husband's "pinchpenny" behavior—his checking on the groceries she brought home to see if she had bought something he thought unnecessary, yelling if she bought the children toys or planned "expensive" birthday parties, refusing to send them to after-school activities because of the cost.

Bob had his own list of grievances. He worked hard for his money, he argued, and she never seemed to have enough. Although he claimed to be giving her a generous amount each month, she managed to spend it all, whereupon she would run up a credit card bill she could not pay and then come to him each month to be "bailed out" with additional cash. According to Bob, if she wanted special activities for the children, he did not object, but she would have to give up other things to live within her budget. Needless to say, they did not agree on what the size of that budget should be. He insisted that it was his right to control the budget because he was the man and the wage earner.

As they talked about themselves, the therapist noted that while Tess came from a middle-class family whose father had gone bankrupt several times, Bob was brought up in a working-class family where he learned to live frugally and watch expenditures. In their early years together, before the children were born, Tess worked in an office, kept her earnings separate from his, and used her own money to buy what she needed. There was little conflict. No thought was given to combining incomes, nor did they see any need to do so since the system they had worked out didn't seem to need fixing. The couple got along well, had a good sexual relationship, spent time with a large social circle, and considered themselves reasonably content and working in partnership.

That changed very soon after the children arrived. Bob complained about his wife's lack of sexual interest, and what he considered her rejection of him in favor of the children. He shouted about her "spendthrift" ways and became livid about the children being overindulged with "things." Tess resented his unwillingness to help with the children, and especially his eating alone, in front of the television set, when he arrived home from work. Soon they slept in separate rooms, she in their bed (in which the children frequently joined her), he on the living room couch, having fallen asleep watching late-night television. Each began to complain to the children about the other, trying to elicit their help to change the other's behavior and to prevent the couple from divorcing.

The therapist reminded them that they once had been able to resolve problems together, and wondered what each needed in order to be able to do so again. He redirected them to consider previous struggles for power and control, recognizing that this was an unresolved issue they had never faced. While they were encouraged to work on a budget—regarding their money as "family" income and outlay they needed to work on collaboratively—the major focus of the therapy turned to helping them gain greater awareness of the process taking place between them. They began to examine how they undermined each other, how seeking alliances with the children was destructive, how their sex life stalemate reflected their unresolved power issues, how they needed to work in partnership if they wished to keep their marriage from self-destructing. He began to comprehend her sense of fatigue and loneliness in raising the children by herself, and she tried to understand his sense of powerlessness and despair in making her hear his point of view. As they listened, fought, defended themselves, each slowly began to understand the viewpoint of the other and to feel less victimized. The therapist continued to build upon their earlier success together, emphasizing their resiliency.

(continued)

BOX 1.4   (*continued*)

Bob returned to their bed, tried to get home early from work on the day of the children's after-school sports events, and said he was willing, if not eager, to provide more money and not try to control her spending about specific items. She, in turn, offered to be more careful about living within a budget they worked on together. Tess gained a better under-standing of their financial situation, and Bob came to realize that the money belonged to both of them, and that together they could decide how best to spend it. As they felt supported by one another, they were able to give up their underlying power struggle and resist reverting to stereotypic gender roles.

sought within the perspective of that school of thought. However, should serious problems arise that do not appear to be explained by the prevailing paradigm, scientific efforts typically occur in an attempt to replace the existing system with a more appropriate rationale. Once the old belief system is replaced, perspectives shift and previous events take on new meaning. The resulting transition to a new paradigm, according to Kuhn (1970), is a scientific revolution. Precisely such a revolution in the thinking of many psychotherapists took place in the 1950s, considered to be the period when family therapy began (Goldenberg & Goldenberg, 2005).

More than simply another treatment method, family therapy represents a "whole new way of conceptualizing human problems, of understanding behavior, the development of symptoms, and their resolution" (Sluzki, 1978, p. 366). The perspective of family therapy demonstrates a paradigm shift, a break with past ideas, calling for a new set of premises and methods for collecting and interpreting forthcoming data. Beyond a concern with the individual's personality characteristics or repetitive behavior patterns, beyond even a concern with what transpires between people (where individuals remain the unit of study), this conceptual leap focuses attention on the family as subject matter. It is the family as a functioning transactional system, as an entity in itself, more than the sum of the inputs of its participants, that provides the context for understanding individual functioning.

By bringing systems theory to the study of families, family therapy represents a major epistemological revolution in the behavioral sciences. Put simply, **epistemology** refers to how one goes about gaining knowledge and drawing conclusions about the world; it is a term commonly used by family therapists to indicate a conceptual framework or belief system. Epistemology refers to the rules used to make sense of experience, the descriptive language used to interpret incoming information. Such rules, not necessarily consciously stated, determine the underlying assumptions we make in our day-to-day behavior as we attempt to understand what is happening around us and how we can bring about change.

A Cybernetic Epistemology

Concerned with patterns and processes, the systems outlook proposes a **cybernetic** epistemology as an alternative to our habitual ways of knowing and thinking. Historically, the science of cybernetics was born during the early 1940s in a series of wartime interdisciplinary conferences in New York City sponsored by the Josiah Macy Foundation and attended by a cross-section of the leading scientists, engineers, mathematicians, and social scientists of the time. The conferees addressed, among other things, the study of communication in reference to regulation and control (for example, the wartime problems of guided missiles and rockets) through the operation of **feedback** mechanisms.

Norbert Wiener (1948), the mathematician who coined the term *cybernetics* and who was to become a principal player in the development of computers, was especially interested in information processing and how feedback mechanisms operate in controlling both simple and complex systems. Wiener chose the term *cybernetics* from the Greek word for "steersman," suggestive of an overall governing or regulating system or organization for guiding or piloting a ship by means of feedback cycles. To Wiener, cybernetics represented the science of communication and control in humans as well as in machines.

These Macy conferences made an important breakthrough by providing a new and exciting epistemology—a new paradigm—for conceptualizing how systems retain their stability through self-regulation as a result of reinserting the results of past performance into current functioning. Perhaps even more significant, a way was becoming available to change patterns of future performance by altering feedback information. Researchers from both the physical and social sciences began to explore how these systems or cybernetics notions could be applied to various fields in which both living and nonliving entities could be governed by self-regulating feedback loops that become activated to correct errors or deviations in the system and thus restore stability in the process of reaching its preprogrammed goal.

Thus, what we now think of as simple or **first-order cybernetics** grew out of communication engineering and computer science as a means of understanding the general principles of how systems of all kinds are self-regulated and thus maintain their stability. Attention was directed toward structure—patterns of organization—and control through feedback cycles; universal laws or codes were sought to explain what governs all systems. It was assumed further that the system being observed was separate from the observer, who could objectively study and carry out changes in the system while remaining outside of the system itself.

It was Gregory Bateson, an English-born anthropologist and ethnologist who worked for the U.S. Office of Strategic Services in India during the war, who took away from these conferences some of these mathematical and engineering concepts and recognized their application to the social and behavioral sciences. Bateson (1972), increasingly concerned with epistemological issues, understood that cybernetics, with its emphasis on self-correcting feedback mechanisms, pointed to the inseparable relationship between stability and change when he later noted:

> All changes can be understood as the effort to maintain some constancy and all constancy as maintained through change. (p. 381)

Although Wiener himself had begun to reformulate psychological constructs (for example, Freud's idea of an unconscious) in information-processing terms, Bateson (1972) deserves the major credit for seeing how cybernetic principles apply to human communication processes, including those associated with psychopathology. Attempting to understand how families in various cultures sustain stability, he introduced the notion that a family might be analogous to a cybernetic system in its use of self-regulating feedback mechanisms to maintain balance and constancy. While Bateson himself remained outside the realm of family therapy, his cybernetic ideas are

© Wadsworth/Thomson Learning

Gregory Bateson, Ph.D.

generally considered to have provided the field of family therapy with its intellectual foundation.

Bateson's later—1956—contributions to a daring **double-bind** theory of schizophrenia as a relationship phenomenon rather than an intrapsychic disorder were monumental in describing an important psychiatric entity in transactional communication terms, specifically in drawing attention to the family context that gave the symptoms meaning. Although this theory regarding the origin of schizophrenia later proved to be incomplete, if not inaccurate, its effort to look beyond the symptomatic person to family transactions was groundbreaking in directing researchers to examine what occurs in the exchange of information and the process of relationships between persons, as in a family. We will return to Bateson and the "double-bind" theory in Chapter 5.

Reciprocal Determinism

Adopting a relationship outlook inevitably shifts attention from *content* to *process*. Rather than dwelling on historical facts as explanations for current problems (Felicite: "Our problem began when my husband, Enrique, lost his job and our son Greg went to work"), this new perspective focuses on the sequence of linked communication exchanges within a cybernetic family system ("With Enrique out of work, our son Greg is contributing more money and seems to be dominating us; I submit to Greg's demands more and more, and I suppose Enrique is resentful"). Note how the latter statement shifts attention from the linear sequential actions of individuals to the transactions occurring between them. The "facts" of the case (content) are static and not nearly as clinically illuminating as is the family interactional pattern (process) and its cultural context.

Content is the language of **linear causality**—the view that one event causes the next in unidirectional stimulus-response fashion. While such a view may be appropriate for understanding simple mechanical situations (where the machinery does not have too many parts, and the parts do not interact much), it is woefully inadequate for dealing with situations exhibiting organized complexity, such as what transpires within a family.

From a cybernetic or systems standpoint, concerned with wholes, a precise part-by-part analysis (such as searching for specific childhood traumatic events as causes of current adult problems) is too reductionistic and inferential to be of much explanatory value. Instead, argue opponents of linear thinking, parts are better understood by the functions they serve in the whole.

In the physical world, the world of Newton, it makes sense to talk of causality in linear terms: A causes B, which acts upon C, causing D. In human relationships, however, this "billiard ball" model, which proposes that a force moves in one direction only and affects objects in its path, rarely—if ever—applies. Consequently, *any search for the "real" or ultimate cause of any interpersonal event is pointless.* A does not cause B, nor does B cause A; both cause each other. Explanations cannot be found in the action of the parts, but in the system as a whole—its communication patterns, complex relationships, and mutual influences.

If content is the language of linear causality, then process is the language of **circular causality.** The emphasis here is on forces moving in many directions simultaneously, not simply a single event caused by a previous one. Within a family, any action by one member affects all other members and the family as a whole; each member's response in turn prompts other responses that affect all other members, whose further reactions provoke still other responses, and so forth. Such a reverberating effect in turn affects the first person, in a continuous series of circular loops or recurring chains of influence.

Problems are not caused by past situations in this view, but rather by ongoing, interactive, mutually influencing family processes. Parents who ask quarreling children, "Who started the fight?" are almost certain to hear, "He (she) started it; I'm only hitting back." Both children are correct, both are incorrect; it all depends on where in the communication loop the parent begins the investigation. Nor is such mutual participation limited to pairs. Within a large family, for example, a multitude of such chains exist. Who started what is usually impossible to decipher, and really of little consequence in resolving the interpersonal conflict. Reciprocity is the underlying principle in all relationships. Change calls for altering the process, not discovering the original culprit.

Note the following contrasts between statements based on linear and circular causality:

Linear: A disturbed mother produces disturbed children.

Implication: Mother's emotional problems cause similar problems in other family members.

Circular: A middle-aged woman, struggling with what she perceives as an inattentive husband, forms an alliance with her 20-year-old son, paying less attention to her teenage daughter. The daughter, feeling rejected, turns to her peers and flirts with promiscuous behavior, to the considerable distress of her parents. The son, not quite ready to become independent, feels he must remain at home because his mother needs his attention. The mother blames her problems on what she considers a distant husband, who in turn feels criticized and excluded from the family. As he protects himself by further distancing himself from her, their sexual relationship suffers. The children respond to the ensuing coldness between the parents in different ways: the son by withdrawing further from friends, remaining at home with his mother as much as possible, and the daughter by pulling away from the family and leaning on a rebellious peer group as models.

Implication: Behavior has at least as much to do with the interactional context in which it occurs as with the inner mental processes or emotional problems of any of the players.

What should be clear from this example is that family processes affect individual behavior, and individuals within the family system affect family processes, in a recursive manner. Within the family context, every action provokes a circular sequence that in turn helps change the original action. The family who brings a defiant adolescent to therapy and wonders why the therapist wants to see all the family members together, is learning that the therapist believes all participants must look at the family context as the locus of the difficulty. To point a finger at one family member as the cause of the family's distress is to ignore dysfunctional patterns between members that perpetuate the problem.

The Identified Patient and the Appearance of Symptoms

Family therapists were among the first to recognize that when a symptom-bearing person (the **identified patient,** or IP) came for help, his or her entire family was hurting and needed help. Early therapists, such as Virginia Satir (1964) contended that the IP was expressing the family's disequilibrium or, in her terms, the family's "pain." Perhaps the IP was expressing what other family members were thinking or feeling, but were unable (or afraid to) acknowledge. Or was the IP's symptomatic behavior (drug addiction, failure to leave home, temper tantrums, dropping out of school) diverting attention from other family problems? The therapist's task became one of refocusing attention, not allowing the symptomatic behavior to obscure other conflicts within the family.

An early thesis was that symptoms had a function; they represented a sign that the family had become destabilized and was attempting to adapt or reestablish equilibrium. This view that symptoms have a protective purpose in helping maintain family stability—in effect, that dysfunctional families need a "sick" member and are willing to sacrifice that person for the sake of family well-being—was initially a mainstay of many family therapy founders. They concluded that the IP's symptoms represented stabilizing devices used to help relieve family stress and bring the family back into the normal range of its customary behavior. In this sense, the IP's actions may be based on a desire, although not usually a planned or premeditated one, to "help" other family members. For example, Haley (1979) described disturbed young people who do not leave home as willingly sacrificing themselves in order to protect and maintain family stability. According to Boszormenyi-Nagy and Ulrich (1981), family loyalty may evoke symptomatic behavior when a child "feels obligated to save the parents and their marriage from the threat of destruction" (p. 169).

Other family therapy pioneers, such as Salvador Minuchin (Minuchin & Fishman, 1981), viewed symptomatic behavior as a reaction to a family under stress and unable to accommodate to changing circumstances, and not particularly as a protective solution to retain family balance. In this view, all family members are equally "symptomatic," despite efforts by the family to locate the problem as residing in one family member. Minuchin sees the IP's symptoms as rooted in dysfunctional family transactions; it is the flawed family structure or inflexibility when new behavior is called for that maintains the symptomatic behavior in the IP. Change calls for the therapist to understand the family context in which the dysfunctional transactions transpire and then to attempt with family members as a group to change that existing context in order to permit new interactional possibilities to emerge.

A less purposeful or deterministic view of the appearance and maintenance of symptoms in a family member was offered by Watzlawick, Weakland, and Fisch (1974), who contend that symptoms or problems arise from repeated use of the same flawed solutions rather than being a sign of family system dysfunction. It was their belief that problems (or symptoms) are created and maintained because of the repeated attempt to apply an unworkable solution that only serves to make matters worse, and that ultimately the attempted solution, repeated without variation, becomes the problem. These authors argue that the family therapist must help the family find new solutions to the original problem if the symptomatic behavior is to be alleviated.

The postmodern view, increasingly popular today among family therapists, represents a break with these cybernetically based notions, raising skepticism regarding the meaning attached to symptomatic behavior. Postmodernists reject the notion that a family member's problems necessarily reflect underlying family conflict. From their **constructivist**[4] perspective, families tell themselves stories and develop beliefs about themselves; these constructions, in turn, organize their experiences and play a powerful role in shaping their lives. In some cases, such stories come to represent dominant and burdensome discourses that lead them to believe they have limited options and are doomed to repeat their self-defeating behavior.

In Michael White's (1989) view, families feel oppressed rather than protected or stabilized by symptomatic behavior in the family. His therapeutic efforts—a form of **narrative therapy** (see Chapter 14), especially his posing of deconstructing questions—represent a collaboration with the family directed at helping explore their ongoing stories and, together with them, co-constructing new stories that hold new possibilities, new ways of seeing and being. By rewriting family stories in such a way that new experiences become possible, White gets family members to unite in order to take back control of their lives from the oppressive set of symptoms. In the process, he believes families are freed to view themselves as a healthy unit struggling against a troublesome external problem rather than seeing themselves as an inherently flawed and disabled group of people.

Second-Order Cybernetics

The clinical thrust of the postmodern perspective, as noted earlier, calls for creating a therapeutic environment in which therapist and family members together can share the subjective ideas, perceptions, beliefs, and interpretations each participant gives to family experiences. As its members explore new information, the family is free to create a new perception of reality, allowing itself to experiment with alternative family narratives. Postmodern family therapists such as social worker Lynn Hoffman (2002) are advocates of **second-order cybernetics,** a post-systems reappraisal of cybernetic theorizing that insists there can be no outside, independent observer of a system, since anyone attempting to observe and change a system is by definition a participant who both influences and in turn is influenced by that system. (In contrast, the first-order cybernetic paradigm conceives of two separate systems—the therapist system and the problem-client family system—in which the therapist remains an external observer, an expert who attempts to effect changes by means of interventions from the outside.)

Second-order cyberneticists contend that in doing family therapy the therapist must be aware that several individuals are present, each with his or her own view of reality and description of the family. Thus these cyberneticists emphasize that objectivity per se does not exist; so-called objective descriptions of families are merely social constructions that may say more about the describer than about the family. Rather than be discovered through so-called objective means, the family's "reality" is nothing more than the agreed-upon consensus that occurs through the social interaction of its members (Real, 1990).

---

[4]*Constructivism* and its related postmodern theory of *social constructionism* (Becvar, 2000) offer new, influential epistemological explanations regarding how we know what we know. The former argues that each of our perceptions is not an exact replica of the world, but rather a point of view seen through the limiting lens of assumptions that we make about people. The latter argues that we cannot perceive a true, objective reality, adding that the reality each of us does construct is mediated through language and is socially determined through our relationships with others and the culture's shared set of assumptions. That is, we experience reality in and through language in terms of the prepackaged thoughts of our society.

From this new perspective, a family is composed of multiple perspectives—multiple realities—and the therapist, no longer seen as an outside observer of (or expert on) the problem situation, has a part in constructing the reality being observed. The therapist does not operate as if he or she or any single family member can reveal the "truth" about the family or its problems. Just as with the other participants, what the therapist sees as existing in the family is a product of his or her particular set of assumptions about families and their problems. There are multiple "truths" about every family, not one universal "truth." The therapist, then, can no longer consider any member's viewpoint as a distortion of some presumably correct interpretation of reality that the therapist (or that a particular family member) alone can see.

In this view humans are seen as observing systems who describe, distinguish, and delineate through the use of language. But since none of us sees an objective universe, each family's interpretation of reality is limited by the "stories" members tell themselves about themselves as individuals or as a family. These "stories" not only reflect but, more importantly, define and give meaning to the family's experiences, and in that sense they are self-perpetuating. Rather than talk of a family's "reality testing," advocates of this view argue that we should speak of "consensus testing." Family therapy in the postmodern era, then, becomes a form of family "conversation" to which the therapist is invited. The therapist and family together generate a new narrative, in effect transforming the pathologizing tale that presumably brought the family to family therapy (Doherty, 1991).

Beginning in the late 1970s, some family therapists sympathetic to the cybernetic ideas of Bateson (1972) began to pay attention to the theories of Chilean biologist Humberto Maturana (1978), cognitive scientist Francisco Varela (1979), cyberneticist Heinz von Foerster (1981), and cognitive psychologist Ernst von Glaserfeld (1987), all of whom urged the abandonment of the simple cybernetic notion that a living system could be observed, studied objectively, and changed from the outside. Instead, they placed the observer in that which was being observed. Family therapists such as Hoffman (1990) applied many of these ideas to their work, adopting a second-order cybernetic model—one in which the observing therapist is an integral and recursive part of the family system being observed, co-constructing with family members the meaning of their lives. Instead of providing answers to the family's problems, the therapist and family members together search for meaning and in the process "re-author" lives and relationships.

While first-order cybernetics might well remain the primary focus for many therapists who see family systems as analogous to mechanical systems, these second-order cyberneticists argue that living systems should not be seen as objects that can be programmed from the outside, but rather as self-creating, independent entities. Slovik and Griffith (1992) maintain that the latter group's efforts represent a backlash against what critics perceive as the potential dangers of controlling, manipulative, and authoritarian intervention tactics and strategies. As Hoffman (1990) illustrates:

> A first-order view in family therapy would assume that it is possible to influence another person or family by using this or that technique: I program you; I teach you; I instruct you. A second-order view would mean that therapists include themselves as part of what must change; they do not stand outside. (p. 5)

Family therapists for the most part continue to practice from a cybernetic approach in some form, although considerable controversy exists over how a troubled and dysfunctional family is best helped to change. Is the family therapist an outside expert, a powerful, take-charge change agent who enters a family to observe, disrupt its customary interactive patterns, and then design strategies to alter the family's self-defeating, repetitive patterns? Or is the family therapist a part of the process necessary for change, with his or her own "reality," who creates a context for change through therapeutic conversation and dialogue in the hope of evolving new meaning by changing family premises and assumptions? Should family therapists be action oriented and push for behavioral change, or focus attention on how language creates a reality for people? Minuchin (1991) questions the extent to which the new approach recognizes the institutions and socioeconomic conditions that influence how people live, pointing out that families living in poverty, for example, have been stripped of much of the power to write their own stories.

SUMMARY

A family is a natural social system that occurs in a diversity of forms today and represents a diversity of cultural heritages. Embedded in society at large, it is shaped by a multitude of factors, such as its place and time in history, race, ethnicity, social class membership, religious affiliation, and number of generations in this country. The way it functions—establishes rules, communicates, and negotiates differences between members—has numerous implications for the development and well-being of its members. Families display a recurring pattern of interactional sequences in which all members participate.

Those considered to be enabled families succeed at balancing the needs of their members and the family system as a whole. Gender roles and ideologies, cultural background, and social class considerations play decisive roles in behavioral expectations and attitudes. The meanings, understandings, and assumptions a family makes about the world reflect the narratives and stories it has created about itself. Its relational resiliency may enable it to confront and manage disruptive experiences; that resiliency is forged through adversity, not despite it.

Adopting a relationship perspective, family therapists do not negate the significance of individual intrapsychic processes, but take the broader view that individual behavior is better understood as occurring within the primary network of a family's social system. Such a paradigm shift from traditional ways of understanding a person's behavior calls for a cybernetic epistemology in which

feedback mechanisms are seen to operate to produce both stability and change. The circular causality involved in what transpires between people within a family forces the family therapist to focus on understanding family processes rather than seeking linear explanations.

Within such a framework, the family symptom bearer, or identified patient, is viewed as merely a representative of a system in disequilibrium. Early family therapists believed the symptom itself acts to stabilize the system and relieve family stress. Others viewed symptomatic behavior more as a reaction to family stress than as a protective solution to restore family balance. In another view, it is the repeated but unworkable solutions that themselves become the problem. From a postmodern perspective, breaking with traditional cybernetic notions, symptoms are seen as oppressive, and the family is urged to unite to take back control of its members' lives from these burdensome symptoms.

While most family therapists adhere to some form of a cybernetic epistemology, there is a developing schism between those who operate from a first-order cybernetic model, in which the therapist remains apart from the system being observed and attempts to change family functioning from the outside, and the second-order cybernetic view in which the therapist is seen as part of the observing system, a participant in constructing the reality being observed. The latter represents the increasingly influential theories of constructivism and social constructionism.

RECOMMENDED READINGS

Bateson, G. (1972). *Steps to an ecology of mind.* New York: Dutton.

Coontz, S. (2005). *Marriage, a history: From obedience to intimacy or how love conquered marriage.* New York: Viking.

Gergen, K. J. (1999). *An invitation to social construction.* Thousand Oaks, CA: Sage.

Walsh, F. (1998). *Strengthening family resilience.* New York: Guilford Press.

Walsh, F. (1999b). *Spiritual resources in family therapy.* New York: Guilford Press.

FAMILY DEVELOPMENT: CONTINUITY AND CHANGE

While family life is an ongoing, interactive process and by no means linear, it exists in the linear dimension of time. From a *multigenerational perspective*, such as the one Carter and McGoldrick (1999) offer, generations have a life-shaping impact on each other as families move through **family life cycle** stages. Within the context of the family's current phase of development, a host of intermingled, intergenerational transactions are occurring concurrently. As one generation deals with issues of aging, another is attempting to cope with children leaving home, while still another may be planning careers or beginning to experience intimate adult relationships. Each generation in this system influences and is influenced by the other.

Because the family life cycle progresses in stages (rather than in a smooth, orderly flow of growth), a family can expect periods of transition and change, perhaps followed by relative stability and then change once again, as together its members attempt to cope with changing life circumstances and demands. In the process, the family's relationship system—roles assigned members, closeness between members, boundary shifts—is continuously being defined and redefined. In this chapter, we adopt a developmental framework in order to broaden our understanding of how families typically advance through a series of milestones, emphasizing the issues and tasks to be dealt with at each stage of family life. A family that falters or loses its developmental momentum may need family therapy in order to move forward in fostering each member's individual development (McGoldrick & Carter, 2003).

SOCIAL FACTORS AND THE LIFE CYCLE

As Kliman and Madsen (1999) observe, the dilemmas that families confront as they negotiate life cycle transitions are not theirs alone, but are embedded in social class and culture-bound narratives. Class determines how many options, opportunities, and privileges are open to family members, as well as the resources on hand for coping with foreseeable transitions (coping with the birth of a first child, arranging child care so both parents can work away from home, dealing with a widowed grandmother) or unforeseen ones (birth of a handicapped child, physical or emotional disability, divorce). Rank (2000) contends that

> Just as family therapy often applies a systemic approach to understanding family dynamics, so too must we appreciate that the family is shaped by its hierarchical position in the system we call socioeconomic status. (p. 238)

Social class lifestyles and cultural background are interlinked; both play vital roles in how a family proceeds through its life cycle. The timing of life cycle stages may vary among families from different cultures, as may the tasks considered appropriate at each phase. Spiritual beliefs and practices, within or outside formal religious boundaries, may help families maintain a connection through generations, ensuring that values are passed along to future generations.

There may be significant cultural differences in traditions, rituals, and ceremonies marking life cycle transitions. Degree of ethnic identification, social class, religion, politics, geography, the length of time the group has been in this country, and the severity of discrimination they experience as a group all influence their attachment to tradition (Hines, Garcia-Preto, McGoldrick, Almeida, & Weltman, 1999). Because acculturation typically occurs over many generations, the beliefs and values of the homeland culture and a migrating family's new culture may continue to mingle for several generations after immigration (Hernandez & McGoldrick, 1999).

Assessing and counseling families from different backgrounds, the family therapist must familiarize himself or herself with the cultural context from which the family emerged, the number of generations that have lived in this country, gender roles, religious influences, and so forth. Otherwise, there is the risk of labeling behavior (a Latina woman's devotion to family above her own welfare, an Asian American man's insistence that his parents live with him, to the consternation of his Caucasian wife) as deviant because it may be contrary to a White middle-class therapist's values and cultural experiences. (On the other hand, the therapist must not simply assume an idiosyncratic family pattern represents a cultural norm without investigating its appropriateness or utility for the family.)

DEVELOPING A LIFE CYCLE PERSPECTIVE

Advocates contend that the family life cycle perspective offers a positive view of the family's capacity to retain its stability and continuity at the same time that it evolves and changes its structure as new relational processes occur. It is not so much that a competent family passes through a particular stage stress-free or without resisting change, but rather that it has the resilience to use its potential strengths, resources, and effective interpersonal processes to master the necessary transitions. The more resilient the family, the more capably it reorganizes to deal with disruptions, and thus the more buoyant it appears in bouncing back after temporarily being thrown off course because of developmental transitions (Glantz & Johnson, 1999). Interpersonal conflicts that develop within a family may signal the family's inability to negotiate a particular life cycle passage or transition point; here the family is thought to have become "stuck" between stages of the life cycle and in need of reorganizing in order to better accommodate to the changing needs of its members.

Different family life cycle stages call for the mastery of specific **developmental tasks** by its members (see Table 2.1 for examples of common tasks from infancy

TABLE 2.1 Examples of Developmental Tasks

Age Period	Task
Infancy to preschool	Attachment to caregiver(s) Language Differentiation of self from environment Self-control and compliance
Middle childhood	School adjustment (attendance, appropriate conduct) Academic achievement (e.g., learning to read, do arithmetic) Getting along with peers (acceptance, making friends) Rule-governed conduct (following rules of society for moral behavior and prosocial conduct)
Adolescence	Successful transition to secondary schooling Academic achievement (learning skills needed for higher education or work) Involvement in extracurricular activities (e.g., athletics, clubs) Forming close friendships within and across gender Forming a cohesive sense of self: identity

Source: Masten & Coatsworth, 1998, p. 207

through adolescence). Note that some tasks are universal (e.g., infant attachment to caregivers) while some may be more culture-bound (e.g., the task of developing an individual identity is less commonly found in cultures that emphasize community commitment over individual advancement); see Masten and Coatsworth (1998). Contemporary middle-class American society expects adolescents to behave differently from younger children or from adults; young adults, economic circumstances permitting, are encouraged to develop independence and autonomy. However, developing competencies in a dangerous inner-city environment may call for survival skills that the larger society may consider inappropriate. Different times, such as periods of war, often require different survival skills.

Developmental tasks define role expectations throughout the life cycle. Newly married couples must develop a process for gaining greater closeness and interdependence; the nature of their involvement with one another inevitably changes once they have a child. Parents must remain involved with young children in a way that would be smothering for adolescents (Minuchin, Lee, & Simon, 1996). Family life cycle advocates argue that the family that has difficulty navigating a particular phase may be temporarily vulnerable—but not necessarily dysfunctional—and may need help before feeling empowered to manage the turning point.

CONCEPTUALIZING THE LIFE CYCLE: SOME PRELIMINARY CAUTIONS

A word of caution before proceeding with the life cycle concepts: As we have emphasized, any generalizations we are about to make should be seen within the context of a particular class, culture, and historical period (early twenty-first-century America), and thus are open to periodic revision as changes occur in the larger society. Differences in language, social experiences, the role of religion and spirituality, degree of acculturation, experiences of different families with family violence, and states of the economy are among the issues that need to be considered.

Most family therapists continue to believe that the life course of families evolves through a predictable sequence of stages that are fairly universal, although such issues as the family's migration history, gender roles, its intergenerational hierarchies, child-rearing attitudes and patterns, and the role of the elderly may be especially relevant in therapeutic work with ethnically diverse families. Young Native Americans, for example, seeking an escape from poverty and finding a lack of employment opportunity on the reservation, frequently move to urban areas, thus weakening their ties to the traditional kinship network of Native American family life and its customary stages of development (Sue & Sue, 1999). In her ecosystemic approach to working with Latino families, for example, Falicov (1998) contends that the family therapy encounter is really an engagement between the therapist's and the family's cultural and personal constructions about family life.

One further caution: It is useful to remember that transitions from one stage to the next are rarely accomplished as neatly in real life as stage theory would suggest. Mastering a significant life cycle transition calls for changes in the family system, not merely rearrangements of accommodations between members (which typically go on unnoticed throughout family life). Most transitions occur over several years, and life stages often merge into one another, so that a family may be trying to cope with the same issues and challenges over several stages. The key point to remember here, as Gerson (1995) observes, is that

> each transition requires a family to change, to reset priorities, and to organize to meet the challenges of the new life cycle stage. Therapists can learn much about a family and how it is coping and functioning by assessing how that family meets the challenges of each life cycle transition. (p. 91)

THE FAMILY LIFE CYCLE FRAMEWORK

Most families, regardless of structure or composition or cultural heritage, progress through certain predictable marker events or phases (such as marriage, the birth of a first child, children leaving home, death of grandparents). Each stage is precipitated by a particular life event—what Zilbach (1989) refers to as a *family stage marker*—demanding change and a new adaptation. These passages may occur because of a sudden major change in family composition (for example, birth of twins) or perhaps due to a major shift in autonomy (a family member starting kindergarten, entering adolescence, moving away from home). In other cases, external factors may be stressing the family and demanding new adaptations—a move to a new community, a change in career, coping with a natural disaster, or perhaps a change in economic circumstances. The family, as a developmental system, typically must attempt to deal with the developmental tasks (or unforeseen set of problems) that require mastery and resolution.

Relationships among and between parents, siblings, and extended family members all undergo transitions as the family proceeds through the life cycle. Table 2.2 proposes a series of discrete stages, starting with single young adults leaving home, marrying, having children, launching those children out into the world, and living

TABLE 2.2 Stages of the Family Life Cycle

Family Life Cycle Stage	Emotional Process of Transition: Key Principles	Second-Order Changes in Family Status Required to Proceed Developmentally
Leaving home: single young adults	Accepting emotional and financial responsibility for self	a. Differentiation of self in relation to family of origin b. Development of intimate peer relationship c. Establishment of self in respect to work and financial independence
The joining of families through marriage: the new couple	Commitment to new system	a. Formation of marital system b. Realignment of relationships with extended families and friends to include spouse
Families with young children	Accepting new members into the system	a. Adjusting marital system to make space for children b. Joining in child rearing, financial and household tasks c. Realignment of relationships with extended family to include parenting and grandparenting roles
Families with adolescents	Increasing flexibility of family boundaries to permit children's independence and grandparents' frailties	a. Shifting of parent-child relationships to permit adolescent to move into and out of system b. Refocus on midlife marital and career issues c. Beginning of shift toward caring for older generation
Launching children and moving on	Accepting a multitude of exits from and entries into the family system	a. Renegotiation of marital system as a dyad b. Development of adult-to-adult relationships between grown children and their parents c. Realignment of relationships to include in-laws and grandchildren d. Dealing with disabilities and death of parents (grandparents)
Families in later life	Accepting the shifting generational roles	a. Maintaining own and/or couple functioning and interests in face of physiological decline: exploration of new familial and social role options b. Support for more central role of middle generation c. Making room in the system for the wisdom and experience of the elderly; supporting the older generation without overfunctioning for them d. Dealing with loss of spouse, siblings, and other peers and preparation for death

Source: Carter & McGoldrick, 1999, p. 2

together in later life. While the stages outlined obviously do not fit every family, especially considering the diverse society in which we now live, the table does serve to draw attention to the multigenerational nature of family life as the family continues to change and evolve.

If every family lives in an ever-changing context, a key question becomes: Is the family under stress flexible enough to allow new interactive patterns to emerge in order to meet the developmental needs of its members? The answer tells us how easily and how well the family manages conflict and negotiates the transitions between stages, and thus has a significant impact on its ability to successfully carry out the tasks of the subsequent stage. Should the family become destabilized as its members struggle to accommodate change (for example, the father and mother develop violent disagreements about how late their teenage daughter may stay out on Saturday night and what friends she may be with), stress will be evident. One or more family members may become symptomatic (the daughter becomes angry and withdrawn; the mother becomes depressed, the father feels isolated and alone, and the parents' marriage deteriorates). The more rigid the family's interactive pattern, the less likely the members will be able to negotiate differences, the more the family will struggle against and be stressed by the need to change, and the more likely symptoms will develop within the family system.

As Zilbach (1989) notes, during each stage, family development proceeds through family task accomplishment, and family characteristics of the previous period are carried over into the next stage. If the carrying out of any particular set of tasks is incomplete, impeded, or disturbed, then development is delayed or suspended and these difficulties are carried into the subsequent stage of family development. For example, parents may experience fears of separating from a young child and allowing that child to move out of the immediate family to day care, preschool, or kindergarten. That same fear, unresolved, may later cause conflict between parents and the child in adolescence as separation again becomes a family issue when the adolescent seeks greater freedom and self-direction; still later, it may delay separation from the family by a young adult.

Both continuity and change characterize the family system as it progresses through time. In some cases the changes are orderly, gradual, and continuous; in others they may be sudden, disruptive, and discontinuous. Both call for transformations in the organization of the system. As an example of the latter, a family may suddenly be confronted by unexpected catastrophic events (serious financial reverses, a terrorist attack, death of a young child by drowning, or a random drive-by shooting). Such crises disrupt the family's normal developmental flow and inevitably produce relationship changes within the family system. As Neugarten (1976) points out, the inappropriate or unanticipated timing of a major event may be particularly traumatic precisely because it upsets the sequence and disturbs the rhythm of the expected course of life. To illustrate the point, Neugarten cites the death of a parent during one's childhood, teenage marriage, a first marriage postponed until late in life, or a child born to parents in midlife.

Certain discontinuous changes are so disruptive and impeding to family life that they suddenly and profoundly shake up and transform a family system so that it never returns to its former way of functioning. Hoffman (1988) points particularly to those events that affect family membership—events representing *family gains* (children acquired through remarriage) or *family losses* (separation of parents, death). Even a natural transition point that requires major shifts in roles (a young mother with a preschool child returns to work outside the home, a husband loses his job and cannot find reemployment) may produce discontinuous changes and have a similar effect on the family system.

As noted earlier, many family therapists believe that symptoms in a family member are especially likely to appear at these periods of change, signaling the family's difficulty in negotiating a transition. However, not all the difficulties a family experiences in coping with change, continuous or discontinuous, inevitably lead to symptomatic behavior. The stress on the family system during a transition may actually give the family an opportunity to break out of its customary coping patterns and develop more productive, growth-enhancing responses to change. In particular, families that have developed effective collaborative ways of coping with adversity and hardship—what Walsh (1999b) calls *relational resilience*—may emerge hardier from crises or persistent stresses or the demands for life cycle transitional changes.

For example, a childless couple who are thinking about becoming parents (considered a continuous life change) may fear, and thus postpone, the event because they view it as restricting mobility, increasing responsibility, interrupting sleep, constricting their social life, and so on; or they may welcome parenthood as a move to strengthen the family and invest in its future. (They may, of course, feel both reluctance and eagerness to become parents.) The discontinuous changes often brought about by remarriage may result in disequilibrium, role confusion, and heightened conflict in the new family, or they may provide a second chance to form a more mature, stable relationship. The family therapist is responsible for helping the family to see the full range of its choices, including the possibilities of generating new solutions; the shared belief of the therapist and family in the adaptability of the family system and its potential for growth and self-healing is crucial in helping families engineer change.

A FAMILY LIFE CYCLE STAGE MODEL

The Developmental Stages

Family sociologists such as Evelyn Duvall and Reuben Hill first proposed a developmental framework for studying families in the late 1940s, in an effort to account for regularities in family life over time (Duvall & Hill, 1948). The major thrust of this early contribution was to plot the stages through which families typically pass, and to predict the approximate time when each stage is reached. Although some variations to this model have been offered over the years, family therapists increasingly have turned to Carter and McGoldrick, who beginning in 1980 have broadened the life cycle concept to include a multidimensional, multicultural, multigenerational perspective. Their latest revision (Carter & McGoldrick, 1999) further expands the concept to include individual, family, and sociocultural perspectives. As these authors have most recently formulated their position, the family life cycle perspective "is the natural context within which to frame individual identity and development and to account for the effects of the social system" (p. 1).

Individual life cycles take place within the family life cycle, and the interplay between the two affects what takes place in each. The relationship system within a family expands, contracts, and realigns over the family's life span, and the family must be flexible enough to sustain the entry and exit of members as well as bolster its members' efforts to move on in their own personal development. Families that become derailed in their life cycle (and correspondingly derail individual efforts at independence) need help in getting back on developmental track. A major goal of family therapy in such situations is reestablishing the family's developmental momentum, utilizing the family's inherent but previously unused strengths.

Courtesy of Monica McGoldrick

Monica McGoldrick, MSW

One final note: the relationship between a family's work life (the prevalence of two-paycheck families having long ago exceeded the long-idealized married couple with a single breadwinner father, a homemaker mother, and two children) and its home life needs to be factored into any consideration of family development. Similarly, high divorce rates, single-parent adoptions, children born out of wedlock to teenagers or later in life to older women, the prevalence of unmarried couples, the increased visibility of gays and lesbians, and numerous stepfamily arrangements have complicated the oversimplified picture of what constitutes normal family development. Nevertheless, the life cycle outlook provides one useful organizing framework for understanding a family's conflicts and negotiations, its flexibility in adapting to changing conditions, and the appearance of problematic or symptomatic behavior at a particularly treacherous crossroad. Perhaps its major value is to establish a template for family difficulties, reveal linkages over generations, and focus on family resilience and continuity.

Family Transitions and Symptomatic Behavior

The family life cycle perspective offers a valuable context for understanding individual and family dysfunction, especially for advocates of the **structural** position (Chapter 10), who argue that problems develop within a family with a dysfunctional structure when the family encounters a transition point but lacks the flexibility to adapt to the changing conditions. For example, a young husband and wife who have not achieved sufficient separation from their parents to be able to establish their own independent marital unit may experience considerable distress, conflict, and confusion when they prepare to enter the next phase of their family life—the birth and rearing of their own children.

Strategists (Chapter 11) also view the appearance of symptoms as a signal that the family is unable to move on to the next stage; as one example, Haley (1979) argues that some families may need therapeutic help in solving problems evoked by a young adult member ready to leave home and embark on a more independent life. In general, Haley views individual symptomatology as arising from an interruption of the family's normal developmental process, and thus he is likely to direct his efforts at helping the family as a whole resolve the impasse that they are experiencing as a group.

Following up on Duvall's (1977) classic formulation of the stages of family development, Barnhill and Longo (1978) differentiate specific transition points that require negotiation as families pass through each stage (see Table 2.3). They contend that families, much like individuals, can become fixated or arrested at a particular phase of development, and thus may fail to make the necessary transition at the appropriate time. Under stress, again like individuals, families may regress to an earlier transition point, when a successful life cycle passage had been made. In Barnhill and Longo's conceptualization, symptoms appearing in any family member (for example, adolescent delinquent behavior) are evidence that the immediate family life task has not been mastered. Anxiety and distress are thought to be at their maximum at transition points as the family tries to cope, rebalance, realign, and restore stability.

McGoldrick and Carter (2003), with a renewed emphasis on both the family and the larger cultural context, provide a more encompassing, intergenerational view of the

TABLE 2.3 Common Transition Points Through the Life Cycle

Duvall Stage	Major Transition to Be Achieved
1. Married couple	Commitment to each other
2. Childbearing family	Developing parent roles
3. Preschool children	Accepting child's personality
4. School children	Introducing children to institutions (school, church, sports group)
5. Teenagers	Accepting adolescence (social and sexual role changes)
6. Launching children	Experimenting with independence
7. Middle-aged parents	Accepting child's independent adult role
8. Aging family members	Letting go—facing each other again
	Accepting old age

Source: Based on Duvall, 1977, and Barnhill and Longo, 1978

impact of multiple stresses on a family's ability to navigate transitions. They believe the flow of anxiety within a family is related to both "vertical" and "horizontal" stressors (see Figure 2.1). Vertical stressors are patterns of relating and functioning transmitted historically through generations—family attitudes, stories[1], expectations, secrets, taboos, and loaded family issues passed along from grandparents to parents to children. Members of all families receive such legacies while growing up, listening to family narratives concerning family experiences that formed the basis for a "family line" or set of prejudgments in viewing new events and situations. The vertical axis also includes any biological heritage, genetic makeup, temperament, and possible congenital disabilities within the family. Any racism, sexism, poverty, homophobic attitudes, as well as family prejudices and patterns of relating carried over from earlier generations add to these vertical stressors. In the words of the authors, the vertical axis represents those aspects of our lives that are "the hand we are dealt. What we do with them is the question."

Horizontal stressors describe the events experienced by the family as it moves forward through time, coping with changes and transitions of the life cycle—the various predictable developmental stresses as well as unexpected, traumatic ones (such as an untimely death, birth of a handicapped child, a serious accident, migration). Traumatic experiences—terrorism, war, economic depression, and natural disasters—are included here, as are social policies affecting the family.

---

[1]As we noted in Chapter 1, in discussing the constructivist view of the appearance of symptomatic behavior in a family member, each family's self-picture is at least partly based on "stories" it has created about itself. These stories often are passed along over generations and may be a source of comfort (how we Sinclairs always come through adversity whatever the odds) or despair (how we Garcias always end up with the short end of the stick, regardless of our efforts). Similarly, a group's history, especially a legacy of trauma, affects future generations (the Holocaust on Jews and Germans, slavery on African Americans and slave-owning groups). The current interest in genealogy represents an effort to feel part of the continuity of one's family's history.

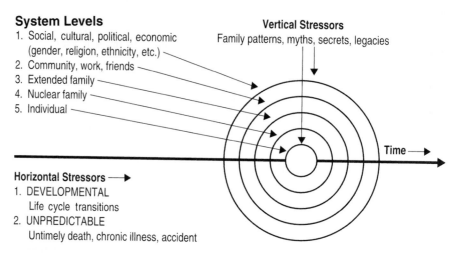

System Levels
1. Social, cultural, political, economic (gender, religion, ethnicity, etc.)
2. Community, work, friends
3. Extended family
4. Nuclear family
5. Individual

Vertical Stressors
Family patterns, myths, secrets, legacies

Time ⟶

Horizontal Stressors ⟶
1. DEVELOPMENTAL
   Life cycle transitions
2. UNPREDICTABLE
   Untimely death, chronic illness, accident

FIGURE 2.1 Horizontal and vertical stressors

With enough stress on the horizontal axis, any family will appear dysfunctional. For a family that is full of stress on the vertical axis, even a small amount of horizontal stress can disrupt the family system. Any amount of horizontal stress (say, the revelation of a teenage girl's pregnancy or the "coming out" of a homosexual adolescent boy) can cause great disruption to a family whose vertical axis is already intensely stressed (excessive family concerns about appearances of moral rectitude). Should such an event occur at a transition point (in our examples, late adolescence), family dysfunction—temporary or longer lasting—is likely to occur. As McGoldrick and Carter (2003) observe:

> The anxiety engendered on the vertical and horizontal axes when they converge, as well as the interaction of the various systems and how they work together to support or impede one another, are the key determinants of how well a family will manage its transitions through life. (p. 381)

In general, the greater the anxiety "inherited" from previous generations at any transition point (say, anxieties over being parents and raising children, passed on by a woman's parents), the more anxiety-producing and dysfunctional this point will be for that young mother expecting her first child. In this example, when horizontal (or developmental) stresses intersect with vertical (or transgenerational) stresses, there is a quantum leap in anxiety in the system. Concurrent external stresses—death, illness, financial setbacks, moving to a new and unfamiliar community—as a family progresses through its life cycle add to the stress. The point where the axes converge, then, becomes a key determinant of how well the family will manage the transition point. What we may conclude is how imperative it is for family therapists to attend not only to a family's current life cycle stresses but also to their connections to family themes handed down over generations.

Critique of the Stage Model

While the stage model of family development just presented offers a valuable context for conceptualizing individual and family dysfunction, its shortcomings too require

BOX 2.1 CLINICAL NOTE

Migration and the Life Cycle

Immigrants to North America are a diverse group in economic background, race, ethnicity, and religious beliefs and practices (Booth, Crouter, & Landale, 1997). In contrast to the early years of the previous century, when most new entrants came almost exclusively from Europe, today's immigrants are primarily from Latin America and Asia. While some come as documented migrants, others, such as those from Mexico and Central America, are frequently undocumented and must attempt to gain entry through illegal means. Nearly 80 percent of all immigrants are people of color. One in five children in the United States today is a child of an immigrant family (Suarez-Orozco & Suarez-Orozco, 2001).

For most immigrant families, migration is a major life event because of its potential peril as they seek refuge in an unfamiliar land. From pre-migration stress (often leaving home and loved ones), to the stress of the migration experience itself (especially for undocumented individuals) to learning to survive in a strange environment, the dislocation process is filled with duress alongside hope for a better future. Post-migration adjustments often involve a struggle and a sense of depletion (Sluzki, 1979). In many cases, familiar family and occupational roles are lost. Family elders may lose status within the family as a result of assimilating more slowly to the language and lifestyle of the new land than do their adolescent family members. For example, a parent who was an engineer or teacher in the old country may be able to find work only in lower-status jobs as a construction worker or manicurist.

The reasons for migration (war, famine, relief from political or religious persecution) are often significant, and its accompanying acculturative consequences (problems with employment, housing, language, xenophobia, and discrimination) may be traumatic and affect life cycle development. Wong and Mock (1997) describe role reversals in immigrant Asian families, as children gain quicker proficiency in the use of English than their parents, undermining traditional cultural norms of parental authority. Falicov (1998) points to the cross-cultural dilemmas as Latino families try to make sense of adapting to American life and raise children according to the style of the dominant culture. Among Mexican American families, migration may be more than a one-time event, as illegal border crossers who have been apprehended and deported try again for entry, or simply leave, returning as work becomes available. Such an ongoing and prolonged process calls for parent-child separations, as parents attempt to immigrate ahead of their children, or in other cases send the children ahead; in either case, the breaking of ties within the nuclear family may have long-term negative consequences (Santisteban, Muir-Malcolm, Mitrani, & Szapocznik, 2002).

Fleeing one's native country is likely to be far more traumatic and to be filled with intense ambivalence than a voluntary relocation seeking a more prosperous life. Whether members of a family migrate together or in sequence may also affect their adaptation. Educational level, social class, gender, age at the time of immigration, community support in the new land, as well as the family's developmental stage of the family life cycle all are significant factors in adaptation. The experience of racial, religious, anti-immigration discrimination, or lack of economic opportunity all negatively influence the migration experience (Falicov, 2003).

acknowledgment. The concept is essentially descriptive rather than explanatory. It purports to offer normative data on intact family life at a time in history when a diversity of lifestyles (delayed marriages, unmarried motherhood, childless families) and a variety of living arrangements (single-parent-led families, cohabiting heterosexual as well as homosexual couples, stepfamilies) are prevalent and functional. The approach fails to take into account individual differences in the timing of nodal events (for example, due to postponed marriages and/or delayed pregnancies). By strongly suggesting that what transpires within the stages is all-important, this approach does a disservice to the equally important—perhaps more important—transitions between stages, which are key periods of change. By attending primarily to intact families, it reflects an ever-decreasing portion of American society. Its arbitrary punctuations of stages tend to obscure the ongoing and relationship-based flow of family life.

Combrinck-Graham (1988) argues that while family development may be linear, family life is anything but—it does not begin at any particular point, nor does it have a clear-cut ending point. Rather, she believes family movement through time is cyclical, or more accurately, proceeds as a spiral. That is, at certain times family members are tightly involved with one another; Combrinck-Graham considers these times of pulling together, as when a new child is born or a serious illness in a family member occurs, as *centripetal* periods. At other times (starting school, beginning a career), individual moves take precedence, and *centrifugal* periods occur. In this formulation there is an oscillation in family life, not the tidy and continuous unidirectional flow suggested by stage theory. At times the family members tend to be oriented inward; at other times they move toward interests outside the family. Combrinck-Graham contends that three-generational families are likely to alternate between centripetal and centrifugal states (keeping members together and pushing them apart, respectively) as events occurring in a particular life cycle period call for greater interdependence or individuation.

Breunlin (1988) agrees that family development is rarely a discrete and discontinuous shift from one life stage to a subsequent stage separated by arbitrary transitions, but rather occurs as gradual oscillations (or microtransitions) between stages as the family makes its way to the next developmental level. He emphasizes that families are far more complex than the stage model suggests, and that in reality development in most families, as we noted earlier, involves multiple simultaneous transitions as various members are undergoing differing degrees of interlocking life changes.

Laszloffy (2002) finds two conceptual flaws in the life cycle approach to studying families. First, defining the specific number, types, and timing of stages perpetuates the assumption of universality—that all families, regardless of composition or culture develop in the same order, ignoring the infinite variations possible between families. Second, she argues that the life cycle approach is biased toward a single generation (such as launching a family member) and fails to attend to the intergenerational and interactional complexities of families (launching and the reciprocal leaving stage).

While these modifications more accurately describe what actually occurs, the life cycle concept nevertheless offers a workable organizing schema for assessing family functioning and planning interventions. Family therapists have attempted to wed a cybernetic epistemology (emphasizing circular causality and feedback loops) to this more sociologically focused developmental framework, going beyond the arbitrary punctuations of stage theory in order to view families as composed of interconnected members engaged in ongoing, interactive processes with one another.

That interconnection may alternate between degrees of closeness and separateness, depending on life circumstances, over the family's life cycle. Family dysfunction may signal that the family is at a developmental impasse. The appearance of symptomatic behavior may thus be seen as a manifestation of the stress the family is experiencing around a transitional event. Or perhaps the family is rigidly organized and cannot change its organizational structure to accommodate new developmental requirements. Continuing to view the family as a process-oriented system comes closer to describing the interconnection of family members over time.

CHANGING FAMILIES, CHANGING RELATIONSHIPS

In this section we attempt to elaborate on common developmental issues of intact families, contrasting these with the unique life cycle experiences of a variety of other families due to divorce, remarriage, adoptions, or same-sex relationships.

Developmental Sequences in Intact Families

Family therapists are apt to depart from the traditional sociological view of the family life cycle commencing at the time of marriage, arguing that single young adults must first complete their primary developmental task: separating from the family of origin without cutting off from them and fleeing to a substitute emotional refuge. Especially in middle-class families, separation from parents is made more difficult today because of longer periods of education leading to prolonged financial dependency, increased housing costs, and so on. Delayed marriages due to career demands, possible fear of sexual experimentation because of sexually transmitted diseases such as AIDS, a general acceptance of later marriages, and apprehension about the longevity of marriage all make commitment to the new relationship more tenuous. In contrast, the poor or working-class African American young man is likely to be further delayed in developing independence because of joblessness and despair about future opportunities, and he often learns to project an external demeanor that masks the disappointment, hopelessness, and helplessness he is experiencing (Hines, 1999).

Becoming an Adult

The primary task of becoming an adult, as Fulmer (1999) puts it, is to leave home but stay connected to one's family of origin. Rather than "breaking ties" and becoming autonomous, young people, regardless of class or cultural background, continue to rely on families for tangible and emotional support as they prepare for work and attachments outside the family. While men have traditionally been expected to work and become self-supporting, women today of all social classes share the goal of finding meaning in work and becoming independent. As a result, more than ever before, White middle- and upper-class women especially are likely to live away from family and on their own before marrying, putting off marriage until they complete their education and launch careers. Working-class people are apt to marry earlier, often viewing marriage as a means of defining themselves as adults (Rank, 2000). Often they move from the family home to a marriage without having experienced living alone and being economically self-sufficient. The same may be true for many Orthodox Jews or Christian fundamentalists.

Poorer African American women, with fewer prospects of pursuing schooling or a subsequent career, may find it hard to imagine that their socioeconomic opportunities will ever improve, and thus may find little reason to delay having children (Ludtke, 1997). Other disadvantaged minorities are apt to have the same reaction to their situation. Among the severely economically impoverished, the likelihood of marriage may be substantially reduced, at least partly due to the paucity of financially secure potential partners.

Coupling

Finding and committing to a partner is, typically, the next developmental task, and in general takes place later than in the past. The pair must move from *independence* to *interdependence* in this stage—what Gerson (1995) labels *coupling*. Whether in a heterosexual union involving marriage or cohabitation or a same-sex pairing (hence the generic term *coupling*), the two people must decide to commit to one another. Especially in the case of a legal marriage, more than a union of two people is involved; the mating represents a change in two established family systems and the formation of a subsystem (the new couple) in each. Less formally bound by family traditions than couples in the past, and thus with fewer models to emulate, today's young, newly married pair must go about differentiating themselves as a couple with primary allegiance to one another and only secondary allegiance to their families of origin. (Both sets of parents must also let go.)

Commitment to the partnership is the key to managing the transition of detaching sufficiently from each of their families and forming a new cohesive paired unit. In some cases, living with a succession of partners may precede finding the ultimate mate. Early marriages may represent a cultural norm (e.g., Latinos) or an effort to escape their families of origin and create a family they never had (McGoldrick, 1999). On the other hand, fear of intimacy and commitment may delay marriage for many men; for older women with careers, there may be fear of losing their independence once married.

Creating a Family

Marriage links two lives through an immense range of experiences; it involves learning to be separate and together, to allocate power, to pool financial and emotional resources, to shape a sexual life, to share intimate as well as mundane feelings, and, most challenging, to rear another generation (Napier, 2000). Ideally, both partners need to feel they are part of a "we" without sacrificing an "I"—a sense of self as separate and autonomous. Even if the couple have lived together before marriage and have established a satisfying and fulfilling sexual pattern, the transition to becoming marital partners represents a significant milestone, with numerous adjustments (negotiating a level of emotional intimacy, working out power arrangements, deciding whether to have children and when, determining their degree of connection to their extended families and friends, as well as which family traditions to retain and which to modify or abandon) required as they become husband and wife (Almeida, Woods, Messineo, & Font, 1998). The adaptational problems may become even more formidable if partners have different ethnic or racial or religious backgrounds and bring different assumptions and expectations into the new marriage.

Each partner in an intact relationship has acquired from his or her family a set of antecedent patterns, traditions, and expectations for marital interaction and family life. In a sense the two have come from separate "cultures" with differing customs, values, rituals, beliefs, gender roles, prejudices, aspirations, and experiences. Parts of both paradigms must be retained so that each person maintains a sense of self; the two paradigms must also be reconciled in order for the couple to have a life in common.

In the process of reconciling these differences, spouses arrive at new transactional patterns—accommodations or tacit agreements to disagree—that then become familiar and ultimately their preferred or habitual way of interacting with each other. For some, such commitment comes easily—they want to be together whenever possible, share private thoughts and intimacies, experience no problem pooling their earnings, call each other at work one or more times a day, and focus on growing closer as a marital couple. For others, such a connection is fraught with hesitations; reluctant to abandon the life they led as single persons, they insist on maintaining separate bank accounts, taking separate vacations, and pursuing weekend activities with friends or separate families of origin rather than spending time together. For this latter group, learning to cooperate and compromise over differences takes a longer time; in some cases it is never achieved.

In creating a family, the partners must not only provide for their basic physical needs but also continually negotiate such personal issues as when and how to sleep, eat, make love, fight, and make up. They must decide how to celebrate holidays, plan vacations, spend money, and do household chores; what to watch on television (and who controls the remote unit) or what other forms of entertainment they both enjoy. They are obliged to decide which family traditions and rituals to retain from each of their pasts and which they wish to generate as their own. Together they need to determine the degree of closeness to or distance from each of their families of origin they wish to maintain. Each has to gain admission to the other's family, in some cases as the first person to do so in many years.

The Arrival of Children

In the case of a married couple, at first the system tends to be loosely organized and the spouses' roles are flexible and often interchangeable. The structure of a family without children allows for a wide variety of solutions to immediate problems. For example, either or both of the partners may prepare dinner at home; they may choose to eat out at a restaurant; they may drop in at a friend's or relative's house for a meal; they may eat separately or together. When there are children to be fed, however, a more formal and specific arrangement will have to be formulated in advance of dinnertime. Beyond making room for children in their lives, psychologically as well as physically, the couple must more clearly define the distribution of duties and division of labor: Who will shop, pick up the children at a nursery or child-care center or at a relative's home, prepare meals, wash the dishes, put their offspring to bed, handle the increased laundry load, and get the children ready in the morning? The commitment of husband and wife, then, to become mother and father represents a significant transition point in a family's life, changing forever the relatively simple playing out of roles between mates who are childless. As Karpel and Strauss (1983) observe, virtually all patterns of time, schedule, expenditures, leisure, use of space in the home, and especially relationships with in-laws and friends are likely to become reorganized around the child.

The arrival of children—the family *expansion* phase (Gerson, 1995)—thus represents the most significant milestone in the life cycle of the family. The partners' lives may not have changed nearly as much when the two first married; this is even more likely if they lived together before marriage and/or established a satisfactory premarital sexual relationship. When husband and wife become parents, however, both "move up" a generation and now must provide care for a younger generation. Other members of the family **suprasystem** also move up a notch—parental siblings become uncles and aunts; nieces and nephews now become cousins; the parents of the new mother and father become grandparents. Overall, a vertical realignment occurs for new family and extended family together. A major task for new parents is to integrate their new relationships to the child with their previously existing relationship with one another. A revised sense of individual identity is likely to occur once the partners become parents, and relative commitments to work and family must be reconsidered.

Making this transition, taking and sharing child-care responsibilities, practicing patience, setting limits, tolerating restrictions on free time and mobility—all of these tasks must be mastered in the expanding family system. Young parents, particularly if both are employed full-time, each must now juggle schedules and attempt to find an acceptable balance between work and domestic responsibilities. At the same time, husband and wife need to redefine and redistribute household and child-care chores, decide how they will earn a living with one breadwinner for a period of time, and determine how best to resume sexual and social activities. The formerly childless couple must find new ways of maintaining and nurturing their relationship, despite the substantial decrease in time and energy for private moments together (Kaslow, Smith, & Croft, 2000).

A young middle-class couple's previously egalitarian role structure and dual earning capacity may break down. They may resort to more traditional male-female divisions of labor, earnings, and power, which may create unexpected conflicts and additional stress. Older parents must learn to accommodate young children in an already established or perhaps fixed pattern of relationships, often without being able to call upon elderly grandparents for support. Regardless of ethnic group or social class, however, the birth of children, as Hines (1999) observes, hastens a young couple's need to connect (or reconnect) to the extended family network—perhaps for occasional child care, and almost certainly for emotional if not financial support. In Latino families, an intricate network of grandparents and other relatives typically helps with child care, in addition to providing "plentiful coaching and advice" (Falicov, 1999, p. 142).

Coping with Adolescence

When children reach adolescence, the family faces new organizational challenges, particularly around autonomy and independence. Parents may no longer be able to maintain complete authority, but they cannot abdicate authority altogether. Here the family is not dealing with entrances and exits into the system but rather with a basic restructuring of interactive processes to allow the teenager more independence (Harway & Wexler, 1996). The task becomes even more complex in immigrant families, as the adolescent's normal striving for self-directed behavior is accelerated through assimilation into mainstream American society, while the parents may continue to adhere to their traditional cultural values of parental authority and control (Santisteban, Muir-Malcolm, Mitrani, & Szapocznik, 2002). In poor African American, Latino, or Asian families, adolescents are often expected to fulfill adult caretaking duties for younger siblings, or to contribute financially to the home, yet to remain obedient and respectful of parents (Preto, 1999). In such cases, becoming independent may not have the same family value that it does for Anglo American middle-class groups.

Rule changing, limit setting, and role renegotiations are all necessary, as adolescents seek greater self-determination, depending less on parents and moving toward their peer culture for guidance and support. Adolescents must strike a balance on their own, forging an identity and beginning to establish autonomy from the family. Teenagers who remain too childlike and dependent or who become too isolated and withdrawn from the family put a strain on the family system. Too rapid an exit from family life by adolescents may also impair a family's ability to adapt. Parents, too, need to come to terms with their teenager's rapidly changing social and sexual behavior. Depending on the spacing of children, parents may find themselves dealing with issues relevant to differing ages and life cycle stages at the same time. Rebellion is not uncommon—in political or religious views, dress, drugs, music, curfew violations, gang behavior, ear piercing, tattoos—as adolescents attempt to gain distance from parental rules.

All of this is likely to occur while simultaneous strains on the system may be taking place: (a) "midlife crises" in which one or both middle-aged parents question not only career choices but also perhaps their earlier marital choices (for some women, this may represent the first opportunity to pursue a career without child-care responsibilities, leading to family dislocations and role changes); and (b) the need to care for impaired grandparents, necessitating role reversals between parents and now-dependent grandparents, perhaps calling for changing caretaking arrangements regarding the older generation.

Leaving Home

Gerson (1995) refers to the next period as one of *contraction;* McGoldrick and Carter (2003) describe this phase of the intact family's life cycle as "launching children and moving on." Unlike in earlier times, today the low birth rate coupled with longer life expectancy means that this stage now covers a lengthy period; parents frequently launch their families almost 20 years before retirement. They must come to accept their children's independent role and eventual creation of their own families. This stage, beginning with the exit by grown children from the family home, proceeds with the later re-entry of their spouses and children into the family system.

Creating adult-to-adult relationships with their children is an important developmental task for parents at this stage, as is the expansion of the family to include the spouses, children, and in-laws of their married children. Once again, assimilated young adults from immigrant families may find their desire for freedom and autonomy in conflict with their parents, such as in Latino families, where children are expected to remain in the parental home until they are married or well into their twenties (Santisteban, Muir-Malcolm, Mitrani, & Szapocznik, 2002).

Reorganizing Generational Boundaries

Parents also need to reassess their relationship with one another now that their children no longer reside at home. Sometimes couples view this change as an opportunity for freedom from child-rearing responsibilities and perhaps, if economically feasible, a chance to travel or explore other activities postponed for financial reasons or time restraints while they cared for their children. Now, in the absence of the care of children, these families see a chance to strengthen their marital bond. In other families, marital strains covered over while they raised children together may resurface with the children gone. Children leaving may in such cases lead to increased marital strife or feelings of depression and loneliness over life becoming empty and meaningless. It is not uncommon for such parents to hold onto their offspring, especially the last child.

Parents now need to cope with moving up a notch to grandparent positions; at the same time, increased caretaking responsibilities for their own needy and dependent parents, especially by women, is likely. In some cases, the renewal of the parent-grandparent relationship provides an opportunity to resolve earlier interpersonal conflicts; in other cases, it may simply exacerbate unresolved conflict from earlier days. A major transition point for the middle-aged adult is apt to revolve around the death of elderly parents.

Another family life cycle stage is reached by the time the children enter their forties, according to transgenerational theorist Donald Williamson (1991), when another level of intimacy is achieved between generations and when the old hierarchical boundaries, ideally, are replaced by a greater peer relationship. Their parents, now in their retirement years, must cope with a dramatic increase in their daily time together—and, frequently, with a reduction in income. Enduring the loss of friends and relatives (and most difficult of all, loss of a spouse); coping with increased dependence on one's children; handling changing relationships with grandchildren; possibly relinquishing power and status; coming to terms with one's own illness, limitations, and ultimate death—these are some of the problems of old age. With the death of one partner, the family must often assume care of the surviving parent at home or in a nursing home, with all family members experiencing a new set of transitional stresses. In some cases, the relationship loss as a result of Alzheimer's disease in an elderly person adds to family caregiver stress.

Retirement and Widowhood

Froma Walsh (1999a) suggests that changes brought about by retirement, widowhood, grandparenthood, and chronic illness/caregiving all represent major adaptational challenges for the entire family system, as it attempts to cope with loss and dysfunction and tries to reorganize itself. Retirement is likely to mean more than a loss of income; loss of identity, status, purpose, and being an important part of a community also are involved, and family relationships must be renegotiated.

A grandparent's death may be the young child's first encounter with separation and loss and, at the same time, may be a reminder to the parents of their own mortality. Illness in elderly parents calls for role reversals with their children; the process is often a source of struggle and embarrassment. In Litwin's (1996) survey of the social network of older persons, he found that those who worked at maintaining a network of relationships with family and friends were likely to live longer, more fulfilled lives.

Developmental Sequences in Other Families

The family developmental approach outlined by sociologists in the 1940s, with its predictable life cycle stages and concurrent developmental tasks, could hardly be expected to have anticipated life circumstances a half century later. Divorce, which was an unusual phenomenon at that time, today has become a familiar and recognized fact of American life, with approximately 1 million divorces occurring annually in this country. Divorce inevitably touches family members at every generation and throughout the nuclear as well as extended families. The divorce process and its sequelae inevitably have a powerful, disruptive impact on all family members, parents and children alike, and all must be taken into account in gaining a full measure of the subsequent dislocations to all participants (Simons, 1996). Most families, however, demonstrate ample rebounding ability in making the necessary adjustments, particularly if the former mates continue mutually supportive co-parenting (Whiteside & Becker, 2000).

The divorce process itself typically occurs over time and in stages, and more likely than not is marked by a great deal of stress, ambivalence, indecision, self-doubt, and uncertainty, even when both partners agree that the marriage is no longer viable. When children are involved, particularly young children, the decision becomes all the more deliberate and painful. Kressel (1985) characterizes the divorce process as "one of the more demanding tasks that rational beings are expected to perform" (p. 4).

Single-Parent-Led Families

One-parent households, which now represent one in four families with children under 18 in the United States, come in a variety of sizes (reflecting the number of children and the number of previous divorces), composition (with or without friends or extended families), and situations (with or without the involvement of ex-mates, with or without financial resources, living alone or with parents) (Anderson, 2003). They are likely to be part of one of the following groupings:

- A divorced person (84 percent women, 16 percent men) with child custody
- An unmarried teenage mother with a planned or unplanned child
- An older unmarried biological mother with a planned or unplanned child
- A single person, male or female, gay or straight, who adopts a child
- An unmarried woman, gay or straight, who chooses impregnation through donor insemination
- A widow or widower with children or stepchildren

Most single-parent-led families are the product of divorce, although in recent years their numbers have swelled due to the general rise in the social acceptance of single women of all socioeconomic situations having children out of wedlock. These include not only teenage mothers but also older women, often in successful professional careers and financially able, who are nearing the end of their childbearing years and wish to experience motherhood (Miller, 1992). Single males who gain custody of their children following a divorce, or who as single parents adopt children—practically unheard of until two decades ago—now represent a significant proportion of all single-parent families (Bianchi, 1995). (We'll consider gay and lesbian adoptions and the use of artificial insemination in the following section.)

In most contemporary post-divorce situations, largely due to efforts of the men's movement, **joint legal custody** is common, so that both ex-partners retain legal authority as parents and share, depending on their ability and willingness to do so, in the decisions regarding the raising of their children. In such situations, members of the extended family—grandparents, aunts, and uncles—often continue to play key supporting roles (Everett & Volgy Everett, 2000). This trend may be especially significant in the case of minority, low-income single families, where a broad support system is common and often may prove essential. Close to half of all African American children live with single parents (Fine, McKenrey, & Chung, 1992), and *informal adoptions* (in which relatives of friends care for children when birth parents are temporarily or permanently unable to do so) have a history that goes back to slavery days. As Lindblad-Goldberg (1989) demonstrated in her work with 126 successful African American, female-headed, single-parent households, many of the social and psychological problems of growing up in a single-parent-led family (and there are many for parent and children alike) are more a function of family poverty than of an inevitable breakdown of the family structure.

Due to a steady high rate of separation and divorce over several decades, adoptions, widowhood, and gay parenting, as well as to the increasing number of out-of-wedlock births to both teenage and older women, single-parent households now represent the fastest growing family type in the United States (Cox, 1996). Close to 20 million children under 18 now live with one parent; Hetherington, Bridges, and Insabella (1998) predict that between 50 and 60 percent of children born in the 1990s will live, at some point, in single-family settings.

The most glaring difference between two-parent families and those headed by divorced or never-married mothers is the disparity in economic well-being; the latter, particularly those with young children, are likely to be worse off financially than any other type of family organization. Mother-headed families especially are characterized by a high rate of poverty, a high percentage of minority representation, relatively low education, and a high rate of downward mobility. As such, they are likely to be over-stressed, with few opportunities for pleasure or relaxation, living in troubled communities which offer few resources and potential danger to their children and themselves (Simons, 1996). Some may take romantic partners into the household for financial, sexual, or protective purposes; in many cases, they find themselves in live-in abusive relationships that they fear leaving because of an inability to survive financially on their own. Many nonresident fathers do not pay child support or do so sporadically; the problem with such so-called "deadbeat dads" is especially severe for single mothers who never married. In some poor families, although regular financial support from fathers is not forthcoming, help in the form of occasional groceries, diapers, baby-sitting, labor around the house, and some small, intermittent monetary contributions may occur.

The divorced mother with physical custody of her children usually must deal not only with lowered economic status but also with grief and self-blame, loneliness, and an inadequate support system. She must also deal with child-care arrangements, custody and visitation problems, and more. Frequently she carries the entire burden of raising a child alone in what is often an emotionally and physically unstable environment (Miller, 1992), balancing the multiple responsibilities of work and family. Despite these obstacles, resiliency is often present, and as Seibt (1996) observes:

> The children raised by single parents can be just as healthy and normal as those raised in the traditional two-parent family. In fact, despite the obstacles, children in most single-parent families are provided with the love and nurturing that all children need and deserve. (p. 41)

Single fathers with custody also experience financial pressures, although these problems are likely to be less severe than those of single mothers, who usually have more limited earning potential. Because commitment to job and career have probably been the highest priority for these single fathers, a shift in focus is necessary, and not being able to spend sufficient time with their children is often a major complaint. Those who opt for a close, nurturing relationship with their children must often learn new roles, change their circle of friends, and rebuild their social lives (Seibt, 1996). Frequently they turn to extended family members, girlfriends, or ex-wives for help with childcare, and as Anderson (2003) observes, in contrast to single mothers, single fathers are often viewed as noble for the parenting efforts.

In the following case, a religious couple splits into two single-parent households following their marital breakup.

BOX 2.2   CASE STUDY

A RELIGIOUS COUPLE DIVIDES INTO TWO SINGLE-PARENT HOUSEHOLDS

Joseph and Sarah, both previously married, were Orthodox Jews who took their religion seriously. The met at temple services, were attracted to one another physically as well as spiritually, and after knowing each other for a year they decided to marry. Joseph, 40, an accountant, had custody of his two daughters from his earlier marriage, and Sarah, 39, childless but eager to have a family, agreed to take on parental responsibility.

Consistent with their religious beliefs, they were eager to have children together, but Sarah found it difficult to get pregnant. By the time she was in her mid-40s, they had attempted a variety of assisted reproduction techniques, mostly ending in failure and frustration. Joseph was ready to give up when Sarah got pregnant with a son, and the following year, using the same reproductive procedure, gave birth to a daughter.

Now the parents of four children, Sarah and Joseph were exhausted—physically, financially, emotionally. Religious beliefs, which had been a cornerstone of their relationship, soon became an area of conflict. Even though their religious devotion had been a source of their original connection to one another, they now began to struggle over its observance; Sarah wanted more strict involvement in religious rituals and synagogue attendance, while her husband was comfortable with his current degree of participation. As she became more critical of him, he withdrew, which led to further angry interaction between them. After ten years of marriage, they got divorced.

One immediate effect was a serious drop in income for both ex-partners. Joseph's older children had moved out with him, creating two single-parent households, and Joseph refused to let Sarah visit with them. She insisted that their younger children continue to attend religious school, but he refused to pay for it, claiming the divorce had strapped him of any money beyond the amount required for daily necessities. Sarah tried turning to the Orthodox community, normally cohesive and supportive, but soon found that community focused on family life, and she felt further isolated. Turning to her parents, she found that they opposed the divorce, blamed her for the breakup, and refused to offer more than the minimal assistance.

Under the stress of being an older mother and single parent, and without feedback from the other parent, Sarah's child-rearing techniques became more fixed and unbending, and frequent mother-child conflicts ensued. The children were distressed by the loss of contact with their half-siblings, as well as the constant bickering over finances whenever the parents were together. Sarah complained of feeling isolated, impoverished, unable to develop a social network. Joseph also felt overwhelmed by the task of raising teenage daughters on his own, although he sometimes asked women friends or his mother for help when he felt particularly burdened. Both parents felt lonely, fatigued, depressed, and discouraged about a future alone.

While sole custody still remains the most common situation, joint legal custody, increasingly awarded by the courts, allows both parents equal authority regarding their children's general welfare, education, and so on. The children may reside with one parent, but both parents have equal access to them. This **binuclear family** (Ahrons & Rodgers, 1987) arrangement, of course, works out best when the former marital partners are each caring and committed parents, are able to cooperate, have relatively equal and consistent parenting skills, and are able to work together without continuing old animosities (Goldenberg & Goldenberg, 2002). The point here is that while the nuclear family no longer lives as one unit, divorce has not ended the family but simply restructured (and frequently expanded) it.

TABLE 2.4 An Additional Stage of the Family Life Cycle for Divorcing Families

Phase		Emotional Process of Transition: Prerequisite Attitude	Developmental Issues
Divorce	The decision to divorce	Acceptance of inability to resolve marital tensions sufficiently to continue relationship	Acceptance of one's own part in the failure of the marriage
	Planning the breakup of the system	Supporting viable arrangements for all parts of the system	a. Working cooperatively on problems of custody, visitation, and finances b. Dealing with extended family about the divorce
	Separation	a. Willingness to continue cooperative co-parental relationship and joint financial support of children b. Work on resolution of attachment to spouse	a. Mourning loss of intact family b. Restructuring marital and parent-child relationships and finances; adaptation to living apart c. Realignment of relationships with extended family; staying connected with spouse's extended family
	The divorce	More work on emotional divorce: overcoming hurt, anger, guilt, etc.	a. Mourning loss of intact family; giving up fantasies of reunion b. Retrieval of hopes, dreams, expectations from the marriage c. Staying connected with extended families
Post-divorce family	Single parent (custodial household or primary residence)	Willingness to maintain financial responsibilities, continue parental contact with ex-spouse, and support contact of children with ex-spouse and his or her family	a. Making flexible visitation arrangements with ex-spouse and family b. Rebuilding own financial resources c. Rebuilding own social network
	Single parent (noncustodial)	Willingness to maintain financial responsibilities and parental contact with ex-spouse and to support custodial parent's relationship with children	a. Finding ways to continue effective parenting b. Maintaining financial responsibilities to ex-spouse and children c. Rebuilding own social network

Source: Carter & McGoldrick, 1999, p. 375

In Carter and McGoldrick's (1999) family life cycle outlook, divorce represents an interruption or dislocation (a "detour") similar to those produced with any shifts, gains, and losses in family membership. As we have noted, relationship changes must be addressed and a new set of developmental tasks dealt with (see Table 2.4) before the divorcing family can move forward. Thus, divorce adds another family life cycle stage, as the family regroups and tries to deal with the physical and emotional losses and changes before rejoining the "main road" in their developmental journey. Should either ex-spouse remarry, then still another stage must occur as all members absorb new members into the family system and go about redefining roles and relationships.

Remarried Families

Remarriage today is nearly as common as first marriages; close to half of all new marriages involve a remarriage for at least one partner, and one in four a remarriage for both (Saxton, 1996). Single life is short-lived for most divorced persons: the median interval before remarriage for previously divorced men is 2.3 years, and for women 2.5 years. About 30 percent of all divorced persons remarry within 12 months of becoming divorced (Ganong & Coleman, 1994). Bray (1995b) estimates that there are more than 11 million remarried households in the United States; one out of every three Americans today is a stepparent, stepchild, stepsibling, or some member of a stepfamily (Booth & Dunn, 1994). Bernstein (1999) predicted that stepfamilies (in which she includes first marriages of single parents and long-term cohabitation of heterosexual as well as gay or lesbian partners) would be the most prevalent family form in twenty-first-century America.

Structurally, remarriage and consequent stepfamily life is complex, since a variety of parental figures, siblings, and extended family members from current and previous marriages are apt to be involved. Children are often called upon to reside in two households for varying periods during an ordinary week, where they must deal with different rules (bedtime, curfew, table manners), ambiguous boundaries, and different roles (an only child in one home, the oldest of several stepsiblings in another). Previous parent-child relationships, which predated the new marriage, inevitably undergo changes as the new system makes room for new members and changing responsibilities and obligations (Ganong & Coleman, 1999). Financial problems may plague a newly remarried family and lead to acrimony and competition between, say, a new (working) wife and a former (nonworking) wife who is receiving monthly spousal support payments.

Adaptation to remarriage becomes still more complex if spouses come from different cultural backgrounds or different individual life cycle phases (for example, an older man with adult children marrying a young woman with no children or young children). Moreover, being an effective stepparent to a young child and to an adolescent is likely to be different because of their different developmental needs (Bray, 1995b). An additional problem often arises because the nonresident biological father (or mother) looms in the background, may remain a major factor in the family system, and may cause loyalty conflicts in children between the absent parent and the stepparent.

Remarriage involves transition from a former household to an integrated stepfamily household, a process Visher, Visher, and Pasley (2003) liken to the acculturation experience of immigrating to a new country. New adaptations become necessary, new situations must be faced, membership in two households must be worked out. New food, new rules, new customs, new loyalties, perhaps new languages and lifestyles, all add to the complex problems of transition. These authors estimate that for many families it may take up to six years before the stepparents can form a solid couple bond and work as a team to deal with the challenges of stepfamily life. Particularly apt to hasten the integration process is the ability and willingness of stepparent and stepchildren to achieve a mutually satisfying relationship (Bray & Kelly, 1998).

Adding to their previous adaptation to a single-parent household, now the entire family must struggle with fears related to investing in new relationships and forming a new family. Visher and Visher (1988) suggest that most stepfamilies have several distinctive problems: They are born out of relationship losses and the abandonment of hopes and dreams in the previous family; they are composed of members with separate family histories and traditions that may be in conflict and need to be reconciled; children are often members of two households, with differing rules and lifestyles; children often experience loyalty conflicts between parents. Goldenberg and Goldenberg (2002) add that there may be difficulties in assuming parental roles with stepchildren, rivalries and jealousies may develop between stepchildren, and competition between the biological mother and the stepmother may occur. Despite these hazards—typically involving disorganization, reorganization, sometimes relocation, and the reassigning of roles (Berger, 2000)—resilient, well-functioning stepfamilies are more the rule than the exception.

From a family life cycle view, more Americans than ever before are experiencing transitions from nuclear family to single-parent or binuclear family, to remarried family or stepfamily, all within a brief time period (Hetherington, 1999). The resulting stepfamilies (far more often a stepfather and custodial mother, rather than the reverse) must undergo an entire new stage of the family life cycle before gaining stability (see Table 2.5). One glimpse of the complexity involved comes from McGoldrick and Carter (1999):

> As the first marriage signifies the joining of two families, so a second marriage involves the interweaving of three, four, or more families, whose previous life cycle courses have been disrupted by death or divorce. (p. 417)

Stepfamily development occurs in stages, and each stage in the process calls for gradually renegotiating and reorganizing a complex and dynamic network of relationships. Those stepparents who demand "instant love" are likely to end up feeling frustrated and rejected. On the other hand, relationships within stepfamilies that are allowed to blossom slowly often lead to caring and loving bonds that last a lifetime (Visher & Visher, 1993). In some cases, the stepparent may provide a model that expands a child's choice of roles in life or that offers a positive view of husband-wife relationships not seen before.

Gay and Lesbian Families

From a life cycle perspective, young gays and lesbians face the same normative demands to become independent adults as do their heterosexual counterparts, but simultaneously they must also learn to cope with the stresses of living in a stigmatizing larger society (Johnson & Colucci, 1999). Frequently, their prolonged unmarried status leads others to consider them not fully functioning adults. (The same is sometimes true of straight men and women.) Especially for those who choose to remain secretive about their homosexuality, they may allow the family of origin's view to be perpetuated that they have not yet found the right opposite-sex partner. When a young gay adult is openly living together with a same-sex partner, some parents may be pleased that their child is in a stable relationship, and less likely to run the risk of indiscriminate sexual encounters, while others may be further distressed since they can no longer deny their gay child's homoerotic commitment.

In developmental terms, adolescence and young adulthood for gays and lesbians is likely to be destabilizing, as the young person with homoerotic interests experiences considerable anxiety, secrecy, and shame over same-sex feelings, all without being able to share these thoughts or feelings with family members or friends. While "coming out" may be painful and occur in stages (sometimes over a lifetime) with

TABLE 2.5 Remarried Family Formation: A Developmental Outline

Steps	Prerequisite Attitude	Developmental Issues
1. Entering the new relationship	Recovery from loss of first marriage (adequate emotional divorce)	Recommit to marriage and to forming a family with readiness to deal with complexity and ambiguity
2. Conceptualizing and planning new marriage and family	Accepting one's own fears and those of new spouse and children about remarriage and forming a stepfamily Accepting need for time and patience for adjustment to complexity and ambiguity of: 1. Multiple new roles 2. Boundaries: space, time, membership, and authority 3. Affective issues: guilt, loyalty conflicts, desire for mutuality, unresolvable past hurts	a. Work on openness in the new relationships to avoid pseudomutuality b. Plan for maintenance of cooperative financial and co-parental relationships with ex-spouses c. Plan to help children deal with fears, loyalty conflicts, and membership in two systems d. Realign relationships with extended family to include new spouse and children e. Plan maintenance of connections for children with extended family of ex-spouse
3. Remarriage and reconstruction of family	Final resolution of attachment to previous spouse and ideal of "intact" family; acceptance of a different model of family with permeable boundaries	a. Restructure family boundaries to allow for inclusion of new spouse-stepparent b. Realign relationships and financial arrangements throughout subsystems to permit interweaving of several systems c. Make room for relationships of all children with biological (noncustodial) parents, grandparents, and other extended family d. Share memories and histories to enhance stepfamily integration

Source: Carter & McGoldrick, 1999, p. 377

different people (family, friends, employers), it is during the young adult period that the struggle to establish a gay identity typically begins (Chandler, 1997). Coupling for gay men may follow a lengthy period of experimentation at locations where gays are known to congregate, and sometimes periods of celibacy (often as protection against AIDS). Young lesbians are apt to bond earlier into stable couplehood than do gay men, and because their identity is partially expressed as part of a partnership, they are more likely than gay men to present themselves as a couple to their families (Fulmer, 1999).

As for gay and lesbian families, with or without children, they are as varied and diverse as heterosexual families: some are childless couples; others are formed after unsuccessful heterosexual marriages (in which prolonged and conflictual custody battles may have taken place). Still others may opt for parenthood by adopting a child; or, in the case of lesbians, may choose artificial insemination or utilize a surrogate in order to have children. They come from all racial, religious, or ethnic backgrounds, and, depending on their community's tolerance for same-sex relationships, may make their relationship visible or keep it private (Ariel & McPherson, 2000). Despite greater public visibility, most are marginalized by the larger heterosexual society, possess limited civil and legal rights, frequently face accusations of immorality, must deal with unwelcoming and unsafe environments, including, at times, the threat of violent assault (Laird, 2003).

Regardless of family genesis, and again like their heterosexual counterparts, gays and lesbians are part of a complex, multigenerational family system populated by their family of origin, an accepting community of like-minded people, and a family of choice consisting of friends, partners, and/or children (Johnson & Colucci, 1999). They are raised with the same cultural norms and beliefs as are heterosexuals, make many of the same assumptions about relationships, negotiate roles and responsibilities, and are likely to belong to mainstream families.

At the same time, their unique experiences with a homophobic and largely unaccepting society (often including members of their family of origin) makes their same-sex family life less comfortably visible to the dominant heterosexual world. With few exceptions, they are still denied the legal benefits and respectability of married life, although this appears to be changing somewhat as some countries and a handful of U.S. states[2] have slowly begun to legally recognize domestic partnerships and in some cases gay marriages. In some states, it remains unlawful for a gay couple to adopt a child together, while other states allow the procedure. If an adoption does occur, according to Adams and Benson (2005), previously rejecting family members may more readily accept their new role (grandparents, uncles, and aunts), perhaps because having children makes the adopting couple seem more like a mainstream family.

It is difficult to determine the exact number of gay or lesbian parents, although the year 2000 census revealed over half a million same-sex unmarried households spread across all counties in the United States (U.S. Census Bureau, (2003). Many more are likely to have remained closeted, keeping their sexual preferences to themselves for fear of negative attitudes or reprisals from neighbors, employers, or co-workers. Laws against adoption by same-sex couples often add to the stress surrounding adoption, with the nonadopting parent often remaining hidden (thus back "in" after having "come out") while his or her mate goes through the lengthy adoption process as a single parent. The applicant may or may not reveal a gay or lesbian lifestyle to the adoption agency. Others, with children and having gone from a heterosexual to a homosexual preference, may find they need to conceal their current partnership from the courts for fear of losing custody or visitation rights. While such factors make exact counts impossible, it is estimated that in the United States there are 1 to 3 million gay fathers (Silverstein & Quartironi, 1996) and perhaps 1 to 5 million

---

[2]Although most states have enacted laws preventing same-sex marriages from being recognized, Vermont in 2000 passed the first "civil union" law granting gays and lesbians most benefits (inheritance rights, joint income tax filings, medical decisions) and protections available to married couples. Vermont remains the state with the highest concentration of same-sex couples, San Francisco the highest among metropolitan areas.

BOX 2.3   CASE STUDY

A LESBIAN COUPLE ADOPTS A CHILD

Many of the problems faced by a same-sex couple adopting an older child, as we illustrate here, are similar to those encountered by heterosexual couples: inexperience as parents, the possibility of pre-adoption trauma to the adoptee, difficulty bonding, special needs of the child or parents, subsequent conflict between the adults. For gay or lesbian parents, there is the additional question of whether the state will recognize the adoption as legal, and how custody and visitation rights will be adjudicated should the couple separate in the future.

Celia, 27, and Brenda, 29, had been lesbian live-in partners for four years and had talked from time to time about adopting a child together. Celia, from San Salvador, had been married briefly eight years earlier, but the marriage had ended in divorce. She had wanted a child while married, but she and her husband had had such a rocky marriage, with numerous separations, that both decided it would not be wise to bring a child into such an unstable situation. Brenda, Australian by birth, had never married, but had been involved in raising two children of a woman friend with whom she had had a previous sexual relationship. Celia and Brenda had been together in an exclusive union since shortly after they met, and both were quite involved in the lesbian community, from which they received considerable social support.

A parenting opportunity arose one day when Dora, Celia's 21-year-old unmarried sister and the mother of a 5-year-old boy, announced that she wanted to return to school and told Celia she was considering putting her son, Richardo, up for adoption.

Not wanting the boy to be placed with strangers, and accustomed to coming to the aid of her younger sister in times of stress, Celia offered to adopt Richardo. Dora, who trusted her older sister and felt burdened raising Richardo by herself (he was the result of a one-night stand when she was 16), readily agreed. Celia and Brenda had had a good relationship with the boy since his birth, and they were certain the transition would be easy, that Richardo would thrive,

and that raising a child together would strengthen their relationship and enrich their lives. Unfortunately, this would not prove to be the case.

Soon after Celia adopted Richardo, she and Brenda began to face the prospects of parenting and the multiple ways in which their lives had begun to change as a result of their new living arrangement.

At first they tried to create a new life and identity for Richardo, offering him his own room in their large house and immediately changing his name to Rick. They instructed him to call them "Mommy" and "Auntie Brenda," and asked him to try to feel a part of this three-member family. Brenda, more experienced with raising children, quit her part-time job at the public library and assumed most of the at-home parenting responsibilities.

Celia continued working full time as a legal secretary to support the household. However, the social support previously offered by the women's network of lesbian and gay friends began to dwindle, as few in the community were involved in raising children.

At first Celia and Brenda were pleased with the parenting arrangement they had worked out together, but after six months or so they began to question its workability. Celia grew envious of Brenda's close relationship with her adopted son, doubting her own ability to deal with Rick in the easy manner that Brenda, more experienced with children, seemed to have. As Celia withdrew from the parenting role, Brenda became increasingly frustrated, resenting that she was carrying out the day-to-day parenting duties with no legal authorization to make decisions regarding Rick. Moreover, Celia's family of origin treated her with suspicion, refusing to acknowledge Brenda's rights regarding child-rearing decisions.

As tensions mounted, Rick began to exhibit problematic behavior at home and at school. He developed various behavioral signs of increased anxiety (sleeping problems, eating problems, discipline problems). Finally, Rick confessed that he was afraid of being "unadopted," of Celia and Brenda separating,

(continued)

BOX 2.3   *(continued)*

and of losing his close relationship with Brenda. His schoolwork suffered accordingly. At a parent-teacher conference attended by both Celia and Brenda, the teacher reported that Rick was easily distractible and hyperactive in the classroom, and that she thought he needed counseling. Recognizing all the signs of increased dysfunction, but knowing they all wanted to stay together, the three made an appointment with a family counselor for the next week. (Goldenberg & Goldenberg, 2002, pp. 17–18)

lesbians who have given birth to children (Gartrell et al., 1996). If we add same-sex couples who have adopted children, and those who have had children through donor insemination or through surrogate mothers, there may be from 12 to 15 million children residing in homes with gay parents in the United States (Goldenberg & Goldenberg, 2005). Nearly a quarter of all gay and lesbian couples are raising children (Adams & Benson, 2005).

Gay and lesbian parents are likely to have life cycle stresses and transitions similar to those of heterosexual families (such as adjusting to new parenthood, sending children off to school) in addition to some unique to their homosexual lifestyle—for example, deciding whether to "come out" or remain "in the closet" to other possibly homophobic parents; figuring out how to help their child fit into the mainstream with his or her peers while preserving the parent's homosexual identity (Carlson, 1996). Contrary to some myths, there is no evidence that gay or lesbian adults are less fit parents than their heterosexual counterparts (Gartrell, Deck, Rodas, Peyser, & Banks, 2005).

Research findings compiled by Patterson (1995) indicate that lesbian women are not markedly different from heterosexual women in their mental health or in their child-rearing practices. Moreover, available research suggests that children raised by these mothers (less data is currently available regarding gay male parenting) develop gender-role behavior patterns similar to those developed by all other children, with no evidence of elevated levels of homosexuality.

Nevertheless, gay parenting does present unique problems throughout the family life cycle. Carlson (1996) indicates that these are likely to arise beginning with the preschool and school-age years, when childhood events (Scouts, sports, dance classes, and so forth) present an endless series of opportunities to parents to "come out" or remain closeted. Later, during adolescence, when conformity to peer group pressures is likely to be particularly strong, children may attempt to distance themselves from their parents. While this is a developmental task common to all adolescents struggling to find their own identities, for children of same-sex marriages, the rejection of their parents' alternate lifestyle may be especially fraught with conflict. Still later, telling a future mate—or possibly worse, his or her parents—about one's gay or lesbian parents is often stressful. Navigating these life cycle stages may be hazardous at times, but doing do successfully may help the children grow up with greater tolerance for diversity than might ordinarily be the case. Nevertheless, the negative impact of marginalization, social disapproval, and discrimination by the majority culture should not be underestimated and has many effects similar to those experienced by other minority groups (Snow, 2004).

SUMMARY

Generations within a family have an enduring, reciprocal, life-shaping impact on one another as they move through family life cycle stages. In this multigenerational view, continuity and change characterize family life as the family system progresses through transitions over time. While the progression is generally orderly and sequenced, certain discontinuous changes may be particularly disruptive. Social class membership and cultural background influence the options, opportunities, and resources available to families for coping with unforeseeable demands for adaptation. The appearance of symptomatic behavior in a family member at transition points in the family life cycle may signal that the family is having difficulty in negotiating change.

The family life cycle perspective, dividing family development into a series of stages through which each family inevitably passes, offers an organizing theme for viewing the family as a system moving through time. Specific developmental tasks are expected to be accomplished at each stage en route. Family therapists, particularly structuralists and strategists, are especially interested in how families navigate transitional periods between stages. Passing expected milestones as well as dealing with unexpected crises may temporarily threaten the family's usual developmental progress, causing realignments in the family's organization. Among immigrant families, migration presents an especially stressful set of circumstances that may be traumatic and negatively affect family life cycle development.

Intact families typically proceed chronologically through a series of family growth phases—coupling (partners moving from independence to interdependence), expansion (accommodating children), and later, contracting (as children move on). Old hierarchical boundaries between parents and children are likely to be replaced by a greater peer relationship as the children reach middle age. Retirement, grandparenthood, widowhood, and chronic illness/caregiving all represent major adaptational challenges for the family system as parents reach old age.

Alternative families, such as those led by single parents (as a result of divorce, adoption, out-of-wedlock births, donor insemination, widowhood) or those for which remarriage has created a stepfamily (most often a stepfather and custodial mother), inevitably experience disruptions in the family life cycle before resuming their orderly development.

Gay and lesbian families are likely to experience life cycle stresses and transitions similar to those of heterosexual families, in addition to those unique to their usually closeted lifestyle. Children raised by gay or lesbian parents are apt to develop patterns of gender-role behavior similar to those developed by all other children.

RECOMMENDED READINGS

Ahrons, C. R., & Rodgers, R. H. (1987). *Divorced families: A multidisciplinary approach.* New York: Norton.

Ariel, J., & McPherson, D. W. (2000). Therapy with lesbians and gay parents and their children. *Journal of Marital and Family Therapy, 26,* 421–432.

Carter, B., & McGoldrick, M. (Eds.). (1999). *The expanded family life cycle: Individual, family, and social perspectives* (3rd ed.). Boston: Allyn & Bacon.

Goldenberg, H., & Goldenberg, I. (2004). *Counseling today's families* (4th ed.). Pacific Grove, CA: Brooks/Cole.

Nichols, W. C., Pace-Nichols, M. A., Becvar, D. S., & Napier, A. Y. (Eds.). (2000). *Handbook of family development and intervention.* New York: Wiley.

Visher, E. B., & Visher, J. S. (1988). *Old loyalties, new ties: Therapeutic strategies with stepfamilies.* New York: Brunner/Mazel.

Walsh, F. (Ed.). (2003). *Normal family processes: Growing diversity and complexity* (3rd ed.). New York: Guilford Press.

CHAPTER 3

GENDER, CULTURE, AND ETHNICITY FACTORS IN FAMILY FUNCTIONING

Any comprehensive attempt to understand personal or family functioning must take into account the fundamental influences of **gender,**[1] **culture,** and ethnicity in shaping the lives and experiences of men and women. These issues have assumed center stage for family therapists in recent years, extending their thinking beyond observing internal family interaction processes to include the impact of these outside social, political, and historical forces on the belief systems and everyday functioning of family members.

Largely fueled by postmodern inquiries into the diversity of perspectives with which to view life, such factors as gender, race or ethnicity, sexual preference, and socioeconomic status are all now recognized as powerful influences on personal and family perspectives and behavior patterns (Goldenberg & Goldenberg, 1999). Kliman (1994) stresses the *interactive* nature of these factors so that one cannot really be considered without the others; for example, the experience of being male or female shapes and is in turn shaped by being working poor or middle class or wealthy and by being Chinese American or African American or a Salvadorian refugee. Gender, culture, ethnicity, and social class must be considered in relationship to one another by a therapist who tries to make sense of a client family's hierarchical arrangement, for example, or perhaps the family's social attitudes, expectations, or feelings of belonging to the majority culture. In short, each of our values, beliefs, and attitudes must be viewed through the prism of our own gender, class position, and cultural experience.

To be fully competent, a therapist must take into account his or her own cultural background, class, race, ethnicity, sexual orientation, religion, life cycle stage, etc., in working with families from different backgrounds, being especially alert to how these factors interact with those same factors in the client family (Hardy & Laszloffy, 1995).

---

[1]It might be useful at the start of this discussion to draw a distinction between *sex* (the biological differences between men and women) and *gender* (the culturally prescribed norms and roles played by men and women). In this chapter we emphasize the latter, as an organizing principle of family relationships, and as the basis of behavior society considers "masculine" or "feminine." Levant and Philpot (2002) offer the useful reminder that gender roles are psychological and socially constructed entities, bring with them certain advantages and disadvantages for men and women alike, and perhaps most important from a therapeutic viewpoint, are not fixed but subject to change.

In the case of gender, both the feminist movement and, more recently, the emergence of men's studies have drawn attention to the limiting and in some cases pernicious effects of sexist attitudes and patriarchal behavior on family functioning; gender inequities have begun to be addressed regarding sex-based role assignments within family groups as well as the wider culture that defines what relationships are possible within families and who is available to participate in those relationships (McGoldrick, Anderson, & Walsh, 1989).

In one well-known treatise on adolescent girls, Mary Pipher (1994) called attention to the increasing number who develop symptoms of depression, addiction, and eating disorders as a result of trying to conform to the culturally-reinforced gender emphasis on female physical appearance over intellect or creativeness.

One result of the societal challenge to fixed gender roles and expectations has been a self-reassessment by family therapists, many of whom have followed theories produced through men's experiences and value systems, not recognizing that women's experiences and values might be different. This male perspective regarding stereotyped gender roles permeated their viewpoint regarding what constitutes "healthy" family functioning and as a consequence, in the view of Philpot and Brooks (1995), therapists too often have acted as agents of a society that has been oppressive toward women. Societal expectations are in transition, however, and family therapists have discovered that many people have begun to define themselves and their family relationships in new, less restrictive ways (Haddock, Zimmerman, & Lyness, 2003).

One consequence of changing views regarding gender by family therapists has been the thrust toward developing a **gender-sensitive family therapy** that, regardless of theoretical approach, attempts to overcome confining sex-role stereotyping by therapists in any clinical intervention efforts. To be gender-sensitive as a therapist is to continue being attuned to the common gender-role messages that clients (and therapists) grow up absorbing; and perhaps more important, to help clients (and oneself) recognize, label, and challenge those sexist-based messages (Philpot, Brooks, Lusterman, & Nutt, 1997).

In addition to greater gender-role awareness in any family assessment effort, a related by-product of the pluralistic outlook of the postmodern movement has been the increased attention to the varied perspectives and lifestyles of the different cultural groups that increasingly make up our society. Just as family therapy theories in the 1950s broke out of the individually focused restrictions of searching for intrapsychic problems, so these more recent efforts to attend to a larger sociocultural context broaden our understanding of cultural influences on family norms, values, belief systems, and behavior patterns. As in the case of a more gender-sensitive outlook, attention to *multiculturalism* has challenged any previously entrenched ethnocentric views by family therapists of what constitutes a "healthy" family. As Goldenberg and Goldenberg (1999) contend, a family therapist today must take a client family's cultural background into account in order to avoid pathologizing ethnic minority families whose behavior is unfamiliar, taking care not to misdiagnose or mislabel family behavior in the process.

GENDER ISSUES IN FAMILIES AND FAMILY THERAPY

A full understanding of family functioning must consider that men and women experience family life both similarly and differently, in their families of origin and in the families they form through marriage. Typically they are reared with different role expectations, beliefs, values, attitudes, goals, and opportunities. Generally speaking, men and women, beginning early in life, learn different problem-solving techniques, cultivate different communication styles, develop different perspectives on sexuality, and hold different expectations for relationships. For example, while women traditionally are socialized to develop attitudes and behavior that derive from a primary value of *affiliation* (cooperation, nurturing, emotional expressiveness, compassion), men are likely to be raised to value *autonomy* (power, aggressiveness, competitiveness, rationality). While both sexes are subject to gender-role expectations, Hyde (1996) suggests that women are more apt to face social disapproval and punishment for refusing to acquiesce to socially determined rules and expectations. A woman may be pejoratively labeled as"ballsy"if she exhibits too much of what is considered the masculine characteristic of assertiveness. Similarly, men may be disparaged as"wimps"if they appear too passive, emotional, sensitive, or vulnerable—qualities that are considered the province of women. The pairing of an overtly"bossy"woman and a"meek, compliant" husband often provokes discomfort in others and subsequent hostile or denigrating remarks precisely because of its unexpected role reversal.

These gender differences in perception and behavior result from a complex interactive process between culture and biological forces. As Levant and Philpot (2002) observe, while the emergence of the "new woman" (assertive, self-sufficient, ambitious, rational, and competitive) has taken place in recent years, many of the traditional values of early gender socialization continue to exist and result in gender-role conflicts and gender identity struggles for many of today's women. In some cases, society's reluctance to accept change has hampered successful adaptation for the many women who strain to juggle work and family responsibilities, to say nothing of balancing expressions of aggression, competitiveness, and similar behaviors with what society has traditionally viewed as acceptable"feminine"behavior.

While men's lives are apt to follow a more or less linear course, largely laid out to them early in life, women's lives in general are more varied, with starts, stops, interruptions, and detours as they are called upon to accommodate to the needs of parents, husbands, children, and other family responsibilities (Shapiro, 1996; Bateson, 2001). Men and women typically enter marriage (or alternative relationships) and, later, parenthood with different ideas of what will be expected of them; not surprisingly, they have different family experiences. Traditionally, it has been the woman who makes the major adjustment to her husband's lifestyle (Goodrich, Rampage, Ellman, & Halstead, 1988). While overlapping perceptions and behavior certainly exist, this gender dichotomy is likely to lead men and women to assign differing priorities to different values, personality characteristics, and behavior patterns. The roles of sex, physical and psychological intimacy, ease and frequency of open communication, relationships with family members, power in the family domain, emotional responsiveness, fidelity, household responsibilities, and financial concerns may all differ in the perceptions of husbands and wives (McGoldrick, 1999). Moreover, those differing experiences and expectations may lay the groundwork for future conflict, clashes resulting from their polarizing gender training, outlook, priorities, and senses of entitlement.

The family therapy field has been relatively slow in recognizing the extent to which the gender-role messages all of us experience during our lifetimes typically affect our current family life (Enns, 1997). As McGoldrick, Anderson, and Walsh (1989) point out, many early family therapists operated in a gender-free fashion, as if family members were interchangeable units of a system with equal power[2] and control (and thus equal responsibility) over the outcome of interactions occurring within the family. The larger social, historical, economic, and political context of family life in a patriarchal society generally was overlooked; therapists by and large felt comfortable taking a neutral stance regarding a family's gender arrangement, thus running the risk of tacitly approving traditional values oppressive to women. The overall result, typically, was for family therapists to perpetuate a myth of equality between men and women within a family seeking their help, ignoring political (that is, power-related) differences between men and women in most relationships (Hare-Mustin & Maracek, 1990).

However, beginning in the late 1970s an increasing number of family therapists, primarily women at first, began to challenge the underlying assumptions about gender that put women at a disadvantage; those assumptions, the therapists claimed, are the basis of the family therapy field (and the culture that created it). Several pioneering studies (Miller, 1976; Hare-Mustin, 1978; Gilligan, 1982; Goldner, 1985; Avis, 1985) faulted existing family therapy models for failing to pay sufficient attention to gender and power differences in male-female relationships, in effect ignoring how these gender patterns influence internal family interaction, the social context of family life. Not yet offering an alternative **feminist family therapy** position[3]—that was to come in the late 1980s—these critics nevertheless argued that family therapists, reflecting the larger society, often (wittingly or unwittingly) reinforced traditional gender roles (Avis, 1996). Underlying such formulations, they asserted, is an endorsement of traditional male/female roles that depreciate qualities (dependency, nurturing, emotional expressiveness) traditionally associated with women while extolling qualities (aggressiveness, competitiveness, rationality) held in high regard by men. Attempting to correct this gender bias, these feminist-informed therapists began to challenge the social, cultural, historic, economic, and political conditions that shaped not only the unique development and experiences of women but also their relationships with men.

Several early noteworthy undertakings deserve special attention. Jean Baker Miller (1976) at the Stone Center for Developmental Services and Studies at Wellesley College, seeking to advance a feminist theory of personality development, addressed the special role that relationships and connections to others play in a woman's sense of her self. To Miller, the center of a woman's development is in her connections to others. Unfortunately that development can become derailed, she contended, in the face of disconnections within families, leading to a woman's sense of loss of empowerment.

---

[2]Power within a family typically is gained in a variety of ways: by gender, age, earning power, respect, or fear. In society at large, power is unequally distributed based on such factors as gender, class, race, religion, ethnicity, age, sexual orientation, profession, and degree of physical ability (Fontes & Thomas, 1996). Although gender roles are in transition, and women have assumed powerful positions (business executives, astronauts, Supreme Court justices, foreign heads of state), Risman (1998) points out that overall men still have more power and status than women in all cultural groups.

[3]There is no single entity labeled feminist family therapy, since there are therapists practicing from all of the approaches we will consider later in this text who may regard themselves as feminist-informed and thus may take a variety of approaches with families. Rather, as Avis (1996) emphasizes, feminist family therapy is a "*perspective* on gender relations, a lens through which a therapist views his or her clients" (p. 223). Regardless of theoretical outlook, all address gender and power imbalances in their clients' lives and all advocate empowerment and egalitarianism as goals (Worell & Remer, 1992; Enns, 1997).

Miller maintained that it was the"non-relational"setting common in many families that led to significant disconnection between its members. In such settings, she observed, children are apt to grow up with a deep sense of isolation and self-blame. Miller and Stiver (1991) posited the following paradox: people (especially women) yearn for connections with others but, protecting themselves, at the same time keep large parts of themselves out of connection, because they fear a replay of early experiences of feeling hurt, misunderstood, or violated.

To Miller, women, as a result of traditional gender-role training, have learned to deal with their subordinate status by stressing skills in cultivating and maintaining relationships, while men more likely seek ways to dominate and control; such female subordination to a male-dominated society is not unlike those behavior patterns developed by all oppressed people, and stifles self-development. Yet, according to Miller, relationship building is crucial for all people, and disconnections serve as a source of psychological distress. Rather than depreciating relatedness as a sign of weakness or dismissing it as exclusively feminine, her more recent work (Miller, Jordan, Kaplan, Stiver, & Surrey, 1997) emphasizes it as a valued strength in men and women alike.

Sandra Bem (1981), an early feminist, was interested in *androgyny*—people having both masculine and feminine traits or characteristics, rather than one or the other, as previous stereotypic thinking of polar opposites would suggest. She argued that what is considered masculine and feminine is developed early in young children[4], and that these socially ingrained and reinforced **gender schema,** applied to themselves, often hamper individual development in both sexes. That is, evaluating one's own behavior or the behavior of others as "unmasculine" or "unfeminine" may reveal an overemphasis on using gender as a schema—a set of enduring beliefs for interpreting and evaluating people and events—rather than other schema that stress uniqueness and individual differences. According to Bem (1983), viewing the world through the prism of gender schemas limits efforts to break out of perceptual sets and stereotypic thinking.

The Women's Project in Family Therapy, co-led by Marianne Walters, Betty Carter, Peggy Papp, and Olga Silverstein—begun in 1977 and recently concluded—represents another ongoing examination of gender patterns in family relationships as well as patriarchal assumptions underlying classic family therapy approaches. Primarily through workshops, these family therapists, despite differences in theoretical outlook and clinical approach, offered a female-informed clinical perspective that challenged the field's conventional wisdom. They argued that a field devoted to families had, paradoxically, relied on outdated blueprints of male-determined, stereotypic sex roles and gender-defined functions within families. Their text, *The Invisible Web* (Walters, Carter, Papp, & Silverstein, 1989), presents a gender analysis of their clinical work, as they describe their experiences in applying a feminist perspective to their understanding of gender- and power-based family issues. Without offering any formal training program, this project has had enormous influence in the field, moving family therapists to look beyond what is occurring within the family and to consider the

---

[4]Psychologist Bem (1998) has more recently described the efforts she and her psychologist husband, Daryl Bem, made to function as egalitarian partners and to raise their children in accordance with gender-liberated ideals.

influence of broader social and cultural forces (Simon, 1997). By calling attention to the constraining experiences of women, the foursome has helped to develop a practical, nonsexist set of therapeutic interventions that take gender considerations into account.

Gender from a Feminist Perspective

Since the field of family therapy was largely defined by men in its earlier years, inevitably male language and attitudes dominated early theories. As McGoldrick, Anderson, and Walsh (1989) observe, one consequence was to consider certain behaviors (for example, emotionality, tenderness) as less mature or less desirable than other behaviors (rationality, objectivity); the result, they noted, was to "unwittingly promote family patterns in which women are devalued, blamed, and made to feel guilty for patterns and lives they have little freedom to change" (p. 10). Hoffman (1990) endorses the notion that a male bias was built into family concepts that take the heterosexual, patriarchal family as the norm, arguing that terms such as "overinvolved mother" or "enmeshed family" are sexist and tend to blame mothers in particular for family problems.

Feminist-informed therapists consider such cybernetic concepts as "circular causality" (to designate a repetitive pattern of mutually reinforcing behavior in a male-female relationship) especially unacceptable. They insist this systems-based concept implies that each participant has equal power and control in a transaction, which they dispute. Particularly in the case of physical abuse (rape, battering, incest) by men against women, they reject the cybernetic notion that both partners are engaging in a mutual causal pattern and that it is the subsequent behavioral sequence, for which they are both responsible, that results in the violent episode (Goldner, Penn, Sheinberg, & Walker, 1990).

Critical of the implication that no one therefore is to blame—a violation without a violator—thus clearing the aggressor of responsibility, feminists emphasize greater masculine power in human relationships, the superior physical strength of men, and the corresponding vulnerability of women. They contend that the cybernetic epistemology tends to blame the victim for colluding in her own victimization either as a co-responsible participant or by remaining in the relationship. Avis (1996) points out that implying that all interactional behavior originates within the interaction itself makes it impossible to search for causes outside the interaction; here she cites such external possible causes as "cultural beliefs about appropriate gender behavior, a pre-existing propensity to use violent behavior, or differences in power with which each partner enters the relationship" (p. 225).

A woman, according to Gilligan (1982), tends to define herself within the context of relationships, on which she in turn relies (while men are more likely to value autonomy, separation, and independence). That is, a woman's sense of self and of morality are likely to be interwoven with caring for other people, and to be embedded in interdependence with them. Gilligan contends that male-dominated theories of psychological development have tended to downplay or devalue that need for affiliation or relatedness, viewing it as a frailty rather than an expression of strength. She believes that such theories, because of their inherent male bias, equate maturity with independence, rationality, individuality, achievement, and action. Such qualities as caring for the needs of others, warmth, compassion, and emotional expressiveness, which our society defines as necessary for feminine behavior, are at the same time

Courtesy of Rachel T. Hare-Mustin

Rachel Hare-Mustin, Ph.D.

given short shrift as expressions of the inferiority of the "weaker sex." To Gilligan, women's traditional caretaking role receives less respect and status than those male-approved roles that emphasize achievement and autonomy. She argues that it is thus difficult for many young women to find a "voice of one's own"—a sense of female identity—without appearing too competent or assertive and thus running the risk of being found unattractive by men.

Rachel Hare-Mustin (1987) describes gender as the "basic category on which the world is organized" (p. 15); according to Judith Avis (1996), gender is "a fundamental dimension of personal and social organization—of personal identity, family relationships, therapeutic relationships, sociocultural privilege and oppression" (p. 221). Hare-Mustin, often credited with being the first to raise feminist issues among family therapists, suggested that commonly observed male-female behavioral differences simply reflect established gender arrangements in society, rather than any essential set of differences in the nature of men and women, as Gilligan proposes. A woman's typically greater concern with relationships, according to Hare-Mustin, can best be understood as a need to please others when one lacks power. In this view, a woman's behavior reflects her less powerful role position vis-à-vis a man's, rather than resulting from an inherent weakness of character. *Where the powerful advocate rules and rationality, the weak espouse relatedness.* Hare-Mustin (1987) offers the following example:

> Thus, in husband-wife conflicts, husbands use logic, wives call on caring. But, in parent-child conflicts, parents, including mothers, emphasize rules; it is the children who appeal for understanding. Society rewards rationality, not emotions, but which is used is associated with who has the power, and not primarily with being male or female. (p. 22)

Gender, Work, and Family Life

The entry of women of all social classes, whether single, married, or heads of single-parent households, into the world of paid work has had a profound effect on evolving male-female relationships. In recent years, women have been marrying later (or choosing not to marry at all) and are having fewer children. Young couples who do decide to become parents, as noted earlier, must rearrange the family system and renegotiate the roles each plays, particularly if the wife continues to work outside the home, as the overwhelming majority do. Working women, especially single mothers or women among the poor, minority, immigrant, and undereducated populations, have always been part of the workforce. What is new, however, is the influx of married women of all social classes and educational levels, including those with young children, into work outside the home (Goldenberg & Goldenberg, 2002); see Box 3.1.

Breaking out of stereotypic male-female roles regarding domestic and work responsibilities is essential. Working wives continue to bear the major responsibility for child care and most household chores, although men now are more involved in the rearing of preschool children and helping with daily domestic tasks than in the past. Women are likely to take on the major obligation of caring for sick children or elderly family members, maintaining contact with the families of origin of both partners, and sustaining friendships.

BOX 3.1   RESEARCH REPORT

CHANGING EDUCATIONAL, WORK, AND FAMILY ROLES

Changes in work and family roles for men and women have occurred at an astonishingly fast pace in the last 30 years. Women now complete graduate and professional schools at a rate equal to or greater than that of men. They now constitute half the U.S. labor force and can expect to spend at least 30 years in the paid workforce. The modal American family today is a dual-earner family, and 40 percent of white, college-educated women earn as much as or more than their husbands (Barnett & Hyde, 2001). The "feminization" of professional ranks (law, medicine, pharmacy, business administration) should continue to increase as older, male-dominated groups retire. However, certain hot-button items remain for many working women: equality of pay, maternity leave, flexible time for family responsibilities (Cox & Alm, 2005).

Men are spending more time on child care and household tasks than in the past, while employed women are doing less. Bond, Galinsky, and Swanberg (1998) predict an equitable sharing of these responsibilities in the near future. Barnett and Hyde (2001) suggest that multiple roles are beneficial for both men and women. Beyond added income, frequently necessary in today's economy, women have opened up opportunities to experience success and to participate in challenging experiences outside the home.

Traditionally, while women's domain has been to manage the home and raise the children, men have taken on the responsibility for financial support and, if necessary, the family's physical protection. Recent studies (Hochschild, 1997; Hawkins, Marshall, & Allen, 1998: Lennon & Rosenfeld, 1994) indicate that while working women may continue to do a greater amount of domestic work than do their husbands, most wives consider the division of labor to be fair if the husband is available when called upon to help, understands and respects the hard work involved in carrying out domestic chores, and listens to his wife's concerns about family work.

With the children out of the house and forming families of their own, men and women may find themselves with differing priorities, according to McGoldrick (1999). She believes that men may wish to seek greater closeness to their wives, while the latter may begin to feel energized about developing their own lives, perhaps through

CLINICAL NOTE

Work is valued in our society, and an important part of each person's identity is tied to his or her occupation. In gathering information during the early phases of family therapy, it may be more conventional to address a man's work situation, but a woman's work history also needs to be assessed. A simple "Do you work?" is inadequate and may imply that if she is a homemaker she is not involved in real work. To ask if she works outside the home is better and more respectful, but nevertheless incomplete, since it overlooks paid work she may have done before staying home to care for children. Inquiring about a previous set of work experiences is more thorough and informative. How she and her partner decided she should devote full time to home care tells us a great deal about how they negotiate and problem-solve together.

resumed careers or other activities outside the home. If serious marital tension leads to divorce, as it sometimes does at this stage, McGoldrick contends that women are especially vulnerable. Not only are they less likely than men to remarry, but their embeddedness in relationships, their orientation toward interdependence, their life-long subordination of achievement to caring for others, and their conflicts over competitive success may make them especially susceptible to despair.

Finally, since women are apt to outlive men, many may find themselves alone and financially impoverished. Very likely they will turn to their daughters (or perhaps daughters-in-law) for support and care, since women in our society shoulder most of the eldercare, with the possible exception of managing finances for the elderly.

Men's Studies and Gender-Role Awareness

To be gender-sensitive (or feminist-informed) is to be aware of the differences in behavior, attitudes, and socialization experiences of growing up masculine or feminine, especially differences in power, status, position, and privilege within the family and in society in general. Brooks (1992) observes that past "gender-blindness" on the part of family therapists was first detected by women—not surprising, considering they were most likely, at least overtly, to be harmed by sexist attitudes—and thus focused principally on the woman's perspective. However, he reminds us that men too have been subjected to substantial role constraints and disadvantages as a result of their masculine socialization experiences. They too may have suffered from sexist therapeutic interventions that have condoned restricting men to a narrow range of family roles (such as breadwinner) while robbing them of the experience of participating in roles (say, child rearing) usually assigned to women. Levant and Philpot (2002) suggest that this type of gender-role restraint is inherently traumatic to men because it truncates their natural emotionality. Brooks (1992) contends that just as the feminist perspective has started to be incorporated into family therapy practices, so should the perspectives of "men's studies" theorists.

Men's studies, a recent addition to the field of gender examination in our society, attempts to extend feminist explorations by attending to role restrictions in men's lives. O'Neil (1982) draws attention to the traditional "masculine mystique" that programs men toward curtailed emotional expressiveness, obsession with achievement and success, restricted affectionate behavior, and concern with power, control, and competition. Homophobia is often a characteristic of such a mystique, resulting in a man's fear that becoming close to another man might cause others to consider him gay. Proof of masculinity from this perspective often derives from the ability to display power and control, most likely at the expense of women and children.

Doyle (1994) identifies five elements that further define common male gender-role socialization experiences: (a) an *antifeminine* element, in which young boys learn to avoid in their own behavior anything considered feminine; (b) a *success* element that values competition and winning; (c) an *aggressive* element, physically fighting when necessary to defend oneself; (d) a *sexual* element, the belief that men should be preoccupied with sex; and (e) a *self-reliant* element, calling for men to be independent and self-sufficient and not to seek help from others. In areas ranging from job performance to sexual performance, athletic skills or mental alertness, men typically compare themselves with other men and concern themselves about how they rank (Philpot, Brooks, Lusterman, & Nutt, 1997).

BOX 3.2   CASE STUDY

A COUPLE CONFRONTS DOMESTIC VIOLENCE

Jim Kull is referred by the Rock County District Attorney's Office to the Rock County Domestic Violence Program. He was arrested two nights ago for an incident in which his wife received several severe bruises on her body and her face. Kris Koeffler, a social worker, has an interview with Mr. Kull. Mr. Kull is an involuntary client and is reluctant to discuss the incident. Ms. Koeffler informs Mr. Kull he has a right not to discuss it, but if he chooses not to, she is obligated to inform the district attorney that he refused services. She adds that in such cases, the district attorney usually files a battery charge with the court, which may lead to jail time.

Mr. Kull reluctantly states that he and his wife had a disagreement, which ended with her slapping him and him defending himself by throwing a few punches. He adds that yesterday, when he was in jail, he was informed she left home with the children and is now staying at a women's shelter. He is further worried she may contact an attorney and seek a divorce.

Ms. Koeffler inquires about the specifics of the "disagreement." Mr. Kull indicates he came home after having a few beers, his dinner was cold, and he "got on" Mrs. Kull for not cleaning the house. He adds that Mrs. Kull then started "mouthing off," which eventually escalated into them pushing and hitting each other. Ms. Koeffler then inquires whether such incidents had occurred in the past. Mr. Kull indicates "a few times," and then adds that getting physical with his wife is the only way for him to "make her shape up." He indicates he works all day long as a carpenter while his wife sits home watching soap operas. He feels she is not doing her "fair share"; he states the house looks like a "pigpen."

Ms. Koeffler asks Mr. Kull if he feels getting physical with his wife is justifiable. He responds with "sure," and adds that his dad frequently told him "spare the rod and spoil both the wife and the kids." Ms. Koeffler asks if his father was at times abusive to him when he was a child. He indicates that he was, and adds that to

this day he detests his dad for being abusive to him and his mother.

Ms. Koeffler then suggests they draw a "family tree," focusing on three areas: episodes of heavy drinking, episodes of physical abuse, and traditional versus modern gender stereotypes. Ms. Koeffler explains that a traditional gender stereotype includes the husband as the primary decision maker, and the wife as submissive to him and primarily responsible for domestic tasks. The modern gender stereotype involves an egalitarian relationship between husband and wife. After an initial reluctance (related to his expressing confusion as to how such a "tree" would help him get his wife back), Mr. Kull agrees to cooperate in drawing such a "tree." (The resulting genogram is presented in Figure 3.1.)

The genogram helps Mr. Kull see that he and his wife are products of family systems that have strikingly different values and customs. In his family, the males tend to drink heavily, have a traditional view of marriage, and tend to use physical force in interactions with their spouse. (Mr. Kull adds that his father also physically abused his brother and sister when they were younger.) On questioning, Mr. Kull mentions he frequently spanks his children and has struck them "once or twice." Ms. Koeffler asks Mr. Kull how he feels about repeating the same patterns of abuse with his wife and children that he despises his father for using. Tears come to his eyes, and he says "not good."

Ms. Koeffler and Mr. Kull then discuss courses of action that he might take to change his family interactions, and how he might best approach his wife in requesting that she and the children return. Mr. Kull agrees to attend Alcoholics Anonymous (AA) meetings, as well as a therapy group for batterers. After a month of attending these weekly meetings, he contacts his wife and asks her to return. Mrs. Kull agrees to return *if* he stops drinking (since most of the abuse occurred when he was intoxicated), *if* he agrees to continue to attend group therapy and AA meetings,

(continued)

BOX 3.2 *(continued)*

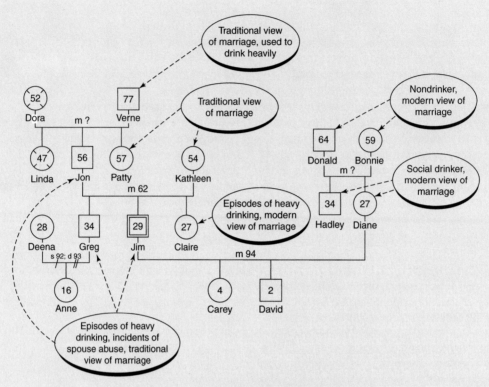

FIGURE 3.1 Sample Genogram: The Jim and Diane Kull Family

and *if* he agrees to go to counseling with her. Mr. Kull readily agrees. (Mrs. Kull's parents, who have never liked her husband, express their disapproval.)

For the first few months, Mr. Kull is on his best behavior and there is considerable harmony in the family. Then one day, on his birthday, he decides to stop for a few beers after work. He drinks until he is intoxicated. When he finally arrives home, he starts to verbally and physically abuse Mrs. Kull and the children. For Mrs. Kull, this is the last straw. She takes her children to her parents' house, where they stay for several days, until they are able to find and move into an apartment. She also files for divorce and follows through in obtaining one.

In many ways, this case is not a "success." In reality, many social work cases are not successful. The genogram, however, is useful in helping Mr. Kull realize that he has acquired, and is now acting out, certain dysfunctional family patterns. Unfortunately, he is not ready to make lasting changes. Perhaps in the future he will be more committed. At the present time he has returned to drinking heavily.

Source: Zastrow, 1999, pp. 188–189

One interpersonal area where gender, asymmetrical power, and control intersect concerns family violence and sexual abuse. Walker and Goldner (1995) and Goldner (1998), writing from a feminist perspective, acknowledge that both partners are involved in woman battering, but that the violent behavior is the man's responsibility and that it is important not to blame the victim (for example, believing that "she provoked it"). Brooks (1992) is especially concerned that the treatment of violence in men ignores the cultural context—and societal sanction—in which violence in men takes place, since for many men socialization toward violence is part of their upbringing. He argues that to be successful, any antiviolence program must be gender-sensitive and include the preventive antiviolence resocialization of men so that they will not rely on violence as an interpersonal strategy. As he observes (Brooks, 1992):

> Just as young girls deserve the opportunity for socialization into achievement and self sufficiency, boys deserve to be freed from the extreme emphasis on physical violence and emotional toughness as proof of masculine worth. (p. 31)

In the previous example, a social worker attempts to deal with a difficult case of wife abuse, using a **genogram** (see fuller discussion in Chapter 8) to help the couple recognize their family histories in regard to the use of alcohol, and in the husband's case, of violence.

Therapy from a Gender-Sensitive Perspective

Gender-sensitive family therapy is intended to liberate and empower both male and female clients, enabling them to move beyond prescribed roles determined by their biological status to ones in which they can exercise choice. In practice this means overcoming internalized social norms and expectations for every client; gender stereotypes in male as well as female clients require examination (Good, Gilbert, & Scher, 1990). Therapy that is gender-aware is action oriented, not merely nonsexist in viewpoint (see Table 3.1).

Whereas nonsexist counseling attempts to avoid reinforcing stereotypical thinking regarding gender roles and power differentials in most male-female relationships, proactive gender-sensitive family therapy goes beyond this goal, deliberately helping clients recognize the limitations on their perceived alternatives imposed by internalizing these stereotypes. As Lewis (1992) observes, clients are better helped when they

TABLE 3.1 Characteristics of Gender-Sensitive Family Therapy

Nonsexist Counseling	Empowerment/Feminist/ Gender-Aware Counseling
Does not reinforce stereotyped gender roles	Helps clients recognize the impact of social, cultural, and political factors on their lives
Encourages clients to consider a wide range of choices, especially in regard to careers	Helps clients transcend limitations resulting from gender stereotyping
Avoids allowing gender stereotypes to affect diagnoses	Recognizes the degree to which individual behaviors may reflect internalization of harmful social standards
Avoids use of sexist assessment instruments	Includes gender-role analysis as a component of assessment
Treats male and female clients equally	Helps clients develop and integrate traits that are culturally defined as "masculine" and "feminine"
Avoids misuse of power in the counseling relationship	Develops collaborative counselor-client relationships

Source: Reprinted with permission from J. A. Lewis, "Gender Sensitivity and Family Empowerment," *Topics in Family Psychology and Counseling,* 1(4), p. 3, © 1992, Aspen Publishers, Inc.

have an opportunity to perceive and overcome social and political barriers. She maintains that the family as a whole can be more effectively empowered if its members work through their assumptions about what is possible for each of them, freely choosing the life—free of role stereotyping—that makes sense to them. Examples of gender-sensitive therapeutic techniques are offered by Philpot, Brooks, Lusterman, and Nutt (1997), four family therapists with differing theoretical orientations who describe how each goes about bridging the separate gender worlds of men and women. Haddock, Zimmerman, and Lyness (2003) have developed a useful Power Equity Guide for training and therapeutic purposes, summarizing the major goals and themes that characterize a gender-informed approach to therapy.

MULTICULTURAL AND CULTURE-SPECIFIC CONSIDERATIONS

Just as an appreciation of gender is essential in gaining a fuller picture of a family's organization, so too understanding families requires a grasp of the cultural context (race, ethnic group membership, religion, social class, sexual orientation) in which that family functions and the subsequent cultural norms by which it lives. Culture—shared, learned knowledge, attitudes, and behavior transmitted from one generation to the next—affects families in a variety of ways, some trivial, others central to their functioning. Language, norms, values, ideals, customs, music, and food preferences are all largely determined by cultural factors (Cuellar & Glazer, 1996).

Culture-Sensitive Therapy

As family therapists have attempted in recent years to apply existing therapy models to previously underserved cultural groups,[5] they have also had to gain greater awareness of their own cultural background and values and to examine the possible impact of these factors in pathologizing ethnic minority families whose values, gender roles, discipline practices, forms of emotional expression, and so forth, are different from theirs or those of the majority culture (Fontes & Thomas, 1996). As a result, efforts are being made to develop a *culture-sensitive therapy* (Prochaska & Norcross, 1999)—one that recognizes, for example, that the white middle-class cultural outlook from which most therapists operate (prizing individual choice, self-sufficiency, independence) is not necessarily embraced by all ethnic groups with which those therapists come into contact. In many Asian families, for example, interdependence within the family is expected, as is the expectation that family members will subordinate their separate needs to those of the family and society at large (McGoldrick, 2003).

The evolving view of cultural diversity recognizes that members of varied racial and ethnic groups retain their cultural identities while sharing common elements with the dominant American culture (Axelson, 1999). In many instances, ethnic values and identifications may influence family life patterns for several generations after immigration to this country. That is, acculturation is an ongoing process that takes place in most cases over many generations, as families confront changing gender-role

---

[5]According to a 1995 California survey of practicing marriage and family therapists, Green (1998) reports that 94 percent were of European American background, while fully 66 percent of their clients were families from other races or ethnic groups.

expectations, child-rearing practices, intergenerational relationships, family boundaries, and so forth, common in the dominant culture to which they have migrated. At the same time, immigrant families often must face changes in social level to lower-status jobs, ethnic prejudice and discrimination, the acceptance of minority status in the new land, and in some cases the fear of deportation.

Clearly, family therapists need to be culturally sensitive to the ever-increasing diversity among client families if they are to deal with such families effectively (Aponte & Wohl, 2000). On the other hand, they must be careful not to blindly adopt an ethnically focused view that stereotypes all members of a particular group as homogeneous and thus responds to a client family as if it were a cultural prototype. Here it is useful to note Falicov's (1995b) reminder regarding ethnically diverse groups, that a variety of other factors—educational level, social class, religion, and stage of acculturation into American society, to name but a few—also influence family behavior patterns. Moreover, individual family members differ from each other in their degree of acculturation as well as in their adherence to cultural values (Sue, 1994).

Developing a Multicultural Framework

A multicultural outlook champions a general, culturally sensitive approach with families and urges therapists to expand their attitudes, beliefs, knowledge, and skills to become more culturally literate and culturally competent (Sue et al., 1998). *Culturally competent* therapists take client cultural histories into account before undertaking assessments, forming judgments, and initiating intervention procedures. They assume

---

CLINICAL NOTE

In training students to work cross-culturally, we often begin by asking them to examine what they believe to be their own ethnic strengths, what cultural groups they know best, with what social class they've had the most experience. How have their life experiences influenced their outlook, belief systems, values, attitudes, and biases toward other groups?

Which ethnic groups do they know least well, have had least contact with, fear, think of in stereotypic terms? What views of these groups did they form growing up, and which of these prejudices remain? Are they careful not to impose their own point of view (e.g., about the age when young adults should leave home, or the extent to which they should remain in close contact with their family of origin after marriage)? Can they see the strengths in other ethnic groups that were missing in their own background?

Are there specific clients with whom they would have trouble working? Child molesters, wife batterers, gays, rural people, cyberspace predators, transsexuals, welfare recipients, immigrants, members of certain racial or religious groups? Why? What can they begin to do to help mitigate these prejudices?

This perspective is intended to alert the family therapist to keep in mind that how he or she assesses, counsels, or in general communicates with families is screened not only through professional knowledge but also through his or her own "cultural filters"—values, attitudes, customs, religious beliefs and practices, and especially outlooks regarding what constitutes normal behavior that stem from the therapist's particular cultural background (Giordano & Carini-Giordano, 1995). In the absence of preparation and information about a family's cultural background, the therapist runs the risk of misdiagnosing or mislabeling an unfamiliar family pattern as abnormal, when the behavior may be appropriate to that family's cultural group heritage (McGoldrick, 1998).

there is no single theory of personality applicable to all families, but instead urge the adoption of a pluralistic outlook that calls for multiple perspectives rooted in, and sensitive to, particular cultures (Prochaska & Norcross, 1999).

More than learning about specific cultures, advocates of multiculturalism such as Pedersen (2000) urge the adoption of an open, flexible attitude about diverse cultures and cultural influences, but not one tied to any specific cultural group. At the same time, they advocate that therapists gain greater awareness of their own values, assumptions, and beliefs, understanding that these are not absolutes but arise from the therapist's own cultural heritage. Sue and Sue (1999) emphasize the importance of adopting a broad viewpoint in working therapeutically with "culturally different" client populations, and the learning of a set of appropriate intervention techniques suited to diverse clients.

Cultural Specificity and Family Systems

Those family therapists who advocate a cultural-specific approach urge more detailed knowledge of common culturally based family patterns of unfamiliar groups.

Courtesy of Kenneth Hardy

Kenneth Hardy, Ph.D.

McGoldrick, Giordano, and Pearce (2005), for example, have brought together several dozen experts to provide detailed knowledge about a wide variety of racial and ethnic groupings. Their description of different lifestyles and value systems underscore that we are increasingly a heterogeneous society, a pluralistic one made up of varying races and ethnic groups, as millions migrate here seeking a better life. One in every four Americans today is a person of color (Homma-True, Greene, Lopez, & Trimble, 1993).

In this regard, Hardy and Laszloffy (1995) have provided a "cultural genogram" to help clients and trainees alike trace their kinship (race, social class, gender, religion, family migration history) networks over several generations. Subjects are asked to explore their personal cultural issues and cultural identities by charting their family ethnicity going back several generations. What were their family's migration patterns? Under what conditions did they enter the United States (immigration, political refugee, slavery, etc.)? Did race play a part? What is the family's dominant religion? How are gender roles defined within the family? What prejudices and stereotypes does their family have about itself and other groups? Answers to these and similar questions help therapists in training to better understand their own culture ("where they are coming from") before attempting to work cross-culturally. In addition, individuals are urged to explore which aspects of their cultural heritage they feel most comfortable "owning" and which ones they have the most trouble "owning." The technique can be used with client families to help broaden their self-understanding.

One way to assess the impact of a family's cultural heritage on its identity is to learn as much as possible about that specific culture before assessing the family. This undertaking is valuable in determining the extent to which its members identify with their ethnic background and to ascertain the relationship of ethnicity issues to the presenting problem (Giordano & Carini-Giordano, 1995). Just as it would be a mistake to judge the family behavior of clients from another culture as deviant because it is unfamiliar, so therapists must also be careful not to overlook or minimize deviant behavior by simply attributing it to cultural differences.

Taking gender, social class position, sexual orientation, religion, and racial or ethnic identification into account, a comprehensive understanding of a family's development and current functioning must assess its cultural group's kinship networks, socialization experiences, communication styles, typical male-female interactive patterns, the role of the extended family, and similar culturally linked attitudinal and behavioral arrangements (Goldenberg & Goldenberg, 1993).

Family therapists must try to distinguish between a client family's patterns that are *universal* (common to a wide variety of families), *culture-specific* (common to a group, such as African Americans or Cuban Americans or perhaps lesbian families), or *idiosyncratic* (unique to this particular family) in their assessment of family functioning. That is, they must discriminate between those family situations where cultural issues are relevant and those where cultural issues are tangential (Falicov, 1988). In this regard, Boyd-Franklin (2002) notes that as is common with many ethnic minority families, and unlike the dominant cultural norms, African Americans adhere to cultural values that stress a collective identity, family connectedness, and interdependence. More specifically, Boyd-Franklin's research (Boyd-Franklin, Franklin, & Toussaint, 2000) with African American parents reveals their special concerns about their children, particularly their sons: survival issues such as racial profiling, the disproportionate number tracked into special education and juvenile justice programs, drugs and alcohol abuse, gangs, violence, and so forth.

Family therapists also must keep in mind that while it is typically helpful to gain awareness of differences that might be attributable to ethnicity or racial characteristics of a specific group, there is also a risk in assuming a sameness among families sharing a common cultural background. Thus, as Fontes and Thomas (1996) caution, a culture-specific family therapy outlook offers useful guidelines, but these guidelines should not be considered recipe books for working with individual families. Even if they share the same cultural background, different families have differing histories, may come from different social classes, or may show different degrees of acculturation. As an example, these authors observe that members of a Mexican American family may identify themselves primarily as Catholic, or Californian, or professional, or Democrat; their country of origin or cultural background may actually be peripheral to the way they live their lives. Ultimately, the therapist's task is to understand how the client family developed and currently views its culture.

Family therapists must exercise caution before using norms from the majority cultural matrix in assessing the attitudes, beliefs, and transactional patterns of those whose cultural patterns differ from theirs. Beyond an appreciation of individual cultural influences, the family therapist must pay attention to what is unique about living as an ethnic minority—the language barriers, the cultural shock, the prejudice and discrimination, the feeling of powerlessness, the suspicion of institutions, the hopelessness, the rage. For example, in working with African American families, Thomas and Sillen (1974) point out that for White therapists to be insistently "color blind" to racial differences is no virtue if it means denial of differences in experiences, history, and social existence between themselves and their clients. The myth of sameness in effect denies the importance of color in the lives of African American families, and thus closes off an opportunity for therapists and family members to deal with sensitive race-related issues (Boyd-Franklin, 2003a).

Further, in working with acculturational and adaptational issues with immigrant families (Berry, 1997), therapists need to take care to distinguish between recently arrived immigrant families, immigrant American families (foreign-born parents, American-born or American-educated children), and immigrant-descendent families (Ho, 1987). Each has a specific set of adaptational problems—economic, educational, cognitive, affective, emotional. In regard to immigrant groups per se, their adaptation or acculturation is likely to be a function of four factors: (a) how long ago they arrived; (b) the circumstances of their arrival; (c) the support system they found upon arrival; and (d) the degree of acceptance by the dominant culture that they found here. An added challenge in working therapeutically with an ethnic family is in understanding the process of change in their values, attitudes, and behavior as they continue to have contact with the new dominant culture and its different values and expectations (Santisteban, Muir- Malcolm, Mitrani, & Szapocznik, 2002).

Ethnicity and the Transmission of Culture

Ethnicity refers to "the unique characteristics of a social grouping sharing national origin and linguistic and cultural traditions, with which members may or may not identify" (Kliman, 1994, p. 29). Members of an ethnic group are likely to share a common ancestry or country of origin, as well as a common group history. As in the case of racial membership, ethnic background profoundly affects a family's everyday experiences; it surely is a fundamental determinant of how families establish and reinforce acceptable values, attitudes, behavior patterns, and modes of emotional expression. Transmitted over generations by the family, ethnicity patterns may surpass race, religion, or national origin in significance for the family, particularly because they represent the individual's and the family's psychological needs for identity and a sense of historical continuity.

Our ethnic background influences how we think, how we feel, how we work, how we relax, how we celebrate holidays and rituals, how we express our anxieties, and how we feel about illness or life and death. Ethnicity patterns, reinforced by family tradition and community membership, may operate in subtle ways, frequently outside of our awareness; but their impact may nevertheless be broad, deep, and potent. These patterns are apt to play a significant role throughout the family life cycle, although that influence may vary between groups as well as within a group itself. In some families who hold on to traditional ways, clinging to cohorts from their religious or cultural background and excluding all others, ethnic values and identifications may be particularly strong and likely to be retained for generations (Goldenberg & Goldenberg, 2002). In Box 3.3 we illustrate a culturally sensitive approach to a family of Mexican heritage. What is presented by the family as a school truancy problem can be seen in a broader social context as a sociocultural problem.

As we noted earlier, even the definition of *family* differs in different ethnic groups. For some (Anglos) the ideal is the intact nuclear family; for others (African American) kinship and the extended community of "brothers" or "sisters" take precedence. Latino American families maintain a web of relationships that extends across generations and provides a support network sustained by rules of mutual obligation. By way of contrast, intergenerational ties are less important for Irish American families, who tend not to call upon extended family members when in need because of a sense of shame or embarrassment (Hines, Garcia-Preto, McGoldrick, Almeida, & Weltman, 1999).

Family loyalty, unity, and honor, as well as family commitment, obligation, and responsibility, characterize most Latino American families, so much so that sacrifices of family members' own needs or pleasures for the sake of the family are often encouraged, if not expected (McGoldrick, Garcia-Preto, Hines, & Lee, 1991). Similarly, the

BOX 3.3   CASE STUDY

COUNSELING A LATINO FAMILY

The Ortiz family, consisting of Roberto, 47, the father; Margarita, 44, the mother; and two daughters, Magdalena, 12, and Rosina, 10, had never been to a counselor before, and they arrived together at the school counseling office for their early evening appointment with little prior understanding of what the process entailed. Unaware that they could talk to a counselor at school about child-related problems at home, they were summoned by the school authorities as a result of poor and sporadic school attendance by the children during the previous six months. Magdalena had actually stopped attending, and her younger sister, Rosina, had recently begun to copy her sister's behavior, although she did go to class some days.

Arranging for the Ortiz family to come to counseling presented several problems. Although Mrs. Ortiz had been in this country for two decades, having arrived from El Salvador by illegally crossing the border at Tijuana, Mexico, with an older brother when she was 25, she spoke English poorly; and she felt self-conscious about her speech in front of the school authorities. Mr. Ortiz, himself an undocumented immigrant from rural Mexico, had been in this country longer and had taken classes in English soon after arriving. He, too, had to be persuaded that all the family members needed to be present. Both parents had recently been granted amnesty under federal immigration regulations and had looked forward to their children having better lives in the United States. Needless to say, both parents were very upset upon learning that their children were school truants.

The school counseling office arranged for Augusto Diaz, one of the counselors, to see the Ortiz family. Of Mexican heritage, Mr. Diaz was a third-generation Latino American who himself had learned Spanish in high school, never having heard it spoken at home growing up. He was sensitive to what each of the Ortiz family members was feeling and to the proper protocol for reaching this family. He began respectfully by addressing the father as the head of the house, thanking him for allowing his family to attend, but indicating that the children could not be allowed to skip school and that there were legal consequences if they continued to do so. Aware that Mrs. Ortiz seemed to be having trouble following his English, Mr. Diaz enlisted Magdalena as translator. From time to time, he used Spanish words or idioms when appropriate, although he himself was quite self-conscious about his Americanized Spanish. He, too, turned to Magdalena when uncertain of whether he had said in Spanish exactly what he had intended.

The first session was essentially designed to familiarize the family with what they could expect from counseling, to build trust in the counselor, and to show them that he was interested in their situation and would try to help. Mr. Diaz encouraged all family members to participate and commented several times on the father's strength in bringing his family in to discuss these issues. They arranged another evening appointment for the following week, at a time that would not interfere with Mr. Ortiz's daytime gardening job or Mrs. Ortiz's daytime occupation as a domestic worker.

When Mr. Ortiz finally felt comfortable enough to share his thoughts, he said that girls did not need higher education, that his daughters already knew how to read and write, and that had he had boys it would have been different. He was upset, however, that they were disobedient and disrespectful in not telling the parents that they were not attending school, but lying instead about how they spent their days. Although Mrs. Ortiz seemed to agree, she also revealed that she herself was suspicious of the school as well as most of what transpired in her adopted country. She hinted that she knew about the truancy, adding that she was afraid for her children in the mixed Hispanic–African American neighborhood in which they lived, and was just as happy that they stayed home rather than being influenced by their rougher classmates. Mrs. Ortiz saw her daughters' being home as an opportunity for some help for her after a long day and as good training for their eventual marriages.

(continued)

BOX 3.3   *(continued)*

Both Magdalena and Rosina, mute unless asked direct questions in the first two sessions, began to open up in the middle of the third family meeting. They admitted feeling isolated at school, especially because their parents would not allow them to bring classmates home or to visit others after dark. They confessed to being intimidated by gangs, something they had been afraid to reveal to their parents, who, they felt, would not understand. Staying away from school had started as a result of Magdalena's being attacked by an older girl on the school playground, after which the girl warned her to stay away or she would be seriously hurt. Rosina usually followed her older sister's lead, and was certain that if her sister was afraid then the danger was real.

By the fifth session the counselor, having gained the respect of the family members, had succeeded in opening up family communication. Mrs. Ortiz expressed an interest in learning English better, and the counselor guided her to a class in English as a second language (ESL) at the high school at night. Mr. Ortiz was persuaded to allow his wife to go out in the evening to attend class with one of their neighbors, another woman from El Salvador. He was pleased that she was trying to improve her English, which would lead eventually to gaining citizenship and thus to greater security for the family. Her mother's learning English would also free

Magdalena from her pivotal role as translator and pseudo-adult in the family. As Mr. Diaz learned of the family's need for other special services, such as filling out various insurance forms and income tax returns, he directed them to the local Catholic church, where some volunteers were helping parishioners with such problems.

The children were given added support by their mother, who walked them to school every day before she left for work. At the counselor's request, the school looked into the situation of the girl who had threatened Magdalena. That older girl still looked menacing, but as Magdalena and Rosina joined other children in the playground rather than being social isolates, they felt safer, and soon the terrorizing stopped. Magdalena joined the school drill team, and Rosina expressed an interest in learning to play an instrument and joining the school band.

The counselor, in an active, problem-solving way, was able to act successfully as a social intermediary among the family, the school, and the church. Mr. Diaz mobilized the Ortiz family to make better use of neighborhood and institutional resources and feel more a part of the overall community, thereby aiding them to solve the presenting truancy problem.

(Goldenberg & Goldenberg, 2002, pp. 331–333)

---

family and its ancestry are typically central in the lives of Asian Americans, with members expected to behave with loyalty and devotion to its values. Filial piety—loyalty, respect, and devotion of children to their parents—is of prime importance in traditional Asian families (del Carmen, 1990).

Family life cycle timing is influenced by ethnic considerations. The Irish wake is a ritual that represents a view of death as the most important transition, freeing humans so that they can go on to a happier afterlife. Polish and Italian American families emphasize weddings, their lengthy celebration reflecting the importance of the family's continuity into the next generation. For Jewish American families, the period of study for the bar or bat mitzvah signifies an adolescent's transition into adulthood, reflecting the high value placed on continued intellectual development (Hines, Garcia-Preto, McGoldrick, Almeida, & Weltman, 1999).

Child-rearing practices also vary greatly. While the dominant American pattern is for parents to have primary responsibility, African Americans may also rely on grandparents and other extended family members to care for children. Roles and boundaries in this kinship network are not rigidly defined, allowing for considerable role flexibility. Beyond actual relatives, other non-blood "relatives" (neighbors, family friends, godparents, preachers) may be intimately involved (Diller, 1999). Especially among the poor, different family members may reside in different households, or two or more families (or parts of families) may live in one household for periods of time. The danger in these generalizations, of course, is that they run the risk of stereotyping. As we have noted earlier, and as Ho (1987) reminds us, there is not only considerable interethnic group diversity but also marked intraethnic group heterogeneity. It is important to remember that some families are more assimilated than others; some have long histories of intermarriage; some individuals rebel against their cultural mandates; and social class differences play a decisive role. The importance of delineating common family patterns is in emphasizing the often-overlooked role of ethnocultural factors in behavior (McGoldrick, Giordano, & Pearce, 2005).

What about families formed by intermarriage between partners from different racial or ethnic groups? In such cross-cultural arrangements, the inevitable accommodations in any marriage may be longer and more complicated as the differences in background between the pair widen (Falicov, 1995a). Diverse outlooks, differing expectations, differing experiences with societal rejection or acceptance or being marginalized, differing culturally determined gender-role experiences, and in some cases differing social class upbringings all need to be considered if the cross-cultural couple is to establish a balanced partnership that acknowledges and respects their cultural similarities and differences. A glimpse at the potential set of misunderstandings can be seen in the following passage:

> An Italian American may interpret her Vermont Yankee husband's and in-laws' (unsolicited) respect for her privacy as cold and unloving; he may respond to his wife's and in-laws' (unsolicited) advice and emotional displays as incursions into his privacy. My WASP husband used to wonder why I phoned my brothers without news to relate; it broke my Jewish heart how rarely he called his sister. Even family members with similar backgrounds may need help in distinguishing assumptions based on culture, class, or family idiosyncrasy. They may interpret similar cultural norms differently, or expect partners and in-laws to share beliefs unique to their own families of origin. (Kliman, 1994, p. 31)

Before closing this section, it is necessary to remind ourselves that each therapist's values are inevitably embedded in that person's gender, ethnic, religious, and social class experiences and current circumstances. Since therapists inevitably expose these perspectives (biases?) in their interactions with their clients, they need to be aware of their own values and beliefs as they help client families to sort out theirs. Rather than oversimplified pictures to be taken at face value, the diverse ethnic profiles presented here are intended to call attention to the rich variety of human experiences and behavior—to emphasize that family therapists cannot ignore the influence of cultural idiosyncrasies in assessing and treating families they might otherwise label deviant or dysfunctional.

Poverty, Class, and Family Functioning

Every cultural group has social class divisions, and each social class is made up of members from different cultural groups. Men and women in each class experience life differently from one another, differently from their counterparts in other classes, and differently from others of the same class but from another cultural group.

No one group is monolithic: not all African Americans are poor; not all Whites are middle-class. In actuality, most of the nation's poor are White, although African Americans and other people of color are disproportionately represented among the poor. Increasingly it takes two parents—and two paychecks—to maintain a household's grip on middle-class status in the United States today.

Social class differences act as primary dividers within a society. Not only do they largely determine access to many resources (including therapy), but they also are influential in shaping beliefs, values, and behaviors (Fontes & Thomas, 1996). As Kliman and Madsen (1999) illustrate, poor families do not expect grandparents to help with down payments, and middle-class families do not expect the parents of 18-year-olds to be their grandchildren's caregivers. Despite our society's cherished myth that we are all middle-class (or have equal opportunity to become middle-class), the facts indicate otherwise: over 14 percent of all American families live below the poverty line, and many more live just above it. According to Columbia University's National Center for Children of Poverty, children living with unmarried mothers are five times more likely to be poor than those living with married parents. However, living with both parents offers no guarantee of clearing the poverty hurdle: more than one-third of children living in poverty were living with both parents (Healy, 1998).

Access to power is also largely determined by class membership. As Aponte (1994) observes:

> The poor are dependent upon and vulnerable to the overreaching power of society. They cannot insulate themselves from society's ills. They cannot buy their children private schooling when the public school fails. They cannot buy into an upscale neighborhood when their housing project becomes too dangerous. When society stumbles, its poorest citizens are tossed about and often crushed. (p. 8)

Poor African American families, embedded in a context of chronic unemployment and discrimination, are particularly limited in their abilities to function in ways that permit family members to thrive. The decline in marriage rates among African Americans, coupled with the increased number of teenage mothers, has added to their family crises.

Marian Edelman (1987), founder of the Children's Defense Fund, argues that the interrelated factors of poverty, male joblessness, and poor, female-headed households operate together to perpetuate generations of membership in America's underclass. In a seemingly endless cycle, the loosening of family structure has led to increased out-of-wedlock births and, correspondingly, increased child poverty; joblessness and its resulting poverty have led to a decline in the number of marriageable males and the further weakening of the family structure. Thus children are poor, according to Edelman's analysis, not only because many live in fatherless homes but also because the single parents with whom they live are likely to be unemployed or, if employed, to earn low wages.

Aponte (1987), too, emphasizes the erosion of family structure and the creation of what he terms *underorganized* (rather than disorganized) families. Living in such situations through generations, families of whatever racial background "learn to view as normal their own impotence" (p. 2). They are forced to accept their dependence upon the community's network of social institutions (welfare, public housing, publicly funded health care) without the necessary political or economic power to influence outcomes. Where fatherless homes predominate, roles lose their distinctiveness, and children may grow up too quickly while being at the same time intellectually and emotionally stunted in development.

Life cycle progression among the poor is often accelerated by teenage pregnancy. Most vulnerable are teenage girls with low academic ability from poor female-headed families. As Coley and Chase-Lansdale (1998, p. 153) observe:

> Life experiences associated with poverty, such as alienation at school, prevalent models of unmarried parenthood and unemployment, and lack of educational opportunities and stable career prospects all serve to lower the perceived costs of early motherhood.

Such early childbearing further decreases these girls' already limited prospects for financial security, steady job expectations, educational attainment, and marital stability.

The stages we have described in Chapter 2 for middle-class, intact families are often fast-forwarded; the "launching" stage for a young mother's children, for example, may occur when she is still at *her* mother's home (Fulmer, 1988). In the same manner, a "single adult" label is not likely to apply to an adolescent mother with children, nor is the parent-child relationship most likely to be the central one around which the family is organized. More probably, grandmother-mother-daughter relationships predominate, and several generations of family are likely to be alive at the same time. The basic family unit in such situations is apt to include extended three- or four-generational networks of kin. Such kinship groups at times function as "multiple-parent families" with reciprocal obligations to one another, sharing meager resources as efficiently as possible.

The family therapist, likely to be middle-class (in viewpoint if not necessarily in origin), must be careful not to regard being poor as synonymous with leading a chaotic, disorganized life, because, for example, long-term planning may not be present. It is essential to distinguish between those families who have been poor for many generations (victims of what Aponte, 1987, calls structural poverty), poor intermittently or temporarily (as students or while divorced but before remarriage), or recently poor because of loss (such as unemployment or the death of the major wage earner). It also helps to be aware that some poor people, including those who are chronically unemployed, share middle-class values (regarding such things as work and education) while others embrace more survival-based values of the working class as a result of their life experiences. Still others, termed the *underclass* by Incan and Ferran (1990), "make their living illegally or otherwise on the fringes of society" (p. 29). Some lead lives that are a series of crises, and others have forged family and social networks that are resourceful and workable. Above all, any efforts to equate poverty with psychological deviance first must take into account the harsh and confining social conditions usually associated with being poor.

SUMMARY

Gender, culture, and ethnicity are three key interrelated factors in shaping lives. In regard to gender, men and women are reared with different expectations, experiences, attitudes, goals, and opportunities, and these differences influence later culturally prescribed role patterns in family relationships. Family therapists have only recently begun to fully recognize the impact of these early patterns on current family life. Feminists contend that psychological research and clinical practice have been filled with outdated patriarchal assumptions and offer a male-biased perspective of sex roles and gender-defined functions within a family. They reject certain cybernetic concepts such as circular causality since such concepts fail to acknowledge differences in power and control between men and women, in effect blaming the victim for her victimization. The entry of women of all social classes in large numbers into the workforce in recent years has also helped break some long-held stereotypic views regarding the distribution of work and family responsibilities between husband and wife. Gender-sensitive therapy is directed at empowering clients, male and female, to move beyond prescribed sex roles based on biological status to ones in which they can exercise choice.

Cultural diversity is increasingly a part of American life, and family therapists have widened their focus from the family to include larger sociocultural contexts that influence behavior. A multicultural emphasis urges therapists to be more culturally sensitive before undertaking assessments, forming judgments, or initiating interventions with families whose backgrounds are different from theirs. Otherwise, therapists risk misdiagnosing or mislabeling unfamiliar family patterns as abnormal.

Gaining greater awareness of their own culturally based values, assumptions, and beliefs should help therapists work more effectively with ethnic families. A culturally specific emphasis asserts the importance of learning about culturally based family patterns of specific groups.

Ethnicity and social class considerations also influence family lifestyles. Ethnic heritage may help determine how families establish values, behavior patterns, and modes of emotional expression, and how they progress through the family life cycle. Living in poverty, whether temporarily or as part of poverty patterns extending over generations, may erode family structure and create underorganized families. In poor families, life cycle progression is sometimes accelerated by teenage pregnancy, which limits educational or financial security and future marital stability.

RECOMMENDED READINGS

Barnett, R. C., & Hyde, J. S. (2001). Women, men, work, and family: An expansionist theory. *American Psychologist, 56,* 781–796.

Boyd-Franklin, N. (2003). *Black families in therapy: Understanding the African-American experience.* New York: Guilford Press.

Falicov, C. J. (1998). *Latino families in therapy: A guide to multiculture practice.* New York: Guilford Press.

Hare-Mustin, R. T. (1987). The problem of gender in family therapy theory. *Family Process, 26,* 15–27.

McGoldrick, M. (Ed.). (1998). *Re-Visioning family therapy: Race, culture and gender in clinical practice.* New York: Guilford Press.

McGoldrick, M., Giordano, J., & Pearce, J. K. (2005). *Ethnicity and family therapy* (3rd ed.). New York: Guilford Press.

Philpot, C. L., Brooks, G. R., Lusterman, D-D, & Nutt, R. L. (1997). *Bridging separate gender worlds: Why men and women clash and how therapists can bring them together.* Washington, DC: American Psychological Association.

INTERLOCKING SYSTEMS: THE INDIVIDUAL, THE FAMILY, AND THE COMMUNITY

Up to this point we have proposed adopting a relationship frame of reference in studying a family's functioning, which involves paying simultaneous attention to its *structure* (the way it arranges, organizes, and maintains itself at any given cross section of time) and its *processes* (the way it evolves, adapts, and changes over time). At the same time, we have underscored the contextual nature of family functioning: not only are the lives of family members interconnected, but the family's structure and processes are themselves embedded in complex extended family, neighborhood, institutional, class, ethnic, and cultural systems. In recent years, therapeutic efforts have begun to be focused on multisystemic approaches that take into account the interactions among the individual, the family, and the surrounding cultural community.

Families are living, ongoing entities, organized wholes with members in a continuous, interactive, patterned relationship with one another extending over time and space. A change in any one component inevitably is associated with changes in other components with which it is in relation. Beyond the relationships of its constituent members, the family itself is continuously linked to larger systems in a bidirectional manner. The interplay between families and those social systems tells us a great deal about the level of success of family functioning.

In this chapter we introduce some of the underlying concepts of **general systems theory,** first proposed by biologist Ludwig von Bertalanffy in the late 1920s and later taken up in the 1940s and early 1950s by early family therapists as founding constructs for the then-new field. Bertalanffy's theory offers a set of assumptions regarding the maintenance of any organism or entity as a result of the complex interaction of its elements or parts. Early family therapists, seeking a scientific model, were particularly attracted to the notion that attention be directed more to the transactions taking place between family members than to the separate qualities or characteristics of each family member. For them, systems concepts became a useful *language* for conceptualizing a family's interactive process. These family therapy pioneers saw themselves as observers outside of the family system attempting to identify and understand what was transpiring within the system.

Both general systems theory and the first-order cybernetics concepts described in Chapter 1 catapulted to scientific attention during the 1940s, the former from the biological sciences and the latter from the mechanical concepts of physics and engineering. Arising at a time ripe for a paradigm change, both models are based on many of the same underlying assumptions regarding self-regulating systems. Indeed, both terms—*general systems theory* and *cybernetics*—often are used interchangeably by family therapists who wish to emphasize that a comprehensive view of family patterns requires looking through an interactive prism rather than focusing on the movements of individual family members.

Systems theory has emerged as an overall concept, encompassing both general systems theory and cybernetics, and focusing on the relationship between elements rather than on the elements themselves. In actuality, according to Constantine (1986), systems terms are not used by therapists with the precision and rigor with which they were originally formulated, but rather simply allude to the idea of a family as a complexly organized, durable, and ongoing causal network of related components.

Indeed, as we elaborate later in this chapter, postmodernists have been particularly rejecting of the systems metaphor both as too mechanical and as a modernistic view[1] that erroneously believes it can discover universal truths about the world that are simply out there and available for observation. Postmodernists content that what we believe to be reality is inevitably subjective, and that rather than discover facts we can only offer subjective perceptions of events (Becvar, 2003). They argue that therapists who think otherwise deceive themselves into believing they can objectively and impartially diagnose families, looking for flaws in their structure rather than, as White (1995) urges, helping families construct new concepts about themselves. Moreover, postmodernists such as de Shazer (1991) criticize systems theorists for reifying concepts—as though families actually possess constructs (rules, feedback, homeostasis) borrowed from cybernetics and general systems theory—rather than simply using the systems metaphor more generally in describing families.

Feminists too have found fault with the systems metaphor for assuming families function according to specific systemic rules divorced from their social, historical, economic, and political contexts. Doing so, as Avis (1996) points out, the systems view, narrowly focused, tends to see family difficulties as arising entirely within a family's interpersonal relationships, missing how gender and power relations in society are mirrored in family life. Feminists argue that systems theory fails to acknowledge the power imbalances between men and women inherent in society.

Nevertheless, although the arguments of these postmodernist and feminist thinkers have merit, and "systems" has become something of a catchword that runs the risk of being taken too literally, the concept should not be undervalued; historically it helped bring about a profound shift in thinking, from a reductionistic search for linear cause-and-effect events to "explain" personal disorder to a broader examination of the ongoing context in which current family dysfunctional patterns occur. For most family therapists today, systems language continues to provide a basic tool for thinking in interactional terms, expanded to emphasize the interaction between the individual, the family, and the surrounding society and culture.

---

[1]Psychological science is essentially based on *modernism,* especially the notion that there is an objectively knowable world and that it can be observed, measured, and understood by a detached, outside observer. As we elaborate in a number of places later in this text, *postmodern* thinkers argue instead that what we perceive of the outside world is a social construction molded by a particular culture, and that our knowledge of the world arises from a social exchange between people, mediated through language and reflecting the current values and outlooks of that culture (Gergen, 2002).

Systems theory lays the foundation for a comprehensive set of therapeutic interventions. At any particular time, a unique feature of systems theory is that it gives the family therapist a paradigm from which to view multiple causes and contexts of behavior (Mikesell, Lusterman, & McDaniel, 1995, p. xv).

Some Characteristics of a Family System

The concepts of **organization** and **wholeness** are keys to understanding how systems operate. If a system represents a set of units that stand in some consistent relationship to one another, then we can infer that the system is organized around those relationships. Further, we can say that the parts or elements of the system interact with each other in a predictable, "organized" fashion. Similarly, we can assume that the elements, once combined, produce an entity—a whole—that is greater than the sum of its parts. It follows that no system can be adequately understood or fully explained once it has been broken down into its component parts and that no element within the system can ever be understood in isolation since it never functions independently.

A family represents one such system, in which the components are organized into a group, forming a whole that transcends the sum of its separate parts. When we speak of the Sanchez family, for example, we are discussing a complex and recognizable entity—not simply the aggregate of Mr. Sanchez plus Mrs. Sanchez plus the Sanchez children.[2] Understanding the dynamic relationships among the components (family members) is far more illuminating than simply summing up those components. The relationships between the family members are complex, and factions, alliances, coalitions, and tensions exist. Causality within the family system is circular and multidirectional.

According to Nichols and Everett (1986), the way in which the family is organized defines its basic structure—its coherence and fit. As these authors illustrate, a family can be organized around a rigid, dominant male head, his acquiescent wife, and rebellious children. Or perhaps the children are compliant and the wife angry or combative. On the other hand, the family may be more matriarchal—a controlling woman, her angrily passive husband, and children who are caught up in the continuous parental struggles. Whatever the arrangement, the family's organization offers important clues as to its consistent or repetitive interactive patterns.

As Leslie (1988) observes, because of the system's wholeness, the movement of each component influences the whole and is explained, in part, by movement in related parts of the system. Focusing on the functioning of one element (member) becomes secondary to understanding the connections or relationships among family members and the overall organization of the system. As an illustration, Leslie notes that a family with two children does not simply add a new member when a baby is born; instead, the family becomes a new entity with accompanying changes in family interactive patterns.

---

[2]In some ethnic groups, such as Italian Americans, there is no such thing as a "nuclear family," since *family* refers to an entire network of aunts, uncles, cousins, and grandparents (Hines, Garcia-Preto, McGoldrick, Almeida, & Weltman, 1999). Together they share holidays and life cycle transitions, and are apt to live in close proximity, if not the same house.

Courtesy of Herbert and Irene Goldenberg

In this family therapy scene, co-therapists work together with a husband and wife who sought help because of their frequent quarrels over disciplining their six-year-old hyperactive daughter.

Should a two-year-old start to engage in hostile outbursts, linear explanations often attribute the new behavior to jealousy or infer the toddler is reacting to the loss of his mother's undivided attention, since she now must devote a great deal of attention to the newborn baby. A systems perspective, on the other hand, might look at how the family has reorganized after the new birth. Perhaps in reorganizing around the infant, the mother has assumed primary care of the infant, and the father the major responsibility for the older children, while the older son has been designated a helper to his mother with the newborn. The toddler may have lost his customary role in the family. From this vantage point, his hostile behavior may be signaling the family that their reorganization is inadequate or perhaps incomplete in meeting the needs of all of its members. To examine the motives of the toddler alone, without addressing the system's interactive patterns, would be to miss the point that the system requires alteration (Leslie, 1988). In the same way, it is imperative that the therapist address broader issues—the mother who may be giving up her work to remain at home with the children, the father who may work longer hours away from home in order to compensate for the income loss, the grandparents who may become involved in caring for the children, the availability of adequate child care, and so on. Adopting a systems view calls for more than viewing the family constellation in isolation.

Family Rules

A family is a cybernetically rule-governed system. The interaction of family members typically follows organized, established patterns, based on the family structure; these patterns enable each person to learn what is permitted or expected of him or her as well as others in family transactions. Usually unstated, such rules characterize, regulate, and help stabilize how—and how well—families function as a unit. They form a

Courtesy of Michael Newman/PhotoEdit, Inc.

This interracial couple, seeking family therapy, momentarily attends to their young child while a daughter from the mother's previous marriage interacts with the therapist.

basis for the development of family traditions, and largely determine expectations of the members vis-à-vis one another. A family's rules, then, reveal its values, help set up family roles consistent with these values, and in the process provide dependability and regularity to relationships within the family system. Rules frequently are carried over from previous generations and often have a powerful cultural component.

The observation that family interactions follow certain persistent patterns—rules—was first made by Don Jackson (1965a), a pioneer in family therapy. He observed that partners in a marriage face multiple challenges as potential collaborators in wage earning, housekeeping, socializing, lovemaking, and parenting. Early in their relationship, they begin to exchange views about one another, as well as express expectations about the nature of their relationship. More or less explicitly, according to Jackson (1965a), they define the rights and duties of each spouse: for example, "You can depend on me to be logical, practical, realistic"; "In return, you can depend on me to be a feeling, sensitive, social person." Such determinations often reflect culturally linked sex roles—in this case, traditional male and female roles, respectively—but variations are frequent.

Family rules determine the way people pattern their behavior; thus, for Jackson, as well as many early family therapists in their first formulations, rules become the governing principles of family life, providing guidelines for future interactive patterns. Addressing the marital dyad, Jackson adopted the still helpful concept of **marital quid pro quo** to describe a relationship with well-formulated rules in which each partner gives something and receives something else in return. Departing from his training in psychoanalysis and the search for intrapsychic conflict in each of the family members, Jackson was beginning to develop a language of interaction, a schema for depicting human exchanges.

BOX 4.1 CLINICAL NOTE

Family Rules and Family Dysfunction

When rules are appropriate for the persons involved, and not too rigid, modifications can be made based on their subsequent experiences together. If rules are flexible and responsive to new information, and carried out while tending to the needs of both, the couple is able to develop a functional division of labor that is intended to help them pursue the sort of life they wish to lead in the future. If, on the other hand, rules are too rigidly defined and fail to take the needs or specific skills of each participant into account, conflict between the couple is likely to follow, leading to family dysfunction.

Extending his observations to family communication sequences, Jackson (1965b) hypothesized that a **redundancy principle** operates in family life, according to which a family interacts in repetitive behavioral sequences. That is, instead of using the full range of possible behavior open to them, members typically settle on a narrow option range or limited redundant patterns when dealing with one another. If, as a therapist, you understand their rules—in some cases rigid, in others loose and vaguely defined— you begin to understand how a family defines its internal relationships. Jackson maintained that it is these rules rather than individual needs, drives, or personality traits that determine the interactive sequences between family members.

Rules may be *descriptive* (metaphors describing patterns of interchange) or *prescriptive* (directing what can or cannot occur between members). They are formulas for constructing and maintaining family relationships. For example, within a family group, descriptive rules may be based on individual prerogatives and obligations determined by age, sex, or generation. Some may be negotiable, while others are not; rigid families may have too many rules, chaotic families too few. Whatever the family structure, all members learn the family's **metarules** (literally, the rules about the rules), which typically take the form of unstated family directives offering principles for interpreting rules, enforcing rules, and changing rules.

Some prescriptive rules are stated overtly—rules such as: "Children allow parents to speak without interruption"; "Children hang up their clothes"; "Parents decide on bedtime"; "Mother makes decisions regarding the purchase of new clothes"; "Father chooses the television programs on Monday night"; "Heavy lifting is done by the males; females do the cooking and cleaning chores"; "Sister helps set the table but Brother helps Dad clear the dinner dishes"; "Younger children go to bed earlier than

CLINICAL NOTE

When working with families who seem to follow unyielding rules, it is important to try to understand what fears underlie the inflexibility. Is a curfew established by parents a reaction to fears of a teenage daughter's drug use, sexual activity, becoming pregnant? Is there a Cinderella fantasy that being home by a certain predetermined hour will be protective? The family needs help in addressing the fears rather than the rules themselves.

older ones"; "Our family does not marry outside our religion"; "Older children are responsible for looking after younger ones."[3]

Most family rules, however, are covert and unstated. That is, they are inferences that all family members draw from the redundancies or repetitive patterns in the relationships they observe at home—for example, "Father is distant due to his frequent absences, so approach Mother if you have a problem"; "It's best to ask Mother for money after dinner, when she's in a good mood"; "Both parents are tired and unavailable, so don't come to them with problems"; "Don't be a crybaby"; "If you lose your glasses, avoid mentioning it as long as possible because they'll both be mad"; "Stay away from their room on Sunday morning, they like to be alone." Children learn and perpetuate these rules.

Parents act according to covert rules of their own: "Daughters in our culture help in the kitchen, but it isn't right to ask a son"; "Boys have later curfews than girls"; "Men in our family can drink, but women can't": "You kids can fight all you want, but don't involve us"; "We can trust our daughter with money, but it seems to burn a hole in our son's pocket." Sometimes a family rule, unstated but understood by all, is that decisions are made by the parents and handed down to the children; in other cases, all family members learn that they may state their own opinions freely. In a well-functioning family, rules help maintain order and stability while at the same time allowing for adjustment to changing circumstances. The issue for such a family is not that it follows the "correct" rules while other, less successful families do not, but rather that its rules are fair, consistent, and clearly communicated to all members.

Virginia Satir (1972), another pioneer in family therapy and an early associate of Jackson's at the Mental Research Institute in Palo Alto, California, also was interested in aiding a family to clarify its communication patterns. She tried to help a family recognize its unwritten rules, especially those rigidly enforced rules that evoke the exchange of hard feelings or that cause family pain. For example, some families forbid discussion of certain topics (mother's drinking problem, or father's unexplained absence from home certain nights, or brother's inability to read, or sister's sexual promiscuity) and consequently fail to take realistic steps to alleviate problems. Other families forbid overt expressions of anger or irritation with each other ("Stop! The children will hear us"; "If you can't say something nice to one another, don't say anything at all"). Still others foster dependence ("Never trust anyone but your mother or father") or enmeshment ("Keep family business within the family") and thus handicap children as they attempt to deal with the outside world.

Satir argued, simply, that dysfunctional families follow dysfunctional rules. Consistent with that view, she attempted to help such families become aware of those unwritten rules that retard growth and maturity. Once these rules have been identified, she believed it may be possible for the family to revise or discard those that are outmoded, inappropriate, or irrelevant, in order to improve the individual self-esteem of members as well as overall family functioning.

---

[3]A small child visiting a friend for the first time is apt to be bewildered by observing a family operating under an alien and unrecognizable set of rules. Mother and father may greet each other with a kiss, may not get into a quarrel over the dinner table, may include children in the conversation. The visiting child is sometimes startled to learn that, according to the rules of the host family, it is not necessary to finish all the food on your plate before you are allowed to have dessert.

Family Homeostasis

Homeostasis refers to the family's self-regulating efforts to maintain stability and resist change. Although the end result is a steady state, the process is hardly a static one. To the contrary, a constantly fluctuating interaction of equilibrating and disequilibrating forces is operating. Early family theorists and researchers—led by Bateson, along with Jackson—recognized the applicability of this cybernetic concept to an upset or threatened family system that initiates homeostatic mechanisms in order to reestablish equilibrium. In their initial formulations, groundbreaking for their time (although more controversial today), researchers saw homeostasis as a way for a family to resist change by returning to its pre-threatened steady state. Most practicing family therapists today would argue that helping families return to previous balanced states shortchanges them by failing to credit them with the resiliency and resourcefulness to regroup at a more highly functioning level.

Homeostatic mechanisms help to maintain the stability of an ongoing arrangement between family members by activating the rules that define their relationships. What happens, however, when a family must change or modify its rules? How adaptive or flexible are the metarules for changing established or habitual patterns in a particular family? As children grow up, they usually put pressure on the family to redefine its relationships. Many adolescents expect to be given money to spend as they wish, to make their own decisions about a suitable bedtime, to listen to music that may be repellent to their parents' ears, to play computer games for unlimited amounts of time, to pursue interests other than those traditionally cared about in the family. They may challenge the family's values, customs, and norms; they insist on being treated as equals. All of this causes disequilibrium in the family system, a sense of loss, and perhaps a feeling of strangeness until reorganization restores family balance.

In most cases, a system tends to maintain itself within preferred and familiar ranges. A demand for deviation or change that is too great, too sudden, or too far beyond the system's threshold of tolerance is likely to encounter counterdeviation responses. In poorly functioning families, demands for even the most necessary or modest changes may be met with increased rigidity as the family stubbornly attempts to retain familiar rules.

While this view of the family operating as a cybernetic system became axiomatic for most family therapists, perhaps the defining metaphor for family therapy in its earlier years, two sets of challenges emerged in the 1980s. One came from feminist family therapists such as Luepnitz (1988), who insisted that power within families is typically asymmetrical; within society at large, different people have differing degrees of power in altering an undesirable situation. Luepnitz believes that cyberneticists and general system theorists fail to take power differentials (particularly between men and women) into account in their homeostatic formulations. While the less powerful may influence the more powerful, the difference between influence and legitimate power is often substantial.

Another set of critics (Dell, 1982; Hoffman, 1981) also argued that the simple homeostasis concept fails to deal with *change*. The earlier homeostatic position, these new epistemologists assert, incorrectly assumes a dualism between one part of the system and another, when in fact all parts together engage in change. More than seeking to maintain the status quo, homeostasis represents a tendency to seek a steady state when a system is perturbed. That new state is always slightly different from the preceding steady state, since all systems continue to change and evolve.

Here the family therapist, as a participant in the system, is called upon to do more than help restabilize a system whose stability has been threatened. Dell (1982) sees the therapist's task in such cases not as helping the family members to return to their former homeostatic balance, but rather as encouraging the family to search for new solutions, in effect pushing the family system out of its old state of equilibrium and into achieving a new level of stability through reorganization and change.

Family stability is actually rooted in change. That is, to the degree that a family is functional, it is able to retain sufficient regularity and balance to maintain a degree of adaptability while preserving a sense of order and sameness. At the same time, it must subtly promote change and growth within its members and the family as a whole. For example, a well-functioning couple dealing with parenthood for the first time may strengthen their partnership and grow more intimate as the family expands to accommodate the new arrival. On the other hand, a less well-functioning couple may grow apart after the birth of the child, with one or the other (or both) feeling unattended to, neglected, angry, and resentful.

Well-functioning families are resilient and able to achieve change without forfeiting long-term stability. An immigrant family, established in their home country but forced to migrate due to war or other social or political events, may face numerous dislocations (new jobs, new language, even a new sense of freedom), but may close ranks and form a stronger bond than before, as together they deal with the changing situation.

Feedback, Information, and Control

Feedback refers to *reinserting into a system the results of its past performance as a method of controlling the system, thereby increasing the system's likelihood of survival.* **Feedback loops** are circular mechanisms whose purpose is to introduce information about a system's output back to its input, in order to alter, correct, and ultimately govern the system's functioning and ensure its viability. Feedback loops help mitigate against excessive fluctuations, thus serving to maintain and thereby extend the life of the system.

Negative feedback (*attenuating* feedback loops) about the performance of the system, fed back through the system, triggers those necessary changes that serve to put the system back "on track" and thus guards the system's steady state, maintaining homeostasis in the face of change. **Positive feedback** (*amplifying* feedback loops) has the opposite effect: it leads to further change by augmenting or accelerating the initial deviation.

Systems require both positive and negative feedback—the former to accommodate to new information and changing conditions, the latter, when appropriate, to maintain the status quo. For example, as children in a family grow into adolescence, they are likely to demand greater independence and self-direction, temporarily destabilizing the family system through their insistence on rule changes. Adaptive or enabling families typically attempt to deal with change by renegotiating teenage privileges and responsibilities and receiving feedback information regarding how easily and appropriately the changes are handled. Positive feedback mechanisms are operating here as the family adapts to change by modifying its structure, and the system's stability is regained. Once the system has been modified, negative feedback mechanisms keep it running on a steady course (until further changes become necessary), and the family has dealt effectively with change while maintaining stability.

In a less functional manner, a family whose repertoire is limited to negative feedback may be inflexible and stifling and consequently engage in restrictive behavior detrimental to a system attempting to deal with changing circumstances. For example, parents may continue to treat the teenager as a child, refusing to acknowledge his or her growing maturity. In a similarly dysfunctional manner, positive feedback, helping to change or modify a system, may reach runaway proportions without the stability provided by negative feedback, forcing the system beyond its coping limits to the point of exhaustion or self-destruction; the adolescent does not know how to handle new freedoms and rebelliously defies all family rules.

No family passes through its life cycle transitions unscathed. Periodic imbalance is inevitable, and feedback loops are called into play that restore stability or escalate conflict. Within a marriage, exchange of information through feedback loops helps maintain equilibrium, as disturbing or annoying patterns are adjusted and new, stabilizing patterns evolve. A misunderstanding can be corrected and minimized (attenuating deviation) or escalated (amplifying deviation). In the latter case, an argument may get out of control, becoming increasingly vicious, ugly, or even violent, reaching the point where neither spouse can (or no longer wants to) control the consequences. However, the conflict may also be resolved through positive feedback as the couple strives for a new level of understanding.

Goldenberg and Goldenberg (2002) illustrate the operation of negative and positive feedback loops in the case of a remarried couple. In the former situation, there is attenuation, or negative feedback:

HUSBAND: I'm upset at the way you talked to that man at the party tonight, especially the way you seemed to be hanging on every word he said.

WIFE: Don't be silly! You're the one I care about. He said he had just come back from a trip you and I had talked about going on and I was interested in what he had to tell me about the place.

HUSBAND: OK. But please don't do it again without telling me. You know I'm touchy on the subject because of what Gina [ex-wife] used to do at parties with other men that drove me crazy.

WIFE: Sorry. I hadn't thought about that. I'll try to remember next time. In the meantime, you try to remember that you're married to me now and I don't want you to be jealous.

In a less blissful situation, instead of the previous attenuation, there is amplification, or positive feedback:

HUSBAND: I'm upset at the way you talked to that man at the party tonight, especially the way you seemed to be hanging on every word he said.

WIFE: One thing I don't appreciate is your spying on me.

HUSBAND: Spying? That's a funny word to use. You must be getting paranoid in your old age. Or maybe you have something to hide.

WIFE: As a matter of fact, I was talking to him about a trip he took that we had talked about, but I don't suppose you'd believe that. Talk about paranoid!

HUSBAND: I give up on women! You're no different from Gina, and I suppose all other women.

WIFE: With an attitude like that, I'm starting to see why Gina walked out on you.

However, positive feedback, while destabilizing, may also be beneficial if it does not get out of control and helps change the system for the better. Consider a third scenario: The couple expands and deepens their relationship by being nondefensive, willing to share their feelings, and reexamining their rules:

HUSBAND: I'm upset at the way you talked to that man at the party tonight, especially the way you seemed to be hanging on every word he said. Can you help me understand what was going on?

WIFE: He said he had just come back from a trip you and I had talked about going on and I was interested in what he had to tell me about the place. Maybe I should have called you over and included you in our conversation.

HUSBAND: No need to invite me. From now on I will come over so I'll know what's happening.

WIFE: I'd like that. Keeping in close contact with you at a party always makes me feel good.

Negative and positive feedback loops are in and of themselves neither good nor bad. In the case of families, both are necessary if stability and continuity are to be maintained despite the vagaries of outside pressures. Notwithstanding the potentially escalating impact of the runaway system in the second example, it should be clear from the third example that not all positive feedback should be thought of as damaging or destructive to the system's operations. Homeostatic does not mean static; as a marriage or a family grows, stability calls for acknowledging change, and change often comes about in a family through breakthroughs that push the family beyond its previous homeostatic level. At times it may be advantageous to propel a family with stagnating or otherwise untenable behavior patterns to new levels of functioning. In these cases, the therapist may seize the opportunity of disequilibrium to promote discontinuity and the restoration of family homeostasis at a new, more satisfactory level for all.

Information processing is fundamental to the operation of any system. If it is faulty, the system is likely to malfunction. The more or less free exchange of information within a family and between the family and the outside world helps reduce uncertainty, thus avoiding disorder. According to Bateson's (1972) elegant definition, information is "a difference that makes a difference." In interpersonal family terms, a word, a gesture, a smile, a scowl—these are differences or changes in the environment comparable to a temperature drop as environmental input. These differences in turn make a difference when the receiver of the new information alters his or her perceptions of the environment and modifies subsequent behavior.

Subsystems

A system, as we have seen, is organized into a more or less stable set of relationships; it functions in certain characteristic ways; it is continuously in the process of evolution as it seeks new steady states. **Subsystems** are those parts of the overall system assigned to carry out particular functions or processes within the system as a whole. Each system exists as part of a larger suprasystem and contains smaller subsystems of which it is the suprasystem.

A family commonly contains a number of coexisting subsystems. The husband and wife dyad constitutes a subsystem; so do the mother-child, father-child, and child-child dyads. In a family, subsystems can be formed by generation (mother and father), by sex (mothers and daughters), by interest (intellectual pursuits), or by function (parental caretakers); see Minuchin (1974). Within each subsystem, different levels of power are exercised, different skills learned, and different responsibilities assigned. For example, the oldest child may have power within the sibling subsystem but must cede that power when interacting with his or her parents.

Because each family member belongs to several subsystems simultaneously, he or she enters into different complementary relationships with other members. For example, a woman can be a wife, mother, daughter, younger sister, older sister, niece, grand-daughter, and so on, simultaneously. Within each subsystem in which she holds membership, she plays a different role and can be expected to engage in different transactional patterns. Consider this example: While giving her younger sister advice about finding a job, a woman is told by her husband to get off the telephone and hurry up with dinner. She decides how to deal with his demand. Some moments later, she remembers not to feel hurt when the children refuse to eat what she has prepared. She even responds diplomatically when her mother, a dinner guest, gives her advice on how to improve the food she has prepared.

The most enduring subsystems are the *spousal, parental,* and *sibling* subsystems (Minuchin, Rosman, & Baker, 1978). The husband-wife dyad is basic; any dysfunction in this subsystem is bound to reverberate throughout the family as children are scape-goated or co-opted into alliances with one parent against the other whenever the parents engage in conflict. The spousal subsystem teaches the children about male-female intimacy and commitment by providing a model of marital interaction. How the marital partners accommodate one another's needs, negotiate differences, make decisions together, manage conflict, meet each other's sexual and dependency needs, plan the future together, and so on, help influence the effectiveness of relationships between all family members. A viable spousal subsystem, one in which the marital partners have worked out a fulfilling relationship with one another, provides both spouses with the experience of intimacy, support, mutual growth, and an opportunity for personal development.

The parental subsystem (which may include grandparents or older children temporarily assigned parental roles) has the major responsibility for proper child rearing, nurturance, guidance, limit setting, and discipline. Through interaction with parents, children learn to deal with authority, with people of greater power, while strengthening their own capacity for decision making and self-direction. Problems within this subsystem, such as serious intergenerational conflicts involving rebelliousness, symptomatic children, or runaways, often reflect underlying family instability and disorganization. In some families, parents share parental authority and responsibility with grandparents, or in other cases with relatives, neighborhood friends, or paid help.

The sibling set represents a child's first peer group. Sibling relationships are typically the longest lasting connections we make, extending over the life span (Cicirelli, 1995). Through participation in this subsystem, a child develops patterns of negotiation, cooperation, competition, mutual support, and later, attachment to friends. Interpersonal skills honed here influence later school or workplace relationships. The influence of this subsystem on overall family functioning depends to a large extent on how viable all family subsystems are. Spousal, parental, and sibling subsystems stand in an overall dynamic relationship, each simultaneously influencing and being influenced by one another. Together, relationships within and between subsystems help define the family's structure.

Other subsystems, most of them less durable than those just outlined, exist in all families. Father-daughter, mother-son, father–oldest son, and mother–youngest child transitional alliances are common. Their protracted duration, however, especially if the alliance negatively affects family functioning, may signal difficulties within the spousal subsystem, alerting the family therapist to the potential instability of the family system.

CLINICAL NOTE

Extreme rivalry between siblings should alert the therapist to the possibility that one or both children view themselves as receiving unfair treatment by one or both parents. Their conflict usually reflects the fighting between the parents, where a parent may draw a child into their conflict to support his or her position. Family members require help to change these inappropriate coalitions.

Boundaries

A **boundary** is an invisible line of demarcation that separates an individual, a subsystem, or a system from outside surroundings. Boundaries help define the individual autonomy of a subsystem's separate members, as well as helping to differentiate subsystems from one another. Within a system such as a family, boundaries circumscribe and protect the integrity of the system, determining who is considered an insider and who remains outside. The family boundary may serve a gatekeeper function, controlling information flow into and out of the system ("We don't care if your friend's parents allow her to stay out until 2 AM; in our family, your curfew is 12 AM"; "Whatever you hear at home you are expected to keep private and not discuss with outsiders").

Within a family itself, boundaries distinguish between subsystems, helping define the separate subunits of the overall system and the quality of their interactive processes. Minuchin (1974) contends that such divisions must be sufficiently well defined to allow subsystem members to carry out their tasks without undue interference, while at the same time open enough to permit contact between members of the subsystem and others. For example, a mother defines the boundaries of the parental subsystem when she tells her 15-year-old son, the oldest of three children: "It's not up to you to decide whether your sisters are old enough to stay up to watch that TV program. Your father and I will decide that." However, she temporarily redefines that boundary to include the oldest child within the parental subsystem when she announces: "I want all of you children to listen to your older brother while your father and I are away from home tomorrow evening." Or she may invite grandparents to join the parental subsystem for one evening only, asking them to check on how the children are getting along or to advise the oldest son on necessary action in case of an emergency.

These examples underscore the idea that the *clarity* of the subsystem boundaries is far more significant in the effectiveness of family functioning than the composition of the family subsystems. While the parent-child subsystem may be flexible enough to include the oldest child, or a grandmother may be pressed into service when both parents are unavailable, the lines of authority and responsibility must remain clear. In most middle-class European American families, a grandmother who interferes with her daughter's management of the children in ways that undermine the parent-child subsystem (and perhaps also the spousal subsystem in the process) is overstepping her authority by being intrusive and crossing family boundary lines. Among poor African American families, however, the lines of authority may deviate from this standard. Here, active grandparent participation in an expanding household is more likely than not to be the norm, as grandparents help provide care for grandchildren, adult children, and other elderly kin (Hines, 1999).

An important issue here involves the *permeability* of the boundaries, since boundaries vary in how easily they permit information to flow to and from the environment. Not only must the boundaries within families be clearly drawn, but the *rules* must be apparent to all. If boundaries are too blurred or too rigid, they invite confusion or inflexibility, increasing the family's risk of instability and ultimate dysfunction.

Open and Closed Systems

A system with a continuous information flow to and from the outside is considered to be an **open system,** while one whose boundaries are not easily crossed is considered a **closed system.** The key point here is the degree of interaction with, and accessibility to, the outside environment. Open systems do more than adapt passively to their surroundings; their social transactions are bidirectional. That is, beyond simply adjusting, they also initiate activities that permit an exchange with the community because their boundaries are permeable. Closed systems, on the other hand, have impermeable boundaries. Thus they fail to interact with the outside environment, lack feedback corrective mechanisms, become isolated, and resist change.

An example of such a closed system is a type of religious cult that closes out the world beyond its borders, specifically to halt the flow of information from the outside world and in that way to control the behavior of its members. Similarly, totalitarian countries that do not permit foreign newspapers, radio or television, or access to the Internet also represent systems deliberately closed to control citizens' behavior.

In family terms, no system is fully open or closed; if it were totally open, no boundaries would exist between it and the outside world, and it would cease to exist as a separate entity; if totally closed, there would be no exchanges with the outside environment, and it would die. Rather, systems exist along a continuum according to the flexibility or rigidity of their boundaries. Families that function effectively maintain the system by developing a balance between openness and closeness, tuned to the outside world so that appropriate change and adaptation are accomplished while changes that threaten the survival of the system are resisted.

All families operate as open systems, but some may appear more closed in the sense of being rigid or insular. The more open the family system, the more adaptable and accessible to change it is. Such a system tends not only to survive but to thrive, to be open to new experiences and to alter or discard no longer usable interactive patterns; thus it is said to have **negentropy,** or a tendency toward maximum order. Such a family system is able to alter its patterns in response to new information calling for a change in family rules, and to discard those established responses that are inappropriate to the new situation.

Due to exchanges beyond their boundaries, open systems—particularly if they have a stable core—increase their chances of becoming more highly organized and developing resources to repair minor or temporary breakdowns in efficiency (Nichols & Everett, 1986). An immigrant family, newly arrived in a new country, that immediately begins learning the customs and language of the adopted land and encourages its children to adapt in a similar manner can be considered to be acting as an open system.

The lack of such exchanges in relatively closed systems decreases their competence to deal with stress. Limited or perhaps even nonexistent contact with others

BOX 4.2   CLINICAL NOTE

Can a Family System Be Too Open?

An open system encourages parents to consider community standards (at what age to drive and under what circumstances, curfew hours, overnight sleepovers) in deciding how much freedom to allow children, but may not permit the unsupervised posting on the Internet of easily accessible private information that could expose children to danger. Allowing a young daughter unfettered access to the computer may lead to her posting her photo and personal information on MySpace.com, increasing the chances of potentially dangerous consequences if she is contacted by cyberspace predators.

outside the family unit may lead to fearful, confused, and ineffective responses in times of crisis. Such closed systems run the risk of **entropy;** they gradually regress, decay because of insufficient input, and thus are prone to eventual disorganization and disorder, particularly if faced with prolonged stress.

Closed systems, then, fail to make enabling adaptations. They are apt to seal themselves off from all but necessary exchanges with the outside world; they maintain strict control on who and what is admitted into the home, screening visitors, restricting computer use, preventing contact with social agencies or uncensored reading matter or television programs, and thus are destined for eventual dysfunction because of insufficient input. For example, recent immigrants or ethnic groups that live in relative isolation, communicating only among their own ethnic group, suspicious of outsiders, and fostering dependence on the family, often tend to hold on to tradition and avoid change, thus operating in the manner of a relatively closed system. Parent-child relationships in such families may encounter problems due in part to culture conflict, and these problems, if serious enough, may lead to the development of an entropic family.

In the following case, a working-class family from India immigrates to the United States. Having been a normal and relatively open family system in their native country, they react to the pressures of immigration by becoming more closed and insular. Feeling unsafe in their adopted country, they resist change. Their children, schooled in the United States, attempt to re-open the system and make the family more flexible and adaptive to their present environment.

BEYOND THE FAMILY SYSTEM: ECOSYSTEMIC ANALYSIS

Adopting an ecosystemic perspective greatly broadens the context, attending to the numerous social systems in which the family functions, not simply intrafamily relationships themselves. Such a view addresses the multiple systems in which families are embedded. In this multidimensional view, attention is directed beyond the family to "external" factors that may be influencing family functioning (Robbins, Mayorga, & Szapocznik, 2003). Beyond helping families improve their coping skills, clinicians with this outlook help empower them to make more effective use of available social and community services. No longer restricted to the consultation room, services may be delivered in schools, homes, community agencies, and elsewhere, at places more

BOX 4.3   CASE STUDY

AN IMMIGRANT FAMILY FACES AN INTERGENERATIONAL CONFLICT

Indira and Sanjay Singh were a sister and brother who came from India to the United States with their parents when they were still of preschool age. Their parents had brought them with the hope that the children's lives would be better than theirs, since neither of the parents had had much education or opportunity in their native land. The parents worked very hard, seven days a week, in a small clothing store they owned, just managing to make a living, and the children were expected to help out as early as six or seven years of age, just as the parents had done with their own parents. Both children were taught to be compliant with adults, to respect their parents' wishes, and to engage in social activities primarily with family or extended family members. Friends from school were discouraged, and Indira and Sanjay, now 17 and 14, respectively, were expected to go places only with each other, never alone or with friends. Television was tolerated but monitored by the parents; for example, the children were not allowed to view scenes of people kissing, which was also not permitted in Indian cinema. When the children objected, the parents reminded them that they were being disrespectful and that if their "insolent" behavior continued, the parents would move them all back to India no matter what the sacrifice to the family.

Loyalty, respect, and family obligation were essential parts of the family code. As in other Indian families they knew, extended family ties were stressed, arranged marriages were the norm, and children were expected to obey their parents, especially their father. The parents did not understand why the children wanted to associate with strangers when family members were available. What class or caste did these strangers belong to? What would happen to her father's plans for her marriage if Indira got into trouble or developed a bad reputation as a result of being in bad company? When Indira asked to go to a party with her high school friends, the parents refused, asking instead why she hadn't proposed helping out in the store so they could get some rest. Despite her protests that she did help but also wanted to have some fun, the parents threw up their hands in despair and told the children how miserable their ungrateful behavior had made their parents.

A teacher who knew something of Indian culture, observing Indira's distress, talked to her about the problems of biculturalism and suggested that such culture conflict was not uncommon between first and second generations in a new country. The teacher suggested family counseling, which the parents first refused to do, expressing shame that intervention by a stranger would be necessary. After the children visited a counselor alone for two sessions, the parents reluctantly came in, and together all four began to deal with the differences between countries and to understand cultural expectations.

Source: Goldenberg & Goldenberg, 2002, pp. 20–21.

convenient to the family. *Home-based services*, an extension of a well-established social service tradition, typically are directed at building and strengthening relationships between the family and the available resources of the community, rather than working directly at repairing family dysfunction (Henggeler & Borduin, 1990). A collaborative venture is encouraged between the family, galvanizing its inherent strengths, and the community's caregivers, who work in partnership to address the needs of the family. In-home therapy, a relatively new phenomenon, is typically short-term and intensive, and usually focuses on ordinarily difficult to reach, multiproblem families—substance-abusing adolescents and their families, teenage mothers, families in which abuse and neglect have occurred, families with severe

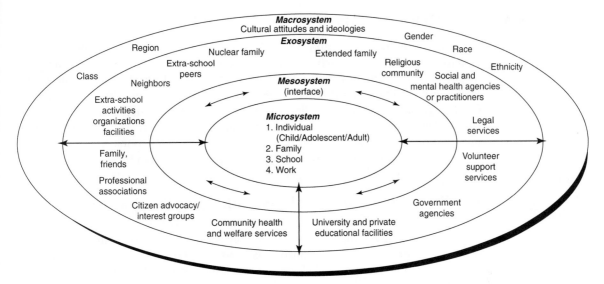

FIGURE 4.1 An ecomap depicting the multiple contexts that influence a person's self-identity and behavior

Source: Based on Knoff (1986).

psychiatric disorders. These at-risk populations are especially vulnerable to break-down and in need of social services; in-home therapy, conducted in the comfort of familiar surroundings, may be less threatening than entering the community to seek help, and thus may lead to more favorable outcomes (Yorgason, McWey, & Felts, 2005).

Individuals and families are nested within multiple but independent social systems that influence how they behave. Bronfenbrenner (1986) proposed a theory of social ecology in which four levels of influence exist, each level containing and influencing the prior level. Thus, the individual is embedded in his or her family system, which is embedded in a neighborhood or religious community, which, in turn is part of an ethnic group or social class, and so forth. Depicted on an ecomap (see Figure 4.1), the *microsystem level* refers to the person and his or her immediate system, the *mesosystem* to the relationships in which members of his or her microsystem take part, the *exosystem* to the larger systems that affect the individual, and the *macrosystem*, the broad social and cultural forces that have the most widespread influence on the individual.

Rather than viewing the family as an isolated, encapsulated system, the ecosystemically oriented therapist is able to intervene at any level to improve family functioning. As Robbins, Mayorga, and Szapocznik (2003) illustrate, problems may be addressed to improve the relationship between family members (microsystem level), to improve a partner's relationship with extended family members (mesosystem level), to work on a behavior-problem child's parent's connection to Alcohol Anonymous (exosystem), or by the therapist serving on a committee to develop treatment practices for victims or perpetrators of domestic violence (macrosystem). Maintaining an ecological focus widens the lens to encourage the development of integrated interventions based on ever-broadening social contexts.

FAMILIES AND LARGER SYSTEMS

All families interact with, and are influenced by, one or more of society's larger systems—health care, church, welfare, probation, schools, the legal system. Low-income families, families with special-needs children, drug abusers, families with members in trouble with the law, families with schizophrenic members, and immigrant families in particular are apt to find themselves caught up in dependence on, and/or conflict with, various social and community agencies. Family interventions sometimes involve a *case management* approach, which typically includes counseling, but in addition advocates for families, helps link them to available community resources and services (medical care, job training, legal services), and monitors their progress.

Family–School Interventions: Enlarging the System

Delivering family services within a school setting can serve as a recognizable example of the interlocking nature of systems. Not only is a child a part of a family that has its own unique structure and relationship patterns, but the family itself is embedded in its culture, ethnic group, social class, and social history. The child is at the same time a member of a school classroom with its own structure and interactive processes; that classroom, in turn, is located within a matrix of a larger school organization. The two major systems in the child's life, home and school, thus interface and form a new larger system with its own characteristics, objectives, priorities, and regularities; moreover, home and school systems may deal with one another in complementary or antagonistic ways.[4] The school child moves between the two, carrying into each the struggles, accomplishments, triumphs, and failures he or she is experiencing in the other (DeHay, 2006).

The school may often be the first to detect a child's emotional or behavioral problem, perhaps reflecting at-home family conflict. In the cases of many low-income, immigrant, or otherwise closed families, who have difficulty accessing mainstream agencies, school-based family services may open the gates to needed psychological, medical, or other social services (Hong, 2006). The family, the school, and the community are all part of this ecosystem (Fine & Carlson, 1992).

The family consultant who is called upon to help assess and treat a schoolchild's behavioral problem (truancy, dropout, low level of commitment, violence, drug use) needs to adopt an ecosystemic approach (Lusterman, 1988), taking into account the interaction of the two systems (home and school) before attempting to sort out whether the child is having difficulties in one or both and to decide how best to proceed. He or she must not only remain aware of the child and the family system but also be familiar with the culture of the school, school law regarding children with special needs, how this school reaches decisions, the role of the school board, and so on (Fine, 1995).

---

[4]Families and school personnel may agree on the child's problem (e.g., a pervasive developmental delay), particularly if their cultural norms are similar. In other cases, they may not agree; the school may perceive a behavioral problem (e.g., hyperactivity) that the family does not agree is problematic, or the family may report a child's behavior as troublesome (stealing from a mother's purse) that the school does not find a particular bother. Ethnic differences often play a part; families and teachers often misperceive each other's intentions and goals because of differences in cultural backgrounds (Rotheram, 1989).

Rotheram (1989) offers the following vignette illustrating one type of problem arising in the interface between family and school:

> An angry parent calls the school, complaining that a seventh-grade teacher has given too much homework and is ruining the family's time together over the weekend, asking too much of a young girl. The teacher is righteously indignant and counters that the parents are encouraging dependence and passivity in their child. She refuses to decrease homework. The next week, the daughter makes a suicide attempt, and the family wants to sue the school. (p. 347)

The liaison-consultant called upon to intervene may be a member of the school system, a therapist brought in by the family, or a social services agency representative. Lusterman (1988) urges "mapping the ecosystem"—evaluating both the school and family before deciding whom to include (child, teachers, school counselors, parents, grandparents, and so on) in the treatment plan. In his view, it is necessary from the outset to make clear that the therapist's task is not advocacy for one group or the other but rather helping to create conditions for change. A systems perspective facilitates the process; if it is carried out successfully, neither party is targeted as causing the presenting problem, and the interactive process between participants becomes the focus of the joint meetings (Rotheram, 1989). An ecosystemic approach is by definition a collaborative undertaking. The family therapist acting as a systems consultant (Wynne, McDaniel, & Weber, 1986) is often able to convene the system, observe interactions, allow differing views of "reality" to emerge, formulate hypotheses, and ultimately facilitate family-school collaboration leading to effective problem solving (Fine, 1995).

Several promising school-related intervention programs, carefully researched and evidence-based, have been developed, illustrating the emerging social-ecological viewpoint. For example, *multisystemic therapy*, first proposed by Scott Henggeler, now at the University of South Carolina (Henggeler & Borduin, 1990), is a family-based treatment program directed at chronic behavioral and emotional problems in adolescents. School-related difficulties are conceptualized as the result of a reciprocal interaction between the schoolchild and the major social systems in which he or she is embedded—family, peers, school, and the neighboring community (Henggeler & Cunningham, 2006). Assessment helps pinpoint the characteristics of the schoolchild's ecology (called "fit factors") that are contributing to the maintenance of the problem behavior. How much of the school problem is associated with characteristics of the *child* (low motivation, learning disability, etc.), the *family* (ineffective monitoring, parental problems interfering with effective parenting), *peers* (drug use, support for truancy), the *school* (poor classroom management practices), the *school-family link* (low trust of each other), and the *community* (criminal subculture that does not value academic success)? Identified strengths, discovered during the assessment, are applied in the subsequent interventions.

The child with a school-related problem, and his or her family, are helped to develop the ability to resolve and manage problems that have a multisystemic set of causal and sustaining factors. Caregiver-teacher-principal meetings, role-playing how best to monitor the child's homework completion, limiting negative peer associations, establishing contingencies at home based on school behavior and performance (providing transportation, increasing privileges), treating individual and family dysfunction, helping the family build a community support system (neighbors, extended family members), helping teachers develop effective classroom behavioral management strategies—this full-court press, integrated approach has proven successful.

BOX 4.4   CASE STUDY

USING AN ECOMAP IN FAMILY ASSESSMENT AND THERAPY

A family who had initially sought the aid of a family therapist for their son Billy's aggressive behavior revealed over the course of therapy that Jim, the father, had been physically abusive to his wife, Cathy. Cathy also disclosed to the therapist that she had been sexually abused, as a child and young adolescent, by her father. The referring family physician knew only of the problems with Billy. By the time they consulted a family therapist, the family had become involved with five larger systems: Jim in a local hospital group for men who batter their wives; Cathy in a program for women who have experienced sexual abuse; Jim and Cathy together in a church counseling program for family violence; Cathy in a women's shelter counseling group; and the entire family in family therapy.

When the family therapist invited the various participants to meet together and coordinate their efforts, differences in approach and fundamental beliefs among the various helpers turned out to be significant. For example, while Jim's group sought the causes of violence within him and from his past experiences, urging a long-term group program, the family therapist took a systemic approach, recommended a short-term approach, and attempted to locate the violence in the context of the couple's ongoing interactions. By contrast, Cathy felt the women's shelter counselors blamed Jim exclusively and thought he was the only one who needed treatment.

Because competing definitions of the problem and approaches to a solution surfaced in this macrosystem, a consultant was needed to help untangle the various family member–helper coalitions that had developed. Imber-Black argues that conflict between specialized "helping" systems may, in many cases such as this one, contribute to or enlarge the very problems the helping systems were created to fix or alleviate. In this case, the consultant highlighted their differences to the helpers, pointing out the impact of these differences on how the couple interacted. Stressing the macrosystem level, she designed an intervention that made the boundaries between helpers clearer and less rigid. At the same time, couple-helper boundaries were clarified and thus became less diffuse and confusing. The restructuring allowed the couple themselves to determine the amount and source of help they needed on a weekly basis.

Family Interventions with Other Populations

For most families, engagements with larger systems are time-limited and proceed, perhaps with occasional exceptions, in ways that are free of long-term problems. However, a significant portion of families frequently become entangled with these larger systems in unfortunate ways, impeding the growth and development of family members while at the same time contributing to cynicism and burnout among helpers. In such cases, as Elizur and Minuchin (1989) illustrate with examples from families where there is mental illness, it is incumbent upon family therapists to look beyond the dysfunctional family itself to a broader view of social systems that encompasses the entire community. To do otherwise, they insist, in many cases is to arrive at "solutions" for the family that, no matter how therapeutically elegant, are inevitably shortsighted because they fail to consider cultural, political, and institutional issues. That is, no matter how effective the family therapy intervention, the social context of treatment must be recognized; the power of organizations in which families are embedded must be understood, lest the frequent inflexibility of

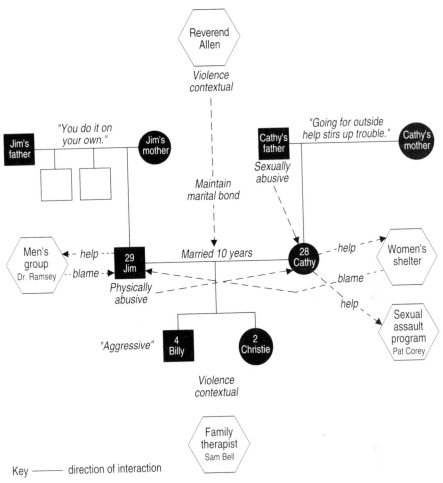

FIGURE 4.2 Conflicting perceptions and interactions in the Lee family case in Box 4.4

Source: Imber-Black, 1988, p. 117

agencies such as psychiatric hospitals, isolating patients from their families, undo any therapeutic gain.

Such problems as physical handicaps or chronic illness or drug abuse or AIDS force some families to spend a significant portion of their lives engaged with larger systems. In the case of long-standing poverty, the relationship with the same public agencies may extend over generations. Problems may develop not only between such families and the agencies in which they often become embedded, but between different public agencies as well. In the case of wife battering just presented in Box 4.4, confusion results from conflicting perceptions by the various professionals attempting to help.

Ecosystemic Assessment

As illustrated in Figure 4.2, **ecomaps** are useful paper-and-pencil assessment devices for diagramming a family's connection to larger social systems. Frequently used by social workers and others to map out and try to coordinate the helping services a family is receiving (Compton & Galaway, 1999), an ecomap is a drawing of the family's social environment, illustrating its simultaneous connections to different agencies. A family receiving child welfare services, for example, might be in contact with the court system, medical services, neighbors, police, attorneys, the school system, foster parents, and various childcare agencies; the ecomap offers a "snapshot" of these relationships at any particular time.

These interlocking programs, if not coordinated, may at times work at cross purposes and result in conflict between specialized helping systems. Ecomaps help organize and clarify both the stresses and supports inherent in the family's environment. As we illustrate here, ecomaps often create a visual presentation of the family's resources, enabling the consultant to call upon as many people as possible in the family's network to develop, in a coordinated fashion, the best and most workable solutions to the family's current predicament (Gilgun, 1999).

SUMMARY

Systems theory, encompassing the contributions of cybernetics and general systems theory, provides the theoretical underpinnings for much of current family therapy theory and practice. The concepts of organization and wholeness in particular emphasize that a system operates as an organized whole that is greater than the sum of its parts, and that such a system cannot be adequately understood if broken down into its component parts.

A family represents a complex relationship system in which causality is circular and multidimensional. Family rules, for the most part unstated but understood by family members, help stabilize and regulate family functioning. Homeostasis is achieved in a family by means of dynamically interacting processes that help restore stability whenever threatened, often by activating the rules that define the relationships. When changes are called for, negative as well as positive feedback loops may help restore equilibrium, in the latter case by promoting discontinuity and necessitating the achievement of homeostasis at a new level. Families need to be able to tolerate change in order to maintain their continuity.

Subsystems carry out specific family functions. Particularly significant are the spousal, parental, and sibling subsystems. Boundaries help separate systems, as well as subsystems within the overall system, from one another. Their clarity and permeability are more germane to family functioning than is their membership composition. Families vary in the extent to which they are open systems; relatively closed systems run the risk of entropy or decay and disorganization.

In recent years, the context for understanding behavior has broadened, as postmodern and ecosystemic thinking have evolved. The assumptions of systems theory, based on a cybernetic model, have been challenged by postmodernists, who accentuate the subjective nature of what we call reality, and by the ecosystemicists, who emphasize the limits of a singularly family-focused outlook and advocate a multisytemic approach. Family systems interact with larger outside social and environmental systems, providing a larger context for understanding diversity of clients and their functioning.

Schools represent an interlocking of systems, in which interventions at various levels can offer a coordinated and successful approach to changing problem behavior. On the other hand, the unbending rules of some institutions may negate any therapeutic gain. Although these systems are often effective in solving problems, confusion may result from competing definitions of the family problem and conflicting solutions offered by different helpers. Ecomaps offer useful visual devices for clarifying the family's relations with interlocking programs, so that better coordination between agencies can provide families with more effective services.

RECOMMENDED READINGS

Bateson, G. (1972). *Steps to an ecology of mind.* New York: Dutton.

Bertalanffy, L. von. (1968). *General systems theory.* New York: Braziller.

Dell, P. F. (1982). Beyond homeostasis: Toward a concept of coherence. *Family Process, 21,* 21–42.

Imber-Black, E. (1988). *Families and larger systems: A family therapist's guide through the labyrinth.* New York: Guilford Press.

Robbins, M. S., Mayorga, B. A., & Szapocznik, J. (2003). The ecosystemic "lens" to understanding family functioning. In T. S. Sexton, G. R. Weeks, & M. S. Robbins (Eds.), *Handbook of family therapy: The science and practice of working with families and couples.* New York: Brunner-Routledge.

Origins and Growth of Family Therapy

In Part I, we established a family relationship framework for viewing and understanding behavior, before offering a developmental outlook based upon life cycle or multigenerational considerations for today's families. We next emphasized that attention needed to be given to gender, culture, and ethnicity factors in any serious effort to fully comprehend family functioning. Finally, to round out this family psychology section, we explored some of the fundamental concepts of interlocking systems that bind individuals, their families, and the greater community together.

In Part II we begin by examining the evolution of family therapy, reviewing some scientific and clinical developments that coalesced in the 1950s to give birth to that movement and then describing its remarkable growth and change over the ensuing decades. Along the way, we intend to note some of the leading players and to describe the sociopolitical climates in which their ideas blossomed. Having provided a background and context for understanding contemporary practice, we next turn to current professional issues, especially the ethical standards of practice today.

Historical Roots of Family Therapy

It is never easy or entirely accurate to pinpoint the start of a scientific endeavor, especially if we adopt a systems outlook with its focus on processes and not sharply delineated beginnings. But most authorities point to the decade following World War II as the period when researchers, later followed by practitioners, first turned their attention to the family's role in creating and maintaining psychological disturbance in one or more family members. The sudden reuniting of families in the aftermath of the war created a number of problems (social, interpersonal, cultural, situational) for which the public sought solutions by turning to mental health specialists. Accustomed to working with individuals, these professionals were now expected to deal effectively with an array of problems within the family. Family members experienced the stress associated with delayed marriages and hasty wartime marriages; the baby boom brought pressures of its own. Changing sexual mores and increasing acceptance of divorce brought new freedoms—and conflicts. Transitions to new jobs, new educational opportunities, increased immigration and the reuniting of families dislocated by the wartime conflict, changing male-female roles, women in the workplace returning to the home, and new homes with mortgages meant new tensions within the family. Adding to all this, the world had entered the nuclear age: the atomic bomb had challenged its basic security. Clearly, the time necessitated changes in thinking and behavior.

In general, psychological intervention became more accessible to people from a broader range of social and educational backgrounds than had been the case in prewar days. Practitioners from many disciplines—clinical psychologists, psychiatric social workers, marriage counselors, pastoral counselors—began to offer such aid, in addition to psychiatrists, who were the primary prewar providers of psychotherapy. The definition of problems considered amenable to psychotherapy, previously dealt with by extended family members and institutions such as the church, expanded to include marital discord, separation and divorce, delinquency, problems with in-laws, and various forms of emotional disturbance not requiring hospitalization. Although most clinicians continued to offer individual treatment only, others began to look at family relationships, at the transactions between members that needed modification if individual well-being was to be achieved.

With enthusiasm high for what science could accomplish, the Macy Foundation Conferences, begun in wartime and continued in peacetime, helped provide some fundamental postulates of the cybernetic theory that was later to prove so central to family therapy formulations depicting families as social systems. Gregory Bateson deserves particular recognition for seeing the relevance of such concepts as feedback loops to the social and behavioral sciences, and ultimately to how human interactive systems work.

In addition to the gradual acceptance of a systems theory framework by many clinicians, with its emphasis on exploring relationships *between* parts that make up an integrated whole, four other seemingly independent scientific and clinical developments during the decade following World War II help set the stage for the emergence of family therapy:

- The investigation of the family's role in the development of schizophrenia in one of its members
- The evolution of the fields of marital and premarital counseling
- The growth of the child guidance movement
- Advances in group dynamics and group therapy

STUDIES OF SCHIZOPHRENIA AND THE FAMILY

What role does a pathogenic family environment play in the development of **schizophrenia**?

In the postwar years, family environment was thought to offer an exciting lead in examining whether specific sets of family dynamics might account for different forms of adult psychopathology, as researchers began zeroing in on the upbringing and family lives of schizophrenics.

Fromm-Reichmann and the Schizophrenogenic Mother

Following the then-prevalent view that the mother's child-rearing behavior established her developing child's emotional stability, some researchers attempted to reconstruct the early mother-child relationships in adult schizophrenics. Maternal rejection was blamed by Frieda Fromm-Reichmann (1948) for the development of male schizophrenia. In a widely quoted paper at the time, this prominent psychoanalyst, known for her work with schizophrenics, introduced the term **schizophrenogenic mother** to denote a domineering, cold, rejecting, possessive, guilt-producing person who, in combination with a passive, detached, and ineffectual father, causes her male offspring to feel confused and inadequate and ultimately to become schizophrenic. Although Fromm-Reichmann emphasized the destructive nature of such parenting, she nevertheless viewed schizophrenia as an intrapsychic disorder, residing within the individual patient; she did not suggest treating the family together, but instead saw the clinician's role as freeing the patient from the parents' noxious influences.

A number of family pathology studies, following Fromm-Reichmann's lead, extended into the late 1950s, narrowly seeking to establish a linear cause-and-effect relationship between pathogenic parents and schizophrenia. These initial efforts to link schizophrenia to family life were ultimately disavowed as too limiting (if not terribly destructive in blaming parents, especially mothers). Researchers today no longer look for a culpable, pathologizing parent and a victimized child, but more commonly search for biological or genetic markers in trying to understand the disorder's origins. Nevertheless, the concept of the schizophrenogenic mother remains historically important in the evolution of family therapy because it directed attention to dysfunctional interactions occurring within a family context and shared by all family members. Family communication difficulties and disturbances in the expression of affect are once again the focus of schizophrenia research today, although precisely how these interactive patterns arise or affect the vulnerable person at risk remains elusive.

Bateson and the Double Bind

During the mid-1950s, a major impetus for family research in the area of schizophrenia came from Gregory Bateson in Palo Alto, California; Theodore Lidz at Yale; and Murray Bowen (and later, Lyman Wynne) at the National Institute of Mental Health. Working independently at first, the investigators did not become fully aware of each other's research until later in the decade.

In 1952, Bateson—then affiliated with the Palo Alto Veterans Administration Hospital—received a Rockefeller Foundation grant to study communication patterns and paradoxes. Soon he recruited Jay Haley, then a graduate student studying communication; John Weakland, a former chemical engineer with training in cultural anthropology; and William Fry, a psychiatrist. Calling upon their broad range of interests, Bateson gave the disparate group free rein; together they examined a variety of communication patterns in humans and animals alike, especially possible contradictions between *levels* of messages—what is communicated and how it is qualified (or in some cases contradicted) by messages from that same person at another level of communication. What ultimately proved most intriguing to this group was the manner and frequency with which schizophrenics sent conflicting and often contradictory feedback messages at one and the same time.

Later, in 1954, with a two-year grant from the Macy Foundation to study schizophrenic communication patterns further, Bateson enlisted Don Jackson, a psychiatrist experienced in working with schizophrenics. Interested in developing an interactional theory around the sequence of exchanges between family members, the research group began to study the possible link between pathological communication patterns within a family and the emergence and maintenance of schizophrenic behavior in a family member.

Utilizing some of the then-emerging cybernetic concepts that Bateson, interested in epistemology, brought to the project, the researchers ultimately hypothesized that the family, when upset and thus threatened, seeks a homeostatic state through feedback mechanisms that monitor the family's behavior in an effort to achieve balance and stability.

Perhaps, they speculated, the appearance of schizophrenic symptoms in a family member interrupted parental conflict when it occurred, and instead united the adversaries in their parental concerns for their child, returning the system to its former level of equilibrium.

Although this description of the emergence of schizophrenic symptoms is viewed now as an oversimplification, these researchers, by attending to family communication sequences, were beginning to *redefine schizophrenia as an interpersonal phenomenon,* challenging the long-held psychodynamic view of schizophrenia as an intrapsychic disorder that subsequently damaged interpersonal relationships. More specifically, they hypothesized that the family might have shaped the strange and irrational behavior of a schizophrenic by means of its contradictory, and thus impossible, communication requirements.

Eager to publish their preliminary results, Bateson, Jackson, Haley, and Weakland (Fry was in the armed services at the time) issued a landmark paper (1956) introducing the double-bind concept to account for the development of schizophrenia in a family member. A double-bind situation occurs when an individual (often a child) receives repeated conflicting injunctions from the same person (say, an adult), with whom the child has an important ongoing relationship. In their exchange, a primary negative injunction by the adult ("Don't do that or you will be punished") is followed by a *conflicting* secondary injunction at a more abstract level (a gesture such as a hug, demanding compliance), again with the threat of punishment if the child disobeys. As a tertiary injunction, the adult demands a response but forbids the child to comment on the contradiction, thus forbidding escape from the confusing situation. The child, perceiving the threat to his or her survival, feels compelled to make some response, but feels doomed to failure no matter what response he or she chooses. Repeated often enough, any part of the sequence can set off upset, panic, or rage in the trapped recipient. Note particularly that the child is faced with more than conflicting messages (where he or she might choose to obey one and disregard the other). In a double-bind situation, the key is in the two conflicting *levels* of messages.

The paper by Bateson and associates reports the following poignant example:

> A young man who had fairly well recovered from an acute schizophrenic episode was visited in the hospital by his mother. He was glad to see her and impulsively put his arm around her shoulders, whereupon she stiffened. He withdrew his arm and she asked, "Don't you love me anymore?" He then blushed, and she said, "Dear, you must not be so easily embarrassed and afraid of your feelings." (p. 259)

Note the sequence of the mother's underlying messages: "Don't touch me" ("Go away"); "Don't trust your feelings in regard to how I respond" ("Come closer"); "Don't challenge the contradictions in my behavior"; "You can't survive without my love"; "You're wrong and at fault no matter how you interpret my messages." The authors report that the distressed patient promptly became violent and assaultive when he returned to the ward.

When a person is confronted by expressions of love and hate, with an invitation to approach and an injunction to stay away issued by the same important figure, Bateson's group hypothesized that he or she is forced into an impossible situation of trying to discriminate correctly between the contradictory messages. Unable to form a satisfactory response (and especially in the case of a child, unable to escape) and unable to comment on the dilemma without being punished further, such a person becomes confused, suspicious that all messages have concealed meanings. It becomes impossible for the person to understand what people really mean or how to communicate or relate to others. Response leads to rejection, and failure to respond leads to the loss of potential love—the classic "damned if you do and damned if you don't" situation. If the important figure (a parent, for example) then denies sending simultaneous contradictory levels of messages, this only adds to the confusion. Once the pattern is established, these researchers hypothesized, only a hint of—or initial step in—the original sequence is enough to set off a panic or rage reaction and, for schizophrenics, may lead to gradual withdrawal from the world of relationships.

Bateson and his colleagues suggested that the typical result of repeated and prolonged exposure to this kind of impossible situation is that the child learns to escape hurt and punishment by responding with equally incongruent messages. As a means of self-protection, he or she learns to deal with all relationships in this distorted manner and finally loses the ability to understand the true meaning of his or her own or others' communications, believing every message contains a concealed meaning. At this point the child begins to manifest schizophrenic behavior. Whether or not this explanation was correct—double-bind communications later proved *not* to be the cause of schizophrenia—the historical importance of this landmark research is its focus on *schizophrenia as a prototype of the consequences of failure in a family's communication system.*

A seminal publication in the history of family therapy, the double-bind hypothesis opposed the psychiatric establishment in its established outlook. By attending to relationships, it challenged the orthodox position that the schizophrenic's problems stemmed from the inner workings of his or her mind, the prevalent psychodynamic view of the time. Not surprisingly, the double-bind idea stimulated much controversy. Particularly troublesome to critics was its gender-biased and linear outlook—the idea that double-bind communication from parents, especially mother toward child, caused schizophrenia. Further research made it clear that double binding occurs at one time or another in most families, without as serious pathological consequences as schizophrenia. Schizophrenia is now seen as a debilitating brain disorder, although one in which communication difficulties and reduced social functioning between family members are often paramount.

Lidz: Marital Schism and Marital Skew

At about the same time that Bateson and his colleagues were studying the family and schizophrenia on the West Coast, Theodore Lidz on the East Coast (at Johns Hopkins University in Baltimore and later at Yale in New Haven, Connecticut) began publishing his findings on the family's role in schizophrenic development of one or more of its children.

A psychiatrist trained in psychoanalysis, Lidz nevertheless rejected the prevalent psychoanalytic notion advanced by Fromm-Reichmann and others that adult schizophrenics were suffering from maternal rejection. Particularly refuting the singling out of rejecting mothers by calling attention to the father's possibly destructive role, Lidz,

Cornelison, Fleck, and Terry (1957a) described five patterns of *pathological fathering* of schizophrenics: rigid and domineering, hostile, paranoid, of little or no consequence at home, passive and submissive.

To these researchers, carrying out longitudinal studies of families with hospitalized schizophrenic members, schizophrenia was a "deficiency disease" resulting from the failure of both parents to play supportive and complementary roles with one another. Lidz and his associates (1957b) described two patterns of chronic marital discord that are particularly characteristic of families of schizophrenics (although each may exist in "normal" families to a lesser extent). **Marital schism** refers to a disharmonious situation in which each parent, preoccupied with his or her own problems, fails to create a satisfactory role in the family that is compatible with and reciprocal to the other spouse's role. Each parent tends to undermine the worth of the other, especially to the children, and they seem to compete for loyalty, affection, sympathy, and support of the children. Neither valuing nor respecting each other, each parent may fear that a particular child (or children) will grow up behaving like the other parent. Threats of separation or divorce are common; it is usual in such families for the father to become ostracized, a virtual nonentity if he remains in the home.

In the pattern of **marital skew,** which these researchers also observed in families with a schizophrenic offspring, the continuity of the marriage is not threatened, but mutually destructive patterns nevertheless exist. The serious psychological disturbance of one parent (such as psychosis) usually dominates this type of home. The other parent, who is often dependent and weak, accepts the situation and goes so far as to imply to the children that the home situation is normal. Such a denial of what they are actually living through may lead to further denials and distortions of reality by the children. Lidz and associates (1957b) concluded that male schizophrenics usually come from skewed families in which there is a dominant, emotionally disturbed mother, impervious to the needs of other family members but nevertheless intrusive in her child's life. At the same time, a skewed family usually has a father who can neither counter the mother's child-rearing practices nor provide an adequate male role model.

Lidz's research searched for family dysfunction (inflexible family role, faulty parental models) as the locus of pathology in schizophrenics. Although his efforts have been criticized by gender-sensitive family therapists and others as emphasizing unbalanced, stereotypic sex roles—fathers should be more forceful, mothers more selfless—he nevertheless pointed the way to the detrimental effect of growing up in a strife-torn family in which the child is split in his or her loyalties.

Bowen, Wynne, and NIMH Studies

First at the Menninger Foundation in Topeka, Kansas, in the early 1950s, and later at the National Institute of Mental Health (NIMH) near Washington, D.C., Murray Bowen, a psychiatrist, broke new ground in the study of schizophrenia. In a dramatic experiment at NIMH, Bowen arranged for mothers to move into cottages on clinic grounds near their hospitalized, schizophrenic children for several months; he was especially interested in identifying unresolved symbiotic mother-child interactions. As he later reported (Bowen, 1960), families of schizophrenics often demonstrate interaction patterns resembling Lidz's findings about marital schism.

Bowen termed the striking emotional distance between parents in such a situation *emotional divorce.* He described relationships of this kind as vacillating between periods of overcloseness and overdistance. Eventually the relationship becomes fixed at a point of sufficient emotional distance between the parents to avoid anxiety; they settle for "peace at any price." One area of joint activity—and, commonly, conflicting views—is the rearing of their children, particularly of children who show signs of psychological disturbance. It is as if the parents maintain contact with each other (and therefore a semblance of emotional equilibrium) by keeping the disturbed child helpless and needy. Thus, adolescence, the period in which the child usually strives for a measure of autonomy, becomes especially stormy and stressful. This is typically the time when schizophrenic behavior first appears.

Bowen proposed the intriguing notion that schizophrenia is a process that spans at least three generations before it manifests in the behavior of a family member. He suggested that one or both parents of a schizophrenic are troubled, immature individuals who, having experienced serious emotional conflict with their own parents, are now subjecting their offspring to similar conflict situations. That child, who is ultimately less well functioning than his parents, seeks out a marital partner with a comparable upbringing (and corresponding psychological disabilities), since Bowen assumed marital choices are typically someone with a similar level of individuation. The couple's child, who in turn is even more vulnerable to dysfunction, passes the deficit on to the next generation, and so on, finally leading to a schizophrenic individual.

When Bowen moved on to Georgetown Medical School in 1956 to found a family therapy training program, he was succeeded as head of the Family Studies Section at NIMH by Lyman Wynne. Wynne, trained both in psychiatry and the social sciences, focused his research on the blurred, ambiguous, and confused communication patterns in families with schizophrenic members. In a series of papers over the next decade (Wynne, Ryckoff, Day, & Hirsch, 1958; Wynne & Singer, 1963), he and his colleagues addressed the social organization of such families, searching for ways in which their communication patterns could be differentiated from those observed in more normal families. For example, observing the families' recurrent unreal, fragmented, and irrational style of communication, these researchers hypothesized that such a family pattern contributes to the schizophrenic member's tendency to interpret events occurring around him or her in blurred or distorted ways. In turn, such confusion or occasional bafflement increases the schizophrenic's social and interpersonal vulnerability, both within and outside the family.

Wynne, a productive researcher and teacher, left NIMH in 1972, but continued his research at the University of Rochester, where he helped organize a family therapy training program. His emphasis on how disordered styles of communication—what he terms *communication deviance*—are transmitted in schizophrenic families provides an interactional vehicle for understanding the development of a thought disorder, the defining characteristic of young schizophrenic adults.

Overview of Early Schizophrenia Family Research

All of the studies described in this section were cross-sectional in design, involving families in which schizophrenia had been diagnosed in a member, usually a young adult, often long before the research was carried out. A common underlying assumption was that disturbances in family relationships are the major cause of mental disorders in general, and that perhaps distinctive patterns of family dynamics can be discovered for each form of psychopathology. Unfortunately, as Goldstein (1988) observes, the major barrier to testing such assumptions is that families were studied long after the major mental disorder such as schizophrenia had affected the family system.

BOX 5.1   RESEARCH REPORT

How Disturbed Families Deal with Emotions

One of the major contributions by Wynne and his colleagues was the observation that schizophrenic families deal with emotions, both positive and negative, in false and unreal ways. Wynne termed these patterns *pseudomutuality* and *pseudohostility.* He labeled as a *rubber fence* the shifting boundaries surrounding these families, allowing some outside information to be introduced but others to be deemed unacceptable and kept out.

Wynne offered the term **pseudomutuality**—giving the appearance of a mutual, open, and understanding relationship without really having one—to describe how such families cover up conflict and conceal an underlying distance and lack of intimacy between their members. Pseudomutuality is a shared family maneuver designed to defend all of the members against separation from one another as well as to avoid pervasive feelings of meaninglessness and emptiness in their lives. One family member typically is designated the "identified patient," permitting the perpetuation of the myth by others that they themselves are normal. A person who grows up in a pseudomutual family setting fails to develop a strong sense of personal identity, since the predominant family theme is

fitting together, even at the expense of developing separate identities. Indeed, the effort to cultivate a separate sense of self is viewed as a threat to family unity. This lack of identity handicaps the person from engaging in successful interactions outside the family and makes involvement within his or her own family system all-important.

Families with **pseudohostility** maintain a relationship by engaging in continuous superficial bickering, masking their deeper need for tenderness and affection. Doing so serves to cover up their need for intimacy, which they have trouble dealing with directly, and impairs gaining a realistic sense of their relationship. Pseudohostility in families represents an effort to disguise underlying chronic conflict and destructive alignments within the family.

Wynne labeled the resistance to outside influences in a pseudomutual family as a **rubber fence,** a changeable situation in which the specific boundaries of the family may shift, as though made of rubber, allowing in certain acceptable information, but unpredictably or arbitrarily closing in order to keep unacceptable information out. Here the rules are in a state of continuous flux, as the family attempts to minimize threatening contact with the outside world.

Despite these deficits in research design, considerable enthusiasm was aroused by this new field of clinical inquiry into the baffling etiology of schizophrenia. A group of schizophrenia/family researchers met for the first time at the 1957 national convention of the interdisciplinary American Orthopsychiatric Association. Although no separate organization was formed by this still-small group of researchers, they did learn of each other's work. The subsequent cross-fertilization of ideas culminated in *Intensive Family Therapy* (Boszormenyi-Nagy & Framo, 1965), a report by 15 authorities on their research with schizophrenics and their families. The clinical investigations that were initiated a decade earlier had laid the groundwork for the emerging field of family therapy.

Marriage and Pre-Marriage Counseling

The fields of marriage and pre-marriage counseling, precursors of family therapy, are based on the concept that psychological disturbances arise as much from conflicts between persons as from conflict within a person. Focusing on some of the unique

BOX 5.2 CLINICAL NOTE

Social Workers and Family Therapy

Social workers are the unheralded pioneers of what later became the field of family therapy. From the founding of the first citywide charity organization in 1877 in Buffalo, N.Y., social workers have been at the forefront of delivering services to needy families. *Family casework* is an integral part of social work preparation; and the Family Service Associations of America, beginning in 1911, have been composed of social work agencies specializing in the treatment of marital and family problems. Broderick and Schrader (1991) suggest that a case could be made that both marriage counseling and family therapy had their origins within the broader field of social casework. Beginning with Virginia Satir, many leading family therapists have come from a social work background (as mentioned throughout this text).

problems of this special form of coupling, early marital counselors (gynecologists and sometimes other physicians, lawyers, social workers, psychologists, and college professors who were family-life specialists), viewed as "experts," attempted to provide answers for people with sexual and other marital difficulties (Broderick & Schrader, 1991). Clergy were especially prominent in offering formal premarital counseling, often as part of an optional or mandatory preparation program before a wedding (Stahmann & Hiebert, 1997).

If we assume that people have always been ready to advise or seek advice from others, informal marriage counseling has certainly existed for as long as the institution of marriage. On the other hand, formal counseling by a professional marriage counselor probably began somewhat over 70 years ago in the United States, when the physicians Abraham and Hannah Stone opened the Marriage Consultation Center in New York in 1929. A year later, Paul Popenoe (a biologist specializing in human heredity) founded the American Institute of Family Relations in Los Angeles, offering premarital guidance as well as aid in promoting marital adjustment. Family educator Emily Mudd started the Marriage Council of Philadelphia in 1932 and later wrote what is thought to be the first textbook in the field (Mudd, 1951). In 1941, largely through Mudd's prodding, the American Association of Marriage Counselors (AAMC) was formed. The AAMC brought together various professionals, primarily physicians, but also others concerned with the new interdisciplinary field of marriage counseling. This organization has led the way in developing standards for training and practice, certifying marriage counseling centers, and establishing a professional code of ethics (Broderick & Schrader, 1991).

Similarly, the first documented premarital intervention program was offered by Ernest Groves (later to be first president of AAMC) in 1924 in a family life preparation course at Boston University. Through the mid-1950s the small quantity of pertinent literature available often focused on such individually oriented topics as physical examinations by physicians as part of premarital counseling efforts. Assistance offered by clergy was apt to be spiritual, educational, and informational, and to have an intrapsychic and religious orientation rather than attend to the couple's interpersonal relationship. If relationship problems were addressed at all, they were likely to be seen as a by-product of a problem within one or both of the prospective newlyweds

(Stahmann & Hiebert, 1997). Rutledge's survey of AAMC members in 1966 found very few professionals performing premarital counseling.

By the mid-1960s, it was still possible to characterize marriage counseling (and pre-marriage counseling) as a set of practices in search of a theory (Manus, 1966). No breakthrough research was being carried out, no dominant theories had emerged, no major figure had gained recognition. The AAMC published no journal of its own. If practitioners published at all, they apparently preferred to submit articles to journals of their own professions. By the 1970s, however, the situation began to change. Among others, Olson (1970) urged an integration of marriage counseling and the emerging field of family therapy, since both focus on the marital relationship and not simply on individuals in the relationship. In 1970 the AAMC, bowing to increased interest by its members in family therapy, changed its name to the American Association of Marriage and Family Counselors (in 1978, it became the present American Association for Marriage and Family Therapy). In 1975, the organization launched the *Journal of Marriage and Family Counseling* (renamed the *Journal of Marital and Family Therapy* in 1979). By then, as Broderick and Schrader (1991) observe, marriage counseling (and by implication pre-marriage counseling) had "become so merged with the more dynamic family therapy movement that it had all but lost its separate sense of identity" (p. 15).

The history of sex counseling parallels that of marriage counseling, and the two disciplines had many of the same practitioners. Moving to become a separate specialty, the American Association of Sex Educators and Counselors was formed in 1967 and set up standards and granted certificates for qualified sex therapists. Since 1970, two journals, the *Journal of Sex and Marital Therapy* and the *Journal of Sex Education and Therapy* have disseminated information in this fast-growing therapeutic movement.

What exactly is marriage counseling—or, as it is more frequently called, marital therapy? Not considered to be as deeply probing, intensive, or as prolonged as psychotherapy, marriage counseling, as initially practiced, tended to be short-term, attempted to repair a damaged relationship, and by and large dealt with here-and-now issues. Unlike psychotherapy, which presumably probed inner meanings, marriage counseling addressed reality issues and offered guidance to troubled couples in order to facilitate their conscious decision-making processes. Early premarital counseling, which tended to be even less attentive to relationship issues or why this couple chose one another, was content to help the pair prepare for marriage by becoming aware of any neurotic individual problems that might cause later hardships.

Couples entering premarital therapy may be doing so as a kind of checkup on the viability of their relationship before marrying—or, more significantly, one or both may fear that some underlying conflict remains unresolved and may lead to a further deterioration of their relationship once married. In some cases, such counseling may be mandated by religious groups to which they belong. When one or the other (or both) has been divorced, particularly if there are children from a previous marriage, such caution is especially pertinent (Goldenberg & Goldenberg, 2002).

Most people who seek help for their marriage are attempting to cope with a crisis (such as infidelity, threat of divorce, disagreements regarding child rearing, money problems, sexual incompatibilities, ineffective communication patterns, conflicts over power and control) that has caused an imbalance in the family equilibrium. Each partner enters marital therapy with different experiences, expectations, and goals and with different degrees of commitment to the marriage. At least one of the partners is

---

CLINICAL NOTE   ⊠

Two persons seeking couples therapy rarely arrive | decision to separate. He or she may continue for a
with the same degree of motivation or identical | brief time to go through the motions to give the
agendas. When therapeutic progress is at a stand- | appearance of making the effort to reconcile, but in
still for no discernible reason, the therapist might | reality is preparing to leave his or her spouse for the
consider that one partner already has made the | therapist to treat individually.

---

usually invested in staying married or they would not seek professional help, but the strength of the determination to stay together may vary greatly between them.

As marital counseling began to focus on the couple's troubled relationship, **conjoint** therapy, in which a couple works with the same therapist together in the same room and at the same time, has replaced earlier efforts to counsel each partner separately.

THE CHILD GUIDANCE MOVEMENT

Two additional streams of thought and clinical development, sometimes overlooked, deserve mention for their influences in the evolution of family therapy. The *child guidance movement*, emerging early in the twentieth century, was based on the assumption that if emotional problems did indeed begin in childhood—as Freud and others were arguing—then early identification and treatment of children could prevent later psychopathology.

Alfred Adler, an early associate of Freud's, was especially cognizant of the key role early family experiences played in determining later adult behavior. Adler helped found the child guidance movement in Vienna in the early 1900s, and while he did not work therapeutically with entire families, he did influence one of his disciples, Rudolph Dreikurs, who later emigrated to the United States, to expand child guidance centers into family counseling centers (Lowe, 1982). In 1924 the American Orthopsychiatric Association, largely devoted to the prevention of emotional disorders in children, was organized. Although child guidance clinics remained few in number until after World War II, they now exist in almost every city in the United States. They provide major settings for identifying and treating childhood psychological disorders, and are especially valuable in involving parents and attending to the larger social systems from which the presenting problem evolved.

Early treatment programs were team efforts, organized around a psychiatrist (psychotherapy), a psychologist (educational and remedial programs), and a social worker (casework with parents and outside agencies). It was standard procedure (and still is in traditional clinics) for the parent (in most cases the more available mother) to visit the clinic regularly for treatment, usually seeing a different therapist from the one working with her child. This collaborative approach has now evolved into conjoint therapy sessions in most clinics, more than likely involving both parents as well as siblings of the identified patient. Rather than viewing the child as the identified patient with intrapsychic problems, or the parents as the source of the child's difficulties, today's outlook focuses on pathology between all the family participants. Child guidance clinics continue to function on the principle of early intervention in a child's family's emotional problems in order to avert the later development of more serious disabilities.

GROUP DYNAMICS AND GROUP THERAPY

Group dynamics and the behavior of small groups served as models of family functioning for some early family therapists such as John Bell (1961). For these therapists, family therapy was a special subset of *group therapy*, except that the participants were not strangers. These practitioners took the position that families are essentially natural groups, and that the therapist's task was to promote interaction, facilitate communication, clarify the group process, and interpret interpersonal dynamics—as any group therapy leader would do. Bell called his approach **family group therapy.**

Group therapy has been practiced in one form or another since the beginning of the twentieth century, but the impetus for its major expansion came from the need for clinical services during and immediately after World War II. The earliest use of the group process in psychotherapy can be credited to the Austrian psychiatrist Jacob Moreno, who, around 1910, combined dramatic and therapeutic techniques to create **psychodrama.** Moreno, whose psychodramatic techniques are still used today, believed that it is necessary to recreate in the therapeutic process the various interpersonal situations that may have led to the patient's psychological difficulties. Since this was hard to accomplish in the one-to-one therapist-patient situation, Moreno, in the role of therapist/director, used a stage on which the patient could act out his or her significant life events in front of an audience. In these psychodramas, various people (frequently, but not necessarily, other patients) represented key persons ("auxiliary egos") in the patient's life. At certain junctures the director might instruct the patient to reverse roles with one of the players, so that the patient could gain a greater awareness of how another person saw him or her. The exploration of a family's interpersonal give-and-take and the resolution of its conflicts through psychodramatic means made this model a natural fit for many family therapists.

Stimulated largely by the theories developed by British psychoanalysts Wilfred Bion and Melanie Klein, considerable interest in group processes developed during the 1930s at the Tavistock Institute in London. Several therapists began experimenting with group intervention techniques (Bion, 1961). In particular, they emphasized dealing with current problems ("here and now") rather than searching for past causes and explanations or reconstructing possibly traumatic early experiences. Samuel Slavson, an engineer by training, began to do group work at the Jewish Board of Guardians in New York City at about the same time; from this work emerged his activity-group therapy technique, in which a group setting encourages disturbed children or adolescents to interact, thereby acting out their conflicts, impulses, and typical behavior patterns (Slavson, 1964). Slavson's approach was based on concepts derived from psychoanalysis, group work, and progressive education. In 1943 the American Group Psychotherapy Association was formed, largely through Slavson's efforts.

In the 1960s, inspired by the emergence of various growth centers around the United States—particularly the Esalen Institute in Big Sur, California—the **encounter group** (part of the human potential movement) made a dramatic impact on the therapy scene and seemed to gain the immediate approval of large numbers of people, mostly from the upper middle class. Today that enthusiasm has waned considerably,

TABLE 5.1 Some Special Advantages of Group Therapy over Individual Therapy

Principle	Elaboration
Resembles everyday reality more closely	Therapist sees patient interacting with others, rather than hearing about it from the patient and possibly getting a biased or distorted picture; adds another informational dimension regarding his or her customary way of dealing with people.
Reduces social isolation	Patient learns that he or she is not unique by listening to others; thus he or she may be encouraged to give up feelings of isolation and self-consciousness.
Greater feelings of support and caring from others	Group cohesiveness ("we-ness") leads to increased trust; self-acceptance is likely to increase when patient is bolstered by acceptance by strangers.
Imitation of successful coping styles	New group members have the opportunity to observe older members and their successful adaptational skills.
Greater exchange of feelings through feedback	Group situation demands expression of feelings, both positive and negative, directed at other members who evoke love, frustration, tears, or rage; patient thus gains relief while also learning from responses of others that intense affect does not destroy anyone, as he or she may have feared or fantasized.
Increases self-esteem through helping others	Patient has the opportunity to reciprocate help, to offer others empathy, warmth, acceptance, support, and genuineness, thereby increasing his or her own feelings of self-worth.
Greater insight	Patients become more attuned to understanding human motives and behavior, in themselves and in others.

Source: Goldenberg, 1983.

although traditional group therapies (Yalom, 1995) and to a lesser extent, encounter groups, continue to exist side by side.

Fundamental to the practice of group therapy is the principle that a small group can act as a carrier of change and strongly influence those who choose to be considered its members. A therapy group is a meaningful and real unit in and of itself, more than a collection of strangers, more than the sum of its parts. Another way of putting it is that the group is a collection of positions and roles and not of individuals (Back, 1974). The Tavistock version of group therapy is a good illustration: The group is treated as if it were a disturbed patient who is hurting because certain functions are not being carried out successfully. In a Tavistock group, the leader helps the group to function in a more balanced, coordinated, and mutually reinforcing way so that the group can accomplish productive work more efficiently. The implications for group therapy with a dysfunctional family are obvious. Table 5.1 summarizes some unique advantages of group therapy.

THE EVOLUTION OF FAMILY THERAPY

The clinical and research endeavors we have described culminated in the field of family therapy. In this section, we describe that evolution.

From Family Research to Family Treatment

Most of the surveys of the family therapy movement (Broderick & Schrader, 1991; Goldenberg & Goldenberg, 1983; Guerin, 1976) agree that the 1950s was its founding decade. It was then that the theories and approaches we have been describing seemed to coalesce. Those ideas, to be sure, pertained more to clinical research than to clinical practice. Observation of the family—particularly one with a symptomatic member—could be justified only if it was presented as a research strategy. Observation of a family as a basis for treatment would have been a direct challenge to the prevailing sanction of confidentiality against a therapist's contact with anyone in the family other than her or his own patient.

Family therapy therefore owes its legitimacy to the facts that (a) it was carried out for scientifically defensible research purposes and (b) the "research" was being done on clinical problems such as schizophrenia that did not respond well to the established psychotherapies of that time (Segal & Bavelas, 1983). As Wynne (1983) notes, Bateson's Schizophrenia Communication Research Project in Palo Alto, the work of Lidz and his co-researchers in New Haven, and Bowen's ambitious effort to hospitalize parents of schizophrenics for residential treatment with their disturbed offspring at the Menninger Clinic (and later NIMH) were all initially research motivated and research oriented. Wynne's own work at NIMH with schizophrenics was based on the use of therapy as a source of experimental data. It was the apparent success of the family research that helped give the stamp of approval to the development of therapeutic techniques.

Who actually deserves credit for first adopting a family therapy approach with client families? Certainly no single person—although Nathan Ackerman, a child psychoanalyst in the child guidance movement, is generally credited with having written the first paper dealing specifically with treating an entire family (Ackerman, 1937). In contrast to the coordinated approach practiced by most child guidance clinics, in which parent and child were seen by separate but collaborating therapists, Ackerman began seeing entire families together at least a decade before other therapists joined him in this approach.

John Bell, an academic psychologist at Clark University in Worcester, Massachusetts, was another major architect of family therapy. Bell (1975) recalled that a casual remark overheard while he was visiting the Tavistock Clinic in London in 1951—to the effect that John Bowlby, a prominent psychoanalyst, was experimenting with group therapy with entire families—stimulated his interest in applying the technique to treat behavior problems in children. Bell assumed that Bowlby was treating the entire family, although this later proved to be an erroneous assumption; actually, Bowlby only occasionally held a family conference as an adjunct to working with the problem child. Based on this misinformation, Bell began to think through the technical implications of meeting with an entire family on a regular basis. Once Bell was back in the United States, a case came to his attention that gave him the opportunity to try out this method as a therapeutic device. Bell's description of his work was not widely disseminated until a decade later (Bell, 1961). That groundbreaking monograph is often thought, along with Ackerman's 1958 text, to represent the founding of family therapy as practiced today. Unlike most of their colleagues in the 1950s, both Bell and Ackerman worked with nonschizophrenic families.

As noted previously, Don Jackson deserves recognition as a family therapy pioneer, introducing an influential if still rudimentary set of descriptive constructs for comprehending family communication patterns (family rules, homeostasis, the redundancy principle) and initiating conjoint treatment to help overcome noxious family interactive patterns. Along with other members of the Palo Alto group, particularly

John Bell, Ed.D.

seminal thinkers Jay Haley and John Weakland, Jackson helped develop innovative ways to influence a family's relationship context in order to produce change. (Bateson, a founder of the field but himself not a therapist, was less concerned with the application of the clinical ideas his group had generated than he was with the philosophy underlying those ideas. His overriding cybernetic view of circular causality focused instead on the process by which people exchange messages, rather than drawing inferences regarding their motives in doing so.)

A list of family therapy trailblazers must also include Murray Bowen, for his organized set of theoretical proposals as well as his innovative technique of hospitalizing families with a schizophrenic member in order to study mother-child symbiotic influences. Carl Whitaker, too, began working with families at Oak Ridge, Tennessee, the site of the secret government plant taking part in the manufacture of the first atomic bomb during World War II.

Pressed into wartime service, Whitaker, a gynecologist, himself had not received the customary psychiatric training, then largely psychoanalytic, and his innovative and often whimsical and idiosyncratic techniques perhaps reflect his less than orthodox training: the use of a co-therapist, the inclusion of intergenerational family members in a patient's therapy, a highly active style with patients.

By organizing a series of family therapy conferences devoted to the treatment of schizophrenia—including a celebrated 1955 event at Sea Island, Georgia—Whitaker was able to bring together many leaders of the emerging family therapy field (including John Rosen and Albert Scheflen from Philadelphia as well as Gregory Bateson and Don Jackson from Palo Alto). The conferences, in which schizophrenics and their families were interviewed while being observed behind a one-way mirror,[1] led to the publication of an early text on the psychotherapy of chronic schizophrenic patients (Whitaker, 1958).

By 1957 the family movement had surfaced nationally (Guerin, 1976) as family researchers and clinicians in various parts of the country began to learn of each other's work. Ackerman, having organized and chaired the first meeting on family diagnosis and treatment at the 1955 American Orthopsychiatric Association, had moved to New York and in 1957 established the Family Mental Health Clinic of Jewish Family Services. In that same year Ivan Boszormenyi-Nagy, having emigrated a decade earlier from Hungary, joined the Eastern Pennsylvania Psychiatric Institute (EPPI) in Philadelphia to conduct research on schizophrenia. Establishing a Family Therapy Department at EPPI, Boszormenyi-Nagy was able to assemble a distinguished group of family-oriented researchers and clinicians and to help make Philadelphia a major early center for family therapy.

By 1959 Don Jackson, remaining a consultant on the Bateson project, had founded the Mental Research Institute (MRI) in Palo Alto; Virginia Satir, Jay Haley, John Weakland, Paul Watzlawick, Arthur Bodin, and Richard Fisch would soon join the

---

[1]The use of a one-way mirror lifted the secrecy from the therapeutic process. Introduced into family therapy by Charles Fulweiler, the mirrors allowed others to observe families in operation as a group, often producing insights into their interactive patterns. Slovik and Griffith (1992) consider the introduction of this observational technique as a significant landmark in the history of family therapy, providing, as it did, clinical confirmation of such concepts as circular causality.

BOX 5.3   THERAPEUTIC ENCOUNTER

WHO ACTUALLY STARTED FAMILY THERAPY?

Ackerman, Bell, Jackson, Bowen, Whitaker—working separately at first and unfamiliar with each other's efforts—gave life to the emerging field of family therapy. During its formative stages, Jay Haley, Virginia Satir, Lyman Wynne, Salvador Minuchin, Ivan Boszormenyi-Nagy, and James Framo played important roles in furthering the field's development. However, it was Christian Midelfort, at the 1952 American Psychiatric Association convention, who presented a paper that was probably the first to report on the treatment of psychiatric patients by including

their families in the therapeutic sessions. Later expanded into a book (Midelfort, 1957), the paper described Midelfort's experiences and results with family therapy in working with relatives and patients in and out of mental hospitals. Unfortunately, Midelfort's pioneering efforts are all but forgotten by most family therapists today, since his geographic location (Lutheran Hospital in La Crosse, Wisconsin) and lack of academic or training center affiliation isolated him from the mainstream of activity and the exchange of ideas and techniques then taking place.

staff. A year later, Ackerman organized the Family Institute in New York (renamed the Ackerman Institute for Family Therapy after the death of its founder in 1971). Representing the East and West coasts, both institutes have played embryonic roles in the evolution of the family therapy field.

The Rush to Practice

Several significant developments in the 1960s indicated that the field of family therapy was gathering momentum. In 1962 Ackerman and Jackson founded the first—and still the most influential—journal in the field, *Family Process,* with Jay Haley as its editor. From its beginnings, the journal enabled researchers and practitioners alike to exchange ideas and identify with the field. In addition, several important national conferences were organized. A meeting in 1964 dealt with the application of systems theory to understanding dysfunctional families (Zuk & Boszormenyi-Nagy, 1967); in 1967 a conference organized by psychologist James Framo was held to stimulate and maintain an ongoing dialogue between family researchers, theorists, and family therapists (Framo, 1972).

Family therapy, gaining professional respectability, was becoming a recognized topic at most psychiatric and psychological meetings. As Bowen (1976) later recalled, dozens of therapists were eager to present their newly minted intervention techniques with whole families. In nearly all cases, this "rush to practice" precluded the development of procedures that were adequately grounded in research or based on sound conceptual formulations. In their clinical zeal—Bowen refers to it as "therapeutic evangelism"—many therapists attempted solutions to family dilemmas using familiar concepts borrowed from individual psychotherapy.

One notable exception to the emphasis on practice over theory and research during this period was Minuchin's Wiltwyck School Project, a pioneering study of urban slum families (Minuchin, Montalvo, Guerney, Rosman, & Schumer, 1967). Minuchin subsequently developed appropriate clinical techniques for successful intervention with male juvenile delinquents, many of whom were Puerto Ricans or African Americans from New York City. From this landmark study of poor, disadvantaged, unstable families, largely without fathers or durable father figures, Minuchin developed an approach he called *structural family therapy* that was pragmatic and oriented toward problem resolution, always mindful of the social environment or context in which the family problems emerged and were maintained.

By 1965 Minuchin had become director of the Philadelphia Child Guidance Clinic, originally in the heart of the African American ghetto, where he focused on intervention techniques with low-income families. His staff included Braulio Montalvo and Bernice Rosman from Wiltwyck, and in 1967 he invited Jay Haley (who, together with John Weakland, had joined the MRI in Palo Alto at the close of the Bateson project)[2] to join them. The Philadelphia center was soon transformed from a traditional child guidance clinic into a large family-oriented treatment and training center. By the late 1960s, the Philadelphia group had begun working with psychosomatic families (with particular attention to families of anorexia nervosa patients), applying some of Minuchin's earlier concepts of boundaries and the interplay of a family's subsystems to psychosomatic problems.

During this highly productive period, the 1964 publication of *Conjoint Family Therapy* by Virginia Satir, then at MRI, did much to popularize the family approach, as did Satir's highly emotional and colorful demonstrations at professional meetings and workshops in many parts of the world. Toward the end of the decade, the character of the work at the MRI changed as the result of Satir's departure to become the director of training at Esalen Institute, a humanistically oriented growth center at Big Sur, California; Haley's move to Philadelphia; and especially Jackson's untimely death in 1968. Although the MRI has continued to focus on family interactional patterns (particularly communication), the Brief Therapy Project, begun in 1967, became its major thrust.

Behavioral family therapy first appeared in the late 1960s. Initially individually focused, often involving amelioration for discrete problems of young children, the techniques introduced relied heavily on learning theory at first. These interventions with families were likely to be derived from empirical studies, and therapeutic procedures were continuously assessed for effectiveness. Consequently, the development of the behavioral approach with families depended less on charismatic leaders or innovative therapists and more on a clinician-researcher collaboration (Falloon, 1991). Nevertheless, some interdisciplinary leaders did emerge—psychologist Gerald Patterson, psychiatrist Robert Liberman, and social worker Richard Stuart.

During the 1960s there were corresponding developments in family therapy outside of the United States. At the psychoanalytically oriented Institute of Family Therapy in London, Robin Skynner contributed a brief version of psychodynamic family therapy (Skynner, 1981). The British psychiatrist John Howells (1975) devised a system for family diagnosis as a necessary step in planning therapeutic intervention. In West Germany, Helm Stierlin (1972) called attention to patterns of separation in adolescence and related these patterns to family characteristics. In Italy, Mara Selvini-Palazzoli (1978), trained in child psychoanalysis but discouraged by her results with

---

[2]The Bateson group had officially disbanded in 1962. Bateson, trained in ethnology and more interested in theoretical ideas regarding communication than in their clinical application to troubled families, moved on to the Oceanic Institute in Hawaii in order to observe patterns of communication among dolphins.

anorectic children, was attracted to the new epistemology proposed by Bateson and the Palo Alto group. Shifting to a systems approach that stressed circularity, she was more successful with resistant cases. In 1967 Selvini-Palazzoli, together with colleagues Luigi Boscolo, Guiliana Prata, and Gianfranco Cecchin, formed the Institute for Family Studies in Milan; the Institute would eventually have a worldwide impact on the field of family therapy—particularly with its use of "long" brief therapy, in which therapy sessions were held at monthly intervals for up to a year.

Innovative Techniques and Self-Examination

For the most part, technique continued to outdistance theory and research in family therapy well into the 1970s. The early part of the decade saw much enthusiasm and a proliferation of family therapy approaches in various parts of the United States:

- In Vermont, treating several families with hospitalized schizophrenic members simultaneously, in group therapy fashion, in a procedure called **multiple family therapy** (Laqueur, 1976)
- In Galveston, Texas, bringing families together for an intensive, crisis-focused two-day period of continuing interaction with a team of mental health professionals, in **multiple impact therapy** (MacGregor, Ritchie, Serrano, & Schuster, 1964)
- In Philadelphia, working in the home with an extended family group including friends, neighbors, and employers, in **network therapy** (Speck & Attneave, 1973)
- In Colorado, treating a family on an outpatient basis in **family crisis therapy** instead of hospitalizing a disturbed, scapegoated family member (Langsley, Pittman, Machotka, & Flomenhaft, 1968)

Behavioral psychologists increasingly began turning their attention to issues related to family matters, such as teaching parents "behavior management skills" to facilitate effective child rearing (Patterson, 1971) and proposing therapeutic strategies for working with marital discord (Jacobson & Martin, 1976) and family dysfunction (Liberman, 1970). The newly available technology of videotape allowed family therapists to tape ongoing sessions either for immediate playback to the family, for later study by the therapist, or for training purposes (Alger, 1976).

In the 1970s, having come of age, and with students and professionals alike now seeking training, the field of family therapy engaged in its first efforts at self-examination. The so-called GAP report (Group for the Advancement of Psychiatry, 1970) presented the results of a survey of practicing family therapists who were asked to rank the major figures in the field according to their influence at that time. The practitioners placed the major figures in this order: Satir, Ackerman, Jackson, Haley, Bowen, Wynne, Bateson, Bell, Boszormenyi-Nagy.

In another kind of effort to bring order and self-awareness to the developing field, Beels and Ferber (1969) observed a number of leading therapists conducting family sessions and studied videotapes and films of their work with families. Beels and Ferber then distinguished two types of family therapists, based on the therapist's relationship to the family group: **conductors** and **reactors.** Conductor therapists are active, aggressive, and colorful leaders who place themselves in the center of the family group. They are likely to initiate rather than respond, to propound ideas vigorously, to make their value systems explicit. Reactors are less theatrical personalities, more subtle and indirect. They observe and clarify the family group process, responding to what the family presents to them, negotiating differences among family members.

Beels and Ferber (1969) contended that each type of therapist is effective in directing and controlling the family sessions and in providing family members with possible new ways of relating to each other; the conductors are more direct in their methods but not necessarily more successful in helping to create a new family experience as the basis for changing its members' interactive behavior patterns.

Further self-examination took the form of outcome research on the effectiveness of family therapy. By the late 1970s the need to take stock was being generally acknowledged. Nevertheless, Wells and Dezen (1978) pointed out after surveying the outcome literature that most family therapy approaches, some of them identified with major figures in the field, "have never submitted their methods to empirical testing and, indeed, seem oblivious to such a need" (p. 266). By the end of the decade there had been some improvement (Gurman & Kniskern, 1981), but the effectiveness of family therapy still required continuing and systematic evaluation.

Perhaps the form of self-analysis that had the most far-reaching impact on the field came from the feminist critique of then-current family therapy systemic ideas and therapeutic techniques. As we noted in Chapter 3, since the mid-1970s a growing number of family therapists, beginning with Hare-Mustin (1978), have argued that family therapy, both as conceptualized and practiced, showed bias in favor of values typically considered masculine—such as autonomy, independence, and control—while devaluing those nurturant and relationship values more customarily associated with females. Moreover, they maintained that developmental schemas typically adopted by family therapists are based on male development, and are assumed to be applicable to women as well. By adopting these schemas, as Slovik and Griffith (1992) point out, therapists tend to devalue qualities such as dependency and caretaking normally linked to women. Moreover, by being insensitive to such issues as gender roles and wife battering, they were, in many cases inadvertently, reinforcing patriarchal attitudes as well as masculine and feminine stereotypes.

The family therapy pioneers, all of whom (with the exception of Satir) were men, have been brought to task for failing to pay sufficient attention to the social and political context in which family members live. Even the venerated Bateson came under fire from feminists. In particular, they contended that his disregard of power and control differences between participants in any transaction, in favor of such cybernetic notions as reciprocity and circularity, assumed a lack of unilateral control by any one participant because the system was in a continuous state of flux. While feminists recognize the circular nature of transactions within a family, they argued that Bateson's formulation is oversimplified in its implication of equal responsibility (and equal blame), particularly in failing to acknowledge the crucial role of power differentiation (men and women; adults and children) in any ongoing relationship.

The feminist critique shook most family therapists out of their growing complacency by insisting that they examine their built-in gender biases regarding fixed male and female roles within a family and society at large. Just as they would later have to deal with developing greater diversity awareness and multiculturalism, so now they were being urged to consider gender-related issues within a family, power differences between husbands and wives, and the individual needs of clients for harmonious family functioning. Perhaps most disturbing of all, family therapists were being directed to examine their own values, attitudes, and beliefs, and to confront sexist views that could prove detrimental to helping all family members, male as well as female, feel empowered.

Professionalization, Multiculturalism, and a New Epistemology

In the 1980s, a number of signs documented the phenomenal growth of the family therapy field. Whereas barely a decade earlier the field had one professional journal of its own, *Family Process*, there were now approximately two dozen family therapy journals, half of them published in English. Once, family therapy centers could be counted on the fingers of one hand; now, in what many consider to be the golden age of family therapy, more than 300 freestanding family therapy institutes existed in the United States alone. (There are fewer such centers devoted exclusively to family therapy today.)

Several organizations now represented the interests of family therapists. In addition to the interdisciplinary American Orthopsychiatric Association (where Ackerman first brought together practitioners interested in family research and treatment), the major groups are as follows:

- The American Association for Marriage and Family Therapy (AAMFT) grew from fewer than 1000 members in 1970 to over 7500 by 1979; to 16,000 by 1989; and to 23,000 by 2006. The AAMFT has the authority to accredit marriage and family therapy training programs, to develop standards for issuing certificates to qualified persons as Approved Supervisors, to publish a code of ethics for its members, and to actively pursue state licensing and certification for marital and family therapists.

- The American Family Therapy Association (now called the American Family Therapy Academy) was founded in 1977. This smaller interest group of approximately 1000 members (by the end of the 1980s) is concerned exclusively with family therapy clinical and research issues as distinct from marriage counseling or marital therapy.

- The International Association of Marriage and Family Counselors (IAMFC), a division of the American Counseling Association, grew from slightly over 100 members when it was founded in 1986 to almost 8000 members in 1996. The IAMFC conducts educational programs and helps develop training standards for marriage and family counseling programs.

- The Division of Family Psychology of the American Psychological Association was established in 1986. Family psychology offers a broader perspective than the clinical emphasis of family therapy, paying special attention to relationship networks within marriage and the family. By the close of the 1990s, membership in the Division of Family Psychology was approximately 1700. In a related matter, the American Board of Professional Psychology, authorized by the American Psychological Association to issue diplomas granting competence in the applied areas of psychology, in the late 1980s added family psychology as a certifiable specialty.

- The International Family Therapy Association (IFTA), made up of therapists, theorists, researchers, trainers, and other professionals working with families, was organized in 1987 and now has more than 500 members from 40 countries around the globe. IFTA conferences, held in various countries, allow for the firsthand exchange of ideas. The organization publishes a semiannual newsletter, the *International Connection*, announcing conferences and offering articles on marriage and family therapy topics.

Family therapy became an international phenomenon in the 1980s, with active training programs and congresses in Canada, England, Israel, Holland, Italy, Australia, West Germany, and elsewhere. The Heidelberg Conference, marking the tenth anniversary of the Department of Basic Psychoanalytic Research and Family Therapy of Heidelberg University in West Germany, took place in 1985, with some 2000 participants from 25 countries attending (Stierlin, Simon, & Schmidt, 1987). Bridging East-West differences in 1987, a family therapy conference attended by over 2500 people from all over the world took place in Prague, Czechoslovakia, followed in 1989 by a similar event in Budapest, Hungary.

Competing models of family therapy, usually associated with one or another of the field's founders, proliferated in the 1980s (Piercy & Sprenkle, 1990). Although each relied on systems theory, differing versions, with differing emphases and perspectives, led to the further evolution, begun a decade or more earlier, of rival "schools" in the field. Nevertheless, the cross-fertilization of ideas continued—helped along by learning from one another through workshops and the videotapes of master family therapists of various persuasions.

Many family therapists broadened the scope of their theories and practices during the 1980s to include collaboration with related disciplines such as medicine. **Medical family therapy** emerged as a subspecialty, and the journal *Family Systems Medicine* (now renamed *Families, Systems & Health*) was founded. Doherty and Baird (1983)—the former a psychologist and the latter a physician—published a landmark book, *Family Therapy and Family Medicine,* in which they argued for the application of a systems approach to treating illness in which members of both disciplines cooperatively act as providers for patients with a variety of medical conditions. Wynne, Shields, and Sirkin (1992) reminded therapists that illness, which many tended to think of as a linear concept, was actually much more than a personal experience; rather, it was transactional and communicative with fellow family members. As these researchers observed, families typically are deeply troubled and burdened by the presence of a member with a serious physical illness.

In addition, psychoeducational programs for families of schizophrenia were introduced in the 1980s (Anderson, Reiss, & Hogarty, 1986), taking the position that they were dealing with a biological disorder, that families should not be blamed, and that the entire family would best profit from help in learning to cope with the disease.

As the feminist challenge continued to influence both theory and practice into the 1980s, so too did the recognition that we live in a pluralistic society, and no "one size fits all" solution is appropriate to all client families. Falicov (1983) led the way in presenting a cultural perspective to family therapy practice. Her work was particularly illuminating in working with Latino families. McGoldrick, Pearce, and Giordano (1982) edited a useful book in which experts from a variety of cultural backgrounds offered insights into working with specific ethnic groups. Boyd-Franklin (1989) presented a systems approach for dealing with African American families in therapy.

Integration, Eclecticism, and the Impact of Constructionism

While differences in philosophy about the nature of families and how best to intervene continued to exist between family therapists throughout the 1990s, "schools" as such became less mutually exclusive. A clear trend emerged toward integration of family therapy models (for example, psychodynamic, cognitive-behavioral, family

BOX 5.4   THERAPEUTIC ENCOUNTER

ADVANCING A NEW EPISTEMOLOGY

One event, destined to have far-reaching consequences for the family therapy field for a decade or more, occurred with the publication of a single issue of *Family Process* early in the 1980s. In it, three sets of family therapists (Dell, 1982; Keeney & Sprenkle, 1982; Allman, 1982) raised important epistemological questions regarding the theoretical foundation, research models, and clinical practice of family therapy. All were critical of the field's rush to put forth new techniques without first rethinking some of the cybernetic notions taken for granted by most family therapists. Dell, for example, objected to the term *homeostasis* as an "imperfectly defined explanatory notion" because it implied a process that returned a system to its previous state, and as such prevented change.

Arguing for what has become known as the *new epistemology*, Keeney and Sprenkle (1982) challenged the field to look beyond its narrow pragmatic approaches (exemplified by designing and carrying out interventions to overcome a family's specific presenting problem) to a broader consideration of overall family functioning. The pragmatic approach, they maintained, had led the field astray, leading to searching for more and better how-to-do-it methods and packageable techniques, but at the expense of more fully appreciating the context in which families live. In these researchers' view, the concern of the pragmatic approach with results such as symptom reduction (behavioral and strategic techniques are examples) limits its vision of what really troubles families and how best to help them find solutions. Moreover, pragmatic views, influenced by early cybernetic notions, place the observer outside the phenomenon being observed, in effect equating families with machines and paying insufficient attention to family interaction and context. Doing so, they argued, erroneously supports a linear notion that such an outsider is in a position to unilaterally manipulate and control a system he or she is observing.

Both Keeney and Sprenkle (1982) and Allman (1982) urged consideration of the *aesthetic* (patterned) dimensions of family therapy. Allman in particular believes the artistry of family therapy is revealed in the therapist's ability to grasp the unifying patterns connecting family members and, if stuck in one pattern they wish to change, to help them rearrange the connecting patterns in order to create new meanings in their lives.

To illustrate the difference between treatment methods reflecting cybernetic concepts and those based on the new epistemology, Keeney and Sprenkle (1982) offer the case of a woman who complains of severe anxiety attacks. The pragmatically oriented therapist might contract with her to engage in a therapeutic effort aimed specifically at alleviating the anxiety symptom. Success could then be evaluated empirically by quantitatively comparing the occurrence of the symptom before and after treatment. An aesthetically oriented therapist would be more concerned with the larger gestalt of family interactive patterns, of which the symptom is but one part. The pragmatic therapist might actually acknowledge that the larger gestalt must change, but would contend that change would follow from symptom removal. The aesthetic therapist, on the other hand, does not argue with the pragmatist's technical considerations, but does not consider them to be primary. In the aesthetic view, instead of being an outside change agent, a therapist's presence should help create a new context—in a sense, a new "family"—so that new behavior may emerge.

By drawing attention to the act of observing what is being observed, and by becoming part of the system thus created, the new epistemological challenge led to the idea of second-order cybernetics, a view that was to gain prominence in the subsequent decade.

systems) into a comprehensive approach (Wachtel, 1997). Therapists continued to view families from different perspectives, but there was greater overlap and frequent borrowing from one another, as the clinical problem demands, even if such borrowing of technique or concept may not always be theoretically justifiable. Broderick and Schrader (1991) note that the field was moving away from the proliferation of narrowly trained specialists. Instead, most therapists were being exposed to an overview of the entire field, developing skills as what these authors call "relational therapists." More than combining models, integrative efforts aim for a more holistic or comprehensive way of assessing and intervening with families.

At the same time, the need for a quicker return to functioning and the restrictions on practice imposed by **managed care** led to a search for brief techniques. The Mental Research Institute (MRI) in Palo Alto and the Brief Therapy Center in Milwaukee are major examples of places that developed different workable brief therapy procedures. Within the last decade, managed care, developed by insurance companies to hold down healthcare costs, has greatly influenced the practice of family therapy (by delineating eligibility for services, number and frequency of sessions, fees, length of treatment, etc.).

By the mid-1990s constructionists had forced family therapists to reexamine not only some cherished systemic theoretical assumptions but also how to most effectively intervene with troubled families. Constructionists believe objectivity is impossible, and that the therapist, presumably an outside observer of a family, in actuality participates in constructing what is observed. Their view helped move the thinking of many family therapists away from theoretical certainties and toward a greater respect for differences in outlook and viewpoints between themselves and individuals within families and between families with different gender, cultural, ethnic, or experiential backgrounds. Multiple narratives by different family members, all equally true, were recognized as part of all family functioning, with no one person (therapist included) perceiving an objective universe. Therapeutically, it meant shifting to a greater collaboration between therapist and family members, all of whom had something to contribute about the current difficulties.

Instead of searching for the "truth" about a family, constructionists argue that each family member has his or her own version of "reality," conditioned by various psychological and biological factors (Maturana, 1978).[3] That is, multiple versions of reality exist within a family, constructed by the individual belief systems each person brings to interpreting a particular problem. The meaning each person derives from an event or situation or relationship is valid for that person; there is no absolute reality, only a set of subjective constructions created by each family member. It is precisely that *meaning*—those assumptions people make about their problems—that interests constructionists.

Assessing a family now called for taking class, ethnicity, and gender roles into account. As Fraenkel (2005) puts it:

> . . . thoughtful therapists, sensitive to the mandates of multiculturalism, feminism, economic differences, and so forth, adopted a not-knowing, exploratory, collaborative stance, turning to families as co-experts in solving their problems. (p. 37)

---

[3]Maturana, a neurobiologist, believes organisms are *structure determined*. That is, they are limited in their functioning by the repertoire of what their nervous system will allow them to see. Thus, their perceptions are defined by their inner states and past experiences as much as by the process they are perceiving. No one, therefore, perceives an objective universe. Learning is at most an accommodation to a new situation and can occur only within strictly defined limits (Guttman, 1991).

In this approach, which stresses a nonpathological orientation to the therapeutic process, all therapists can do is help family members understand and reassess the assumptions and meanings each participant has constructed about a common family problem.

The therapist does not try to change the family's structure, nor is he or she able to change the social conditions that help determine family functioning. Rather, change occurs as a result of a family reexamining its belief systems. Therapists can help by introducing information intended to change patterns, but, from this viewpoint, cannot predict or design the exact nature of any subsequent changes. Family therapy, from this new perspective, becomes the collaborative creation of a context in which family members share their constructions of reality with one another, in the hope that the new information thus obtained will facilitate changes in perceptions among the members. As new meaning is co-constructed in conversation, new options and possibilities emerge (Friedman, 1993).

While still controversial, the epistemologies of constructionism and second-order cybernetics have become the cutting edge of family therapy. Instead of attempting to change family members, here efforts are directed at engaging families in "conversations" about their problems (Anderson & Goolishian, 1988), as a result of which they can begin to feel empowered to change themselves by becoming aware of, and accommodating to, each other's needs, wishes, and belief systems.

This clinical effort to make family therapy more focused on creating meanings through language rather than on behavioral sequences or family interactive patterns has been led by Paul Watzlawick (1984), Michael White (1989), and Lynn Hoffman (1990), as well as Harlene Anderson and Harry Goolishian (1988). Tom Andersen (1987), a Norwegian psychiatrist, employs an egalitarian technique he calls a *reflecting team*, in which a clinical team first watches a family and therapist behind a one-way mirror, then reverses roles and holds an open forum regarding what they have just seen while the family observes their discussion behind the one-way mirror. The idea is to offer a variety of new perceptions to the family, and for them to select those that appear to them to be meaningful and useful. The therapist team reflections are meant to stimulate new conversations within the family and ultimately, for each family member, to provoke greater understanding of oneself, one's surroundings, and one's relationships (Andersen, 1993).

In addition to gender and cultural awareness, today's family therapists are paying closer attention to spiritual and religious resources in the lives of their clients (Walsh, 1999b). Spirituality and religion play important roles in all cultures, as people seek a sense of purpose, meaning, and morality in their daily existence. In family assessment as well as therapeutic interventions, spiritual values, related or not to formal religious institutions, may be central in the lives of many families, and may act as major determinants of family attitudes and beliefs.

Ecological Context, Multisystemic Intervention, and Evidence-Based Practice

One challenge of this new century calls for moving beyond simple systems theory and furthering our understanding of the roles that larger sociopolitical and cultural issues play in people's lives. Sexton, Weeks, and Robbins (2003) suggest that every client is more than a member of a single group who can be summarized under a single label (gay, elderly, divorced, Latino, Black, etc.) Rather, each of us is a multicultural person, someone who identifies with multiple groups that provide us with sets of specific values, and particular sets of experiences. They urge therapists to attend to both their client's and their own "ecological niche"—locating individuals and families in terms of race, class, religion, sexual orientation, occupation, migration experiences, nationality, and ethnicity.

Family therapy, always concerned with context in understanding behavior, is broadening that context, moving beyond simply examining relationships within a family to adding an ecosystemic view concerned with social systems in which families function in order to more fully understand the current diversity of family experiences. In order to do so, many family therapists are moving outside of the consultation room and into the community, and they are taking their view of systems within systems with them into outside social agencies and organizations.

An additional challenge calls for better informing clinical practice with relevant research. Toward this end, researchers have begun to develop empirically supported psychological interventions, when feasible, in an effort to advance the scientific basis for clinical assessments and treatment. Still in its early stages, the goal of such evidence-based practices goes beyond merely proving that family therapy works, but more specifically addresses what change mechanisms most effectively lead to positive outcomes, with what client populations or sets of clinical problems, under what circumstances and in what settings. All provide useful information for therapy planning with a specific family. The overall goal here is to improve the quality and cost-effectiveness of such interventions and to enhance accountability by practitioners (APA, 2005).

SUMMARY

Five seemingly independent scientific and clinical developments together set the stage for the emergence of family therapy: *systems theory,* exploring how relationships between parts of a system make up an integrated whole; *schizophrenic research,* helping establish the role of the dysfunctional family in schizophrenia and setting the stage for studying interaction patterns in other kinds of families; *marital and premarital counseling,* bringing couples into conjoint treatment to resolve interpersonal conflicts rather than treating the participants separately; the *child guidance movement,* focusing on intervention with entire families; and *group dynamics* and *group therapy,* employing small-group processes for therapeutic gain and providing a model for therapy with whole families.

Stimulated by the research-oriented study of families with schizophrenic members, the family therapy movement gained momentum and national visibility in the 1950s. However, technique continued to outpace theory and research well into the 1970s. Innovative therapeutic techniques were introduced, including behavioral approaches to family-related problems. By then the field was growing at a rapid rate, and a number of efforts aimed at self-awareness and self-evaluation were undertaken. Most noteworthy was the feminist critique of family therapy, challenging familiar family therapy tenets that reinforce sexist views and stereotypical sex roles.

In the 1980s marital therapy and family therapy became an all-but-unified field. Practitioners from a variety of disciplines made "family therapist" their primary professional identification when joining interdisciplinary organizations. A new epistemology, challenging the early cybernetic notions, gained attention. Medical family therapy was introduced, increasing collaborative efforts with physicians. Psychoeducational programs, especially with schizophrenics and their families, gained prominence, as did efforts to develop cultural competence in working with diverse ethnic groups.

The trend, begun in earnest in the 1990s, was away from strict adherence to "schools" of family therapy and toward integration. Today the constructionist paradigm concerns itself more with helping families examine their belief systems than with intervening in order to change their underlying structure or behavior patterns. At the same time, managed care has imposed limitations on the customary ways of practicing family therapy. Today's family therapists are paying closer attention to gender and cultural issues, to ecosystemic analyses as well as spiritual and religious considerations in the lives of their clients. Evidence-supported interventions are being sought, by researchers, practitioners, consumers, and insurance company payers, in an effort to improve the quality and cost-effectiveness of clinical services.

RECOMMENDED READINGS

Ackerman, N. W. (1958). *The psychodynamics of family life.* New York: Basic Books.

Bateson, G., Jackson, D. D., Haley. J., & Weakland, J. (1956). Towards a theory of schizophrenia. *Behavioral Science, 1,* 251–264.

Bowen, M (1960). A family concept of schizophrenia. In D. D. Jackson (Ed.), *The etiology of schizophrenia.* New York: Basic Books.

Broderick, C. B., & Schrader, S. S. (1991). The history of professional marriage and family counseling. In A. S. Gurman & D. P. Kniskern (Eds.), *Handbook of family therapy* (Vol. II). New York: Brunner/Mazel.

Dell, P. F. (1982). Beyond homeostasis: Toward a concept of coherence. *Family Process, 21,* 21–42.

PROFESSIONAL ISSUES
AND ETHICAL PRACTICES

In this chapter we focus on the everyday issues of contemporary clinical practice. More specifically, we concern ourselves with two continually evolving sets of professional issues—how to ensure the highest quality of professional competence at the least cost to society and how to remain alert to ethical standards, particularly as practice shifts attention from the individual client to the family system as a whole.

PROFESSIONAL ISSUES

The License to Practice

Most established professions seek some form of legal statute to gain public acceptance and respectability. Statutes in each state in the United States and in all Canadian provinces control and regulate professional practice (e.g., medicine, law, clinical psychology, clinical social work), and since 1970 there has been a concerted effort to seek similar legal standards for credentialing marital and family therapists (MFTs). These therapists have sought legal recognition primarily because licensure has become synonymous with professionalism (Huber, 1994) and because reimbursements from health plans for providing clinical services are paid only to licensed providers. While licenses do not ensure competence, they help assure potential consumers of counseling that the practitioner has met certain educational standards, had two years of post-degree supervisory training experiences, and been screened and credentialed by a professional certifying board.

Several important premises support efforts at licensure (Corey, Corey, & Callanan, 2007): (a) Licensure protects the public by establishing minimum standards of service and holding professionals accountable if they do not measure up; (b) it protects the public from its ignorance or naiveté regarding mental health services, helping potential consumers choose practitioners more judiciously; (c) it increases the likelihood that practitioners will be competent, having met the standards to obtain a license; (d) it makes mental health services more affordable, since clients going to licensed practitioners may be partly reimbursed; (e) it upgrades the profession by gathering together practitioners committed to improving and maintaining the highest standards of excellence; and (f) it allows the profession to define itself and its activities more clearly, thus becoming more independent. As noted earlier, licensing assures the public that the practitioner has completed an approved educational program, has had an acceptable number of hours of supervised training, and has successfully gone through some screening or evaluative program. Advocates of licensing thus maintain that the consumer's welfare is better safeguarded when legal regulations exist.

Possessing a license, of course, does not ensure competency. Licenses are generic in the sense that they do not specify what client problems the licensee is competent to work with nor what techniques he or she is trained to use. So, for example, a practitioner may be trained to work with individuals while lacking the experience or skills for family interventions. Ethically, that person should seek additional training and supervision before undertaking clinical work in a new modality. In practice, however, the therapist accustomed to working with individuals may sometimes erroneously convince himself or herself of competence with families without being up-to-date regarding new developments in the family field or familiar with the cultural backgrounds of families seeking services.

An individual seeking professional status in marital and family therapy may earn a graduate and/or professional degree from a university or obtain professional preparation at a center offering specialized training in marital and family therapy. A person who follows the academic route and has obtained the requisite training supervision in a program accredited by the appropriate professional association (for example, the American Psychological Association—APA) may seek either **licensing** or **certification** (according to the law governing practice in a particular state or province) in his or her discipline.

A state licensing law, more restrictive than certification, regulates who may practice (for example, licensed psychologist, licensed physician, licensed clinical social worker) by defining education and experience criteria, administering qualifying examinations, and stating the conditions under which a license may be revoked (thereby terminating the right to practice) for ethical or other reasons. Favored by most professionals in that discipline, it restricts both who may use the title (say, MFT) and who may engage in practice (as a marital and family therapist) (Sweeney, 1995).

A state certification law, a weaker and less comprehensive form of regulation, simply certifies who has the right to use a particular professional title. Such a law does not govern practice or define permissible activities but simply guarantees that the title (for example, "psychologist") will be used only by people who meet the standards established by the law. Like the licensing laws, certification laws set up criteria for issuing and revoking certificates; in that sense they help to monitor practice, at least regarding use of the title. Less desirable than licensing, state certification may represent what advocates of a particular discipline are able to achieve in the state legislature, often because of opposition from other mental health occupations.

Regulatory boards and legislatures in some states have mandated the successful completion of specific **continuing education** (CE) courses (for example, child abuse, human sexuality, chemical dependency, supervisory competence), plus requiring a minimum number of CE hours (attending lectures, conferences, workshops, local and national conventions) as a condition of renewing a license or certificate. These mandates are an effort to ensure that practitioners keep abreast of advances in theory and practice, so they can offer the most up-to-date services (Nagy, 2005) and retrain if they wish to change areas of practice. Practitioners are most likely to attend annual meetings of the American Association for Marital and Family Therapy (AAMFT), the American Family Therapy Academy (AFTA), the Family Therapy (now Psychotherapy) Networker Symposium in Washington, D.C., and the multidisciplinary American Orthopsychiatric Association (AOA) meetings, in addition to conventions of their mother organization (American Psychological Association, National Association of Social Workers, American Counseling Association).

After a slow start, licensing of MFTs is now proceeding swiftly in the United States. One reason for the earlier lag in licensure was that it is easier to establish criteria for licensing the graduates of recognized university programs than those from newly established training programs in freestanding family institutes. In addition, some members of the established mental health professions initially opposed an independent profession of marital and family therapy; according to their view, marital and family therapy is but a subspecialty of psychotherapy. However, MFTs argue that they are a separate profession and that university preparation in the mental health field generally does not sufficiently emphasize work with families; graduates of such programs should themselves seek additional training and acquire a license in marital and family therapy if they wish to practice in the field. The subject remains controversial, touching on professional issues such as eligibility for third-party payments from health insurance plans[1] to cover the treatment of marital or family dysfunction as well as the updating of professional skills and conceptual knowledge. Clearly, practitioners accustomed to working with individual clients need further training before working with families. On the other hand, MFTs may lack the requisite grounding to treat individuals.

Efforts to gain recognition for marriage and family therapists in every state and Canadian province have been led by the AAMFT in conjunction with local practitioner groups. By mid-2005, 48 states plus the District of Columbia regulated marriage and family therapy practice, and other state legislatures and Canadian provinces were considering regulatory bills.

Requirements may vary between states, although all require that those licensed or certified as marriage and family therapists meet certain educational and clinical experience criteria, usually comparable to the standards for Clinical Membership in AAMFT. There were approximately 48,000 licensed or certified MFTs in the United States and Canada in 2005.

Peer Review

Monitoring, examining, or assessing the work of one's colleagues, or having one's own work reviewed by one or more colleagues, is hardly new for anyone who has completed a training program in any of the disciplines involved in marital and family therapy. By the time someone has become a professional, he or she probably has presented work samples in numerous case conferences, to say nothing of having been

---

[1]Freedom-of-choice laws in most states permit consumers to choose among various licensed practitioners, including marital and family therapists, disallowing third-party payors from discriminating against any one discipline. Consequently, most insurance programs, as well as the government-sponsored CHAMPUS (Civilian Health and Medical Program of the Uniformed Services) program for armed forces retirees and dependents of active military personnel, now recognize various providers (MFTs, social workers, psychologists, psychiatrists) as authorized mental health service providers.

BOX 6.1   RESEARCH REPORT

CORE COMPETENCIES IN PRACTICING FAMILY THERAPY

Current efforts are under way to define the core competencies necessary to practice family therapy. Assuming the fledgling therapist has fulfilled the proper educational and internship requirements, been supervised by one or more licensed and experienced family therapists, and received his or her license, how do we know if the clinician is competent to perform effectively?

Marrelli (1998) suggests that competency in general is composed of four elements: *knowledge*, *skills*, *abilities*, and *personal characteristics*. The clinician must be informed, must understand the concepts, principles, and guidelines to carry out the professional task, and must possess the skills and cognitive ability needed to successfully achieve a desired outcome. Personal characteristics refer to those values, attitudes, and traits needed to carry out work assignments and develop good relations with others.

The AAMFT Marriage and Family Therapy Core Competencies Task Force (AAMFT, 2004) has identified six domains specific to family therapy competence:

- *Admission to treatment* (interactions with clients before establishing a therapeutic contract)
- *Clinical assessment and diagnosis* (identifying the issues to be addressed in therapy)

- *Treatment planning and case management* (directing the course of treatment)
- *Therapeutic interventions* (activities designed to ameliorate the identified clinical issues)
- *Legal issues, ethics, and standards* (awareness of current statutes, regulations, values, and mores related to family therapy)
- *Research and program evaluation* (knowledge of systematic analysis of therapy and how to assess its effectiveness)

Six subdomains spell out what five processes are involved in acquiring the core competencies: conceptual skills, perceptual skills, executive skills, evaluative skills, and professional skills (Northey, 2005).

Nationally, the American Board of Family Psychology (a division of the American Board of Professional Psychology) has defined stringent measures of competency before issuing board certification as a "diplomate" in family therapy. In this voluntary program, specific educational, training, and number of years of relevant experience with couples and families are required before candidates are eligible for this prestigious certification. The process itself calls for the candidates to demonstrate competence by providing written transcripts of their work with a specific case and to pass a rigorous oral examination in family psychology.

---

videotaped or observed through a one-way mirror working with families. No doubt cases have been dissected by supervisors and classmates while in training. Having become a professional, a therapist may seek further consultation when therapeutic impasses arise, in dealing with otherwise difficult or sticky clinical procedures, or whenever upcoming ethical decisions need scrutiny. Therapists in private practice often seek such self-regulating **peer review** and peer support by belonging to peer-consultation groups, where they seek help and support from colleagues in dealing with problematic cases, discuss ethical and legal issues that arise, or simply exchange experiences to counter feelings of loneliness that are an inevitable part of functioning as a sole practitioner (Greenburg, Lewis, & Johnson, 1985). Borders (1991) views structured peer groups as valuable for practitioners, regardless of years of experience, particularly in gaining instructional feedback from others, honing skills, and monitoring the therapist's own outlook and behavior.

Managed Care and Professional Practice

Undoubtedly, the major change in professional practice in recent years has come about due to the unprecedented growth of managed care. In contrast to practices prior to the 1980s, whereby independent practitioners billed insurance carriers ("third-party payors") on a fee-for-service delivery basis (and health costs soared[2]), today's employers, who pay the major portion of healthcare bills for their employees, are more mindful of controlling the escalating costs (Hersch, 1995). As a result, managed care has become the dominant economic force in healthcare delivery in the United States for the moment—and as Cummings (1995) observes, has forced mental health workers to reassess cherished attitudes regarding professional practice.

Managed care organizations contract with employers, insurance companies, or union trusts to administer and finance their health benefit programs. Increasingly, employers who offer health benefits have opted for managed care programs for their employees—prepaid health insurance coverage in which, in addition to employer contributions, a fixed monthly fee is collected from each member enrolled who has voluntarily chosen to participate in a particular medical (including mental health) plan as a subscriber.

Such a system for delivering mental health services, sometimes but not always including marital and family therapy, has at its core a contract between a therapist (usually referred to as a *provider*), or a group of therapists, and a *health maintenance organization* (HMO), a type of managed care system. In exchange for being admitted into the provider network and agreeing to accept referrals by being part of the HMO roster, the professional agrees under contract to provide services for a previously negotiated fee (usually significantly lower than the customary rates of fee-for-service providers in the community) and to abide by the managed care organization's explicit provisions. Managed care groups believe that by monitoring practitioner decisions and insisting on time-limited interventions, they are increasing provider accountability and ensuring efficient and effective treatment. Critics, on the other hand, argue that the quality of care is frequently sacrificed by organizational decisions based primarily on financial considerations (MacCluskie & Ingersoll, 2001).

In an attempt at cost containment, managed care plans typically call for preauthorization before the therapist may begin treatment, and further authorization after a previously approved number of sessions (with annual and lifetime cost caps) if the therapist can justify additional treatment to the satisfaction of the managed care group's peer reviewer. Typically, only a limited number of sessions per designated time period are approved (whether or not short-term therapy is the provider's treatment of choice), and the client's choice of therapist is restricted to providers on the managed care roster. To keep costs down, managed care programs may limit services and contract with less qualified providers who often are expected to rely on treatment manuals for short-term interventions.

---

[2]There are, of course, many reasons for the rise in healthcare costs: an aging population utilizing more services, improved technology resulting in more costly equipment, rising expectations in the general population for available healthcare, more medical malpractice suits (Davis & Meier, 2001). However, in the area of psychotherapy, Cummings (1996) holds practitioners more accountable, contending that before managed care they had few incentives for making their interventions more efficient and thus reducing the length (and cost) of their services.

According to critics Seligman and Levant (1998), this determination to favor brief therapy and the use of manuals may benefit some clients, especially in simple cases; but it ignores the needs of others, when cases are complicated and when the therapist judges that longer-term, intensive treatment is necessary to achieve therapeutic gains. Miller (1996) sees an overall decline in the quality of mental health services due to the inherent economics of managed care. He contends that in the name of efficiency, essential services have been cut and access to treatment denied for a significant portion of the population with moderate to serious problems. In his view, underdiagnosis, undertreatment, and overly restrictive hospital admissions and hospital stays belie the claim of improved quality of care. Indeed, wide differences exist in the policies of different health maintenance organizations—in the variety of services approved, in the number of sessions authorized, and in the freedom allowed providers. As larger companies swallow up smaller HMOs, service contracts and approved providers may change for consumers, sometimes during treatment.

Managed mental health care programs usually include a fixed number of mental health practitioners (individually or as part of a provider network); others are excluded when the panel of providers is full—a particular problem for newly licensed practitioners attempting to enter the field. Referrals are made to providers within defined geographic areas; in many plans the practitioner must be available for emergencies on a 24-hour basis.

Whether a client can be seen, for how many visits, at what fee, covering what services, for what problems or conditions—all are negotiated with the managed care organization. Peer reviewers or case managers (usually but not always professionals) act as "gatekeepers," carrying out *utilization reviews,* the conclusions of which often conflict with the practitioner's ideas about how best to manage the case. Such utilization reviews, ostensibly directed at determining the necessity and appropriateness of the practitioner's services, occur at regular intervals throughout treatment. They may thus represent an implicit threat of termination of benefits before the practitioner believes the client or family is ready to stop treatment. Justifying the continuation of treatment for an additional number of sessions often requires considerable supporting documentation in the form of paper reviews or lengthy telephone conversations with a managed care reviewer (Davis & Meier, 2001).

Cost containment, a primary goal of managed care groups, appears to take precedence over quality of care. Since HMOs are competitive for employer contracts, reimbursement rates are likely to continue to decrease and services be further restricted to cut costs. Although the case manager's decision can be appealed either by the client or the provider who believes the client will experience direct harm from discontinuing treatment, in practice such appeals are most often denied.

Under managed mental health care contracts, therapists are thrust into carrying out new (and especially for older therapists, unfamiliar) tasks. Typically, the practitioner must regularly submit to case managers a written treatment plan for each client or family, establishing therapeutic goals and justifying procedures, before being authorized to begin (or continue a previously submitted treatment plan) for a finite number of sessions. It is the therapist's responsibility to explain why services are necessary and to account for procedures carried out; the lengthy paperwork and frequent reimbursement conflicts with reviewers are often a source of stress and potential burnout for clinicians with heavy managed care caseloads (Rupert & Baird, 2004).

As noted, managed care plans support short-term, directive, problem-solving therapy aimed at returning clients to their previous levels of functioning (rather than optimal functioning); see Shueman, Troy, and Mayhugh (1994). That is, these plans aim to limit treatment to whatever it takes to return clients to a functional level as soon as possible, but nothing more. A secondary goal is to prevent recurrence of the presenting symptoms. Just how much treatment is enough remains a debatable issue, although long-term therapy is typically denied by case managers, regardless of its justification in the therapist's opinion.

Most managed care organizations require subscribers to sign an information release form, permitting their therapist to disclose private information ordinarily kept confidential. Thus, while the therapist traditionally seeks to protect the clients' privacy, as an HMO provider he or she is called upon to share information—diagnosis, types of services provided, duration of treatment—that compromises all previously determined ideas regarding **confidentiality.** Because therapists can no longer assure clients of confidentiality, clients may withhold vital information from the therapist or, in more extreme cases, refuse to seek treatment when needed (Acuff et al., 1999).[3]

The option of remaining a solo private practitioner who wishes to provide fee-for-services outside of managed care organizations is becoming less and less economically feasible. Cummings (1995), a former American Psychological Association president, recognized the inevitability of this "rapid industrialization" of health care early, and for a decade has been critical of the APA's initial resistance; in his view, such opposition prevented the organization's participation in health economics decisions. He argues for retraining therapists in time-limited therapeutic procedures, urging them to engage in personally conducted outcome research to measure and justify what works in what they do. Cummings believes the mental health profession is undergoing perhaps its greatest change, as many practitioners are forming large group practices in order to provide an integrated system of care, acquire an arsenal of time-effective techniques, and learn which of their interventions are most effective through outcome research in their group practice.

Managed care has challenged therapists to reexamine their professional ethics, rethink how best to allocate professional resources, come to terms with accounting for what they do with clients, and develop speedier and more effective interventions. The situation regarding how best to deliver professional services is likely to remain turbulent for many years to come, although clearly managed care in some form is here to stay.

Legal Liability

Every practitioner is exposed to the possibility of financial liability—the possibility that the therapist intentionally or unintentionally harmed a client in some specific manner, and consequently may be financially accountable. While such suits are still

---

[3]Due to numerous complaints regarding the loss of privacy, Congress passed the Health Insurance Portability and Accountability Act (HIPAA), effective in 2003. Among its provisions are efforts to establish standards for safeguarding the privacy of patient information (e.g., in transmitting electronic healthcare claims) and for developing privacy procedures for practitioners, including the protection of patient records such as psychotherapy notes. Managed care companies are prohibited from making the disclosure of such therapy notes a condition for paying claims.

BOX 6.2 RESEARCH REPORT

EVIDENCE-BASED CLINICAL PRACTICE

One positive result of managed care's effort to require brief but efficient therapeutic intervention has been the need to develop techniques and procedures of proven effectiveness with specific sets of client problems. Although researchers in medicine, psychology, and other health-related professions have focused on the problem of establishing a scientific base for clinical practice for decades, it came into prominence in the 1990s, in part due to the pressures exerted by managed care programs. Chambless and his associates (1996; 1998) first provided criteria for identifying empirically validated treatments for psychological disorders. Greeted enthusiastically by some as the best demonstration of the scientist-practitioner model long advocated in clinical psychology, and as the most ethical way to practice, it also had its detractors, who criticized any reliance on standardized treatment manuals as simplistic and mechanistic. Opponents also decried its early exclusive focus on specific treatment techniques as opposed to common factors, such as relationship issues, that

account for much of the variance in outcomes across various disorders, and its initial lack of attention to ethnic, race, or cultural factors (APA, 2005).

Evidence-based practice in psychology addresses "what works for whom" (Roth & Fonagy, 2004). That is, what specific clinical interventions have been shown through research to be most effective with what specific problems or diagnoses (Deegear & Lawson, 2005)? As Norcross (2002) observes, such interventions are most likely to be effective if they attend to the client's specific problems, but also his or her strengths, personality characteristics, and the sociocultural context in which he or she lives. Such variables as age, gender identity, race, religious beliefs, and sexual orientation must also be taken into account, further complicating the task. While still in its early stage, the development of empirically supported treatments calls for therapists to be up-to-date on research findings, as these treatment methods may well represent the future trend in individual and family therapy.

relatively rare,[4] there remains the possibility, especially in an increasingly litigious society, that clients may file a legal malpractice suit against a therapist for one or more of the following reasons: breach of confidentiality, sexual misconduct, negligence, breach of contract (regarding such items as fees, promised availability), failure to protect clients from a dangerous person's conduct, or even for exercising undue influence over a patient. Bringing such charges into civil court, the client or family may sue for compensatory damages (compensating them for their loss) as well as punitive damages (punishing the therapist for reckless, wanton, or heinous behavior); see Vesper and Brock (1991).

Malpractice, either deliberately or through ineptitude or carelessness, represents the most likely form of alleged wrongful behavior to produce client litigation. Here the

---

[4]According to available data from the American Psychological Association Insurance Trust, the probability of a psychologist being sued is extremely small—less than half of 1 percent (Bennett, Bryant, VandenBos, & Greenwood, 1990). Nevertheless, litigation remains an ever-present possibility; certain cases, such as sexual contact with clients, suits over repressed memories presumably induced by a therapist, or whether the risk of a patient's suicide could have been foreseen and prevented, are increasing. All practitioners maintain professional liability insurance, in varying amounts of coverage, for safety as well as peace of mind.

therapist is accused of failing to render professional services or exercise the degree of skill ordinarily expected of other professionals in a similar situation (Corey, Corey, & Callanan, 2007). That is, professional negligence is said to have occurred; the claim is that the therapist departed from usual practices or did not exercise sufficient care in carrying out his or her responsibilities. (One important note: Practitioners are not expected always to make correct judgments or predict the future, but they are expected to possess and exercise the knowledge, skills, and standards of care common to members of their profession.)

If therapists are sued for malpractice, they will be judged in terms of actions appropriate to other therapists with similar qualifications and duties. However, if they acted in good faith but the client failed to make progress, they are not liable if they made a mistake that knowledgeable and skilled colleagues, similarly trained, could ordinarily make. However, even if the suit fails, and the therapist is exonerated, he or she has inevitably invested considerable time and money, and experienced consider-able distress, in mounting a defense.

Common types of malpractice suits include the following:

- Failure to obtain or document **informed consent** (including failure to discuss significant risks, benefits, and alternative procedures) prior to commencing treatment
- Misdiagnosis (as when a client attempts suicide)
- Practicing outside of one's area of competence
- Negligent or improper treatment
- Abandonment of a client
- Physical contact or sexual relations with a client
- Failure to prevent dangerous clients from harming themselves or others
- Failure to consult another practitioner or refer a client
- Failure to adequately supervise students or assistants

Perhaps the most common grounds for a malpractice suit is sexual contact (Pope & Vasquez, 1998), and some states have now declared such activity to be a felony. The number of sexually based complaints is increasing, although it is unclear whether the incidence of sexual relations with clients is accelerating or whether clients are more likely to come forward today than in the past. In either case, as attorneys Stromberg and Dellinger (1993, p. 8) note, "for therapists who have engaged in sexual intimacies with patients, a *finding of liability against the therapist is highly likely*" (italics theirs). Any initial consent by the patient is not a defense, since it is assumed that the client may be experiencing emotional distress, feel low self-esteem, and thus be in a posi-tion of greater vulnerability to sexual exploitation than under normal circumstances. A history of emotional or sexual abuse may increase vulnerability and compound the subsequent damage inflicted (Pope, 1994).

Under such circumstances, the courts reason that refusing the overtures of an unscrupulous therapist, whose motives the client wants to trust, may be difficult— especially if the therapist labels such advances as "therapeutic" for relieving the client's problems (Welfel, 2006). Suicide attempts, hospitalizations, and prolonged symptoms of posttraumatic stress may occur; moreover, following the experience, the client may be reluctant to reenter therapy with another therapist precisely when such treatment is most needed (Bates & Brodsky, 1989). If the therapist is found guilty by the court, the likelihood of a suspended or lost license is substantial, as is the probability of

CLINICAL NOTE

Ways of avoiding a malpractice suit include keeping accurate and complete records of treatment plans, following informed consent procedures, protecting confidentiality of client records to the extent possible, consulting with colleagues when in doubt, operating within an area in which one was trained or studied later in order to maintain a level of competency, taking professional responsibilities seriously and not abandoning a difficult or frustrating case, making referrals when appropriate, and making certain that clients will be seen in emergency situations when the therapist is away.

losing a malpractice suit amounting to hundreds of thousands of dollars (Reaves & Ogloff, 1996).

Beyond lawsuits for sexual misconduct, claims of malpractice are likely to involve participating in nonsexual dual or multiple relationships (such as going into a business venture with a client) or performing incorrect treatment (incompetence in choosing a treatment plan); see Pope and Vasquez, 1998). Failure to prevent suicide by a client and breaches in confidentiality are also frequent causes for malpractice suits (Welfel, 2006). Assessing the risk of suicide typically involves inquiring about previous suicide attempts, about thoughts or impulses regarding killing oneself, prior incidents of self-harm, the development of a specific suicide plan, or a family history of attempted or completed suicides (Baerger, 2001).

In general, for a malpractice suit to succeed, four elements must be present: (a) a professional relationship existed, so that the therapist incurred a legal duty to care; (b) there is a demonstrable standard of care that was breached when the practitioner performed below that standard; (c) the plaintiff suffered harm or injury, physical or psychological; and (d) the professional's breach of duty due to negligence or injurious actions was the direct cause of the harm done the plaintiff. The plaintiff must prove all four elements exist in order to win the malpractice litigation (Bennett, Bryant, VandenBos, & Greenwood, 1990). Corey, Corey, and Callanan (2007) offer this example: In the case of suicide, could a practitioner have foreseen the suicide risk (that is, made a comprehensive risk assessment and documented his or her findings), and did he or she take reasonable care or precautions, again well documented, to prevent the self-destructive act? Liability arises if the therapist failed to act so as to prevent the suicide, or did something that contributed to the suicide attempt.

Professional liability insurance is necessary for all family therapists (unless the organization for which they work carries malpractice insurance covering them) if they are to afford the costs of litigation. Most professional organizations, such as the APA, NASW, and the AAMFT, offer group professional liability (malpractice) insurance for purchase by their members.

MAINTAINING ETHICAL STANDARDS

Beyond legal regulation through licensing or certification, professions rely on self-regulation through a variety of procedures—state-mandated continuing education as prerequisite for license renewal, peer review, consultation with colleagues, and so forth—to monitor the professional activities of their members. Codes of ethics, in particular, offer standards whose potential violation may provoke both informal and formal discipline (Huber, 1994). The former involves pressures exerted by colleagues upon violators through consultations regarding questionable practices; the latter may involve censure by professional associations, in some cases barring violators from continued membership.

Professional Codes of Ethics

Every major organization devoted to providing counseling or therapeutic services has its own code of ethics to guide professional practices and uphold professional standards (e.g, APA, 2002; NASW, 1999; AAMFT, 2001). (We reproduce the AAMFT code as one example, in Appendix A.) These codes undergo periodic updating as changing community standards and changing technologies arise (such as computerized record keeping or therapy offered over the Internet). Beyond those codes, governmental regulatory agencies, state licensing boards, specialty organizations, and local professional associations offer their own guiding principles for acceptable professional conduct. The national organizations also publish recommendations for working with specific populations (e.g., guidance on cultural diversity, on dealing with gay and lesbian clients, on the need for accurate record keeping). Each organization typically appoints or elects an ethics committee to monitor the conduct of its members; protects the public from unethical practices; and considers alleged violations of its code concerning one of its members.

Should an ethics committee, in response to a colleague or client complaint, determine that a practitioner has violated the code of ethics of his or her profession, a range of sanctions may be imposed. Generally speaking, the degree of seriousness of the violation is the major determinant of what level of sanction an ethics committee might impose. These code violations range from behavior reflecting poor judgment compared with prevailing standards but without malicious intent (for example, advertising infractions; inappropriate public statements), which calls for educative resolutions, to those cases where substantial harm to others has resulted from the practitioner's behavior and that person is not prone to rehabilitation (defrauding insurance carriers; sexual exploitation), which call for expulsion from the professional organization. Ethics committees may be lenient toward a non-malevolent first offender, offering him or her an educative solution; that same offense, committed repeatedly by an experienced but recalcitrant practitioner, would be greeted with more severe sanctions.

Ethical codes define standards of conduct subscribed to by members of the profession, aiding members in their decision making with clients whenever possible areas of conflict arise. Through membership in a professional organization, the member pledges to abide by a set of ethical standards that helps reassure the public that he or she will demonstrate sensible and responsible behavior (Woody & Woody, 2001). The codes obviously do not cover all situations, but merely offer general guidelines for responsible behavior. As Fisher (2003) notes, the competency and judgment gained through education, training, supervision, experience, and consultation with colleagues represents the linchpin for fulfilling one's ethical responsibilities.

The AAMFT code covers eight areas (see Appendix A):

- Responsibility to clients
- Confidentiality
- Professional competence and integrity
- Responsibility to students and supervisees

- Responsibility to research participants
- Responsibility to the profession
- Financial arrangements
- Advertising

Ethical Issues in Couples and Family Therapy

Some unique and complex ethical issues arise as therapy shifts from an individual focus to one that involves a marital and family system. For example, to whom and for whom does the therapist have primary loyalty and responsibility? The identified patient? The separate family members as individuals? The entire family? Only those members who choose to attend family sessions? Suppose different family members have conflicting goals or conflicting self-interests. Is the primary goal one of increasing family harmony or maximizing individual fulfillment? (See Patten, Barnett, & Houlihan, 1991.)

To address the multiple interests of family members, Gladding, Remley, and Huber (2001) suggest the therapist focus treatment on the family system rather than acting as an advocate of any one member or group of members. At the same time, these authors urge therapists to assist families in negotiating which values they collectively wish to conserve, modify, or reject in the interest of fairness and family harmony.

Most family therapists struggle at one time or another with the ethical dilemma of family needs versus individual needs. More than academic hairsplitting is involved here. Early feminist thinking represented by Hare-Mustin (1980) warned that "family therapy may be dangerous to your health"; that is, the changes that most benefited the entire family were not always in the best interests of each of its members. Hare-Mustin was especially concerned that female family members be influenced by therapists to subjugate their individual rights for the sake of family needs, further perpetuating society's gender roles. Margolin (1982) too was concerned that family therapists might endorse—and thus perpetuate—some familiar sexist myths concerning women: that remaining in a marriage is usually best for women, that a woman's career deserves less attention than her husband's, that child rearing is a mother's sole responsibility, and in general that a husband's needs are more significant than a wife's. Now two decades after these warnings, one would hope that family therapists have become more gender-sensitive and informed, and are better trained from the start to address gender issues.

Family therapists inevitably engage in an active valuing process with families, whether intentionally or not. As Doherty and Boss (1991) point out, the notion of value neutrality by the therapist is naive and no longer even debatable. They maintain that family therapists take value positions continually in their thinking as well as their interventions with families. As the authors put it, values and ethics are closely related; values are the beliefs and preferences undergirding the ethical decisions made by individuals and groups. For therapists, as for everyone else, values are the cherished beliefs and preferences that guide human decisions.

Because specific therapist values (attitudes toward divorce, extramarital affairs, nontraditional lifestyles, cross-cultural issues, gender-defined roles in the family or society at large) may be enormously influential in the process of marital or family therapy—guiding decision making—therapists must examine their own attitudes closely. The danger here is that the therapist might be biased against families whose attitudes, culture, and sexual orientation differ radically from his or her own, or might side with one family member (say, a father) against the behavior and stated attitudes of other members (an adolescent), not by situation but by identification with being a parent. In another scenario, a family therapist—deliberately or unwittingly, consciously or unconsciously—may attempt to sustain a failing marriage, when one or both partners wish to divorce.

Whether the family therapist's values are such that he or she chooses to be responsible to the individual as opposed to, say, the marriage, may have significant consequences. To cite a common problem described by Bodin (1983), suppose a husband is contemplating divorcing his wife, an action his wife opposes. The husband may feel his individual happiness is so compromised by remaining in the marriage that he hopes the therapist attaches greater importance to individual well-being than to maintaining some abstraction called the "family system." The wife, on the other hand, hopes the therapist gives higher priority to collective well-being, helping individuals adjust their expectations for the sake of remaining together. Many therapists caught in such a situation take the position that a strife-torn marriage all but guarantees unhappiness for everyone, including the children. Others argue that the stress and uncertainty of separation and divorce may do irreparable damage to the children and thus the maintenance of family life, imperfect as it is, is preferable to the breakup of the family. As Bodin observes, the therapist's position may have a profound impact not only in terms of the rapport established with the various family members but also with regard to the therapist's formulation of the problems, goals, and plans for treatment.

How should therapists deal with family secrets? Should parental secrets (for example, sexual problems) be aired before the children or be brought up in a separate couple's session? How should an extramarital affair—hidden from the spouse but revealed to the therapist in an individual session—be handled by the therapist? What about family secrets—incest between the father and teenage daughter, or inferred physical abuse of the wife or young children, or child neglect?

Here the therapist has legal responsibilities that supersede confidentiality; he or she must report the suspicion of abuse or neglect to the police or child welfare authorities, even in the absence of proof. In such a situation, the therapist must carefully observe family interactions, formulate an ethical course of action, and take steps to ensure the safety and well-being of family members.

Undertaking therapeutic work with a family, then, poses a variety of complications with respect to the therapist's professional responsibilities. The help offered to one family member may temporarily deprive or disturb another, especially in a rigid family system. A preference for one or the other spouse implies favoritism and, potentially, the loss of necessary impartiality. As Margolin (1982) observes:

> Attempting to balance one's therapeutic responsibilities toward individual family members and toward the family as a whole involves intricate judgments. Since neither of these responsibilities cancels out the importance of the other, the family therapist cannot afford blind pursuit of either extreme, that is, always doing what is in each individual's best interests or always maintaining the stance as family advocate. (p. 790)

Confidentiality

When a client enters a professional relationship with a therapist, the latter takes on the ethical responsibility of safeguarding the former from revealing what was discussed

BOX 6.3   CASE STUDY

A THERAPIST REPORTS PARENTAL ABUSE

Ned, Alice, and their four children all appeared to be living a happy, upper-middle-class life in a large western city. Ned was a successful attorney, a partner in a national firm, and Alice, a stay-at-home mom, was busy raising their children, ages 4 to 10, and actively involving herself in their school activities. Beneath the surface impression, however, the couple was engaged in an ongoing destructive interaction with one another that permeated the entire family system.

The most obvious sign of disturbance, and the ostensible reason they contacted a family therapist, was the difficulty both parents were having with Brandon, their oldest son, whom they described over the telephone as "obstinate and defiant." The therapist asked to see all six family members, and they agreed to participate. The parents signed an informed consent form, which included the therapist's obligation to report a case of child abuse, should that be discovered.

Initially undisclosing for several sessions, the children ultimately began describing the daily battles at home, especially between Alice and Brandon. Soon Ned chimed in, backing up what the children had reported and indicating he had been afraid to bring it up because he feared his wife's wrath. One particularly egregious event, all five agreed, involved Alice locking the boy out of the house, in the winter cold, for four hours because he refused to take a bath. That event, according to Alice, represented her desperation after a series of conflicts over Brandon's "misbehavior." When the therapist asked Ned where he was during the melee, all he could reveal was that he was frightened and withdrew to his study.

The therapist believed both parents were involved in child abuse, Alice through her rage and Ned through neglect. She told the couple she would have to report it to Children's Protective Services, which enraged the mother further but was accepted by the father. After consulting the therapist, that agency recommended anger management and a parent training class for the mother. The father also was ordered to take these classes, since his suppressed anger seemed to have led to his withdrawal and ineffective parenting.

The parents acknowledged that there was abuse in the family and that their unexamined life as a couple required scrutiny. They agreed that the therapist had been tough on them, but that she was fair and impartial, and that they would continue to see her as a couple to try to deal with their long-brewing issues. Together, the three worked on how the family system sustained the abuse and needed change.

during the therapeutic relationship. Confidentiality, protecting the client from unauthorized disclosures of personal information by the therapist without prior client consent, has long been a hallmark of individual psychotherapy. Its rationale is based on encouraging clients to develop the trust necessary for them to make full disclosures without fear of exposure outside the consultation room.

In marital and family therapy, some therapists take the position that they must ensure that information given to them in confidence by a family member will be treated as it would be in individual therapy, and thus not be divulged to a spouse or other family member (although the therapist may encourage the individual to share his or her secret in a subsequent conjoint session). Other therapists, in an effort to avoid an alliance with a family member, refuse to see any member separately, in effect insisting that secrets be brought out into the open to the marital partner or family in sessions together. Still other therapists, if they individually see—or talk to by telephone, or receive a written message from—a family member, tell the informant beforehand that whatever is divulged may be communicated to the others, if in the

BOX 6.4 CLINICAL NOTE

Computer Technology and Confidentiality

The increasingly common use of computers to store case notes, psychological test results, and patient financial records makes those records vulnerable to theft, duplication, or loss of privacy when others have access to the files, and thus calls for extraordinary efforts to protect confidentiality (Sampson, Kolodinsky, & Greeno, 1997). The exchange of information regarding clients through e-mail, facsimile machines, voice mail, answering machines, cell phones, and so on, runs similar risks.

In most clinic or hospital situations today, where computers are networked, stored data that can be retrieved by a variety of viewers are often coded (e.g., Clarence Jones, social security number 123-45-6789, becomes J6789) and backup files may be stored on separate disks. Pseudonyms may replace actual names. Encryption methods reduce the risk of unauthorized access to e-mail communications (Welfel, 2006).

The national Health Insurance Portability and Accountability Act (HIPAA) represents an effort by Congress to protect the security and confidentiality of health information transmitted by practitioners over electronic networks to managed care agencies. The HIPAA, requiring therapist compliance, is primarily directed at protecting patient privacy by requiring his or her permission to release personal data. In addition, for security purposes, the law mandates that the therapist perform a risk analysis of his or her practice by documenting that computer systems are secure and accessible only to authorized persons. As part of that analysis, each practitioner must review routine practices to prevent unintended or inappropriate disclosures through breaches in security when transmitting confidential information in electronic form for healthcare claims.

therapist's judgment it would benefit the couple or family. Whatever the procedure, it is essential to ethical practice that the therapist makes his or her stand on all aspects of confidentiality clear to each family member from the outset of therapy.

Confidentiality is intended to ensure the right to privacy, and a therapist is ethically obligated to refrain from revealing private client information obtained in therapy unless given client authorization to do so. However, there are exceptions where confidentiality can be breached (Corey, Corey, & Callanan, 2007):

- When mandated by law, as in reporting child abuse, incest, child neglect, or elder abuse
- When necessary to protect clients from harming themselves or when they pose a danger to others
- When the family therapist is a defendant in a civil, criminal, or disciplinary action arising from the therapy
- When a waiver has previously been obtained in writing

If the therapist should use material about a family in teaching, writing, or lecturing, he or she is obligated to preserve the clients' anonymity. As we observed earlier in this chapter, the increased use of third-party payors for therapeutic services often calls for disclosure of personal information to an insurance company or managed care organization. This loss of privacy may become a therapeutic issue—clients holding back information—when peer reviews or utilization reviews of therapeutic procedures require therapists to inform clients that some information may be revealed

BOX 6.5 CLINICAL NOTE

Limits of Confidentiality

Confidentiality represents a clinical responsibility that must be maintained unless circumstances demand disclosure to protect the welfare of a client or the public at large. Those extenuating circumstances include the following situations:

- When a client gives informed consent to disclosure
- When a therapist is acting in a court-appointed capacity
- When there is a risk of suicide or some other life-threatening emergency
- When a client initiates litigation against the therapist
- When a client's mental health is introduced as part of a civil action

- When a child under the age of 16 is the victim of a crime
- When a child requires psychiatric hospitalization
- When a client expresses intent to commit a crime that will endanger society or another person (duty to warn)
- When a client is deemed to be dangerous to him- or herself
- When required for third-party billing authorized by the client
- When required for properly utilized fee collection services

Source: Falvey, 2002, p. 93

(Miller, 1996). Box 6.5 presents a list compiled by Falvey (2002) regarding the limits of confidentiality.

The duties of protecting clients from harming themselves, and protecting others from potentially dangerous clients, are especially important professional responsibilities (Swenson, 1997). In the former, therapists must intervene—call in family members and/or the police, or get the client to a hospital emergency room—if they believe a client is seriously considering suicide.

A therapist who determines that there is clear and imminent danger to someone the client vows to harm must take personal action and inform the responsible authorities; the therapist also has a *duty to warn* and protect the intended victim because the courts have ruled (*Tarasoff* decision) that "the rights of clients to privacy end where the public peril begins" (Perlin, 1997). Adopted in California in 1976, the ruling has become a national standard of practice (Falvey, 2002). However, in practice it often poses a serious dilemma for therapists—how to determine when a client is sufficiently dangerous to an identifiable victim (not just letting off steam about someone) that reasonable steps to warn that person must be taken, thus breaching confidentiality (Ahia & Martin, 1993). While no therapist is expected to make perfect predictions of calculable danger, care is necessary in making the assessment of risk to a potential victim; good written records should be kept, and discussions with supervisors, consultants, or even attorneys are advisable (Monahan, 1993). Some states protect therapists from malpractice lawsuits for breaching confidentiality if they can establish having acted in good faith to protect third parties (Stromberg, Schneider, & Joondeph, 1993).

Similarly, mandatory reporting laws, while they differ from state to state, all require therapists to disclose suspicions of incest or child abuse to the proper child protective agency. A therapist is held liable for failing to do so if he or she has reason to suspect (or a child discloses) abuse or neglect. Once again, states provide immunity from civil lawsuit for reporting suspected abusers. Sometimes problems arise because the therapist has previously failed to inform clients of this limitation on confidentiality (Nicolai & Scott, 1994), and sometimes therapists, in violation of the law, choose not to report suspected abusers for what they consider to be therapeutic reasons (Kalichman & Craig, 1991).

The limits of confidentiality should be spelled out by the therapist at the start of therapy, lest family members agree to proceed while operating under wrong assumptions. The issue is linked to informed consent, to be discussed with the family at the beginning of treatment, so that their decision to continue indicates their acceptance of the confidentiality ground rules (Smith, 1999).

Informed Consent

Matters of informed consent and the right to refuse treatment have become critical ethical issues in the practice of marital and family therapy. Most family therapists agree that before families enter therapy, they must be adequately informed concerning the nature of the process they are about to undertake (Haas & Malouf, 1995; Malley & Reilly, 1999). The purposes of the sessions, typical procedures, risks of possible negative outcomes (divorce, job changes), possible benefits, costs, what behavior to expect from the therapist, the limits of confidentiality, information provided to third-party payors, the conditions that might precipitate a referral to another therapist or agency, available alternative treatments—these issues all require explanation at the outset, before each client agrees to participate. Two principles are operating here (Welfel, 2006)—full disclosure by the therapist so the client can decide whether to proceed, and free consent (deciding to engage in an activity without coercion or pressure). In some cases, therapists provide written documents ("Patient's Rights and Responsibilities") to accompany their oral presentations, to be read, signed, and kept at home for future reference.

How should a therapist deal with family members who refuse treatment? Doherty and Boss (1991) focus on the issue of *coercion* regarding reluctant adults or children, as in the case where therapists insist that all members attend before family therapy can get under way. Willing members are thus in a position of being coerced by denying them access to treatment unless they successfully persuade the others to participate. Both these authors, as well as Margolin (1982), agree that a therapist with such a policy would do well to have a list of competent referral sources to which the family members willing to take part might go for help.

Children present another thorny issue. Family therapists need to inform children, at the child's level of understanding, what is likely to transpire in family therapy and then ask for their consent to participate. Consent should also be obtained before videotaping, audiotaping, or observing families behind a one-way mirror. The entire issue of informed consent is gaining prominence, fitting in as it does with current concerns over patient and consumer rights.

Privileged Communication

Privileged communication offers clients even more protection from forced disclosure of private matters discussed with their therapist than does confidentiality. A legal

Informed Consent/Office Policies

Welcome Statement: Welcome to my office. As a licensed therapist, I am governed by various laws and regulations and by the code of ethics of my profession. The ethics code requires that I make you aware of specific office policies and how these procedures may affect you. However, many of these policies will be unrelated to our work together.

Patient's Rights: Our relationship is strictly voluntary and you may leave the psychotherapy relationship anytime you wish.

Limits of Confidentiality: Sessions between a psychologist and patient are strictly confidential, except under certain legally defined situations involving threats of self-harm or harm to another, and situations of child abuse, elder abuse, or abuse of otherwise dependent individuals. In the case of danger to others, I am required by law to notify the police and to inform any intended victim(s). In the case of self-harm, I am ethically bound to inform the nearest relative, significant other, or to otherwise enlist methods to prevent self-harm or suicide. In instances of child abuse, elder abuse, or dependent abuse, I must notify the proper authorities.

Payment, Fees & Insurance: It is customary to pay for sessions at the time of the session or at the end of each month, unless otherwise arranged. Fees will be increased once yearly. Fee for court attendance or writing a psychological report is based upon the hourly session fee.

Phone Accessibility & Emergency Procedures: I will return calls as soon as possible should you need to speak to me between sessions. However, I cannot guarantee an immediate return call when left a voicemail message. Efforts are made to return calls within four hours. If you have an immediate emergency, call 911 for help. In the event of a lengthy telephone session, you will be charged at the hourly session fee.

Cancellation Policy: If you need to cancel or reschedule an appointment, please notify me as soon as possible, at least 24 hours in advance, so that I might fill the hour; if so, you will not be charged. This is necessary because a professional time commitment is set aside and held exclusively for you. If you cannot guarantee a specific time, we can arrange different times each week based upon our schedules.

I have read, understood, and agreed to the conditions stated above.

<hr>

Name

<hr>

Date

FIGURE 6.1 A Sample Informed Consent Form

right to privacy, privileged communication protects a client from having prior confidences revealed by a therapist from the witness stand during court proceedings without his or her prior consent (Glosoff, Herlihy, Herlihy, & Spence, 1997). Thus, therapists cannot be forced to produce client records in court, or in general answer questions about private matters revealed to them by clients, without client permission. However, since the privilege belongs to the client, the client's waiving that privilege of privacy leaves the therapist with no legal grounds for withholding the information. All states have some form of therapist-client privilege statute, although the specific details vary by state. The issue, however, is less clear in couple or family therapy; indeed, these therapeutic activities are not subject to privileged communication in many states (Corey, Corey, & Callanan, 2007), and clients and therapists alike need to be informed of their state's laws regarding both confidentiality and privileged

CLINICAL NOTE

It is best when the therapist states a position regarding his or her willingness to go to court prior to beginning therapy with a couple contemplating divorce or anticipating a child custody conflict. A therapist who is forthright about not feeling comfortable choosing sides in a possible court battle or not competent as a forensic expert to appear in court, allows the couple to choose another therapist before starting treatment, if they so desire. Should they decide to remain, establishing such neutrality at the beginning of the relationship keeps later conflict to a minimum.

communication at the start of treatment. One sticky problem is, exactly who is the client: the individual, the couple, the family? In the case of a divorcing pair, suppose one spouse seeks testimony from the therapist while the other does not wish the information revealed?

Generally speaking, the therapist, careful about protecting client privacy, should always demand permission in the form of a written release from a client before revealing any information to others. In the case of suspected child or elder abuse, however, the therapist is mandated by law to report his or her suspicions, and the rules regarding privileged communication do not apply.

Maintaining Professional Competence

Whether a novice or widely experienced in working with couples and families, all therapists need periodic upgrading of their clinical skills. Continuing education is required to keep abreast of new developments in the field (for example, gender-sensitive therapy, postmodern therapeutic approaches, psychoeducation, multicultural considerations) and new populations served (AIDS patients and their families; substance abusers; the homeless). Belonging to professional organizations and attending lectures at local and national conventions, taking workshop classes, consulting with colleagues, keeping up with the family therapy clinical and research literature, and so forth—all help maintain the lifelong learning necessary to remain a competent professional.

Exceeding the bounds of one's competence and experience in assessing and treating marital or family problems is considered unethical. Therefore, therapists must know the boundaries of their own competence and refer to fellow professionals those clients who require services beyond the therapist's professional training or experience. Reaching a prolonged therapeutic impasse with a family should also alert a therapist that a reassessment is in order, and that a referral or a consultation with a peer who has expertise in the particular troublesome area might help resolve the problem and move the therapeutic process forward.

Clients with whom therapists experience serious and unresolvable conflicts in values should also be directed to other therapists competent to deal with their problems. Even highly experienced family therapists seek the input of a consultant for purposes of verifying diagnostic impressions or confirming therapeutic strategies. In addition, psychiatric consultants may be called upon to administer medication (for example, antidepressant drugs) or hospitalize a client if the family therapist lacks hospital privileges or has not dealt with hospitalization in his or her training.

SUMMARY

Professional practice in marital and family therapy is regulated by legal statutes (licensing or certification) and self-regulated by ethical codes, peer review, continuing education, and consultation. Core competencies in the practice of family therapy are under development. Forty-eight states currently license marriage and family therapists as qualified healthcare providers. Managed care organizations, dedicated to containing costs and insisting on therapist accountability, increasingly are administering and financing the delivery of mental health services in the United States. One consequence is that therapists who are managed care providers can no longer ensure strict confidentiality, since most contracts call for subscribers to grant permission for therapists to disclose requested information to case managers.

All therapists have legal and ethical responsibilities to maintain high levels of professional competence. The ethical code of professional organizations, defining standards of conduct for members of the profession, offers guidance in identifying clinical situations in which the therapist must make ethical decisions, and offers principles on which those decisions can best be based. New technology has called for new efforts to protect privacy, and the Health Insurance Portability and Accountability Act offers safeguards for ensuring confidentiality. Family therapists frequently must deal with the ethical dilemma involved in concerning themselves with individual needs versus family needs.

Preserving confidentiality of a client's disclosures, providing clients with informed consent (e.g., about the limits of confidentiality) before commencing treatment, and assuring clients of their legal protection through privileged communication are common ethical concerns aimed at protecting client privacy.

RECOMMENDED READINGS

Bennett, B. E., Bryant, B. K., VandenBos, G. R., & Greenwood, A. (1990). *Professional liability and risk management.* Washington, DC: American Psychological Association.

Corey, G., Corey, M. S., & Callanan, P. (2007). *Issues and ethics in the helping professions.* Pacific Grove, CA: Brooks/Cole.

Cummings, N. A. (1995). Impact of managed care on employment and training: A primer for survival. *Professional psychology: Research and practice, 26,* 10–15.

Pope, K. S., & Vasquez, M. J. T. (1998). *Ethics in psychotherapy and counseling: A practical guide for psychologists* (2nd ed.). San Francisco: Jossey-Bass.

Welfel, E. R. (2006). *Ethics in counseling and psychotherapy: Standards, research, and emerging issues* (3rd ed.). Belmont, CA: Thomson/Brooks/Cole.

PSYCHODYNAMIC MODELS

Family therapists share a view of the family as the context for relationships as well as a therapeutic commitment to address the process of family interaction. Under the umbrella of systems theory, they attempt to examine what lies both within and outside the system—its multiple inputs and possible paths of actions—being careful not to neglect what transpires within the individual participants. Gender and cultural considerations, as well as the interface between the family and the broader community in which it is embedded, figure prominently in the thinking and clinical approaches of contemporary family therapists.

While noteworthy differences continue to exist in the theoretical assumptions each school of thought makes about the nature and origin of psychological dysfunction, in what precisely they look for in understanding family patterns, and in their strategies for therapeutic intervention, in practice the trend today is toward eclecticism and integration in family therapy (Moultrop, 1986; Mikesell, Lusterman, & McDaniel, 1995; Lebow, 1997). In this postmodern age that emphasizes that all knowledge is inescapably relative and subjective, there is less and less acceptance of the erstwhile belief in the endless possibilities of a single model, universally applicable to all client problems and appropriate for all families regardless of cultural background or family type. The prevalence of a wide variety of family configurations (single parents, gay couples, remarried families) and culturally diverse groups reinforces the idea that no single theory or set of interventions is likely to fit all equally well. Today's family therapists, including many who identify themselves as disciples of a particular school, are apt to be less doctrinaire in practice than their theoretical differences suggest, incorporating contributions from "rival" schools (sometimes unwittingly) in their treatment approaches when appropriate, in order to achieve optimal results. Greater acceptance of a diversity of ideas within the field allows for a greater range of choices in what specific set of therapeutic interventions to adopt in specific situations or kinds of family problems in order to achieve maximum effectiveness.

Prochaska and Norcross (1999) contend that the modal orientation of family therapists today is eclecticism/integration. They note that the *psychotherapy integration movement*, as it is now called, is rapidly accelerating for individual as well as family therapists, as psychotherapy has matured and the "ideological cold war" between theoretical systems has abated. Many clinicians of various theoretical persuasions have

BOX 7.1   CLINICAL NOTE

Eclecticism and Integration in Current Family Practice

Eclecticism and *integration* are related but not interchangeable notions. The former refers to the selection of concepts or intervention techniques from a variety of theoretical sources, usually based on the experiences of a clinician that a specific approach works with a certain set of presenting problems. Thus eclecticism is usually pragmatic and case based. Examples of eclecticism include functional family therapy for adolescent delinquents and substance abusers (Alexander, Waldon, Newberry, & Liddle, 1990) or the family psychoeducational treatment of severe psychiatric disorders (McFarlane et al., 2003). Multisystemic therapy (Henggeler & Borduin, 1990) represents an empirically supported, family-based treatment program, based on systems theory and Bronfenbrenner's (1986) social ecology theory, which has been directed at treating juvenile offenders and their families. Goldner's (1998) approach to treating violent couples represents still another effort aimed at a specific clinical problem.

Integration, more controversial, represents a paradigm shift and calls for an extensive combining of discrete parts of theories and treatment processes into a higher-level theory that crosses theoretical boundaries and uses intervention techniques in a unified fashion. While no one integrative theory has yet emerged as predominant, a number of efforts have appeared, such as Dattilio's (1998) endeavor to combine systemic and cognitive perspectives, Pinsof's (1995) attempt to synthesize family, individual, and biological therapies, and Wachtel's (1997) bid to integrate psychoanalysis, behavior therapy, and the relational world of family therapy. Integrative couples therapy (Jacobson & Christensen, 1996) represents a successful combination of a humanistic outlook and communication training, added to the problem-solving techniques of behavioral therapy.

Lebow (2003) contends that the practice modes of most family therapists are now integrative or eclectic. No one school or therapeutic approach has a monopoly on effectiveness, although efforts to establish evidence-based techniques are under way in some approaches, especially emotionally focused couple therapy or cognitive-behavioral family therapy. Seeking the common factors that lead to successful interventions, regardless of theoretical model, represents another effort toward integration.

joined together recently to form the Society for the Exploration of Psychotherapy Integration.

While the unadulterated practice of a single form of family therapy is becoming less common, and therapists today are likely to selectively borrow concepts and techniques from one another that cross theoretical boundaries, there nevertheless are important distinguishing theoretical constructs between the various traditional schools of family therapy. While there may no longer be slavish devotion in practice, a therapist's theory helps organize what information to seek and how to go about seeking it, how to formulate a therapeutic plan, make interventions, and understand what transpires. Because of this selectivity factor, each theory is also necessarily limited and one-sided; further, no single theory can explain and predict all the behavior patterns observed or provide a treatment rationale for all behavioral, intrapsychic, or interpersonal problems.

In this and the following six chapters in Part III, we look at the classical approaches to family theory and clinical practice, grouping those models that are primarily psychodynamic (concerned with insight, motivation, unconscious conflict, early infant-caregiver attachments); those that emphasize the experiential-humanistic viewpoint (emotional engagement, self-growth, self-determination); those that pay special attention to the family as a system (transaction patterns, alliances, boundaries)—the transgenerational, structural, strategic, and systemic models; and those that are cognitive-behavioral in their approach (emphasizing learning skills and behavioral change).

Later in the text, in Part IV (Chapters 14–16), we present some evolving theories and therapeutic techniques that challenge these entrenched models. Here we offer some fresh outlooks, such as solution-focused and narrative therapy, largely influenced by the postmodern proposition that people invent rather than discover reality. Such considerations have tended to deconstruct the field's complacent notions of objectivity and therapeutic certainty regarding what causes family dysfunction and how best to help families get back on track. We also include psychoeducational approaches to family therapy, which represent another shift in our thinking of what causes problems, symptoms, or disabilities in individual family members; rather than look to the family as the source of the difficulties, therapeutic efforts are directed at maximizing the functioning of families to whom problems, such as schizophrenia in a family member, have occurred.

THE PLACE OF THEORY

The theoretical foundation of the field of family therapy demands to be strengthened lest it become merely a set of clever, even flashy, empirically derived intervention techniques. Important and seemingly effective as some of these techniques may be, they require the kind of rationale or justification that only a coherent, unified theory can provide. Acknowledging the usefulness of employing a variety of therapeutic techniques as called for by the needs of a specific family, Patterson (1997) nevertheless argues that a clear theoretical position provides the structural underpinnings for assessment and treatment planning to occur. He maintains that a therapist must accurately identify the major theoretical orientation from which he or she operates before utilizing congruent intervention methods within it.

While techniques relevant to helping a specific family may be borrowed by an eclectic therapist, there remains considerable controversy over whether an integrated supertheory is ever likely to emerge, since, as Grunebaum (1997) points out, there are too many inherent incompatibilities in the central theoretical constructs of the major theories for such a conceptual integration to occur. As we are about to see, different schools of family therapy make different assumptions about human nature, have different goals, and use different criteria for evaluating what constitutes a successful outcome (Liddle, 1982).

All theories, of course, are inevitably speculations or hypotheses offered in the hope of shedding light or providing fresh perspectives on the causes of family dysfunction. They are never, in and of themselves, true or false; rather, some are more useful than others, particularly in generating research hypotheses that can be verified through testing. All of these theories are tentative; all are expendable in the sense that useful theories lead to new ways of looking at behavior and to the discovery of new relationships that in turn lead to new sets of theoretical proposals.

At this stage in the development of family therapy, we need to examine the usefulness of the various contributions that have already been made to our understanding of family development and functioning. Some models have come from the research laboratory, others from the consultation room of a clinician working with seriously disturbed or merely temporarily troubled families. In evaluating each of the models presented in this and subsequent chapters, keep in mind the following criteria of a sound theory:

- Is it *comprehensive*? Does it deal with understanding family functioning and avoid being trivial or oversimplified? Is it generalizable to all families as they behave in all situations (not, for example, only to white middle-class families or only to the ways families behave in special psychotherapeutic situations)?
- Is it *parsimonious*? Does it make as few assumptions as necessary to account for the phenomena under study? If two competing theoretical systems both predict the same behavior, is the theory chosen the one with fewer assumptions and constructs?
- Is it *verifiable*? Does it generate predictions about behavior that can be confirmed when the relevant empirical data have been collected?
- Is it *precise*? Does it define concepts explicitly and relate them to each other and to data (avoiding relying solely on figurative, metaphorical, or analogical language)?
- Is it *empirically valid*? Do systematic empirical tests of the predictions made by the theory confirm the theory?
- Is it *stimulating*? Does it provoke response and further investigation to enhance the theory or even to demonstrate its inadequacies?

SOME HISTORICAL CONSIDERATIONS

Psychoanalysis, both as theory and a form of practice, deserves recognition for playing the central role in establishing and defining the nature of psychotherapy (Sander, 1998). Initially focused on treating neurotic individuals by examining and reconstructing childhood conflicts, generated by the colliding forces of inner drives and external experiences, psychoanalysis became the dominant ideology in American psychiatry after World War II. Shortly before the war, a large number of European clinicians (including Erik Erikson and Erich Fromm), psychoanalytic in their orientation, had come to this country to escape the Nazi regime. The American public had been receptive to Freud's ideas since early in that century. With the arrival of these clinicians, psychoanalysis began to gain greater acceptance among medical specialists, academicians, and clinicians in the psychology community, as well as among sociologists and psychiatric social workers. Indeed, many of family therapy's pioneers—Ackerman, Bowen, Lidz, Jackson, Minuchin, Wynne, Boszormenyi-Nagy—(all men, incidentally), were psychoanalytically trained. Some, such as Jackson and Minuchin, moved far from their psychoanalytic roots in favor of systems thinking, while others (Bowen, Lidz, Wynne) continued to produce theories that reflected some of their earlier allegiances.

Freud's Impact on Family Therapy

Sigmund Freud, founder of psychoanalysis at the turn of the twentieth century, had been aware of the impact of family relationships on the individual's character formation, particularly in the development of symptomatic behavior. For example, in his famous case of Little Hans, a five-year-old boy who refused to go out into the street for fear that a horse might bite him, Freud hypothesized that Hans was displacing anxiety associated with his Oedipus complex. That is, Freud believed Hans unconsciously desired his mother sexually but felt competitive with, and hostile toward, his father, as well as fearful of his father's reaction to his hostility. Hans had witnessed a horse falling down in the street, and Freud speculated that he unconsciously associated the scene with his father, since he wanted his father hurt too. According to Freud, Hans unconsciously changed his intense fear of castration by his father into a phobic symptom about being bitten by the horse, whom Hans had previously seen as innocuous. Having substituted the horse for his father, Hans was able to turn an internal danger into an external one. The fear was displaced onto a substitute object, which is prototypically what takes place in the development of a phobia. In this celebrated 1909 case (Freud, 1955), the boy was actually treated by the father, under Freud's guidance.

Historically, the case of Little Hans has conceptual as well as technical significance. Conceptually, it enabled Freud to elaborate on his earlier formulations regarding psychosexual development in children and the use of **defense mechanisms** (such as displacement) as unconscious **ego** devices a person calls on as protection against being overwhelmed by anxiety. Moreover, the case supported Freud's emerging belief that inadequate resolution of a particular phase of psychosexual development can lead to neurotic behavior such as phobias. Note, however, that Freud chose not to work with either the child or the family but encouraged Hans's father, a physician, to treat his own son under Freud's supervision.[1] Ultimately, Hans was relieved of his phobic symptom.

From the case of Little Hans and similar examples from among Freud's published papers, we can appreciate how family relationships came to provide a rich diagnostic aid to Freud's psychoanalytic thinking. He recognized that the family provided the early environment—or context—in which neurotic fears and anxieties developed, although he failed to take matters one step further to identify how current or ongoing family relationships helped maintain the maladaptive or problematic behavior. His therapeutic efforts thus concentrated on the family of origin as the client remembered it, and not how his current family functioned.

Four years earlier, in 1905, Freud had written that psychoanalysts were "obliged to pay as much attention . . . to purely human and social circumstances of our patients as to the somatic data and the symptoms of the disorder. Above all, our interest will be directed toward their family circumstances" (Freud, 1959, pp. 25–26). In practice, however, as we have pointed out, Freud preferred working therapeutically with individuals; both his theories and techniques stress the resolution of intrapsychic

---

[1]Here, Freud was anticipating a technique used by many of today's family therapists—using family members, especially parents, as agents of change.

conflicts rather than restructuring interpersonal or transactional phenomena within a family. So strongly was he opposed to working with more than one family member at a time that his negative assessment became virtually an unquestioned doctrine among psychoanalysts, who for many years accepted the prohibition against analyzing members of the same family (Broderick & Schrader, 1991). In fact, as Bowen (1975) notes, one psychoanalytic principle that may have retarded earlier growth of the family therapy movement was the isolation of the therapist-patient relationship and the related concern that contact with the patient's relatives would "contaminate" the therapist. Bowen reported that some hospitals had one therapist deal with the patient's intrapsychic processes while another handled practical matters and administrative procedures, and a third team member, a social worker, talked to relatives. According to Bowen's early experiences, failure to respect these boundaries was considered "inept psychotherapy." It was only in the 1950s that this principle began to be violated—more often for research than for clinical purposes—and that family members began to be seen therapeutically as a group.[2]

Adler and Sullivan: Contributing Pioneers

Another psychoanalytic influence on family therapy is the work of Alfred Adler, an early associate of Freud's in Vienna. As we indicated in Chapter 5, Adler helped found the child guidance movement in the early 1900s. A physician originally interested in ophthalmology, Adler later began to specialize in neurology and psychiatry, especially in treating childhood disorders. Adler was one of the first to be invited by Freud to join the Vienna Psychoanalytic Society, which he did in 1902. Although initially he published psychoanalytically oriented articles in medical and educational journals, Adler eventually developed views divergent from psychoanalytic theory, emphasizing the importance of social (including family) factors as opposed to Freud's **drive theory** (Scharf, 2000). More holistic in studying the whole person and less concerned with unconscious motivations than his mentor, Adler particularly challenged Freud's lack of attention to social elements in personality formation. Instead, he offered a theory rooted in social relationships: All behavior is purposive and interactive, and the basic social system is the family (Carlson, Sperry, & Lewis, 1997). Thus having broken with Freud's insistence on a biologically based drive theory—substituting social, purposeful, and developmental determinants—Adler moved on to form the Society for Individual Psychology in 1914, a group that underscored the importance of the total individual in any therapeutic undertaking.

Adler insisted that an individual's conscious personal and social goals as well as subsequent goal-directed behavior could be fully understood only by comprehending the environment or social context, especially the family, in which that behavior originated and was displayed. Adlerian concepts such as sibling rivalry, family constellation, and style of life attest to Adler's awareness of the key role of family experiences in influencing adult behavior. His holistic view of the person as unpartitionable has applicability to the systems outlook of today's family therapists. Adler's direct family therapy connection can be seen today in such psychoeducational efforts as marriage enrichment

---

[2]Just how much change has occurred since the 1950s? Today family therapists demonstrate their work with families before large professional audiences, without benefit of one-way mirrors or other devices to shield participants from viewers. Most families report that any initial self-consciousness is quickly overcome.

Nathan Ackerman, M.D.

programs, in parent education undertakings aimed at facilitating adult-child understanding and cooperation (Dinkmeyer, McKay, Dinkmeyer, & McKay, 1997), and in integration of Adlerian concepts with some of the major approaches in family therapy (Sherman & Dinkmeyer, 1987).

Another important theorist, American psychiatrist Harry Stack Sullivan, was psychoanalytically trained but was also influenced by sociology and social psychology. Throughout a career that began in the late 1920s, he stressed the role of interpersonal relationships, within the family and with outsiders, in personality development. Sullivan (1953) argued that people are essentially products of their social interactions; to understand how people function, he urged the study of their "relatively enduring patterns of recurrent interpersonal situations" (p. 110).

Sullivan, at the Washington School of Psychiatry, stressed the importance of peer relationships in personal and social development, believing that the seeds for later disturbance were sown in early dealings with others. He emphasized the crucial nature of the early mother-child dyad, arguing that these formative experiences lead to viewing parts of oneself as good me, bad me, and not me—later, as we shall see, consistent with object relations theory. Working mostly with schizophrenics, much of the time at the Sheppard and Enoch Pratt Hospital in Baltimore, Sullivan noted that the disorder frequently manifested itself during the transitional period of adolescence, leading him to speculate about the possibly critical effects of the patient's ongoing family life in producing the confusion that might lead ultimately to schizophrenia (Perry, 1982). Sullivan (1940) described his way of engaging patients as acting as a *participant observer*, anticipating by several decades the current second-order cybernetic idea of the therapist being part of the ongoing therapeutic system.

Don Jackson and Murray Bowen, both of whom were later to become outstanding figures in the emerging field of family therapy, trained under Sullivan and his colleague Frieda Fromm-Reichmann. Jackson's work was clearly influenced by Sullivan's early notion of redundant family interactive patterns. Bowen's theories, especially those pertaining to individual pathology emerging from a faulty multigenerational family system, can be traced to Sullivan's influence.

But it is Nathan Ackerman, a psychoanalyst and child psychiatrist, who is generally credited with deliberately adapting psychoanalytic formulations to the study of the family. In what may have been the first paper to deal specifically with family therapy, published as the first article in the Bulletin of the Kansas Mental Hygiene Society, Ackerman (1937) emphasized the influence of the family as a dynamic *psychosocial unit* in treating one of its emotionally disturbed members. The constant interaction between the biologically driven, inner conflicted person (a psychoanalytic concept), the family, and the social environment (a person-systems concept) was to preoccupy him for more than three decades, as he struggled to apply an intrapsychic vocabulary to family diagnosis and treatment. As he summed it up in a paper published shortly after his death (Ackerman, 1972):

> Over a period of some thirty-five years, I have extended my orientation to the problems of behavior, step-by-step, from the inner life of the person, to the person within family, to the family within community, and most recently, to the social community itself. (p. 449)

The Psychodynamic Outlook

For the remainder of this chapter, we intend to consider three aspects of psychodynamic theories:

- The classical psychoanalytic drive theories first introduced by Sigmund Freud
- Object relations theory, a revision of earlier psychoanalytic formulations with an emphasis on the search for satisfying human relationships
- The self psychology theory of Heinz Kohut, with its emphasis on the role of narcissism (love of self) as an organizing determinant of personality development and as a necessary precursor for love of others

Classical Psychoanalytic Theory

The **psychodynamic** view of individual behavior, derived from Freud's psychoanalytic model, focuses on the interplay of opposing innate forces (or drives) within a person as the basis for understanding that person's motivation, conflicts, and symptomatology. That is, drives motivate behavior by means of bodily demands that take the form of unconscious wishes and impulses seeking satisfaction. Freud contended that each drive has four components: an aim (say, the release of sexual or aggressive tension), a source (in the case of hunger, for example, the bodily need for nourishment), an impetus (the pressure or urgency of the drive), and an object (the person or thing or condition that will satisfy the drive: food, sexual intercourse, etc.). An object choice, then, as first articulated by Freud, may be a significant person or anything that is a target of another person's feelings or drives (St. Clair, 2000). It is important here to note that it is not the real object per se, nor how that object or person behaves in real life, that is at issue, but rather the *fantasies about the object the perceiver experiences.* So, falling in love with another person, according to Freud, primarily involves investing energy in one's inner thoughts or mental representations of that special person.

Although Freud also acknowledged a subordinate role played by the environment, especially the parents, in individual personality formation—what we have been describing as the family context—he nevertheless was insistent that treatment be individually focused,[3] viewing the presence of family members as an obstacle to psychoanalytic intervention.

As we indicated early in this chapter, most of the family therapy pioneers were psychoanalytically trained, and in their initial zeal in the 1960s and 1970s, having discovered systems thinking, they seemed to dismiss individually focused psychoanalytic ideas as antiquated and, in the linking of adult pathology to childhood developmental conflicts, hopelessly linear. By the mid-1980s, however, a more integrated view was being advocated by many family therapists, who urged that systems thinkers not neglect the individual family member's personal conflicts and motivation (Slipp, 1984; Nichols, 1987). Today, the interlocking systems of the individual, the family, and the community are at the forefront; many Freudian ideas about the needs and conflicts of individual family members are being revisited alongside family relationship patterns and the impact of community life.

---

[3]Freud is quoted by Sander (1998) as having questioned how psychoanalytic treatment, which he compared to a surgical procedure, could succeed "in the presence of all the members of the patient's family, who would stick their noses into the field of the operation and exclaim aloud at every incision" (p. 429).

Deviations from the Classical View

An attempt at specifically integrating psychodynamic and family systems concepts has been offered by Bentovim and Kinston (1991) and by Slipp (1991). The former, British family therapists, present a model called focal family therapy. Consistent with the development of family therapy in the United Kingdom—where, unlike the United States, family therapy had its origins almost exclusively in child guidance and child psychiatric clinics—this approach is developmentally oriented and looks for family disturbances, especially traumatic events to family members that have led to intrapsychic and interpersonal disturbance within the family. In formulating a focal hypothesis about a family's conflict, these therapists consider the family's response to the symptom in the identified patient, the function of symptom in family functioning, what keeps the family from facing their conflicts directly, and any link to past trauma.

Samuel Slipp (1991), a psychiatrist trained in both psychoanalysis and family therapy, sees the two as potentially complementary and both involved in the genesis and maintenance of psychopathology. As a result, he attends to any significant childhood development of the participants while addressing ongoing family interaction using the framework of object relations theory. Both individual and family diagnoses are part of Slipp's treatment plan in his effort to integrate psychoanalytic and systems concepts and therapeutic methods.

As Nichols (1987) notes, in arguing for the restoration of individual dynamics into psychodynamic family therapy, no matter how much our attention is focused on the entire family system, individual family members remain separate flesh-and-blood persons with unique experiences, private hopes, ambitions, outlooks, expectations, and potentials. At times, people may react out of personal habit and for private reasons. Psychoanalytically oriented therapists who accept Nichols's holistic view—what he calls interactional psychodynamics—are urged to remain attentive to the circular nature of personal and family dynamics.

As family therapy has moved beyond early cybernetic formulations, which were viewed as too mechanistic, and as renewed efforts attempt to include individual experiences and outlooks in any comprehensive understanding of family functioning, there has been a corresponding revival of interest in psychodynamic postulations. The new look, however, is relationship based, and seeks not only to discover how the inner lives and conflicts of family members interlock but also how the binding together affects disturbances in family members.

In a major, highly influential set of deviations from classical psychoanalysis, psychoanalytically oriented therapists practicing **object relations therapy** have become more relationship focused, instead of remaining a **blank screen** (the classical position) on which the patients projects their fantasies. As we shall discuss shortly, these therapists try to participate in a *holding environment* (a safe, nurturing setting), caring for family members while remaining aware of any transference processes. In the "shared holding" process, the family is encouraged to feel free to interact safely in front of a trusted therapist.

A form of psychodynamically oriented therapy that first flourished in Britain in the 1950s, object relations therapy emphasizes the fundamental need in people for attachments and relationships. (Objects, as we noted earlier, refer to persons or things to which a person relates or otherwise gains gratification.) In object relations family therapy (Scharff & Scharff, 1987), the interacting forces both within and between individuals are explored in the process of treatment. In particular, efforts are directed at examining thwarted relationship experiences early in life, particularly mother-child interactions, that become internalized and that shape a child's inner world and later adult relationships and experiences (St. Clair, 2000).

Heinz Kohut (1971, 1977), an American psychiatrist born and educated in Vienna, was responsible for a major development in contemporary psychoanalysis. Kohut published a provocative if controversial series of books challenging some basic tenets of classical psychoanalysis, such as its drive theory. Based on his work in analyzing patients with **narcissistic personality disorders**—patients Freud considered unanalyzable because they were not able to invest or engage in a relationship with the analyst—Kohut developed a **self psychology**. In his self psychology theory, Kohut argued that narcissistic personality difficulties (as well as others) result from a failure in childhood to develop confident feelings about oneself as the result of poor experiences with inadequate or unavailable parents. As a result, narcissists, self-centered and with a powerful need for attention and admiration, are likely to see themselves as the center of all relationships in which they engage. As St. Clair (2000) notes, Kohut's work helps explain why narcissistic persons do not necessarily withdraw interests from outside objects, but rather are unable to rely on their own inner resources, instead creating intense attachments with others. We'll return to a further discussion of Kohut's work shortly.

As we present various family approaches that reflect a psychodynamic perspective, keep in mind that each one simultaneously addresses two levels of understanding and intervention: the motives, fantasies, unconscious conflicts, and repressed memories of each family member and the more complex world of family interaction and family dynamics.

Psychoanalysis and Family Dynamics (Ackerman)

As early as the 1930s, Nathan Ackerman, a psychoanalytically trained child psychiatrist in the child guidance movement, began to attend to the family itself as a social and emotional unit whose impact on the child needed exploration. By the 1940s, he was making clinical assessments of entire families (Green & Framo, 1981) and devising clinical techniques for applying psychoanalytic principles to treating preschool children and their families (Ackerman, 1956). In contrast to the collaborative approach practiced by most child guidance clinics, in which parent (usually mother) and child were seen by separate but collaborating therapists, Ackerman, as head of the Child Guidance Clinic at the Menninger Clinic in Topeka, Kansas, started to experiment with seeing whole families together for both diagnostic and therapeutic purposes. As part of his effort to obtain as complete a picture of family functioning as he could, especially among families suffering economic hardships during the Great Depression, Ackerman had members of his staff make home visits with client families (Guerin, 1976).

Although he continued to work with both individuals and families for a decade, by the 1950s Ackerman had moved explicitly into family therapy. In New York City in 1960, he opened the Family Institute, soon to become the leading family therapy training and treatment center on the East Coast. One of the earliest pioneers in assessing and treating families, Ackerman remained throughout his long career a boldly direct, provocative, confrontational therapist, who, true to his psychoanalytic background, never lost sight of the individual family member's needs, wishes, and longings.

Ackerman (1970), who is regarded by some as the "grandfather of family therapy," saw the family as a system of interacting personalities; each individual is an important subsystem within the family, just as the family is a subsystem within the community. He grasped early on that fully understanding family functioning calls for acknowledging input from several sources: the unique personality of each member; the dynamics of family role adaptations; the family's commitment to a set of human values; and the behavior of the family as a social unit. At the individual level, the process of symptom formation may be understood in terms of intrapsychic conflict, an unconscious defense against anxiety aroused by the conflict, and the resulting development of a neurotic symptom (a classical psychoanalytic explanation). At the family level, the symptom is viewed as part of a recurring, predictable interactional pattern intended to assure equilibrium for the individual, but actually impairing family homeostasis by producing distortions in family role relationships. In family terms, an individual's symptom becomes a unit of interpersonal behavior reflected within a context of shared family conflict, anxiety, and defenses. Conceptualizing behavior in this way, Ackerman was beginning to build a bridge between psychoanalytic theory and the then-emerging systems theories.

A "failure of **complementarity**," to use Ackerman's terms, characterizes the roles played by various family members with respect to each other. Change and growth within the system become constricted. Roles become rigid, narrowly defined, or stereotyped—or shift rapidly, causing confusion. According to Ackerman (1966), the family in which this occurs must be helped to

> accommodate to new experiences, to cultivate new levels of complementarity in family role relationships, to find avenues for the solution of conflict, to build a favorable self-image, to buttress critical forms of defense against anxiety, and to provide support for further creative development. (pp. 90–91)

For a family's behavior to be stable, flexibility and adaptability of roles are essential; roles within the family, which change over time, must allow for maturing children to gain an appropriate degree of autonomy.

Conflict may occur at several levels—within an individual family member, between members of the nuclear family, between generations including the extended family, or between the family and the surrounding community. Inevitably, according to Ackerman's observations, conflict at any level reverberates throughout the family system. What begins as a breakdown of role complementarity may lead to interpersonal conflict within the family and ultimately to intrapsychic conflict in one or more individual members; the individual's conflict deepens if the internalized family conflicts are persistent and pathogenic in form. One of Ackerman's therapeutic goals was to actively interrupt this sequence by extrapolating intrapsychic conflict to the broader area of family interaction.

Should the conflict between members become chronic, the family is at risk of reorganization into competing factions. The process often gets under way when one individual—often noticeably different from the others—becomes the family scapegoat. As that individual is singled out and punished for causing family disunity, various realignments of roles follow within the family. One member becomes "persecutor," while another may take the role of "healer" or "rescuer" of the "victim" of such "prejudicial scapegoating." Families are thus split into factions, and different members may even play different roles at different times, depending upon what Ackerman considers

BOX 7.2 THERAPEUTIC ENCOUNTER

ACKERMAN'S ACTIVE, CHALLENGING INTERVENTIONS: A CLINICAL VIGNETTE

To watch Ackerman on film or videotape is to see an honest, warm, straightforward, provocative, charismatic person at work in the very midst of the family, challenging a prejudice, coming to the aid of a scapegoated child, helping expose a family myth or hypocrisy, vigorously supplying the emotional ingredients necessary to galvanize a previously subdued family. No topic is taboo or off limits, no family rules so sacred they cannot be broken, nothing so shameful as to be unmentionable. Labeled as a "conductor" type of family therapist by Beels and Ferber (1969), Ackerman was said to lend the family "his pleasure in life, jokes, good sex, and limited aggression."

The following brief excerpt is from a therapy session with a family whose crisis was brought on when the 11-year-old daughter threatened to stab her 16-year-old brother and both parents with a kitchen knife. The explosive attack was precipitated by the girl's discovery of a conspiracy among the family members to say that her dog had died when in reality the mother had taken him to the dog pound. Members of the family indulge in many small lies, then cover up and deny their feelings. Note how Ackerman will have none of this charade. He reveals his own feelings in order to cut through the denial and open up the family encounter. The left-hand column is the verbatim account; the right-hand column is Ackerman's analysis of what is taking place.

Source: Ackerman, 1966, pp. 3–4.

Transcript	Comments
Dr. A: Bill, you heaved a sigh as you sat down tonight.	Therapist instantly fastens on a piece of nonverbal behavior, the father's sigh.
Father: Just physical, not mental.	
Dr. A: Who are you kidding?	Therapist challenges father's evasive response.
Father: I'm kidding no one.	
Dr. A: Hmmm . . .	Therapist registers disbelief, a further pressure for a more honest response.
Father: Really not . . . Really physical. I'm tired because I put in a full day today.	
Dr. A: Well, I'm very tired every day, and when I sigh it's never purely physical.	An example of therapist's use of his own emotions to counter an insincere denial.
Father: Really?	
Dr. A: What's the matter?	
Father: Nothing. Really!	
Dr. A: Well, your own son doesn't believe that.	Therapist now exploits son's gesture, a knowing grin, to penetrate father's denial and evoke a deeper sharing of feelings.
Father: Well, I mean nothing . . . nothing could cause me to sigh especially today or tonight.	
Dr. A: Well, maybe it isn't so special, but . . . How about it, John?	Therapist stirs son to unmask father.

(continued)

BOX 7.2   *(continued)*

Transcript	Comments
Son: I wouldn't know.	Now son wipes grin off his face and turns evasive, like father.
Dr. A: You wouldn't know? How come all of a sudden you put on a poker face? A moment ago you were grinning very knowingly.	Therapist counters by challenging son, who took pot shot from sidelines and then backed away.
Son: I really wouldn't know.	
Dr. A: You . . . Do you know anything about your pop?	
Son: Yeah.	
Dr. A: What do you know about him?	
Son: Well, I don't know, except that I know some stuff.	
Dr. A: Well, let's hear.	

Source: Ackerman, 1966, pp. 3–4.

the shared unconscious processes going on within the family at any particular period of time. Typically, observed Ackerman, such family alliances and interpersonal conflicts begin with a failure of complementarity within the marital dyad; the family is precluded from functioning as a cooperative, supportive, integrated whole. In cases such as these, Ackerman's therapeutic mission was to shift a family's concern from the scapegoated person's behavior to the basic disorder of the marital relationship.

In an early paper, Ackerman (1956) presented a conceptual model of interlocking pathology in family relationships. Concerned with the impact of the family environment on the development of childhood disorders, Ackerman was one of the first to note the constant interchange of unconscious processes taking place between family members as they are bound together in a particular interpersonal pattern. Accordingly, any single member's behavior can be a symptomatic reflection of confusion and distortion occurring in the entire family. With notions such as "interlocking pathology," Ackerman—trained as a Freudian, but personally inclined to attend to social interaction—was able to wed many of the psychoanalytic concepts of intrapsychic dynamics to the psychosocial dynamics of family life.[4]

---

[4]The pattern of interlocking pathology had long been known to therapists, many of whom made the disquieting observation that sometimes when a patient improved, his or her marriage failed (Walrond-Skinner, 1976). This seemed to suggest that prior to treatment the patient had felt locked into a neurotic relationship; after treatment, he or she was no longer willing to take part in the dysfunctional interaction and felt free—and able—to leave the marriage. If in the course of psychoanalytic treatment a spouse became upset in response to the changes occurring in the patient, individual therapy with another therapist was the usual recommendation. It is not surprising that under this approach, a patient's "improvement" was viewed as a threat to other family members who might proceed to subtly undermine the therapeutic progress. It was not until conjoint family therapy began to be practiced that all of the persons involved in a family were treated together.

Ackerman's broadly based therapeutic approach used principles from biology, psychoanalysis, social psychology, and child psychiatry. Unaffected and deceptively casual in manner, Ackerman tried through a series of office interviews and home visits to obtain a firsthand diagnostic impression of the dynamic relationships among family members. Hearty, confident, freewheeling, unafraid to be himself or to disclose his own feelings, he was apt to bring out these same qualities in the family. Soon the family was dealing with sex, aggression, dependency, and family secrets, the issues it had previously avoided as too threatening and dangerous.

Trained as a psychoanalyst, Ackerman clearly retained his interest in each family member's feelings, fantasies, and unconscious conflicts. However, influenced by social psychology, he was impressed by how personality is shaped by the particular social roles people are expected to play. In his approach to families, Ackerman was always interested in how people define their own roles ("What does it mean to you to be a father?") and what they expect from other family members ("How would you like your daughter to react to this situation?"). When all members delineate their roles clearly, family interactions proceed more smoothly, he maintained. Members can rework alignments, engage in new family transactions, and cultivate new levels of complementarity in their role relationships.

Ackerman believed the family therapist's principal job is that of a catalyst who, moving into the "living space" of the family, stirs up interaction, helps the family have a meaningful emotional exchange, and at the same time nurtures and encourages the members to understand themselves better through their contact with the therapist. As a catalyst, the therapist must play a wide range of roles—from activator, challenger, and confronter to supporter, interpreter, and integrator. Unlike the orthodox psychoanalyst who chooses to remain a neutral, distant, mysterious blank screen, Ackerman as family therapist was an open, vigorous, passionate person who engaged a family in the here and now and effectively made his presence felt. He moved directly into the path of family conflict, influenced the interactional process, supported positive forces and counteracted negative ones, and withdrew as the family began to deal more constructively with its problems.

Diagnostically, Ackerman attempted to fathom a family's deeper emotional currents—fears and suspicions, feelings of despair, the urge for vengeance. Using his personal emotional responses as well as his psychodynamic insights, he gauged what the family was experiencing, discerned its patterns of role complementarity, and probed the deeper, more pervasive family conflicts. By "tickling the defenses" (gently provoking participants to openly and honestly express what they feel), he caught members off guard and exposed their self-justifying rationalizations. In due course, he was able to trace significant connections between the family dysfunction and the intrapsychic anxieties of various family members. Finally, when the members were more in touch with what they were feeling, thinking, and doing individually, Ackerman helped them expand their awareness of alternate patterns of family relationships through which they might discover new levels of intimacy, sharing, and identification.

Throughout his long career, Ackerman remained staunchly psychodynamic in outlook; his death in 1971 removed one of the major proponents of this viewpoint in family therapy. A collection of his published papers with commentary by the editors (Bloch & Simon, 1982), called *The Strength of Family Therapy*, attests to his trailblazing efforts as well as his broad range of interests (child psychoanalysis, group therapy, social and cultural issues, marriage, and more). According to these editors, Ackerman practiced what he held dear in theory—namely, not to be bound by professional conventions unless they had some definite theoretical or clinical value for the problem at hand. He was among the first to demonstrate his work with families before a professional audience, breaking the traditional psychoanalytic code of secrecy about what really went on during therapeutic sessions.

Nevertheless, despite Ackerman's importance in the early years of family therapy, and notwithstanding the exhilaration he created while demonstrating the skills of a superb clinician at work, few therapists today would say their approach follows Ackerman's style. Nor did Ackerman leave behind any semblance of a carefully worked out theory of family processes or guidelines for clinical interventions. The Family Institute (renamed the Ackerman Institute in his memory), while acknowledging his pioneering efforts, does not operate from a psychodynamic perspective today. Systems theory (and more recently, strategic, Milan-school, and postmodern approaches) has largely replaced psychoanalytic thinking for its staff clinicians. While many therapists continue to be interested in the "psychodynamics of family life," and use psychoanalytic concepts, the psychodynamic view is currently best expressed by object relations theory, to which we now turn.

OBJECT RELATIONS THEORY

Classical psychoanalysis is considered to be a drive theory—inborn sexual and aggressive impulses emanate from what Freud termed the *id*. Having created an excitation, these impulses lead to unconscious fantasies as the individual endeavors to achieve gratification through discharge of these drives. However, the drive's behavioral expression may lead to perceived danger or a fear of punishment. The resulting structural conflict—between the id impulses and those parts of the personality Freud labeled ego and superego—is the soil from which psychopathology grows (Slipp, 1988). Acting out an impulse unconsciously becomes associated with the danger of reprisal—physical punishment, loss of love—from parents or other key parent figures in the child's life. Note that while the psychoanalytic emphasis is on the single individual's internal world of fantasies, the resulting anxiety or depression is initially developed in relationship with significant others.

It is precisely this combined attention to individual drives (motives), the development of a sense of self (wishes, fears, internal conflicts), and unconscious relationship seeking that object relations theory addresses and that helps explain the revived interest in psychoanalytic formulations by some family therapists. While systems theory has dominated family therapy for several decades, especially its focus on interactions within families, some are rediscovering the value of basic psychodynamic concepts that draw attention to the inner lives and conflicts of individual family members.

Object relations theory views the infant's experiences in relationship to the mother as the primary determinant of adult personality formation. According to this theory, the infant's need for attachment to the mother is the foundation for the development of the self—the unique psychic organization that creates a person's sense of identity (Scharff & Scharff, 1992). Bowlby (1969) considers issues of attachment and loss to be central to functioning in humans and all higher mammals; he argues that how people resolve these issues determines personality development and possible psychopathology.

While Freud first used the term *object* in relation to instinctual drives, in the context of early mother-child bonds, other theorists have expanded on object relations to refer to internal, largely unconscious views of an individual from past experiences in

BOX 7.3 RESEARCH REPORT

ATTACHMENT THEORY AND ADULT INTIMACY PATTERNS

Attachment refers to the early emotional bond that develops (or fails to develop adequately) between infants and their caregivers. According to John Bowlby (1969), infants develop a secure attachment when certain core needs in the developmental process are met. When secure, the infant who becomes frightened or feels threatened, a normal occurrence, will reach out to the caregiver (usually but not necessarily the mother) for responsiveness, comfort, and protection, confident that it will be forthcoming. On the other hand, those infants who experience rejection or indifference when feeling in jeopardy are likely to internalize insecure or anxious attachment relationships. For the latter group, separation from the persons with whom they have formed an attachment can lead to the emotional distress seen in infant separation anxiety.

In addition to Bowlby's (1969) pioneering work on this subject, Mary Ainsworth and her associates (1978) have described the complex interactive process by which mother and child communicate. Rather than being passive recipients, babies cry, smile, fuss, gaze, grasp, babble, reach, and so forth, and so actively participate in the mother-infant relationships for survival and pleasure. According to Ainsworth's research, most infants form *secure attachments*, upset if the mother leaves but easily calmed when she returns. Others, less fortunate, display an *anxious-ambivalent attachment*, loudly protesting her departure and not particularly comforted by her return. A third group demonstrate *avoidant attachment*, seeking little connection to the mother, not distressed when she leaves, and often rejecting offers of comfort. The attachment style each person develops is profoundly influenced by the attachment style of the caregiver (Scharff & Scharff, 2003). Early infant experiences with maternal unavailability (due to illness, death, high stress levels, trauma, abuse, etc.) frequently leads to impaired relationships later in life.

Object relations therapists believe these early attachment patterns represent a cornerstone of intimate relations in adult life. They contend that those individuals who grow up with a history of insecure attachments often unconsciously choose intimate partners to repair their earlier deprivation, only to reenact their earlier failed attachment experience. Sensitive to the slightest signs of annoyance or disappointment from others, and angered by what they perceive to be rejection, they sometimes go from relationship to relationship seeking to heal old wounds.

Hazan and Shaver (1987) theorize that romantic love is an attachment process, and that each person's attachment history will be reflected in his or her adult relationships, thus reenacting earlier bonding with primary caregivers. These authors propose that secure adults are able to trust others and not fear abandonment, anxious-ambivalent adults fear rejection and abandonment, and avoidant adults have difficulty establishing a close and confident connection to others. Although Hazan and Shaver's survey research has lent support to their proposals, their conclusions remain controversial. Less debatable is Scharff and Scharff's (2003) observation in regard to attachment styles in insecure adults: that they may be insecure in various ways—preoccupied with and dependent on close relationships, dismissive of the need for closeness and compulsively self-reliant, or downright fearful of rejection.

childhood that shape his or her current relationships with others (St. Clair, 2000). Thus, an individual interacts not only with the actual other person but also with this subjective, internalized representation of the other, likely a distorted version of some actual person from the past.

The early theoretical work of Melanie Klein, a British psychoanalyst who emigrated from Vienna in 1926, provided much of the foundation of object relations theory. Her insights into the preverbal, inner world of the child's object relations are often considered to represent the start of the movement. Klein's contribution focused attention on the infant's innate or instinctual makeup, as containing elements of love as well as hate. Because the infant's inner life, beginning at birth, involves a world of fantasy, he or she first experiences objects, such as the mother, through fantasies. It is on the basis of such prior fantasies that the infant filters real-life experiences. Working directly with children—in contrast to Freud, whose theories about childhood came from the recollections of neurotic adult patients—Klein was able to delve into the fantasies of young clients and to expand previous psychoanalytic formulations to cover the earliest phases of life. Freud saw drives as originally objectless; gratification came first, and it did not matter, initially, what the object was. Klein, on the other hand, argued that drives (urges, instincts) are inherently directed at objects. To Klein, then, drives are relational (St. Clair, 2000).

Following Klein's lead, object relations theory was developed further by members of the British Middle School[5] (Michael Balint, Ronald Fairbairn, Harry Guntrip, Donald Winnicott). While their theories take somewhat different forms, in general they hold that an infant's primary need is for attachment to a caring, nurturing mother (or, in more recent formulations, to any person primarily responsible for the infant's daily care). This is offered in contrast to Freud's intrapsychic, drive-oriented theory, which also focused on the infant's mothering experiences, but which theorized that the infant's basic struggle is in coming to terms with sexual and aggressive impulses aimed at acquiring gratification from a parent (J. S. Scharff, 1989).

W. R. D. Fairbairn (1952), a psychiatrist in Edinburgh, Scotland, who worked therapeutically with **schizoid** adults from the late 1930s to the 1950s, followed up on Klein's work but rejected her acceptance of Freud's drive motivation in favor of purely psychological explanations. His innovative theory of personality development was based strictly on the consideration of object relations (Grotstein & Rinsley, 1994). To Fairbairn, the basic human drive is to relate to outside objects, and those objects inevitably are people.

Fairbairn maintained that because the infant experiences different sets of encounters with a mother—sometimes nurturing, sometimes frustrating—and cannot control the circumstances or leave the relationship, he or she creates a fantasy world to help reconcile the discrepant experiences. In this process, called **splitting** by Fairbairn, the child within the first year of life internalizes an image of the mother into a good object (the satisfying and loving mother) and a bad object (the inaccessible and frustrating mother), forming distinct internal relationships with the separate objects. The former becomes an idealized object and allows the child to feel loved, the latter a rejecting

---

[5]The British Middle School is so named because it functioned as an independent group, beginning in the 1950s, attempting to maintain a balance between the orthodox or classical psychoanalysts and the followers of Klein, in order for the British Psychoanalytic Society to avoid splitting into rival factions (Slipp, 1988). Klein, because of her work dating back to the late 1920s, is usually credited as the first object relations theorist, since she hypothesized that infants were capable of orienting themselves to "objects" from birth—thus, earlier than Freud postulated. However, Klein did not challenge Freud's emphasis on the instinctual basis of development (Sutherland, 1980). It fell to some of her followers, especially Fairbairn, to elaborate on many of the ideas concerning the effects of mother-child interactions on the infant's later intrapsychic and interpersonal functioning. To Fairbairn, the fundamental drive in people is not to gratify an impulse but to develop satisfying human (i.e., object) relationships.

BOX 7.4   THERAPEUTIC ENCOUNTER

THE CINDERELLA STORY: A CASE OF SPLITTING?

Let us suppose that Cinderella comes to a therapist because she has problems in her marriage to the prince. A traditional Freudian might investigate Cinderella's repression of her sexual instincts and unresolved oedipal feelings she had for her parents. This therapist or analyst would analyze Cinderella's problems in terms of defenses and conflicts between the structures of the ego and the id.

A therapist working with an object relations perspective would note that Cinderella suffered early psychological deprivation from the loss of her mother. Possibly this loss caused Cinderella to make use of the psychological defense mechanism of splitting, by which she idealized some women (such as her fairy godmother) and saw other women as "all bad" (her stepsisters and stepmother). She idealized the prince, despite knowing him for only a short time. A marriage based on such distorted inner images of herself and others is bound to run into problems as she sooner or later must deal with the prince as a real person with human flaws. In object relations theory, the issue would center on the discrepancy between Cinderella's inner world and the persons and situations of the actual world. (St. Clair, 2000, p. 3)

---

object that leads to anger, a feeling of being unloved, and a longing to regain that love. Part of her is loved, another part hated; because she is not seen yet as a whole person, one or the other part dominates at different times. Most children are able to integrate the two images by the second year of life. However, the degree to which a person resolves this conflict provides the basis for how well he or she develops satisfying human relationships later in life. If unresolved, the splitting is likely to lead to labile feelings as an adult as a result of viewing people (or the same person at different times) as "all good" or "all bad."

To illustrate the concept of splitting, and to demonstrate how classical psychoanalytic and object relations therapists might deal with a familiar "case," St. Clair (2000) offers the case of Cinderella in Box 7.4. Note especially how the latter therapists view the problem in terms of developmental arrest, while the former look for structural (id, ego, superego) conflicts.

To Fairbairn, these internalized split objects become part of one's personality structure: good-object **introjects** (imprints of parents or other significant figures) remain as pleasing memories, bad-object introjects cause intrapsychic distress. Psychological representations of these introjects unconsciously influence future relationships, since current experiences are interpreted through the filter of one's inner object world of good-bad images. As a result, the person may grow up with distorted expectations of others, unconsciously forcing intimates into fitting the internal role models. As Fairbairn illustrates, the earlier the split (resulting, for example, from an early loss of a parent), the more likely it is that the person will yearn for merger with loved ones so that they become a part of him or her. At the same time, he or she may also yearn for independence and separation, a normal part of growing up, although too much distance may lead to feelings of loneliness and depression.

British psychologist Henry Dicks (1967), at the Family Psychiatric Unit of the Tavistock Clinic in London, expanded Fairbairn's object relations conceptualizations by proposing that marriages were inevitably influenced by each spouse's infantile experiences. To Dicks, one basis for mate selection was that the potential partner's personality unconsciously matched split-off aspects of oneself. That is, while two people make conscious marital choices based upon many factors, including emotional compatibility, physical and intellectual attraction, background similarities, and so forth, Dicks believed that unconscious motives were also operating; in Jill Scharff's (1995) observation, at the unconscious level, they seek an "extraordinary fit, of which they are unaware" (p. 169). Each one thus hopes for integration of the lost introjects by finding them in the other. Dicks suggested that in a troubled marriage each partner relates to the other in terms of unconscious needs; each partner perceives the other to a degree as an internalized object, and together they function as a joint personality. In this way each partner attempts to rediscover, through the other, the lost aspects of his or her primary object relations that had split off earlier in life. This is achieved through the operation of the defense mechanism of **projective identification,** an interactive mental process in which marital partners unconsciously defend against anxiety by projecting or externalizing certain split-off or unwanted parts of themselves onto their partners, who in turn are manipulated to behave in accordance with this projection. Consequently, each person attempts to reestablish contact with missing or repudiated parts of themselves. As Dicks (1967) states:

> The sense of belonging can be understood on the hypothesis that at deeper levels there are perceptions of the partner and consequent attitudes toward him or her as if the other was part of oneself. The partner is then treated according to how this aspect of oneself was valued; spoilt and cherished, or denigrated and persecuted. (p. 69)

To put it succinctly, object relations theorists believe we relate to people in the present partly on the basis of expectations formed by early experiences (Nichols, 1987). That is, the past is alive in people's memories, and unconsciously continues to influence their lives in powerful ways. People continue to respond to others based largely on their resemblance to internalized objects from the past, rather than how these others may truly behave. Thus a family member may distort the meaning or implication of another member's statement or action, perhaps misreading or overreacting because of unconscious, emotion-laden, inner images developed early in life with parents or other important caretaker figures. To resolve current problems with others, it becomes necessary to explore and repair those faulty unconscious object relationships internalized since infancy. Gaining insight is seen as helping overcome the impasse.

Family therapists are especially interested in how this plays out in marital relatedness. According to advocates of the object relations view, the two individuals joined by marriage each bring to the relationship a separate and unique psychological heritage. Each carries a personal history, a unique personality, and a set of hidden, internalized objects into all subsequent transactions with one another. Inevitably, the dyadic relationship bears resemblances to the parent-child relationships the partners experienced in their families of origin. As Meissner (1978) observes: "The capacity to successfully function as a spouse is largely a consequence of the spouse's childhood relationships to his (or her) own parents" (p. 26). The relative success that marital partners experience, as well as the manner in which they approach and accomplish developmental tasks throughout the life cycle, is largely determined by the extent to which they are free from excessive negative attachments to the past.

Object relations family therapists view troubled marriages as contaminated by the pathogenic introjects from past relationships with members of the previous generation residing within each partner. Moreover, the partners' unresolved intrapsychic

BOX 7.5 CLINICAL NOTE

Monads, Dyads, and Triads

Traditional psychoanalytic theory is considered *monadic*—explanations of an individual's disturbed thoughts or behavior are based on the characteristics of that person. (Arthur experiences frequent guilt feelings because he has a punishing superego.) Object relations theory moves the focus to a *dyadic* one—the interaction between two persons. (Arthur experiences frequent guilt feelings because of his early dealings with a critical mother.) Most family therapists operate from a *triadic* viewpoint. (Arthur experiences frequent guilt feelings because his divorced mother insists he reject his father by refusing to spend time with him during weekend visitation opportunities.)

problems not only prevent them from enjoying a productive and fulfilling marital experience but also are passed along to their children, who eventually bring psychic disturbances into their own marriages. Object relations therapists contend that only by gaining insight into, and thus freedom from, such burdensome attachments to the past can individuals—or couples—learn to develop adult-to-adult relationships in the present with members of their families of origin.

Object relations family therapy, primarily developed in England, represents a revision of classical psychoanalytic theory to include an emphasis on early infant-caregiver attachments and unconscious relationship-seeking. Moving beyond drive theory and its concern exclusively with intrapsychic processes, its two-person (nurturing figure–infant) emphasis makes it more consistent with the interactional views favored by systems-oriented family therapists. At the same time, individual intrapsychic issues and past experiences are not overlooked. What is added is the consideration of the development of the self in relation to others—that from birth onward, a person needs to bond, to form attachments, to relate to others. Furthermore, declare the advocates of object relations theory, this powerful relationship-seeking need is so great as to be the fundamental driving force throughout life.

Slipp (1988) suggests that the object relations perspective also supplies an important reminder, sometimes underattended to by family therapists, that individuals may bring serious personal emotional problems into a relationship, and that pathology need not exist mysteriously only in the transactions between people.

OBJECT RELATIONS THERAPY

Object relations therapists are a diverse group, although they all accept the idea that internal images or psychic representations derived from significant relationships in the past may produce faulty or unsatisfying or distorted current dealings with people. We will elaborate on two such approaches.

Object Relations and Family-of-Origin Therapy (Framo)

Another first-generation family therapist whose training and early orientation was psychoanalytic, James Framo (1981) stressed the relationship between the intrapsychic and the interpersonal, offering an amalgam of psychodynamic and systems concepts. Framo,

James Framo, Ph.D.

one of the few psychologists in the early family therapy movement, was affiliated for two decades, beginning in the mid-1950s, with the Eastern Pennsylvania Psychiatric Institute (EPPI) in Philadelphia, before beginning an academic career at Temple University. For the last 20 years of his long career, ending in his death in 2001, Framo worked in San Diego as both teacher and practitioner. Among the founders of the family therapy movement, Framo is particularly celebrated for his advocacy of couples groups.

Not wishing to disregard the significant contributions made by psychoanalysis to our understanding of an individual's intrapsychic world, Framo nevertheless believed psychoanalytic theory had not paid sufficient attention to the social context of a person's life, particularly the early crucial role played by family relationships in shaping individual behavior. Framo refused to polarize the intrapsychic and the interactional, maintaining that both are essential to understanding the dynamic aspects of family life. As he pointed out in the introduction to a collection of his papers (Framo, 1982), his orientation to marital and family theory and therapy emphasized

the psychology of intimate relationships, the interlocking of multi-person motivational systems, the relationship between the intrapsychic and the transactional, and the hidden transgenerational and historical forces that exercise their powerful influences on current intimate relationships. (p. ix)

At EPPI Framo began to view family dysfunction as rooted in the extended family system. Ultimately he developed a set of intervention techniques that helped couples in marital therapy deal with unresolved issues each partner brings to the marriage from his or her family of origin. Consistent with the view of object relations theorists, Framo believed that insoluble intrapsychic conflicts derived from one's family of origin continue to be acted out or replicated with current intimates, such as a spouse or children. Indeed, Framo (1981) contended that efforts at the interpersonal resolution of inner conflict (for example, harshly criticizing a spouse for failing to live up to one's wildly inappropriate expectations) are at the very heart of the kinds of distress found in troubled couples and families.

Extrapolating from Fairbairn's proposals regarding splitting, Framo (1976) theorized that a young child who interprets parental behavior as rejection, desertion, or persecution is in a dilemma; the child cannot give up the sought-after object (the parents), nor can he or she change that object. Typically, the ensuing frustration is dealt with by internalizing aspects of the "loved-hated" parents in order to control the objects in the child's inner world. According to Framo, the most powerful obstacle to change is people's attachments to their parental introjects. The more psychologically painful the early life experience, the greater the investment in internal objects, the more an adult will engage in an unconscious effort to make all close relationships fit the internal role models.

Framo's interest in dealing with marital discord reflects in part Fairbairn's emphasis on the impact of splits and introjects on adult relationships and in part the work of Dicks (1967), who argued that marital partners choose one another on the basis of their primary object relations, which they have split off, and which, in interacting with their spouse, they experience once again as a result of projective identification. Framo (1992) insisted that people *usually do not select the partner they want; they get the one that they need.*

That is, each is drawn to someone who recreates the childhood dream of unconditional love, but also is enough like the bad inner object to allow old hatreds to be projected. According to Framo (1992, p. 115):

> A partner is chosen who, it is hoped, will cancel out, replicate, control, master, live through, or heal, in a dyadic framework, what could not be settled internally. Consequently, one's current intimates, one's spouse and children, are, in part, stand-ins for old images, the embodiments of long-buried introjects.

One major source of marital disharmony results from projective identification—spouses who project disowned aspects of themselves onto their mates and then fight these characteristics in the mate. Similarly, children may be assigned inappropriate family roles based on parental introjects. Such roles may even be chosen for them before they are born (for example, conceiving a baby in the belief that the offspring will save a shaky marriage).

Therapeutically, Framo began by treating the entire family, especially when the presenting problem involved the children. However, symptomatic behavior in a child may simply be a means of deflecting attention from a more basic marital conflict. In such cases, once the child's role as identified patient is made clear and the child is **detriangulated** from the parents, Framo typically dismissed the children and proceeded to work with the marital dyad.

Framo's unique contribution to family therapy technique was his process of guiding a couple through several treatment stages: conjoint therapy; couples group therapy; and, finally, family-of-origin (intergenerational) conferences. The couples group, in which many couples participate soon after beginning treatment, allowed Framo to use many of the positive aspects of group therapy, especially the therapeutic feedback from other couples, to assist his therapeutic efforts. In many cases it is far more enlightening and potent for a couple to see its own interaction patterns acted out by another couple than to hear a therapist merely comment on the same behavior, with no one else present. The group experience, to Framo's way of thinking, had a secondary function of reducing the individual's resistance to the next stage of treatment, which involved a number of family members meeting together.

In a daring therapeutic maneuver, Framo (1992) involved each individual (without the partner present) in sessions with his or her family of origin (parents, brothers, and sisters). Here, instead of the customary working out of past or current problems with these family members via a relationship with the therapist, Framo's family-of-origin approach provided a direct opportunity for clearing up past misunderstandings or sources of chronic dissatisfaction. In some cases, misinterpretations based upon childhood misperceptions could be straightened out. Clients were encouraged to face their family of origin in order to present their views, perhaps not aired before; the session was not intended to be an opportunity for indictment, blame, recrimination, or condemnation.

Often conducted with a co-therapist, family-of-origin sessions were usually divided into two 2-hour sessions with a break in between (varying from several hours to an overnight interruption). Two major goals were involved—to discover what issues or agendas from the family of origin might be projected onto the current family, and to have a corrective experience with parents and siblings. Framo cogently reasoned that if adults were able to go back and deal directly with both past and present issues with their original families—in a sense, to come to terms with parents before they die—then they would be liberated to make reconstructive changes in their present marriage or family life. Usually held toward the end of therapy, family-of-origin conferences enabled individuals to gain insight into the inappropriateness of old attachments, rid themselves of "ghosts," and respond to spouses and children as individuals in their own right—not as figures on whom they project unresolved issues and introjects from the past.

Instead of dealing with introjects with a therapist, family-of-origin sessions take the problems back to their original etiological source. Dealing with family members as real people frequently loosens the hold and intensity of these internalized objects and exposes them to current realities. As Framo (1992) warned, family-of-origin therapy may not change people's lives drastically, nor is it likely to fulfill all fantasies of what clients can get from parents and siblings. However, it often has a restorative function, reconnecting family members to one another, allowing participants to see one another as real people and not simply in their family-assigned roles. Old rifts may be healed by more accurate readings of one another's intentions, or perhaps as past events are reinterpreted from an adult perspective. The intergenerational encounter provides a forum for forgiveness, compromise, acceptance, and resolution. At its best, it helps family members learn techniques for the future betterment of family relationships.

Object Relations Family Therapy (Scharff & Scharff)

An object relations approach more faithful to orthodox psychoanalysis comes from the collaboration of David Scharff and Jill Savege Scharff, husband and wife psychiatrists affiliated for many years with the Washington School of Psychiatry, and now directors of their own institute—the International Institute of Object Relations Therapy—in Washington, D.C.

In the Scharffs' therapeutic approach, unconscious themes expressed in dreams and fantasies are evoked and investigated, family histories are explored as they relate to current relationships, interpretations are made to the family, insight is sought, and **transference** and **countertransference** feelings are explored in an effort to arrive at greater understanding and growth. Consistent with drive theory, the Scharffs attempt to aid the couple in overcoming resistance in order to become aware of repressed impulses.

Unlike individual psychoanalysis, however, here the focus is on the family as a nexus of relationships functioning in ways that support or obstruct the progress of the family or any of its separate members as they proceed through the developmental stages of family life (Scharff & Scharff, 1987; 1997). Marriage is seen as similar to each partner's earlier child-mother relationship in that, as adults, each seeks a permanent attachment to a caring figure. In the following case, both partners view the maternal image as powerful.

Building upon Freud's classical psychoanalytic formulations, but departing from the strict insistence on an instinctual basis of understanding behavior, the Scharffs make use of the object relations contributions of Klein and Fairbairn. Historical analysis of current individual as well as relationship difficulties are central components of this technique, since it is assumed that intrapsychic and interpersonal levels are in continuing interaction. Helping family members gain insight by becoming conscious of precisely how they internalized objects from the past, and how these objects continue to intrude on current relationships, is an indispensable part of providing understanding and instigating change.

BOX 7.6   CASE STUDY

OBJECT RELATIONS THERAPY WITH A DISTRESSED COUPLE

A shy, timid man always felt inferior because, although he was tall and handsome, he was not athletic, didn't have many friends, and could never get a date for the prom. He met a small but assertive, opinionated, athletic woman who was his company's softball coach. He saw in her qualities that he would have liked to have in himself. She felt much less attractive than he was, but she enjoyed a challenge and invited him out on a date. She soon recognized that he had problems with self-esteem. She disavowed them in the same way that she pushed past her own vulnerabilities. It turned out that they were attracted to each other physically and felt happy together and sexually fulfilled, but they stayed together for unconscious reasons. Both shared the unconscious assumption that the woman was more important, stronger, and more dependable than the man. In his close-knit, Old World immigrant family, the man continued to revere the mother, even though he wanted distance from the old-fashioned family culture. The woman was close to her mother, a modern, divorced, professionally achieving woman, and she had been deeply hurt by her father's abandonment. In marriage, the man found another woman to adore and serve, and the woman found a father who would stay with her.

Then she became pregnant, and their sex life stopped. He thought that his male role was to stay out of the way so she could carry out her supremely maternal function. She felt that he had abandoned her now that she was to have a child, just as her father had done to her mother. The more passive and withdrawn he became, the more she overfunctioned, recreating with her daughter the exclusive relationship she had with her mother and hating her husband for abandoning her emotionally as her father had done. All her rage at her father came out in relation to her husband. Envious of the exclusive attention given to the baby, he felt inferior and unworthy of love, and his self-esteem plummeted.

The projective identificatory system, in which the strong woman was admired and which was the basis for their bond during courtship, became a divisive force in the child-rearing years of their marriage. In Object Relations Couple Therapy, the couple learned about this basic assumption and how disabling it had been. The husband and wife reviewed their family histories and let go of the working models they had developed in their families of origin. They freed each other to create a more equal appreciation of mother and father, traditional and contemporary lifestyles, and male and female contributions to their marriage and family.

Source: Scharff & Scharff, 2003, pp. 68–69.

Confirming their object relations credentials, the Scharffs emphasize the fundamental human need for attachment, to be in a relationship, and the possible destructive effects of early separation from caring figures. Any anxiety resulting from such separation experiences is assumed to lead to repression, permitting less of the ego to relate freely to others. Because the repressed system is by definition out of contact with the outside world, thus operating as a closed system, new experiences do not provide an opportunity for growth. In adulthood, such individuals continue to seek outlets for their repressed object relationships through repetition of their earlier, unsatisfying infantile experiences. Responding to introjects from the past, family members cannot respond to one another as they are in reality. Instead they respond to an internal object, as though reacting to powerful forces—psychic representations—from the past. Thus unconscious, but also conscious, systems of relationships within individuals as well as families become the subject matter of analysis (J. S. Scharff, 1989).

According to the Scharffs, interpretation by the therapist in order to provide insight is essential. While they oppose the blank-screen stance of classical psychoanalysts, they do adopt a neutral stance of involved impartiality, helping provide a shared holding environment,[6] thus creating a therapeutic climate allowing each family member to project onto the therapist his or her own unfinished problems from the past. In contrast to the second-order cybernetic views of many current family therapists—that the therapist inevitably becomes a part of the family system—the Scharffs believe they are able to remain outside the family system, and thus are in a position to offer comments on what is happening to them as well as on what they observe taking place within the family.

That is, the Scharffs make use of the transference, which they view broadly as occurring between family members, between each family member and the therapist, and particularly between the family as a group and the therapist. This is an essential part of treatment, since it evokes in the therapeutic sessions, in response to the therapist's neutrality, an "object hunger"—a replay of infantile relating with caretakers in the family of origin. At the same time, the therapist experiences countertransference in responding to the family struggles, unconsciously evoking his or her own internal struggles from the past. If sufficiently worked through in previous personal analysis and training, and with supervision, this shared venture of object relations may evoke greater empathy from the therapist with family vulnerabilities and struggles. As David Scharff (1989) points out, in this way object relations therapists allow themselves to "be the substrate for a newly emerging understanding, which they then feed back to the family in the form of interpretation" (p. 424).

In forming a therapeutic alliance with a family, the Scharffs create a nurturing climate in which family members can rediscover lost parts of the family as well as their individual selves. This holding environment, an atmosphere intended to create trust and caring among all participants, is a key element in the Scharffs' approach, as the therapist offers empathy and a safe environment while attending to the psychological processes each participant is experiencing separately as well as with one another and with the therapist. Each partner is encouraged to examine his or her early nurturing or caring—what the Scharffs call "holding"—experiences, and how images retained from those experiences affect the couple's current marital relationship and their view of the therapist. The family's shared object relations are assessed, as are the family's stage of psychosexual development and its use of various mechanisms of defense against anxiety. Observing family interaction, encouraging members to express their separate viewpoints as well as observe the views of one another, obtaining a history of internalized objects from each member, feeding back therapist observations and interpretations—these are all ways of joining the family. Later, helping family members work through chronic interaction patterns and defensive projective identifications is necessary if they are to change patterns and learn to deal with one

---

[6]Holding environment is a rather imprecise concept, but an important one in Scharff and Scharff's therapeutic approach. The notion was first used by British pediatrician Donald Winnicott (1965), a member of the British Middle School of object relations theorists, to describe the needs of an infant to avoid feeling abandoned or annihilated. Unlike Freud, who was aware of parental influences but stressed the infant's inner world and instinctual drives, Winnicott underscored the significance of the infant's environmental needs, especially for the parents to provide sufficient care and attention for the infant to experience a good start in life. Successful holding experiences result from being brought up in a caring and nurturing home climate, and lead to feeling whole, real, an effective person, someone with self-esteem.

another in a here-and-now fashion attuned to current realities rather than unconscious object relations from the past (D. Scharff, 1989).

Successful treatment is measured not by symptom relief in the identified patient, but rather by the family's increased insight or self-understanding and its improved capacity to master developmental stress. A fundamental goal of object relations family therapists is for the family to support one another's needs for attachment, individuation, and growth.

KOHUT AND SELF PSYCHOLOGY

Many contemporary psychoanalytic thinkers, following the lead of Heinz Kohut (1971, 1977), have retreated from Freud's strict drive theory and thus have been more receptive to the idea that both intrapsychic forces (gratifying the needs of the Self) and interpersonal forces operate in a reciprocal fashion. These ideas are now at the forefront of today's practice for many clinicians with psychoanalytic or object relations views.

Kohut, a physician trained in Vienna, spent most of his professional career in the United States, at the Chicago Institute for Psychoanalysis. There he formulated his influential ideas regarding self psychology, emphasizing the relationship between the self (the person's personality core or center of initiatives) and outside objects as the defining organizational principle of human lives. Kohut, working in the middle of the twentieth century, believed that changing family lifestyles and new family forms had left much of Freudian theory in need of reexamination. From his viewpoint, conflict within the person (and between people) arises early in life from a lack of sense of self, rather than from instinctual conflict.

Without rejecting classical psychoanalytic concepts completely, Kohut focused specifically on how early relationships, especially with the caretaker mother, are crucial in forming the child's later sense of who he or she is and in affecting how well that person can make and sustain relationships later in life. Kohut contends that initially the infant does not view its parents as separate persons or objects; rather, the parents are seen narcissistically, as **selfobjects,** extensions of the infant represented by attention and praise coming from its environment. That is, the infant makes no distinction between itself and its mother's praise (although it may not view her as a real object as yet).

Kohut maintains that the infant does not yet have a self, even if the parents think otherwise. That core self begins to emerge from interactions with and responses from selfobjects. Ideally, according to Kohut, young children start to develop a core cohesive self when they experience two qualities from their attentive parents—empathy (validating how they feel) and idealization of parents (being proud to have good parents and to be part of them). As a result of internalizing parental appreciation, the child forms an autonomous self, characterized by self-acceptance and self-esteem. Such fortunate children are said by Kohut to have their needs *mirrored* by their parents and the idealization met by satisfying interaction with parents who themselves feel self-esteem. Less fortunate children—those whose parents fail to demonstrate sufficient appreciation or themselves have little self-esteem—continue to crave admiring attention throughout life.

Narcissism, then, is ever-present, especially among infants and young children, and represents a stage of development. It is not a pathological condition of self-absorption (as Freud maintained), but a necessary motivating organizer of development in which love of self precedes love for others. All adults continue to have narcissistic needs they wish to fulfill, and continue to need the mirroring of the self by selfobjects throughout life (St. Clair, 2000). As Kohut (1971) illustrates, even as adults, seeking a connection with someone who is unresponsive or indifferent often makes us feel empty, unloved, with lowered self-esteem, and in Kohut's view, filled with narcissistic rage.

Based on his work with patients, Kohut (1971) contended the infant's core is likely to contain a self-centered, grandiose-exhibitionistic part, especially if the parent offers unconditional admiration. Because the child will inevitably be frustrated at not receiving everything wished for, the conflict at this early stage is often between doing what the child wants and believes he or she deserves (the self-assertive, grandiose self) and what the child believes the idealized parent wants him or her to do (the idealized selfobject), says Kohut (1977). Tantrums at being frustrated thus represent narcissistic rages—the removal of the mirroring selfobject. Kohut considers such tantrums as a normal sequence in development and a precursor of object love. Such mature love is likely to involve mutual mirroring and idealization.

Working therapeutically with patients with narcissistic personality disorders, Kohut contends that they are experiencing a defect in the structure of the self, not having successfully completed the integration of the grandiose and idealized object into a reality-oriented self. He found that those who grow up feeling insufficiently admired or attended to will seek such acceptance in exaggerated narcissistic cravings, experiencing others as selfobjects. To the narcissistic adult, then, a selfobject is a person undifferentiated from oneself who serves the needs of the self. He or she sees everyone as an extension of self, and as existing to serve the self. Within a marriage, he or she may continue to search for the idealized partner—determined to be in control, rageful if not—forever seeking merger with the unconditional availability of the mirroring selfobject or idealized object (St. Clair, 2000).

Nevertheless, unlike classical psychoanalysis, which looks at narcissism as the inability to love or otherwise relate to others, Kohut believes narcissism, in its less severe form, can represent healthy development. He contends that no person is ever completely independent of selfobjects, but rather requires throughout life a milieu of empathetically responding selfobjects in order to function (St. Clair, 2000). If no one is ever completely free of the need for attention from others, narcissistic personalities can be said to have an excessive, at times outlandish need to be attended to and adored, constantly seeking admiration. These individuals react to criticism or rejection—even indifference—with exaggerated rage, shame, and humiliation. Relations with others are inevitably flawed due to the narcissist's self-absorption and unending sense of entitlement.

For analysis to be effective, according to Kohut, the reactivation of the original developmental tendencies must take place with the therapist. Persons with self disorders must be mirrored (respected, attended to) and permitted to idealize the authentic, empathetic therapist. Thus meeting the person's narcissistic needs, the therapist can begin to develop a mirroring or idealizing transference. Once transference is established, therapist interpretations provide the patient with insights into the seeking of narcissistic relationships, helping them to see that they are inevitably frustrating and unsatisfying. The goal is for the person (or the couple) to develop more autonomous selves. Box 7.7 illustrates such a therapeutic situation.

BOX 7.7   THERAPEUTIC ENCOUNTER

CINDERELLA REVISITED: A CASE OF A SELF-DISORDER?

In Box 7.4 we illustrated the use of object relations therapy in the case of Cinderella, described by St. Clair (2000) as representing a case of splitting. The same author differentiates the object relations view from the self psychology of Kohut with the following:

A therapist or analyst working within the framework of self psychology would attend to the experience that Cinderella had of herself in therapy as this experience is manifested in the transference to the therapist. Analysis of her transference might reveal an impoverished self that needed a powerful and idealized object. Cinderella's search for such an object reflects her lack of self-esteem and her need to be affirmed by such an idealized object, whether in the form of the fairy godmother, the prince, or the therapist. She needed to fuse with the idealized prince out of hope for a feeling of well-being. Out of touch with her own inner emptiness and angry feelings, Cinderella might either idealize her therapist or view the therapist the way she viewed her stepmother. (p. 3)

SUMMARY

Current trends favor eclecticism and integration in family therapy, as therapists borrow concepts and techniques that cross theoretical boundaries. However, distinguishing theoretical constructs remain between traditional schools, and controversy remains regarding the possibility of ever creating an integrated supertheory of family therapy. The psychodynamic viewpoint, based initially on a psychoanalytic model, focuses on drive theory and the interplay of opposing forces within an individual. While treatment based on this model appears to be exclusively concerned with the personality of the single individual patient, the role of family context in personality formation is an essential element of the theory.

Nathan Ackerman, a family therapy pioneer, attempted to integrate psychoanalytic theory (with its intrapsychic orientation) and systems theory (emphasizing interpersonal relationships). He viewed family dysfunction as a failure in role complementarity between members and as the product of persistent unresolved conflict (within and between individuals in a family) and prejudicial scapegoating. His therapeutic efforts were aimed at disentangling such interlocking pathologies.

The psychodynamic position today is largely based on object relations theory. In contrast to Freud's intrapsychic, instinctual theory, here the emphasis is on the infant's primary need for attachment to a caring person, and the analysis of those internalized psychic representations—objects—that continue to seek satisfaction in adult relationships.

Two examples of object relations therapeutic approaches are provided by Framo and Scharff and Scharff. Framo believed that insoluble intrapsychic conflict, derived from the family of origin, is perpetuated in the form of projections onto current intimates such as a spouse or children. He concerned himself with working through and ultimately removing these introjects; in the process he saw couples alone, then in a couples' group, and finally held separate sessions with each partner and the members of his or her family of origin.

Scharff and Scharff utilize a therapeutic approach that is heavily psychoanalytic, creating a holding environment, evoking unconscious material, making interpretations, providing insight, relying on transference and countertransference feelings in helping families learn how past internalized objects intrude on current family relationships. A fundamental goal is for family members to support one another's needs for attachment, individuation, and personal growth.

Also at the forefront of today's psychodynamically oriented theory and practice is Kohut's work with self psychology. His focus was on early infant relations with a caretaker mother, particularly in the view of the mother as an extension of himself or herself (a selfobject). Kohut emphasized the development of a core self, mirrored by parents, as well as the idealization of parents; he viewed both processes as essential to forming an autonomous self. Narcissism represents a stage of early development, and may persist as a personality disorder into adulthood.

RECOMMENDED READINGS

Ackerman, N, W. (1966). *Treating the troubled family.* New York: Basic Books.

Dicks, H. V. (1967). *Marital tensions.* New York: Basic Books.

Framo, J. L. (1992). *Family–of-origin therapy: An intergenerational approach.* New York: Brunner/Mazel.

Kohut, H. (1977). *The restoration of the self.* New York: International Universities Press.

Scharff, D., & Scharff, J. S. (1987). *Object relations family therapy.* New York: Jason Aronson.

CHAPTER 8

TRANSGENERATIONAL MODELS

Transgenerational approaches offer a psychoanalytically influenced, historical perspective to current family living problems by attending specifically to family relational patterns over decades. Advocates of this view believe current family patterns are embedded in unresolved issues in the families of origin. That is not to say that these problems are caused by earlier generations, but rather that they tend to remain unsettled and thus persist and repeat themselves in ongoing patterns that span generations. How today's family members form attachments, manage intimacy, deal with power, resolve conflict, and so on, may mirror to a greater or lesser extent earlier family patterns. Unresolved issues in families of origin may show up in symptomatic behavior patterns in later generations.

A number of pioneering family therapists—Murray Bowen, Ivan Boszormenyi-Nagy, James Framo, Carl Whitaker—incorporated generational issues in their work with families. As we noted earlier, Framo typically brought each partner's family members in for family-of-origin sessions in which current differences got discussed, and Whitaker invited extended family members such as grandparents as "consultants" to an ongoing family session. However, we have chosen to place both Framo and Whitaker elsewhere in the text—Framo with the object relations therapies and Whitaker with the experiential therapies—because their efforts are also strongly influenced by these other outlooks and procedures. The remainder of this chapter focuses on the multigenerational views of Murray Bowen and Ivan Boszormenyi-Nagy.

BOWEN'S FAMILY THEORY

By turning first to Murray Bowen, one of the foremost original thinkers in the field, we intend to expound on a theory that represents the intellectual scaffolding upon which much of mainstream family therapy has been erected. Bowen, the developer of **family systems theory,** conceptualized the family as an emotional unit, a network of interlocking relationships, best understood when analyzed within a multigenerational or historical framework.

His theoretical contributions, along with their accompanying therapeutic efforts, represent a bridge between psychodynamically oriented approaches that emphasize self-development, intergenerational issues, and the significance of past family relationships, and the systems approaches that restrict their attention to the family unit as it is presently constituted and currently interacting. His therapeutic stance with couples involved a disciplined, unruffled but engaged professional, careful not to be triangled into the couple's emotional interaction. By attending to the process of their interactions, and not the content, Bowen hoped to help the partners hear each other out (sometimes for the first time without their customary passion and accusations of blame) and thus learn what each must do to reduce anxiety and build their relationship.

Unlike many of his fellow pioneers in family therapy, who struggled at first to stretch classical psychoanalytic theory to fit family life—Ackerman comes to mind here—Bowen recognized early on that most psychoanalytic concepts were too individually derived and not readily translatable into the language of the family. Rather than attempt to adapt such concepts as *unconscious motivations* to family interactive patterns, Bowen believed the driving force underlying all human behavior came from the submerged ebb and flow of family life, the simultaneous push and pull between family members for both distance and togetherness (Wylie, 1990b). *This attempt to balance two life forces—family togetherness and individual autonomy—was for Bowen the core issue for all humans.* Successfully balanced, such persons are able to maintain intimacy with loved ones while differentiating themselves sufficiently as individuals so as not to be swept up by what is transpiring within the family.

A key figure in the development of family therapy, Murray Bowen remained, until his death in 1990, its major theoretician. Since his early clinical work with schizophrenics and their families at the Menninger Clinic as well as at the National Institute for Mental Health (NIMH), Bowen stressed the importance of theory for research, for teaching purposes, and as a blueprint for guiding a clinician's actions during psychotherapy. He was concerned with what he considered the field's lack of a coherent and comprehensive theory of either family development or therapeutic intervention and its all-too-tenuous connections between theory and practice. In particular, Bowen (1978) decried efforts to dismiss theory in favor of an intuitive "seat of the pants" approach, which he considered to be especially stressful for a novice therapist coping with an intensely emotional, problem-laden family.

Leading Figure

By educational background and training, Bowen was imbued with the individual focus of psychoanalysis. But his professional interest in the family began early in his career when, after wartime military service, he trained as a psychiatrist and remained on the staff at the Menninger Clinic in the late 1940s. There, under the leadership of Karl Menninger, innovative psychoanalytic approaches were being tried in treating hospitalized persons suffering from severe psychiatric illnesses. Intrigued, from a research perspective, by the family relationships of inpatients, especially schizophrenics, Bowen became particularly interested in the possible transgenerational impact of a mother-child **symbiosis** in the development and maintenance of schizophrenia. Extrapolating from the psychoanalytic concept that schizophrenia might result from an unresolved symbiotic attachment to the mother, herself immature and in need of the child to fulfill her own emotional needs, Bowen began studying the emotional *fusion* between schizophrenic patients and their mothers. In 1951, in order to view their relationship close up, he organized a research project in which mothers and their schizophrenic children resided together in cottages on the Menninger grounds for several months at a time.

In 1954, Bowen was eager to put his new ideas regarding family dynamics into clinical practice. However, stifled by what he saw as the prevailing emphasis on conventional individual psychiatry at the Menninger Clinic, he moved his professional research activities to the NIMH in Bethesda, Maryland. Soon, in what surely was a radical idea for its time, Bowen had entire families with schizophrenic members living for months at a time in the hospital research wards, where he and his associates were better able to observe ongoing family interaction. Here Bowen discovered that the emotional intensity of the mother-child interaction was even more powerful than he had suspected. More important, the emotional intensity seemed to characterize relationships throughout the family,[1] not merely those between mother and child. Fathers and siblings too were found to play key roles in fostering and perpetuating family problems, as triangular alliances were continually formed and dissolved among differing sets of family members.

The reciprocal functioning of all the individual members within the family became so apparent that Bowen began to expand his earlier mother-child symbiosis concepts to now viewing the entire family as an unbalanced emotional unit made up of members unable to separate or successfully differentiate themselves from one another. Although he did not adopt a cybernetic epistemology per se, nor was he interested especially in directly changing a family's ongoing interactive patterns, Bowen had moved from concentrating on the separate parts (the patient with the "disease") to a focus on the whole (the family).

© Wadsworth/Thomson Learning

Murray Bowen, M.D.

Now he began to direct his attention particularly to what he called the *family emotional system*—a kind of family guidance system shaped by evolution that governs its behavior—for him a workable descriptive framework for understanding human interaction. The conceptual shift was to prove to be a turning point in his thinking, as Bowen increasingly viewed human emotional functioning as part of a *natural system,* following the same laws that govern other systems in nature, no less valid than the laws of gravity. Bowen, dissatisfied with what he considered the subjectivity of most psychoanalytic conceptualizations, began the process of making the study of human emotional functioning a more rigorous science. In the forefront of his field, Bowen was beginning to formulate nothing less than a new theory of human behavior.

When the NIMH project ended in 1959, Bowen moved to the Department of Psychiatry at Georgetown University in Washington, DC; the university was a place more conducive to his theoretical bent. He remained there for 31 years, until the end of his career. Working in an outpatient setting, and with families many of whom had less severe problems than schizophrenia, Bowen continued to formulate a comprehensive family systems theory that could be applied to processes occurring in all families, functional

---

[1]Bowen's early observations of the emotional intensity of families with schizophrenic members have been confirmed by recent research on the role of expressed emotions such as anger and hostility on the course of the schizophrenic disorder. Studies of schizophrenics following hospital release indicate that lowering expressed emotion in the family is a major way of reducing relapse (Miklowitz, 1995).

as well as dysfunctional. At the same time, he proposed a method of therapy based on a solid theoretical foundation (in contrast to those techniques that were evolving on an experiential basis). Developing a training program in family therapy while continually refining the concepts he first developed in the 1960s, he published *Family Therapy in Clinical Practice* in 1978, detailing his theoretical formulations and offering therapeutic techniques consistent with that theory. In 1977, Bowen became the first president of the newly formed American Family Therapy Association, an organization he helped found to pursue interests in research and theory.

Other Leading Figures

Several updated explications of Bowen's theoretical ideas as well as their clinical applications have been offered by Michael Kerr (Kerr & Bowen, 1988) and Daniel Papero (1990, 2000), both at the Georgetown Family Center in Washington, D.C. Also in Washington, Edwin Friedman (1991), a rabbi trained by Bowen, was able to apply family systems theory to pastoral counseling. (Friedman died in 1996.) Philip Guerin, an early disciple of Bowen's who founded the Center for Family Learning in New Rochelle, New York, has been especially active in devising interventions tailored to the intensity and duration of the marital conflict (Guerin, Fay, Burden, & Kautto, 1987) and in working with family relationship triangles (Guerin, Fogarty, Fay, & Kautto, 1996). Peter Titelman (1998) in Northampton, Massachusetts, has demonstrated the applicability of Bowen's work to a variety of emotionally dysfunctional families (e.g., families with phobias, depression, alcoholism). Betty Carter (Director Emerita of the Family Institute in Westchester in White Plains, New York) and Monica McGoldrick (1999) at the Multicultural Institute in Highland Park, New Jersey, authors of the influential multigenerational work on family life cycles, are Bowenian in orientation. The latter two also have paid close attention to the powerful influences of culture, class, gender, and sexual orientation on family patterns (McGoldrick & Carter, 2001).

Family Systems Theory

Family systems theory (sometimes referred to as *natural systems theory* to differentiate it from cybernetically based family systems theories) is derived from the biological view of the human family as one type of living system. As Friedman (1991) points out, the theory is not fundamentally about families, but about life (or what Bowen referred to as the "human phenomenon"), and it attempts to account for humanity's relationship to other natural systems. As Wylie (1990b, p. 26) explains, Bowen "considered family therapy a by-product of the vast theory of human behavior that he believed it was his real mission to develop." According to the theory, the human family is seen as appearing due to an evolutionary process in nature. Thus, like all living systems (ant colonies, the tides, the solar system), humans and the human family are guided by processes common in nature. In particular, the theory concerns itself with a special kind of natural system—the family's emotional system (Kerr & Bowen, 1988).

EIGHT INTERLOCKING THEORETICAL CONCEPTS

In its present state of refinement, Bowen's theory of the family as an emotional relationship system consists of eight interlocking concepts. Six of the concepts address emotional processes taking place in the nuclear and extended families; two later concepts, emotional cutoff and societal regression, speak to the emotional process across generations in a family and in society. All eight constructs are interlocking in the sense that none is fully understandable without some comprehension of the others.

All of the following concepts are tied together by the underlying premise that *chronic anxiety* is omnipresent in life. While it may manifest itself differently, and with different degrees of intensity, depending on specific family situations and differing cultural considerations, chronic anxiety is an inevitable part of nature—a biological phenomenon that Bowen believed humans have in common with all forms of life (Friedman, 1991). From this natural systems perspective, chronic anxiety is transmitted from past generations, whose influence remains alive in the present, as each family grapples with balancing togetherness and the self-differentiation of its separate members.

Anxiety—arousal in an organism when perceiving a real or imagined threat—stimulates the anxious-prone person's emotional system, overriding the cognitive system and leading to behavior that is automatic or uncontrolled (Papero, 1990). In family terms, anxiety is inevitably aroused as families struggle to balance the pressures toward togetherness as well as toward individuation. If greater togetherness prevails, imbalance results and the family moves in the direction of increased emotional functioning and less individual autonomy. As a by-product of decreased individual autonomy, the person experiences increased chronic anxiety. Chronic anxiety, then, represents the underlying basis of all symptomatology; its only antidote is resolution through differentiation (see next section), the process by which an individual learns to chart his or her own direction rather than perpetually following the guidelines of family and others.

According to family systems theory, the eight forces shaping family functioning are

1. Differentiation of self
2. Triangles
3. Nuclear family emotional system
4. Family projection process
5. Emotional cutoff
6. Multigenerational transmission process
7. Sibling position
8. Societal regression

Differentiation of Self

The cornerstone of the carefully worked out family systems theory is the notion of forces within the family that lead to individuality and the opposing forces that make for togetherness. Both intrapsychic and interpersonal issues are involved here. In the former, the person must, in the face of anxiety, develop the ability to separate feelings from thinking, and to choose whether to be guided in a particular instant by intellect or emotion. In the latter, he or she must be able to experience intimacy with others but separate as an autonomous individual from being caught up in any emotional upheaval sweeping the family. Put more positively, the well-differentiated person is able to balance thinking and feeling (and thus adhere to personal convictions while expressing individually initiated emotions) and at the same time to retain objectivity and flexibility (and thus remain independent of his or her family's emotional pressures).

The degree to which a **differentiation of self** occurs in an individual, says Bowen, reflects the extent to which that person is able to distinguish between the intellectual process and the feeling process he or she is experiencing. That is, differentiation of self

BOX 8.1 CLINICAL NOTE

A Feminist Challenge

Some feminists such as Hare-Mustin (1978) and Lerner (1986) dispute Bowen's contentions regarding the differentiation of self. They argue that what Bowen seems to value here are qualities—being autonomous, relying on reason above emotion, being goal directed—for which men are socialized, while simultaneously devaluing those qualities—relatedness, caring for others, nurturing—for which women typically are socialized.

However, Bowenians McGoldrick and Carter (2001) maintain that by distinguishing between thinking and feeling, Bowen was addressing the need for controlling one's emotional reactivity in order to control behavior and think about how we choose to respond, and was not arguing for the suppression of authentic or appropriate emotional expression.

is demonstrated by the degree to which a person can think, plan, and follow his or her own values, particularly around anxiety-provoking issues, without having his or her behavior automatically driven by the emotional cues from others. The degree to which one can separate emotionally from parents in growing up is the key: in extreme cases, the attachment is so complete that a symbiosis exists in which parents and child cannot survive without one another. Such unresolved emotional attachment is equivalent to a high degree of undifferentiation in a person and in a family (Papero, 1995). (In other cultures, particularly those that focus on family togetherness, individuality and differentiation may be expressed differently.)

The ideal here is not to be emotionally detached or fiercely objective or without feelings, but rather to strive for balance, achieving self-definition but not at the expense of losing the capacity for spontaneous emotional expression. The theory does not assume that rational behavior should be pursued at the expense of feelings, nor is it necessary to suppress emotional expression. Rather, individuals should not be driven by feelings they do not understand. A balance of feelings and cognition remained the goal of self-differentiation. As family systems theory uses the term, *differentiation* refers more to a process than to an achievable goal—a direction in life rather than a state of being (Friedman, 1991).

As Papero (1990, p. 48) notes, any individual's level of differentiation can best be observed under anxious family circumstances:

> To the degree that one can thoughtfully guide personal behavior in accordance with well defined principles in spite of intense anxiety in the family, he or she displays a level or degree of differentiation.

As an example, suppose a college student, living away from home during the academic year, goes home midyear to attend his sister's wedding. Amid the tensions typically occurring around such an event, to what degree is he drawn into family feuds, conflicts, coalitions, or emotional turmoil? His degree of differentiation can be gauged by the degree to which he is able to remain sufficiently involved to partake in and enjoy the pleasures of this landmark family event, but also sufficiently separated so as not to be drawn into the family emotional system.

Individuals with the greatest **fusion** between their thoughts and feelings (for example, schizophrenics dealing with their families) function most poorly; they are likely to be at the mercy of automatic or involuntary emotional reactions and tend to become dysfunctional even under low levels of anxiety. Just as they are unable to differentiate thought from feeling, such persons have trouble differentiating themselves from others and thus merge easily with whatever emotions dominate or sweep through the family. To the extent to which such automatic emotional attachments to one's family remain intact, the individual is handicapped from differentiating from the family and becoming an effectively functioning human being. Highly fused persons, with few firmly held positions of their own, are apt to remain emotionally "stuck" in the position they occupied in their families of origin (Bowen, 1978).

Bowen (1966) early on introduced the concept of **undifferentiated family ego mass,** derived from psychoanalysis, to convey the idea of a family emotionally "stuck together," one where "a conglomerate emotional oneness . . . exists in all levels of intensity" (p. 171). For example, the classic example of the symbiotic relationship of interdependency between mother and child may represent the most intense version of this concept; a father's detachment may be the least intense. The degree to which any one member is involved in the family from moment to moment depends on that person's basic level of involvement in the family ego mass. Sometimes the emotional closeness can be so intense that family members feel they know each other's feelings, thoughts, fantasies, and dreams. This intimacy may lead to uncomfortable "overcloseness" and ultimately to a phase of mutual rejection between two members.

In other words, within a family system, emotional tensions shift over time (sometimes slowly, sometimes rapidly) in a series of alliances and splits. What Bowen had initially characterized in psychoanalytic terms—*undifferentiated family ego mass*—he later recast in systems language as *fusion-differentiation.* Both sets of terms underscore the theory's transgenerational view that maturity and self-actualization demand that an individual become free of unresolved emotional attachments to his or her family of origin.

For illustrative purposes, Bowen (1966) proposed a theoretical scale (not an actual psychometric instrument) for evaluating an individual's differentiation level. As noted in Figure 8.1, the greater the degree of undifferentiation (no sense of self or a weak or

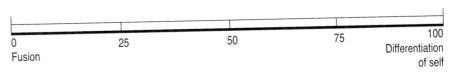

FIGURE 8.1 The theoretical differentiation-of-self scale, according to Bowen's conception, distinguishes people according to the degree of fusion or differentiation between their emotional and intellectual functioning. Those at the lower level (0–25) are emotionally fused to the family and others and lead lives in which their thinking is submerged and their feelings dominate. The lives of those in the 25–50 range are still guided by their emotional system and the reactions of others; goal-directed behavior is present but carried out in order to seek the approval of others. In the 50–75 range, thinking is sufficiently developed so as not to be dominated by feeling when stress occurs, and there is a reasonably developed sense of self. Those rare people functioning between 75 and 100 routinely separate their thinking from their feelings; they base decisions on the former but are free to lose themselves in the intimacy of a close relationship. Bowen (1978) considers someone at 75 to have a very high level of differentiation and all those over 60 to constitute a small percentage of society.

unstable personal identity), the greater the emotional fusion into a common self with others (the undifferentiated family ego mass). A person with a strong sense of self ("These are my opinions . . . This is who I am . . . This is what I will do, but not this") expresses convictions and clearly defined beliefs. Such a person is said to be expressing a *solid self.* He or she does not compromise that self for the sake of marital bliss or to please parents or achieve family harmony, or through coercion.

People at the low end of the scale are those whose emotions and intellect are so fused that their lives are dominated by the feelings of those around them. As a consequence, feeling anxious, they are easily stressed into dysfunction. Fearful and emotionally needy, they sacrifice their individuality in order to ensure acceptance from others. They are expressing an undifferentiated *pseudo self,* which they may deceive themselves into thinking is real, but which is composed of the opinions and values of others. Those far fewer individuals at the high end are emotionally mature; they can think and feel and take actions on their own despite external pressures to fall in line. Because their intellectual or rational functioning remains relatively (although not completely) dominant during stressful periods, they are more certain of who they are and what they believe, and thus more free to make judgments and decisions independent of any emotional turmoil around them. In the midrange are persons with relative degrees of fusion or differentiation. Note that *the scale eliminates the need for the concept of normality.* It is entirely possible for people at the low end of the scale to keep their lives in emotional equilibrium and stay free of symptoms, thus appearing to satisfy the popular criteria for being "normal." However, these people not only are more vulnerable to stress than those higher on the scale but also, under stress, are apt to develop symptoms from which they recover far more slowly than those at the high end of the scale.

To summarize:

- Below 50 (low differentiation): tries to please others; supports others and seeks support; dependent; lacks capacity for autonomy; primary need for security; avoids conflict; little ability to independently reach decisions or solve problems.
- 51–75 (midrange differentiation): has definite beliefs and values but tends to be overconcerned with the opinions of others; may make decisions based on emotional reactivity, especially whether decisions will receive disapproval from significant others.
- 76–100 (high differentiation): clear values and beliefs; goal directed; flexible; secure; autonomous; can tolerate conflict and stress; well-defined sense of solid self and less pseudo self. (Roberto, 1992)

Any person's level of differentiation reflects that individual's degree of emotional independence from the family as well as from others outside the family group. A moderate-to-high level of differentiation permits interaction with others without fear of fusion (losing one's sense of self in the relationship). While all relationships ranging from poorly to well-differentiated ones are in a state of dynamic equilibrium, the flexibility in that balance decreases as differentiation decreases. Figure 8.2 illustrates the varying degrees to which a person's functioning can be influenced by the relationship process.

Family systems theory assumes that an instinctively rooted life force in every human propels the developing child to grow up to be an emotionally separate person, able to think, feel, and act as an individual. At the same time, a corresponding life

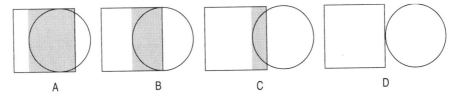

FIGURE 8.2 Relationship A is one where the functioning of each person is almost completely determined by the relationship process. The degree to which individual functioning is either enhanced or undermined by the relationship is indicated by the shaded area. The clear area indicates the capacity for self-determined functioning while in a relationship. Relationships B and C are progressively better differentiated. Individual functioning, therefore, is less likely to be enhanced or undermined by the relationship process. Relationship D is theoretical for the human. It represents two people who can be actively involved in a relationship yet remain self-determined.

Source: Kerr & Bowen, 1988, p. 71

force, also instinctively rooted, propels the child and family to remain emotionally connected. Because of these counterbalancing forces, no one ever achieves complete emotional separation from the family of origin. However, there are considerable differences in the amount of separation each of us accomplishes, as well as differences in the degree to which children from the same set of parents emotionally separate from the family. The latter is due to characteristics of the different parental relationships established with each child, which we elaborate on later in this section.

How valid is Bowen's differentiation of self concept? Despite the vast attention the theory has received, there have been few programmatic attempts to test its validity with respect to personality functioning or the quality of interpersonal relations between persons with differing degrees of differentiation, or even to changes as a result of Bowenian therapy. Skowron and Friedlander (1998) have made a useful start in this direction, developing a self-report instrument, the Differentiation of Self Inventory, focusing on adult significant relationships both with family-of-origin members and with outsiders. In these authors' preliminary study, adults with scores reflecting less emotional reactivity and less fusion showed lower chronic anxiety and greater marital satisfaction.

Triangles

In addition to its interest in the degree of integration of self, family systems theory also emphasizes emotional tension within the individual or in that person's relationships. The greater the couple's fusion, the more difficult is the task of finding a stable balance satisfying to both. One way to defuse such an anxious two-person relationship within a family, according to Bowen (1978), is to triangulate—draw in a significant family member to form a three-person interaction. Triangulation, then, is a common way in which two-person systems under stress attempt to achieve stability (Guerin, Fogarty, Fay, & Kautto, 1996).

The basic building block in a family's emotional or relational system is the **triangle,** according to Bowen. During periods when anxiety is low and external conditions are calm, the dyad or two-person system may engage in a comfortable back-and-forth exchange of feelings. However, the stability of this situation is threatened if one or both participants get upset or anxious, either because of internal stress or from stress external to the twosome. When a certain moderate anxiety level is reached, one or both partners will involve a vulnerable third person.

According to Bowen (1978), the twosome may "reach out" and pull in the other person, the emotions may "overflow" to the third person, or that person may be emotionally "programmed" to initiate involvement. This triangle dilutes the anxiety; it is both more stable and more flexible than the twosome and has a higher tolerance for dealing with stress. When anxiety in the triangle subsides, the emotional configuration returns to the peaceful twosome plus the lone outsider. However, should anxiety in the triangle increase, one person in the triangle may involve another outsider and so forth until a number of people are involved. Thus, triangles extend and interlock into ever-larger groups as tension increases (Roberto, 1992). Sometimes such triangulation can reach beyond the family, ultimately encompassing social agencies or the courts.

Generally speaking, the higher the degree of family fusion, the more intense and insistent the triangulating efforts will be; the least-well-differentiated person in the family is particularly vulnerable to being drawn in to reduce tension. (In this triadic setup, a child making an inadequate attempt to resolve tensions between his or her parents may get the label of identified patient.) The higher a family member's degree of differentiation, the better that person will manage anxiety without following the triangulating process (Papero, 1995). Beyond seeking relief of discomfort, the family relies on triangles to help maintain an optimum level of closeness and distance between members while permitting them the greatest freedom from anxiety.

Bowen (1976) refers to the triangle as the smallest stable relationship system. By definition, a two-person system is unstable and forms itself into a three-person system or triad under stress, as each partner attempts to create a triangle in order to reduce the increasing tension of their relationship. When anxiety is so great that the basic three-person triangle can no longer contain the tension, the resulting distress may spread to others. As more people become involved, the system may become a series of *interlocking triangles,* in some cases heightening the very problem the multiple triangulations sought to resolve. For example, a distraught mother's request for help from her husband in dealing with their son is met with withdrawal from the father. As the mother-son conflict escalates, she communicates her distress to another son, who proceeds to get into conflict with his brother for upsetting their mother. What began as a mother-son conflict has now erupted into interlocking conflicts—between mother and son, brother and brother, and mother and father.

Thus, triangulation does not always reduce tension. Kerr and Bowen (1988) point out that triangulation has at least four possible outcomes: (a) a stable twosome can be destabilized by the addition of a third person (for example, the birth of a child brings conflict to a harmonious marriage); (b) a stable twosome can be destabilized by the removal of a third person (a child leaves home and thus is no longer available to be triangulated into parental conflict); (c) an unstable twosome can be stabilized by the addition of a third person (a conflictual marriage becomes more harmonious after the birth of a child); and (d) an unstable twosome can be stabilized by the removal of a third person (conflict is reduced by getting a third person, say a mother-in-law, who has consistently taken sides, out of the picture).

To give another familiar example, note that conflict between siblings quickly attracts a parent's attention. Let us assume that the parent has positive feelings toward both children who, at the moment, are quarreling with each other. If the parent can control his or her emotional responsiveness and manage not to take sides while staying in contact with both children, the emotional intensity between the siblings will diminish. (A parallel situation exists when parents quarrel and a child is drawn into the triangle in an attempt to dilute and thus reduce the strain between the combatants.) Generally speaking, the probability of triangulation within a family is heightened by poor differentiation of family members; conversely, the reliance on triangulation to solve problems helps maintain the poor differentiation of certain family members. As McGoldrick and Carter (2001) observe, involvement in triangles and interlocking triangles represents a key mechanism whereby patterns of relating to one another are transmitted over generations in a family.

A similar situation exists when a couple visits a marital/family therapist. Following from this theory, if the therapist—the third person in the triangle—can remain involved with both spouses without siding with one or the other, the spouses may learn to view themselves as individual, differentiated selves as well as marital partners. However, if the third person loses emotional contact with either of the spouses, the twosome will proceed to triangulate with someone else.

Nuclear Family Emotional System

Bowen (1978) contends that people choose mates with equivalent levels of differentiation to their own. Not surprisingly, then, the relatively undifferentiated person will be attracted to a person who is equally fused to his or her family of origin. It is probable, moreover, that these poorly differentiated people, now a marital dyad, will themselves become highly fused and will produce a family with the same characteristics. According to Bowen, the resulting **nuclear family emotional system** will be unstable and will seek various ways to reduce tension and maintain stability. The greater the nuclear family's fusion, the greater will be the likelihood of anxiety and potential instability, and the greater will be the family's propensity to seek resolution through fighting, distancing, exploiting the impaired or compromised functioning of one partner, or banding together over concern for a child (Kerr, 1981).

More specifically, Kerr and Bowen (1988) regard three possible symptomatic patterns in a nuclear family as the product of the intense fusion between partners (see the following list). The greater the level of fusion in the marital dyad, the more frequently are these mechanisms likely to occur. Similarly, in a family living with a high level of chronic anxiety, these mechanisms are at work continuously, their intensity or frequency changing in response to acute anxiety being experienced at the moment (Papero, 1990).

Each pattern described here is intensified by anxiety and, when the intensity reaches a sufficient level, results in a particular form of symptom development. The person (or the relationship) who manifests the specific symptom is largely determined by the patterns of emotional functioning that predominate in a family system. The three patterns are as follows:

1. *Physical or emotional dysfunction in a spouse,* sometimes becoming chronic, as an alternative to dealing directly with family conflict; the anxiety generated by the undifferentiated functioning of every family member is being absorbed disproportionately by a symptomatic parent.

2. *Overt, chronic, unresolved marital conflict,* in which cycles of emotional distance and emotional overcloseness occur; both the negative feelings during conflict and the

positive feelings for one another during close periods are likely to be equally intense in roller-coaster fashion; the family anxiety is being absorbed by the husband and wife.

3. *Psychological impairment in a child,* enabling the parents to focus attention on the child and ignore or deny their own lack of differentiation; as the child becomes the focal point of the family problem, the intensity of the parental relationship is diminished, thus the family anxiety is being absorbed in the child's impaired functioning; the lower a child's level of differentiation, the greater will be his or her vulnerability to increases in family anxiety and thus to dysfunction.

Furthermore, dysfunction in one spouse may take the form of an *overadequate-underadequate reciprocity,* in which one partner takes on most or even all family responsibilities (earning a living, caring for the children, cooking, shopping, arranging a social life, and so on) while the other plays the counterpart role of being under-responsible (can't drive without becoming anxious, can't choose clothes, can't have friends to the house). Fused together, the two pseudo selves develop an arrangement in which one partner increasingly underfunctions while the other takes up the slack by assuming responsibility for them both. When the tilt gets too great, according to Singleton (1982), the one giving up more pseudo self for the sake of family harmony becomes vulnerable to physical or emotional dysfunction.

In some cases, this pattern intertwines with marital conflict, the underadequate one complaining of dominance, inconsiderateness, and so forth from the spouse. The overadequate one is more comfortable with the arrangement until the underadequate one complains or becomes so inadequate as to cause difficulties for the overadequate one. When this occurs, the problem is likely to be seen by the unsophisticated eye as belonging to the unhappy underadequate spouse, rather than as a relationship problem for which both need help.

Almost any family will have one child who is more vulnerable to fusion than the others, and thus likely to be triangulated into parental conflict. Any significant increase in parental anxiety triggers this child's dysfunctional behavior (in school, at home, or both), leading to even greater anxieties in the parent. In turn, the child's behavior becomes increasingly impaired, sometimes turning into a lifelong pattern of poor functioning.

The nuclear family emotional system is a multigenerational concept. Family systems theorists believe individuals tend to repeat in their marital choices and other significant relationships the patterns of relating learned in their families of origin, and to pass along similar patterns to their children. The only effective way to resolve current family problems is to change the individual's interactions with his or her family of origin. As that person changes, others in emotional contact with him or her will make compensatory changes (McGoldrick & Carter, 2001). Only then can differentiation proceed for others, as all the individuals involved become less overreactive to the emotional forces sweeping through the family.

Family Projection Process

Parents do not respond in the same way to each child in a family, despite their claims to the contrary. That is, they pass on their level of differentiation to the children in an uneven fashion: some emerge with a higher level than their parents, some with a lower level, and others with a more or less identical level (Papero, 1995). In particular, those children more exposed to parental immaturity tend to develop greater fusion to the family than their more fortunate siblings and have greater difficulty separating smoothly from their parents. Responding to their mother's anxiety, they remain more vulnerable to emotional stresses within the family and consequently live lives more governed by emotional upheavals than do their brothers or sisters.

The fusion-prone, focused-on child is the one most sensitive to disturbances and incipient signs of instability within the family. Bowen (1976) believed that poorly differentiated parents, themselves immature, select as the object of their attention the most infantile of all their children, regardless of his or her birth order in the family; Bowen calls this the **family projection process.** This process provides the means by which the parents transmit their own low level of differentiation onto the most susceptible child. In many cases, this child is physically or mentally handicapped or psychologically unprotected in some fashion, and pays the price by becoming poorly self-differentiated.

The projection process operates within the mother-father-child triangle; the transmission of undifferentiation occurs through the triangulation of the most vulnerable child into the parental relationship. The sibling positions of the parents in their families of origin offer possible clues as to which child will be chosen in the next generation. As the child most emotionally attached to the parents of all the children within a family, he or she will have the lowest level of differentiation of self and the most difficulty in separating from the family. Moreover, Kerr (1981) believes that the greater the level of undifferentiation of the parents and the more they rely on the projection process to stabilize the system, the more likely it is that several children will be emotionally impaired. This process of projecting or transmitting parental undifferentiation may begin as early as the initial mother-infant bonding.

The intensity of the family projection process is related to two factors: the degree of immaturity or undifferentiation of the parents and the level of stress or anxiety the family experiences. In one triangulating scenario described by Singleton (1982), the child responds anxiously to the mother's anxiety, she being the principal caretaker; the mother becomes alarmed at what she perceives as the child's problem, and becomes overprotective. Thus a cycle is established in which the mother infantilizes the child, who in turn becomes demanding and impaired. The third leg of the triangle is supplied by the father, who is frightened by his wife's anxiety and, by needing to calm her but without dealing with the issues, plays a supportive role in her dealings with the child. As collaborators, the parents have now stabilized their relationship around a "disturbed" child, and in the process perpetuated the family triangle. That person will be less able to function autonomously in the future.

Emotional Cutoff

Children less involved in the projection process are apt to emerge with a greater ability to withstand fusion, to separate thinking and feeling. Those who are more involved try various strategies upon reaching adulthood, or even before. They may attempt to insulate themselves from the family by geographic separation (moving to another state), through the use of psychological barriers (cease talking to parents), or by the self-deception that they are free of family ties because actual contact has been broken off. Bowen (1976) considers such supposed freedom an **emotional cutoff**—a flight of extreme emotional distancing in order to break emotional ties—and not true emancipation. In Bowen's formulation, cutting oneself off emotionally from one's family of origin often represents a desperate effort to deal with unresolved fusion with one or both parents—a way of managing the unresolved emotional attachment to them. More likely than not, the person attempting the cutoff tends to deny to himself or herself that many unresolved conflicts remain with family-of-origin members. Kerr (1981) contends that emotional cutoff *reflects* a problem (underlying fusion between generations), *solves* a problem (reducing anxiety associated with making contact), and *creates* a problem (isolating people who might benefit from closer contact). As McGoldrick and Carter (2001) note, cutting off a relationship by physical or emotional distance does not end the emotional process, but actually intensifies it. Cut off from siblings or parents, those individuals are apt to form new relationships (with a spouse or children) that are all the more intense and that may lead to further distancing and cutoffs from them.

Cutoffs occur most often in families in which there is a high level of anxiety and emotional dependence (Bowen, 1978). As both factors increase and greater family cohesiveness is expected, conflicts between family members may be disguised and hidden. Should the fusion-demanding situation reach an unbearable stage, some members may seek greater distance, emotionally, socially, perhaps physically, for self-preservation. When a family member insists on communication, it is apt to be superficial, inauthentic, and brief (short visits or phone calls during which only impersonal topics are discussed).

Bowen insisted that adults must resolve their emotional attachments to their families of origin. In a revealing paper delivered in 1967 to a national conference of family researchers and therapists (1972), he openly described his personal struggles to achieve a differentiation of self from his own family of origin. Without this differentiation, Bowen argued, family therapists may unknowingly be triangulated into conflicts in their client families (much as they were as children in their own families), perhaps overidentifying with one family member or projecting onto another their

---

BOX 8.2   THERAPEUTIC ENCOUNTER

BOWEN'S SELF-DIFFERENTIATION FROM HIS FAMILY OF ORIGIN

Bowen's self-revealing article, "Toward a Differentiation of Self in One's Family" (1972) was published under an anonymous authorship because Bowen was describing real people whose anonymity he wished to protect. Actually, the entire process of achieving greater self-differentiation from his family of origin represents a deliberate effort by Bowen to confront entrenched and complex patterns of family interaction. Given an opportunity to return home for the funeral of a distant relative, Bowen decided to apply his newly formulated ideas about fusion, triangles, and so on, at a time when family members were experiencing anxiety and thus might be more open to change. Purposely provoking a response by raising old family emotional issues, he managed to remain detached and undefensive, to calm his family's anxieties, and in the process to differentiate himself once and for all. Wylie (1990b) reports Bowen's exhilaration about successfully carrying out the visit without becoming triangulated or fused into the family's emotional system. Bowen's self-differentiation efforts have sometimes been compared to Freud's self-analysis. Therapists training to practice Bowen's techniques work on differentiating themselves from their families of origin, much as candidates wishing to become psychoanalysts have a training analysis (Titelman, 1987).

own unresolved difficulties. Family therapists need to get in touch with and be free of their own internalized family so that unfinished business from the past does not intrude on current dealings with client families.

Multigenerational Transmission Process

In perhaps his most intriguing formulation, Bowen (1976) proposed the concept of a **multigenerational transmission process,** in which severe dysfunction is conceptualized as the result of chronic anxiety transmitted over several generations. Two earlier concepts are crucial here—the selection of a spouse with a similar differentiation level and the family projection process that results in lower levels of self-differentiation for that invested, or focused offspring particularly sensitive to parental emotional patterns. By contrast, children less involved in parental overfocusing can develop a higher level of differentiation than their parents (Roberto, 1992).

Assume for a moment that the least well-differentiated members of two families marry—as Bowen's theory would predict—and that at least one of their children, due to the projection process, will have an even lower differentiation level than theirs, increasing his or her anxiety. The eventual marriage of this person—again, to someone with a similarly poor differentiation of self—passes along the reduced level of differentiation to the members of the next generation, who in turn pass it along to the next, and so forth. As each generation produces individuals with progressively poorer differentiation ("weak links"), those people are increasingly vulnerable to anxiety and fusion, and as noted, spousal dysfunction, marital conflict, or child impairment are likely to result. If the parents focus their anxiety on the most vulnerable offspring, that poorly differentiated person will grow up having a difficult time managing emotional reactions and maintaining autonomy.

Although the process may slow down or remain static over a generation or two, ultimately—it may take as many as eight or ten generations—a level of impairment is reached that is consistent with dysfunction—schizophrenia, chronic alcoholism, or other manifestations of psychological impairment (Papero, 1990). If the family encounters severe stress and anxiety, however, serious dysfunction may develop in an earlier generation. In some less stressful cases or under favorable life circumstances, poorly differentiated people may keep their relationship system in relatively symptom-free equilibrium for several generations longer. This process may be reversed, of course, should someone in this lineage marry a person considerably higher on the differentiation-of-self scale. However, as noted earlier, Bowen contended that most persons choose mates at more or less their own level of differentiation.

Sibling Position

Bowen credits Toman's (1961) research on the relationship between birth order and personality with clarifying his own thinking regarding the influence of **sibling position** in the nuclear family emotional process. Toman hypothesized that children develop certain fixed personality characteristics based on their birth order in the family. He offered ten basic personality sibling profiles (such as older brother, younger sister; younger brother, older sister; only child; twins), suggesting that the more closely a marriage duplicates one's sibling place in childhood, the better will be its chance of success. Thus, a first-born would do well to marry a second-born, for example. He maintained further that, in general, the chances for a successful marriage are increased for persons who grew up with siblings of the opposite sex rather than with same-sex siblings only.

Bowen realized that interactive patterns between marital partners may be related to the position of each partner in his or her family of origin, since birth order frequently predicts certain roles and functions within one's family emotional system. Thus, an oldest child who marries a youngest may expect to take responsibility, make decisions, and so on; that person's mate also expects this behavior based on his or her experiences as the youngest in the family. Two youngest children who marry may both feel overburdened by responsibility and decision making; the marriage of two oldest children may be overly competitive because each spouse is accustomed to being in charge (Kerr, 1981). Note, however, that it is a person's *functional* position in the family system, not necessarily the actual order of birth, that shapes future expectations and behavior.

Societal Regression

In a final concept, **societal regression,** Bowen extended his thinking to society's emotional functioning. In the least well developed of his theoretical formulations, he argued that society, like the family, contains within it opposing forces toward undifferentiation and toward individuation. Under conditions of chronic stress (population growth, depletion of natural resources) and thus an anxious social climate, there is likely to be a surge of togetherness and a corresponding erosion of the forces intent on achieving individuation. The result, thought Bowen, was likely to be greater discomfort and further anxiety (Papero, 1990).

It was Bowen's (1978) pessimistic view that society's functional level of differentiation had decreased over the last several decades. He called for better differentiation between intellect and emotion in order for society to make more rational decisions rather than act on the basis of feelings and opt for short-term "Band-Aid" solutions.[2]

FAMILY SYSTEMS THERAPY

Family systems therapy occurs in stages. Adopting a neutral and objective role in order to remain untriangled into the family, the therapist first attempts to assess the family's emotional system, past and present, through a series of evaluation interviews and measurement techniques, before intervening therapeutically with the family. Ultimately, therapeutic goals for changing the relational system include helping family members manage their anxiety, helping them detriangulate from three-person systems, and most important, aiding each family member to increase his or her basic differentiation of self.

The Evaluation Interview

The appraisal of a symptomatic family begins with the initial telephone contact. Kerr and Bowen (1988) caution the therapist against being drawn into the family emotional system by overresponding to the caller's forceful, charming, or theatrical presentation of the family's problem. Throughout the subsequent therapy, they warn, the therapist

---

[2]Although Bowen tried to remain current in dealing with society's influences on family life, his efforts thirty years ago did not anticipate the current interest in how gender, race, ethnicity, sexual orientation, etc., affect attitudes, beliefs, behavior patterns, and the transmission of family values over generations. As we emphasize throughout this text, those factors are at the forefront of contemporary family psychology and family therapy.

must guard against becoming incorporated into the family's problem, taking sides in disputes, or becoming overly sympathetic with one member or angry at another. A therapist who thus becomes fused with the family's emotional system, or allows himself or herself to be triangulated into their conflicts, or becomes engulfed by their anxiety, can have a divisive influence on family functioning and fail to promote further differentiation among family members. While the family must become convinced that the therapist cares and remains interested in them, the therapist must resist their efforts to get him or her overinvolved emotionally. As Friedman (1991, p. 151) advises,

> if you, as a therapist, allow a couple to create a triangle with you, but take care not to get caught up in the emotional process of that triangle either by overfunctioning or being emotionally reactive, *then, by trying to remain a nonanxious presence in that triangle, you can induce a change in the relationship of the other two that would not occur if they said the same things in your absence.* (author's emphasis)

Objectivity, as opposed to emotional reactivity, should characterize the therapist's behavior in this system of family therapy. It is important to stay connected to all participants without taking sides or becoming too subjectively involved. Bowen believed that the more a therapist has worked on becoming differentiated from his or her own family of origin, the more the therapist can remain detached, unswayed, and objective. Actually, as Friedman (1991) points out, it is the therapist's presence—engaging without being reactive, stimulating without rescuing, teaching a way of thinking rather than using any specific behavior or therapeutic intervention technique—that is the ultimate agent of change.

Family evaluation interviews are carried out with any combination of family members: a parent, husband and wife, the nuclear family, perhaps including extended family members. Since Bowen viewed family therapy as a way of conceptualizing a problem rather than as a process that requires a certain number of people to attend the sessions, he was content to work with one family member, especially if that person was motivated to work on self-differentiation from his or her family of origin. In fact, according to Kerr and Bowen (1988), while conjoint sessions are generally useful, at times seeing people together may impede the progress of one or the other. Instead, they argue, if one parent can increase his or her basic level of differentiation, the functioning of the other parent as well as the children will inevitably improve.

Family evaluation interviews begin with a history of the presenting problem, focusing especially on the symptoms (physical, emotional, social) and their impact on the symptomatic person or relationship. If more than one person is present, the therapist is interested in each member's perception of what created and what sustains the problem for which they seek relief, why they seek such help now, and what each hopes to get from the experience. Through a series of such process questions,[3] the therapist

---

[3]Process Questioning directed at individuals ("What happens to you when your husband . . .") or at a couple ("How do the two of you deal with . . .") is a major technique for family systems therapists, since it represents a way of remaining in touch with client problems without directing client behavior or taking responsibility for fixing their dilemmas. Friedman (1991) believes such questioning allows the therapist to maintain objectivity and a differentiation-promoting position with clients.

attempts to assess the pattern of emotional functioning as well as the intensity of the emotional process in the nuclear family of the symptomatic person. What is the relationship system like in this family? What are the current stressors? How well differentiated are the family members? What is the family's adaptive level? How stable is the family, and how (and how successfully) does it handle anxiety? What three-person (or more) triangles exist? Are emotional cutoffs operating? The initial interview, which may extend over several sessions, seeks information on all of these issues in assessing the degree of family dysfunction associated with the presenting symptoms, which may appear in one or more family members.

Consistent with a transgenerational outlook, Bowenians are particularly interested in the historical pattern of family emotional functioning, the family's anxiety levels at varying stages of its life, and the amount of stress experienced in the past compared with current functioning. Of special interest too is whether one spouse's functioning has improved significantly—and the other spouse's has declined significantly—over the course of their relationship. By probing the history of the symptoms in each family member, therapists search for clues as to where the various pressures on the family have been expressed and how effectively the family has adapted to stress since its inception. At this point in the evaluation, the focus has begun to expand beyond the symptomatic person to an examination of the relationship network of the nuclear family.

The final part of the evaluation interview attempts to understand the nuclear family in the context of the maternal and paternal extended family systems. Here the therapists are interested in multigenerational patterns of fusion, the nature of the nuclear family's relationship with the extended families, and the degree of emotional cutoff of each spouse. Parallels in relationship patterns between the husband and wife and his or her parents may offer important clues of poor differentiation from the families of origin. The therapist's goal with this undertaking is to develop a road map of the family's emotional system, since each nuclear family is believed to embody the emotional processes and patterns of preceding generations.

The Genogram

Since Bowen believed multigenerational patterns and influences are crucial determinants of nuclear family functioning, he developed a graphic way of investigating the genesis of the presenting problem by diagramming the family over at least three generations. To aid in the process and to keep the record in pictorial form in front of him, he constructed a family genogram in which each partner's family background is laid out. Worked out with the family during early sessions, it provides a useful tool for allowing therapist and family members alike to examine the ebb and flow of the family's emotional processes in their intergenerational context. Each individual's family's biological, kinship, and psychosocial makeup can be gleaned from perusing this visual graph (Roberto, 1992).

Figure 8.3 offers a partial set of commonly used genogram symbols. Together, the symbols provide a visual picture of a family tree: who the members are, what their names are, ages, sibling positions, marital status, divorces, adoptions, and so on, typically extending back at least three generations for both partners. When relevant, additional items of information such as religious affiliation, work histories, ethnic origins, geographic locations, socioeconomic status, noteworthy health issues, and perhaps significant life events may be included. More than providing a concise pictorial depiction of the nuclear family, the genogram may suggest certain

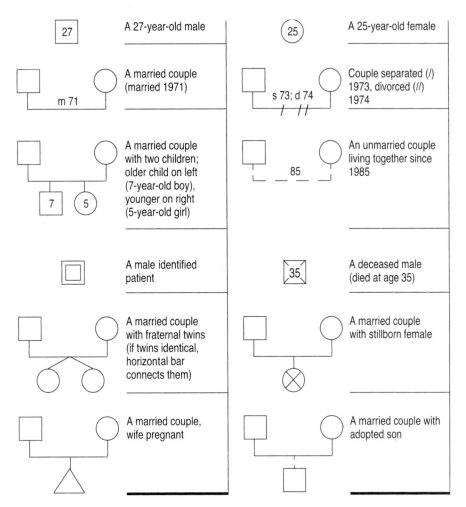

FIGURE 8.3 A partial set of commonly agreed-upon genogram symbols.
Source: Based on McGoldrick & Gerson, 1985

emotional patterns in each partner's family of origin, thus providing data for assessing each spouse's degree of fusion to extended families and to one another.

McGoldrick and Gerson (1985), strongly transgenerational in outlook, suggest that family patterns tend to repeat themselves; what happens in one generation will often occur in the next, as the same unresolved emotional issues are replayed from generation to generation. A recently updated and expanded version of their text (McGoldrick, Gerson, & Shellenberger, 1999) contains numerous computer-generated genograms of multigenerational processes in 32 notable families, ranging from Sigmund Freud to Bill Clinton, Thomas Jefferson to the Roosevelts, and including various celebrities from the entertainment world.

Genograms often give families their first inkling of intergenerational family relationship patterns. Goldenberg and Goldenberg (2002) offer the following example of just such a situation (see Figure 8.4):

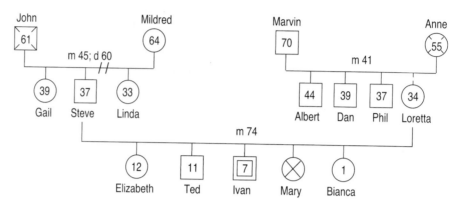

FIGURE 8.4 Genogram of three generations of a family.
Source: Goldenberg & Goldenberg, 2002, p. 61

A family contacted a counselor in 1988 because their son, Ivan, was having school difficulties, disrupting class activity and generally being inattentive. The genogram revealed that his mother, Loretta, was adopted, after her adoptive parents had tried unsuccessfully to have a daughter after three sons. She married early, at 20, soon after the death of her adoptive mother. Steve, a middle child whose parents divorced when he was a preteenager, lived in a single-parent household with his mother and two sisters until he married Loretta. Steve and Loretta started their own family before either was 25, perhaps in an effort to create some stability in contrast to what either had known growing up.

The fact that they now have four children (one died in childbirth) suggests a strong involvement in family life, especially because the children's ages are spread over more than ten years. Are the parents being overprotective, perhaps to compensate for what they felt deprived of as youngsters? What has been the effect of Loretta's pregnancies over the last several years on the other children? To what extent does Ivan feel he is being displaced as the youngest child by the birth of Bianca? (p. 59)

Note how many hypotheses spring from the genogram, to be explored with the family subsequently. Fusion-differentiation issues in the family of origin, the nuclear family emotional system, emotional cutoffs by the parents, sibling positions, and many other of Bowen's concepts appear as possibly relevant to Ivan's presenting symptoms. When evaluation interview data are put into schematic form in a family genogram, therapist and family together are better able to comprehend the underlying emotional processes connecting generations. In a sense the family genogram is never completed, as information uncovered during the course of therapy sheds new light on basic patterns of emotional reactivity in both the nuclear and extended families. Major turning points for the family (such as the unexpected death of a key family member) may mark the start of a series of family problems that may reverberate across generations (Papero, 1990). Genograms are thus a relatively emotion-free way of collecting information that makes sense to the family and connects them to the therapeutic exploratory process.

CLINICAL NOTE

Even the most intense, quarrelsome family often quiets down during the process of constructing a genogram together. Typically there is high interest paid by all members as their family history unfolds, family secrets are revealed, and generational patterns are identified.

Therapeutic Goals

Family systems therapy, no matter the nature of the presenting clinical problem, is always governed by two basic goals: (a) management of anxiety and relief from symptoms; and (b) an increase in each participant's level of differentiation in order to improve adaptiveness (Kerr & Bowen, 1988). Generally speaking, the family needs to accomplish the former goal first, before the latter can be undertaken. Ultimately, however, overreactive emotional interactions with the extended family must be changed, leading to greater self-differentiation for nuclear family members. In the case of marital conflict, for example, the therapist *tracks* the emotional process between the spouses and then *shifts* the emphasis from the *marital* level to the *self level* as each partner differentiates from the spouse. In the process, equal attention is paid to historical ways in which previous generations have created family patterns as well as current manifestations of those patterns throughout the family system (Aylmer, 1986).

In the following case, a rural couple in conflict must deal with their deteriorating economic situation. However, the possibility of the wife going to work outside the home collides with the instilled roles, traditions, and values from their families of origin, and contradicting these time-honored family norms is a source of anxiety. Among the beliefs passed down over generations are that employment of women outside the home is incompatible with family life and that the husband must be the family's primary breadwinner. Family cohesion is at stake.

Bowen's standard method of conducting family therapy was to work with a system consisting of two adults and himself. Even when the identified patient was a symptomatic child, Bowen asked the parents to accept the premise that the basic problem was between the two of them—the family's emotional system—and that the identified patient was not the source of the problem. In such a situation, Bowen might never see the child at all. As Kerr (1981) explains, "A theoretical system that thinks in terms of family, with a therapeutic method that works toward improvement of the family system, is 'family' regardless of the number of people in the sessions" (p. 232).

Back Home Visits

To help remove an adult client from a highly charged emotional triangle with parents, solo visits to the family of origin may be arranged. Typically these structured visits are prepared for beforehand by telephone or letter, in which the client makes known those issues causing personal distress. The client is instructed to maintain an "observer" stance as much as possible at first, monitoring distressing emotional and behavioral patterns while retaining a sense of separateness despite surrounding tensions and anxiety. Later, the now more self-directed client can decline getting

BOX 8.3   CASE STUDY

A FARMING COUPLE FACES A DILEMMA

Martha and her husband, Jacob, were at great odds. Tradition in their farm families held that women should not work but instead should rear children. Jacob prided himself on providing adequately for his family, even with the small parcel of land that was his share of their family farm. But the tobacco crop had not done well this year, and they were having great difficulty even keeping their children clothed. Both Martha and Jacob's parents volunteered to help financially to see them through poor times. Martha's pride was too great to accept handouts, and having been reared with a strong work ethic, she accepted a job as a clerk in a bookstore at the town shopping mall, without consulting Jacob. Jacob took her action as a personal affront. Both sets of parents were so distraught that they were barely speaking to Martha. In fact, Jacob's parents were so disturbed they refused to look after the children for the few hours after school before Martha returned from work. They firmly believed the children would suffer. They saw the role of women as remaining in the home, rearing children, keeping the house, and helping with the farm as needed.

Referred by a new friend at her job, Martha came willingly to conjoint marital therapy. Jacob came with much reluctance. There was a very cold tension between them. Jacob preferred not to reveal their family problems to an outsider. Martha believed this was their only chance to bring the family back together. In efforts to build a therapeutic alliance and create an atmosphere where it was safe to reveal feelings, the therapist acknowledged Jacob's hesitations to come to therapy and validated his reasons for reluctance; likewise, the therapist reflected understanding of Martha's belief that therapy was their only hope of reuniting the family.

The next task of therapy was to explore the differences between the couple. Guided by the therapist in a very structured mirroring dialogue that helped the couple to feel safe with each other, Jacob admitted he blamed the group of farm women, of which Martha was a member, for influencing her decision to go to work. He saw her involvement as disloyal to him and disrespectful of what he was trying to do for the family. Martha argued that it was only the desperate financial situation that had propelled her to go against Jacob's will. Eventually she disclosed that she was not satisfied with staying home and had often yearned for work outside the home. Using the genogram as a tool, the therapist explored family-of-origin issues with the couple. Jacob revealed the shame he felt for not sufficiently providing for the family and the resentment he harbored toward his father for giving up so much of their family land for development rather than preserving it for succeeding generations. With improved communication, the couple became more accepting of each other, and Jacob began to acknowledge how Martha's income benefited the family.

Next, the couple was coached in talking to their respective families. They felt the need to convince their families that employment for Martha was best for their family. The therapist guided them in presenting their newly found common perspective to both families. As Jacob's parents began to see their son as a willing participant in the new arrangement and to realize that he was even proud of Martha's work, they were able to discuss the guilt they had been feeling for not having more land to give Jacob and to become less protective of him. Martha's family was less accepting but nevertheless acknowledged the couple's right to make their own decision.

Source: Shellenberger & Hoffman, 1995, pp. 464–465

caught up in old patterns and negotiate for more functional and supportive relationships (Roberto, 1992).

Because Bowen was particularly concerned that his clients develop the ability to differentiate themselves from their families of origin, the focus of much of his work was on extended families. In this respect Bowen resembled Framo (1981),[4] although Bowen sent clients home for frequent visits (and self-observations) after coaching them in their differentiating efforts, while Framo brought members of the families of origin into the final phases of therapy with his clients. Going home again, for Bowen, was directed at greater self-differentiation from one another—not at confrontation, the settlements of old scores, or the reconciliation of long-standing differences. Reestablishing emotional connectedness with the family of origin—especially when rigid and previously impenetrable boundaries have been built up—is a critical step in reducing a client's residual anxiety due to emotional cutoff, in detriangulating from members of that family, and in ultimately achieving self-differentiation, free of crippling entanglements from the past or present.

Family Therapist as Coach

Bowen presented himself as a researcher helping the family members become objective researchers into their own ways of functioning. The term he preferred was *coach* (having moved during his career, in his own words, "from 'couch' to 'coach'")—an active expert who calmly assists family members, through low-key, direct questions, in defining and clarifying their emotional responsivity to one another. In the process, family members were encouraged to listen, think about their situation, control their emotional reactivity, and learn to express self-defining "I-positions." When the coach has taught them successfully, often by modeling "I-positions," the individual family members are responsible for the actual work of changing. Their self-differentiation, the basic goal of the therapy, must come from them and not the therapist, on the basis of a rational understanding of the family's emotional networks and transmission processes.

Bowen (1976) took the position that the successful addition of a significant other (a friend, teacher, clergyman) to an anxious or disturbed relationship system can modify all relationships within the family. The family therapist can play this role as long as

---

[4]Several other family therapists, notably Norman Paul and Donald Williamson, endorse the transgenerational viewpoint that certain unfinished issues with one's family of origin must be addressed directly before family therapy is terminated. Paul (1974), a family therapy pioneer, has been particularly concerned that unresolved issues over death, loss, and grief be dealt with therapeutically, arguing that a family's rigid or otherwise dysfunctional behavior patterns are often tied to an earlier denied or inappropriately expressed grief over the death of a loved one. He advocates uncovering the loss and helping family members complete the unresolved mourning process together. Williamson (1991) believes that by the fourth decade of their lives—middle adulthood—grown children should have terminated the earlier hierarchical power structure with their aging parents, and the family should have begun to redistribute power on a more equitable basis between generations. Failure to do so, he hypothesizes, may lead to marital and family behavior in the second generation that becomes dysfunctional and symptomatic, as these adult children fail to take on "personal authority" with their families. Williamson contends that the renegotiation is essential if one is to differentiate from one's parents, gain a sense of personal authority, and begin an eventual mourning process for the parents. After careful preparation with selected clients (writing an autobiography, taping phone conversations with parents, and so forth), Williamson arranges several office visits extending over three days between the adult child and the parents, aimed at shifting power and achieving peerhood between generations. Williamson's efforts are consistent with the social construction view of rewriting one's family story as a way of creating a more egalitarian and intimate narrative with one's parents.

CLINICAL NOTE

Learning to make "I-statements" ("I'm upset at what you're doing now") rather than accusations ("Why do you enjoy picking fights?") is apt to lead to a more honest exchange than blaming the other person. When both partners take responsibility for their feelings and express them directly, the chances of resolving conflict are greatly improved.

---

he or she manages to stay in nonanxious emotional contact with the two most significant family members (usually the parents) but remains uninvested in (or detriangulated from) the family conflict. Bowen's insistence that the therapist not engage with the family system—maintaining what Aylmer (1986) calls a *detached-involved position*—is dramatically different from the "total immersion" approach of family therapists such as Ackerman. Here the therapist remains unsusceptible, calm, objective, detriangulated from the emotional entanglements between the spouses. If the therapist can maintain that kind of stance—despite pressures to be triangulated into the conflict—Bowenians believe tension between the couple will subside, the fusion between them will slowly resolve, and other family members will feel the positive repercussions in terms of changes in their own lives—all adding to the likelihood of each member achieving greater self-differentiation.

Family systems therapists may choose one partner, usually the one more mature and better differentiated, and focus on that individual for a period of time. This person is assumed to be the member of the family most capable of breaking through the old emotionally entangling patterns of interaction. When that person succeeds in taking an "I-stand," the others will shortly be forced into changing, subsequently moving off in their own directions. A stormy period may follow before a new equilibrium is reached, but the former pathological ties are broken and each person has achieved a greater sense of individuality.

Doing family therapy by *coaching* individual family members to change themselves in the context of their nuclear and parental family systems (McGoldrick & Carter, 2001) has become a prominent part of Bowenian family systems therapy. After defining the crisis that brought the family into therapy, the individual member is tutored to define himself or herself both in the family and the family of origin. By guiding that person to avoid triangles and getting embroiled in family emotional processes, the coach is helping change his or her emotional functioning in the family, eventually helping change the entire system. Genograms sometimes help define that person's role in the system. Process questioning also helps to clarify for the client his or her role in the family's emotional life. Successful coaching helps the individual reenter the system by developing authentic emotionally engaged relationships with other family members, rather than repeating old, dysfunctional family patterns. McGoldrick and Carter (2001) describe the process as follows:

> The basic idea of coaching is that, if you can change the part you play in your family and hold it despite the family's reaction while keeping in emotional contact with family members, you maximize the likelihood (not a guarantee!) that they will eventually change to accommodate your change. (p. 291)

Box 8.4 illustrates a coaching procedure with a young African American woman.

BOX 8.4   CASE STUDY

COACHING FOR FAMILY REENTRY

Cheryl, a 30-year-old African American social worker who had not seen her father for many years, spent several sessions describing her current marital and in-law conflicts, which had led her to seek help. She had not corresponded with her father since he left the family to live with a girlfriend years before. She had had a distant relationship with her mother since she left home at 17 to live with an aunt and attend college. She considered her mother "hopeless" for having stayed so long with her father, who was cold and critical, and then with a boyfriend, whom she was still supporting. She saw both parents as irrelevant to her current life and problems.

After discussing the striking patterns of marital conflict, in-law problems, and emotional cut-offs on her genogram, she was encouraged to undertake a coaching process to explore her role in her family of origin as a way to gain more flexibility for her marriage. She explored the cut-off with her parents and became aware with the coach that her issue with her mother was much less intense than the one with her father. As her first move of reentry, she decided to write a letter to her father in which she referred briefly and regretfully to their cut-off and then went on in a low-key way to express interest in his life, his wife, and young son (whom she had never met), and to bring him up-to-date about her life. To her mother, for whom she realized she had fewer conflictual feelings, she wrote in more depth about her life and proposed to visit her in the near future.

Source: McGoldrick & Carter, 2001, p. 289

A Controlled, Cerebral Approach

Family therapy sessions for Bowenians tend to be controlled and cerebral. Each partner talks to the therapist rather than talking directly to the other. Confrontation between the partners is avoided to minimize emotional reactivity between them. Instead, what each partner is thinking is externalized in the presence of the other. Interpretations are avoided. Calm questioning defuses emotion and forces the partners to think about the issues causing their difficulties. Rather than allowing partners to blame each other or ignore their differences in a rush of intimacy, Bowenians insist that each partner focus on the part he or she plays in the relationship problems.

CONTEXTUAL THERAPY

Relational Ethics and the Family Ledger

Another influential family therapy approach that addresses multigenerational patterns of connection within a family comes from the work of Ivan Boszormenyi-Nagy and his associates. His **contextual** therapy, as elaborated in a collection of his papers

CLINICAL NOTE

The technique of having each partner in a marital conflict speak directly to the therapist is used frequently when the therapist wishes to de-escalate the level of emotional intensity taking place between the partners when they attempt to address one another directly.

spanning 30 years (Boszormenyi-Nagy, 1987), is heavily influenced by Fairbairn's (1952) object relations theory, existential philosophy, and Sullivan's interpersonal psychiatry (1953), to which is added an *ethical perspective*—trust, loyalty, transgenerational indebtedness and entitlements, as well as fairness in relationships between family members. Although he acknowledges the family as a social system, Boszormenyi-Nagy believes that the burdens for today's families are complex, and a comprehensive picture of their functioning must go beyond a simple appreciation of the interactional sequences occurring between members. What also demands attention, in his view, is the impact of both intrapsychic and intergenerational issues within families, especially each member's subjective sense of claims, rights, and obligations in relation to one another. To function effectively, family members must be held ethically accountable for their behavior with one another and must learn to balance *entitlement* (what one is due or has come to merit)[5] and *indebtedness* (what one owes to whom).

A core concept in contextual theory, **relational ethics** focuses attention on the long-term, oscillating balance of fairness among members within a family, whereby the welfare interests of each participant are taken into account by the others. Relational ethics encompasses both individual psychology (what transpires within the person) and systems characteristics (roles, power alignments, and communication sequences within the family). A marital couple, for example, must develop a symmetrical give-and-take, balancing rights and responsibilities, merits and obligations, toward one another, in order to maintain and continue to build their relationship. When the needs of the partners conflict, which is inevitable in any relationship, they must be able, openly and honestly, to negotiate differences that maintain overall fairness. Fairness, decency, consideration of every family member's needs, loyalty, equality, reciprocity, caring, accountability—these together help determine the direction, form, and freedom of action within a family (Boszormenyi-Nagy, Grunebaum, & Ulrich, 1991). Symptoms may appear when trustworthiness and caring within a family break down. Destructive entitlements may occur within a family, for example, when parents exploit a child's loyalty by expecting the child to be available as a mature adult—parentification—or by hampering or preventing the child's growth—infantilization (Ducommun-Nagy, 1999).

To contextual therapists, the patterns of relating within a family that are passed on from generation to generation are keys to understanding individual as well as family functioning. *Trust* is the fundamental property of relationships, and it can be depleted or restored depending on the capacity of family members to act upon a sense of loyalty and indebtedness in their give-and-take with one another. Instead of focusing on symptomatic behavior or family pathology, the contextual therapist attends to relational resources as leverages for change; relationships are viewed as trustworthy to the extent that they permit dialogue among family members regarding issues of valid claims and mutual obligations.

---

[5]In some cases, "destructive entitlements" exist. As Ulrich (1998) notes, the hurt or deprived child may attempt to wrest from innocent parties what he or she failed to receive from parents, or perhaps to punish innocent parties for his or her own wounds. While such claims may be legitimate, clearly the chosen targets are not.

Leading Figures

Ivan Boszormenyi-Nagy, a psychiatrist with psychoanalytic training who emigrated to the United States from Hungary in 1948, founded the Eastern Pennsylvania Psychiatric Institute (EPPI) in Philadelphia in 1957 as a research center for studying schizophrenia. (James Framo, along with Geraldine Spark, Gerald Zuk, and David Rubenstein, were early associates at this state-sponsored training and research institute.) After a long series of unsuccessful attempts to find biochemical clues to explain the etiology of the disorder, Boszormenyi-Nagy and his colleagues began to focus on the behavioral and psychological aspects of schizophrenia, ultimately turning to transgenerational issues within the family. When the EPPI closed in 1980 due to the loss of state funding, the researchers continued to refine contextual theories at nearby Hahnemann University Medical School.

Boszormenyi-Nagy joined initially with Spark, a psychiatric social worker with an extensive psychoanalytic background and experience in child guidance centers.

Together the pair (Boszormenyi-Nagy & Spark, 1973) advanced a theory based upon **invisible loyalty** within a family, in which children unconsciously take on responsibilities to aid their parents, often to their own detriment (e.g., become a failure to confirm parental forecasts).

In addition, Boszormenyi-Nagy and Spark proposed a set of therapeutic techniques that pertained to uncovering and resolving family "obligations" and "debts" incurred over time. The researchers introduced such new (non-psychoanalytic) terms as family *legacy* (expectations handed down from previous generations concerning what is expected, say, of men and women) and family *loyalty* (allegiances in children based on parental fairness) in order to emphasize that family members inevitably acquire a set of expectations and responsibilities toward each other.

Fair and equitable parental behavior engenders loyalty in the children; unfair demands or an exaggerated sense of obligation may produce invisible loyalties in which the child unconsciously continues, endlessly, to pay off a debt to parents, frequently to his or her own disadvantage or self-harm as it takes priority over all other concerns.

Besides Boszormenyi-Nagy, leading exponents of this view include psychologist David Ulrich (1998) in Greenwich, Connecticut, as well as psychiatrist Catherine Ducommun-Nagy (1999), wife of the founder, at the Institute for Contextual Growth in Ambler, Pennsylvania.

Ivan Boszormenyi-Nagy, M.D.

© Wadsworth/Thomson Learning

Legacies, Debts, and Entitlements

Figuratively speaking, each person has a sense of unsettled accounts, how much he or she has invested in relationships within the family, and whether there has been a fair balance between what has been given and received. While this is hardly a strict bookkeeping system and seldom if ever perfectly balanced, confronting and redressing imbalances is viewed as essential if a family is to stay vital and avoid stagnation. Ulrich (1983) cites a temporary imbalance: A wife works at an unsatisfying job so her husband can finish law school—but with the expectation that what she has invested in the common fund will eventually be replaced, for their mutual enrichment.

Obligations may be rooted in past generations and need not be consciously recognized or acknowledged to influence the behavior of family members in the present. In a sense, every family maintains a *family ledger*—a multigenerational accounting system of what has been given and who, psychologically speaking, still owes what to whom.

Boszormenyi-Nagy and Krasner (1986) argue that traditional interventions, either individually or family focused, consistently ignore family balances due, either owed or deserved, especially intergenerational ones. Yet people, in or out of therapy, constantly raise such questions as: "What do I owe, and to whom?" "What do I deserve, and from whom?" "What relationships do I need and want?" "What relationships am I obliged to retain, whether or not I need or want them?"

Whenever injustices occur, there is the expectation of some later repayment or restitution. Problems in relationships develop when justice comes too slowly or in an amount too small to satisfy the other person. From this perspective, dysfunctional behavior in any individual cannot be fully understood without looking at the history of the problem, the family ledger, and examining unsettled or unredressed accounts. A symptom that develops might represent an accumulation of feelings of injustice that has grown too large.

The family legacy, then, dictates debts and entitlement. One son may be slated to be successful ("We expect you'll be good at anything you try"), another to become a failure ("We don't think you'll ever amount to much"). A son may be entitled to approval, the daughter only to shame. Because of such family imperatives, as Boszormenyi-Nagy and Ulrich (1981) point out, the children are ethically bound to accommodate their lives somehow to their legacies. Ulrich (1983) gives the following graphic example:

> A son whose familial legacy is one of mistrust among family members, angrily confronts his wife every time she spends any money without his prior approval. He is convinced, and he tries to convince her, that her untrustworthy, spendthrift behavior is going to bankrupt them. (p. 193)

In fact, the wife, who works full-time as well as tending to their child, may temporarily unbalance the week's budget, but her overall efforts contribute to the family's solvency. If her response to his anger is fear—a legacy she carries from her own family—she may hide her purchases. His discovery of such concealment reinforces his mistrust; his subsequent anger strengthens her fears. Together their legacies have had a corrosive effect on their marriage. In ledger terms, he is still making payments to his mother's injunction that a wife is not to be trusted. By "overpaying" his mother, he is robbing his wife. She, in turn, may be paying off similar debts. Contextual therapy would direct them to reassess all their relationships, pay off legitimate filial debts, and free themselves from oppressive obligations.

Therapeutic Goals

While the reduction of stress is an important goal in this, as in all therapies, the fundamental goal of contextual therapy is in the improvement in the family members' capacity for relatedness, rebalancing the give-and-take and emotional ledgers between family members. Thus, contextual therapists help families reopen the often conflicting claims of who owes what to whom; some of these claims may have lain dormant for generations. Once the claims are addressed, the therapist aids family members in taking reparative steps to regain a balance and restore fairness and trust in their relationships (Ulrich, 1998). Well-functioning families are characterized by their ability to negotiate imbalances and especially by their ability to maintain a sense of fairness and accountability in their interactions with one another.

Contextual therapists do not focus on pathology but rather attend to the family's relational resources (Ducommun-Nagy, 1999). That is, they help each family member explore the possibility of earning entitlements from others by appropriate giving to them. Advocates of this view insist that individual autonomy cannot be achieved without a genuine consideration of others. Clients are encouraged to consider the interests of others as ultimately benefiting both giver and receiver.

The Ethical Connection

The ethical dimension gives contextual therapy its uniqueness. Insisting that they are not moralizing or taking a judgmental position, practitioners of this approach contend that they offer a realistic strategy for preventing individual and relational imbalance and eventual breakdown. They argue that effective therapeutic intervention must be grounded in the therapist's conviction that trustworthiness is a necessary condition for reworking legacy assessments and allowing family members to feel they are entitled to more satisfying relationships. Practitioners of contextual therapy maintain that families cannot be fully understood without an explicit awareness of family loyalty—who is bound to whom, what is expected of all family members, how loyalty is expressed, what happens when loyalty accounts are uneven ("We were there for you when you were growing up and now we, your aging parents, are entitled to help from you").

Contextual therapy helps rebalance the obligations kept in the invisible family ledger. Once these imbalances are identified, efforts can be directed at settling old family accounts (for example, mothers and daughters "stuck" in lifelong conflict), "exonerating" alleged culprits, or transforming unproductive patterns of relating that may have existed throughout the family over many past generations. The major therapeutic thrust is to establish or restore trustworthiness and relational integrity in family relationships. Parental behavior may be reassessed (and forgiven) in light of its roots in the past.

In the example offered in Box 8.5, a therapist helps a family split by dissension and conflicting loyalties learn fairer and more ethically responsible ways of dealing with one another. In the process of overcoming a stagnating relationship with her mother, the woman gains a more trustworthy level of relating to her husband and daughter.

BOX 8.5   CASE STUDY

A CONTEXTUAL THERAPIST ELICITS A FAMILY'S RELATIONAL RESOURCES

Mr. and Mrs. Jones were seeking help for their marriage. The presenting problem had to do with Mrs. Jones's angry outbursts at her husband and mother. An intelligent and compulsively neat person, Mrs. Jones was resentful of the fact that her mother had humiliated and frustrated her. Their relationship, she claimed, was characterized by mistrust and manipulation. She handled her rage through long-distance calls to her parents that inevitably resulted in tortuous arguments with her mother; or else she ignored her parents for prolonged periods of time.

His wife's hostile outbursts rendered Mr. Jones helpless. A hardworking, meticulously responsible salesman, he was deeply discouraged and never knew what he would face when he came home from work. On some occasions, Mrs. Jones would try to ruin the garden equipment that he so highly prized. On other occasions, she would throw out his favorite books. On

(continued)

BOX 8.5 *(continued)*

the other hand, there were times when their marriage seemed to be all right. For example, they could function as a team whenever members of their extended family were in real need. During their brief respite, they could enjoy each other and reported that their sexual relations were good.

However, the couple was often at war over their only child. Sheila, age 12, was chronically caught between them and lived in constant jeopardy of being split in her loyalties to them. Mrs. Jones would greet her husband at the door with complaints about their daughter. He resented being cast into the unfair role of referee and retaliated by forming a subversive alliance with Sheila. In therapy sessions, the couple finally consented to hear each other out. Together the three family members began to work toward fairer ways of relating.

Mr. and Mrs. Jones and Sheila seemed comforted by the therapist's capacity to elicit the justifications of each of their sides (multi-directed partiality). Yet, Mrs. Jones was openly annoyed at any attempts to offer fair consideration to her mother. In the interim, things went better for the family. Until now Mrs. Jones had lacked the security to look for a job commensurate with her intelligence and ability. For a long time she had invested her energies in compulsive housekeeping. Suddenly she found a job that she liked.

Immediately, tensions eased as her world widened and opened up. Mr. Jones learned to distance himself from his wife when she regressed into outbursts of anger. And Mrs. Jones began to exchange letters with her mother and managed some pleasant visits with both of her parents.

On occasion, some of the vindictiveness previously channeled toward her parents was now transferred to the therapist. At one point, Mrs. Jones refused to accompany her husband to their therapy session, arguing that the therapist "didn't care" about her. Two weeks later, though, she left an emergency message with the answering service: Her mother had died suddenly, unexpectedly. Overcome by the intensity of her emotions, she expressed profound gratitude. What would have happened to her, she wondered, if the therapist had not enabled her to find a way to her mother? What if she had failed to repair their relationship before it was too late?

Source: Boszormenyi-Nagy & Krasner, 1986, pp. 45–46

SUMMARY

Family systems theory, developed primarily by Murray Bowen, has a transgenerational outlook and is based on a natural systems perspective in which human behavior is seen as the result of an evolutionary process and as one type of living system. The major theoretician in the family therapy field, Bowen conceptualized the family as an emotional relationship system and offered eight interlocking concepts to explain the emotional processes taking place in the nuclear and extended families over generations.

These include differentiation of self, triangles, the nuclear family emotional system, the family projection process, emotional cutoff, multigenerational transmission process, sibling position, and societal regression. Chronic anxiety is seen as an inevitable part of nature and as transmitted from previous generations as families attempt to balance togetherness and differentiation.

Family evaluation interviews stress objectivity and neutrality, as therapists make an effort to remain outside, and thus not become triangled into, the family's emotional network. Genograms offer helpful pictorial depictions of the family's relationship system over at least three generations. Therapeutically, Bowenians work with marital partners in a calm and carefully detriangulated way, attempting to resolve the fusion between them; their goals are to reduce anxiety and resolve symptoms, and ultimately to maximize each person's self-differentiation within the nuclear family system—and from the family of origin. Coaching individual family members to redefine themselves and detriangulate from parents is a prominent part of contemporary practice.

Contextual family therapy, developed primarily by Ivan Boszormenyi-Nagy, focuses on relational ethics and transgenerational legacies, exploring how influences from the past have a bearing on present-day functioning in all members. In this view, families have invisible loyalties—obligations rooted in past generations—and unsettled accounts that must be balanced. Contextual therapy attempts to rebuild responsible, trustworthy behavior, taking into account the entitlements of all concerned. Its goal is to help dysfunctional families rebalance the give-and-take and emotional ledgers between members and develop a sense of fairness, trust, and accountability in interactions with one another.

RECOMMENDED READINGS

Bowen, M. (1978). *Family therapy in clinical practice.* New York: Jason Aronson.

Guerin, P. J., Fogarty, T. F., Fay, L. E., & Kautto, J. G. (1996). *Working with relationship triangles: The one-two-three of psychotherapy.* NewYork: Guilford Press.

Kerr, M. E., & Bowen, M. (1988). *Family evaluation: An approach based on Bowen theory.* NewYork: Norton.

Toward a differentiation of self in one's family. In J. L. Framo (Ed.), *Family interaction: A dialogue between family researchers and family therapists.* NewYork: Springer.

EXPERIENTIAL MODELS

Experience, encounter, confrontation, intuition, process, growth, existence, spontaneity, action, the here-and-now moment—this is the vocabulary used by those family therapists who, in general, minimize theory (and especially theorizing) as a therapeutic hindrance, an artificial academic effort to make the unknowable knowable. They argue that change resides in a *nonrational therapeutic experience,* one that establishes the conditions for personal growth and unblocks family interaction, rather than merely offering intellectual reflection or insight into the origins of problems. It is the immediacy of the relationship between the family and an involved therapist and the process in which they engage together that catalyzes the growth of individual family members as well as the family system as a whole.

Experiential family therapy is an outgrowth of the **phenomenological** techniques (Gestalt therapy, psychodrama, Rogerian client-centered therapy, the encounter group movement), so popular in the individual therapy approaches of the freewheeling 1960s, applied to family problems. Expanding experiences, unblocking suppressed impulses and feelings, developing greater sensitivity, gaining greater access to one's self, learning to recognize and express emotions, achieving intimacy with a partner—these are some of the **humanistic** goals for champions of this viewpoint. Early advocates aimed at nothing less than personal fulfillment, in contrast to what they perceived to be the then-prominent (psychoanalytic) goal of resolving childhood-formed neuroses. Less systemic in their thinking than were most other first-generation family therapists, and definitely out of step with the more currently popular cognitively based and social constructionist approaches such as solution-focused therapy and narrative therapy, the experiential family therapists focus attention on current ("in the moment") emotionality. That view suffered a serious setback (although hardly a deathblow) with the passing in the last decade or so of two of its illustrious leaders, Carl Whitaker and Virginia Satir.

Today, despite having fewer advocates than in its 1960s halcyon days, a new experiential wave is represented by, among others, Susan Johnson and Leslie Greenberg, whose **emotionally focused couple therapy (EFCT)** emphasizes emotional engagement between partners, identifying the feelings that define the quality of their relationship, and helping them create secure attachment bonds. This approach is more accepting of the place of theory than was its experiential forebears, while continuing to emphasize client awareness of inner experiences over intellectual understanding. In a research endeavor particularly conspicuous because of its rarity among experiential therapists, they (Johnson, 2003; Johnson, Hunsley, Greenberg, & Schindler, 1999; Greenberg, 2002) have spelled out replicable procedures and developed outcome studies to measure the effectiveness of their therapeutic undertakings.

A SHARED PHILOSOPHICAL COMMITMENT

Rather than endorsing a single technique, experiential interventions are, by definition, uniquely fitted to the individual client or family by a personally involved therapist. Each of the approaches we will consider in this chapter engages families in different ways, although they share certain philosophical tenets. All emphasize choice, free will, and especially the human capacity for self-determination and self-fulfillment, thus accentuating the client's goals over any outcomes predetermined by the therapist. Disordered or dysfunctional behavior is viewed, especially by the early experientialists, as the result of a failure in the growth process, a deficiency in actualizing one's capabilities and possibilities. Because each person (and by extension, each family) is unique, each must be helped to become aware of and reach his or her (or its) potential, discovering in the process the solutions to current problems.

Psychotherapy, then, with individuals or with families, must be an interpersonal encounter in which therapist and client(s) strive to be real and authentic. Acquiring sensitivity, gaining access to feelings and their expression, and learning to be more spontaneous and creative (by engaging in nonrational experiencing) are typical avenues clients take for arriving at their goals. If the therapeutic intervention succeeds, the results should facilitate growth for all participants, clients and therapists alike.

The primacy of emotional experience over rational thought and especially intellectualization is underscored in each of the approaches we are about to discuss. Human growth potential and the importance of the therapeutic alliance are stressed. Consequently, therapists in each approach are active, often self-disclosing, and likely to make use of a variety of evocative procedures to help clients get closer to their feelings, sensations, fantasies, and inner experiences. Sensitivity to one's here-and-now, ongoing life experiences is encouraged throughout therapy; denying impulses and suppressing affect is viewed as dysfunctional and growth-retarding. In the case of emotionally focused approaches to couples, empathic attunement and responsivity to one's partner is stressed so that each person feels understood. Helping partners overcome constricted emotional expressions that prevent empathic responses becomes a key underlying skill to be mastered by both participants.

Experiential family therapists strive to behave as real, authentic people (rather than acting as blank screens or wearing therapeutic masks or maintaining therapeutic neutrality). By having direct encounters with clients, they attempt to expand their own experiences, often having to deal with their own vulnerabilities in the process (which, when appropriate, they are likely to share with clients). Their therapeutic interventions attempt to be spontaneous, challenging, and, since personalized, often idiosyncratic, as they attempt to help clients gain self-awareness (of their thoughts, feelings, body messages), self-responsibility, and personal growth. The experiential family therapist takes on the task of enriching a family's experiences and enlarging the possibilities for each family member to realize his or her unique and extraordinary potential.

The Experiential Model

As noted, experiential family practitioners tailor their approach to the unique conflicts and behavior patterns of each family with whom they work. There are probably as many ways to provide an experience for accelerating growth as there are variations in family dysfunction. The work of some experiential therapists such as Carl Whitaker (1976) clearly reflects the psychodynamic orientation of their training,[1] though they are careful, as far as possible, not to impose any preconceived theoretical suppositions or techniques upon families. Others, such as Kempler (1981), show evidence of their training in Gestalt therapy. Virginia Satir, a warm, intuitive, highly empathic therapist, was an early member of the Mental Research Institute in Palo Alto, who utilized her humanistic outlook to draw out the positive growth potential in each family member with whom she worked.

David Kantor, along with Fred Duhl and Bunny Duhl, represent other early influential experiential family therapists. All three co-founded the Boston Family Institute in 1969, and together (Duhl, Kantor, & Duhl, 1973) were instrumental in developing some useful expressive techniques, such as **family sculpting,** a nonverbal communication method whereby a family member can physically place other members in a spatial relationship with one another, symbolizing, among other things, his or her perception of the family members' differences in power or degrees of intimacy with one another.

Experiential therapists deal with the present rather than uncovering the past. Their emphasis is on the here and now, the situation as it unfolds from moment to moment between an active and caring therapist and a family. The interactions among family members and with the therapist are confronted in an effort to help everyone involved in the encounter develop more growth-enhancing behavior. Rather than offer insight or interpretation, as psychoanalysts espouse, the therapist provides an emotionally charged experience—an opportunity for family members to open themselves to spontaneity, freedom of expression, and personal growth. The interpersonal experience rather than the reliance on technique is, in itself, the primary stimulus to growth in this here-and-now approach to psychotherapy.

Symbolic-Experiential Family Therapy (Whitaker)

Symbolic-experiential family therapy (S-EFT), pioneered by Carl Whitaker, is a multigenerational approach that addresses both individual and family relational patterns in the process of therapy. Oriented toward personal growth (rather than stability) and family connectedness, the therapist assumes a pivotal role in helping family members dislodge rigid and repetitive ways of interacting by substituting more spontaneous and flexible ways of accepting and dealing with their impulses. Several generations of a family are typically included in the therapeutic process, since practitioners of S-EFT consider the influence of extended families, past and present, to be omnipresent in

---

[1]Whitaker's early training in child psychiatry and his original orientation with individual patients was influenced by the work of Otto Rank, an early associate of Freud's who emphasized allying himself with the patient's search for growth and providing a"here and now"therapeutic learning experience. British object relations theorist Melanie Klein's insistence that psychopathology represents the patient's efforts toward self-healing was another important early influence on Whitaker's conceptualizations (Neill & Kniskern, 1982).

BOX 9.1 CLINICAL NOTE

Symbolic-Experiential's Distinguishing Features

- A pragmatic, nontheoretical approach to psychotherapy
- A steadfast effort to depathologize human experience
- The replacement of preplanned therapeutic technique with the therapist's spontaneous creativity
- An emphasis on emotional experience and affectively engaging families

- A commitment to client self-access, self-fulfillment, expanded experiences, and family cohesiveness
- The use of self by the therapist (drawing upon images, fantasies, and personal metaphors from one's own life)
- The use of symbolic, nonverbal methods or play
- The use of co-therapy

the family's unverbalized *symbolic* experiences. Why symbolic? Keith and Whitaker (1982) explain it this way:

> We presume it is experience, not education that changes families. The main function of the cerebral cortex is inhibition. Thus, most of our experience goes on outside of our consciousness. We gain best access to it symbolically. For us "symbolic" implies that some thing or some process has more than one meaning. While education can be immensely helpful, the covert process of the family is the one that contains the most power for potential changing. (p. 43)

To understand how symbolic-experiential family therapy evolved, beginning in the 1940s, we must first trace the career of Carl Whitaker, an unconventional, colorful, and iconoclastic psychiatrist who, right up until his death in 1995, was the epitome of an experiential family therapist. He first made his national influence felt with his innovative (often radical) work in individual psychotherapy, especially his trailblazing efforts to redefine a schizophrenic's symptoms as signs that an individual was "stuck" in the process of growth (rather than suffering from a deteriorative condition) and was attempting to apply "creative" solutions to vexing interpersonal problems. Coauthor of a landmark book, *The Roots of Psychotherapy* (Whitaker & Malone, 1953), Whitaker was an early champion of becoming an active therapist, pushing for growth and integration (maturity) in his patients and not simply offering insight or understanding to facilitate their "adjustment" to society. In this publication, Whitaker and psychologist Malone broke ranks with the then-prevalent orthodox psychoanalytic position by advocating an epistemological shift away from the search for internal conflict to experientially dealing with the patient's interactional dysfunction (Roberto, 1991).

In his work with schizophrenics Whitaker took the audacious position, never before espoused, that each participant in therapy is to some degree simultaneously patient and therapist to the other. Both invest emotion in the process, both are vulnerable, both regress, both grow as individuals as a result of the experience. Both expose themselves to the risks of change. Each takes responsibility for his or her own maturing process, but not for one another. The therapist must be committed to his or her own growth, personally as well as professionally, if he or she is to catalyze growth in others.

The Use of Co-therapy with Schizophrenics

Raised in relative rural isolation on a dairy farm in upstate New York, and perhaps less bound by customary social convention than most people, Whitaker early on pursued an unorthodox career path. Trained originally as an obstetrician/gynecologist in the early 1940s, Whitaker found himself interested in the psychological aspects of that field. In an unconventional move, he spent his final year of training at a psychiatric hospital, working largely with schizophrenic patients. He received further training at the Louisville Child Guidance Clinic and at the nearby Ormsby Village, a live-in treatment center for delinquent adolescents. There he learned to develop here-and-now techniques for reaching patients ordinarily resistant to more customary forms of psychiatric intervention (Neill & Kniskern, 1982).

As the United States entered World War II in 1941, Whitaker, a civilian, was called upon to treat patients in Tennessee at Oak Ridge Hospital, a closed community located where the secret U.S. atomic bomb was being assembled. Perhaps because of the heavy workload (Whitaker is said to have treated 12 patients per day in half-hour, back-to-back sessions), or perhaps because he believed he lacked sufficient experience with adult patients, or perhaps because he wished to share his intense personal involvement in the therapeutic process, Whitaker began working with colleagues such as John Warkentin as part of a **co-therapy** team. In any event, following the war, he was asked to establish and chair the psychiatry department at the medical school at Emory University in Atlanta, Georgia. There, together with associates such as Warkentin (who possessed a doctorate in psychophysiology but with additional training as a child therapist) and later Thomas Malone (trained in psychoanalytic work with adults), Whitaker continued his earlier unconventional co-therapy treatment of schizophrenics. The technique allowed one therapist to serve as an observer while the other engaged the client more directly.

As Whitaker pursued his unorthodox approach to treating schizophrenics, he became increasingly aware of the key role played by the family in the etiology of the disorder. As he later put it, he became intrigued with the idea that "there is no such thing as a person, that a person is merely the fragment of a family" and, in typical Whitaker provocative style, that "marriage is not really a combination of two persons; rather it is the product of two families who send out a scapegoat to reproduce themselves" (Whitaker & Ryan, 1989, p. 116).

Broadening his earlier perspective, Whitaker began to conceptualize schizophrenia as both an intrapsychic and interpersonal dilemma and to treat his schizophrenic patients along with their families. The multiple-therapist team—an extension of Whitaker's earlier reliance on co-therapy—was an innovation that helped to prevent a single therapist from becoming entangled in what Whitaker found to be a powerful, enmeshing family system.

Two or more therapists working together afforded this protection and at the same time provided a model for desirable interpersonal behavior for the entire family (for example, disagreeing in front of the family, but in a constructive manner).

The Symbolic Aspects of Family Therapy

By the mid-1960s Whitaker had resigned from Emory University, where he had been under political pressure because of his unorthodox administrative and educational procedures. Joined by colleagues Warkentin, Malone, and Richard Felder (a psychiatrist),

Whitaker formed the Atlanta Psychiatric Clinic, a private practice group, to pursue working with individuals, including chronic schizophrenics, and their families. In 1965, now defining himself as a family therapist, Whitaker moved to the University of Wisconsin School of Medicine in Madison and began—first with August Napier, a psychologist now in practice in Atlanta, and later with David Keith, a child psychiatrist now in Syracuse—to elaborate his ideas about affectively engaging a variety of families, not simply those with psychotic members (Napier & Whitaker, 1978; Keith & Whitaker, 1982). Moreover, Whitaker was starting to pay closer attention to what he personally was experiencing in the treatment process; he saw the potential for using that awareness to press for changes in his patients at the same time that he himself continued to benefit by investing in the therapeutic encounter.

Symbolic-experiential family therapists insist that both real and symbolic curative factors operate in therapy. They liken the symbolic aspect of therapy to the infrastructure of a city; while not apparent on the surface, what runs underneath the streets and buildings is what permits life on the surface to go on (Whitaker & Bumberry, 1988). Reflecting a psychodynamic influence, these therapists believe our personal subterranean worlds are dominated by the flow of impulses and evolving symbols, even if not always conscious; indeed, they believe it is these "emotional infrastructures" that ensure the flow of our impulse life. Since they contend that the meaning we give to external reality is determined by this internal reality, it follows that helping expand the symbolic inner worlds of families can aid in their leading fuller, richer lives.

The Therapist's Use of Self

Symbolic-experiential family therapists attempt to understand a family's complex world of impulses and symbols by looking for and giving voice to similar underlying impulses and symbols within themselves. Not willing to settle for material from the surface world of thinking and reasoning, they probe into the covert world beneath the surface words, trying to sense the far more important symbolic meanings of what transpires between themselves and the client family. By showing ease with accepting and voicing their own impulses and fantasies, they help family members become more comfortable in recognizing, expressing, and accepting theirs. The growth and development of individual members, according to S-EFT, is stimulated when members feel themselves to be a part of an integrated family. Once they experience this sense of security and belongingness, they can later feel free ("unstuck") enough to psychologically separate from the family and develop autonomy as unique individuals.

Normalizing Human Behavior

Throughout therapy, advocates of S-EFT listen, observe, stay in immediate touch with what they are experiencing, and actively intervene to repair damage, without being concerned over *why* the breakdown occurred. They make an effort to depathologize human experience, as suggested earlier by Whitaker's view of schizophrenia. Dysfunction is viewed in both its structural and process aspects.

Structurally, perhaps disorganized or impermeable family boundaries have resulted in nonfunctional subsystem operations, destructive coalitions, role rigidity, and separation between generations. Process difficulties may have led to a breakdown in negotiation between family members to resolve conflict, perhaps to the

Carl Whitaker, M.D.

© Wadsworth/Thomson Learning

loss of intimacy or attachment or trust, as individual relationship needs remain unmet. In general, these therapists assume that symptoms develop when dysfunctional structures and processes persist over a period of time and interfere with the family's ability to carry out its life tasks (Roberto, 1991).

In these therapists' view, "psychopathology" arises from the same mechanisms that produce "normal" behavior. Consequently, following Whitaker's lead, they are not afraid to encourage "craziness" (unconventional, childlike, socially unacceptable behavior) in family members or, for that matter, in themselves, believing that new outlooks and creative solutions typically follow as the family is freed to stretch and grow. Through his sometimes quirky and irrepressible "right brain" style, Whitaker was often able to help sensitize the family to its own unconscious or symbolic life.

For practitioners of S-EFT, the focus of therapy is the process— what occurs during the family session—and how each participant (therapist included) experiences feelings, exposes vulnerabilities, and shares uncensored thoughts. Whenever an individual or family system seeks to grow, the therapist (or co-therapists) can take advantage of this inherent drive toward fulfillment and maturity to engage that person or group in an existential encounter free from the usual social restraints and the role playing that customarily characterize doctor-patient or therapist-client relationships. The encounter is intended to shake up old ways of feeling and behaving and thus to provide an unsettling experience to reactivate the seemingly dormant but innate process of growth.

Establishing Therapeutic Goals

The family therapist's mission, as S-EFT sees it, is to help the three-generational family (family-of-origin members as well as adults and children in the current family) to simultaneously maintain a sense of togetherness along with a sense of healthy separation and autonomy. Family roles, while largely determined by generation, should remain flexible, and members should be encouraged to explore, and on occasion even exchange, family roles. Healthy families, according to Whitaker and Keith (1981), develop an "as if" structure that permits latitude in role playing, often allowing each family member to try on new roles and gain new perspectives:

> For example, the 6-year-old son says to daddy, "Can I serve the meat tonight?" and daddy says, "Sure, you sit over on this chair and serve the meat and potatoes and I'll sit over in your place and complain." (p. 190)

For practitioners of S-EFT, this exchange is an opportunity to develop a healthy, straight-talking communication, in which all family members are able to look at themselves and grow both as individuals and as a family. Consistent with this experiential perspective, Whitaker viewed family health as an ongoing process of *becoming*, in which each member is encouraged to explore a full range of family roles in order to develop maximum autonomy. Growth as a goal takes precedence over achieving stability or specific planned solutions, and symbolic-experiential therapists may terminate therapy still leaving the family uncertain about future direction, but with better tools for finding their own way.

The Therapeutic Process

Symbolic-experiential family therapy sets itself the goal of encouraging individuation and personal integrity of all family members at the same time that it helps the family members evolve a greater sense of family belonging. Rather than attend to symptoms in an identified patient, here the family therapist immediately engages the entire family, forcing it as a group to examine the basis of their existence as a family unit.

In Whitaker's colorful description of the therapeutic process, "the journey of family therapy begins with a blind date and ends with an empty nest" (Whitaker & Bumberry, 1988, p. 53). In its initial stages, the therapist must deal with the inevitable *battle for structure,* as the family sizes up the therapist and his or her intentions and attempts to impose its own definition of the upcoming relationship: what's wrong with the family, who's to blame, who requires treatment, how the therapist should proceed. In S-EFT, therapists insist on controlling the ensuing structure, from the first telephone contact onward, so therapy can begin on a productive note and the therapist does not compromise his or her own needs, beliefs, or standards. If the therapist loses this initial struggle, the family will then bring into therapy the identical behavioral patterns that are likely creating their current problems in the first place.

In the process, the therapist is establishing an "I" position with the family, stimulating them, ultimately, to piece together an identifiable "we" position as a family. For example, by insisting on his own autonomy, Whitaker was telling the family that he is interested in his own growth as a result of their experience together, and that they need not be concerned about protecting him. Real caring, for Whitaker, requires distance, partially achieved by caring for himself and not only for his client family. Whitaker and Bumberry (1988) emphasize dealing with the family on a symbolic level in a "metaposition"—establishing what each can expect from the other. Whitaker, who frequently used sports analogies, saw himself as a coach. He was not interested in playing on the team, only in helping it play more effectively. By stepping in to play first base, he argued, he would be indicating he did not think much of the first baseman they already have, a destructive message. Instead, as coach, he encouraged them to develop their own resources. The therapist, who starts out in an all-powerful position, eventually becomes a facilitator and resource person as the family increasingly takes the initiative for how it wishes to change (Keith, 2000).

If the therapist must win the battle for structure, the family must be victorious in the *battle for initiative* (Napier & Whitaker, 1978). Just as the battle for structure defines the integrity of the therapist, so the battle for initiative defines the integrity of the family. It is they who are in charge of their lives and responsible for decisions about the direction they wish, as a group, for their lives to go. That is, any initiative for change must not only come from the family but also be actively supported by its members. These therapists shun responsibility for changing a family, and especially for seeking family leadership.

Practitioners of S-EFT insist the family convene as a group with all members present, underscoring their sense of a family unit as well as acknowledging that the family itself is the client. Together they are encouraged to probe their relationships—in Whitaker's words, "to ante up"—despite efforts to identify specific members as the problem. Rather than comfort or reassure, the therapist is apt to be outspoken and take risks, shaking up entrenched family patterns. Keith (1998) suggests an initial goal of increasing family anxiety ("It's really much worse than you think") in order to force family members to take more responsibility for the living pattern they have created.

BOX 9.2   THERAPEUTIC ENCOUNTER

Whitaker Destabilizes a Family System

In the following case offered by Whitaker, a mother, father, and six-year-old girl attend the first session. The daughter is described as school-phobic, the mother obese, the father a hard-driving executive. Mother and father deny relationship struggles, despite his working nearly 75 hours a week and frequently staying out late.

CARL: You mean he's totally lost interest in you?

MOM: Well, no, it's not that. It's just that his way of contributing to the family is to make sure that we have everything we need.

CARL: Except a husband and father.

MOM: No. He's a good father.

CARL: (turning to the daughter) Sarah, do you think that Mommy worries that Daddy might be kissing the secretary? You know, he's gone at work so much. Maybe he gets lonely too.

SARAH: No. Daddies don't get lonely. Just Mommies, but since Mommy has me, she doesn't have to be lonely either.

CARL: Well, I'm sure glad you take such good care of your Mommy but I still worry about Daddies. It's very hard to tell when they're lonely.

Here Whitaker is beginning to get them to think about family relationships, without specifically suggesting that Sarah's dedication to Mom may be related to her refusal to go to school, or that she may be expressing through remaining at home her desire to help Mom hide from her depression. Later in the same session, Mom begins to complain about her inability to play tennis with her high-powered husband because of her weight.

CARL: (turning to Dad) Do you worry about her weight, too, or do you prefer playing with other partners?

DAD: Of course I'd love her to pick up the sport, but it's just not possible. It would be dangerous for her to exert herself with so much excess weight.

CARL: So you don't want to feel like you killed her by pushing tennis. I suppose I can understand that. How is it that you manage to live with the knowledge that she's slowly committing suicide via her obesity? (Whitaker & Bumberry, 1988, pp. 62–64)

Note how the therapist has started them thinking beyond the presenting symptoms of separate individuals, expanding the symptom framework to include possible extramarital affairs, self-destructive overeating, and a relationship gap between the parents.

Each member's participation in the lives of the other members is in the process of becoming clarified under Whitaker's provocative (and destabilizing) comments. While they may not yet make the necessary connections to stabilize at a higher functioning level, they leave the session with new ideas to consider, all within a relationship or interpersonal perspective. In future sessions, having set the therapeutic structure, the therapist must be careful to get the family to take responsibility for facing themselves, winning the battle for initiative, and through an experiential exchange with him, to come alive and cease playacting.

In Whitaker's view (1977), then, family therapy occurs in stages:

1. *A pretreatment or engagement phase* in which the entire nuclear family is expected to participate; the therapist or co-therapists establish that they are in charge during the sessions but that the family must make its own life decisions outside of these office visits (the latter is intended to convey the message that a therapist does not have better ideas for how family members should run their lives than they themselves do).

2. *A middle phase* in which increased involvement between both therapists and the family develops; care is taken by the therapist not to be absorbed by the family system; symptoms are seen and relabeled for the family as efforts toward growth; and

the family is incited to change by means of confrontation, exaggeration, anecdote, or absurdity.

3. *A late phase* in which increased flexibility in the family necessitates only minimal intervention from the therapist or therapy team.

4. *A separation phase* in which the therapists and family part, but with the acknowledgment of mutual interdependence and loss. In the final phase, the family uses more and more of its own resources, and assumes increased responsibility for its way of living. With separation—the "empty nest"—there is joy mingled with a sense of loss.[2]

Symbolic-experiential change-producing interventions have a covert, implicit quality. Symptoms are rarely attacked directly. Insight seems to follow rather than precede changes in feelings and behavior. History taking is occasionally important but not carried out routinely; in any case, it must not be allowed to impede this approach's major therapeutic thrust—forming a close and personal alliance with the family as a whole and providing an experience that is symbolic to the family but does not reinforce its distress (Keith & Whitaker, 1982). What the family therapist has most to offer, Whitaker believed, is his or her personal maturity; the stage of the therapist's personal development influences the kind of support or assistance he or she gives to the family. Whitaker maintained that the therapist who does not derive benefit, therapeutically, from his or her work has little to give, therapeutically speaking, to client families. The use of co-therapists adds another dimension; the ability of both therapists to join together, have fun together, disagree, or even quarrel with each other, and perhaps to go off on different tangents—one acting "crazy" and the other providing stability—is a model for spontaneous and productive interaction.

GESTALT FAMILY THERAPY (KEMPLER)

All of the family therapy approaches we are considering in this chapter are, to a greater or lesser extent, *existential* in character. More an orientation to understanding human behavior than a formal school of psychotherapy, existentially influenced therapies are concerned with entering and comprehending the world as it is being experienced by the individual family members as well as the family as a functioning whole. The therapies have in common an emphasis on the meaning the patient gives to existence, to *being*. Because people define themselves through their current choices and

---

[2]Napier and Whitaker (1978) provide an intriguing full account of family therapy with the Brice family (two parents; a suicidal, runaway teenager; an adolescent son; and a six-year-old daughter) in their book, *The Family Crucible.*

BOX 9.3   THERAPEUTIC ENCOUNTER

WHITAKER: THE PERSON OF THE THERAPIST

Throughout his work with individuals and families, Whitaker stressed his personal need to "stay alive" as a human being and as a therapist. He frequently asserted that "nothing worth knowing can be taught," insisting that the therapist must uncover his or her own belief system and symbolic world, and then use that self (rather than specific therapeutic techniques) to grow and help families do the same. Three decades ago he offered a loosely formulated set of rules for therapists that still seem applicable today (Whitaker, 1976, p. 164):

1. Relegate every significant other to second place.
2. Learn how to love. Flirt with any infant available. Unconditional positive regard probably isn't present after the baby is three years old.
3. Develop a reverence for your own impulses, and be suspicious of your behavior sequences.
4. Enjoy your mate more than your kids, and be childish with your mate.
5. Fracture role structures at will and repeatedly.
6. Learn to retreat and advance from every position that you take.
7. Guard your impotence as one of your most valuable weapons.
8. Build long-term relations so you can be free to hate safely.
9. Face the fact that you must grow until you die. Develop a sense of the benign absurdity

of life—yours and those around you—and thus learn to transcend the world of experience. If we can abandon our missionary zeal we have less chance of being eaten by cannibals.

10. Develop your primary process living. Evolve a joint craziness with someone you are safe with. Structure a professional cuddle group so you won't abuse your mate with the garbage left over from the day's work.
11. As Plato said, "practice dying."

In effect, these "rules" urge therapists to be sure to take care of their own needs in the process of caring for others. They need to open themselves up to others, allowing themselves to love without insisting on perfection in their love object. They need to trust their own wishes and desires but not necessarily how they play out in behavior. Their mate—more than children, parents, and so on—should represent their primary love object. Whitaker urged therapists to abandon rigid rules because they inhibit growth, and to try to remain flexible and available for new experiences without insisting on always knowing the right answer. Strong relationships, says Whitaker, are worth cultivating, and once developed can endure angry conflict. Let go; you can't fix everything!

Learn to play—both at home and at work—and live every day to its fullest measure!

---

decisions, action in the present, not reflection on the past, is the key to understanding for the existentialist. Even the future—what people choose to become—is charged with more influence than the past and the conflicts associated with the past. In existential therapies, clients are urged to examine and take responsibility for their lives. Unconscious material may be brought forth but is not automatically assumed to be any more meaningful than the conscious data of life.

Psychotherapy in this framework is an *encounter* between two or more persons who are constantly developing, evolving, and fulfilling their inner potential. Technique is de-emphasized to preclude one person seeing the other as an object to be analyzed. In contrast to the common therapeutic belief that understanding stems from technique, existentialist therapists believe that technique follows understanding. Formal and conventional doctor-patient roles are replaced by a more egalitarian and open arrangement in which each participant opens his or her world to the other as an existential partner. The emphasis is on presence; in a real, immediate, ongoing relationship between two or more persons, each tries to understand and experience as far as possible the being of the other(s).

If existentialism is concerned with how humans experience their immediate existence, Gestalt psychology focuses on how they perceive it. Having accepted the therapeutic implications of existentialism along with much of the rhetoric of Gestalt psychology, Frederick (Fritz) Perls is generally credited with launching the Gestalt therapy movement in the United States. For Perls (1969), who worked with individuals, change is facilitated when the client's thoughts and feelings become congruent. A major treatment goal, then, is for the client to achieve greater self-awareness in order to become more self-directed, more centered, more congruous. By removing blocks and especially entrenched, intellectualized thinking patterns, the client often was aided to break through to his or her emotionally rooted inner experiences. (Perls enjoyed putting it this way: Lose your mind and come to your senses.) Extrapolating from the individual focus, Gestalt family therapists focus attention on the immediate—"What people say, how they say it, what happens when it is said, how it corresponds with what they are doing, and what they are attempting to achieve" (Kempler, 1982, p. 141). Here the goal is to bring discordant elements (within oneself or between family members) into a self-disclosing confrontation and ultimate resolution.

Gestalt family therapy, popularized in the 1970s and 1980s, is likely to appear dated today, but we include it as a forerunner of contemporary therapeutic direction for the following reasons: (1) it encourages open and honest expression of all emotions (hopes, fears, wishes, anxieties), a forerunner of many of today's therapeutic approaches aimed at achieving authenticity and connection to others; (2) it emphasizes individual growth and the development of the Self, within family systems, again a contemporary view; and (3) it rests heavily on therapist modeling of desired behavior, on being a genuine person, on utilizing the therapist's personality to effect change, a part of many current collaborative procedures.

Leading Figure

The most prominent Gestalt family therapist is undoubtedly Walter Kempler, whose techniques stem from his adaptation of the individual work of Perls, with whom he studied. Kempler, a physician trained in Texas, practiced general medicine in Los Angeles for several years before returning for a psychiatric residency at the UCLA Neuropsychiatric Institute in the late 1950s. Several years later he established the Kempler Institute for the Development of the Family, first in Los Angeles and later in other areas of southern California. Kempler traveled extensively until his recent retirement, especially in the Scandinavian countries, lecturing and giving demonstrations of his prodding, confrontational interventions with family members. Antitheoretical, much like Whitaker, Kempler's therapeutic efforts are aimed at helping clients expand their awareness, take responsibility for their actions, and gain a sense of autonomy and authenticity. Again like Whitaker, Kempler contends that the family holds the key to the personal development of its members.

A Gestalt Family Therapy Credo

Kempler (1981) insists that an effective therapeutic encounter meet the following four demands:

1. A clear knowledge of "who I am" at any given moment. This requires a dynamic awareness of what I need from moment to moment.

2. A sensitive cognition or appraisal of the people I am with and the context of our encounter.
3. The development and utilization of my manipulating skills to extract, as effectively as I am capable, what I need from the encounter.
4. The capability of finishing an encounter. (p. 38)

The Therapeutic Encounter

Employing a personally interactive way of working with families, **Gestalt family therapy** represents an effort to blend some of the principles and procedures of family and Gestalt therapies in order to help people reach beyond their customary self-deceptive games, defenses, and facades. To do so, the therapist relies on the forthright expression of what he or she is experiencing, in order to assist clients to become aware of and release previously unrecognized or bottled-up feelings.

Kempler's (1981) therapeutic efforts are provocative, highly personal, uncompromisingly honest, and powerful. He presses for self-disclosure by family members, expecting that the wish or need to resolve their problems or improve relationships will give them the courage to expose their vulnerabilities. He actively and directly insists that everyone, himself included, become more intensely aware of what they are doing or saying or feeling. Like the mechanic who would rather listen to a troublesome engine than hear a description of it, Kempler first starts up a family conversation:

Transcript	Comments
Mother: Our 15-year-old son Jim has been making a lot of trouble for us lately.	The healthier the family, the more readily they talk to each other. For instance, should Jim respond immediately to his mother's charge with "That's not true!" it would indicate that he has both self-confidence and the hope of being heard. Let's assume Jim doesn't leap in.
Therapist (to Jim evocatively): Do you agree that the number one problem in this family is that you are a troublemaker?	
Jim: Not really.	
Therapist: Tell her what you think is.	
Jim: It's no use.	
Therapist (to Mother): Do you have anything to say to his hopelessness?	

Transcript	Comments
Mother: I think we've said all there is to say.	Family members are often reluctant to engage one another, particularly initially. The therapist perseveres by offering himself, if necessary.
Therapist (to Jim): I'd like to know what you think is the problem, Jim.	
Jim: They are too rigid.	The battlelines often have both parents on one side. It is better when it is a free-for-all.
Therapist: Both of them identical?	
Jim: Mother more than Father.	
Therapist: Then, maybe you can get some help from him.	
Jim: He's too weak. He always gives in to her.	
Therapist (to Father): Do you agree with him?	
Father: Of course not.	
Therapist: You didn't tell him.	

Source: Kempler, 1974, pp. 27–28

Kempler is interested in what each person wants and from whom, expressed in the most specific terms possible. Participants are forced to talk to each other, in face-to-face, encounter-group-like fashion. If a wife complains to Kempler that her husband lacks understanding or sensitivity, Kempler directs her to tell that to her husband, not the therapist, and to be specific in her complaint. If she argues that it will do no good, Kempler insists she tell *that* to her husband. If she then breaks down, admits her feelings of hopelessness, and begins to cry—all without provoking a response from her husband—Kempler will point out his silence and invite him to answer her. From the initial interview through the subsequent sessions, the focus remains the immediate present. Self-disclosure and open, honest exchanges with others are basic ground rules for family members to follow if they are to untangle a family problem or overcome an impasse.

Viewing the individual within his or her functional context—the family—Gestalt family therapists attempt to help each family member achieve maximum individuation at the same time that they promote more vital relationships among the various members. Thus, the traditional goals of the Gestalt therapist working with an individual client (growth of the individual and the development of a distinct sense of self) are combined with objectives for the family group as a whole. First helping family members to explore how their awareness is blocked, the therapist then channels the increased awareness so that they may engage in more productive and fulfilling processes with one another (Kaplan & Kaplan, 1978).

The Gestalt therapist facilitates self-exploration, risk taking, and spontaneity. Since such undertakings are all but impossible if an individual or family fears that self-discovery could be harmful, it is essential that the therapist provide an unchecked and unequivocal model for self-disclosure. To strike the familiar pose as a benevolent and accepting therapist only plays into the client's fantasies that disapproval is dangerous, according to Kempler (1982). By contrast, Kempler is emotionally intense, assertive, genuine, challenging, sometimes brutally (if refreshingly) frank; in short, he expresses whatever he is feeling at the moment in the hope of making an impact on the family.

As the following excerpt from a couple's therapy session begins, Kempler has just completed a moving exchange with the wife, during which the husband remained silent. Kempler now turns to the husband because he wants his participation.

Transcript	Comments
Therapist: Where are you?	
He: I don't know, (pause) I was thinking of something else. (pause) I don't understand what is going on. I guess that's it (pause) partly thinking what I had to do today.	He was always inarticulate, always speaking haltingly and tentatively. His eyes blinked nervously as if he were being buffeted. I had mentioned this before. On past occasions I had confronted him with his inarticulateness and his blinking, but we had made no progress with it. It seemed that I had tried everything I knew to no avail.
Therapist: Damn, that makes me angry. You're a clod. That's the word I want to buffet you with. Damn you. So insensitive. No wonder you've got problems in your marriage. (Then, cooling down enough to make an "I" statement instead of the "you" accusations, I continued) I want you to hear; I want you to join in; I want you to at least acknowledge our presence some way other than leaving. At best, I'd want you to appreciate us in what happened, at worst, to tell us you don't like us for being inane, but not just to abandon us.	
He: (Thoughtful) Earlier I was aware of something like envy (pause) resentment (pause) I don't know.	
Therapist: (Still angry) You never know. That's your standard answer. Now I don't know. I don't know what the hell to do with you to get in touch with you.	
He: I'm sorry. (pause) I always say I'm sorry. I guess I'm sorry. I was envious. (pause) I felt angry 'cause I was envious.	He was trying to be with me now, and I wanted to try harder myself. I decided to try clarifying and/or intensifying his statement.
Therapist: Try on: "I long to be close to both of you, but I never learned how."	I felt my own sadness when I said that and knew I was on target—or else I would not have been so angry with him. His tears were confirmation as he choked up trying to say the sentence.
Therapist: You don't have to, but I wish you could talk to us now.	
He: I can't. It's too sad.	
Therapist: It?	
He: The sentence . . .	

Transcript	Comments
Therapist: Then try to include all the words "I'm so sad when I think of how I long to be close and can't because I never learned."	I kept wanting to return to this key phrase and yet I did not want my urging to become more central for him than his experiencing his longing. He sat thoughtfully, still tearing and saying nothing. Several minutes passed.
Therapist: I'm suddenly aware of my own difficulty in speaking about longing. I could debate with you more easily than I can speak of feeling the longing to be close. I realize I still haven't spoken to mine and can only hesitantly speak about yours.	I began to cry. He was now trying harder to look at me through his tears. I found myself smiling through my tears.
This feels better than debating or idly chatting but it sure is sad. I feel closer to you in our sadness.	"It," I thought. How clever. He nodded, still unable to speak.
He: (Finally) I can do it with my car—feeling close by racing people. . . . I'm so safe that way. I can't just be close.	
Therapist: (I seemed finished with me for the moment and was free to turn once again to him. I offered the sentence again—modified.) "I long to be close but never learned how, but now I'm learning finally."	

He began to cry more heavily as he nodded his head and turned inward again, looking down. His wife reached out warmly. "This reminds me of the time that you . . ." I interrupted her, "Leave him alone now. You can talk to him later." She grasped, or at least readily accepted, my command. I wanted him to be wherever he was with his feelings, not diverted to some other time and place. Her comment sounded like an "aha" announcement and I felt no compunction to honor it. She could keep it to and for herself.

I left them and was visiting my father, fluttering through historical scenes like a hummingbird. His lovingly tousling my hair—the only times he ever touched me that I could recall. His angrily shouting at me. His intellectual lectures to teach me something. I became painfully aware of his absent touch and never being spoken to affectionately by him. He never told me he loved me or even that he liked me. I recalled the surprise I once felt when I overheard him admiring me to one of his friends. I am sad. Of course, I long.

I came back to our session and was aware of this couple once again. They were both looking at me. I shared my thoughts. Then he related clearly, articulately his own longings, recalling, smiling through his fresh tears, his father teaching him to drive, the only closeness he knew with his father. To intensify his experience, I suggested that he envision his father. He couldn't. He just cried. "Tell him," I suggested, "how you longed to be close to him but just didn't know how because you never learned." After a long pause, he replied: "I used to feel angry and frustrated. I realize now he never learned either."

He was integrating and I was pleased. I became vacant, and we all sat silently, alone and close. (Kempler, 1981, pp. 11–13)

Kempler's demand for a complete and honest emotional encounter with and between family members reflects his Gestalt heritage. Although far less popular today than in the heyday of encounter groups and sensitivity training three decades ago, this technique offers a useful counterweight to the currently fashionable concerns with cognitive analyses and behavior change.[3] No holds are barred, no feelings stifled. As noted earlier, the therapist is a real flesh-and-blood person who knows who he is, what his needs are, and what he is experiencing from moment to moment during the shared therapeutic encounter with the family. At the same time, he expects—nay, insists—that all participants search for, uncover, and express what they are experiencing *now*, since to Gestaltists, *nothing exists except in the now*. He urges clients to stay with the experience as it is happening, and until they recognize and "own" what they are feeling from moment to moment. All efforts to avoid this awareness are counteracted by Kempler as soon as they occur; it is in the now, say Gestaltists, that people are or are not growing, are or are not enhancing their coping abilities, are or are not in touch with themselves and with reality.

THE HUMAN VALIDATION PROCESS MODEL (SATIR)

The human validation process model, experiential in nature, emphasizes the collaborative efforts of therapist and family members to achieve family "wellness" by releasing the potential viewed as inherent in every family (Satir & Bitter, 2000). Clear, congruent communication is stressed in maintaining a balanced and nurturing family system, and the building of self-esteem is considered essential if all members are to thrive as individuals and as part of a functional system. Especially important to this model—as is the case for all experiential approaches—is the personal involvement of a caring therapist who demonstrates, often through self-disclosure, his or her own honest and spontaneous feelings. More specifically, the therapist, as a resource person, encourages family members to develop a process for directly expressing emotions, in many cases learning to change embedded rules that discourage or in some cases prohibit dealing with one another at a feeling level.

Leading Figure

Virginia Satir's central place in the history of the family therapy movement has been noted several times earlier in this book. In the 1950s, among the founding parents of the family therapy movement, Satir was in the unique position of being both a woman and a social worker among predominantly white male psychiatrists. Actually, she probably preceded most of her male counterparts in working with families, reportedly having seen her first family in therapy in 1951 and having offered the first training program ever in family therapy in 1955 at the Illinois State Psychiatric Institute (Satir, 1982). It was several years later that she read of a group engaging in family research efforts in Palo Alto, California (Bateson, Jackson, Haley, & Weakland, 1956); having contacted them, she was invited by Jackson to help him start what became the Mental Research Institute (MRI). More interested in training than in research, Satir soon set about demonstrating her techniques with families, culminating in the first published description of conjoint family therapy (Satir, 1964), truly a groundbreaking text for therapists and students alike.

---

[3]Kempler and Whitaker both seek open, honest, uncensored expression. Whitaker's assertions reflect his efforts to be in tune with his unconscious impulses, while Kempler's statements reflect his insistence that he and the clients stay in the moment. For Kempler, "staying in the moment" helps strip away the defense of escaping into talking about the past, changing the subject, or perhaps asking questions of others instead of expressing one's own thoughts and beliefs.

Over a 30-year span, until her death in 1988, Satir continued to be a prolific writer. She is especially celebrated for her inspiring family therapy demonstrations (said to number between 400 and 500) around the world. Although linked to the communication approach because of her early MRI affiliation, Satir's work during the 1960s at Esalen, a growth center, encouraged her to add a humanistic framework and emphasize a number of growth-enhancing techniques (sensory awareness, dance, massage, group encounter techniques) to evoke feelings and clarify family communication patterns. In her later writing, Satir (1986) identified her approach as a Human Validation Process Model in which the therapist and family join forces to stimulate an inherent health-promoting process in the family. Open communication and emotional experiencing were the mechanisms that helped achieve that end, as family members, following the therapist's lead, learned to take the risk of expressing feelings openly, congruently, and without defensiveness.

Virginia Satir was a charismatic leader, truly an original; no discussion of experiential family therapy would be complete without paying homage to her vision. She presented herself to families (often in demonstrations and without prior contact with the family) as a dynamic, nurturing, folksy, genuine person, someone with belief in the goodness of people and in the "healing power of love" (Satir & Baldwin, 1983). While the latter made her appear simplistic and Pollyannaish to critics, she nevertheless was revered by followers and profoundly touched those families with whom she worked. The "love" she practiced with clients and that she postulated as a necessary condition for actualizing one's capabilities was based on her assumptions about what best facilitates change.

Satir assumed people want to be whole, authentic, sensitive, and genuine with one another. Thus, she looked for and found in people signs of their healthy *intentions*, even when these were embedded in unhealthy behavior (Lawrence, 1999). Symptomatic behavior, for Satir, was "adaptive attempts gone awry" rather than fixed characteristics of the person (Waters & Lawrence, 1993). Summaries of her underlying philosophical assumptions and therapeutic techniques can be found in Woods and Martin (1984), Brothers (1991), Andreas (1991), Satir, Banmen, Gerber, and Gomori (1991), and Satir and Bitter (2000).

Symptoms and Family Balance

Satir concerned herself with the family as a balanced system. In particular, she wanted to determine the "price" each part of the system "pays" to keep the overall unit balanced. That is, she viewed any symptom in an individual member as signaling a blockage in growth, and as having a homeostatic connection to a family system that to keep its balance requires blockage and distortion of growth in some form in all of its members.

A presenting symptom in a family member gave Satir (1982) the initial clues for "unraveling the net of distorted, ignored, denied, projected, unnourished, and untapped parts of each person so that they can connect with their ability to cope functionally, healthily, and joyously" (p. 41).

Individual Growth and Development

Satir believed that all humans strive toward growth and development, and that each of us possesses all the resources we need for fulfilling

© Wadsworth/Thomson Learning

Virginia Satir, M.S.W.

BOX 9.5 CLINICAL NOTE

Satir's Eight Aspects of the Self

Satir (1986) contended that the self—the core of every person—consists of eight separate but interacting elements or levels, which together exert a constant influence on a person's well-being. Satir searched for the varying degrees of strength in each of these parts of the person. In tapping an individual's nourishing potentials, she attempted to work at one or more of the following levels:

Physical (the body)
Intellectual (thoughts, logic, processing of facts, left-brain activity)

Emotional (feelings, intuition, right-brain activity)
Sensual (sound, sight, touch, taste, smell)
Interactional (I-Thou communication between oneself and others)
Contextual (colors, sound, light, temperature, movement, space, time)
Nutritional (solids and fluids ingested to furnish energy)
Spiritual (one's relationship to life's meaning, the soul, life force)

our potential, if only we can gain access to these resources and learn to nourish them. More specifically, she pointed to three types of factors influencing human development: (a) unchangeable genetic endowment, determining our physical, emotional, and temperamental potential; (b) longitudinal influences, the result of learning acquired in the process of growth; and (c) the constant mind-body interaction.

Longitudinal influences—the sum of learning since birth—are especially significant. Here Satir emphasized the child's experiences of the *primary survival triad* (father, mother, child) as the essential source of self-identity. Adult self-worth or self-esteem evolves from the relative proportion of constructive to destructive interaction experiences arising from this triad. The child also learns to decipher parental messages; discrepancies between words, tone, touch, and looks help shape future adult communication patterns.

Another important factor in individual growth is the *mind, body, feeling triad.* Body parts may often take on metaphoric meaning; each part usually has a positive or negative value attached to it by its owner. Some are liked, others disliked, some need awakening. In what Satir called a therapeutic *parts party,* clients are encouraged to become aware of these parts and learn to use them "in an harmonious and integrated manner" (Satir & Baldwin, 1983, p. 258).

As noted, Satir believed all persons possess all the resources they need for positive growth, if she could help them harness their potential to nourish themselves. Building self-esteem, promoting self-worth, expanding awareness, exposing and correcting discrepancies in how the family communicates—these were the issues Satir tackled as she attempted to help each member of the family develop "wellness" and become as "whole" as possible. The extent to which they could identify and practice new possibilities determined their chances to integrate change into their family life. With success based upon family resiliency, family members would discover new solutions to their problems.

Family Roles and Communication Styles

Satir contended that the way the family communicates reflects the feelings of self-worth of its members. Dysfunctional communication (indirect, unclear, incomplete, unclarified, inaccurate, distorted, inappropriate) characterizes a dysfunctional family system. One of Satir's lasting contributions is her simple—but far from simplistic—classification of styles of communication, especially apparent in dealing with stress. She argued that under such stressful conditions, a person in a relationship with another person communicates in one of five ways (Satir, 1972). These styles are expressed through body position and body language as much as through verbal behavior. The *placater* acts weak, tentative, self-effacing; always agrees, apologizes, tries to please. The *blamer* dominates, invariably finds fault with others, and self-righteously accuses. The *super-reasonable* person adopts a rigid stance, remains detached, robot-like, calm, cool, maintaining intellectual control while making certain not to become emotionally involved. The *irrelevant* person distracts others and seems unable to relate to anything going on, afraid to offend or hurt others by taking a position on an issue. Only the *congruent communicator* seems real, genuinely expressive, responsible for sending straight (not double-binding or otherwise confusing) messages in their appropriate context.

Various combinations of these styles exist in most families. For example, take the case of a blaming wife, a blaming husband, and a placating child triad: "It's the school, they don't teach anything anymore"; "It's the child down the street, that's where she's learned those bad words"; "It's the way you've raised her, she's just like you"; "I'll try to do better, Daddy, you're absolutely right. I'll stop watching TV tomorrow, go to the library . . . leave the dishes and I'll do them tomorrow after school." In a blamer/super-reasonable couple, the wife might complain bitterly, "We hardly ever make love anymore; don't you have any feelings for me?" The husband might respond coldly, "Of course I do or I wouldn't be married to you. Perhaps we define the word *love* differently." In the case of a conversation between a super-reasonable parent ("Let's discuss precisely why you seem to be having difficulties with your math problems tonight") and the irrelevant child ("It's time for my television program now"), nothing gets settled or resolved; the tension is maintained if not increased. Table 9.1 illustrates Satir's four-stance model of dysfunctional family communication. Only the congruent person maintains self-esteem under stress, making certain that his or her inner feelings are matched by clear and direct outer communication and behavior (Satir & Bitter, 2000).

Satir maintained that these roles are essentially poses that keep distressed people from exposing their true feelings because they lack the self-esteem that would allow them to be themselves. Placaters are afraid to risk disapproval if they speak up or disagree or act in any way independent of a parent or spouse. Blamers also feel endangered and react by attacking in order to cover up feeling empty, unworthy, and unloved themselves. Super-reasonable people feel safe only at a distance and rely on their intellect to keep from acknowledging that they too have feelings and are vulnerable. Irrelevant people (often the youngest child in a family) gain approval only by acting cute and harmless. Satir, a warm, caring, nurturing person—but also capable of being fearlessly direct—inevitably tried to facilitate straight talk between family members, encouraging them to be congruent in their communications, matching words to feelings to body stance, without qualification.

TABLE 9.1 Four Dysfunctional Communication Stances Adopted Under Stress (Satir)

Category	Caricature	Typical Verbal Expression	Body Posture	Inner Feeling
Placater	Service	"Whatever you want is okay, I'm just here to make you happy."	Grateful, boot-licking, begging, self-flagellating	"I am like a nothing. Without you I am dead. I am worthless."
Blamer	Power	"You never do any-thing right. What is the matter with you?"	Finger pointing, loud, tyrannical, enraged	"I am lonely and unsuccessful."
Super-reasonable	Intellect	"If one were to observe carefully, one might notice the workworn hands of someone present here."	Monotone voice, stiff, machine-like, computer-like	"I feel vulnerable."
Irrelevant	Spontaneity	Words unrelated to what others are saying. For example, in midst of family dispute: "What are we having for dinner?"	In constant movement, constant chatter, distracting	"Nobody cares. There is no place for me."

Source: Based on Bandler, Grinder, & Satir, 1976

The "Seed" Model

In her workshops, Satir often presented two contrasting views of the world, which she labeled the "Threat and Reward" model and the "Seed" model. Relationships in the former suppose a hierarchy in which some people define rules for others to follow without question. The hierarchy is based on roles that powerful individuals hold on to for life. While those on top are not necessarily malevolent, their behavior helps create individuals who feel weak and have low self-esteem. Conformity is expected in the Threat and Reward model, whether based on gender or lower-status positions in society. The cost of nonconformity is guilt, fear, or rejection. Resentment and hostile feelings also are common, and for some people feelings of hopelessness may be present.

In the Seed model, *personhood* rather than role determines identity, and every person is born with a potential that may be fulfilled. While roles and status differences exist (parent-child, doctor-patient), they define relationships only within certain contexts and are not based on permanent status or role differences outside of that context. In the Seed model, change is viewed as an ongoing life process and an opportunity for growth. Satir was a strong advocate of the Seed model, insisting that given the proper conditions of nurture, children, like seedlings, can develop into healthy adults.

CLINICAL NOTE

A useful exercise for families fixed into rigidly defined roles for their members is to ask each person to play an unaccustomed role for 10 minutes during the session. The results are often eye openers and may lead to joint efforts to change their communication styles.

Family Assessment and Intervention

Satir tried to help people feel good about themselves, often as a result of her own boundless, optimistic approach to life. She was less concerned with conducting a formal assessment or zeroing in on the specific content of presenting problems than she was with getting to work clarifying and improving family communication. Her diagnostic understanding of the family came out of her developing relationship with each of its members. She tended to work with families in terms of their members' day-to-day functioning and their emotional experiences with each other. She taught people congruent ways of communicating by helping to restore the use of their senses and the ability to get in touch with and accept what they were really feeling. Thus, she helped individuals (and families) build their sense of self-worth; she opened up possibilities for making choices and bringing about changes in relationships (Bandler, Grinder, & Satir, 1976).

Because Satir believed human beings have within them all the resources they need in order to flourish, she directed her interventions at helping families gain access to their nourishing potentials—and then learn to use them. This is a growth-producing approach in which she encouraged people to take whatever risks were necessary in taking charge of their own lives. Early in the therapy process, Satir would present herself as a teacher introducing the family to a new language, helping them to understand their communication "discrepancies," blocking the kinds of repetitive sequences that end with members falling into the incongruent family communication styles discussed earlier.

Satir's primary talent was as a therapist and trainer rather than a theory builder or researcher. She aimed at accessibility in her writing style, consistent with her desire for clear and direct communication, although her concepts (self-esteem, family pain, family health) often lacked precision. She was a vigorous, nurturant, compassionate, down-to-earth, massively perceptive person who engaged a family authoritatively from the first session onward. She spoke simply and directly, kept up a running account of what she was doing with the family, tried to pass along her communication skills to family members, then arranged encounters between members according to the rules she had taught them.

In the following example from her early, if somewhat dated work (Satir, 1967), the parents and their children, Johnny (age 10) and Patty (age 7), are being seen together; Johnny, the identified patient, is having behavior problems at school. Satir wants to clarify what ideas each member has about what to expect from therapy and why each is there. Note how she tries to help the family members (a) recognize individual differences among them by having each member speak for himself or herself; (b) accept disagreements and differing perceptions of the same situation; and most important, (c) say what they see, think, and feel in order to bring disagreements out into the open.

In this brief excerpt we also see Satir's effort to build self-esteem in each family member and to emphasize that each person is unique and has the right to express his or her own views without another person (for example, a parent) answering for him or her. She lets the family know her goals, thus enabling them to know what to expect as they work together. Warm and caring herself, with a strong set of humanistic values, Satir stressed the role of intimacy in family relationships as a vehicle for growth among all family members. A healthy family, to Satir, is a place where members can ask for what they need, a place where needs are met and individuality is allowed to flourish. Dysfunctional families do not permit individuality, and their members fail to develop a sense of self-worth. If parental messages to one another or to their children

---

BOX 9.6 THERAPEUTIC ENCOUNTER

SATIR CLARIFIES FAMILY COMMUNICATION

PATTY: Mother said we were going to talk about family problems.

THERAPIST: What about Dad? Did he tell you the same thing?

PATTY: No.

THERAPIST: What did Dad say?

PATTY: He said we were going for a ride.

THERAPIST: I see. So you got some information from Mother and some information from Dad. What about you, Johnny. Where did you get your information?

JOHNNY: I don't remember.

THERAPIST: You don't remember who told you?

MOTHER: I don't think I said anything to him, come to think of it. He wasn't around at the time, I guess.

THERAPIST: How about you, Dad? Did you say anything to Johnny?

FATHER: No, I thought Mary had told him.

THERAPIST: (to Johnny) Well, then, how could you remember if nothing was said?

JOHNNY: Patty said we were going to see a lady about the family.

THERAPIST: I see. So you got your information from your sister, whereas Patty got a clear message from both Mother and Dad. (Shortly, she asks the parents what they remember saying.)

THERAPIST: How about that, Mother? Were you and Dad able to work this out together—what you would tell the children?

MOTHER: Well, you know, I think this is one of our problems. He does things with them and I do another.

FATHER: I think this is a pretty unimportant thing to worry about.

THERAPIST: Of course it is, in one sense. But then we can use it, you know, to see how messages get across in the family. One of the things we work on in families is how family members communicate—how clearly they get their messages across. We will have to see how Mother and Dad can get together so that Johnny and Patty can get a clear message.

(Later, she explains to the children why the family is there.)

THERAPIST: Well, then. I'll tell you why Mother and Dad have come here. They have come here because they were unhappy about how things were going in the family and they want to work out ways so that everyone can get more pleasure from family life. (Satir, 1967, pp. 143–145)[4]

---

are incongruent or confusing, then family communication across generations tends to be similarly unclear or confounded. Parents with low self-esteem communicate poorly and contribute to feelings of low self-esteem in their children.

In an early technique, Satir initiated a family's treatment by compiling a **family life fact chronology** to understand the history of the family's development by depicting key elements in its evolution, beginning with the birth of the oldest grandparents. Her goal was to force family members to think about characteristic family patterns and especially about the relevant concepts that had formed the basis for their developing relationships.

---

[4]A more detailed description and analysis of Satir's work with a family can be found in Satir and Baldwin (1983). The major portion of the book is devoted to a transcript of one of Satir's family therapy demonstrations, including a step-by-step explanation of her techniques and interventions.

While she shares with Whitaker the idea that the therapist makes use of himself or herself in dealing with a family, his methods were more apt to reflect his psychodynamic beginnings, while hers revealed her debt to Carl Rogers and the humanistic movement's striving for fulfillment and self-actualization. Satir believed the therapist must be a resource person who shows the family how to change, how to get in touch with their own feelings, how to listen to others, how to ask for clarification if they do not understand another person's message, and so on. Through her gentle, caring, matter-of-fact questioning, Satir enabled parents to listen to their children's statements and opinions, perhaps for the first time; she also helped the children to understand their parents' views and behavior. In time, through such a feedback process, congruent communication replaces the blaming, placating, super-reasonable, and irrelevant family communication styles described earlier.

Family Reconstruction

Another therapeutic innovation developed by Satir in the late 1960s, **family reconstruction** attempts to guide clients to unlock dysfunctional patterns stemming from their families of origin. The technique blends elements of Gestalt therapy, guided fantasy, hypnosis, psychodrama, role playing, and family sculpting (as noted earlier, physically molding family members into characteristic poses representing one family member's view of family relationships at a particular moment—say, after the death of a grandmother). The idea is to shed outgrown family rules and dislodge early misconceptions. Used with families as well as in group therapy settings (Nerin, 1986), family reconstruction is a process that takes family members through certain fixed stages of their lives. By reenacting their family's multigenerational drama, members have an opportunity to reclaim their roots, and in the process perhaps view old perceptions in a new light, thereby changing entrenched perceptions, feelings, and beliefs (Nerin, 1989).

Generally speaking, family reconstruction has three goals: (a) to reveal to family members the source of their old learning; (b) to enable them to develop a more realistic picture of the personhood of their parents; and (c) to pave the way for members to find their own personhood. The technique is said to be especially useful for dealing with family issues when there is little or no access to the real family of origin.

Within a group setting, usually with enough members so that separate actors can portray each family member, the client (here called the Explorer) elicits the aid of others to play key family roles in the history of the Explorer's extended family across at least three generations. With the therapist acting as the Guide, the Explorer works through lingering family conflicts (for example, "healing" a relationship between him and his mother) in an effort to reconstruct the past mysteries of his or her life, come away with a new understanding of past events, and as a result become free to maximize his or her potential.

The Guide leads the Explorer through the reconstruction, asking questions based on a chronological account of the family history extending over several generations. A trusting relationship between Guide, Explorer, and auxiliary members is essential if the Explorer is to maximize learning from the process.

Satir is quoted (Nerin, 1989) as saying:

> When one views human life as sacred, as I do, family reconstruction becomes a spiritual as well as a cognitive experience to free human energy from the shackles of the past, thus paving the way for the evolvement of being more fully human. (p. 55)

The Avanta Network

For the last decade of her life, Satir's influence waned in the family therapy movement, probably because of conflict with other leaders and her interest in changing larger systems. She moved away from the mainstream of the family therapy movement.[5] While continuing to travel around the world as a kind of roving emissary of humanistic family therapy, Satir was persuaded to try to supply a systematic rationale for her interventions, so that her style could be learned by others and not merely represent a technique unique to her. With two colleagues who had analyzed and devised a model of Satir's linguistic style with families (Bandler, Grinder, & Satir, 1976), she began to identify the key elements in her therapeutic approach: challenging the built-in expectations in the family's existing communication patterns; helping the family members work together to understand what they want in terms of change; preparing the family for a new growth experience; helping the members learn a new family process for coping; and providing the tools they will need to continue the change process after therapy. Most important, these researchers' linguistic analysis indicated that Satir taught the actual skills necessary to communicate differently as a family. Having learned these skills, family members presumably would be able to cope more creatively and effectively with any new problem or crisis using the strategies they themselves developed during family therapy.

Having developed a worldwide following, Satir turned her attention to larger systems. In 1977, as an outgrowth of her humanistic orientation, she formed the Avanta Network (*avante* is Italian for "moving ahead"; thus, Avanta referred to "going beyond"), a nonprofit organization for training others in her therapeutic outlook and procedures.

Despite Satir's enormous influence on the field—she was judged during her lifetime to be one of the best family therapy teachers in the world (Braverman, 1986)—her artistically intuitive way of working with families has a dwindling number of followers today. Possibly this is because many continue to perceive her interventions to be more a manifestation of her personality and clinical inventivenss—and thus hard to learn—than a systematic set of therapeutic procedures based on a theoretical structure. Some efforts are under way, however, to integrate her approach with emotionally focused therapy that is solidly grounded in explicit theory, relationship principles, and therapeutic skills and processes (Brubaker, 2006).

Her contributions—an insistence on the importance of open and direct communication, her effort to help clients build self-esteem, her belief in the resiliency of every family—were essential to family therapy's early development and a needed balance

---

[5]One event hastening Satir's departure—according to Pittman (1989), who was present—occurred in Venezuela in 1974, at a meeting of board members of the influential journal *Family Process*. In a heated debate with Salvador Minuchin regarding the future direction of family therapy, Minuchin criticized what he regarded as Satir's evangelical approach, insisting that more than the healing power of love was involved in repairing dysfunction within a family. Satir argued otherwise, calling on her colleagues to join her crusade for nothing less than the salvation of humankind through family therapy. When it became clear to all assembled that Minuchin's position represented the direction in which the field was headed, Satir, dissatisfied with its limited mission, directed her efforts away from mainstream family therapy and focused her energies on the Avanta Network and similar organizations.

to rival approaches less concerned with emotionality. Beyond that, Cheung (1997) suggests that Satir's emphasis on the prime importance of language, her belief that people have the potential to change and make their own choices, and her view of the therapist as participant-facilitator may represent an early influence consistent with current social construction theories. In Cheung's view, family reconstruction resembles a narrative approach that affords an opportunity to reexamine beliefs and reconstruct meanings regarding one's past experiences.

EMOTIONALLY FOCUSED COUPLE THERAPY (GREENBERG AND JOHNSON)

What's new in experiential family therapy are efforts to integrate its focus on the Self with a systems outlook, presenting a model grounded in explicit theory and supported by effectiveness research. Emotionally focused therapy views couples in both intrapsychic and interactional terms, helping them gain access to what is emotionally significant for each of the partners. At the same time, it helps them examine what guides their experiences and actions, and assists their explorations through the ongoing transactions occurring in the close, personal therapist-client(s) relationship.

EFCT's focus is on the process between people, not what is inherent in each person. Each partner learns to examine how his or her interactions with the other set off cues that maintain distress and dysfunction between the pair. Here the emphasis is on helping clients explore their moment-to-moment inner experiences and relationship events, especially the rigid patterns that block *emotional engagement*. The therapist's role becomes one of a facilitator, knowing how to help clients explore particular kinds of experiences, rather than the expert who knows *what* the client is experiencing (Greenberg, Rice, & Elliott, 1996). Greenberg (2002) has described the therapist's task as "coaching" clients to work through their feelings rather than control or avoid them.

Leading Figures

Susan Johnson (2002; 2004) a Canadian psychologist at the University of Ottawa, is also director of the Center for Emotionally Focused Therapy and the Ottawa Couple and Family Institute. Les Greenberg (1999, 2002), a psychologist at York University in Toronto, Canada, is the director of that university's Psychotherapy Research Center. Together, the two are the originators and main proponents of Emotionally Focused Couples Therapy, considered to be among the best empirically validated couples interventions currently available. In addition to their separate publications, the two have written books together (Greenberg & Johnson, 1988) and each has published numerous books, articles, and chapters with others over the past twenty years.

A Brief, Integrative Approach

This short-term (8-10 sessions) experiential approach is an outgrowth of humanistic therapy, especially the client-centered procedures of Carl Rogers (creating a safe therapeutic environment and modeling active *empathic* understanding), and Fritz Perls's Gestalt therapy (directing clients toward greater awareness by engaging in resolution-enhancing *affective processes*). Add to this mix the contribution of Satir, particularly her emphasis on *congruent communication* and closeness in the therapist-client relationship, as well as an adaptation of Bowlby's contribution of *attachment theory* directed at adult love relationships.

EFCT practitioners believe that we humans have an inherent tendency to maximize our capabilities, to actualize ourselves. We also organize what we see and give it meaning, filtered through our current emotional states and the ways in which we organize our experiences. If a couple can be helped to change their negative emotional patterns, to bond to one another with positive, caring emotion, and learn to restructure their relationship so that they become more attuned and responsive to each other, then therapeutic changes can occur. A sudden surge of emotional intensity in a couple's interactions alerts the therapist that the couple is "caught in dealing with an attachment injury" (Johnson, Makinen, & Millikin, 2001, p. 147).

The Change Process

The thrust of emotionally focused couples therapy becomes, first, helping couples identify repetitive negative interactive sequences that restrict accessibility to one another, and second, aiding them to redefine their problem in terms of its underlying and compelling emotional blocks. As the therapist helps them reprocess and restructure these rigid patterns, each partner is better able to form a secure sense of attachment and emotional connectedness to the other. Greenberg and Johnson (1988) believe change occurs as partners gain new experiences, on an emotionally meaningful level, of new aspects of themselves, of their partners, and of the new interactions.

Courtesy of Susan Johnson

Susan Johnson, Ed.D.

Skills for enhancing empathic exploration and understanding of one another are taught, and specific exercises are directed by EFCT practitioners to aid couples in recognizing and identifying their own and their partner's internal cognitive, emotional, and bodily processes. Brubaker (2006) suggests that what Satir was able to achieve intuitively, such as seemingly magically unearthing positive intentions and resources in all presenting problems, EFCTers try to do systematically, offering a step-by-step series of therapeutic tasks, in manual form, to facilitate emotional change.

Specifically, EFCT focuses on helping clients restructure negative interactive patterns (attacking-withdrawing, pursuing-distancing) that have become habitual and have created emotional removal or remoteness or have led to attack-attack engagement. In distressed relationships, these patterns become rigid and laden with affect, consequently acting to curtail closeness or trust and precluding the evolution of new patterns or responses. The emotionally focused therapist tries to modify the key emotional experiences of both partners, the positions they take in this relationship dance, and the relationship events that define the quality of their attachment in order for them to build secure emotional bonds (Johnson & Greenberg, 1995).

Outlining the EFCT Change Process

Greenberg and Johnson (1986, p. 261) illustrate the change process in this way:

1. An individual perceives himself or herself differently by bringing into focal awareness experiences not previously dominant in this person's view of self. For example, "I see and accept my vulnerability."
2. The spouse, upon witnessing the partner's new affective expressions, perceives the partner in a new way. For example, "I see your need for caring and contact rather than your hostility."
3. The individual's personal reorganization leads to different behavior in the interaction with the spouse. For example, "I now ask you for reassurance from a position of vulnerability."

4. The spouse's new perception of the partner leads to different responses. For example, "I comfort you rather than withdraw."
5. As a function of their partner's new behaviors, individuals come to see themselves in a new way. For example, "Since I can fulfill your needs, I see myself as valuable and necessary to you."

Put simply by Wetchler and Piercy (1996, p. 87), "as Mary begins to see John's withdrawal as a fear of being emotionally hurt and John understands that her anger is due to her fear of being abandoned by him, they will begin to talk differently to each other and develop a more stable bond."

Attachment Theory and Adult Relatedness

Attachment theory[6] (Bowlby, 1969) plays a central role here in offering a basis for explaining how adult relationships become troubled and dysfunctional. Each of us needs the predictable emotional accessibility and responsiveness of significant others in order to achieve a sense of personal security, to experience a sense of trust and safety, to feel self-confident. If not forthcoming, there is no emotional engagement, and the seeker is left feeling disconnected, frustrated, angry, depressed, and ultimately detached. Under such conditions of despair, destructive interactive patterns are almost sure to follow.

As Johnson (2003) observes:

> . . . when one partner fails to respond at times when the other partner's attachment needs become urgent, these events will have a momentous and disproportional negative impact on the affective tone of the relationship and its level of satisfaction. Conversely, when partners are able to respond at such times, this will potentiate the connection between them. (p. 266)

Marital distress, then, signals the failure of an attachment relationship to provide security, protection, or closeness, resulting in anxiety and a sense of vulnerability in one or both partners. Couples may hide their *primary emotions* (their real feelings, such as

---

[6]The concept of attachment is used somewhat differently here than in object relations theory. Acknowledging that early attachment bonds provide the model for later adult relationships, emotionally focused therapists view all humans as needing security and protection; in distressed relationships, these essentially healthy attachment needs are thwarted due to the couple's rigid pattern of interaction. EFCT tries to help partners in close relationships create secure attachment bonds (Johnson, 2003).

CLINICAL NOTE

A rageful spouse who declares he or she has been betrayed by a mate is likely experiencing a powerful attachment injury. The partner, attending a significant family event such as a birthday party or funeral, was seen as emotionally unavailable or unresponsive or inattentive at a key moment when support or other signs of caring were urgently needed. If unresolved, the injured partner is likely to bring the incident up repeatedly, sometimes over many years, as a symbolic example of the other's untrustworthiness and lack of caring.

fear of rejection) and in their place display defensive or coercive emotions (*secondary, reactive emotions* such as expressing anger or blaming when afraid), leading to *negative interactions* in which each partner fears revealing his or her primary emotions. Repeated over time, this pattern builds fears of trusting one's partner enough to exhibit honest primary emotions, which in turn become buried even further. EFCT therapists use the therapeutic relationship to help the couple access and reprocess the primary emotions underlying their interactional positions, enhance their emotional bond, and change their negative interactional sequences toward increased attachment security.

Steps in the Treatment Manual

In contrast with the other forms of experiential family therapy described in this chapter—which typically rely heavily on the charisma of the practitioner—here Johnson and Greenberg (1995) offer a step-by-step treatment manual for conducting EFCT so others can replicate the therapy process:

1. Delineating conflict issues in the core struggle
2. Identifying the negative interaction cycle
3. Accessing the unacknowledged feelings underlying interactional positions
4. Reframing the problem in terms of underlying feelings, attachment needs, and negative cycles
5. Promoting identification with disowned needs and aspects of self, and integrating these into relationship interactions
6. Promoting acceptance of partner's experiences and new interaction patterns
7. Facilitating the expression of needs and wants, and creating emotional engagement
8. Establishing the emergence of new solutions
9. Consolidating new positions

A Final Comment

In addition to spelling out these clinical procedures, EFCT has provided data-based studies demonstrating the effectiveness of this approach in a variety of clinical situations with at-risk populations (e.g., trauma victims, marital distress, various family mental health problems) (Baucom, Shoham, Mueser, Daiuto, & Stickle, 1998; Dunn & Schwebel, 1995; Johnson, Hunsley, Greenberg, & Schindler, 1999). These combined efforts—operationalizing therapeutic intervention procedures, supported by research demonstrating successful outcomes—augur well for the revitalization of the experiential approach to family therapy.

SUMMARY

Experiential family therapists use the immediacy of the therapeutic encounter with family members to help catalyze the family's natural drive toward growth and the fulfillment of individual members' potentials. Early experiential efforts were essentially nontheoretical and nonhistorical, stressing action over insight or interpretation, primarily by providing a growth-enhancing experience through family-therapist interactions. Attention to moment-by moment emotional experiences remains a defining feature of this form of family therapy.

The major practitioners of the experiential approach have been Carl Whitaker, Walter Kempler, and Virginia Satir. Whitaker, who some 50 years ago began redefining a schizophrenic's symptoms as signs of arrested growth, continued in his work with families to stress both intrapsychic and interpersonal barriers to development and maturity. His family therapy approach, often involving a co-therapist, was designed to capitalize on both the real and symbolic experiences that arise from the therapeutic process, and was aimed at bringing personal growth. Claiming that his interventions were largely controlled by his unconscious, he sought a growth-producing experience for himself, believing that a therapist who does not personally benefit, therapeutically speaking, from the encounter has little to give to client families.

Kempler, a practitioner of Gestalt family therapy, is adamant in dealing only with the *now*—the moment-to-moment immediacy shared by the therapist and the family members. Like most Gestalt therapists, Kempler guides individuals to reach beyond their customary self-deceptive games, defenses, and facades. Uncompromisingly honest himself, he confronts and challenges all family members to explore how their self awareness is blocked and to channel their increased awareness into more productive and fulfilling relationships with each other.

The most celebrated humanistically oriented family therapist was Virginia Satir. Her demonstrations with families were known around the world. Her approach to families combined her early interest in clarifying communication "discrepancies" between family members with humanistically oriented efforts to build self-esteem and self-worth in all the members. Believing that human beings have within themselves the resources they need in order to flourish, Satir viewed her task as one of helping people gain access to their nourishing potentials and teaching people to use them effectively.

Experiential family therapy today is best represented by emotionally focused couples therapy (EFCT), developed by Leslie Greenberg and Susan Johnson. Systemic in outlook, and based on client-centered and Gestalt therapy principles, this approach aids couples to change negative interactive patterns at the same time that they build secure emotional bonds. Attachment theory provided its theoretical base. Therapeutic procedures are offered in a step-by-step treatment program that is easy to emulate, and data-based outcome studies have been carried out to demonstrate its clinical effectiveness.

RECOMMENDED READINGS

Greenberg, L. S., & Johnson, S. M. (1988). *Emotionally focused therapy for couples.* New York: Brunner/Mazel.

Kempler, W. (1981). *Experiential psychotherapy with families.* Brunner/Mazel.

Satir, V. M., & Baldwin, M. (1983). *Satir step by step: A guide to creating change in families.* Palo Alto, CA: Science and Behavior Books.

Whitaker, C. A., & Bumberry, W. M. (1988). *Dancing with the family: A symbolic experiential approach.* New York: Brunner/Mazel.

The Structural Model

Many of the basic concepts of the structural approach to family therapy are already familiar to the reader: family rules, roles, coalitions, subsystems, boundaries, wholeness, organization. The very fact that these constructs are part of the everyday vocabulary of family therapy—and so readily come to mind in thinking of family relationships and interactional patterns—underscores the historical prominence of this model. In particular, its clearly articulated theory of family organization and the guidelines for applying that theory offered by Salvador Minuchin and his associates (Minuchin, 1974; Minuchin & Fishman, 1981; Minuchin, Rosman, & Baker, 1978; Minuchin & Nichols, 1993; Minuchin, Lee, & Simon, 1996) have helped ensure that a legion of systems-oriented family therapists would adopt the structural viewpoint. Indeed, in the 1970s, the carefully crafted structural view for working with a family first helped popularize family therapy to many professionals and the public alike.

The Structural Outlook

Structural family therapy shares with other family systems approaches a preference for a *contextual* rather than an individual focus on problems and solutions. Its uniqueness, however, results from its use of *spatial and organizational metaphors,* both in describing problems and identifying solutions, and its insistence on *active therapist direction* (Colapinto, 1991).

The model's major thesis—that an individual's symptoms are best understood as rooted in the context of family transaction patterns, that a change in family organization or structure must take place before the symptoms are relieved, and that the therapist must provide a directive leadership role in changing the structure or context in which the symptom is embedded—has had great impact on the practices of many family therapists. The learning experiences involved in mastering structural techniques have been described by Minuchin and nine of his supervisees (Minuchin, Lee, & Simon, 1996).

As the major determinants of the well-being of a family's individual members, structural theorists emphasize

- The *wholeness* of the family system
- The influence of the family's *hierarchical* organization
- The interdependent functioning of its *subsystems*

It is the family's underlying organizational structure (that is, its enduring and regulating interactional, rule-setting patterns) and its flexibility in responding to changing conditions throughout the family life cycle that help govern the appearance of functional or dysfunctional patterns. Minuchin (1984) views families as going through their life cycles seeking to maintain a delicate balance between stability and change; the more functional the family, the more open to change during periods of family transitions, and the more willing to modify its structure as changing conditions demand.

Structural therapists actively strive for organizational changes in the dysfunctional family as their primary goal, assuming that individual behavioral changes as well as symptom reduction will follow as the context for the family's transactions changes. They reason that when the family's structure is transformed, the positions of its members are altered, and each person experiences changes as a result. It is the structural therapist's primary role, then, to be an instrument of change—to actively engage the family as a whole, to introduce challenges[1] that force adaptive changes, and to support and coach family members as they attempt to cope with the ensuing consequences (Colapinto, 1991).

Leading Figure

Born and raised in Argentina of European immigrant parents, Minuchin set out to practice pediatrics following his medical training. When Israel declared itself a state in 1948, Minuchin, guided by his sense of social purpose (still present today in his consultative work), volunteered his services to Israel and served as an army doctor for 18 months in the war with the Arab nations. After subsequent training as a child psychiatrist in the United States, a good part of which was under the tutelage of Nathan Ackerman, Minuchin returned to Israel in 1952 to work with displaced children from the Holocaust and then with Jewish immigrants from the Arab countries.

Back in the United States once again in 1954, Minuchin began psychoanalytic training at the William Alanson White Institute (where Sullivan's interpersonal psychiatry ideas held sway), eventually becoming the intake psychiatrist at the Wiltwyck School, a residential school for delinquent adolescents outside New York City. Inspired further by an article by Don Jackson in 1959, Minuchin began to look beyond the individual children, primarily low-income African American and Puerto Rican youngsters from New York's inner city, and to focus on examining and analyzing their family predicaments. Because these families often had multiple problems and disconnected family structures, Minuchin and his therapeutic team started developing a theory and set of special intervention techniques for working with these underorganized poor families. Increasingly, he turned to a sociological analysis of social context—just how the experience of living under poverty conditions affected family functioning. To effect change, Minuchin and his coworkers began to search for therapeutic ways of changing family context rather than directing their efforts at individually troubled adolescents with personality or behavioral problems.

---

[1]One famous challenging technique is the "stroke and kick," a restructuring maneuver in which the therapist first says something positive and reinforcing (for example, saying to a substance abuser working at recovery, "You're doing a good job of trying to deal with your problem," and then turning to his wife, whom the husband has neglected, and asking her, "How does it feel to be without a husband this last six months?"

Salvador Minuchin, M.D.

Finding that the use of long-term, interpretive psychoanalytic techniques with a passive, head-nodding therapist was ineffective with this challenged population, Minuchin and his associates proceeded to devise many brief, direct, concrete, action-oriented, and problem-solving intervention procedures to effect context change by restructuring the family. (Nathan Ackerman's influences regarding interlocking pathology and his provocative, charismatic presence with families are clear here.) The results of Minuchin's eight years at Wiltwyck, during which he developed many highly original and action-oriented techniques for working with poor, disadvantaged families, were described in *Families of the Slums* (Minuchin, Montalvo, Guerney, Rosman, & Schumer, 1967) and earned Minuchin widespread recognition (Simon, 1984). The Wiltwyck experience, especially its revelation of the need for family reorganization and for some effective form of hierarchy among family members, laid the cornerstone for structural family therapy.

In 1965, now desirous of testing his techniques with a wider cross section of families, including both working-class and middle-class populations, Minuchin took on the directorship of the Philadelphia Child Guidance Center. To assist with training, he brought along social worker Braulio Montalvo from Wiltwyck and also recruited Jay Haley from Palo Alto.[2] Originally a small clinic with a staff of ten located in the heart of the African American ghetto, the Philadelphia Child Guidance Clinic blossomed under Minuchin's boldly imaginative leadership until it grew into the largest facility of its kind ever established. The clinic soon occupied an elaborate modern complex, had close to 300 people on its staff, and became affiliated with Children's Hospital on the campus of the University of Pennsylvania. The clinic has the distinction of being the first clinic in the United States where ghetto families represented a majority of the clients served. In 1974, Minuchin published the widely read *Families and Family Therapy,* an elaboration of ideas concerning change in families through structural family therapy.

After stepping down as director of the Philadelphia Child Guidance Center in 1975, and as director of training there in 1981, Minuchin spent most of his professional time teaching, consulting, supervising, writing, and demonstrating his dramatic techniques in front of professional audiences around the world. In 1981 he founded and, until 1996, led a small group called Family Studies, Inc. (now renamed the Minuchin Center for the Family) in New York City, offering consultative services to community organizations, particularly those dealing with poor families (Minuchin, Colapinto, & Minuchin, 1998). Minuchin has now retired to Florida, but continues to lecture around the world.

---

[2]The cross-fertilization of ideas between these three, some of it said to have transpired while they were carpooling to and from work together, was extensive and enriching to all concerned, as Minuchin acknowledged in his classic text (Minuchin, 1974). Montalvo, born and raised in Puerto Rico, is credited by Minuchin as his most influential teacher, and is one of the unheralded pioneers in family therapy. He introduced many innovations to the live supervisory process (see Appendix B) and helped train minority paraprofessionals who had no prior educational or therapeutic experience. Haley, who was also to make an impact on Minuchin's thinking, gave priority to teaching trainees concrete, step-by-step skills rather than emphasizing any underlying theory. Haley's *Problem-Solving Therapy,* a popular 1976 text, began to take form first as a syllabus for training paraprofessionals (Simon, 1984).

Other Leading Figures

Over the years, Minuchin has surrounded himself with many clinicians from various disciplines who themselves have contributed significantly to shaping structural family theory and therapy. Psychiatrist Charles Fishman (1993), social worker Harry Aponte (1999), and psychologist Marion Lindblad-Goldberg (Lindblad-Goldberg, Dore, & Stern, 1998), all of Philadelphia, have contributed to advancing the structural viewpoint through offering family therapy training, typically with economically needy families.

Marianne Walters, a social worker in Washington, D.C., is best known for the groundbreaking work she and her associates (Walters, Carter, Papp, & Silverstein, 1989) produced as part of the long-running Women's Project, employing the lens of gender to examine family relationships. Psychiatrist Jorge Colapinto (2000) is Director of the Foster Care Project at the Ackerman Institute in New York. The original Philadelphia Child Guidance Center, having trained thousands of family therapists, was closed a decade ago, and now has been replaced by a more modest Philadelphia Child and Family Guidance Training Center, still structurally oriented, under Lindblad-Goldberg's direction.

Psychosomatic Families

Shortly after assuming directorship of the Philadelphia Child Guidance Clinic in 1965, Minuchin turned his attention to the role of family context in psychosomatic conditions, especially such urgent medical problems as diabetes and anorexia. More specifically, no medical explanations could be found for the unusually large number of diabetic children who required emergency hospitalization for acidosis (a depletion of alkali in the body), nor would they respond to individual psychotherapy directed at helping them deal with stress. As Minuchin and his coworkers began to accumulate research and clinical data and to redefine the problem in family terms, successful interventions involving the entire family became possible. Later research expanded to include asthmatic children with severe, recurrent attacks as well as anorectic children; the additional data confirmed for Minuchin that the locus of pathology was in the context of the family and not simply in the afflicted individual.

As proposed in *Psychosomatic Families*, which Minuchin wrote with research psychologist Bernice Rosman and pediatrician Lester Baker (Minuchin, Rosman, & Baker, 1978), families of children who manifest severe psychosomatic symptoms are characterized by certain transactional problems that encourage somatization. *Enmeshment* is common, *subsystems* function poorly, and *boundaries* between family members are too diffuse to allow for individual autonomy. A psychosomatic family was found to be overprotective, inhibiting the child from developing a sense of independence, competence, or interest in activities outside the safety of the family. The physiologically vulnerable child, in turn, feels great responsibility for protecting the family. The manifestation of symptoms typically occurs when stress overloads the family's already dysfunctional coping mechanisms. Thus, the symptoms are regarded as having a regulating effect on the family system, the sick child acting as a family conflict defuser by diverting family attention away from more basic, but less easily resolved, family conflicts.

Unlike the underorganized, often single-parent-led, family population they found at Wiltwyck, at the Philadelphia Child Guidance Center Minuchin and his colleagues were dealing primarily with middle-class, intact families that, if anything, appeared to be too tightly organized. Therapeutic intervention, while attending to family context, had to be modified to first destructure the family's rigid patterns, and then restructure them in order to permit greater flexibility. In the process, therapeutic efforts were directed not only at changing the structure of relationships within the family but also at helping the family develop clearer boundaries, learn to negotiate for desired changes, and deal more directly with hidden, underlying conflicts. According to Colapinto (1991), the Minuchin team's family-focused success in treating anorexia nervosa—which, unlike diabetes or asthma, has no physiological basis—drew many family therapists to the structural model.

Structural Family Theory

As Minuchin (1974) describes his viewpoint:

> In essence, the structural approach to families is based on the concept that a family is more than the individual biopsychodynamics of its members. Family members relate according to certain arrangements, which govern their transactions. These arrangements, though usually not explicitly stated or even recognized, form a whole—the structure of the family. The reality of the structure is of a different order from the reality of the individual members. (p. 89)

Like most systems theorists, the structuralists are interested in how the components of a system interact, how balance or homeostasis is achieved, how family feedback mechanisms operate, how dysfunctional communication patterns develop, and so forth. Consistent with Minuchin's background in child psychiatry, he influenced his associates to observe too how families cope with developmental tasks as the family matures, and particularly how families, as complex systems, make adaptive changes during periods of transition. Structuralists pay special attention to family transactional patterns because these offer clues to the family's structure, the permeability of the family's subsystem boundaries, and the existence of alignments or coalitions—all of which ultimately affect the family's ability to achieve a delicate balance between stability and change. Before an individual's symptoms can be reduced or extinguished, according to this model, structural changes must first occur within the family.

Family Structure

Just as is the case with all adapting organisms, families need some form of internal organization that dictates how, when, and to whom to relate; the subsequent transactional patterns make up the structure of the family (Colapinto, 1991). Put another way, a family's structure is the invisible or covert set of functional demands or codes that organizes the way family members interact with one another (Minuchin, 1974). In essence, the structure represents the sum of the *operational rules* the family has evolved for carrying out its important functions. It provides a framework for understanding those consistent, repetitive, and enduring patterns that reveal how a particular family organizes itself in order to maintain its stability and, under a changing set of environmental conditions, to seek adaptive alternatives. Typically, once established, such patterns are self-perpetuating and resistant to change. They are unlikely to change until a family's changing circumstances cause tensions and imbalance within the system.

For example, an interactive routine may evolve in a family whereby the young son refuses to comply with his mother's pleading to clean up his room, but will submit to his father's request without hesitation. Repeated over time, and in a variety of situations, a basic family structure may emerge in which the father is seen in the family as the ultimate authority and the mother as possessing insufficient power or clout to be obeyed.

Subsequent transactional patterns between family members are likely to reflect this now-established interactive blueprint. These patterns serve to arrange or organize the family's component subunits into more or less constant relationships (Umbarger, 1983) and thus regulate the family's day-to-day functioning. However, structure in and of itself should not necessarily be thought of as static or fixed. On the contrary, certain temporary structures (a mother-son coalition in which the father is kept in the dark, say, about erratic school attendance or a bad grade) may occur but not persist beyond a brief arrangement, and thus must be considered to be dynamic. It's the structural therapist's task to watch for any repeatable family processes in action during therapy sessions, because they lead to detecting faulty or problematic or ineffective patterns that together reveal where the family's need for restructuring exists.

A family's transactional patterns regulate the behavior of its members, and are maintained by two sets of constraints: *generic* or universal rules, and *idiosyncratic* or individualized rules (Minuchin, 1974). With regard to the former, structuralists contend that all well-functioning families should be hierarchically organized, with the parents exercising more authority and power than the children, and the older children having more responsibilities as well as more privileges than their younger siblings.

In addition, there must be *complementarity* of functions—the husband and wife, for example, operate as a team and accept their interdependency. The degree to which the needs and abilities of both spouses dovetail and reciprocal role relations provide satisfaction are key factors in harmonious family functioning. In some cases, family balance is achieved by different family members' being assigned complementary roles or functions (good child–bad child; tender mother–tough father). Thus, complementarity or reciprocity between family roles provides a generic restraint on family structure, allowing the family to carry out its tasks while maintaining family equilibrium. Complementarity takes the form of teamwork in well-functioning families. Idiosyncratic constraints apply to specific families, and involve the mutual presumptions of particular family members regarding their behavior toward one another.

While the origin of certain expectations may no longer be clear to the persons involved, buried in years of implicit and explicit negotiations, their pattern of mutual accommodation, and thus functional effectiveness, is maintained (Minuchin, 1974). The evolved rules and subsequent behavioral patterns of a particular family's game become a part of the family's structure, ensuring that the system will maintain itself.

Here some feminists take exception to Minuchin's insistence on family hierarchies, claiming that they run the risk of reinforcing sex role stereotypes. Luepnitz (1988) argues that Minuchin bases many of his ideas regarding family organization on the work of the influential functional sociologist Talcott Parsons (Parsons & Bales, 1955), who saw normal family life neatly organized according to gender roles, family functions, and hierarchical power. Parsons maintained that adaptation to society requires that husbands perform an "instrumental" role (e.g., making managerial decisions) in the family, and that wives perform "expressive" roles (caring for the family's emotional needs). Hare-Mustin, as quoted by Simon (1984), believes Minuchin himself models the male executive functions while working with families, in effect demanding that the father resume control of the family and exert leadership much as Minuchin leads and directs the therapeutic session.

Colapinto (1991) contends that the stereotypic division of instrumental vs. expressive roles is not held up as an ideal by Minuchin, but rather that Minuchin believes all families need *some* kind of structure, *some* form of hierarchy, and *some* degree of differentiation between subsystems. Thus, a family will try to maintain preferred patterns—its present structure—as long as possible. While alternate patterns may be considered, any deviation from established rules that goes too far too fast will be met with resistance, as the family seeks to reestablish equilibrium. On the other hand, the family must be able to adapt to changing circumstances (a child grows into a young adult; mother goes to work outside the home; grandmother comes to live with them). It must have a sufficient range of patterns (including alternatives to call upon whenever necessary) and must be flexible enough to mobilize these new patterns in the face of impending change, if members are to continue to exist as a family unit. The family must be able to transform itself in ways that meet new circumstances, while at the same time taking care not to lose the continuity that provides a frame of reference for its members.

Family Subsystems

As we pointed out in Chapter 4, families carry out their basic functions in part by organizing themselves into coexisting subsystems, often arranged in hierarchical order. Typically, family subsystem divisions are made according to gender (male/female), generation (parents/children), common interests (intellectual/social), or function (who is responsible for what chores). Beyond these more obvious patterns, various possibilities (older children vs. younger; boys vs. girls; parents vs. teenagers) spring up in most families. All families contain a number of coexisting but separate subsystems.

Subsystems, then, are components of a family's structure; they exist to carry out various family tasks necessary for the functioning of the overall family system. Each member may belong to several subgroups at the same time, and families are capable of organizing themselves into a limitless number of such units. Each person may have a differing level of power within different subgroups, may play different roles, may exercise different skills, and may engage in different interactions with members of other subsystems within the family. Complementarity of roles (Ackerman's influence again) is a key here—as Minuchin (1974) points out, a child has to act like a son so his father can act like a father, but he may take on executive powers when he is alone with his younger brother.

Subsystems are defined by interpersonal *boundaries* and rules for membership; in effect, they regulate the amount of contact with other subsystems. Such boundaries determine who participates and what roles those participants will have in dealing with one another and with outsiders who are not included in the subsystem. They may be based on temporary alliances (mother and daughter go shopping together on Saturday afternoon) and may have rules concerning exclusion (fathers and brothers are unwelcome). Or they may be more enduring (based on generational differences in roles and interests between parents and children) with clearly defined boundaries separating the two generations (one watches public television documentaries, the other MTV). Subsystem organization within a family provides valuable training in developing a sense of self, in the process of honing interpersonal skills at different levels.

The spousal, parental, and sibling subsystems are the most prominent and important subsystems in the family. The strength and durability of the *spousal subsystem* in particular offers a key regarding family stability. How husband and wife learn to negotiate differences and eventually accommodate to one another's needs and develop complementary roles tells us a great deal about the likelihood of family stability and flexibility to adapt to changing circumstances.

While the arrival of children forces the couple to transform their system to now become a *parental subsystem* grappling with new responsibilities, complementarity of roles remains essential, as the couple negotiates differences in parenting attitudes and styles. Those accommodations to one another's individual perspectives are apt to continue and get renegotiated as children grow and require different parental responses at different stages of their lives. It is crucial at the start and throughout parenting that, whatever the demands of child rearing and the efforts expended toward the evolvement of an effective parental subsystem, the parents continue to work at maintaining and strengthening their spousal subsystem, which is fundamental to family well-being.

The *sibling subsystem* offers the first experience of being part of a peer group and learning to support, cooperate, and protect (along with compete, fight with, and negotiate differences). Together, the children comprising this subsystem learn to deal with the parental subsystem in order to work out relationship changes commensurate with the developmental changes they are going through. In a well-functioning family, all three subsystems operate in an integrated way to protect the differentiation, and thus the integrity, of the family system.

Boundary Permeability

The specific composition of any subsystem is not nearly as important as the clarity of its boundaries. Put another way, boundaries within a family vary in their flexibility or **permeability,** and that degree of accessibility helps determine the nature and frequency of contact between family members. *Clearly defined boundaries* between subsystems within a family help maintain separateness and at the same time emphasize belongingness to the overall family system. In an ideal arrangement, the clarity enhances the family's overall well-being by providing support and easy access for communication and negotiation between subsystems whenever needed, while simultaneously encouraging independence and the freedom to experiment by the members of the separate subsystems. The autonomy of members is not sacrificed, but at the same time the boundaries remain flexible enough so that care, support, and involvement are available as needed. An important benefit of such clarity becomes apparent whenever the family attempts to make structural changes over time to accommodate to changing life circumstances.

Excessively *rigid or inflexible boundaries* lead to impermeable barriers between subsystems. In this case, the worlds of parents and children—the generational hierarchy—are separate and distinct; the members of neither subsystem are willing or able to enter into the other's world. With parents and children unable to alter or cross subsystem boundaries when necessary, autonomy may be maintained, but nurturance, involvement, and the easy exchange of affection with one another are typically missing. While the child in such a family may gain a sense of independence, it often comes at the price of feeling isolated from others and unsupported during critical times.

Diffuse boundaries are excessively blurred and indistinct, and thus easily intruded upon by other family members. Here, parents are too accessible, and contact with their children may take the form of hovering and the invasion of privacy. Children run the risk of becoming too involved with their parents, in the process failing to develop independent thinking and behaving or to learn the necessary skills for developing relationships outside the family. Because there is no clear generational hierarchy, adults and children may exchange roles easily, and a member's sense of self or personal identity becomes hard to establish for later adulthood. Here children may feel supported and cared for by parents, but it is often at the expense of feeling free to take independent (and possibly disapproved of) actions.

In a well-functioning family, clear boundaries give each member a sense of "I-ness" along with a group sense of "we" or "us." That is, each member retains his or her individuality but not at the expense of losing the feeling of belonging to a family. Most family systems fall somewhere along the continuum between **enmeshment** (diffuse boundaries) and **disengagement** (rigid boundaries); see Minuchin et al., 1967. Most families are neither totally enmeshed nor totally disengaged, although they may contain enmeshed or disengaged subsystems. Minuchin and Nichols (1993) describe a familiar, if troubled, middle-class family pattern in which a disengaged father is preoccupied with work and neglectful of his wife and children, and an enmeshed mother is overinvolved with her children, her closeness to them serving as a substitute for closeness in the marriage.

Enmeshment refers to an extreme form of proximity and intensity in family interactions in which members are overconcerned and overinvolved in each other's lives. In extreme cases, the family's lack of differentiation between subsystems makes separation from the family an act of betrayal. Belonging to the family dominates all experiences at the expense of each member's self-development. Whatever is happening to one family member reverberates throughout the system: a child sneezes, his sister runs for the tissues, his mother reaches for the thermometer, and his father becomes anxious about sickness in the family.

Subsystem boundaries in enmeshed families are poorly differentiated, weak, and easily crossed. Children may act like parents, and parental control may be ineffective. Excessive togetherness and sharing leads to a lack of separateness; members, overly alert and responsive to signs of distress, intrude on each other's thoughts and feelings. Members of enmeshed families place too high a value on family cohesiveness, to the extent that they yield autonomy and have little inclination to explore and master problems outside the safety of the family. As we indicated earlier in this chapter, enmeshment is common in psychosomatic families.

At the other extreme, members of disengaged families may function separately and autonomously but with little sense of family loyalty. Interpersonal distance is great, the members frequently lacking the capacity to be interdependent or to request support from others when needed. Communication in such families is strained and guarded, and the family's protective functions are limited. When an individual family member is under stress, the enmeshed family responds with excessive speed and intensity, while the disengaged family hardly seems to look up, offer emotional support, or even respond at all. As Minuchin (1974) illustrates, the parents in an enmeshed family may become enormously upset if a child does not eat dessert, while in a disengaged family they may feel unconcerned about the child's hatred of school.

Alignments, Power, and Coalitions

While boundaries are defined by how a family is organized, **alignments** are defined by the way family members join together or oppose one another in carrying out a family activity.

Power within a family has to do with both authority (who is the decision maker) and responsibility (who carries out the decision). Thus, alignments refer to the emotional or psychological connections family members make with one another. Power, on the other hand, speaks to the relative influence of each family member on an operation's outcome.

Aponte and Van Deusin (1981) believe that every instance of a family transaction makes a statement about boundaries, alignments, and power. As we have noted, the boundaries of a subsystem are the rules defining who participates and what roles they will play in the transactions or operations necessary to carry out a particular function. (For example, should the sex education of young children be carried out by father, mother, older siblings, or be a shared responsibility? Or should the task be left to the schools?) Alignments refer to how supportive or unsupportive of one another the play-ers are in carrying out an operation. (For example, does father agree or disagree with his wife's disciplinary actions with the children?) Power is seldom absolute but is related to the context or situation. (For example, the mother may have considerable influence on her adolescent daughter's behavior at home but minimal influence over the daughter's social contacts outside the home.) Power is also related to the way family members actively or passively combine forces. (For example, the mother's authority depends on her husband's support and backing as well as on the acquiescence of her children.)

Certain alignments are considered by structuralists to be dysfunctional. In what Minuchin (1974) calls **triangulation,** each parent demands the child ally with him or her against the other parent. Whenever the child does side with one parent, however, the other views the alignment as an attack or betrayal and, in such a dysfunctional structure, the child is in a no-win situation. Every movement the child makes causes one or the other parent to feel ganged up on and assailed. Because the problems fail to be worked out between the parents, a third person is brought in (similar to Bowen's concept of triangles) and becomes part of the process taking place.

© Rob Van Patten/Digital Vision/Getty Images

Mealtime rituals often provide an opportunity for open communication, helping to ensure boundary permeability between generations.

In this simulated scene, a mother's whispered secret strengthens her alliance with one child but may have an undermining effect on overall family functioning.

Coalitions (Minuchin, Rosman, & Baker, 1978) are alliances between specific family members against a third member. A *stable coalition* is a fixed and inflexible union (such as mother and son) that becomes a dominant part of the family's everyday functioning. A *detouring coalition* is one in which the pair hold a third family member responsible for their difficulties or conflicts with one another, thus decreasing the stress on themselves or their relationship.

Alignments, power, boundaries, and coalitions are interrelated phenomena within a family system. Power often results from alignments between members, and can be an important determinant of functional or dysfunctional living. Structuralists believe that power resulting from a strong parental alignment is often beneficial to child rearing and limit setting. On the other hand, coalitions between a parent and a child against the other parent can have an undermining effect on family functioning. Detouring, while it may give others the impression of family harmony, may often be destructive to maintaining clear boundaries.

Structuralists believe that for parents to achieve a desired outcome in the family, there must be

- *Clearly defined generational boundaries* so that parents together form a subsystem with executive power
- *Alignments between the parents* on key issues, such as discipline
- *Rules related to power and authority*, indicating which of the parents will prevail if they disagree and whether the parents are capable of carrying out their wishes when they do agree

Note that strong generational boundaries also prohibit interference from grandparents as much as they prevent children from taking over parenting functions. Alignments must function properly or individuals will cross generational boundaries—go to Grandmother for permission if Mother says no—to get what they want.

Family Dysfunction

Rosenberg (1983) summarizes the structural position succinctly when he concludes that "when a family runs into difficulty, one can assume that it is operating within a dysfunctional structure" (p. 160). Perhaps the family, proceeding along normal developmental lines, has hit a snag in entering a new developmental stage or in negotiating a particular life cycle crisis such as the birth of another child, children leaving for college, or retirement.

Perhaps the family members have become overinvolved or enmeshed with each other (parental behavior that seems supportive and loving to a preadolescent is experienced as suffocating and intrusive by a teenager). Or, at the other end of the continuum, perhaps we are dealing with the dilemma of disengagement (parents' detachment permits growth and encourages children's resourcefulness, but at the same time represents parents' unavailability and lack of support in time of crisis). Dysfunction suggests that the covert rules that govern family transactions have become (perhaps temporarily) inoperative or inappropriate and require renegotiation.

A dysfunctional family by definition has failed to fulfill its purpose of nurturing the growth of its members (Colapinto, 1991). In the Wiltwyck families (Minuchin et al., 1967), typically burdened by severe external stressors brought about by poverty, five dysfunctional family structures were differentiated: (a) enmeshed families; (b) disengaged families; (c) families with a peripheral male; (d) families with noninvolved parents; and (e) families with juvenile parents. A sense of feeling overwhelmed and helpless was common to these families, often led by single mothers, who struggled to control or guide their delinquent children.

Just as the social context as stressor was apparent in the Wiltwyck population, so the inadequate internal responses to stress—the other component of the dysfunctional equation—played a key role for the Philadelphia working-class and middle-class families suffering from psychosomatic disorders (Colapinto, 1991). Here the problem stemmed from inflexibility, particularly the family's inability to confront and seek to modify those transactional patterns that had ceased to satisfy the needs of family members. The result was an inadequate and stereotypical family response to stress, as the family persisted in employing obsolete patterns as new situations arose. For example, a couple having negotiated a complementary relationship before the arrival of children, but one not allowing for much open conflict, failed to adapt readily to becoming parents, where a change from their implicit contract was in order due to differing circumstances. To cite another example, parents accustomed to dealing with young children were unable to adapt to growing teenagers who now demanded more autonomy. Fear of oneself or one's partner departing from established patterns often led to rigid repetition of failed patterns.

Disengagement or enmeshment—avoiding contact with one another or continuous bickering—were both directed at circumventing change, thus failing to achieve conflict resolution. Overprotection of the sick child by the entire family helped cover up underlying family conflicts and tended to discourage the development of a sense of competence, maturity, or self-reliance on the part of the symptomatic child.

Minuchin (1974) reserves the label of *pathological* for those families who, when faced with a stressful situation, increase the rigidity of their transactional patterns and boundaries, thus preventing any further exploration of alternatives. Normal families, in contrast, adapt to life's inevitable stresses by preserving family continuity while remaining flexible enough to permit family restructuring.

STRUCTURAL FAMILY THERAPY

The structural approach has made two particularly noteworthy contributions to family therapy practice, according to Aponte and DiCesare (2000): demonstrating that (a) poor families, including those living in "chaotic slums," can benefit from family therapy and (b) examining a family's structure, including those families that have become fragmented or underorganized, can be a powerful means for treating family dysfunction. The model recognizes the influence of social factors in family functioning and in working within the community's larger systems.

Therapeutic Goals

Because structuralists view symptoms in a family member as emerging from, and as being maintained by, a family structure unable to adapt to changing environmental or developmental demands, they consider that they have reached their therapeutic goal when the family has restructured itself and thus freed its members to relate to one another in nonpathological patterns (Prochaska & Norcross, 1999). As these authors go on to point out, changing a family's structure calls for changing its rules for dealing with one another, and that in turn involves changing the system's rigid or diffuse boundaries to achieve greater boundary clarity.

Structural therapeutic efforts are geared to the present and are based on the principle of action preceding understanding. That is, action leads to new experiences, to insight and understanding, to rearranged structures. The major therapeutic thrust of structural family therapy is to actively and directly challenge the family's patterns of interaction, forcing the members to look beyond the symptoms of the identified patient in order to view all of their behavior within the context of family structures (the covert rules that govern the family's transactional patterns). The aim here is to help the family change its stereotyped interactive patterns and redefine its relationships, thus aiding members to better deal with the stresses in their lives (Colapinto, 2000).

As Minuchin and Nichols (1998) observe, in a marital relationship, for example, one partner's behavior is yoked to the other's. Their actions are codetermined, subject to reciprocal forces that support or polarize. The structural therapist's task is to disentangle the pair from their automatic yoked reactions, and in the process help each partner discover his or her individuality, power, and responsibility.

Structuralists offer the family leadership, direction, and encouragement to examine and discard rigid structures that no longer are functional and to make adaptive changes in structure as family circumstances and family developmental stages change. For example, changes in the relative positions of family members may be in order, such as more proximity between husband and wife or more distance between mother and son.

Hierarchical relationships in which the parents customarily exercise authority may be redefined and made more flexible in some cases and reinforced in others. Alignments and coalitions may be explored, embedded conflicts acknowledged, alternative rules considered. To use an example offered by Colapinto (1982), a mother may be urged to abstain from intervening automatically whenever the interaction between her husband and son reaches a certain pitch, while father and son may be encouraged not to automatically abort an argument just because it upsets Mom. For structuralists, the most effective way to alter dysfunctional behavior and eliminate symptoms is to change the family's transactional patterns that maintain them.

Although they are not always so neatly separated in practice, the therapeutic efforts of structuralists typically follow this order:

1. Joining and accommodating
2. Assessing family interactions
3. Monitoring family dysfunctional sets
4. Restructuring transactional patterns

Joining and Accommodating

In an attempt to disarm family members who may be suspicious or fearful of being challenged or blamed, structuralists typically begin by adjusting to the family's affective style. With a constricted family, the therapist tries not to be too demonstrative; with an expansive family, he or she is more open and uses expressive movements. The therapist greets each member by name and encourages him or her to participate, but does not insist on a response or confront silent or resistant members. The therapist shows respect for the family hierarchy by asking first for the parents' observations. (If the children are addressed first, the parents may feel the therapist is blaming them for family problems, and they will likely reject future therapist efforts as biased.) Nonthreatening, friendly, ready to help without being pushy, the structural therapist is at the same time adapting to the family organization, assimilating the family's language patterns, interactive style, and commonly used terms—and gaining a sense of family patterns and structures.

As a therapist, Minuchin (1974) describes himself as acting like a distant relative, **joining** a family system and respectfully **accommodating** to its style. As the therapist links with the family and begins to understand family themes and family myths, to sense a member's pain at being excluded or scapegoated, to distinguish which persons have open communication pathways between them and which closed, he or she is beginning to obtain a picture of the family hierarchical structure, subsystems operations, boundaries, coalitions, and so on.

Mimesis (Greek for "copy") refers to the process of joining the family by imitating the manner, style, affective range, or content of its communications in order to solidify the therapeutic alliance with them. The therapist might tell of personal experiences ("I have an uncle like that") or mimic a family member's behavior (taking off his coat, sitting in a particular position, playing with the baby). These efforts are sometimes spontaneous, sometimes planned; whatever the case, they often have the effect of increasing kinship with the family and building trust as the therapist becomes part of the system.

Joining, then, lets the family know that the therapist, a nonpermanent but concerned member, understands and is working with and for them in a common search for alternate ways of dealing with what has likely become a family impasse. In the process, the structural therapist is encouraging the family to feel secure enough to explore other, more effective ways of interacting and solving problems together. Acknowledging their areas of pain or stress, the therapist lets family members know that he or she will respond to them with sensitivity, and that it is safe for them to confront the distressing—and thus previously avoided—issues.

Affiliating with the family, the therapist might make *confirming statements* regarding what is positive about each member; this technique helps build self-esteem and may also allow other family members to see that person in a new light. Another way of confirming that the therapist is tuned in is to describe an obviously negative characteristic in one family member while at the same time "absolving" that individual of responsibility for the behavior. One effect may be for that person to rebel or begin to seek changes against being controlled by the other person. Minuchin and Fishman (1981) give the following illustrations:

> To a child, the therapist might say: "You seem to be quite childish. How did your parents manage to keep you so young?" To an adult, the therapist could say: "You act very dependent on your spouse. What does she do to keep you incompetent?" (p. 34)

Through this technique, the person feels recognized in a problem area without feeling criticized or guilty or to blame about it. As a result, that individual more readily acknowledges the dysfunctional behavior rather than denying it or becoming defensive. By identifying the dysfunction as interpersonal, the family is being prepared to think of their transactions in circular terms (instead of what were probably previous linear explanations) and to attend to the complementarity of family relations. In this simple, nonpathologizing way, the therapist also is subtly suggesting that the participants are capable of (structural) change if they work together to reprogram how they deal with one another—in a word, that they have the power and resiliency to initiate a structural change in their transaction patterns.

Assessing Family Interactions

Assessment overlaps with joining the family. From the start, structuralists attempt to assess a family by attending primarily to its organizational structure and ongoing transaction patterns, paying special notice to the social context in which any dysfunctional behavior has manifested itself. Their ultimate concerns in any family appraisal are the family's hierarchical organization, the ability of its subsystems to carry out their functions, the family's possible alignments and coalitions, the permeability of its current boundaries, and its pliability or rigidity in meeting the needs of individual members as circumstances command. Structuralists are interested in how flexibly the family adapts to developmental changes as well as unexpected situational crises, and how well—and how easily—family members join together to resolve conflict.

Overall, the thrust of the assessment effort, from the initial session onward, is to evaluate the family's ability to change obsolete or no longer workable interactive patterns within the family, helping the family replace these outmoded patterns with ones more consistent with ongoing family development. However, the major purpose of the early assessment, for the structuralists, is not so much to diagnose family weaknesses as it is to develop a *road map* for entering the family, adjust to its customary style of dealing with problems, and once inside, plan restructuring interventions.

Assessment is an integral and ongoing part of structural family therapy. Immediately upon joining the family—sometimes before meeting them, based on intake sheet information—the therapist is forming hypotheses about the family's structural arrangement.

These early hunches, subject to refinement and revision, help guide early probing into the family's organization. What part of the system appears to be underfunctioning? Why, and how badly, has the system broken down? Why now? Which family interactive patterns seem especially problematic? What latent adaptive structures can the family call upon from their past efforts to cope with crises? These and similar questions are likely to occur to the structural therapist experiencing the family's trans-actions, as he or she begins to form a tentative diagnosis of family functioning.

Having joined the family, structuralists are likely to want to learn about coalitions, affiliations, the nature of family conflict, and the ways in which this family resolves conflict. One technique is to direct their attention to the family's current organization, which they diagram in graphic form in order to map out relationship patterns within the family. Just as Bowenian family systems therapists, consistent with a transgenerational theory, utilize genograms to chart family relationships extending back at least three generations, structuralists use family diagramming to depict a family's *current* transactional patterns. While the Bowenians seek clues regarding the family's intergenerational influences, the structuralists concern themselves with conveying information, through lines and spatial arrangements, about the family's current organizational structure, boundaries, and behavioral sequences.

Structuralists make use of a simple pictorial device called a *structural map* to formulate hypotheses about those areas where the family functions well and other areas where dysfunction may be occurring. Used as an assessment device, **family mapping** often helps provide an organizing schema for understanding complex family interactive patterns—especially which particular subsystem is involved in perpetuating a problem—and as such may be invaluable in therapeutic planning. As Minuchin and Fishman (1981) point out:

> The family map indicates the position of family members vis-à-vis one another. It reveals coalitions, affiliations, explicit and implicit conflicts, and the ways family members group themselves in conflict resolution. It identifies family members who operate as detourers of conflict and family members who function as switchboards. The map charts the nurturers, healers, and scapegoaters. Its delineation of the boundaries between subsystems indicates what movement there is and suggests possible areas of strength or dysfunction. (p. 69)

Figure 10.1 illustrates some common symbols structuralists use to delineate the clarity of family boundaries (clear, diffuse, rigid), subsystem operations, and family

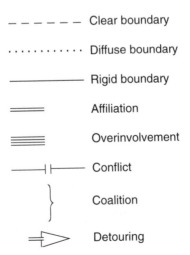

FIGURE 10.1 Minuchin's symbols for family mapping
Source: Minuchin, 1974, p. 53

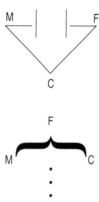

FIGURE 10.2 The effect of stress on the subsystem boundaries of a family. In the top diagram, a father (F) and mother (M) both stressed at work come home and criticize each other, but then detour their conflict by attacking the child (C). In the bottom diagram, the husband criticizes the wife, who seeks a coalition with the child against the father. Note the rigid cross-generational subsystem of mother and child; their coalition has the effect of excluding the father. Minuchin refers to this as a cross-generational dysfunctional pattern.
Source: Minuchin, 1974, p. 61

transactional styles. Figure 10.2 offers two examples of the use of structural mapping in depicting family conflict. The upper figure exemplifies a familiar detouring coalition within a family in which parents cope with direct conflict with one another by directing the problem they are having onto their child. The lower figure, again familiar, is a simple notation by a structural therapist of an intergenerational coalition in a family with diffuse mother-child boundaries.

Mapping offers an almost endless number of possible combinations for picturing family boundaries, alliances, affiliations, coalitions, detouring strategies, and so on. For example, family enmeshment may be illustrated by the symbol of overinvolvement; a coalition of several members against another can be shown by brackets. Family mapping, although a simple shorthand device, has two especially useful purposes: it graphically describes how the family is organized, and it helps the therapist detect the family subunit requiring restructuring (Umbarger, 1983). Figure 10.3 diagrams an overinvolved parent-child bond as well as a family coalition against the other parent. Structural maps are created throughout therapy and are revised or discarded as new family information becomes available.

Monitoring Family Dysfunctional Sets

Monitoring and helping to modify troubled or problematic transaction patterns is the crux of the structural intervention process. Once structuralists have gained entrance into the family, they begin to probe the family structure, looking for areas of flexibility and possible change. For example, a family has come for therapy because the teenage daughter is shy, withdrawn, and has difficulties in her social life. The therapist may observe for diagnostic purposes how the family enters the therapy room: The girl sits next to her mother, and they move their two chairs close together. When the therapist

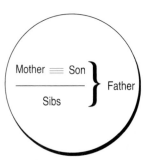

FIGURE 10.3 This diagram shows a closed-family-unit boundary with an overinvolved mother and son comprising the parental subsystem. Between them and the other children is a rigid boundary, yet apparently under enough control so that all are in a coalition against the father.
Source: Umbarger, 1983, p. 36

asks what the problem is, the mother answers, ignoring her daughter's attempts to add her thoughts on the matter. The mother makes comments that suggest she has too intimate a knowledge of her adolescent daughter's personal life—more knowledge than is usual. Within a few minutes after starting, the structural therapist makes the first intervention, asking the mother and father to change chairs. Structural therapy has begun: As the father is brought into the picture, the family flexibility is being tested; with the implication of pathology in the mother-daughter dyad, the family's reason for seeking therapy for the teenager is already being reframed or relabeled as a problem with a larger focus.

Two structural techniques are operating in this example. **Boundary making** represents an effort to create greater psychological distance between the enmeshed mother and daughter, and by bringing the marginalized father closer, to begin to modify the family's customary transactional patterns. The daughter, in turn, gains a greater chance of developing more independence as the diffuse boundary with her mother is starting to be clarified. The strengthened parental subsystem increases the likelihood of greater differentiation between parents and children in the family. At the same time, the therapist is using the technique of **unbalancing**—attempting to change the hierarchical relationship between members of the parental subsystem by having the father take on an expanded role in the family. By seeming to side with the father, the therapist is upsetting the family homeostasis and making an initial move to change preexisting family patterns by first unbalancing and then realigning the system. In boundary making, then, the therapist tries to change the distance between subsystems; in unbalancing, the goal is to change the hierarchical relationships of the members of a subsystem (Minuchin & Fishman, 1981).

Through **tracking,** the structural therapist adopts symbols of the family's life gathered from members' communication (such as life themes, values, significant family events) and deliberately uses them in conversation with the family. The therapist's effort to confirm that he or she values what family members say, without soliciting the information, is also a way of influencing their later transactional patterns; Minuchin (1974) calls this "leading by following." Tracking a particular family theme may also reveal clues to the family structure. For example, in working with an enmeshed family, Minuchin noted the father's statement that he disliked closed doors. Tracking the door issue, Minuchin discovered that the children were not permitted to close the doors of their rooms, that a brother slept in his older sister's room, and that the sex lives of the parents were curtailed because their own bedroom door remained open. Later, Minuchin was able to use the metaphor of the doors to help the family clarify its boundaries. Thus, tracking can be used as a restructuring strategy.

An **enactment** is a staged effort by the therapist to bring an outside family conflict into the session so that the family members can demonstrate how they deal with it. The therapist can then observe the conflict sequence and begin mapping out a way to modify the members' interaction and create structural changes. Using this technique, the therapist actively creates a scenario during a session in which the players act out their dysfunctional transactions rather than simply describe them (Colapinto, 2000). To use an example offered by Rosenberg (1983), a mother complained that her two-year-old daughter had tantrums and embarrassed her in front of grandparents, on buses, and in other situations. The daughter remained well behaved during the early sessions despite (or maybe because of) her mother's insistence that she engaged in this awful behavior away from the therapist. During the third or fourth session, when the child asked for gum, Rosenberg saw his chance: he asked the mother not to give her daughter the gum, because lunchtime was approaching.

As the child's whimper turned to crying, to begging, and finally to falling on the floor and undressing herself—and as the mother considered giving in—Rosenberg encouraged the mother to hold firm, despite the by-now deafening noise. More than a half hour later, the child came to a whimpering stop; she seemed fine, although both mother and therapist were exhausted. However, the mother had asserted her control during the enactment, thus learning she could be competent and more resolute than she had previously thought. From a structural viewpoint, the child's problematic behavior was redefined in transactional terms; the generational boundaries were reestablished; effective alternative transactional patterns were introduced; the proper hierarchical order was put into place (mother was again in charge); and the daughter, whose tantrums at home ceased shortly thereafter, was comfortable in knowing that her mother could handle her.

Structuralists deliberately take on a decisive role with families, since they view the therapist, rather than any techniques or interpretations or prescriptions, as the ultimate instrument of change (Colapinto, 1991). Therapeutically, they actively challenge the rigid, repetitive transactional patterns by which some families unsuccessfully attempt to organize themselves and cope with stress, and then, by deliberately "unfreezing" these patterns and unbalancing the system, create an opportunity for the family to structurally reorganize. Generally, this therapeutic effort involves a push for clearer boundaries, increased flexibility in family interactions, particularly at transition points in family life, and most important, modification of the dysfunctional structure.

Here it is important to note that while essentially focused on family transactional patterns, structuralists nevertheless make certain they do not lose track of what is happening to each family member; as Minuchin, Rosman, and Baker (1978) caution, therapists would be committing a serious error by "denying the individual while enthroning the family" (p. 9). That is, while they believe problematic or symptomatic behavior typically arises when families, whether enmeshed or disengaged, rigidly resist change, they remain aware that certain individuals may bring physical, emotional, behavioral, or learning disabilities to the family situation, and that these disabilities must be accommodated in facilitating family restructuring.

Any dysfunctional hierarchical issues within the family typically are explored since structuralists insist, for families to be functional, not only that parents are in charge of their children but also that differentiation exists between subsystems. Parents together must form and maintain an executive coalition, a parental subsystem; they have the responsibility to care for and protect and help socialize their children. They also have rights to make decisions (selection of schools, home relocation) they believe are best for the survival of the overall family system. However, as the children grow and their needs change, the parental subsystem must change accordingly, sharing opportunities for decision making and self-direction with the children. Disengaged families need to loosen their boundaries and increase family interaction. Enmeshed families need to develop clear yet flexible boundaries to encourage individuation and distinct differentiation between subsystems.

Siblings too must develop a working subsystem of peers; within the sibling system they must learn to negotiate, cooperate, compete, make friends, deal with enemies, and develop a sense of belonging. Spouses, aside from being parents, must also receive support from one another and together develop a subsystem that serves as a model for expressing affection, helping each other deal with stress, and dealing with conflict as equals. If there is a major dysfunction within the spousal subsystem, it will likely reverberate throughout the family (Minuchin & Fishman, 1981).

Minuchin (1974) conceives of family pathology as resulting from the development of *dysfunctional sets.* Dysfunctional sets are the family reactions, developed in response to stress, that are repeated without modification whenever there is family conflict. A husband experiencing stress at work comes home and shouts at his wife. The wife counterattacks, escalating the conflict that continues without change until one partner abandons the field. Both parties experience a sense of nonresolution. In another example, a mother verbally attacks an adolescent son, the father takes his side, and the younger children seize the opportunity to join in and pick on their older brother. All family members become involved, and various coalitions develop; but the family organization remains the same, and the dysfunctional sets will be repeated in the next trying situation.

Restructuring Transactional Patterns

Structuralists assume that any family seeking treatment is experiencing some stress that has overloaded the system's adaptive and coping mechanisms, handicapping the optimum functioning of its members in the process. Consequently, they set themselves the task of helping families rearrange their organization—restructuring the system that governs its transactions—so that the family functions more effectively and the growth potential of each member is maximized. Restructuring involves changes in family rules and realignments, changes in the patterns that support certain undesirable behaviors, and changes in the sequences of interaction. We have noted several techniques structuralists employ to facilitate structural changes—enactments, boundary making, unbalancing. To highlight a particular transaction and get the message across to family members, the therapist may also increase the *intensity* of a remark (by heightening its affective component—"It's essential that you as parents agree about this"; by frequently repeating it in different contexts—to a child resisting growing up: "But how *old* are you?"; or by using it in regard to different transactions).

One particularly useful technique, **reframing,** changes the original meaning of an event or situation, placing it in a new context in which an equally plausible explanation is possible. The idea is to relabel what occurs in order to provide a more constructive perspective, thereby altering the way the event or situation is viewed. As used by structuralists, reframing is directed toward relabeling the problem as a function of the family structure. Typically, within the context of an enactment, the therapist first redefines a presenting problem. For example, in the case of an adolescent daughter's self-starvation, the anorectic girl is labeled as "stubborn" and not "sick," forcing the family members to reconsider their earlier view that she is ill and thus not responsible for what is occurring.

Giving new meaning to the girl's behavior creates a new context that can ultimately change the family's transactional patterns, perhaps helping to modify dysfunctional coalitions or alter poorly working boundaries and subsystems. The fact of the daughter's not eating has not changed, only the *meaning* attributed to that behavior. Not intended to deliberately deceive, reframing rather is used by structuralists and other family therapists (especially strategic therapists) to change family perspectives and ultimately to change family behavior patterns based on the new options and alternatives.

Structural interventions frequently *increase the stress* (another restructuring technique) on the family system, perhaps even creating a family crisis that unbalances family homeostasis. But they also open the way for transformation of the family structure. Now the family has no choice but to face the chronically avoided conflict. In an enmeshed family system, for example, members often believe the family as a whole can neither withstand change nor adapt to it; consequently, the system demands that certain members change (develop symptoms) in order to maintain the dysfunctional homeostasis.

When the danger level of family stress is approached, the symptom bearer is activated as part of a conflict avoidance maneuver; the family system reinforces the continuance of the symptoms that help maintain the system's balance and status quo. It is the structural therapist's job to make everyone aware, often through reframing, that the problem belongs and pertains to the family, not an individual; that the implementation of new functional sets must replace the habitual repetition of the dysfunctional ones; and that the family, having located and identified the problem, together can resolve the underlying conflict by making the necessary structural modifications.

The therapeutic tactics employed by structuralists are often dramatic and at times theatrical. Like stage directors, they set up a situation, create a scenario for enactment, assign roles and tasks to the family, and then observe the family in action (Colapinto, 2000). For example, in treating an anorectic adolescent who is self-starving and refusing to eat, Minuchin arranges to meet the family at lunch for the first session (Minuchin,

Rosman, & Baker, 1978). He creates such an enactment deliberately, to foster a crisis around eating and to experience what the family members are experiencing. He observes the parents pleading, demanding, cajoling, becoming desperate, and feeling defeat.

He watches the adolescent girl demonstrate hopelessness and helplessness, pathetically asserting through her refusal to eat that she has always given in to her parents at the expense of herself, but will do so no longer. While the daughter has been labeled as the problem, Minuchin, reframing, helps the family see that the symptoms of **anorexia nervosa** are a response to family dysfunction, not simply the adolescent's defiant behavior. All the family members are locked into a futile pattern of interaction that has become the center of their lives; each member has a stake in maintaining the disorder.

In turn, the syndrome plays an important role in maintaining family homeostasis. Structural family therapy helps each person in the family to recognize the syndrome and take responsibility for contributing to it. By creating a family crisis, Minuchin forces the family to change the system, substituting more functional interactions.

Typical of Minuchin's directive, unyielding, crisis-provoking approach is his insistence in this case that the parents force the emaciated girl to eat. They coax, cajole, threaten, yell, and finally stuff food down her throat until their daughter collapses in tears. Minuchin believes she will now eat. As he later explains it:

> The anorectic is obsessed with her hopelessness, inadequacy, wickedness, ugliness. I incite an interpersonal conflict that makes her stop thinking about how terrible she is and start thinking about what bastards her parents are. At that demonstration, I said to the parents, "Make her eat," and when they did she had to deal with them as people. Previously, the parents had been saying "We control you because we love you." In the position I put them in, they were finally saying "God damn it, you eat!" That freed her. She could then eat or not eat; she could be angry at them as clearly delineated figures. (Malcolm, 1978, p. 78)

With this approach, Minuchin has been able to show that the anorectic symptom is embedded in the faulty family organization. Changing that organization eliminates the potentially fatal symptom. As the family members begin to experience themselves and each other differently, the stage is set for new transactional patterns to emerge. The emergence of new structures is intended to aid the identified patient along with the family as a whole. From this viewpoint, a symptomatic person's presenting problem is embedded in the family's dysfunctional rules; as inappropriate or constricting rules are replaced, and family members are released from stereotyped positions and functions, the symptom is no longer needed to maintain family homeostasis, and it becomes unnecessary (Colapinto, 1982). Because of family reorganization, future symptom development should become less likely as the opportunity is increased for all members, and the family as a whole, to enhance their growth potential.

In Box 10.1 we offer a detailed case concerning the triangulation that occurs when a child from a former marriage comes to live with a newly married couple. Note particularly how the therapist employs various structural family therapy techniques (family mapping, reframing, reestablishing boundaries, strengthening the spousal subsystem) in helping the family alter its previously destructive path.

BOX 10.1 CASE STUDY

STRUCTURAL THERAPY WITH A DIVIDED STEPFAMILY

Joyce and David Oliver had been married only eight months when they contacted a family counselor as a last resort. Both partners were in their late 20s: Joyce, never married, had established a career in business; David, previously married, had been divorced for about a year when he met Joyce at a ski resort. They had a great time together and, after seeing each other daily for several months when they returned to the city, decided to marry. David had spoken briefly of Kiri, his four-year-old daughter who lived with his ex-wife in another state; but Joyce did not see the child as having much to do with her, since Kiri lived with her mother. Joyce had met her future stepdaughter only once before the wedding ceremony.

The family problems began shortly after the wedding when Rhonda, David's ex-wife, announced that she was having some personal problems—including some with Kiri—and was sending her to live with David and Joyce. For David, who took his parental responsibilities very seriously, this was a welcome opportunity to see Kiri daily and take an active part in her upbringing. At last he would have the perfect family he had always dreamed of, the perfect harmony that he had failed to achieve in his previous marriage. Joyce, having no experience with children, wasn't sure what to expect; but she was eager to share parental responsibilities if it made her new husband happy.

Unfortunately, David's dreams failed to materialize, in no small part due to his own behavior—as well as Kiri's. She was not an easy child to live with, having been suddenly whisked away from an over-close mother. Confused and frightened, Kiri clung to her father, quickly becoming overattached to him and excluding her stepmother. David, in turn feeling guilty over his child's obvious upset, became very attached to Kiri—so much so that Joyce sometimes felt he preferred the child's company to hers. Instead of learning to live with her new husband, Joyce soon felt she was saddled with an instant family in which she felt like an outsider in her own home. David called Kiri daily before leaving work to see if she needed him to bring anything home. When his wife objected and complained of feeling "frozen out," David defended himself by saying he was merely acting like any concerned parent would, adding that Joyce's jealousy forced him to do even more for Kiri than he might have if Joyce had done more.

At night David put Kiri to bed; if he stayed more than the 10 minutes he had promised Joyce, she became depressed, withdrew, and did not talk to him the rest of that evening. According to David, Joyce was a spoiled child herself, being competitive with a four-year-old; he was losing respect for her. During their joint sessions with a family counselor, he spoke of being raised by a widowed mother as an only child, and how central to his life was the feeling of family closeness. Joyce, on the other hand, insisted that David did not allow her to develop a relationship with Kiri, expecting her to instantly love someone because he did, but doing nothing to instill in Kiri that they had to reorganize the family to include all three of them. She herself had been raised by a divorced mother in a relatively disengaged family where all three children lived relatively separate lives.

The conflict between them had reached the boiling point by the time the couple contacted the counselor. David labeled his wife a "wicked stepmother," whom he threatened to leave unless she "corrected her behavior." She, in turn, accused her husband of having a "romance" with his daughter, strongly implying that there might be more to the father-daughter relationship than was evident. Neither was willing to listen to what the counselor was saying, each apparently eager to win his favor and favorable judgment regarding who was right. Joyce would hear of nothing short of sending Kiri back to her mother; David insisted he would not be given an ultimatum regarding how to deal with his own child. While the counseling was in its early stages, Rhonda announced that she had gotten remarried, to a man named Mel, and that she was pregnant.

The counselor began by indicating he was not there to judge who was right, but to help David and Joyce gain some tools for understanding what was happening to them. It was clear that both were miserable, and Kiri undoubtedly was also. If the couple continued this way, they would almost certainly get divorced—an unfortunate circumstance for both of them, since their marriage had not had a chance.

To reduce the white heat between the couple so that counseling might proceed, the counselor attempted two early interventions. One was to reduce the tension by asking them to describe their own histories of child rearing. The information would be useful later, and for the moment would help each spouse begin to grasp that they had come into parenting with different experiences and expectations. As another initial intervention ploy, the counselor asked whether they would be willing to listen to what the other had to say without condemning it, getting defensive, or resorting to name-calling. The counselor thus appealed to their rational selves; since each spouse was anxious not to be labeled the difficult or unreasonable one, the two agreed.

Each spouse proceeded to discuss his or her view of child rearing. They had clear disagreements based on different experiences of their own, and the counselor helped each of them to listen and try to understand. Joyce's rejecting behavior toward Kiri was reframed by the counselor as inexperience rather than wickedness; David's overinvolvement was reframed as eagerness to be a good father. Joyce acknowledged that she could learn from David since she had known little parental attention and affection growing up, but she insisted that he try to be less critical of her if he really wanted

her to make the effort. David acknowledged he might be overdoing the parenting, since he had not had a father of his own at home as a model. The counselor helped him understand that fathers who obtain custody often have unrealistic expectations of how a stepmother should behave. In this case, David was willing to relinquish some parenting chores as he became convinced that Joyce was willing to try. He was encouraged to avoid any coalitions with Kiri against Joyce.

The next phase of the counseling dealt with reestablishing boundaries. The counselor explained that stepfamily blending does not come automatically or instantly, but only through a gradual rearrangement of the new family's structure. It was agreed that David would allow Joyce to do more of the parenting in the best way she saw fit—even if it differed from his way. He would explain to Kiri that although Rhonda was still her mother, Joyce would be taking over the day-to-day job, with his approval, when Kiri lived with them. That is, Kiri was told that Joyce was not replacing her biological mother, only supplementing her. Kiri could visit her mother whenever it could be arranged—something Kiri expressed an interest in doing, especially after her stepsister was born. Together, David and Joyce told Kiri that she was a member of two households; she could feel free to move between the two without loyalty conflicts.

David and Joyce had their own loyalty issues to resolve. As he came to understand that he had given

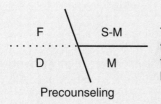

F   S-M   The diffuse boundary between father and daughter indicates
·················   they have formed an overinvolved or enmeshed relationship;
D   M   the stepmother is isolated and excluded, as is the absent
                      biological mother.
Precounseling

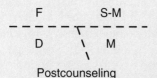

F   S-M   A restructuring has occurred, and a clear boundary now
– – – – – – – – –   exists between the united parents and the daughter, as well
D   \   M   as between the daughter and her biological mother.

Postcounseling

FIGURE 10.4   Pre- and postcounseling structural mapping of the Oliver family.

(continued)

BOX 10.1   (*continued*)

his daughter his first loyalty—primarily out of guilt over the impact on Kiri of his failed marriage—David recognized that he was contributing to the diminution of his current marital relationship. Joyce recognized that because she felt in a secondary position, she struggled against the child excessively, forcing David to defend Kiri; thus she, too, contributed to the deteriorating marriage. The counselor helped the pair untangle these difficulties, focusing them on working to strengthen their separate identity as a couple and their primary loyalty to each other. They were encouraged to spend more time alone as a couple, sharing activities that did not include Kiri. As this occurred, the couple's bond grew; differences between them, although still present, began to be negotiated more openly rather than through a father-daughter versus stepmother conflict. New rules and happier solutions followed as David, Joyce, and Kiri began to develop their own traditions and to define themselves as a family.

Note the counselor's goals in this case:

1. Reduce the accusations and blame fixing between the adults.
2. Reframe or relabel the behavior each finds objectionable in the other as well intentioned, thereby diffusing some of the self-righteous rage and indignation.
3. Appeal to each adult's wish to be seen as reasonable and fair in hearing out the spouse's contentions.
4. Define the problem as a systems one to which each member, including the child, is contributing.
5. Strengthen the spousal subsystem, encouraging their loyalty to each other and their common purpose and family identity.
6. Consolidate parental authority and unity in regard to the child without her experiencing loss of her biological mother.
7. Help reduce loyalty conflicts for the child and adults.
8. Keep the remarried system an open system with permeable boundaries, so that the child not only derives a sense of security from the home where she lives but also retains membership in her other household.
9. Help the family members to tolerate differences among themselves or from some ideal intact family model.
10. Encourage the development of new rules, behavior patterns, and family traditions.

Source: Goldenberg & Goldenberg, 2002, pp. 195–198

SUMMARY

The structural approach in family therapy is primarily associated with Salvador Minuchin and his colleagues, first at the Wiltwyck School and later at the Philadelphia Child Guidance Center. Systems-based, structural family theory focuses on the active, organized wholeness of the family unit and the ways in which the family organizes itself through its transactional patterns. In particular, the family's subsystems, boundaries, alignments, and coalitions are studied in an effort to understand its structure. Dysfunctional structures point to the covert rules governing family transactions that have become inoperative or in need of renegotiation.

Structural family therapy is geared to present-day transactions and gives higher priority to action than to insight or understanding. All behavior, including symptoms in the identified patient, is viewed within the context of family structure. Structural interventions are active, carefully calculated, even manipulative efforts to alter rigid, outmoded, or unworkable structures. To achieve such changes, families are helped to renegotiate outmoded rules and to seek greater boundary clarity.

By joining the family and accommodating to its style, structuralists gain a foothold to assess the members' way of dealing with problems and with each other, ultimately helping them to change dysfunctional sets and rearrange or realign the family organization.

Family mapping provides a simple observational technique for charting the family's ongoing transactional patterns.

Enactments (having the family demonstrate typical conflict situations in the therapy session), *boundary making* (realigning inappropriate or outdated boundaries), *unbalancing* (supporting one member to interfere with family homeostasis), and *reframing* (the therapist's relabeling or redefining a problem as a function of the family's structure) are therapeutic techniques frequently used to bring about a transformation of the family structure. The ultimate goal is to restructure the family's transactional rules by developing more appropriate boundaries between subsystems and strengthening the family's hierarchical order. A final case study illustrates some structural techniques.

RECOMMENDED READINGS

Aponte, H. J., & DiCasare, E. J. (2000). Stuctural therapy. In F. M. Dattilio & L. J. Bevilacqua (Eds.), *Comparative treatments for relationship dysfunction*. New York: Springer.

Colapino, J. (1991). Structural family therapy. In A. S. Gurman & D. P. Kniskern (Eds.), *Handbook of family therapy* (Vol. II). New York: Brunner/Mazel.

Minuchin, S. (1974). *Families and family therapy*. Cambridge, MA: Harvard University Press.

Minuchin, S., & Fishman, H. C. (1981). *Family therapy techniques*. Cambridge, MA: Harvard University Press.

Strategic Models

Strategic therapies offer an active, straightforward set of therapist interventions aimed at reducing or eliminating the presenting set of family problems or behavioral symptoms. Less focused on the meaning of the symptom or its origins, strategists typically issue a series of directives or tasks to the family, directed at changing those repetitive interactive sequences within families that lead to cross-generational conflict. Whereas other approaches rely on interpretation or relationship building, strategists zero in on those behavioral sequences within the family that perpetuate the problem, then offer directives to provoke the family to change the way they deal with one another, sometimes without their cooperation or knowledge that they are being manipulated into doing so. Among the greatest virtues of strategic family therapy is its insistent attention to the task at hand—removing the disturbing symptom or dysfunctional behavioral sequence—continuous tracking of the family's patterns of interpersonal exchanges, and its use of assignments of tasks to achieve therapeutic ends.

Strategic therapies derive from the work of the Palo Alto research group projects of 1952–1962 on family communication described earlier in the text. The seminal ideas of Gregory Bateson, Don Jackson, Jay Haley, John Weakland, Paul Watzlawick, and their associates helped shape the family therapy field and are fundamental to how practitioners view family relationships even today. Feedback loops, the redundancy principle, double binds, family rules, marital quid pro quo, family homeostasis—all are such familiar and basic concepts that young family therapists today might assume they were always known. They were not; they are part of communication theory, which emerged when Bateson and his colleagues set out to study communication patterns in families with schizophrenic members.

THE COMMUNICATIONS OUTLOOK

Communication theorists concern themselves with how verbal and nonverbal messages get exchanged within a family. They pay attention to the question of *what* is occurring rather than *why* it is occurring—to the ongoing *process* between and among people within a system and the ways in which they interact, define, and redefine their relationships, and not to drawing inferences about each participant's inner conflicts. Communication patterns—the style or manner in which information is exchanged (that is, coded and encoded) within a family; the precision, clarity, or degree of ambiguity of the transmission; and the behavioral or pragmatic effect of the communication, as much as the *content* of what is communicated—help determine those relationships.

In shifting the locus of pathology from the individual to the social context and the interchange between individuals, these family therapy pioneers were not denying that intrapsychic mechanisms influence individual functioning (although an examination of these mechanisms was played down in practice). Rather, they were giving greater credence to the power of family rules to govern interactive behavior; to them, a breakdown in individual or family functioning follows from a breakdown in rules. Feedback loops revealed a great deal about how family members communicated with one another, how they went about resolving conflict, what chain of command existed within their ranks. To this day, the strategic therapist's primary way of viewing problems is to attend to the family's *sequence of interactions* and its *hierarchy of interactions* (Keim, 1998).

Communication theorists argue that a circular interaction continues between people because each participant imposes her own **punctuation;** each arbitrarily believes that what she says is caused by what the other person says. In a sense, such serial punctuations between family members resemble the dialogue of children quarreling:"You started it!" ("I'm only reacting to what you did.")"No, you started it first!" and so on. As Weakland (1976) contends, it is meaningless to search for a starting point in a conflict between two people because it is a complex, repetitive interaction, not a simple, linear, cause-and-effect situation with a clear beginning and end.

Once considered iconoclastic if not radical, this view of redundant patterns of communication within the family as offering clues to family dysfunction provided a linguistic leap forward for the emerging field. While its early view of the therapist as an authoritative expert strategically directing—manipulating—families to change is largely out of fashion today (replaced by the collaborating therapist or coach without fixed ideas of how the family should change), the communication perspective itself has undergone considerable revision as it has evolved over four decades; current proponents also can be considered to represent the strategic approach. For clarity of presentation, however, we have separated four outlooks: the original Mental Research Institute (MRI) interactional view, the brief therapy principles and therapeutic procedures that characterize current MRI activities, the strategic therapy refinements advanced primarily by Jay Haley and Cloé Madanes, and the strategic-related efforts developed in Milan, Italy, by Mara Selvini-Palazzoli and her associates. The last group's labors, much of which have evolved in the social construction direction, are discussed more fully in the next chapter.

THE STRATEGIC OUTLOOK

Efficiency and technical parsimony are the hallmark of these models; all are change oriented, brief in duration, and view families in non-pathological terms. All four approaches involve active therapists who tailor their novel strategies or interventions specifically to a family's presenting complaint and terminate therapy as soon as that complaint is resolved. Their specific aim is to help the family resolve its presenting problem; they are less concerned with promoting personal growth or working through any underlying family emotional issues or teaching families specific problem-solving skills (Shoham, Rohrbaugh, & Patterson, 1995). The family receives help for what they came for, without the therapist speculating on whether other, as yet unidentified problem areas might still exist or that further therapy perhaps is called for.

While there are noteworthy differences in the four approaches, we group them together because all represent, in varying degrees of refinement, elaborations on the theme that clients determine what the problem is and *therapists are responsible for change.* Therapists can initiate interventions to change the family's problem-solving management or strategies without attending to, or providing insight into, why that behavior occurred in the first place. Specific, reachable goals are delineated clearly at the outset of treatment, and the family and therapist together recognize when such concrete goals are met.

MRI INTERACTIONAL FAMILY THERAPY

Leading Figures

Founded by Don Jackson in 1959, and initially with a small staff consisting of social worker Virginia Satir and psychiatrist Jules Riskin, the Mental Research Institute in Palo Alto at first existed side by side with the neighboring Bateson Project. When the Bateson team ended its research endeavors in 1962, Haley, Weakland (coauthors, along with Bateson and Jackson, of the double-bind theory), and briefly, Bateson himself, joined the MRI as research associates; also at MRI were psychologists Paul Watzlawick and Arthur Bodin and psychiatrist Richard Fisch. Other prominent family therapists discussed elsewhere in this text—John Bell, Carlos Sluzki, Cloé Madanes, and Steve de Shazer come to mind—have been affiliated with this outstanding training center at one time or another over the years.

Developing a Communication Paradigm

In the decade ending not long after Jackson's death in 1968 at the age of 48, the theoretical groundwork for the interactional approach of the MRI was laid, based largely on ideas derived from general systems theory, cybernetics, and information theory. Moving beyond their original formulations regarding the familial origins of schizophrenia, these researchers zeroed in on the family interaction sequences in all families in an effort to understand how faulty communication patterns might lead to family dysfunction. Watzlawick, Beavin, and Jackson's (1967) *Pragmatics of Human Communication* is considered the classic pioneering text in the communication field, drawing the attention of family therapists to the need for the simultaneous study of *semantics* (the clarity of meaning between what is said and received), *syntax* (the pattern as well as manner or style in which information is transmitted), and *pragmatics* (the behavioral effects or consequences of communication). These authors presented a series of axioms regarding the interpersonal nature of communication:

- *All behavior is communication at some level.* Just as one cannot *not* behave, so one cannot not communicate. The wife who complains in utter frustration that her husband "refuses to communicate" with her but instead stares at the television set all evening is responding too literally to his failure to talk to her. On a nonverbal level, she is receiving a loud and clear message that he is rejecting her, withdrawing from her, may be angry or bored with her, wants distance from her, and so on.

- *Communication may occur simultaneously at many levels*—gesture, body language, tone of voice, posture, intensity—in addition to the content of what is said. In some cases, the message at one level contradicts one at another level. People can say one thing and mean another, modifying, reinforcing, or contradicting what they have just said. In other words, they are both communicating ("How are you?") and at another level communicating about their communications ("I do not really expect you to answer, nor do I especially want to know the answer, unless you say you are fine"). All communication takes place at two levels—the surface or content level and a second level called **metacommunication,** which qualifies what is said on the first level. Problems may arise when a message at the first level ("Nice to see you") is contradicted by a facial expression or voice tone that communicates another message ("How can I make a quick getaway from this boring person?") at the second level.

• *Every communication has a content (report) and a relationship (command) aspect.* Every communication does more than convey information; it also defines the relationship between communicants. For example, the husband who announces "I'm hungry" is offering information but also, more important, is telling his wife that he expects her to do something about it by preparing dinner. He is thus making a statement of his perceived rights in the relationship; he expects his wife to take action based on his statement. The way his wife responds tells him whether she is willing to go along with his *definition of the relationship* or wants to engage in what could be a struggle to redefine it ("It's your turn to make the dinner tonight" or "Let's go out to a restaurant tonight" or "I'm not hungry yet").

• *Relationships are defined by command messages.* These messages constitute regulating patterns for stabilizing relationships and defining family rules. In operation, the rules preserve family homeostasis. In a family, when a teenager announces she is pregnant, or parents decide to get a divorce, or a handicapped child is born, or a family member becomes schizophrenic, it has an effect similar to flinging open a window when the home heating system has been warmed to the desired temperature. The family goes to work to reestablish its balance.

• *Relationships may be described as symmetrical or complementary.* If it is a relationship based on equality the interactive pattern is **symmetrical;** if the context of the behavioral exchange is oppositional, the pattern is **complementary.** In the former, participants mirror each other's behavior; if A boasts, B boasts more grandly, causing A to boast still further, and so on in this one-upmanship game. By definition, complementary relationships are based on inequality and the maximization of differences. In this form of reciprocal interaction, one partner (traditionally the male) takes the "one-up" position and the other (traditionally the female) assumes the submissive "one-down" position. However, despite appearances, these positions need not be taken as an indication of the partners' relative strength or weakness or power to influence the relationship.

• *Symmetrical relationships run the risk of becoming competitive.* In this case, each partner's actions influence the reactions of his or her partner in a spiraling effect called **symmetrical escalation.** Quarrels may get out of hand and become increasingly vicious as a nasty jibe is met with a nastier retort, which prompts the first person to become even more mean and ill-tempered, and so on. Squabbling partners may continually vie for ascendance over one another, neither willing to back down nor to concede a point. (In one Woody Allen movie, an exchange between a bickering couple goes something like this: "The Atlantic is the best ocean"; "You're crazy—the Pacific is a much better ocean"; "You're the one who's crazy and doesn't know what he's talking about"; and so on.) Clearly, in this transaction, the content of the argument is meaningless; it's the escalating conflict that is notable. The process of the exchange rather than its content defines the relationship.

- *Complementary communication inevitably involves one person who assumes a superior position and another who assumes an inferior one* (a bossy wife, a submissive husband, or vice versa). One partner's behavior complements the other's; if A is assertive, B becomes submissive, encouraging A to greater assertiveness, demanding still more submissiveness from B, and so on.

- *Each person punctuates a sequence of events in which he or she is engaged in different ways.* Such punctuations organize behavioral events taking place into each participant's view of cause and effect and thus are vital to ongoing interactions.

- *Problems develop and are maintained within the context of redundant interactive patterns and recursive feedback loops.* Haley, who had been a graduate student in communication when first recruited for the Bateson project, underscored the struggle for power and control in every relationship that is inherent in the messages that sender and receiver exchange. Who defines the relationship? Will that person attempt to turn it into a symmetrical or complementary one? Who decides who decides? Observe a couple discussing how to allocate expenditures, or what television program to watch, or who will answer the telephone, balance the checkbook, go to the refrigerator to get a snack, or pick up the dirty socks and underwear from the bedroom floor, and in each of these see if you do not learn a great deal about how the partners define their relationship.

Paradoxical Communication

The communication theorists were the first to point out that there is no such thing as a simple message. People continually send and receive a multiplicity of messages by both verbal and nonverbal channels, and every message may be qualified or modified by another message on another level of abstraction (Weakland, 1976). Not infrequently, the receiver can become confused when contradictions appear between what is said and what is expressed in tone or gesture.

A double-bind message is a particularly destructive form of such a **paradoxical injunction.** As we described it in Chapter 5, a double-bind message is communicated when one person, especially someone in a powerful position, issues an injunction to another that simultaneously contains two levels of messages or demands that are logically inconsistent and contradictory, producing a paradoxical situation for the recipient. In addition, the person receiving the paradoxical message is unable to avoid the incongruity or to comment on the impossibility of meeting its requirements, resulting in confusion.

Paradoxical injunctions are forms of communication that must be obeyed but that must be disobeyed to be obeyed! Two conditions typically must exist: (a) the participants must have a close complementary relationship; and (b) the recipient of the injunction cannot sidestep or otherwise avoid responding to the communication or metacommunication.

Consider the following injunction from a person in a position of authority:

IGNORE THESE INSTRUCTIONS

To comply with the instructions, a person must *not* follow instructions, since one message denies or negates the other ("I order you to disobey me"). Unable to discriminate which order or level of message to respond to, the recipient nevertheless is called upon to make some response. He or she is thus caught in a bind, being called upon to make a response but doomed to failure with whatever response is chosen. Although initially speculated to be the type of paradox that might be responsible for schizophrenia in a child who repeatedly receives such double-bind communications, it is now assumed that double binding, while still considered damaging, may exist at varying times and with varying degrees of serious consequences in all families.[1] Admittedly a linear construct, the double-bind concept (Bateson, Jackson, Haley, & Weakland, 1956) nevertheless was truly groundbreaking and heralded a breakthrough in the psychotherapy field by providing a new language and set of assumptions regarding relationships reflected in communication patterns to account for symptomatic behavior.

Therapeutic Assumptions

Led primarily by the innovative thinking of Paul Watzlawick (Watzlawick, 1978; Watzlawick, 1984; Watzlawick, Weakland, & Fisch, 1974), a longtime researcher into interpersonal communication and the language of change, the MRI therapeutic model emphasizes that, ironically, the solutions people use in attempting to alleviate a problem often contribute to the problem's maintenance or even its exacerbation. That is, people are not being difficult or resistant to change, but rather are "stuck" in repeating inappropriate and non-workable solutions. In this view, problems may arise from some ordinary life difficulty, perhaps coping with a transition such as the birth of an infant or an older child going off to school for the first time. Most families handle such transitions with relative ease, although occasionally the difficulty turns into a problem, particularly when mishandled or allowed to remain unresolved while the family persists in applying the same "solution" despite its previous failure to eliminate the difficulty. Ultimately the original difficulty escalates into a problem "whose eventual size and nature may have little apparent similarity to the original difficulty" (Fisch, Weakland, & Segal, 1982, p. 14).

In a pragmatic, therapist-directed approach, aimed at solving the current problem for which the family came seeking help, the task is to break into the family's repetitive but negatively self-perpetuating cycle. Confronted with family members engaged in repetitive and often mutually destructive behavior patterns, the MRI therapist wants to know what makes the behavior persist, and what he or she must do to change it (Watzlawick, Weakland, & Fisch, 1974), but not what in the past caused it, or how the family needs insight or restructuring.

First, the therapist must carefully delineate the problem in clear and concrete terms. Next, solutions previously attempted by the family must be scrutinized. The therapist is now prepared to define, again as precisely and concretely as necessary, just what change is sought, before implementing a strategy or therapeutic plan for achieving change (Watzlawick, 1978). As a general rule, the interactional therapist is seeking

---

[1]The double-bind situation is no longer believed to be the cause of schizophrenia, although it remains a historically significant formulation in that it drew attention to the possible role of family communication patterns in developing and maintaining family dysfunction. Today it is assumed that many families engage in such flawed communication at times; perhaps this is excessively so in families with severe but unacknowledged interpersonal conflict. Having lost its original pathological referent to schizophrenia, the double-bind concept is currently used loosely to refer to a variety of interactive communication patterns whose messages leave the receiver confused.

BOX 11.1   CASE STUDY

TREATING AN ALCOHOLIC SYMPTOM

In the following case, the therapist asks the patient to make what seems to be a small alteration in how he handles his drinking problem. Seeing it as a minor adjustment, he accepts the directive easily, not aware that he is beginning the process of modifying his "solution" to the problem. Therapy is concluded when the presenting symptom is eliminated or the presenting problem resolved, despite the fact that other problems remain.

Don was a 38-year-old high school teacher who had contacted the therapist 10 years earlier with indecisions over a career. This time, his anxious call for an appointment alerted the therapist that some crisis had occurred, and when Don appeared in her office the next day he was agitated and distraught. He told her how he had embarrassed himself and his wife and teenage children at a family wedding. Ordinarily a meek, mild-mannered person, he drank too much and got into a physical fight with a stranger. He reported that his family was angry with him, that he was determined to quit drinking, and he was ready to start working on the problem now.

The therapist recommended a self-help, 12-step AA program, but Don insisted he could conquer the problem on his own. The therapist was skeptical, however, and encouraged him to at least enlist the support of his older brother, who had quit drinking, and to talk to him as a "sponsor" every day.

After several sessions of weekly therapy, Don suffered a relapse, when his wife, Gwen, invited him to stop for a drink on their way home after he had picked her up at the airport. Gwen also had a drinking problem, which she claimed was under control, and by now it had become clear to the therapist that drinking was a core part of their relationship. When Gwen was asked to attend the therapy sessions with Don, she resisted, explaining that he was the one with the uncontrollable problem.

The therapist's initial efforts to provide insight into the connection between the use of alcohol and their relationship did not seem to help or lead to change. Deciding to concentrate on the presenting symptom—Don's drinking—the therapist suggested that he make a small change: to only drink together with Gwen, and at no other time. Since she was going on a business trip, and he had sole responsibility for caring for the children, he had earlier decided himself he would not drink during her absence, so he agreed to the directive.

Later, he told the therapist that her assignment was not hard to comply with, and that he had not had drinks with the other teachers after school on Friday, as had been the group's custom. He was even more gratified by realizing he had voluntary control over when he drank. He did continue drinking with Gwen when she returned, as he had been directed to do, but recognized there needed to be more to their relationship than being drinking buddies. They began to discuss their relationship—for the first time in years—and Gwen decided to seek help for her drinking. When Don called the therapist six months later, he seemed proud to report that the drinking was under better control and that he and his wife and children had become closer.

---

ways to change outmoded family rules, reveal hidden personal agendas, and modify or attempt to extinguish paradoxical communication patterns.

First-Order and Second-Order Changes

One especially useful set of concepts introduced by Watzlawick, Weakland, and Fisch (1974) concerns the level of change sought by the therapist. **First-order changes** are superficial behavioral changes within a system that do not change the structure of the system itself. These changes are apt to be linear and little more than cosmetic or perhaps simply a reflection of a couple's good intentions—for example, not to raise their voices and argue anymore.

These first-order changes are likely to be short-lived; even if the symptom is removed—the couple tries to control their quarreling—the underlying systemic rules governing the interaction between them have not changed, and the cease-fire is likely to be violated sooner or later.

Second-order changes require a fundamental revision of the system's structure and function. Here the therapist moves beyond merely helping remove the symptom, also striving to help the family alter its systemic interaction pattern—not just calling a halt to fighting, but changing the rules of the family system and consequently reorganizing the system so that it reaches a different level of functioning. If the therapy is successful, the old rules are discarded as obsolete; as a result the family may become temporarily confused, but then will attempt to reconstitute itself in a new way.

According to Watzlawick (1978), therapy must accomplish second-order changes (a change in viewpoint, often due to a therapist's reframing of a situation) rather than mere first-order changes (a conscious decision by clients to behave differently).

The Therapeutic Double Bind

Interactional therapists (and strategic therapists in general) argue that it is their responsibility, as outsiders, to provide the family with an experience that will enable the members to change their rules and metarules concerning their relationships with one another and with the outside world. Couples need to learn how each punctuates an interaction (who each thinks is responsible for what), and how conflict often follows differences in such perceptions. Families must examine their patterns of communication (including report and command functions) and especially the context in which communication occurs.

More specifically, faulty but persistent solutions to everyday difficulties must be examined to learn if the family (a) ignores a problem when some action is called for; (b) overreacts, taking more action than is necessary or developing unrealistic expectations from actions taken; or (c) takes action at the wrong level (making cosmetic first-order changes when second-order changes are necessary). As we demonstrate shortly, the MRI Brief Therapy Center approach incorporates this time-limited, highly focused therapeutic effort toward problem resolution.

While focusing on the presenting problem and helping the family develop clear and concise goals, strategists often try to induce change by offering explicit or implicit directives—therapeutic tasks aimed at extinguishing ineffective interactional sequences (examples are given later). To the therapist, these are clever maneuvers designed to subtly gain control over the presenting symptoms and force families to attempt different solutions; to the family these directives often appear to fly in the face of common sense, but family members nevertheless put themselves in the hands of the expert and follow instructions. The overall purpose of such paradoxical approaches is to jar or interrupt the family's established, but ineffective, pattern of interaction by powerful indirect means. Since second-order change is the goal, the therapist is attempting to circumvent family resistance to altering the interactive patterns that maintain the problematic behavior.

One direct outgrowth of research on the pathological double bind has been the notion of the *therapeutic double bind,* a general term that describes a variety of paradoxical techniques used to change entrenched family patterns. Just as a pathological double bind places an individual in a no-win predicament, so a therapeutic double bind is intended to force that person (or couple or family) into a no-lose situation: A symptomatic person is directed by the therapist not to change (for example, a depressed person is told not to be in such a hurry to give up the depression) in a context where the individual is expecting to be helped to change. In effect, the therapist's directive is to change by remaining the same. The person thus is caught in a trap: If the directive not to do anything is defied and the individual tries to lift the depression, he or she learns to acquire control of the symptom and this constitutes desired therapeutic change; if the person complies and does not attempt to change, he or she acknowledges a voluntary exercise of control over the symptoms. Since symptoms, by definition, are beyond voluntary control, the person can no longer claim to be behaving symptomatically through no fault of his or her own. Either way, the person gains control over the symptom; the symptom no longer controls the person. The symptoms have fallen under therapeutic control.

In a form of therapeutic double bind called **prescribing the symptom,** strategists try to produce a runaway system by urging or even coaching the client to engage in or practice his or her symptoms, at least for the present time. A family is instructed to continue or even to exaggerate what it is already doing (for example, a mother and daughter who continually fight might be directed to have a fight on a regular basis, every evening for fifteen minutes immediately after dinner). Since the family has come in desperation for help from the therapist (who seems to have high qualifications and to know what he or she is doing) and since the directive not to change appears easy to follow because the symptomatic behavior (the fighting) is occurring anyway, the family attempts to comply.

The therapist, asked to help them change, appears to be asking for no change at all. Such an assignment, however, undermines family members' fearful resistance to anticipated efforts to get them to change by rendering such opposition unnecessary. The therapist is actually on the way toward outwitting any resistance to change. At the same time, the therapist is challenging the function or purpose of the symptom, suggesting the family behaves that way because it serves to maintain family balance. In our example, confronted with the repugnant task of fighting on a regular basis, thereby exercising voluntary control over a previously uncontrolled situation, the mother and daughter resist the directive and begin to interact in a different manner. The unstated rules by which they operated before may become clearer to them, as does the notion that their quarreling does not "just happen" involuntarily but can be brought under voluntary control.[2] Since their interactive pattern no longer serves the family function of providing balance, the entire family must seek new ways of interacting with one another.

---

[2]Maurizio Andolfi (1979), director of the Family Therapy Institute in Rome, Italy, is particularly adept at unbalancing rigid family systems, often through effective use of "prescribing the symptom." In a family in which an anorectic adolescent girl controls family communication and defines all relations, including the relationship between her parents, Andolfi will forbid the girl to eat during a lunch session when the therapist and family eat together normally. Since her symptom (not eating) is now involuntary, it no longer serves as a means of controlling family interactions. At the same time, the family can no longer use its typically incongruent message, "Eat, but don't eat." The prescription interrupts the family game based on the daughter's eating problem and helps expose the rules of the anorectic family system.

CLINICAL NOTE

Relabeling works best when there is an aspect of truth in the directive. Thus, "What you call your wife's nagging is merely her wishing to have things put away so the two of you will have a neater home to enjoy."

Another form of therapeutic double bind, **relabeling** (essentially changing the label attached to a person or problem from negative to positive) attempts to alter the meaning of a situation by altering its conceptual and/or emotional context in such a way that the entire situation is perceived differently. That is, language is used to alter the interpretation of what has occurred, and thus invites the possibility of a new response to the behavior. The situation remains unchanged; but the meaning attributed to it, and thus its consequences, are altered.

The classic example comes from Mark Twain's Tom Sawyer, who relabeled as pleasurable the drudgery of whitewashing a fence and thus was in a position to ask other boys to pay for the privilege of helping him. Relabeling typically emphasizes the positive ("Mother's not being overprotective; she merely is trying to be helpful") and helps the family redefine disturbing behavior in more sympathetic or optimistic terms. Relabeling provides a new framework for looking at interaction; as the rules by which the family operates become more explicit, the family members become aware that old patterns are not necessarily unchangeable. The goal of relabeling, like that of the other therapeutic double-bind techniques, is to change the structure of family relationships and interactions.

MRI Brief Family Therapy

Brief therapy calls for finding alternative ways of facilitating beneficial changes that are relatively quick and inexpensive, and that are especially suited at symptomatic junctures in the life cycle of individuals and families (Peake, Borduin, & Archer, 1988). Typically they are active, highly focused, short-term methods that attempt to enable the family system to mobilize its underutilized resources to solve or resolve the problem(s) that led them to seek help.

The MRI version of brief therapy focuses on resolving problems that result from prior attempts to solve an ordinary difficulty. After identifying the family's more-of-the-same solutions that prolong the problem, the MRI brief therapist tries to discover the family rules and communication sequences that maintain and perpetuate the problem. Interventions then are directed rather specifically at changing the rules that sustain the problem the family wants fixed. Once the problem is eliminated, the therapist's task is completed; no effort is made to seek further changes, unless requested by the family. The focus of all clinical interventions at the Brief Therapy Center is on solving specific problems and/or reducing presenting symptoms, rather than seeking changes in the overall family system. If client families change what they are doing to solve a problem, then changes in the presenting problem can be achieved, since it is assumed that their attempted solutions are feeding the problem and thus perpetuating it (Schlanger & Anger-Diaz, 1999). Thus it can be said that the focus is on *treating the solution*, not treating the problem.

Brief family therapy as practiced at the MRI[3] is a time-limited (usually no more than 10 sessions), pragmatic, non-historical, step-by-step strategic approach based on the notion that most human problems develop through the mishandling of normal difficulties in life. In the MRI view, the attempted "solutions" imposed by families become the problem, as people persist in maintaining self-defeating "more of the same" attempts at problem resolution. Thus, from the MRI behavioral perspective, *the client's complaint is the problem, not a symptom of an underlying disorder,* as more psychodynamic approaches might theorize.

Put in more graphic interpersonal terms, the client is like a person caught in quicksand, grabbing onto someone else: The more he or she struggles, the more likely he or she is to sink and pull others in; the more he or she sinks, the more the struggling escalates and the more others are caught in the quicksand. In other words, ineffective attempts persist, and now the "solution" itself only makes matters worse. According to advocates of this approach, it is only by giving up solutions that perpetuate the problem and attempting new solutions that are different *in kind* that changes can occur in the self-perpetuating behavior.

The time limitations of this approach force clients to specifically define their current problem ("We believe our teenage boy is using drugs") rather than speak in generalities ("We're having family problems"). Here the therapist is interested in how, exactly, this problem affects every participant's life, and why they are seeking help just now (rather than earlier or later).

The strategically oriented brief therapist tries to obtain a clear picture of the specific problem as well as the current interactive behavior that maintains it, then devises a plan for changing those aspects of the system that perpetuate the problem (Segal, 1987). By restraining people from repeating old unworkable solutions (and by altering the system to promote change), the therapist can help them break out of their destructive or dysfunctional cycle of behavior.

Brief therapy advocates argue that most therapists, in attempting to help a distressed person, encourage that person to do the opposite of what he or she has been doing—an insomniac to fall asleep, a depressed person to cheer up, a withdrawn person to make friends. These approaches, by emphasizing opposites or negative feedback, only lead to internal reshuffling; they do not change the system. Watzlawick and associates (1974) call such moves superficial first-order changes, effecting change within the existing system without changing the structure of the system itself. Real change, however, necessitates an alteration of the system itself; it calls for a second-order change to make the system operate in a different manner. First-order changes, according to Watzlawick, Beavin, and Jackson (1967), are "games without end"; they are mistaken attempts at changing ordinary difficulties that eventually come to a stalemate by continuing to force a solution despite available evidence that it is precisely what is *not* working (Bodin, 1981).

Three Types of Misguided Solutions

MRI therapists take this position on problem formation—that complaints typically presented to a therapist arise and endure because of the mishandling of those normal,

---

[3]Several brief therapy approaches currently exist side by side, no doubt stimulated in part by the restrictive reimbursement practices instituted by managed care companies. Consequently, many agencies set limits on the number of sessions provided. In Chapter 14 we contrast the MRI problem-focused approach with that of the Brief Family Therapy Center in Milwaukee's solution-focused effort.

everyday difficulties occurring in all of our lives. Repeatedly employing unsatisfactory solutions only produces new problems, which then may increase in severity and begin to obscure the original difficulty. From the MRI perspective, there are three ways in which a family mishandles solutions so that they lead to bigger problems: (a) some action is necessary but not taken (for example, the family attempts a solution by denying there is a problem—the roof is not leaking, sister is not pregnant, money is no problem even though father has lost his job); (b) an action is taken when it is unnecessary (for example, newlyweds separate soon after the wedding ceremony because their marriage is not as ideal as each partner fantasized it would be); (c) action is taken at the wrong level (for example, marital conflicts or parent-child conflicts are dealt with by "common sense" or first-order changes, such as each party agreeing to try harder next time, when revisions in the family system—second-order changes—are necessary). The third type is probably most common, since people with problems attempt to deal with them in a manner consistent with their existing frame of reference. Repeated failures only lead to bewilderment, frustration, and intensification of the same responses.

Paradoxical interventions, especially reframing, are emphasized in order to redefine the family's frame of reference so that members conceptualize the problem differently and change their efforts to resolve it. As we saw in our earlier discussions of the structural approach to therapy, reframing involves a redefining process in which a situation remains unchanged but the meaning attributed to it is revised so as to permit a more constructive outlook. Reframing allows the situation to be viewed differently and thus facilitates new responses to it. As language changes about a problem, changes in feelings are likely to follow.

MRI Brief Therapy in Action

As practiced at the MRI, brief therapy, presented to the clients as being of short-term duration, sets up a powerful expectation of change. At the same time, the therapists tend to "think small," to be satisfied with minor but progressive changes. They also urge their clients to "go slow" and to be skeptical of dramatic, sudden progress; this restraining paradoxical technique is actually designed to promote rapid change as the family is provoked to prove the therapist wrong in his or her caution and pessimism. In general, the therapists do not struggle with the client's resistance to change, neither confronting the family nor offering interpretations to which the members might react negatively or defensively. Brief therapy aims to avoid power struggles with the family while it reshapes the members' perspectives on current problems and on their previous attempts to overcome difficulties.

MRI brief therapists do not insist that all family members attend sessions; they are content to deal only with those members motivated enough to do so. An important aspect of their work is first to collect data on previously failed solutions so as not to repeat them. They then set up specific goals of treatment, formulating a case plan and implementing interventions whenever there is an opportunity to interrupt earlier repetitive attempted solutions that merely serve to perpetuate the problem (Segal, 1991).

The MRI brief therapy program is a team effort. Although each family is assigned a primary therapist who conducts the interviews, other team members may watch from behind the one-way mirror and telephone the therapist with advice, feedback, and suggestions while treatment is in progress—all efforts directed at speeding up a change in family interactive patterns. In special cases (for example, a therapist-family

---

BOX 11.2   THERAPEUTIC ENCOUNTER

STRATEGICALLY DESIGNING A NOVEL SOLUTION FOR A CHRONIC PROBLEM

The author (Segal) and Dr. Fritz Hoebel studied and treated 10 families in which the husbands had suffered a major heart attack but were still continuing to engage in high-risk behaviors: poor diet, smoking, lack of exercise, and excessive consumption of alcohol. All of these families were referred by cardiologists, or by the staff of a cardiac rehabilitation program, who had given up on these individuals, fearing they were on a suicide course. In all 10 cases the identified heart patient would have nothing to do with any further treatment or rehabilitation efforts.

Rather than wasting a lot of time and energy trying to convince the patient to come for treatment, we worked with their spouses. Using a five-session limit, we focused our attention on the way the wives had attempted to reduce their husbands' high-risk behavior—our aim was to change the system—that is, the husband's behavior—by getting the wives to change their attempted solutions. In most cases the wives struggled, argued, and nagged their men to change, so our primary effort was getting the wives to back off from this position. In one

case that worked particularly well, on our instructions the wife returned home and told her husband that she had been doing a lot of thinking about him.

She said she had decided that he had a right to live out the rest of his life in his own style, no matter how short that might be. Her primary concern now was herself and the children and how they would be provided for when he died. She then insisted that her husband go over all the life insurance and estate planning, instructing her how to handle things after his death. She also called life insurance agencies and asked whether there was any way her husband's life insurance could be increased. As instructed, she told them to call back at times she knew she would not be home but her husband would be there to take the calls. Within two weeks after she had begun to deal with him this way, the husband had resumed his participation in the cardiac rehabilitation exercise program and was watching his diet.

Source: Segal, 1982, pp. 286–287

---

impasse) one of the team members may enter the room and address the primary therapist or the clients, perhaps siding with the client to increase the likelihood that forthcoming directives from the observer will be implemented. Families are not screened prior to treatment and are taken into the program on a first-come, first-served basis. Team discussions precede and follow each session after the initial family contact. Telephone follow-ups, in which each family receiving treatment at the center is asked by a team member other than the primary therapist to evaluate change in the presenting problem, take place 3 months and 12 months after the last interview.

The cybernetic nature of both problem formation and problem resolution, with its recursive feedback loops and circular causality metaphors, is basic to MRI thinking and therapeutic endeavors. Ineffective solutions to everyday difficulties lead to symptomatic behavior; once a family member manifests a symptom, the family, believing it has the best way to deal with the problem, responds by repeating the interactive behavior that produced the symptom in the first place. The further repetition of poor solutions intensifies the original difficulty, as the family clings to behavior patterns that are no longer functional or adaptive (Peake, Borduin, & Archer, 1988). Therapists, then, must direct their efforts at helping families substitute new behavior patterns (new solutions) to replace the old ones.

Schlanger and Anger-Diaz (1999), directors of the Latino Brief Therapy Center at the MRI, outline the following steps in their brief therapy approach in response to the client's initial phone call:

- Defining the problem
- Identifying the attempted solutions
- Determining the position of the client
- Designing an intervention
- Selling the intervention to the client
- Assigning homework
- Doing a homework follow-up
- Terminating

The case description in Box 11.2 (Segal, 1982) illustrates the effectiveness of the MRI brief therapy approach. The therapy team helps a concerned wife to revise her earlier self-defeating solutions to a problem and thus to institute second-order changes in her interactions with a resistant husband.

STRATEGIC FAMILY THERAPY (HALEY AND MADANES)

If the original MRI communication/interaction approach drew the greatest attention from family therapy professionals in the 1960s, and Minuchin's structural model was the most consistently studied and emulated in the 1970s, then it is fair to say that the various strategic approaches took center stage in the 1980s (and that social constructionist and narrative approaches gained ascendance in the 1990s and into the present century). As we've noted, the main characteristic of this approach is that the therapist takes responsibility for devising a strategy for solving the client's presenting problem. Typically their interventions involve creating novel ways of disrupting those entrenched family interactive sequences that help produce and maintain the problem the family comes to therapy to alleviate.

The Haley-Madanes strategic approach defines a presenting problem in such a way that it can be solved; goals eliminating the specific problem are clearly set; therapy is carefully planned, in stages, to achieve these goals; problems are defined as involving at least two and most likely three people, thus allowing for an examination of problematic family structures (broken hierarchical rules, cross-generational coalitions) and dysfunctional behavioral sequences. The thrust of the intervention is to shift the family organization so that the presenting problem or symptom no longer serves its previous function in the family. Change occurs not through insight and understanding, but through the process of the family carrying out directives issued by the therapist.

Leading Figures

The career of Jay Haley plays an important part in the development of the strategic approach to family therapy. Haley was a key member of Bateson's schizophrenia research project in the 1950s, and helped develop the double-bind concept. Bateson himself was interested in the concept's theoretical significance, as a description of interaction, but not in the clinical issues of interpersonal influence within a family.

Haley (1963), however, saw its clinical application; he took the position that implicit in every interpersonal transaction is a struggle for control of the *definition* of the relationship. He viewed symptomatic behavior in one partner as a maladaptive control strategy, warning that the therapist must maintain control of the therapy relationship, lest the client gain control and perpetuate his or her difficulties in order to "continue to govern by symptomatic methods" (Haley, 1963, p. 19).

In 1953 Haley, along with John Weakland, became interested in understanding the communication occurring in hypnosis between hypnotist and subject, and with

Bateson's encouragement began to attend workshops on that subject led by Milton Erickson. Pursuing that interest further, but now more intrigued by Erickson's metaphoric therapeutic style for issuing indirect suggestions, Haley and Weakland visited Erickson regularly in Phoenix over a period of several years. Erickson's influence on many of the underlying assumptions and subsequent therapeutic techniques of strategic therapy is great; Haley (1973; 1976) actually credits his mentor as the inventor of the general approach of strategic family therapy.

Erickson's therapy was brief, active, directive, and carefully planned. Taking responsibility for change, he tailored a novel approach for each case, typically looking for the person's area of resourcefulness and putting it to work (Hoffman, 2002). His use of hypnotic techniques, typically focused on symptom removal, required the therapist to assume full charge of the treatment and to issue directives (however subtle or indirect) as a way of gaining leverage for eliminating the troublesome symptom. Joining with patients, believing in their inherent wisdom to help themselves once shown how, and gaining their trust, Erickson set about through indirect suggestions to encourage them to break out of their old behavior patterns and, in the process, abandon their presenting symptom. Erickson argued that an effective therapist needs to be a strategist who approaches each new client with a specific therapeutic plan, sometimes a simple directive or a paradox, fitted to that individual and intended to solve his or her problem. Erickson's unorthodox but artful stratagems, extraordinary feats of observation, and seemingly uncanny ability to tap unrecognized and previously untapped resources in his clients (usually individuals rather than families) have been chronicled by Haley (1973) as well as by Zeig (1980). Jeffrey Zeig has continued Erickson's legacy, founding and directing the Milton H. Erickson Foundation in Phoenix, dedicated to promoting and advancing Erickson's ideas by offering training programs in hypnosis and psychotherapy worldwide.

Noted for his creative and unconventional hypnotic techniques, Erickson was particularly skilled at "bypassing client resistance" through the use of *paradoxical directives.* That is, he was able to persuade patients to hold onto a symptom (by not fighting it or insisting the client work at giving it up) and then subtly introduce directions to induce change. Thus he was able to avoid direct confrontation with the symptom, a tactic likely to have been met with resistance, and to use the client's own momentum to force symptom abandonment. This technique, developed so that the hypnotic subject would not experience a loss of control to the hypnotist, became the later basis for many of Haley's strategic interventions in working with families. The family's fear of relinquishing control to the therapist often makes it resistant to change. The therapist's not directly confronting such resistance lessens family members' fear that they will be

Milton Erickson, M.D.

required to do things against their will. Once they feel safe, and with the aid of a therapist jumpstarting the change process, people can begin to call upon their own resources to attempt new ways of thinking and behaving.

Haley was also influenced by his long association (1967–1973) as trainer and theory builder with Salvador Minuchin and Braulio Montalvo at the Philadelphia Child Guidance Center. Mitrani and Perez (2003) actually classify Haley's position as a structural-strategic approach; Minuchin himself points out that there are obvious similarities between the structural and strategic outlooks (Simon, 1984). Haley's concern with maintaining family generational hierarchies and avoiding disabling coalitions[4] (joint action by two family members against a third) allies him with the structural group, while his interest in paradoxical directives and other unobtrusive ways of managing resistance identifies him with the latter.

By 1975 Haley and Cloé Madanes, then his wife, who had trained at the MRI before moving on to the Philadelphia Child Guidance Clinic, together formed the Family Therapy Institute of Washington, D.C., a highly respected training program for family therapists. Haley, a prolific writer, described his strategies for changing the way a family is organized in *Problem-Solving Therapy* (1976); the following decade he published *Ordeal Therapy* (1984), an account of treatment based on the premise that if a client is maneuvered into a position where he or she finds it more distressful to maintain a symptom than to give it up, the client will abandon the symptom. In addition to Haley and Madanes (1981), leading strategic therapists today include social worker James Keim (1998, 2000) in Colorado and Jerome Price (1996) in Michigan, both formerly affiliated with the Family Therapy Institute in Washington, D.C. Their efforts, as well as those of like-minded therapists, are frequently described in the *Journal of Strategic and Systemic Therapies* (now renamed the *Journal of Systemic Therapies*).

The Meaning of Symptoms

Although the generally accepted view at the time was that symptoms were by definition involuntary and maladaptive, Haley early on (1963) took the position that a symptom, rather than representing behavior beyond one's control, is a strategy, adaptive to a current social situation, for controlling a relationship when all other strategies have failed. All participants are caught up in the repetitive sequence that keeps the process going. The symptomatic person simply denies any intent to control by claiming the symptom is involuntary. ("It's not that I am rejecting you. It's my headache that keeps me from wanting to be sexually intimate with you tonight.") Thus, symptoms often control another person indirectly, and this oblique way of communicating through symptom formation may serve a function for the overall family system.

Power and control are at the very core of Haley's thinking about family functioning. Jockeying for control occurs in all families and in every relationship between two or more people. ("You can't boss me around anymore; I'm not a baby" is a familiar

---

[4]As Mitrani and Perez (2003) observe, coalitions are especially detrimental to family functioning because they detour conflict and do not allow relationships to develop fully between the three participants. If Julia and Samantha have a conflict they cannot manage directly, and Emily enters the fray by aligning herself with one against the other, the original two do not have an opportunity to work out their problem, and their relationship does not develop. Haley is interested in changing the repeated sequence of interaction in such a triangle.

BOX 11.3 CLINICAL NOTE

Symptoms: Voluntary or Involuntary Efforts at Control?

Haley cites the case of a woman who insists her husband be home every night because she suffers anxiety attacks if left alone. She does not recognize her demand as a means of controlling his behavior, but explains it as a function of her anxiety attacks over which she presumably has no control. The husband faces a dilemma; he cannot acknowledge that she is controlling his behavior (the anxiety attacks are at fault for that), but he cannot refuse to let her control his behavior (after all, she has anxiety attacks).

Symptoms are thus seen as adaptive and under the client's voluntary control. By acting helpless, the wife gains considerable power and control over the relationship. Without offering insight or otherwise sharing the view of voluntary control over symptoms with the clients, the strategist seeks to change the situation—perhaps help the couple redistribute power and responsibilities—so that the symptom is no longer necessary to control the husband.

taunt, challenging the family's hierarchy, heard from a teenager trying to change family rules.) Most couples develop suitable upfront means of dealing with issues of control; according to Haley, people who present symptoms are resorting to subtle, indirect methods. It is his contention that control struggles in a relationship are inevitable; one cannot not try to define a relationship or attempt to control an outcome. Haley considers the maneuver pathological only if one or both participants deny trying to control the other's behavior and/or exhibit symptomatic behavior in the process of doing so.

All strategists contend that communication defines the nature of the relationship between partners. If a husband is willing to discuss only the weather when he and his wife are together in the evening, he may be defining the relationship as one where they talk only about conventional or impersonal matters. If the wife refuses to comment on tomorrow's forecast but instead expresses the idea that they seem distant from each other this evening, she is attempting to redefine the relationship on more personal and intimate terms. *Their conflict is not a struggle to control another person, but a struggle to control the definition of the relationship.* As we have noted, in some marriages a partner's symptoms (for example, anxiety attacks, phobias, depressions, heavy drinking) control what takes place between the partners—where they go, what they do together, whether one can leave the other's side for any length of time, and so on.

Strategists thus *define symptoms as interpersonal events*, as tactics used by one person to deal with another. In their view, the therapist's goal is to maneuver the client into developing other ways of defining relationships so that the symptomatic methods will be abandoned.

Triangles, Sequences, and Hierarchies

In the Haley-Madanes approach, problems involve the interaction of at least three parties (with a coalition of a minimum of two against at least one other). While larger numbers may of course exist in a family, they argue that the triangle is the preferred way of describing family interaction (Keim, 1999). Thus, presented with a case of marital conflict, the strategic therapist is apt to view this presenting problem as not merely

CLINICAL NOTE

Therapists need to take care to be evenhanded, and not be tempted to form coalitions with family members low in the family hierarchy (e.g., overprotecting children or the identified patient) against those with higher authority or power.

an issue between spouses; rather, he or she will look at the effect of others (children, in-laws, work associates) on the couple. Strategic therapists also track interactional sequences of events, which of course are likely to be circular. Keim (1999) cites the case of shoplifting by a teenager as more than an individual act; it is a sequence of events involving peers and parents. Rather than focus on treating the individual offender, strategists focus on changing the relevant interactional sequence of the presenting problem, helping the family replace any painful or escalating sequences between members who care about each other with a calmer and more conciliating sequence.

Hierarchy within a family, so central to Minuchin's structural ideas, is incorporated into strategic thinking, no doubt influenced by Haley's work with Minuchin at the Philadelphia Child Guidance Clinic. Without viewing a client family's hierarchical structure as functional or dysfunctional, strategists want to know what roles each member plays and whether problems arise because people are unhappy with their roles. As Keim (1999) illustrates, a child who is functioning as an adult within a family is not a problem in and of itself, according to strategic thinking; but the child's role becomes a problem if unhappiness develops in the family because he or she is assuming the adult role. Strategic therapists are especially attuned to oppositional behavior that may develop in a family when assigned or ascribed roles are uncomfortable or no longer fit and conflictual communication and behavioral sequences follow.

Developing Therapeutic Strategies

Strategic family therapists direct their interventions at a specific presenting problem, deal with the present ways the problem is maintained, and customize strategies (straightforward or indirect directives) designed to track and ultimately alter problem-related interactive sequences. Rather than offer interpretation or provide insight or insist the family reorganize its overall set of relationships—the family usually resolves a problem without knowing why or how—strategic therapists respectfully attempt to change only those aspects of the family system that are maintaining the problematic or symptomatic behavior. The emphasis in strategic therapy, according to Madanes (1981), is not on devising a therapeutic method applicable to all cases, but rather on designing a unique strategy for each specific presenting problem. The focus throughout is on artfully alleviating the presenting problem, not exploring its roots or buried meanings. Thus, Haley-Madanes strategic therapy is likely to be short-term, since it is limited to specific problems and tailored to solutions.

Criticized for his manipulative style, Haley (1963) points out that therapists and patients continually maneuver with each other in the process of all forms of family treatment. Family members, fearful of change, may try to manipulate, deceive, exclude, or subdue a therapist in order to maintain the homeostatic balance they have achieved, even if it is at the expense of symptomatic behavior in one of their members. They do so not to torment a therapist, but rather because they are frightened of altering their behavior, clinging to what they believe is the only solution to their problem. The strategic therapist, therefore, must take an authoritative stance. Haley (1976) sees his task as taking responsibility for changing the family organization and resolving the problem that brought the family to see him. He is highly directive, giving the family members precise instructions or directives and insisting that they be followed. For example, Haley cites the case (1976) of a grandmother siding with her grandchild (age 10) against the mother. He saw the mother and child together, instructing the child to irritate the grandmother and instructing the mother to defend her daughter against the grandmother. This task forced a collaboration between mother and daughter and helped detach the daughter from her grandmother, releasing the family to develop a more appropriate hierarchical structure.

As we can see from this example, strategists typically cast problems in triadic terms (in this case, child, mother, grandmother), focusing especially on the effects of their directives on the behavioral sequences that follow between the participants. As active, take-charge therapists, their aim is to issue directives that alter dysfunctional sequences. Typically, as in this example, those sequences revolve around one's family hierarchy, since a family's confused hierarchical setup is often thought to be the root of symptomatic behavior in a family member. Haley advocates that therapists intervene when they see the need to do so (rather than when the family requests therapist input), comment openly about the family's efforts to influence or control them, give directions and assign tasks, and assume temporary leadership of the family group. Strategic therapists attempt to avoid getting enticed into coalitions within the family; however, they may develop a coalition with one or more members to overcome an impasse but quickly disengage before becoming entangled with one or another family faction.

Another strategic tactic is to emphasize the positive, usually by relabeling previously defined dysfunctional behavior as reasonable and understandable. In one often-quoted example, allegedly attributed to Haley, he boldly (and at first glance, outrageously) told a wife whose husband had chased after her with an ax that the man was simply trying to get close to her. Here, Haley was simply following a principle of communication theory described earlier; namely, that all communication occurs at two levels, and that the message at the second level (metacommunication) qualifies what takes place on the surface level.

What Haley was communicating by the relabeling, and what the wife also sensed, was that the husband indeed did want to connect with her, but his rage got in the way of doing so in any constructive manner. (In everyday exchanges, a remark made by a sender in normal conversation can be taken as a joke or an attack, as praise or as blame, depending on the context in which the receiver places it.) By addressing the metamessage—he wanted to get close—Haley changed the context, freeing the participants to think and therefore behave differently in the new context.

The Initial Interview

Haley (1976) contends that the first interview, which he insists the whole family attend, sets the stage for the entire course of therapy. Proceeding systematically through stages, strategists negotiate with the family to decide what specific problem requires attention, then formulate a plan of action to change the family's dysfunctional sequences or faulty hierarchy in order to eliminate the problem. Typically, in the opening *brief social stage,* strategists create a cooperative and relaxed atmosphere while observing family interaction and trying to get all members to participate, thus indicating all are involved (not merely the identified patient) and should have a voice in the therapy.

Next, in this highly structured process, Haley-influenced strategists shift to the *problem stage,* getting down to the business of why (for example, to solve what specific presenting problem) the family is there. They pose such questions as "Why do you seek help now? What would each of you like to change? Quickly or slowly? Do you wish to realize what is happening or just to change? Are you willing to make sacrifices to change?" (Haley, 1988). In this information-gathering phase, in which all members are urged to participate, conversation is directed at the therapist, who displays an interest but does not interpret the thoughts and feelings being expressed. How each family member views the presenting problem is particularly noteworthy here.

The *interactional stage,* during which the family discusses the problem aloud with one another in the presence of the therapist, permits the therapist to observe any dysfunctional communication sequences, coalitions, problematic hierarchies, conflicts between any duos, and so forth, thereby offering clues about future therapeutic interventions.

The fourth segment of the first interview, the *goal-setting stage,* gives the therapist and family together an opportunity to precisely determine the presenting problem they wish to solve or eliminate. This phase results in a contract that clearly defines goals, allowing all participants to measure change or gauge the success of their efforts as therapy progresses.

In the final or *task-setting stage,* the strategic therapist ends the initial interview with the first set of simple homework assignments or directives, beginning the process of changing sequences of interaction within the family. If the initial interview is done successfully, the family members feel comfortable with the therapist and committed to working together for change (Haley, 1976).

The Use of Directives

Directives, or assignments of tasks to be performed outside of the therapeutic session, play a key role in strategic family therapy, and are given for several reasons: (a) to get people to behave differently so they will have different subjective experiences; (b) to intensify the therapeutic relationship by involving the therapist in the family's actions during the time between sessions; and (c) to gather information, by their reactions, as to how the family members will respond to the suggested changes. Advice, direct suggestions, coaching, homework, even assignments of ordeal-like behavior to be followed if a symptom appears, are examples of straightforward directives by the therapist aimed at changing an unworkable system and achieving problem solution. They are typically prepared with care, tailored to the family's style, and issued in a precise manner, with the expectation that the family will report back at the next session about carrying out the task.

As Madanes (1991, p. 397) emphasizes, "The directive is to strategic therapy what the interpretation is to psychoanalysis. It is the basic tool of the approach." In some cases, strategists issue a straightforward directive (simultaneously a report and a command) to family members to take specific action (for example, instructing a mother to stop intruding when the father and son try to talk to each other) because they want or expect them to follow it in order for them to change their behavior toward one another. However, asking someone to stop engaging in certain behavior is a difficult directive to enforce; its success depends upon the status of the therapist giving the instruction, the severity or chronicity of the behavior, how often the directive is repeated, and the willingness of family members to cooperate with the therapist in accomplishing the task. This last point regarding motivation is a particularly essential factor determining whether the therapist will succeed in this direct approach.

Frequently, the direct approach is unsuccessful. (If direct suggestion were successful, the chances are great that the family would have followed advice from friends and not come to a therapist's office.) Another kind of task assignment, more indirect, is one by which the therapist attempts to influence clients to take some action without directly asking them to do so. Often couching the task in paradoxical form (see Table 11.1), the strategic therapist hopes to provoke the family to rebel or resist him or her so that they give up the symptom. Assignment of paradoxical tasks can be directed at individual family members, pairs of people, or at the family system (Weeks & L'Abate, 1982).

To be used with relative infrequence, as when a client is in crisis or especially resistant to change, paradoxical directives commonly take one of two forms— *prescriptive* or *descriptive*. Prescriptive paradoxes ask the client(s) to do something, while descriptive paradoxes relabel something already being done by giving it a positive meaning or connotation.

As Wachtel and Wachtel (1986) illustrate the former, a client seeking help for his procrastination is asked not to try to accomplish more in the coming week between sessions, but rather to record the various ways he wastes time each day and how long each takes. The changing set, or perhaps the unpleasant task, often leads to a reduction of procrastination. The client may report that there was little to write down the previous week because he got his work done. Or in the case in which a list is made, the client will often gain greater awareness of his self-defeating behavior or perhaps learn that he is less a procrastinator than overdemanding or expecting too much from himself. We offered an example of a descriptive paradox earlier in this section in Haley's relabeling the ax-wielding of the husband as a loving act.

As used by strategists, and borrowed from Erickson's hypnotic techniques, a paradoxical directive asks clients to *restrain from change*, and is designed to provoke defiance in the recipient. The client is told to continue to do what he or she came to therapy to get over doing (that is, to continue having the symptom). The therapist, on the other hand, is trying indirectly to get the client or family to decide that they won't do what they have now been directed to do. Confused, the family members perceive that through the assignment of such a task the therapist is asking them not to change at the same time that the therapist has declared the intention of helping them change.

For example, an intelligent son, failing in school, is told to continue to fail so that his less well-educated father can feel good about himself. If the boy conforms to the directive, he admits control and acknowledges how his behavior contributes to family secondary gain (an advantage or benefit, such as reassuring the father, that arises due to an illness or appearance of a symptom). If he rebels against the directive to continue to fail, he gives up the symptom. This paradoxical prescription subtly reveals the secondary gain that the patient's symptomatic behavior (poor grades) provides for the family, covertly suggesting change is both possible and desirable.

Paradoxical interventions[5] represent a particularly ingenious way of maneuvering a person or family into abandoning dysfunctional behavior. Similar to "prescribing the symptom," this technique is particularly appropriate for strategists because they assume that families who come for help are also frightened and therefore resistant to the help being offered. The result may be a standoff, a power struggle with the therapist trying to help family members change but in doing so destabilizing their previous homeostatic balance, and the family trying to get the therapist to fail but to go on trying because they realize something is wrong. Andolfi (1979), who is also considered a structural-strategic therapist, describes such an encounter as a game into which the therapist is drawn, and in which every effort by the therapist to act as an agent of change is nullified by the family group. If not careful, Andolfi warns, the therapist can easily get entangled in the family's contradictory logic of "help me to change, but without changing anything." The strategic paradoxical approach, aimed at families who defy compliance-based interventions and based on putting clients in a double bind, encompasses several stages.

First, the therapist attempts to set up a relationship with the family in which change is expected. Second, the problem to be corrected is clearly defined; third, the goals are clearly stated. In the fourth stage, the therapist must offer a concrete plan; it is helpful if a rationale can be included that makes the paradoxical task seem reasonable. In the fifth stage, the current authority on the problem (such as a physician or a parent) is disqualified as not handling the situation the right way; in the sixth stage, the therapist issues the directive. In the seventh and last stage, the therapist observes the response and continues to encourage the usual problem behavior in order to maintain the paradox.

It is of utmost importance for the therapist using a paradoxical intervention that prescribes the symptom to carefully encourage the member(s) with the behavior to be changed to continue that behavior unchanged—a domineering wife to continue to run everything in the family; a daughter refusing to attend school to stay home; an adolescent boy masturbating in public to continue doing so but to keep a chart of how often, what days he enjoyed it most, and so on. Strategists might tell a couple who always fight unproductively to go home and fight for three hours. The issue becomes one of control. The domineering wife no longer runs everything if the therapist is telling her what to do, and if she resists his directive she will become less domineering

---

[5]By now the reader is aware that this approach is employed by many family therapists, especially in dealing with defiant or resistant families. We particularly underline its use in our discussion of those therapeutic approaches that emphasize clear communication, because a paradoxical injunction (for example, "Be spontaneous") is a prototype of a double-bind situation. To command someone to be spontaneous is to demand behavior that cannot be spontaneous because it is commanded. Thus, with seeming innocence, the sender is trapping the receiver into a situation where rule compliance also entails rule violation (Watzlawick, Weakland, & Fisch, 1974). The receiver is faced with two conflicting levels of messages, is bewildered, and cannot respond effectively. As Haley, Watzlawick, Erickson, and others use the paradox therapeutically, the family is told, in effect, "Disobey me." As in the case of commanding someone to be spontaneous, instructing the person to disobey what you are saying creates a paradox. Thus, the family told not to change in effect defies the therapist's injunction; the family begins to change to prove the therapist wrong in assuming it could not change. If the therapist allows himself or herself to be put down as wrong and even suggests that the change is very likely to be temporary and a relapse probable, the family will resist relapse and continue to change to prove the therapist wrong again. It is essential that the therapist never claim credit for helping the family—indeed, the therapist remains puzzled by the change—in order to preclude the family's need to be disobedient in the form of a relapse.

TABLE 11.1 Common Examples of Paradoxical Interventions

Reframing	"He checks on your whereabouts several times a day not because he's jealous but because he's thinking about you all the time."
Relabeling	"Your wife is being helpful by reminding you about unfinished tasks around the house because she wants to make a nice home for you."
Prescribing the symptom	"Practice quarreling with each other as soon as you wake up."
Restraining	"Don't do anything about the problem this week so we can see how really bad it is."
Offering prescriptions	"Keep a list of everything that might worry you during the day and set aside an hour every night to go over them and become a competent worrier."
Offering descriptions	"The two of you, as a married couple, are to be commended for avoiding confronting your differences. It would be too risky to change things now."
Predicting a relapse	"The two of you got along better this week but you're probably going to have a major blowup soon."
Declaring hopelessness	"You're probably right. There's nothing you can do. It would be a disservice to you to allow you to continue therapy."

Source: Weeks & L'Abate, 1982; Seltzer, 1986

in relation to her husband. Similarly, strategists assume in the other cases that the symptom presented, originally a way of gaining an advantage, will be resolved if the symptom now places the person at a disadvantage. In the case of the couple, strategists expect them to stop fighting; people do not like to make themselves miserable because someone else tells them to do so.

Should the individual or family follow instructions and continue the problematic or symptomatic behavior, the therapist has been given the power and control to make the symptom occur at his or her direction. Should the individual or family resist the paradoxical intervention, the symptomatic behavior is, in the process, given up (and, again, the therapist retains power and control). Strategic therapists devote a great deal of time to devising *nonharmful*, if sometimes seemingly absurd, paradoxical tasks appropriate to the problem of the person desiring to change or get rid of a disturbing symptom. We catalogue some common paradoxical interventions in Table 11.1.

In another form of prescriptive directive called *ordeal therapy* (Haley, 1984), once again based on the work of Erickson, the strategic therapist will instruct a client to carry out an unpleasant chore (for example, rising in the middle of the night to wax the kitchen floor) whenever the symptom appears during the day, thus making the distress of the consequences a greater hardship than the distress of the original symptom. By selecting a harmless or mildly noxious task, but one consistent with a client's desires (say, keeping a spotless house) yet like an ordeal in its execution, Haley again tries to make it more difficult for the client to have the problem or symptom than to give it up. Ordeal therapy calls for a clear statement of the problem or symptom to be addressed and a commitment to change on the part of the client even if suffering is required, as well as a promised willingness to follow a therapist's directive regardless of its logic or relevance to the presenting problem.

There are three major steps in designing a paradox, according to Papp (1983): *redefining, prescribing,* and *restraining.* Redefining is intended to change the family's perception of the symptom. Toward this end, behavior that maintains the symptom is defined as benignly motivated, loving gestures the family employs to preserve its stability. Thus, anger may be relabeled as caring, suffering as self-sacrifice, distancing as a way of reinforcing closeness. Instead of trying to change the system directly, the therapist appears to be supporting it, respecting the emotional logic upon which it runs. Next, the wording of the prescription ("Practice being depressed"; "Continue being rebellious against your parents") must be brief, concise, and unacceptable (in order for the family to recoil at the instruction), but the therapist must appear sincere by offering a convincing rationale for the prescription. Later, when the family members press for change, the therapist attempts to regulate the pace of change by urging restraint, pointing out to them what new difficulties might arise. At the same time, the therapist seems to be cautiously allowing the family to change despite these anticipated difficulties.

Restraining strategies ("go slow") are efforts to emphasize that the system's homeostatic balance is in danger if improvement occurs too rapidly. If the directive is presented with a creditable rationale ("Change takes time and must proceed step by step; otherwise there is danger of relapse if too much change occurs too fast"), the client is likely to go along with it. The tactic is intended to prepare clients for change, to acknowledge their reluctance to change, and to solidify change once it begins (Shoham, Rohrbaugh, & Patterson, 1995). "Go slow" messages, according to Fisch, Weakland, and Segal (1982), provide the additional benefit of reducing the client's sense of urgency about finding new solutions. Such messages have the added effect of normalizing relapse should it occur, without the family becoming demoralized or giving up trying.

Haley (1976) inquired, in a case of a young, middle-class couple concerned that their young child soiled his pants, what the consequences would be if he began to go to the toilet normally. (This move suggested that Haley could help them with the problem but would rather not until he was sure of the positive consequences to the entire family.) When the couple returned the next week and indicated that they could think of no adverse consequences, the therapist suggested some possibilities: for example, could the mother tolerate being successful with her child? This effort to challenge the mother's involvement with her child and reframe her behavior contained messages at several levels: (a) Haley thought she could tolerate success; (b) he was benevolently concerned so he wanted to make sure she could tolerate it; and (c) the mother would find the suggestion of not tolerating success to be unacceptable. No mother is likely to think she cannot be successful with her own child, as Haley well knew. Thus provoked (the father was similarly confronted), both parents became highly motivated to solve their problem to prove they could tolerate being normal; the boy's problematic behavior ceased.

Effectiveness of Strategic Approaches

Is strategic therapy effective? Unfortunately, rigorous research is lacking, and the advocates of this approach rely heavily on anecdotal case reports. In some early studies (Watzlawick et al., 1974) a telephone follow-up at regular intervals after ending therapy found favorable results: 40 percent claimed complete symptom relief, 32 percent considerable relief, 28 percent no long-term help. Stanton, Todd, et al. (1982) offered a well-designed and carefully controlled study in which structural-strategic techniques were successfully employed for treating families with an adult member who engaged in heroin addiction, and positive results were found in follow-ups. Szapocznik,

BOX 11.4 RESEARCH REPORT

NEW DIRECTIONS: A HUMANISTIC SET OF STRATEGIES?

Two approaches call attention to a less provoking or authoritarian form of strategic family therapy. Madanes (1981, 1984), developed some **pretend techniques** that are paradoxical in nature but less confrontational than Haley's. As such, they are less apt to invite defiance and rebelliousness, but still are helpful in overcoming family resistance. Based on playfulness, humor, and fantasy, these gentler approaches would have a therapist suggest, for example, that a symptomatic child (say, one who is a periodic bed wetter or has recurring stomachaches) "pretend" to have a symptom at this moment and that the parents "pretend" to help. In effect, the therapist, changing the context, is subtly asking the clients to voluntarily control behavior (by turning it on and off) that they presumably regard as involuntary and thus, by definition, uncontrollable. By maneuvering the family through this kind of paradoxical intervention, Madanes manages to work out in make-believe what once produced an actual symptom. In

many cases, if the family is pretending, then the actual symptom cannot be real and can be abandoned at will.

In recent years strategic family therapists have moved away from issues over power and control with families. Today they are more likely to take a soothing, protective, and more respectful role with families. Keim (1999), acknowledging this more humanistic influence, demonstrates its effectiveness with families in which oppositional behavior in children or adolescents is the presenting problem. In what he calls the "soft side" of hierarchy, Keim directs parents to retain authority while urging them to avoid power struggles within the family. Being coached to resist being drawn into confrontations, parents are helped to create a new, more generally satisfying system of positive and negative consequences with their children. Children, feeling better understood, are helped to achieve an emotional state wherein they feel safe discussing their problems within the family.

Kurtines, et al. (1989) utilized similar techniques to reduce drug reliance in adolescent substance abusers. Stanton and Shadish (1997), in a more recent comprehensive survey, found that structural-strategic family therapy produced more favorable outcomes than non-family-based interventions. However, the overall effectiveness of this approach with a variety of problems (marital conflict, intergenerational conflict) awaits further research examination.

SUMMARY

Communication theories, emerging from the research at the Mental Research Institute in Palo Alto in the 1950s, have had a major impact on the family therapy field by recasting human problems as interactional and situational (tied to a set of circumstances that maintains them). The introduction of this epistemology by Bateson, Jackson, and others laid the foundation for the original interactive therapeutic approach of the MRI, now conceived as strategic family therapy. Particularly characteristic of this approach is the

use of therapeutic double binds or paradoxical techniques for changing family rules and relationship patterns.

Paradoxes—contradictions that follow correct deductions from consistent premises—are used therapeutically to direct an individual or family not to change in a context that carries with it the expectation of change. The procedure promotes change no matter which action—compliance or resistance—is undertaken. "Prescribing the symptom," as used by

Jackson, Watzlawick, and other strategists, is a paradoxical technique for undermining resistance to change by rendering it unnecessary.

The interactional view of the MRI is today best exemplified by its Brief Therapy Center activities. Here, the flawed or misguided solutions attempted by families are considered to be the problem, and interventions are directed at treating those previously failed solutions by offering novel, therapist-designed directives.

Haley and Madanes offer a related version of strategic family therapy. Their approach is characterized by carefully planned tactics and the issuance of directives for solving a family's presenting problems. Haley in particular uses straightforward directives or task assignments as well as indirect paradoxical interventions; the latter force the willing abandonment of dysfunctional behavior by means of the family defying the directive not to change.

Madanes employs paradoxical principles in the form of "pretend" techniques, nonconfrontational interventions directed at achieving change without inviting resistance. Strategic therapists now take a softer, more soothing approach, as in the case of working with families where there is oppositional behavior in children or adolescents.

RECOMMENDED READINGS

Fisch, R., Weakland, J. H., & Segal, L. (1982). *The tactics of change: Doing therapy briefly*. San Francisco: Jossey-Bass.

Haley, J. (1973). *Uncommon therapy*. New York: Norton.

Haley, J. (1984). *Ordeal therapy*. San Francisco: Jossey-Bass.

Keim, J. (1999). Strategic therapy. In D. M. Lawson & F. F. Prevatt (Eds.), *Casebook in family therapy*. Pacific Grove, CA: Brooks/Cole.

Madanes, C. (1981). *Strategic family therapy*. San Francisco: Jossey-Bass.

Watzlawick, P., Beavin, J. H., & Jackson, D. D. (1974). *Pragmatics of human communication*. New York: Norton.

THE MILAN SYSTEMIC MODEL

Made up originally of card-carrying members of the strategic school, particularly those who were attracted to the early MRI model described in the previous chapter, the Milan group in Italy underwent several transitions in viewpoint and emphasis during its heyday in the 1970s and 1980s, ultimately paving the way for the collaborative approaches to family therapy that dominated the 1990s. Based initially on first-order cybernetic ideas, with its emphasis on family rules and homeostasis-seeking interactive patterns, this strategically related approach went on to spawn a number of significant new postmodern developments, sometimes referred to as post-Milan, that attempt to understand the implications of second-order cybernetics and build them into family therapy theory and practice (Campbell, Draper, & Crutchley, 1991).

In short, the work of this group shifted the focus of treatment for many family therapists away from observing interactive sequences and patterns, and toward questioning family belief systems. Therapeutically, they moved away from creating strategies to help families change their behavior to helping them examine their thoughts, attitudes, beliefs, and the meanings they attach to their own behaviors as well as those of other family members. Families thus were helped not only to become aware of the repetitive patterns in which they were caught, but also to see themselves within a relational context (i.e., from the perspective of fellow family members). Moving beyond their earlier, typically linear perceptions of family interactions, each family member was now in a stronger position to examine a variety of perspectives that provide more alternatives for solving problems.

The notion that the therapist as observer is part of what is being observed—and thus is inescapably a part of the system to which he or she is offering therapy—redefines the therapist as someone who, like the other participants, has a particular perspective but not a truly objective view of the family or what's best for them. One consequence of this thinking is to take "truth" away from the therapist and make goal setting a participatory process that therapist and family members engage in together. Doing so empowers the family to make changes (or not make them) as they see fit. The therapist as a *nonhierarchical collaborator* (although hopefully a knowledgeable and inventive one who is both curious and impartial), allows the family to investigate and decide about its future in its own way and at its own pace. The theoretical and therapeutic implications of this very contemporary viewpoint helped catapult the contributions of members of the original Milan group, especially Luigi Boscolo and Gianfranco Cecchin, to the forefront of 1990s family therapy thinking and practice.

Milan Systemic Family Therapy

Three major related approaches to family therapy were strongly influenced by the theorizing of Gregory Bateson: the MRI interaction model, the strategic model developed by Haley and Madanes (both described in detail in Chapter 11), and the model put forth by a group of family therapists in Milan led by Mara Selvini-Palazzoli. All three approaches view problems as arising from the family's interactional sequences, but in practice both the MRI and strategic therapeutic approaches were also inspired by the clinical methods of Milton Erickson; the Milan group's model was the most consistent, conceptually and methodologically, with Bateson's original ideas concerning circular epistemology (MacKinnon, 1983). The Milan approach, as it continued to evolve, remained focused on information, much as Bateson (1972) did—as exemplified in his famous definition of information as "a difference that makes a difference." Characterized by a systematic search for differences—in behavior, in relationships, in how various family members perceive and construe an event—and by efforts to uncover the connections that link family members and keep the system in homeostatic balance, the approach has come to be known as **systemic family therapy.**

Leading Figures

Trained as a child psychoanalyst, Mara Selvini-Palazzoli in the late 1960s set about organizing a team of eight fellow psychiatrists—including Luigi Boscolo, Gianfranco Cecchin, and Guiliana Prata—to treat families of severely disturbed children, many of whom were suffering from anorexia nervosa. However, the team's initial efforts to apply psychoanalytic concepts to the family proved to be very time-consuming and produced limited results. Turning to the published accounts of the works of the Palo Alto group, particularly the book *Pragmatics of Human Communication* (Watzlawick, Beavin, & Jackson, 1967), four of the team members—Selvini-Palazzoli, Boscolo, Cecchin, and Prata—formed a study group to better understand strategic theories and techniques in the hope that such an outlook would increase their prospects for success in helping families with entrenched interactive patterns.

By 1971, the four together split off from their more psychoanalytically oriented colleagues and formed the Milan Center for the Study of the Family in order to work more exclusively with family systems. While Watzlawick was their major consultant in these early years, visiting them periodically in Italy, over the next decade the group gradually developed their own theory and set of strategic intervention techniques (Boscolo, Cecchin, Hoffman, & Penn, 1987). They published their first article in English in 1974 (Selvini-Palazzoli, Boscolo, Cecchin, & Prata, 1974), introducing a team approach along with a set of powerful and innovative intervention techniques such as *positive connotation* and *rituals* (both of which we describe in detail later in this chapter) designed to overcome therapeutic impasses and change stalemated family interactive sequences.

What is now referred to as the "classic" Milan approach—initially the clinical application of some of the theoretical concepts formulated in *Pragmatics of Human Communication*—quickly captured the imagination of many family therapists around the world. Working with families who were dealing with a wide range of the most severe emotional problems, the Milan group reported particular success in treating anorectic children as well as schizophrenics with their team approach. The first comprehensive exposition of their work in book form in English can be found in *Paradox and Counterparadox: A New Model in the Therapy of the Family in Schizophrenic Transaction* (Selvini-Palazzoli, Boscolo, Cecchin, & Prata, 1978).

After a decade of work together, the four separated into two autonomous groups (Selvini-Palazzoli and Prata; Boscolo and Cecchin) in 1980, each set pursuing differing emphases in their thinking and practices although retaining similar (but not identical) systemic outlooks. Selvini-Palazzoli and Prata later engaged in family systems research, particularly directed at developing techniques for interrupting the destructive games they believe are played by psychotic individuals and their families. Their intervention techniques, as we shall see, represent a return to some of their earlier strategic and structural ways of working (Simon, 1987).

In the United States the systemic outlook, especially its more recent modifications by Boscolo and Cecchin, found a particularly receptive audience among some members of the Ackerman Institute for Family Therapy in New York, particularly Peggy Papp (1983), Peggy Penn (1982), and Joel Bergman (1985). Lynn Hoffman, formerly at Ackerman, has since relocated to New England and adopted a post-Milan, collaborative, social constructionist viewpoint (Hoffman, 2002). In England, Elsa Jones (1993) as well as David Campbell and Rosalind Draper (1985) are enthusiastic supporters of the Milan viewpoint, as is Brian Cade (Cade & O'Hanlon, 1993) in Cardiff, Wales. In Canada, Karl Tomm of the University of Calgary is a leading interpreter of the Milan (and post-Milan) systemic approach, and has himself moved in the direction of a more social constructivist/narrative view (MacCormack & Tomm, 1998) in his therapeutic work with families. A description of Boscolo and Cecchin's work can be found in *Milan Systemic Family Therapy* (Boscolo, Cecchin, Hoffman, & Penn, 1987). Selvini-Palazzoli's later work, carried out in collaboration with a new group of colleagues, is called *Family Games* (Selvini-Palazzoli, Cirillo, Selvini, & Sorrentino, 1989); in it she proposed a universal intervention said to be particularly applicable to breaking up repetitively resistant patterns in families with severely disturbed members.

The Early Milan Model: Paradoxes, Counterparadoxes, Rituals, and Positive Connotations

Showing the strong influence of strategic techniques on their thinking, especially the use of paradoxical prescriptions intended to loosen rigid family transactions, Selvini-Palazzoli and her associates initially began to focus on the *rules of the game* in psychotic families—tactics by which family members struggle against one another as, together, they act to perpetuate unacknowledged family "games" in order to control each other's behavior. (The reader will recognize Haley's focus on power tactics within families here.) That is, they conceptualized the family as "a self-regulating system which controls itself according to the rules formed over a period of time through a process of trial and error" (Selvini-Palazzoli, Boscolo, Cecchin, & Prata, 1978, p. 3). The therapist's task, then, was to help disrupt, expose and ultimately interrupt the destructive "games" in which all family members participate together.

Selvini-Palazzoli and colleagues asserted that the schizophrenic family, trapped by the rules of the game, is powerless to effect change. That is, the rules of the family's game, rather than any individual input, define and sustain its members' relationships.

What remained paradoxical was that all family members, presumably seeking therapy in order to change, nevertheless continued to behave in ways that prevented any change from taking place. As Tomm (1984a) observed, it was as though the family were asking the therapist to change its symptomatic member, at the same time insisting that the rest of the family was fine and had no intention of changing.

Assuming that symptomatic behavior in a family member helped maintain the system's homeostatic balance through an unacknowledged network of coalitions and alliances, developed over generations, the team began by *prescribing no change* in that behavior. In this way, they were adapting the MRI technique of paradoxical intervention to their own systemic formulations that all of the family's attitudinal and behavioral patterns were mere moves designed to perpetuate the family game, and thus could not be confronted or challenged head-on. Through the subsequent use of therapeutic **counterparadoxes**—essentially therapeutic double binds—the family was warned against premature change, allowing the members to feel more acceptable and unblamed for how they were, as the team attempted to discover and counter the family's paradoxical patterns, thus interrupting repetitive, unproductive games.

In the language of the Milan group, the family's behavior was given a **positive connotation**—positive motives were ascribed to all family transactions, which were reframed to appear to be carried out in the name of family cohesion and thus as functioning purposefully to maintain family homeostasis. At the same time, each family member's behavior was connoted as related to the identified patient's symptoms, thereby tacitly getting their acknowledgment of overall implication in the "family game." Subsequent interventions typically prescribing assigned rituals were aimed at forcing behavior change in the system. (We elaborate on these powerful applications of paradoxically inspired techniques, along with examples, shortly.)

Long Brief Therapy

Two distinguishing characteristics of the original Milan systemic family therapy were its *spacing of therapeutic sessions* and its use of a *team of therapists* who work together with a family. The original Milan team method has been described as "long brief therapy" (Tomm, 1984a), since relatively few sessions (generally about 10) were held approximately once a month and thus treatment might extend up to a year or so. Initially, this unusual spacing of sessions was instituted because so many of the families seen at the Center in Milan had to travel hundreds of miles by train for treatment.

Later, the therapy team realized that their interventions—often in the form of paradoxical prescriptions aimed at changing the way an entire family system functioned—took time to incubate and finally take effect. Once the frequency was determined, the therapists did not grant an extra session or move up a session to shorten the agreed-upon interval. Such requests by families are seen as efforts to disqualify or undo the effects of a previous intervention (Selvini-Palazzoli, 1980). Early systemicists were adamant in their insistence that the therapist not submit to the family's "game" or become subjugated to its rules for maintaining sameness and controlling the therapeutic relationship. Even under pressure from the family, these therapists would remain unavailable in the belief that a request for an exceptional meeting actually meant the family was experiencing rapid change and needed the time to integrate any subsequent changes in family rules.

During most of the 1970s, the Milan group worked in an unconventional but consistent way developed from their strategic-based research. One or sometimes two

Mara Selvini-Palazzoli, M.D.

therapists (typically a man and a woman) saw the entire family together, while the remainder of the team watched from behind a one-way mirror to gain a different perspective. From time to time during the session, the observers summoned one of the therapists out of the room in order to change therapeutic direction. Conferring with the therapist, the observers would offer suggestions, opinions, and observations, often issuing directives that the returning therapist could then share with the family.

Following this strategy conference, the therapist rejoined the family group, discussed what had transpired with the other team members, and assigned the family members a task, usually a paradoxical prescription. Sometimes such an intervention took the form of a *paradoxical letter,* a copy of which was given to every family member. If a key member missed a session, a copy of the letter would be sent by mail, frequently with comments (again, often paradoxically stated) regarding his or her absence. Prescriptions took the form of opinions ("We believe Father and Mother, by working hard to be good parents, are nevertheless . . .") or requests that certain behavioral changes be attempted by means of rituals carried out between sessions ("The immediate family, without any other relatives or outsiders, should meet weekly for one hour, with each person allowed fifteen minutes to . . ."). By addressing the behavior of all the members, the therapists underscored the connections in the family patterns. Prescriptions usually were stated in such a way that the family was directed not to change for the time being. Box 12.1 offers a typical paradoxical letter with subsequent analysis keyed to specific statements.

Structured Family Sessions

The classic Milan therapeutic interview format thus was divided into five segments: the presession, the session, the intersession, the intervention, and the postsession discussion. Family therapy began with the initial telephone call from the family. The team member who took the call talked to the caller at length, recording the information on a fact sheet. Who called? Who referred the family? What is the problem? How disturbed is the caller's communication? What tone of voice is used? What is the caller's attitude regarding the forthcoming treatment? What special conditions, if any, does the caller attempt to impose (specific date or time)? These intake issues were then taken up with the entire team in the presession, prior to the first interview, in a lengthy and detailed way, and various team members proposed tentative *hypotheses* regarding the family's presenting problem. Particularly noteworthy is that the referring person or agency was kept involved throughout treatment, in recognition of their part in the larger system.

In a similar fashion, such team conferences occurred before each session, as the group met to review the previous session and together planned strategies for the upcoming one. All of these tactics affirmed the Milan therapists' belief that the family and therapist(s) are part of one system. During the session itself, a major break in the family interview (the intersession) occurred as the observer team had an active discussion with the therapist outside of the family's hearing, during which hypotheses were validated or modified; the therapist then returned to offer the team's intervention (usually a prescription or ritual) to the family. The team's postsession discussion focused on an analysis of the family's reaction to the intervention and gave the therapists a chance to plan for the following session (Boscolo, Cecchin, Hoffman, & Penn, 1987).

BOX 12.1   THERAPEUTIC ENCOUNTER

A Paradoxical Letter

Dear Norma, Sara, Ann, and Dave:

I was very impressed with the sadness and hurt in your family in our last session. I am glad the two of you were able to express your sadness.[1] It is important when you are sad and hurt to be able to share your feelings with other family members. Family members who share their hurts really love one another.[2] However, I have grave misgivings about how much you should share at this time. I think it is much too soon for you to communicate these feelings to each other.[3] Instead each of you should continue to protect the family from its sadness by distracting or keeping each other busy.[4] You might even select one family member on whom you can focus all of your attention, or maybe someone in the family has already decided to take this role. This person could be responsible for starting fights and misbehaving.[5] The person selected should be a very responsible and local member of the family; this should make the choice easy because one of you already is acting in an overtly responsible manner (but enjoying it).[6]

Your family is also in a silent crisis.[7] Someone has changed recently, which has the family confused and uncertain about the future. The confusion and chaos in the family are actually part of the preparation for the family's forthcoming growth and change.[8]

Warning: The family should be prepared for a big fight on Wednesday night.[9]

1. *Cryptic statement:* Raises the question of who expressed sadness, and is designed to unite the family in guessing who it was.
2. *Relabeling:* Sharing hurt is equated to love.
3. *Restraining:* Previous statement tells the family members it is good to share hurt, but now they are warned that it may be risky.
4. *Positive connotation:* Distraction is said to protect the family, which puts them all on the same level.
5. *Prescription:* The fighting is prescribed.
6. *Relabeling:* The most distracting member of the family is relabeled as the one who is responsible and loyal.
7. *Cryptic statement:* What is a "silent crisis"?
8. *Relabeling:* Remember, this is a chaotic family; there is no predictability or certainty; the confusion is relabeled as preparation for growth.
9. *Paradoxical question:* Our next session is scheduled for Thursday; the oldest daughter said she would not return; hence we expect a fight about her attendance on Wednesday night, if not earlier.

Source: Weeks and L'Abate, 1982

In this earlier version of the Milan model there is more concern with family processes than family structure. Members of dysfunctional families were seen as engaging in unacknowledged destructive, repetitive sequences of interaction. No one seemed able to extricate himself or herself from the family's self-perpetuating "games" in which members tried to control each other's behavior. The identified problem is seen as serving the system in the best way possible at the moment. Why, then, can the family not find a better way to survive and function, one that does not involve sacrificing one of its (symptomatic) members? Perhaps the rules governing the system are too rigid, tolerating an extremely narrow range of behavior. Since the family members, through their communication patterns, maintain the system's rules and thus perpetuate the transactions in which the symptomatic behavior is embedded, the therapist must try to change the rules in order to change that behavior (Selvini-Palazzoli, Boscolo, Cecchin, & Prata, 1978).

Put more succinctly, systemic therapy tried to discover, interrupt, and thus change the rules of the game before the behavior of the players (the symptomatic member as well as other family members) could change. For example, the therapist working with a family with an anorectic daughter must break the code inherent in the following family game, as each parent both insists upon and denies family leadership (Selvini-Palazzoli, 1978):

MOTHER: I don't let her wear miniskirts because I know her father doesn't like them.
FATHER: I have always backed my wife up. I feel it would be wrong to contradict her. (p. 208)

Note the trap the therapist is drawn into if he or she tries to change such confusing and disqualifying statements. Direct interventions are likely to bring forth countermoves, as the family members fight off any challenge to their rules. Following Bateson's earlier work, Selvini-Palazzoli and her colleagues in their early formulations contended that a family double-bind message, a paradox, could be undone only by a therapeutic double bind, which they call a counterparadox.

Positive Connotations and Ritual Prescriptions

Two interviewing techniques that emerged from this early Milan period deserve special attention.

Positive connotation is a form of reframing the family's problem-maintaining behavior in which symptoms are seen as positive or good because they help maintain the system's balance and thus facilitate family cohesion and well-being. By suggesting a good motive for behavior previously viewed as negatively motivated ("The reason your child refuses to go to school is that he wants to provide companionship for his lonely mother"), the systemic therapist is indicating to the family that the symptomatic behavior formerly looked upon negatively may actually be desirable. Instead of being considered "bad" or "sick" or "out of control," the symptomatic child is considered to be *well intentioned* and to be *behaving volitionally*. Note that it is not the symptomatic behavior (school refusal) that is connoted to be positive, but rather the intent behind that behavior (family cohesion or harmony).

All members are considered to be motivated by the same positive desire for family cohesion, and thus all are linked as participants in the family system. Because the positive connotation is presented by the therapist as an approval rather than a reproach, the family does not resist such explicit confirmation and accepts the statement. As a result of reframing, the symptomatic behavior is now viewed by the family as voluntary, greatly enhancing the possibilities for change. However, the positive connotation has implicitly put the family in a paradox: Why must such a good thing as family cohesion require the presence of symptomatic behavior in a member?

CLINICAL NOTE

Overly intense families, intent on fighting and not listening to one another, often quiet down and attend to what each other is saying when the therapist reframes their statements as positively motivated and well intentioned.

One other important function of positive connotation deserves mention: It prepares the family for forthcoming paradoxical prescriptions. That is, when each member's behavior is connoted as positive, all view one another as cooperative and thus are more willing to join in complying with any tasks they may be assigned by the therapist, reducing family resistance to future change. If the therapist adds a no-change prescription—"And because you have decided to help the family in this way, we think that you should continue in this work for the time being" (Tomm, 1984b, p. 266)—an additional paradox of "no change in the context of change" further increases the impact of the intervention. The seemingly innocuous phrase "for the time being" implies that the current family pattern need not always occur in the current manner, leaving open the possibility of future spontaneous change. The family is left to resolve the paradoxical absurdities on its own.

Family **rituals,** such as weddings, birthday parties, baptisms, bar mitzvahs, graduations, funerals, and so forth, often play a central role in a family's life. Such transitions are designed to mark and facilitate family developmental transitions and changes. Therapeutically, they may be designed to intervene in established family patterns, promoting new ways of doing things, which in turn may alter thoughts, beliefs, and relationship options (Imber-Black, Roberts, & Whiting, 1989). As Campbell, Draper, and Crutchley (1991) put it:

> The purpose of a ritual is to address the conflict between the family rules operating at the verbal level and those operating at the analogic level by a prescription to change behavior rather than an interpretation to provide insight. (p. 327)

Rather than offer a direct prescription, which the family may fear or resist or otherwise oppose, ritualizing the prescribed behavior offers a new context and is thus more likely to be carried out by the family. Rituals usually are assigned in paradoxical prescriptions describing in detail what act is to be done, by whom, when, and in what sequence. Typically, carrying out the ritual calls for the performance of a task that challenges some rigid, covert family rule.

Rituals address aspects of family relationships that the therapist or team hypothesizes as significant for family functioning, based on how the team views the family's current difficulty. Generally, they are ceremonial acts proposed by the therapist in a tentative way as suggestions or family experiments that are not expected to become a permanent part of family life. The therapist does not insist that the ritual be carried out, but indicates that he or she believes the gesture to be useful.

Generally speaking, the purpose of a ritual is to provide clarity where there might be confusion in family relationships; the clarity is gained by the family's enactment of the directive (Tomm, 1984b). Take the case of parents who are inconsistent or competitive with one another in attempting to maintain behavioral control of a disruptive child. An alternating-day ritual might be suggested in which Mother takes full charge of discipline on odd days (with father observing and taking exact notes on the ensuing mother-child interaction) and Father takes charge on even days (with mother playing the counter-role). Each parent is directed to carry out the assigned roles for a certain number of days, and to behave "spontaneously" for the remaining days of the week. Carrying out the ritual clarifies differences in approach for the parents and provides greater awareness of how their differences can cause confusion in their child. It thus highlights the importance of two-parent consistency as a goal if the child is to achieve the comfort level necessary to abandon the disruptive behavior.

BOX 12.2 CLINICAL NOTE

Assigning Rituals as Therapeutic Strategies

Strategic therapists, including the early Milan group, frequently use assigned rituals in working with individuals as well as families to help them break out of rigid behavioral patterns. Fisch, Weakland, and Segal (1982) report the case of a perfectionist who was given the task of making one deliberate mistake a day. In this case, a woman potter who expressed various complaints about her creations was directed to produce imperfect pottery for one hour on an agreed-upon day. Similarly, directing a rigid or compulsive person to fail purposely (to say something stupid or socially inappropriate, to behave in a clumsy or gauche way) often produces a liberating effect.

Drawing attention to crucial distinctions is thus an important aspect of a ritual. In some cases the message the therapists wish to convey is sufficiently critical that they prepare a written statement for the family to read before carrying out the task. As Tomm (1984b) observes, rituals often enable the family to clarify chaotic patterns and confront inherent but previously unrecognized contradictions.

An Evolving Model: Hypothesizing, Neutrality, and Circular Questioning

Continuing to flesh out their ideas, by 1980 the Milan group was beginning to reduce the use of paradoxes. In a landmark paper, "Hypothesizing-circularity-neutrality: Three guidelines for the conductor of the session" (Selvini-Palazzoli, Boscolo, Cecchin, & Prata, 1980), they revealed their thinking to be moving in a systemic direction and away from strategic techniques. Most significant in this new therapeutic course was the prominence given the interviewing process per se (especially the technique of circular questioning) and the de-emphasis on issuing directives (positive connotations and rituals) as therapeutic strategies.

The three landmark intervention strategies—hypothesizing, circularity, and neutrality—developed near the end of the original Milan group's collaboration are central to post-Milan technical innovations. Circular questioning in particular became the cornerstone of Boscolo and Cecchin's later modifications of the original systemic outlook. When systemic therapists speak of circularity they are referring both to interactional sequences within the family and, because the therapist is part of the system, to the therapist's interactional relationship with the family. The therapist's hypotheses lead to questions, and the family's responses lead to refined hypotheses and new questions, all leading to changes in the family's belief system.

Central to the revised Milan approach and thus the first act of this type of therapy is **hypothesizing.** Milan systemicists contend that hypothesizing, a continual interactive process of speculating and making assumptions about the family situation, provides a guide for conducting a systemic interview. Such a guide to the family system is not true or false, but rather is useful as a starting point, open to revision or abandonment by the family as well as the therapist as new data accumulate. The technique allows the therapist to search for new information, identify the connecting patterns that sustain family behavior, and speculate on how each participant in the family contributes to systemic functioning. Beginning with the family's first telephone

BOX 12.3   THERAPEUTIC ENCOUNTER

AN ANORECTIC ADOLESCENT AND THE FAMILY GAME

Consider the following hypothesis about how the symptom of anorexia might provide a clue about the family game:

A 13-year-old girl whose mother has recently returned to work goes on a diet to lose her "baby fat" and continues food refusal to the point of developing symptoms of anorexia. These symptoms and the resulting danger to the girl's health require that her mother leave her newly acquired job and become active in monitoring her daughter's eating habits. The father, who is nine years older than the mother, encourages his wife in this diligent detective-like behavior.

When viewed within the context of this family's relationship pattern, the child's self-destructive behavior can be seen as an ingenious attempt, covertly supported by the father, to keep her mother dependent and tied into the role of wife and mother. Alternately it can be seen as supporting the mother's ambivalence regarding obtaining employment, and her need to pull the father closer to home with worries. Finally, as Selvini-Palazzoli (1986) recently argued, the child's behavior may represent the culmination of concerted efforts among all family members to prove that competition leads nowhere. (Gelcer, McCabe, & Smith-Resnick, 1990, pp. 52–53)

contact, and continuing throughout the therapeutic process, hypothesizing represents therapeutic formulations regarding family functioning.

Systemicists believe that unless the therapist comes to the family session prepared with hypotheses to be checked out, there is the risk that the family may impose its own definition of the problem and its resolution, which is likely to be faulty and to perpetuate the presenting problem. Hypothesizing involves the active efforts the team makes during the presession to formulate in advance of the family session what they believe might be responsible for maintaining the family's presenting symptoms. Diagnostically useful in formulating a "map" of the family's "game," hypothesizing also orients the therapist to ask the kinds of questions that will elicit answers confirming, necessitating revision of, or refuting the suppositions.

Hypotheses formulated by the team typically take the form of systemic or relational statements, linking all family members, and thus offer a circular structure regarding family rules and interactive behaviors. They help the team organize forthcoming information from the family and begin to comprehend why the symptomatic behavior manifested itself in this family at this time. Hypotheses are carefully constructed to elicit a picture of how the family is organized around the symptom or presenting problem. Circularity throughout the family system is stressed. Asked for a description of the problem at the start of the first interview, the family might point to the symptom bearer as the one with the problem. The Milan therapist will ask, "Who noticed the problem first?" This redefines the problem as relational—it does not exist without a "noticer," and thus it does not belong to one person alone. Moreover, the problem is depicted as an event between two or more family members, thus involving the wider family system (Boscolo, Cecchin, Hoffman, & Penn, 1987).

Hypothesizing permits the therapist to present a view of the family's behavior that is *different*—not true or false, but simply different from the family's own established self-picture. The therapist is thus offering a conceptualization—of the family's

---

BOX 12.4   THERAPEUTIC ENCOUNTER

A CLINICAL VIGNETTE: A MILAN-STYLE INITIAL INTERVIEW

The Parker family referred themselves for family therapy following a son's school suspension of eight days for fighting after basketball practice. The mother is a homemaker, the father sells retirement programs, the twin boys are 16. A sister, 20, lives in another city and did not attend. The interview is conducted by a female, doctoral-level therapist. Graduate students observe behind a one-way mirror and are part of the therapy team but are not involved in this segment.

THERAPIST: Tell me what brings you here today?

MOM: Well, it's just the straw that broke the camel's back, you know. Alex is the one who got in trouble this time, but they have both been problems and it's getting out of hand.

THERAPIST: So Alex and Andrew got you here equally.

MOM: Well, they didn't get us here. I got us here. I had to threaten to get them here.

THERAPIST: And they went along with your threats?

MOM: Well, yes.

THERAPIST: What about you, Dad? Do you have to be threatened, or did you come on your own?

DAD (laughs): Oh, she threatens me all the time. But I know I have to do what she says.

THERAPIST: So do you agree with Mom that Alex and Andrew got you here, or did you come because Mom threatened?

DAD (mumbles and laughs): Well, I don't really know. I just . . . I don't know.

THERAPIST: Don't quite know why you are here?

DAD: Well, yes, they are problems, but you know that's just how kids are, and they are 16 and very active guys. They both play basketball and . . . (shrugs and throws up his hands)

THERAPIST: So Mom is pretty sure of herself and takes strong steps to get things done. Dad is not so sure but is willing to go along with Mom.

MOM: Well, I wouldn't say he always goes along with me. He gets upset all on his own. He just gets mad at different things, and then he gets out of control and hollers.

THERAPIST: Oh? What kinds of things upset Dad?

MOM: Well, little things, like if the papers are left on the floor and not put up immediately.

THERAPIST: So Mom and Dad both get upset but over different things. What about you, Alex; what upsets you?

ALEX: Mom is crazy.

---

communication patterns, the meaning of a member's symptoms, how the family organizes itself to deal with problems, the family game, and so forth. In doing so, the therapist identifies himself or herself as an active participant—someone who does not necessarily have all the answers but, with his or her unique view of the family's reality, may open family members up to considering a new perspective on their lives.

As Burbatti and Formenti (1988) contend, *the goal of therapeutic hypotheses is change, not truth.* In the Batesonian tradition, hypothesizing offers information, allowing family members to choose or reject the therapeutic message from an active therapeutic partner. If, instead, the therapist were simply a passive observer, the Milan group believes the family would impose its own punctuations and resume its own games; little if any new information would be forthcoming to initiate change, and the system would tend toward entropy. Hypothesizing, on the other hand, offers a structured viewpoint, organizing data provided by the family, encouraging family members to rethink their lives and together begin to form new hypotheses (for example, regarding previously denied coalitions) about themselves and their "games."

THERAPIST: Oh? What kind of crazy things does Mom do?

ALEX: She's always upset over any little thing. Always nagging us.

THERAPIST: So Mom gets more upset than Dad?

ALEX: Oh, yeah.

THERAPIST: Who tends to notice first when Mom gets upset?

ALEX: Well, it depends on what she does. If I come home and she's going nuts because I screwed up, then I notice. But I ignore it if I can.

THERAPIST: How does she get you to notice when you are trying to ignore her?

ALEX: Well, sometimes it works. I just say yeah, man, and go on and say I gotta go practice or like that.

THERAPIST: So you do that pretty well. What about Dad? Is he better than Mom at getting upset?

ALEX: Well, he's harder to ignore for sure.

THERAPIST: And what about Andrew? How often does he get upset? Less than Mom? Less than Dad?

ALEX: Andrew?

THERAPIST: Yes, that guy right there.

ALEX: Well . . . really never.

THERAPIST: Andrew, is that right?

ANDREW: I get upset some.

THERAPIST: At who? Who do you get upset with the most?

ANDREW: Dad and Mom. Mom more because she's around. It's hard to get mad at Dad because he's never there. But when Dad blows, he blows and, oh man, watch out.

THERAPIST: Sounds like you agree with Alex. Dad can be a volcano when he wants to and you have to sit up and take notice.

Note how in this initial session the therapist avoids discussing the content of the presenting problem (how the boys get in trouble, whether Mom is indeed "crazy") but instead sets the stage for a systemic view of the family by identifying a theme (getting upset) and asking questions about behaviors in which all members participate. The therapist offers a positive connotation (Mom is pretty sure of herself and takes strong steps to get things done, and Dad is not so sure but willing to go along with her) rather than saying to them that Mom is upset and Dad uninvolved. She also solicits everyone's opinions, uses circular questioning (Who notices first? Who gets more upset?). The therapist is developing hypotheses to be checked out and revised if necessary as therapy progresses.

Source: Prevatt (1999, pp. 192–194

Neutrality, a systemicist therapeutic stance, is different from noninvolvement; it means the therapist is interested in, and accepts without challenge, each member's unique *perception* of the problem (if not necessarily accepting the problem itself). No one family member's view is seen as more correct than that of any other. Thus, each family member may repeatedly experience the therapist as being allied with one or another member as that person's views are elicited, but never as allied with any one participant.

All perceptions by family members are considered to be legitimate and accepted without judgment by the therapist. By hearing all views, the family is in a better position to pinpoint the problem affecting all its members and to begin to develop a range of alternative solutions (Prevatt, 1999).

To Milan therapists, neutrality refers to efforts to remain allied with all family members, avoiding getting caught up in family coalitions or alliances. Such a position, typically low-key and nonreactive, gives the therapist maximum leverage in achieving change by not being drawn into family "games" or appearing to side with one family member against another. More concerned with curiosity about how the family system works than with attempting to change it, the neutral therapist assumes that the system the family has constructed makes sense; the family members could not be any other way than they are at the moment. By not offering suggestions as to how the family should be, the therapist activates the family's capacity to generate its own solutions (Boscolo, Cecchin, Hoffman, & Penn, 1987).

Again we emphasize that therapeutic neutrality does not imply being inactive or indifferent. Actually, the therapist might display neutrality by listening without prejudice to what is being said, but at the same time asking thought-provoking, relationship-focused questions. A report that the family argues a lot might be accepted by the neutral therapist as interesting information. Without joining the family in assuming arguing is bad, the therapist might inquire, "Who enjoys fighting the most?" or "What would be missing if all the arguing suddenly stopped?" (Tomm, 1984b). (Note that a hypothesis that the family is getting something out of the fighting is subtly being explored.) Nor should the therapist become too committed to the family's changing. As Selvini-Palazzoli has observed, "If you wish to be a good therapist it is dangerous to have too much of a desire to help other people" (quoted in Simon, 1987, p. 28). Rather, the therapist's goal should be to *help the family achieve change in its ability to change*. They also have the right not to change. Neutrality precludes taking a position for or against any specific behavioral goals from therapy or assuming that the therapist must somehow be the one to effect change.

Cecchin (1987) characterized the notion of neutrality as *curiosity*, in response to the widespread misunderstanding that neutrality demonstrated coldness or aloofness. As the term is currently used, the curious therapist is open to numerous hypotheses about the system, and invites the family to explore hypotheses that increase the number of options or possibilities for the changes they seek. Curiosity and inquisitiveness offer hope of change rather than focusing on what has gone wrong with the family (Cecchin, Lane, & Ray, 1992).

Circular questioning involves asking each family member questions that help address a difference or define a relationship between two other members of the family. These differences are intended to reveal the multiple perspectives of different family members and to expose recursive family patterns. Here the therapist is trying to construct a map of the interconnections between family members, and is assuming that asking questions about differences in perception—and questions derived from the feedback from previous questions about differences—is the most effective way of creating such a map (Campbell, Draper, & Crutchley, 1991). One major gain is that each family member is continually exposed to feedback from the others throughout the therapy.

One particularly significant accomplishment of this revised Milan approach was to translate Bateson's earlier view of the key role of circular causality in understanding relationships into an exquisite interviewing technique. As Selvini-Palazzoli, Boscolo, Cecchin, and Prata (1980) define it in their landmark paper:

> By circularity, we mean the capacity of the therapist to conduct his investigation on the basis of feedback from the family in response to the information he solicits about relationships and, therefore, about differences and change. (p. 3)

Underscoring the notion of feedback loops, the team developed guidelines for asking questions that led to the construction of a map of the interconnections between family members. More specifically, rather than relying on a free-form set of therapeutic questions, based loosely on previously formulated hypotheses, Boscolo, Cecchin, Hoffman, and Penn (1987, p. 11) insisted on questions that (a) probed differences in perceptions about relationships ("Who is closer to Father, your daughter or your son?"); (b) investigated degrees of difference ("On a scale of one to ten, how bad do you think the fighting is this week?"); (c) studied now-and-then differences ("Did she start losing weight before or after her sister went off to college?"); and (d) sought views of family members on hypothetical or future differences ("If she had not been born, how would your marriage be different today?"). The idea was to search for mutually causal feedback chains underlying family interactive patterns, and to incorporate these findings into systemic hypotheses, which in turn would form the basis for asking further circular questions, leading to further refined hypotheses, and so forth. The technique is particularly ingenious in that it allows very little room for a refusal to answer, since questioners are given choices.

The technique focuses attention on family connections rather than individual symptomatology, by framing every question so that it addresses differences in perception by different family members about events or relationships. Asking a child to compare his mother's and father's reactions to his sister's refusal to eat, or to rate each one's anger on a 10-point scale, or to hypothesize what would happen if they divorced—these are all subtle and relatively benign ways to compel people to focus on differences. By asking several people the same question about their attitude toward the same relationship, the therapist is able to probe deeper and deeper without being directly confrontational or interrogating the participants in the relationship (Selvini-Palazzoli, Boscolo, Cecchin, & Prata, 1980).

Family members reveal their connections by communicating information, expressed verbally as well as nonverbally. Information about the family lies in differences in meaning each participant gives an event. Such differences in turn reflect views of family relationships. Circular questioning aims at eliciting and clarifying confused ideas about family relationships and introducing information about such differences back to the family in the form of new questions. Table 12.1 provides examples of common types of circular questions.

Such triadic questioning (addressing a third person about the relationship between another two) often produces change in the family in and of itself, as well as providing information to the therapist. Families learn in the process to think in circular rather than linear terms, and to become closer observers of family processes. Another member's perspective may prove enlightening when compared with one's own view of an event or relationship.

QUESTIONING FAMILY BELIEF SYSTEMS

Despite the continuing evolvement of the Milan team's ideas, their basic therapeutic mission has remained constant: to help families recognize their choices and to assist members in exercising their prerogatives of choosing. Fundamental to accomplishing these goals is the creation of a therapeutic climate wherein family members can hear each other's perspectives as each answers therapist questions. If differences in viewpoint continue to exist, at least members listen and learn to accept other viewpoints or belief systems as viable (Gelcer, McCabe, & Smith-Resnick, 1990). Questioning family members, hypothesizing about the family game, and constantly feeding back information to the family have remained the key methods of achieving those goals.

As we have noted, heavy use of the paradox-counterparadox phenomenon characterized the early Milan team efforts. Dysfunctional families with a symptomatic member, presumably seeking change, themselves seemed to behave paradoxically—the

TABLE 12.1 Circular Questions

Category	Definition/Function	Examples
Differences in relationship	Establish interpersonal relationships, subsystems, and alliances.	Who are you closest to in the family? Who do you confide in the most?
Differences in degree	If a problem can be more or less intense, then it also has the potential to cease.	Who worries more about your son? Is the fighting worse or is the running away worse? On a scale of 1 to 5, how much does that worry you?
Differences in time	If a problem has a beginning, then it can have an end.	Does she cry more now that you are separated, or did she cry more when you were together? Who noticed first? Who was cooperative before he became cooperative? Are you closer now than you used to be?
Hypothetical/ future	Establish a sense of control over actions.	If you were to leave, what would he do? When your daughter leaves for college, how will your husband react?
Observer-perspective	Help individuals to recognize how their own reactions, behaviors, and feelings may serve as links in the family interactions.	Who agrees that this is a problem? How does your father express love? Who is your mother likely to get support from? How would your daughter describe your discipline style?
Normative-comparison	Promote healthy functioning by establishing a healthy frame of reference. Allow individuals identified as the problem to feel less abnormal.	Does your family fight more or less than other families? Is your family more or less tightly knit than other families? Is your son rowdier than the other boys his age? Do you and your husband argue more than other couples you know?
Hypothesis introducing	Help move the family toward new insights or solutions by imbedding a working hypothesis into a question.	If you get angry to cover up your vulnerability, does your family interpret that as your being hostile? Do you see your shyness as a way of not getting close to others or as a way of being selective about who you want to be friends with?
Linear	Noncircular questions used when history or specific information is desired.	Where are you employed? How long have you been married? What other problems do you see? How long has he been gone? How do you punish him when he misbehaves?

Source: Prevatt, 1999, p. 191

moves each member of the system made seemed to keep change from occurring. In effect their common message was that they had a problematic member who needed to change, but as a family the rest of the members were fine and did not intend to change.

Recognizing from a systems perspective that it is impossible for a part to change without a complementary change in the whole, the Milan group began to design interventions in the form of counterparadoxes directed at breaking up such contradictory patterns, thus freeing up the family to change. One common counterparadox, as we have seen, was to declare that although they were change agents, they did not wish to upset what appeared to be a workable family homeostatic balance and therefore would prescribe no change for now (Selvini-Palazzoli, Boscolo, Cecchin, & Prata, 1978). Thus, the therapist might say, "I think the family should continue to support Sophia's behavior for the present."

In a later revision that shifted their thinking away from the MRI version of families as self-correcting systems governed by rules, the Milan team began to think of systems as evolving and unfolding rather than seeking a return to a previous homeostatic level. Extrapolating from Bateson's (1972) work, they theorized that dysfunctional families are making an "epistemological error"—they are following an outdated or erroneous set of beliefs or "maps" of their reality; that is why they appear to be "stuck" or in homeostatic balance. Put another way, the family was having problems because they had adopted a set of beliefs that did not fit the reality in which they were living their lives. In effect, they were being guided by an outdated map; the signs and streets had changed since the map's publication.

In fact, according to this new perspective, the family's beliefs about itself were not the same as the actual behavior patterns of its members. They only gave the impression of being "stuck"; in reality, their behavior was changing continuously. The Milan group decided they needed to help families differentiate between these two levels— meaning and action. Therapeutically, they began to introduce new information, new distinctions in thought and action, carefully introducing a difference into the family's belief system.

Relying now on circular questioning to present differences for the family to consider, the team attempted to activate a process in which the family creates new belief patterns and new patterns of behavior consistent with those beliefs (Tomm, 1984a). New information was given the family explicitly through reframing or implicitly through the prescription of family rituals.

By uncovering connecting patterns, by revealing family "games," by introducing new information into the system through opinions or requests that certain family rituals be carried out between sessions, Milan therapists were trying to bring about a transformation in family relationship patterns. Note that unlike Haley, whom we discussed in Chapter 11, they did not issue prescriptions to arouse defiance and resistance. Rather, they offered "information" about family connectedness and the interrelatedness of members' behavior. By deliberately trying not to provoke resistance to change, they were offering input in the form of information in order to help the family discover its own solutions (MacKinnon, 1983).

Milan therapeutic procedures also changed over time. The classic method—male and female co-therapists, two team members behind the one-way mirror—was amended so that a single therapist was likely to work with the family while the rest of the team (often students learning the technique) observed. The observers were free to call the therapist out of the room to share ideas and offer hypotheses. The fixed monthlong interval between sessions became more flexible, depending on feedback from the family and consultants. Generally speaking, a 10-session limit extended over an indeterminate period of time still qualifies the approach as long brief therapy (Jones, 1993).

In offering a case study in which acting-out children "provide a shield for marital difficulties," Prevatt (1999) outlines the following steps in her work with the family:

1. Constructing a working hypothesis
2. Exhibiting a therapeutic stance of neutrality
3. Using circular questioning as both an assessment and therapeutic technique
4. Working with a team to monitor the process
5. Identifying the labels used by the family
6. Identifying openings or themes to be explored
7. Using positive connotation for problematic behaviors
8. Using an end-of-session intervention

The Invariant Prescription

In their evolving therapeutic approach, Selvini-Palazzoli and Prata sought to avoid employing hit-or-miss end-of-session prescriptions for each new family by specifically seeking a *universal prescription* that would fit all families. Their research focused on finding similarities in the games that "crazy" families play, and formulating countermoves so that the therapist can interrupt these games and force a change in family interactive patterns (Pirrotta, 1984).

In a later therapeutic modification, developed from research begun with Prata, Selvini-Palazzoli (1986) focused on the impact of a single sustained intervention to unhinge collusive parent-child patterns. Seeking a way to successfully intervene with chronically psychotic adolescents and adults, she and a new set of associates (Selvini-Palazzoli, Cirillo, Selvini, & Sorrentino, 1989) began to elaborate on her earlier conceptualization of severely dysfunctional behavior as linked to a specific power struggle "game" within the family. Reacting to a struggle between parents, psychotic and anorectic family members were thought to have developed symptoms in an effort to defeat one of the parents in favor of the other. To break up the game, Selvini-Palazzoli and associates now offered the controversial proposal that therapists offer a specific ritual for the parents. Later, Selvini-Palazzoli proposed that this universal or invariant prescription be applied to all families with schizophrenic or anorectic children. This method calls for a more directive therapist in control of the sessions. Its underlying paradoxical message is that a family member's (say, a child's) symptoms represent understandable motives but contribute to the damaging family games.

The **invariant prescription** is based on a six-stage model of psychotic family games. Selvini-Palazzoli contends that a single process takes place in all schizophrenic and anorectic families, beginning with a stalemated marriage (stage 1) in which a child attempts to take sides (stage 2). Eventually drawn into the family game, the child erroneously considers the actively provoking parent to be the winner over the passive parent, and sides with the "loser." The subsequent development of disturbed behavior or symptomatology in the child (stage 3), requiring parental attention, represents a demonstration to the passive parent of how to defeat the "winner." Instead of joining the child, however, the passive parent or "loser" sides with the "winner" parent (stage 4) in disapproving of the child's behavior. The child, in this scenario, feels betrayed and abandoned and responds by escalating the disturbed behavior, determined to bring down the "winning" parent and show the "loser" what can be done (stage 5). Ultimately the family system stabilizes around the symptomatic behavior (stage 6), with all participants resorting to "psychotic family games" as each tries to turn the situation to his or her advantage (Selvini-Palazzoli, 1986).

A provocative therapeutic strategy in such a situation is to offer the parents an invariant prescription—a fixed sequence of directives they must follow if the therapist is to help them interrupt the family game. After an initial family interview, the therapist sees the parents separately from the child and gives them the following prescription intended to introduce a clear and stable boundary between generations (Selvini-Palazzoli, 1986):

> Keep everything about this session absolutely secret at home. Every now and then, start going out in the evenings before dinner. Nobody must be forewarned. Just leave a written note saying, "We'll not be home tonight." If, when you come back, one of your (daughters) inquires where you have been, just answer calmly, "These things concern only the two of us." Moreover, each of you will keep a notebook, carefully hidden and out of the children's reach. In these notebooks each of you, separately, will register the date and describe the verbal and nonverbal behavior of each child, or other family member, which seemed to be connected with the prescription you have followed. We recommend diligence in keeping these records because it's extremely important that nothing be forgotten or omitted. Next time you will again come alone, with your notebooks, and read aloud what has happened in the meantime. (pp. 341–342)

The parental alliance, reinforced by joint action and by secretiveness, is strengthened by the prescription (Selvini-Palazzoli, Cirillo, Selvini, & Sorrentino, 1989; Prata, 1990) and previously existing alliances and family coalitions are broken. Parental disappearance exposes and blocks family games, over which none of the players had complete control but which nevertheless perpetuated psychotic behavior. The overall therapeutic thrust, then, is to separate the parents from the rest of the family, alter previous family interactive patterns, and then reunite the family in a more stable alliance at the conclusion of the treatment.

Although Selvini-Palazzoli (1986) initially claimed a high success rate for this powerful intervention technique, the therapeutic power of a single prescription for all disturbed families has yet to be established. Selvini-Palazzoli herself, in the early 1990s, again reflecting her restless desire for change and new exploration, seemed to downplay the use of brief techniques, including the invariant prescription, by returning to long-term, intergenerational family therapy. Nevertheless, this description of the psychotic process occurring in certain families is intriguing, and the use of this potent intervention procedure aimed at strengthening parental alliances and dislodging family coalitions is an admirable effort to break up a rigid, destructive family game and force family members to invent more flexible ways of living together.

A Post-Milan Systemic Epistemology

Taking a different path, Boscolo and Cecchin continued to elaborate the systemic ideas first presented in the hypothesis-neutrality-circularity paper. Departing from strategic interviewing techniques, these therapists developed a post-Milan collaborative therapeutic intervention style based on the interviewing process itself, particularly the use of circular questioning. By listening to the differing views of the same situation

Luigi Boscolo, M.D.

presented by various family members, each participant is helped to see his or her own behavior in a relational context, rather than from a linear or narrow self-centered perspective.

Consistent with those views, Boscolo and Cecchin's most recent efforts were directed at fine-tuning such *questioning techniques* in order to aid family members in hearing and attempting to understand the family's relational context from the perspective of fellow family members. In seeking to advance a new systemic epistemology, these therapists have become central players in advancing the constructivist and narrative approaches that now are so popular in the family therapy field worldwide.

Boscolo and Cecchin, in their training seminars, turned increasingly to developing ways of introducing new ideas and new patterns of thinking to family members (Pirrotta, 1984). Unlike Selvini-Palazzoli's direct, take-charge therapeutic style, offering parents prescriptions, Boscolo and Cecchin's efforts emphasize neutrality as a more effective device for quietly challenging an entire family to reexamine its epistemology. In effect, they temporarily join the family, becoming part of a whole system from which they can begin to offer information and perspectives on reality. In essence, the therapists and family members influence one another, producing the opportunity for change as a by-product.

Expanding on earlier cybernetic ideas, Boscolo and Cecchin argue that by becoming part of the observing system, the observer loses all objectivity, and there no longer exists a separate observed (family) system. Having adopted such second-order cybernetic concepts, they observe that

> first-order cybernetics pictured a family system in trouble as a homeostatic machine.
> Jackson's model based on the concept of family homeostasis is such a case. According to Jackson, a symptom plays an important part in maintaining the homeostasis of the family.
> This model was, perhaps, an advance over nineteenth-century models for psychopathology . . . but still separated the therapist from the client. A second-order model conceptualizes the treatment unit as consisting of both the observer and the observed in one large bundle. This cannot be achieved easily as long as pathology is assumed to be in a container: as in a . . . "dysfunctional family system." (Boscolo, Cecchin, Hoffman, & Penn, 1987, p. 14)

Boscolo and Cecchin argued that perhaps it is better to do away with the concept of family systems entirely, and think of the treatment unit as a *meaning system* in which the therapist is as active a contributor as anyone else. Any intervention, then, should not be directed at a particular outcome, but rather should be seen as jarring the system that then will react based on its own structure. For Boscolo and Cecchin, the system does not create the problem. Rather, the problem creates the system; it does not exist apart from the "observing systems" that reciprocally and collectively define the problem. Thus, therapists cannot change families through therapeutic interventions but can merely coexist in a therapeutic domain in which they may perturb the system through interaction but that will only lead to therapeutic change if the structure of the family system allows the perturbations to have an effect on its organization (Campbell, Draper, & Crutchley, 1991, p. 336).

Consistent with postmodern ideas, therapists do not have the answers but, together with the family, can co-construct or co-evolve new ways of looking at the family system, deconstructing old family assumptions and creating the possibility of new narratives or versions of reality that are less saturated with past problems or past failed solutions.

Tomm's Reflexive Questioning

Karl Tomm, in a series of papers (1987a, 1987b, 1988), has elaborated on these second-order cybernetics ideas, arguing that the presence of the therapist in the enlarged therapist-family system calls for him or her to carry out continuous "interventive interviewing." More than simply seeking workable interventions, Tomm (1987a) urges therapists to attend closely to the interviewing process, especially their own intentionality, adopting an orientation in which everything an interviewer does and says, and does not do and say, is thought of as an intervention that could be therapeutic, nontherapeutic, or countertherapeutic.

Tomm thus adds "strategizing" to the original set of Milan techniques of hypothesizing, circularity, and neutrality. His circular questions are carefully constructed, not simply for information-gathering purposes but also as a change-inducing technique, activating reflective thinking about one's belief system and the meanings given to events. Tomm is interested in the therapist's ongoing cognitive activity, evaluating the effects of past therapeutic actions, developing new plans of action, anticipating the consequences of possible interventions, and deciding, moment to moment, how to most effectively achieve maximum therapeutic influence. More specifically, Tomm concerns himself with the kinds of questions a therapist asks to help families extract new levels of meaning from their behavior, in the service of enabling them to generate new ways of thinking and behaving on their own.

Of greatest relevance are what Tomm (1987b) refers to as *reflexive questions.* Intended to be facilitative, they are designed to move families to reflect on the meaning they extract from their current perceptions, actions, and belief systems, stimulating them to consider alternative constructive cognitions and behavior. Tomm differentiates eight groups of reflexive questions:

1. *Future-oriented questions* (designed to open up consideration of alternate behavior in the future) ("If the two of you got along better in the future, what would happen that isn't happening now?")
2. *Observer-perspective questions* (intended to help people become self-observers) ("How do you feel when your wife and teenage son get into a quarrel?")
3. *Unexpected counterchange questions* (opening up possibilities of choices not previously considered by altering the context in which the behavior is viewed) ("What does it feel like when the two of you are not fighting?")
4. *Embedded suggestion questions* (allowing therapist to point to a useful direction) ("What would happen if you told her when you felt hurt or angry instead of withdrawing?")
5. *Normative-comparison questions* (suggesting problem is not abnormal) ("Have any of your friends recently dealt with the last child leaving home, so that they would understand what you are going through now?")
6. *Distinction-clarifying questions* (separating the components of a behavior pattern) ("Which would be more important to you—showing up your boss's ignorance or helping him so that the project can be successfully completed?")

7. *Questions introducing hypotheses* (using tentative therapeutic hypotheses to generalize to outside behavior with others) ("You know how you become silent when you think your husband is angry with you? What would happen if next time you told him how you felt?")

8. *Process-interrupting questions* (creating a sudden shift in the therapeutic session) ("You just seemed to get quiet and upset, and I wonder if you thought I was siding with your wife?")

Tomm's classification of questions represents an attempt to alert therapists to what can and should be asked of families, as well as what impact a series of circular questions is likely to have on families. These questions permit the therapist to plan interventive interviewing, ever mindful of the intention behind the questions they construct. Through a series of such questions, Tomm intends for families to break free of their current fixed ideas and achieve new meaning as they go about reorganizing their behavior.

As Tomm has moved in the direction of a social constructionist/narrative view (MacCormack & Tomm, 1998), he has concentrated his efforts on helping individuals and families bring forth their *healthy interpersonal patterns (HIPS)* and replace *pathologizing interpersonal patterns (PIPS); see* Hoyt (2001b). This simple typology refers to interaction patterns that generate or promote healing between people as opposed to pathology. To Tomm, it is the interaction pattern (e.g., domination and control vs. submission and compliance) that is contaminated in PIPS, not the persons who have drifted into the habitual pattern. If HIPS open up space (welcoming others into one's life and nurturing the relationship), then PIPS close off growth, promote defensiveness, and cut off relatedness.

Clients are encouraged to reflect upon the pattern in which they are immersed and to identify and seek out alternatives to patterns of giving meaning or taking action. Tomm (MacCormack & Tomm, 1998) views the therapist as a coach or resource in the social construction of new patterns of interaction, conversation, and relationship.

SUMMARY

The Milan team practices systemic family therapy, an outlook based on Bateson's circular epistemology. The technique has undergone some changes over the years as the original four principals—Selvini-Palazzoli, Boscolo, Cecchin, and Prata—presented many innovative interviewing techniques aimed at counteracting sustained and entrenched family games. Initially emphasizing paradoxical therapeutic measures, the four later introduced hypothesizing, circular questioning, and therapist neutrality as guidelines for conducting sessions, helping each family member become exposed to information about the perceptions of the other members, and interrupting destructive family interactive patterns. Positive connotations and the use of prescribed rituals are other Milan therapeutic trademarks.

The four separated into two groups in 1980—Selvini-Palazzoli and Prata continued to engage in research directed at interrupting destructive family games, while Boscolo and Cecchin pursued the development of training models, seeking to advance a new systemic epistemology. The interviewing process itself, especially the use of circular questioning, has become the cornerstone of Boscolo and Cecchin's modification of the original Milan systemic method of working with families.

Selvini-Palazzoli and Prata have developed an invariant prescription for forcing change in the interactive patterns of severely disturbed families.

Boscolo and Cecchin have been influential in stimulating interest in second-order cybernetic ideas, developing a post-Milan view that has greatly influenced postmodern therapeutic efforts. Tomm has elaborated on the thinking of Boscolo and Cecchin, cataloguing sets of circular questions aimed at encouraging families to reflect on the meaning of their life patterns in an effort to trigger families to consider new cognitive and behavioral options.

The notion that the therapist as observer is part of what is being observed—and thus is inescapably a part of the system to which he or she is offering therapy—redefines the therapist as someone who, like the other participants, has a particular perspective but not a truly objective view of the family or what's best for it. One consequence of this thinking is to take "truth" away from the therapist and make goal setting a participatory process that therapist and family members engage in together.

RECOMMENDED READINGS

Boscolo, L., Cecchin, G., Hoffman, L., & Penn, P. (1987). *Milan systemic family therapy.* New York: Basic Books.

Selvini-Palazzoli, M. (1986). Towards a general model of psychotic games. *Journal of Marital and Family Therapy, 12,* 339–349.

Selvini-Palazzoli, M., Boscolo, L., Cecchin, G., & Prata, G. (1978). *Paradox and counterparadox.* New York: Jason Aronson.

Tomm. K. (1987). Interventive interviewing: Part I. Strategizing as a fourth guideline for the therapist. *Family Process, 26,* 3–14.

CHAPTER 13

BEHAVIORAL AND COGNITIVE-BEHAVIORAL MODELS

The models of family therapy we are about to describe are relatively recent additions to the field, since it is only within the last 30 years or so that the application of **behavioral** concepts has been extended to the couple or family unit. The use of therapeutic behavioral methods with individuals, however, goes back to the early 1960s when, largely as a reaction against what was perceived as unverifiable psychodynamic theory and technique, a movement began to bring the scientific method to bear upon the psychotherapeutic process. **Cognitive** therapies, especially as applied to families, emerged in the early 1980s as an expansion of earlier behavioral approaches to couples in conflict (Dattilio, 2001).

BEHAVIORAL THERAPY AND FAMILY SYSTEMS

Early efforts to modify behavior involved the application of learning theory and other experimentally based principles to changing undesired client behavior. In these initial formulations, family members when considered at all were assumed to be a part of the client's natural environment; as such, in seeking ways to extinguish the client's problematic or maladaptive behavior, the therapist observed the manner in which family members stimulated or aroused that behavior in the client. While it was assumed that modifying an individual's deviant behavior necessitated changing the behavior of key family members, therapeutic intervention directed at the family as a whole was rarely attempted.

Leading Figures

Three pioneers in attempting to modify undesired behavior came from related disciplines—social worker Richard Stuart (1969), psychologist Gerald Patterson (1971), and psychiatrist Robert Liberman (1970). These early behaviorists were more apt to address specific behavioral problems in families (poor communication between spouses, acting-out behavior in children and adolescents), identified in a family assessment process, than attempt to gain a comprehensive picture of family dynamics (Sanders & Dadds, 1993). Limiting their therapeutic efforts to behavior they could observe, and without inferring intrapsychic or interpersonal causality, these therapists attempted to extinguish or otherwise manipulate certain targeted behaviors by means of **reinforcements.**

As Falloon (1991) illustrates, a therapist observing a child's deviant behavioral patterns assumed that the maintenance of the troublesome behavior resulted at least in part from the reinforcement (the consequences immediately following and contingent upon that behavior) provided by other family members. While therapeutic efforts remained individually focused, the behavior therapist nevertheless attempted, simultaneously, to instruct key family members on how best to change or modify their behavior so they would not participate in sustaining the client's deviant behavior. Patterson (Patterson & Brodsky, 1966) in particular developed **behavioral parent training** (often carried out in the client's home), clinically adapting learning principles from the laboratory in order to modify the behavior of a multiple-problem child as well as the reinforcing responses of his parents.

Adopting a Family Framework

Behavior therapists working with couples or entire families adopted a similar role (teacher, coach, model) as well as a corresponding set of intervention procedures directed at imparting skills (for example, in problem solving or communication) involving the mutual exchange of positive behavior, thus altering earlier maladaptive patterns. Liberman (1970) and Stuart (1969), working independently, were early proponents of **behavioral couples therapy.** Both offered interventions based on **operant conditioning,** relying on the Skinnerian principle that certain voluntarily emitted responses can be strengthened by selectively rewarding or reinforcing those responses, so that in the future they will occur more frequently than other responses that have not been rewarded.

Liberman, at UCLA, also pioneered what is now considered a psychoeducational approach to working with families with mentally disordered members. Stuart, working primarily with distressed couples, offered a **contingency contract,** a written schedule describing the terms for the exchange of mutually reinforcing behaviors between individuals in a family, aimed at reducing undesired or problematic behavioral exchanges. Other early behavioral therapists, such as Joseph Wolpe (1958), a psychiatrist then living in South Africa, advanced a set of desensitization techniques based upon the earlier **classical conditioning** laboratory studies of Ivan Pavlov and John Watson.

Box 13.1 lists the major assumptions of behavior therapy, initially based on the principles of learning theory derived from experimental psychology. Such an approach has remained oriented toward families presenting specific behavioral problems. Note especially the emphasis on a scientifically based methodology, the continuous interplay between assessment of family functioning and treatment planning, the introduction of interventions to diminish specific problematic behavior patterns, and the use of feedback information from the implementation of interventions to measure changes of targeted behaviors.

A GROWING ECLECTICISM: THE COGNITIVE CONNECTION

By the late 1970s some behaviorists, less determined to keep mental activities out of the equation than in the past, began to acknowledge that cognitive factors (attitudes, thoughts, beliefs, attributions, expectations) also influence behavior, and they sometimes introduced an auxiliary cognitive component to supplement the main behavioral treatment, especially directed at couples in conflict. Increasingly, since that

BOX 13.1   CLINICAL NOTE

Ten Underlying Assumptions of Behavioral Therapy

1. All behavior, normal and abnormal, is acquired and maintained in identical ways (that is, according to the same principles of learning).
2. Behavior disorders represent learned maladaptive patterns that need not presume some inferred underlying cause or unseen motive.
3. Maladaptive behavior, such as symptoms, is itself the disorder, rather than a manifestation of a more basic underlying disorder or disease process.
4. It is not essential to discover the exact situation or set of circumstances in which the disorder was learned; these circumstances are usually irretrievable anyway. Rather, the focus should be on assessing the current determinants that support and maintain the undesired behavior.
5. Maladaptive behavior, having been learned, can be extinguished (that is, unlearned) and replaced by new learned behavior patterns.
6. Treatment involves the application of the experimental findings of scientific psychology,

with an emphasis on developing a methodology that is precisely specified, objectively evaluated, and easily replicated.
7. Assessment is an ongoing part of treatment, as the effectiveness of treatment is continuously evaluated and specific intervention techniques are individually tailored to specific problems.
8. Behavioral therapy concentrates on "here-and-now" problems, rather than uncovering or attempting to reconstruct the past. The therapist is interested in helping the client identify and change current environmental stimuli that reinforce the undesired behavior, in order to alter the client's behavior.
9. Treatment outcomes are evaluated in terms of measurable changes.
10. Research on specific therapeutic techniques is continuously carried out by behavioral therapists.

Source: Goldenberg, 1983, p. 221

breakthrough, **cognitive-behavioral therapy,** emphasizing the importance of cognitive and behavior interactions among family members, has been embraced by many family therapists, in no small part because of its empirically supported, research-based effectiveness (Baucom, Shoham, Mueser, Daiuto, & Stickle, 1998). Today, cognitive-behavior couples therapy has been subject to a greater number of controlled outcome studies than any other therapeutic modality (Dattilio & Epstein, 2005).

Leading Figures

Albert Ellis, a New York psychologist, and Aaron Beck, a psychiatrist in Philadelphia, are generally considered to have offered the earliest cognitive slants on intimate couple relationships. According to Ellis's (1979) A-B-C theory of dysfunctional behavior, it is not the activating events (A) of people's lives that have disturbing consequences (C), but the unrealistic interpretation they give to the events, or the irrational beliefs (B) about what has taken place that cause them trouble. Thus, a partner might have unrealistic expectations about a relationship, "catastrophizing" a commonplace disagreement and indoctrinating herself with negative evaluations ("I am worthless, a failure") afterward. Ellis suggested it is not the quarrel per se, but the exaggerated, illogical, or otherwise flawed interpretation that causes havoc and leads to negative views of oneself or the future of the relationship. He contended that **cognitive restructuring** would help the client modify her perceptions and allow her to produce new self-statements ("It's really upsetting that we don't agree, but that doesn't mean I'm a failure as a person or that our marriage is doomed").

If Ellis's outlook is that couple conflict occurs when partners maintain unrealistic beliefs and expectations about their relationship, Beck's viewpoint is more expansive and inclusive, attending in greater depth to family interactive patterns. Family relationships, cognitions, emotions, and interactive behavior are all seen as mutually influencing one another; thus, Beck's view is more consistent with the systems perspective (Dattilio, 2001). Beck, originally trained as a psychoanalyst, first began to deviate from that position as a result of his research with depressed patients, in which he concluded that they felt as they did because they committed characteristic *errors of thinking* (negative thoughts about themselves, the world, the future). Beck (1976) hypothesized that earlier in life these depressed people had, through various unfortunate personal and interpersonal experiences, acquired negative **schemas** (enduring sets of core beliefs and attitudes about people, relationships, and so on, that organize subsequent thoughts and perceptions) that are reactivated when a new situation arises that resembles, in their thinking, conditions similar to those under which the schema was learned. Cognitive distortions follow, leading to a misperception of reality. Beck's therapeutic efforts were then directed at providing patients with experiences, both during therapy sessions and outside the consultation room, that disconfirm negative conclusions (such automatic thoughts as "It's hopeless"; "I'm to blame") and attempt to alter negative schemas. Beyond changing current distorted beliefs, Beck advocated that therapist and client work together to teach the client new methods he or she can use in the future for evaluating other beliefs, all leading to changing dysfunctional behaviors.

Applying Beck's theory to families, each member's set of schemas include attributions about why certain events occurred in the family, how the spousal relationship should operate, what types of problems to expect in a marriage, what responsibilities each family member should have, how best to raise children, and similar cognitions about family life (Schwebel & Fine, 1994). These schemata greatly influence how each person thinks, feels, and behaves within the family. Family schemas represent jointly shared beliefs about what is occurring within the family, and of course are open to errors, distortions, and omissions impacting how family members respond, emotionally and behaviorally, to one another. Therapeutically, the task becomes helping families restructure the family's dysfunctional beliefs and, as a consequence, helping alter their behavioral patterns.

Many of the ideas initially proposed by Ellis's rational-emotive therapy[1] and Beck's cognitive therapy were originally considered too simplistic by family therapists when compared to the more complex systems theory then at the height of its popularity, and consequently they received little attention. By the late 1980s, however, due to a great deal more systems-friendly research on the role of the partners' perceptions, thoughts, and expectations regarding each other's actions, cognitive interventions in

---

[1]Ellis (1995) has rechristened his approach Rational Emotive Behavior Therapy (REBT) to acknowledge its affinity to the behavioral outlook. According to Ellis, REBT is a more accurate description of the interaction between thinking/feeling/wanting and behaving. Cognitive therapists believe that how we think determines how we feel and behave.

marital and family therapy had gained a foothold. Today's major figures include Frank Dattilio (2005), at the University of Pennsylvania School of Medicine, Norman Epstein (1992) at the University of Maryland, and Donald Baucom at the University of North Carolina (Epstein & Baucom, 2002).

Cognitive Restructuring

Acknowledging that some problematic responses within a family are mediated by distorted or dysfunctional beliefs (schemas), attitudes, and expectations, many behaviorists now have broadened their outlook to include the use of cognitive restructuring procedures. This was done in order to help clients explore dysfunctional interpretations, modify automatic thoughts and assumptions, and alter hampering schemas ("My husband left the toilet seat up. He's inconsiderate of my feelings." "My parents are grounding me this weekend because they hate to see me have a good time with my friends." "My children never appreciate my efforts around here."). It is especially in the area of marital or couples therapy that cognitive theory and research has made its strongest contribution to date. Just as behaviorists have integrated cognition into behavior therapy, Dattilio (1998) has attempted to use cognitive-behavioral theories and techniques as integrative components with other models of couple and family therapy.

The Cognitive-Behavioral Outlook

Cognitive-behaviorists view people as neither exclusively driven by inner conflicts (the orthodox psychoanalytic stance) nor helplessly buffeted by outside forces (the orthodox behavioral position). Instead, they understand personal functioning to be the result of continuous, reciprocal interaction between behavior and its controlling social conditions.

While once behaviorists sought exclusively to change the environmental conditions that maintain undesired behavior, most now also emphasize the importance of *self-regulation* and *self-direction* in altering behavior. Cognitive-behavioral therapy attempts to modify thoughts and actions by influencing an individual's conscious patterns of thoughts. Donald Meichenbaum (1995), a leading cognitive-behaviorist with a special interest in stress management, contends that cognitive-behavioral therapies have attempted to integrate the clinical concerns of psychodynamic and systems-oriented psychotherapies with the technology of behavior therapy.

Although attending less exclusively to observable behavior than advocates of **radical behaviorism,** as well as trying to modify a client's thinking processes, cognitive-behavioral therapists continue to "place great value on meticulous observation, careful testing of hypotheses, and continual self-correction on the basis of empirically derived data" (Lazarus, 1977, p. 550). Gambrill (1994) actually defines behavioral practice as "an empirical approach to personal and social problems in which the selection of assessment and intervention methods is based whenever possible on related research" (p. 32).

The unique contribution of this approach, then, lies not in its conceptualizations of psychopathology or adherence to a particular theory or underlying set of principles, or even to a unique set of interventions, but in its insistence on a rigorous, data-based set of procedures and a regularly monitored scientific methodology.

Although the traditional behavioral viewpoint continues to focus on the identified patient as the person having the problem, and in that sense remains largely linear in approach, there are efforts by many former behaviorally oriented therapists (for example,

Alexander & Parsons, 1982; Jacobson & Christensen, 1996) to accommodate a systems/behavioral/cognitive perspective.[2] Most cognitive-behavioral family therapists today continue to view family interactions as maintained by environmental events preceding and following each member's behavior. These events or contingencies, together with mediating cognitions, are what determine the form as well as the frequency of each family member's behavior (Epstein, Schlesinger, & Dryden, 1988).

THE KEY ROLE OF ASSESSMENT

Behavioral therapists and more cognitively oriented therapists share these features, according to Beck (1995):

> They are empirical, present-centered, problem-oriented, and require explicit identification of problems and the situations in which they occur as well as the consequences resulting from them. (p. 232)

Behavioral family therapists strive for precision in identifying a problem, employ quantification to measure change, and conduct further research to validate their results. They design programs that emphasize a careful assessment of the presenting problem (a **behavioral analysis** of the family's difficulties) and include some direct and pragmatic treatment techniques to alleviate symptoms and teach the family how to improve its skills in communication and self-management.

A behavioral analysis might include an objective recording of discrete acts engaged in by family members, along with the behaviors of others that serve as antecedent stimuli, as well as the interactional consequences of the problematic behavior (Epstein, Schlesinger, & Dryden, 1988). In doing so, the interviewer is attempting to pinpoint exactly which behavior needs to be altered, and what events precede and follow manifestation of the behavior. For instance, working with a distraught family in which the presenting problem is a four-year-old boy's "temper tantrums," the behavioral therapist might want to know exactly what the family means by "tantrums," the frequency and duration of such behavior, the specific responses to the behavior by various family members, and especially the antecedent and consequent events associated with these outbursts. By means of this inquiry, the behavioral therapist attempts to gauge the extent of the problem and the environmental factors (such as the presence of a particular family member, a particular cue such as parents announcing bedtime, a particular time and place such as dinnertime at home) that maintain the problematic behavior. The assessment of environmental circumstances is especially crucial, since the behavioral therapist believes that all behavior (desirable and undesirable) is maintained by its consequences.

Similarly, cognitive-behaviorists use many of the same assessment and treatment techniques as other behavioral therapists, supplemented by special attention to belief systems and how couples, for example, process the same information. A typical

---

[2]A particularly interesting conversion involves Gerald Patterson, once a strict behaviorist, who modified many of his views after studying systems theory with Salvador Minuchin. James Alexander was another strict behaviorist who expanded his thinking to include strategic ideas when he developed *functional family therapy*. Jacobson and Christenson found traditional behavioral couples therapy too confining and developed a more integrative approach to treating couples in distress.

assessment (Dattilio & Bevilacqua, 2000) may start with a joint interview with both partners, listening to how each conceptualizes the presenting problem. Questionnaires and personality inventories, filled out separately, may be added for greater clarification of their thinking about their situation and relationships. Individual visits with each may follow, reviewing their responses to those inquiries, before conjoint sessions commence. Since assessment is an ongoing process, questionnaire/inventories may be administered several times during the therapy in order to assess progress. Cognitive-behavioral therapy typically calls for a limited number of sessions, making it particularly attractive to managed care insurance payors.

As Dattilio and Padesky (1990) point out, cognitive therapists work at three interconnected levels: (a) the most accessible level of *automatic thoughts* (ideas, beliefs, images) that people have regarding a specific situation ("My husband is late. He doesn't care about how I feel"); (b) at a deeper level, *underlying assumptions* (rules that are the roots of automatic thoughts: "You can't count on men to be there for you"); and (c) at the core, basic beliefs or *schemas* (inflexible, unconditional beliefs for organizing information: "I'll always be alone"). Beginning with the automatic erroneous belief, the woman has jumped to the extreme or inappropriate conclusion of anticipated lifelong loneliness. Such a set of beliefs influences her appraisal of her husband's subsequent behavior, in turn causing an emotional and behavioral response. Before introducing a cognitive restructuring program, cognitive-behaviorists assessing relationship distress are especially interested in identifying the frequency and reciprocal patterns of both positive and negative behaviors in which couples exchange.

A Behavioral Assessment

Falloon (1991) suggests that a behavioral assessment of family functioning typically occurs at two levels: (1) a **problem analysis** that seeks to pinpoint the specific behavioral deficits ("Seven-year-old Michael steals from his mother's purse"; "Eleven-year-old Joan can't seem to pay attention in school") underlying the problem areas that, if modified, would lead to problem resolution; and (2) a **functional analysis** directed at uncovering the interrelationships between those behavioral deficits and the interpersonal environment in which they are functionally relevant. Functional analyses seek understanding of the immediate antecedents and consequences of the problem behavior: ("We've tried to stop Michael from watching television [ground Joan on weekday nights] but then we stop enforcing the rules after a few days").

Here the therapist is interested not only in increasing positive interaction between family members by altering the environmental conditions that oppose or impede such interaction but also in training family members to maintain the improved behavior. No effort is made to infer motives, uncover unconscious conflicts, hypothesize needs or drives, or diagnose inner pathological conditions producing the undesired behavior; the individual or family is not necessarily helped to gain insight into the origin of current problems. Instead, emphasis is placed on the environmental, situational, and social determinants that influence behavior (Kazdin, 1984). Those therapists who are more strictly behavioral attempt to train a person's behavior rather than probe those dimensions of personality that, according to other models, underlie behavior.

A Cognitive-Behavioral Assessment

Cognitive-behavioral therapists, by contrast, include a functional analysis of *inner experiences*—thoughts, attitudes, expectations, beliefs. Less linear in outlook, they see individuals as interactive participants, interpreting, judging, and influencing each other's behaviors. Typically, they gather such data using three main forms of clinical assessment: self-report questionnaires, individual and joint interviews, and direct behavioral observations of family interaction (Epstein & Baucom, 2002). As an example of a family self-report, parents complaining about their child's resistance to a bedtime schedule might be asked to keep logs at home, monitoring and recording specific acts and their specific responses ("For the last four nights, our eight-year-old has gone from one of us to the other until his father finally agrees he can stay up past his bedtime and watch the TV program"). In the case of adult relationship problems, specific tests (for example, Eidelson and Epstein's [1982] Relationship Belief Inventory or Fincham and Bradbury's [1992] Relationship Attribution Measure) might be employed, tapping unrealistic beliefs about close relationships in the first example, or attributions (inferences about the cause of events in their relationship) such as a partner's perceived overcriticalness (Dattilio, Epstein, & Baucom, 1998).

As for interview-based data, the therapist might probe automatic thoughts—*beliefs* ("He avoids talking to me at night"), *expectancies* ("I hate to make plans with friends because he's always late"), or *attributions* ("The reason he acts as he does is because he doesn't care about my feelings") as clients report upsetting experiences with one another. Direct observations of couples, for example, might focus on a couple's communication skills deficits as they are directed to plan a night out away from the children, or perhaps their deficits in negotiation skills as their failure to compromise escalates conflict. On the other hand, when asked by the therapist to solve a problem together in the therapist's office, they may discover that they possess heretofore untapped problem-solving skills. Such structured tasks (for example, role-playing an adolescent's request for a later curfew) are often used by cognitive-behavioral therapists to check on progress in reaching the desired changes in targeted behaviors (Epstein, Schlesinger, & Dryden, 1988). Box 13.2 offers various types of cognitive distortions frequently found among couples.

BEHAVIORALLY INFLUENCED FORMS OF FAMILY THERAPY

The behaviorally oriented family therapist is more likely than most systems-based family therapists to use distinct clinical procedures (such as skills training) and not to insist on participation of the entire family. Sometimes the family is brought in when individual procedures fail, or when behavioral observation suggests that family members are helping maintain the individual's symptomatic behavior; the family is excused after that phase of therapy is completed, and the therapist continues to implement individually oriented procedures.

Extended family members are far less likely to be involved in behavioral therapy. In general, behavioral family therapists view the family as burdened by the patient, or perhaps as unwittingly responding in ways that support and maintain his or her problem behavior, while most systems-oriented family therapists assume that family involvement is always present and plays an active part in symptom maintenance (Todd, 1988).

Moreover, as noted earlier, purely behavioral family therapists tend to adopt a linear rather than a circular outlook on causality. For instance, a parent's inappropriate, inconsistent, or otherwise flawed response to a temper tantrum is believed to cause as well as maintain a child's behavioral problem (contrary to the more commonly held

BOX 13.2 CLINICAL NOTE

Some Common Cognitive Distortions Among Couples

Arbitrary inferences: Conclusions drawn in the absence of supporting substantiating evidence. ("She's late from work. She must be having an affair.")

Selective abstractions: Information taken out of context, highlighting certain details and ignoring others. ("He didn't say good morning when we woke up. He must be angry.")

Overgeneralization: An isolated incident or two is allowed to serve as representative of all similar situations, related or not. ("She turned me down for a date Saturday night. I'll always be rejected.")

Magnification and minimization: A case or circumstance is perceived in a greater or lesser light than is appropriate. ("Our checkbook is out of balance. We're financially ruined.")

Dichotomous thinking: Experiences are codified as complete successes or complete failures. (A husband asks his wife how his paperhanging job is going. She questions the smoothness of one seam, to which he replies, "I can't do anything right in your eyes.")

Mind reading: Knowing what the other is thinking without asking, and as a consequence ascribing unworthy intentions to the other. ("I know what's going on in her mind. She's trying to figure out a way to dump me.")

Biased explanations: A suspicious type of thinking about a partner, especially during times of interpersonal stress, assuming his or her negative intent. ("He's acting real 'lovey-dovey' because later he'll ask me to do something he knows I hate to do.")

Source: Adapted from Dattilio & Bevilacqua (2000)

systems view among family therapists that the tantrum constitutes an interaction, including a cybernetic exchange of feedback information, occurring within the family system). Predictably, the behavioral family therapist is likely to aim his or her therapeutic efforts at changing dyadic interactions (for example, a mother's way of dealing with her child's having a tantrum) rather than adopting the triadic view more characteristic of systems-oriented family therapists, in which the participants in any exchange are simultaneously reacting to other family transactions (for example, a mother who feels neglected by her husband and who attends too closely to the slightest whims of her child; a father who resents his wife taking so much attention away from him in order to interact with their son).

While some of the leading behavioral family therapists such as Gerald Patterson, Robert Liberman, Richard Stuart, and James Alexander do view the family as a social system (whose members exercise mutual control over one another's social reinforcement schedules), others remain far from convinced. Gordon and Davidson (1981), for example, acknowledge that in some cases a strained marital relationship may contribute to the development and/or maintenance of deviant child behavior (or vice versa), but they argue that systems theorists have exaggerated the prevalence of the phenomenon. Their experiences lead them to conclude that deviant child behavior may occur in families with and without marital discord; they state that "the simple presence of marital discord in these families may or may not be causally related to the child's problems" (p. 522).

BOX 13.3   CLINICAL NOTE

Some Characteristics of Behavioral Family Therapies

The work of behavioral family therapists (including cognitive-behaviorists) has several characteristics that distinguish it from the approaches taken by the systems-oriented family therapists we have considered:

- A direct focus on observable behavior, such as symptoms, rather than an effort to hypothesize causality interpersonally
- A careful, ongoing assessment of the specific, usually overt, behavior to be altered

- A concern with either increasing (accelerating) or decreasing (decelerating) targeted behavior by directly manipulating external contingencies of reinforcement
- A striving to teach and coach communication and problem-solving skills
- An effort to train families to monitor and modify their own reinforcement contingencies
- A standard of empirically evaluating the effects of therapeutic interventions

Behavioral Couples Therapy

Not long after the behavioral approach in psychology began to be applied to clinical problems (e.g., phobias) in individuals, interest grew in adapting this perspective to problems of marital discord. By the end of the 1960s, Robert Liberman and Richard Stuart separately had published their early efforts in this regard, each offering a straightforward, step-by-step set of intervention procedures in which some basic operant conditioning principles were applied to distressed marital relationships, effectively increasing partner satisfaction and relationship stability in many cases. From its inception, the basic premise of behavioral marital therapy (BMT), according to Holtzworth-Munroe and Jacobson (1991), has been that the behavior of both partners in a marital relationship is shaped, strengthened, weakened, and modified by environmental events, especially those events involving the other spouse (p. 97).

Manipulating the Contingencies of Reinforcement

Liberman's (1970) approach began with a behavioral analysis ("What behaviors would each like to see changed in themselves or their partners?""What interpersonal contingencies currently support the problematic behavior?"), followed by an effort to restructure the reciprocal exchange of rewards between the partners. That is, after assessing what needed fixing, Liberman attempted to increase certain target behaviors and decrease others by directly manipulating the external contingencies of reinforcement.

The couple, in turn, was expected to monitor and modify their own reinforcement contingencies. Liberman's goals were simple and straightforward, and especially in their early form focused strictly on behavior change: to guide couples to increase their pleasing interactions and decrease aversive interactions.

Robert Liberman, M.D.

Stuart (1969) developed a set of therapeutic procedures he called **operant interpersonal therapy,** especially the use of contingency contracting, to try to get couples to maximize the exchange of positive behaviors. He argued that successful marriages can be differentiated from unsuccessful ones by the frequency and range of reciprocal positive reinforcements the partners exchange ("I'll be glad to entertain your parents this weekend if you accompany me to the baseball game [or ballet performance] next month"). Although this technique today is considered by most family therapists to be an oversimplified, heavy-handed, and mechanical approach to a complex marital exchange, Stuart was beginning to blend Skinner's operant learning principles with *social exchange theory* (Thibaut & Kelley, 1959). Relationship satisfaction was recast as reward-cost ratios: If missing but potentially rewarding events can be identified and maximized and displeasing events occurring in excess can be identified and minimized, then the reward-cost ratio should increase greatly, and each partner should not only feel more satisfied but also be more willing to provide more rewards for the other partner. As part of Stuart's approach, he had each partner record the number of instances and the type of caring behavior he or she offers each day. Table 13.1 offers a sample of such "caring days" requests.[3]

The use of contingency contracting and the teaching of behavioral exchange strategies characterized the approach of behavioral marital therapists during the 1970s, particularly Jacobson and Margolin (1979). Contingency contracting remained the focal point of the approach, both to enhance the quality and quantity of mutually pleasing interactions and, by nonreinforcement, to diminish the frequency of arguments, provocations, and generally negative communication sequences (Falloon & Lillie, 1988).

From Reinforcements to Skill Building

Communication/problem-solving training was often introduced in the 1980s with the intent of teaching couples to negotiate resolutions of their conflicts (present and future) in noncoercive ways, thus creating positive relationship changes. In some cases, **therapeutic contracts**—written agreements between spouses stipulating specific behavioral changes—were negotiated. Here, each spouse explicitly states what behavior he or she wants increased, thus avoiding the all-too-familiar marital plea for mind reading: "If you really loved me, you'd know what I want." Note how the agreement developed by Stuart (1980) in Table 13.2 offers each partner a range of constructive choices, any one of which can satisfy their reciprocal obligations. By not creating the expectation that reciprocation should be forthcoming immediately ("I'll do this if you do that"), a contract can increase the likelihood of spontaneous reciprocation. Stated briefly, the dynamic interplay of any couple's behavior is often overlooked (Atkins, Dimidjian, & Christensen, 2003).

---

[3]In *Helping Couples Change,* Stuart (1980) spelled out in greater detail his "caring days" technique for building commitment in a faltering marriage. All requests must meet the following criteria: (1) they must be positive ("Please ask how I spent my day" rather than "Don't ignore me so much"); (2) they must be specific ("Come home at 6 p.m. for dinner" rather than "Show some consideration for your family"); (3) they must be small instances of behavior that can be demonstrated at least once daily ("Please line up the children's bikes along the back wall of the garage when you get home" rather than "Please train the children to keep their bikes in the proper place"); and (4) they must not have been the subject of recent intense conflict (since neither spouse is likely to concede major points at this stage of treatment).

TABLE 13.1   A Sample Request List for Caring Days

Wife's Requests	Husband's Requests
1. Greet me with a kiss and hug in the morning before we get out of bed.	1. Wash my back.
2. Bring me pussywillows (or some such).	2. Smile and say you're glad to see me when you wake up.
3. Ask me what recording I would like to hear and put it on.	3. Fix the orange juice.
4. Reach over and touch me when we're riding in the car.	4. Call me at work.
5. Make breakfast and serve it to me.	5. Acknowledge my affectionate advances.
6. Tell me you love me.	6. Invite me to expose the details of my work.
7. Put things away when you come in.	7. Massage my shoulders and back.
8. If you're going to stop at the store for something, ask me if there is anything that I want or need.	8. Touch me while I drive.
9. Rub my body or some part of me before going to sleep, with full concentration.	9. Hold me when you see that I'm down.
10. Look at me intently sometimes when I'm telling you something.	10. Tell me about your experiences at work everyday.
11. Engage actively in fantasy trips with me—e.g., to Costa Rica, Sunshine Coast.	11. Tell me that you care.
12. Ask my opinion about things you write and let me know which suggestions you follow.	12. Tell me that I'm nice to be around.
13. Tell me when I look attractive.	
14. Ask me what I'd like to do for a weekend or a day with the desire to do what I suggest.	

Source: Stuart, 1976

TABLE 13.2   A Holistic Therapeutic Marital Contract

It is understood that Jane would like Sam to:	It is also understood that Sam would like Jane to:
wash the dishes;	have dinner ready by 6:30 nightly;
mow the lawn;	weed the rose garden;
initiate lovemaking;	bathe every night and come to bed by 10:30;
take responsibility for balancing their checkbooks;	call him at the office daily;
invite his business partners for dinner once every six or eight weeks;	plan an evening out alone for both of them at least once every two weeks;
meet her at his store for lunch at least once a week.	offer to drive the children to their soccer practice and swim meets;
	accompany him on occasional fishing trips.

It is expected that Sam and Jane will each do as many of the things requested by the other as is comfortably manageable, ideally at least three or four times weekly.

Source: Stuart, 1980, p. 248

Despite modifications from its earlier exclusive focus on behavior, the basic premises and practices of behavioral marital therapy, as outlined by Liberman and Stuart, remained tied to basic learning principles. However, critics charged that some of its earlier assumptions were too simplistic: that both partners, as rational adults, will not resist change but will follow the therapist's suggestions; that a focus on overt behavior change is sufficient, without attending to underlying perceptual processes and interpersonal conflicts; that marital disharmony derives from the same sources, such as insufficient reciprocity, throughout the marital life cycle; that displeasing behavior, such as anger, should simply be held in check without exploring the covert reasons for conflict; that the couple-therapist relationship can be ignored (Gurman & Knudson, 1978).

Increasingly based on **social learning theory** (learning that occurs due to interaction with other people) as well as behavioral-exchange principles, behavioral couples therapy became less technological and more flexible over time. In addition to encouraging the increased exchange of pleasing behaviors (and the diminution of aversive behaviors), therapists such as Jacobson and Margolin (1979) also aimed to reduce problems by teaching couples more effective problem-solving skills. Such problem solving is broken down into two separate phases: *problem definition* (learning to state problems in clear, specific, non-blaming ways; learning to acknowledge one's own role in creating or perpetuating the problem; attempting to paraphrase the other's view, even if it is inconsistent with one's own); and *problem resolution.* Brainstorming solutions together and negotiating compromises (which later may be put in writing) often facilitate problem resolution. Rather than the accusatory "You don't love me anymore," the therapists suggest that couples use the more concrete, less provocative, more self-revealing statement, "When you let a week go by without initiating sex, I feel rejected" (Jacobson & Margolin, 1979, p. 230).

Recognizing that behavior changes will lead to greater marital satisfaction, practitioners of behavioral couples therapy attempt to create behavior change in two ways: (a) by encouraging partners to define the specific behaviors they wish their partners to exhibit, then instructing them in how to increase the frequency of those behaviors; and (b) by teaching couples communication and problem-solving skills so that they can produce those changes (Eldridge, Christensen, & Jacobson, 1999).

Broadening the Outlook: The Cognitive Perspective

As cognitive-behavioral therapy gained prominence during the late 1980s its proponents began to argue that distress and conflict in a relationship are influenced by an interaction of cognitive, behavioral, and affective factors, and that a strictly behavioral approach is too linear and does not fully address such dynamic interplay (Epstein, Schlesinger, & Dryden, 1988). Consequently, they contended, behavior change alone is insufficient in effecting permanent resolution of conflict between partners, particularly if that conflict is intense and ongoing. To resolve the likely escalating antagonistic and provocative behavior between them, couples need to acquire skills for recognizing and defining problems clearly, identifying mutually acceptable problem-solving strategies, and implementing these solutions quickly and effectively (Dattilio, Epstein, & Baucom, 1998).

Cognitive-behavioral family therapy is directed at restructuring distorted beliefs (schemas) learned early in life from the family of origin, cultural traditions, the mass media, and relationship experiences growing up. In turn, these schema affect automatic

BOX 13.4   CLINICAL NOTE

Homework Assignments as Therapeutic Aids

Many couple and family therapists assign tasks to be performed outside of the consultation room and then discussed at the following session. Cognitive-behaviorists in particular use such techniques in an effort to keep the therapy session alive during the time between meetings, making therapy a 24-hour experience and part of daily living. Actually changing undesired behavior or thoughts replaces simply talking about doing so during the therapy session or trying to recollect each time what was discussed at the previous session. Bevilacqua and Dattilio (2001) and Schultheis, O'Hanlon, and O'Hanlon (1999) have provided useful brief family therapy homework planners.

Homework assignments may take a variety of forms:

1. Assigned readings (e.g., Markman, Stanley, & Blumberg's *Fighting for Your Marriage*, 1994)
2. Audiotaping and especially videotaping of sessions, to be played back at home for a review of the interactions that occurred during the session
3. Trying out unfamiliar activities together in order to observe the couple's interactions and learn improved ways of dealing with one another
4. Practicing techniques (assertiveness exercises, pleasing behaviors) learned during therapy to alter undesired behavior

thoughts and emotional responses to others (Dattilio & Epstein, 2003). Partners also develop schemas specific to their current relationship. Within a family, for example, cognitive distortions may result in one member being scapegoated—singled out to be blamed for all family problems and thus deserving of family scorn or rejection. Whatever that person does, the others selectively view a portion of that behavior as further proof of their original belief in his or her malevolent intent, and the person remains demonized.

Working with the marital pair, cognitive therapists try to modify each spouse's unrealistic expectations about what they should expect from the relationship, and teach them how to decrease destructive interactions. Distortions in evaluating experiences, derived from negative automatic thoughts that flash through one's mind ("I notice her looking at other men whenever we go out; she must be thinking she'd be better off with someone else"), are labeled as beliefs that in effect are *arbitrary inferences* in the absence of supporting evidence. Sometimes such automatic thoughts, which couples are taught to monitor, may take the form of *overgeneralizations* (the housewife who forgets to pick up her husband's shirts at the laundry is labeled by him as "totally undependable"). In other cases, *selective abstractions* may be operating ("You're good at finding the one thing I forgot to do, but you never seem to notice the things around here that I do"). By identifying and exposing each partner's underlying schema about themselves, their partner, and the marital relationship, the therapist helps the couple accept responsibility together for the distress they are experiencing (Epstein & Baucom, 1989). Sometimes "homework" assignments to be carried out away from the session are made by the therapist; these often replace Stuart's (1980) therapeutic contracts but have the same goal: creating a written agreement to decrease specific negative behaviors by substituting specific positive behaviors each partner stipulates as desirable in the other, and reviewing the performance of each partner at the next therapy session.

Integrative Couples Therapy

Neil Jacobson (at the University of Washington) and UCLA's Andrew Christensen (Jacobson & Christensen, 1996; Christensen, Jacobson, & Babcock, 1995; Eldridge, Christensen, & Jacobson, 1999) developed behaviorally based therapeutic strategies for promoting more accommodating and collaborative attitudes—"partner acceptance"— in addition to the more traditional behavioral techniques for helping couples attain behavior change. Jacobson (1991) described the therapeutic process directed at helping couples achieve interactional or contextual change as follows:

> By promoting an intimate conversation about the differences between them that make desired changes impossible, the partners are getting much of what they need from the conversation itself, and thus the original problem becomes less important. (p. 444)

In this eclectic approach, strategic techniques (reframing) and humanistic/ experiential techniques (empathic joining of the couple around the problem, self- care) are added to the more traditional behavioral methods (use of assessment instru- ments, therapist modeling, behavioral exchange interventions, communication/problem- solving training) in an effort to promote intimacy and understanding in place of anger and blame (Jacobson & Christensen, 1996). Combinations of these techniques are directed at overcoming each participant's tendency to see the problem between them as emanating exclusively from the other person, and subsequently attempting (unsuc- cessfully) to change that person's behavior where changes are not feasible. Instead, **integrative couples therapy** delineates various procedures designed to help couples see certain differences between them as inevitable, helping foster tolerance (rather than resignation) concerning perceived negative behaviors in a partner, and accept- ance of those behaviors especially resistant to change. By acknowledging each other's emotional vulnerabilities and personality differences, Christensen and Jacobson (1999) contend that couples have taken a large step toward active acceptance of each other's feelings and actions, and as a consequence have moved away from blaming and toward *reconcilable differences*. Two key themes in this therapeutic approach involve promoting acceptance and promoting change (Jones, Christensen, & Jacobson, 2000).

Integrative couples therapy represents a return to a more traditional behavioral emphasis on the functional analysis and external determinants of behavior (Christensen, Jacobson, & Babcock, 1995). However, its therapeutic interventions rep- resent a departure from traditional behavioral couples therapy. Historically, those approaches have focused on achieving *change,* since excesses or deficits in the behav- ior of one partner were considered to be the causes of distress in the other. Such change was typically generated by behavioral exchange strategies or communication/ problem-solving techniques, directed at helping couples change the *rules* of their behavior (the husband learns to kiss his wife upon arriving home since the therapist instructed him to increase positive behaviors leading to the wife's greater satisfaction).

Unfortunately, the underlying *theme of the problem*—that he still "doesn't get it" about being generally more attentive and caring, and that she finds that intolerable— does not get addressed, since it would be impossible to review every one of their interactions where change is desired. In other cases, the rule-governed behavior feels fake or contrived or insincere, so it backfires and is abandoned. Rule-governed processes may lead to change, argue these therapists, but additional strategies are needed when the couples are unable or unwilling to make the changes the other desires.

Emotional acceptance refers to situations where behavior change either fails to occur, or else occurs but not to the extent the partner would like. Instead of demanding more of what was deemed insufficient (or less of what was excessive), here the partners are urged to alter their reactions to the behavior previously seen as intolerable or unacceptable in their partner, in effect *balancing change with acceptance* of those behaviors not open to change. Acceptance may be enhanced in two ways: (a) by experiencing the problem in a new way, say as a common enemy (from joint empathic understanding of the problem or perhaps from detachment from the problem so it becomes less offensive); or (b) by reducing the aversiveness of the partner's actions, either through greater tolerance of those actions or through the increased ability to take care of oneself when confronted with the partner's negative behaviors (Christensen, Jacobson, & Babcock, 1995). The partner may still not like the behavior or wish it were different, but nevertheless learn to consider it a part of the package of qualities (many appealing, some bothersome) in their mate. In effect, instead of seeking to change aversive behavior in order to achieve relationship satisfaction, this approach also fosters acceptance of that behavior where change is unattainable, so that it is experienced in a new way, as less aversive (Eldridge, Christensen, & Jacobson, 1999).

Behavioral Research in Couples Therapy

Behavioral couples therapy is arguably the most studied approach in couples' therapy (Sexton, Robbins, Holliman, Mease, & Mayorga, 2003). Howard Markman (1992), a psychologist who focuses his longitudinal research with couples on what causes marital distress, concludes that it is not so much the differences between people that matter, but rather how those differences are handled (that is, how couples learn to communicate and manage conflict). In a four- to five-year follow-up of a marital distress prevention program directed at teaching more effective communication and conflict management skills, Markman and colleagues (Markman, Renick, Floyd, Stanley, & Clements, 1993) found that those couples functioning at a higher level had maintained more positive communication patterns while those functioning more poorly exchanged more negative communication and showed greater marital violence.

Markman, a prominent longitudinal researcher, has, along with his colleagues, investigated the impact of couples' exchange of negative affect before parenthood on their later marital and family functioning (Lindahl, Clements, & Markman, 1997). Observing and coding the communication patterns of 25 couples before becoming parents and again five years later, these researchers wanted to know how the couples' earlier ability to handle marital conflict predicted how they would handle the competing needs of children and deal with later marital conflict. Using behavioral observations and videotapes of mother-child and father-child interactions, results indicated that the way in which couples handle negative affect with one another after parenthood is a more salient factor in how they manage and regulate negative affect with their children than would have been predicted from pre-child marital functioning. However, the husband's pre-child angry and conflictual behavior and the couples' negative escalation were predictive of marital conflict and the triangulation of the child into their discord. In general, how couples regulate negative affect early in marriage, while not decisive in itself, appears to set the tone for future parent-child interactions. We'll return to the work of Markman and his associates (Floyd, Markman, Kelly, Blumberg, & Stanley, 1995; Silliman, Stanley, Coffin, Markman, & Jordan, 2002) on preventive intervention and relationship enhancement when we discuss psychoeducational programs for couples and families.

John Gottman, perhaps today's most prolific marriage researcher, has been especially active in attempting to develop a scientific basis for helping couples in conflict (Gottman, Ryan, Carrere, & Erley, 2002). Beyond his academic credentials at the University of Washington, he is the founder and director of the Gottman Institute in Seattle, a marriage clinic in which intake procedures, treatment plans, and follow-up methods are employed to test out his empirically research-based conclusions regarding the components of a happy and successful marriage.

Gottman (1994) has offered several studies on those aspects of marital interactive processes that discriminate between happily married and unhappily married couples. Using video cameras, EKG monitors, galvanometer sensors, and specially designed observational instruments, Gottman and his research team (Gottman & Krokoff, 1989; Gottman, Coan, Carrere, & Swanson, 1998) compared how couples communicate, both verbally and nonverbally, microsecond by microsecond. In their sequential analysis, the researchers studied such indicators as body movements, facial expressions, gestures, even the couple's heart rates during conflict with one another, attempting to identify those behavioral and physiological responses essential to a stable marriage as well as those that predict the couple is headed for divorce (Gottman, 1996).

According to Gottman's findings, and contrary to popular opinion, it is not the exchange of anger that predicts divorce, but rather four forms of *negativity* that Gottman calls "The Four Horsemen of the Apocalypse"—*criticism* (attacking a spouse's character), *defensiveness* (denying responsibility for certain behavior), *contempt* (insulting, abusive attitudes toward a spouse), and *stonewalling* (a withdrawal and unwillingness to listen to one's partner). In a typical demand-withdrawal transaction, women were found more likely to criticize while men were likelier than women to stonewall. Using these four variables, Gottman and his associates were able to increase their prediction of marriage dissolution by 85 percent. In addition, a second *distance and isolation cascade* (emotionally flooding, viewing problems as severe, not wanting to work out problems with a spouse, living parallel lives, and experiencing loneliness) increase the prediction of dissolution to more than 90 percent (Gottman, Ryan, Carrere, & Erley, 2002). Clearly it is positive affect that plays a pivotal role in the development of satisfying and lasting relationships.

According to Gottman (1994), there are three types of stable couples: (a) *volatile couples* (those who are emotionally expressive, may bicker frequently and passionately, but are more romantic and affectionate than most couples); (b) *validating couples* (harmonious but less emotionally expressive, these couples listen to one another and try to understand each other's viewpoint); and (c) *conflict-avoiding couples* (those low in emotional expressiveness, who typically resolve problems by minimizing or avoiding them, emphasizing the positive aspects of their relationship and accepting negative aspects as unchangeable).

Gottman's findings indicate a greater climate of agreement in these happily married couples: in all three stable couples, the researchers observed the exchange of five positive responses to one negative response, while the positive-to-negative ratio in unstable marriages was 0.8:1 (that is, more negativity than positivity). Gottman and Krokoff (1989), in a well-designed longitudinal study, found that while *conflict engagement* (that is, direct, if angry, expressions of dissatisfaction) between partners might cause marital distress in the short run, such confrontation is likely to lead to long-term improvement in marital satisfaction by forcing couples, together, to examine areas of disagreement.

Behavioral Parent Training

Behaviorists have offered intervention primarily directed at teaching parents specific behavioral strategies for diminishing or extinguishing problematic behavior in their children, by and large addressing a grab bag of discrete observable behavioral problems (bed-wetting, temper tantrums, chore completion, compliance with parental requests, hyperactivity, sleep problems, and bedtime fears) rather than more global sets of personal or interpersonal problems of children (Dangel, Yu, Slot, & Fashimpar, 1994).

For example, Gerald Patterson, a pioneer in the field of parent training, argues that while out-of-control children are angry, fail in school, lack self-esteem, and have poor relationships with their parents, these factors are secondary by-products of an ongoing process and not the causes of delinquency. Advocating parent training for conduct problems, he contends:

> Aggression in children and adolescents is a behavioral problem, not a mental health problem. The causes lie in the social environment, not in the minds of the youngsters. (Forgatch & Patterson, 1998, p. 85)

Learning Family Management Skills

© Wadsworth/Thomson Learning

Gerald Patterson, Ph.D.

Most behavioral parent training (BPT) advocates have had as their goal the alteration of the undesirable behavior in the child, accepting the parents' view that the child is the problem. By changing parental responses, the behavioral therapist hopes to produce a corresponding change in the child's behavior. Psychologists at the Oregon Social Learning Center, under the direction of Gerald Patterson and John Reid, led the way in developing a series of treatment programs, based on social learning principles, teaching parents how to reduce and control disruptive behavior in children (Patterson, Reid, Jones, & Conger, 1975). Initially focused exclusively on parent training, these researchers later acknowledged that teaching parents to change their child-rearing behavior produces parental resistance. Along with educating parents, they now attempt to resolve parental resistance, recognizing that both factors are prime determinants of successful intervention (Patterson, 1985).

Should parents be trained how to most effectively deal with a specific problem from which they seek relief ("Our daughter argues whenever we ask her to do anything"), presumably generalizing learned skills on their own to subsequent problems? Or should they be instructed in a standardized package of skills using behavioral management practices to increase prosocial behavior and decrease problematic behavior in their children, regardless of the presenting problem? Advocating the latter approach, Dangel, Yu, Slot, and Fashimpar (1994) believe in the efficacy of parents acquiring a set of skills that can be used to address a wide range of problems, applicable to a variety of childhood problems and settings such as home or school. More than resolving a particular problem, the skills-building model increases the likelihood that parents will apply the skills to other existing problems or ones that occur in the future or with other children.

Parent skills training has many practical features to recommend it. It is cost effective in the sense that less time is needed for assessing and developing a specific intervention procedure, because the treatment plan is standardized. Its focus is on family
empowerment. It minimizes the family's reliance on qualified professional therapists,
who may be in short supply. Skills learned with one child may be applicable to his or
her siblings should similar conditions arise. Without diminishing parental authority,
the training process, if successful, builds competence and a feeling of confidence in
parents. Intervention generally begins early, correcting an established problem; parent training thus has a preventive aspect. Perhaps most important, parents possess the
greatest potential for generating behavior change because they have the greatest control over the significant aspects of the child's natural environment (Gordon &
Davidson, 1981). The use of parents as trainers makes it easier for children to actually
use the new behavior they learn, since they do not have to go through the process of
transferring what they have acquired from a therapist to their home situation.

The initial request for treatment rarely if ever comes from the child. It is likely to
be the parents who are concerned about their child's disturbed (and disturbing) behavior (see Table 13.3) or failure to behave in ways appropriate to his or her age or sex.

According to Patterson and Reid (1970), a faulty parent-child interaction pattern
has probably developed and been maintained through *reciprocity* (a child responding
negatively to a negative parental input) and *coercion* (parents influencing behavior
through the use of punishment). BPT intervention aims to change this mutually
destructive pattern of interaction, usually by training parents to observe and measure
the child's problematic behavior and then to apply social learning techniques for
accelerating desirable behavior, decelerating undesirable behavior, and maintaining
the consequent cognitive and behavioral changes.

As is true of all cognitive or behavioral interventions, parent training begins with
an extensive assessment procedure. Before teaching parenting skills, the behavioral
therapist relies on interviews, questionnaires, behavioral checklists, and naturalistic
observations of parent-child interactions in order to identify the specific problem
behavior along with its antecedent and consequent events. Through such a behavioral
analysis, the therapist is able to pinpoint the problem more exactly; evaluate the form,
frequency, and extent of its impact on the family; and systematically train parents to
use social learning principles to replace the targeted behavior with more positive,
mutually reinforcing interaction.

The actual training of parents in skills acquisition and knowledge of behavioral
principles may be as direct as instructing them, individually or in parent groups, by written material (books, instructional pamphlets), lectures, computer software programs,
videotapes, or role-playing demonstrations (Dangel, Yu, Slot, & Fashimpar, 1994). Such
focused education is apt to emphasize how, when, and under what circumstances to

TABLE 13.3 Behavior Problems Described as "Severe" by over 4000 Parents During Ten Years of PBT Workshops

Behavior Problem	Percentage Rating as "Severe"
Disobedience; difficulty in disciplinary control	52
Disruptiveness; tendency to annoy and bother others	49
Fighting	45
Talking back	43
Short attention span	42
Restlessness; inability to sit still	40
Irritability; easily aroused to intense anger	37
Temper tantrums	35
Attention seeking; "show-off" behavior	35
Crying over minor annoyances	33
Lack of self-confidence	33
Hyperactivity; "always on the go"	33
Distractibility	33
Specific fears; phobias	17
Bed wetting	16

Source: Falloon & Liberman, 1983, p. 123

enforce rules or act consistent, or how to apply behavioral deceleration procedures such as **time out** from positive reinforcement, or acceleration procedures such as home **token economy** techniques (Gordon & Davidson, 1981).

In *Families*, Patterson (1971) first outlined procedures for parents to acquire "behavior management skills" geared toward more effective child management. Presumably, many adults come by these skills "naturally," that is, without deliberately following a prescribed program. For less well-equipped parents, Patterson spelled out a plan for observing a child's behavior to establish a **baseline**, pinpointing the specific behavior the parents wish to change, observing and graphing their own behavior, negotiating a contract with the child, and so on. Figure 13.1 represents a checklist constructed for a boy who displayed a wide range of out-of-control behavior. The parent-child contract, jointly negotiated, stipulated that the parent would check with the teachers daily to get the necessary information and would regulate the consequences for the child's behavior. These consequences included mild but fair punishment for continued problem behavior, in addition to "payoffs" (such as no dishwashing chores, permission to watch TV) for adaptive behavior. In establishing the contract, the child helps set the "price" in points for each item, sees the results daily (the program is posted in a conspicuous place at home, such as the refrigerator door), and negotiates the backup reinforcers (for example, TV programs) for the accumulated points.

The parents are rehearsed and then supervised in the use of these procedures; additional performance training, such as demonstrations by the therapists, may be

Dave's Program						
	M	T	W	T	F	S
Gets to school on time (2)	2					
Does not roam around the room (1)	0					
Does what the teacher tells him (5)	3					
Gets along well with other kids (5)	1					
Completes his homework (5)	2					
Does homework accurately (5)	3					
Behaves OK on the schoolbus (2)	2					
Gets along well with brothers and sisters in evening (3)	0					
Total	13					

1. If Dave gets 25 points, he doesn't have to do any chores that night and he gets to pick all the TV shows for the family to watch.
2. If Dave gets only 15 points, he does not get to watch TV that night.
3. If Dave get only 10 points, he gets no TV and he also has to do the dishes.
4. If Dave gets only 5 points or less, then he gets no TV, washes the dishes, and is grounded for the next two days (home from school at 4:00 and stays in yard).

FIGURE 13.1 A parent-child negotiated contract checklist indicating specific duties to be performed and a point system based on the degree of goal achievement.
Source: Patterson, 1971

provided for those having difficulties in carrying out the program. Gordon and Davidson (1981), surveying the literature on the usefulness of the procedure, concluded that "it is an effective intervention for discrete, well-specified behavior problems. In cases of more complex deviant behavior syndromes, the research is encouraging but not conclusive" (p. 547). A major concern, of course, is how long therapeutic changes are maintained after treatment ceases; longer-range follow-up studies are indicated.

The behavioral therapist may also work through the parents when the target for intervention is an adolescent's behavior. By observing the natural interaction between family members (sometimes in a home visit, as popularized by TV's Super Nanny), the therapist performs a functional analysis of the problem behavior, determining what elicits it, what reinforces and maintains it, and how the family members' interaction reflects their efforts to deal with it (passive acceptance, resignation, anger, bribes, encouragement, and so forth). Such an analysis calls for systematic observation of family behavior, typically recording concrete instances of which behaviors were displayed by which family members in response to which other bits of behavior. Behavioral intervention strategies chosen by the therapist are apt to be specific and directed at helping to resolve or eliminate the problem.

Constructing Contingency Contracts

Contingency contracting, based on operant conditioning principles, may be a particularly useful "give to get" technique in reducing parent-adolescent problems. The technique is simple and straightforward, usually involving a formally written agreement or contract spelling out in advance the exchange of positively rewarding behaviors between the teenager and his or her parents. Although initially offered by Stuart (1969) in the treatment of marital discord, this reciprocity concept seems especially applicable to parent-adolescent conflict where the previous excessive use of aversive controls by parents (nagging, demanding, threatening) has been met by equally unpleasant responses from the adolescent. The goal here is to acknowledge the power of both sets of participants to reverse this persistent negative exchange by means of a mutual exchange of positive and cooperative giving of pleasurable behavior (Falloon, 1991).

A contract is negotiated wherein each participant specifies who is to do what for whom, under which circumstances, times, and places. Negotiations are open and free from coercion; the contract terms are expressed in clear and explicit statements. For example, a contract negotiated between parents and an adolescent with poor grades specifies that she will "earn a grade of 'C' or better on her weekly quiz" rather than "do better in school." The second statement is too vague and open to different interpretations by the participants; by that kind of definition the adolescent may believe she has done better and fulfilled her part of the agreement, while the parents believe the gain is insignificant, so the conflict between them over school performance remains unresolved. By the same token, the rewards must be specific ("We will give you $15 toward the purchase of new clothes for each week your quiz grade is 'C' or better") and not general or ambiguous ("We'll be more generous about buying you clothing if you get good grades"). The point here is that each participant must know exactly what is expected of him or her, and what may be gained in return.

A contract (Figure 13.2) is an opportunity for success, accomplishment, and reward. However, the desired behavior, such as a "C" grade, must be realistic and within the grasp of the contractor. In addition, each member must accept the idea that privileges are rewards made contingent on the performance of responsibilities. Behavioral therapists believe that a family member will exchange maladaptive behavior for adaptive behavior in anticipation of a positive consequence, a desired change in the behavior of the other. The teenager's responsibility (that is, better grades) is the parents' reinforcer, and the parents' responsibility (money) is the teenager's reinforcer. BPT helps a family set up a monitoring or record-keeping system that enables the contractors and the therapist to assess the reciprocal fulfillment of the contract terms. Bonuses are given for consistent fulfillment of the terms, and penalties are imposed for failure to adhere to them. Note that as in all behavioral procedures, the success of treatment can be measured by the extent to which the contract works for all parties.

Contingency contracting is not an end in itself, but merely one motivating and structuring device among a variety of family intervention techniques (for example, modeling, **shaping,** time out, use of tokens, and other operant reinforcement strategies) used in the BPT approach. Contracting may open up communication within a family and help members express for the first time what each would like from the others. In some cases, the contracting process even makes family members aware of wishes or desires they had not previously recognized within themselves. Finally, an important aspect of this approach is its focus on goals and accomplishments. Contingency

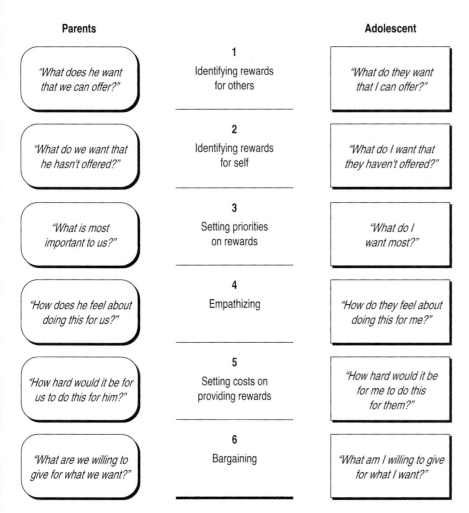

Parents   **Adolescent**

1
Identifying rewards
for others

"What does he want
that we can offer?"

"What do they want
that I can offer?"

2
Identifying rewards
for self

"What do we want that
he hasn't offered?"

"What do I want that
they haven't offered?"

3
Setting priorities
on rewards

"What is most
important to us?"

"What do I
want most?"

4
Empathizing

"How does he feel about
doing this for us?"

"How do they feel about
doing this for me?"

5
Setting costs on
providing rewards

"How hard would it be for
us to do this for him?"

"How hard would it be
for me to do this
for them?"

6
Bargaining

"What are we willing to
give for what we want?"

"What am I willing to give
for what I want?"

FIGURE 13.2   Steps in negotiating a contingency contract between parents and an adolescent. The family contracting exercise is a structured learning experience conducted by the behaviorally oriented family therapist to help family members, stepwise, to identify their needs and desires (rewards) for themselves and each other, to set priorities for rewards for self, to empathize with others, to set costs of providing rewards to others, and finally to bargain and compromise.

Source: Weathers & Liberman, 1975

contracting formalizes the family's natural expectations into concrete actions. By giving recognition for achievement, the family becomes more positive in its interactions. By improving specific interactions between certain family members, the behavioral therapist is teaching a way of negotiating that may serve as a model for conflict resolution in other areas of family life.

FUNCTIONAL FAMILY THERAPY

Based on a clearly stated set of principles, and strongly supported by evidence-based findings, **functional family therapy,** or FFT, (Alexander & Parsons, 1973; Sexton & Alexander, 1999) is designed to bring about both cognitive and behavioral changes in individuals and their families. The model, which purports to integrate learning theory, systems theory, and cognitive theory, goes beyond most behavioral models by attempting to do more than change overt behavior; it posits that clients need help first in understanding the *function* the behavior plays in regulating relationships. Since its inception over 30 years ago, FFT has emerged as a family-based intervention program used widely to treat adolescent behavioral problems, especially underserved youth with problems over violence, delinquency, and substance abuse from a variety of ethnic and cultural backgrounds.

Parents in troubled families often blame their difficulties on their child's negative traits (laziness, selfishness, irresponsibility), feeling powerless in the process to effect change. As we noted earlier, simply teaching the parents a parent skills technology, which inevitably includes an examination of their own behavior, may be met with resistance. As developed by Alexander and Parsons (1982), functional family therapy aims at creating a non-blaming relationship focus, providing explanations for the causes of all members' behaviors that do not impute their motives (Morris, Alexander, & Waldron, 1988). By urging adoption of this new perspective, the functional therapist tries to modify the attitudes, assumptions, expectations, labels, and emotions of the entire family. New perceptions and, ultimately, new behaviors are apt to follow these cognitive changes.

To functional family therapists, such as James Alexander at the University of Utah, *all behavior is adaptive*. Rather than being thought of as "good" or "bad," the individual's behavior is viewed as always serving a function, as representing an effort to create a specific outcome in interpersonal relationships. While the interpersonal payoffs or functions for family members may appear to take a variety of forms (a child elicits parental attention by having a tantrum; a teenager creates independence by having himself thrown out of the house; a husband avoids arguments by busying himself at work for long hours into the evening), they are seen in this view, ultimately, as behaviors that serve to define and create interpersonal relationships.

Without placing a prior value on the usefulness or desirability of the behavior, the functional therapist tries to comprehend why the behavior exists, and how and why it is maintained by others within the family. Alexander and Parsons (1982) offer the following illustration of the function of behaviors within the family context:

> Mother reports that Debbie, 14 years old, has been receiving increasingly poor grades for 18 months. Within the past 12 months she has begun smoking dope; has been having sexual relations with her 19-year-old boyfriend; has almost stopped going to school; and rarely comes home except late at night. At home she is sullen, argumentative, occasionally hysterical, and rarely truthful. (p. 14)

Looking at the family context, the functional family therapist might speculate on the interpersonal payoffs Debbie's behavior offers each of the family members. One guess is that a function of Debbie's behavior for her is creating justification for running away. What's in it for Debbie's mother that might prompt her to go along with her daughter's behavior, while at the same time protesting that it makes her miserable? The authors infer several possible functions for the mother: her daughter's behavior (a) enables the mother to justify coercing her withdrawn husband into becoming more involved with what is happening at home, thus joining her more actively in parenting; (b) removes her from her overwhelming responsibility because the father is brought in as final authority; (c) arouses a response from the father, which the mother does not ordinarily receive if she handles the situation herself; and (d) keeps her in the mothering role, despite her adolescent daughter's becoming more self-sufficient.

Thus, whatever the misery, interpersonal payoffs may exist for the mother (as well as the father), perpetuating Debbie's behavior. The functional family therapist, having attempted to understand which interpersonal functions are served for whom by the problem behavior (for instance, increased closeness between the spouses), might then offer help to the family in finding more effective ways to accomplish the same result. Note that the *therapist does not try to change the functions, but rather the specific behaviors used to maintain these functions.*

Functional family therapy proceeds in stages. In the initial assessment stage, the therapist is interested in determining the functions served by the behavioral sequences of various family members. Are they creating greater distance, or are they becoming closer through their interpersonal patterns? The second stage, instituting change in the family system, aims at modifying attitudes, expectations, cognitive sets, and affective reactions. Family members typically enter therapy with a punitive, blaming explanation for their problems ("My mother bugs me; she still thinks I'm a baby"; "My daughter is a chronic liar; she creates all the tension in the house"). The therapist's task during this phase of treatment is to change the focus from an individualistic, blaming outlook to one in which all participants understand that together they form a system and share responsibility for family behavior sequences.

Working with at-risk adolescents and their families, the functional family therapist seeks to uncover *the risk and protective patterns* characteristic of their interaction. The "problem" behavior is not viewed as the source of the family's troubles; rather, the way the problem behavior is managed within the family relationship system is what creates the difficulty (Sexton & Alexander, 2003).[4] Thinking of clinical problems in risk and protective terms allows the FFT therapist to attend to the family's relationship patterns rather than to determine who is at fault for the family difficulties. Discovering the "function" of these patterns for this family leads the way toward interventions designed to alter the family system. FFT therapists do not attempt to change the family's relational experiences; the adolescent may still seek attention, but the earlier means of doing so (getting himself thrown out of the house) is likely to change. In the case of the at-risk adolescent, FFTers insist on changing the *means* (drugs, gang membership) by which the young person attains what he or she seeks, especially if such means damage others. Research data indicate a greater reduction in recidivism with FFT than with other similar programs (Alexander, Sexton, & Robbins, 2000).

CONJOINT SEX THERAPY

Both behavioral and cognitive-behavioral techniques have been applied to the field of sex therapy, especially in treating many forms of sexual dysfunction in a relatively quick and effective manner (Kleinplatz, 2001). Generally speaking, these intervention procedures take the form of brief, intensive treatment of symptoms, regardless of origin or underlying psychological or emotional causes. More specifically, treatment, whether

---

[4]This outlook is consistent with the MRI strategic view that problems are the result of misguided solutions.

BOX 13.5 THERAPEUTIC ENCOUNTER

Conducting a Sexual Status Examination

An essential part of any evaluation of a couple's sexual problems includes the sexual status examination (Kaplan, 1983) in which the interviewer tries to discover the immediate causes of the presenting problem and the possible parts played by medical or psychological factors. Here the interviewer must help both partners feel comfortable going into detail about their sexual activities, before launching into questions about their most recent sexual encounter. When did the experience occur? Where? Under what circumstances? Who initiated the encounter? How

did the other person respond? What, if any, problems (e.g., premature ejaculation in a man, a non-orgasmic response in a woman) arose, and how did each participant react? What feelings and thoughts did each have before, during, and after intercourse?

In some cases, it may be instructive to question masturbatory practices, dreams, or fantasies, since these may provide leads to the immediate causes of the couple's problems, and aid in developing suitable out-of-session behavioral assignments (Plaut & Donahey, 2003).

applied to men or women, is apt to be aimed at reducing or eliminating any mechanical problems in sexual performance. In recent years, as early enthusiasm over these techniques has gradually waned because few outcome studies were able to replicate earlier findings, there has been a corresponding medicalization of the field with the introduction of drugs such as sildenafil (Viagra) (Donahey & Miller, 2001).

Sexual problems may be a metaphor for the dynamics of a couple's relationship, in which case the therapist focuses on helping them repair their interpersonal struggles, or it may be a problem in and of itself, requiring sex education, cognitive restructuring, or the learning of behavioral skills (Mason, 1991). More than likely, elements of both are involved, since sexual functioning is increasingly seen as a biopsychosocial phenomenon (Plaut & Donahey, 2003).

The clinician (family therapist and/or sex therapist) must evaluate the psychological, physical, and interpersonal nature of any sexual dysfunction, while remaining sensitive to the distress (shame, embarrassment, loss of self-worth, fear of rejection) one or both partners may feel because of the dysfunction. Therapeutic strategy calls for an assessment of the relationship regarding the commitment of each partner: their sexual histories and expectations; their ability to communicate their feelings about sex and other matters openly, as well as to negotiate for what they want or what gives them pleasure; and their degree of comfort in problem solving together (Walen & Perlmutter, 1988).

CLINICAL NOTE

While it is desirable to conduct a conjoint sexual status examination so that both partners hear each other's versions, the situation may at times prove to be too uncomfortable for one or the other, forcing the procedure to be done separately for each partner. Here the therapist should suggest that the information be revealed at a later joint session for a fuller exploration of the couple's sexual problems.

Sex therapists frequently make the assumption that some marriages flounder primarily because of sexual difficulties or incompatibilities per se. According to Kaplan (1979), these dysfunctions are of several types, grouped according to stages of the sexual response cycle: *desire disorders* (ranging from low sexual desire to sexual aversion), *arousal disorders* (difficulty achieving sexual excitement), *orgasm disorders* (premature, delayed, or unpleasant orgasms), *sexual pain disorders* (pain involved in sexual activity), or *problems with sexual frequency* (disparities between partners regarding desired frequency).

Prior to 1970, individuals or couples experiencing any of the sexual dysfunctions listed above either relied on folk cures or sought psychodynamically oriented therapies to obtain insight into the early origin of their current problems, usually with questionable results (Heiman, LoPiccolo, & LoPiccolo, 1981). However, with the breakthrough publication by Masters and Johnson (1970) of *Human Sexual Inadequacy*, based on 11 years of clinical research, sex therapy came of age. Seen within the context of the sexual revolution occurring at the time, this monumental study not only advanced the open discussion of sexual dysfunction but also pinpointed specific learning-based remediation plans for such sexual dysfunctions as impotence or premature ejaculation in males and non-orgasmic female responses (heretofore pejoratively labeled frigidity) and dyspareunia (painful intercourse) in women. In effect, Masters and Johnson demonstrated that sexual problems could arise from a variety of prior experiences (or lack of experiences), did not necessarily mean that the symptomatic person was struggling with neurotic conflict, and could be treated successfully (i.e., sexual performance improved) without much attention to their underlying causes (Burg & Sprenkle, 1996).

A basic assumption in the Masters and Johnson (1970) approach, and what puts it into a systems framework, is that there is no such thing as an uninvolved partner in a relationship in which some form of sexual inadequacy exists. Using what was an innovative idea for its time, research-oriented gynecologist William Masters and psychologist Virginia Johnson treated couples conjointly to emphasize that inevitably, any dysfunction is partly a relationship problem rather than one that belongs to only one partner.

In their original sex therapy model, Masters and Johnson offered a two-week residential program of daily sessions[5] that began with an extensive assessment; a detailed sexual history was taken from each partner, not only regarding chronological sexual experiences but also, more important, in respect to sexually oriented values, attitudes, feelings, and expectations. Next a medical history was taken, and each partner underwent a thorough physical examination. On the third day, the co-therapists and the marital partners met to review the accrued clinical material and to begin relating individual and marital histories to current sexual difficulties. During the next several days, the therapists concentrated on giving the couple instructions, to be practiced outside the therapy session.

The therapists taught the marital partners *sensate focus*—that is, learning to touch and explore each other's bodies and to discover more about each other's sensate

---

[5]The Masters and Johnson Institute in St. Louis still recommends daily sessions, away from the participants' everyday routines; but in practice this suggestion is rarely followed elsewhere today because of its impracticality for most couples. According to Heiman, Epps, and Ellis (1995), most of the sexual desire treatment programs now utilize weekly sessions.

areas, but without feeling any pressure for sexual performance or orgasm. Sensate focus exercises are designed to offer both partners pleasure in place of the anxiety previously accompanying a demand for sexual arousal or intercourse; their ultimate value is in eliciting future increased levels of arousal—and progressively increasing degrees of intimacy—without anxiety over sexual performance. This desensitization technique is based on behaviorist Joseph Wolpe's (1958) earlier application of classical conditioning procedures for learning to deal with phobic objects and situations.

According to Masters and Johnson, a primary reason for sexual dysfunction is *performance anxiety*—the participant is critically watching (they refer to it as "spectatoring") his or her own sexual performance instead of abandoning himself or herself to the giving and receiving of erotic pleasure with a partner. Masters and Johnson point out that in order to fully enjoy what is occurring, partners must suspend all such distracting thoughts or anxieties about being evaluated (or evaluating oneself) for sexual performance. Although Masters and Johnson were not cognitive-behaviorists themselves, their treatment efforts involved some therapeutic ingredients (sex education, communication training, behavioral exercises, a focus on symptom remission rather than a search for explanations from the past) that fit comfortably with cognitive-behavioral principles and intervention procedures (Heiman & Verhulst, 1990).

Psychiatrist Helen Singer Kaplan (1974), in attempting to integrate a psychodynamic model with Masters and Johnson's behavior model, described a variety of personal and interpersonal causes of sexual dysfunction in a couple attempting intercourse (sexual ignorance, fear of failure, demand for performance, excessive need to please one's partner, failure to communicate openly about sexual feelings and experiences).

She pointed out that there may be various intrapsychic conflicts (such as early sexual trauma, guilt and shame, repressed sexual thoughts and feelings) within one or both partners that impede satisfying sexual activity. Finally, Kaplan cited a third set of psychological determinants of sexual dysfunction—namely, factors arising from the relationship such as various forms of marital discord, lack of trust, power struggles between partners, and efforts to sabotage any pleasure being derived from the sexual experience. In combination or singly, any of these problems or conflicts can lead to distressing sexual symptoms that threaten a marriage by heightening tensions and can even lead to its dissolution.

Unlike Masters and Johnson, who required participating couples to spend two weeks in residential treatment, Kaplan, as a solo therapist, successfully treated couples on an outpatient basis once or twice a week with an integrated set of procedures based on miscellaneous behavioral interventions (systematic desensitization, sensate focus, relaxation techniques), cognitive therapy (cognitive restructuring), psychodynamic psychotherapy, anti-panic medication, and family systems interventions. Throughout her "psychosexual therapy," she emphasized the relational or interpersonal nature of the treatment. More recently, Kaplan (1995) described her integrated efforts to treat sexual desire disorders (sometimes referred to as inhibited or hypoactive sexual desire), ordinarily the type of sexual problem most resistant to treatment. Weeks and Gambescia (2002) have provided an updated version for treating hypoactive sexual desire in which they integrate principles of sex and couples therapy.

Sex therapists today employ a number of familiar techniques—sensate focus, systematic desensitization using a hierarchy of relaxing/sensual images as sexual situations are presented, communication training to educate partners in initiating and refusing sexual invitations, and communicating during sexual exchanges, all directed at overcoming disorders of sexual desire. In general, cognitive-behaviorists plan specific exercises for each partner that are aimed at overcoming negative, self-defeating feelings and images regarding sexual experiences (Heiman & Verhulst, 1990).

In addition, as sex therapy has become more "medicalized" (Rosen & Leiblum, 1995) in recent years, drugs (such as Viagra), penile injections of testosterone, or vacuum devices for erectile disorders (failure to achieve or maintain an erection) have gained favor with some men for improving erectile function leading to successful sexual intercourse. (Testosterone for women has also been used in treatment.) Critics argue, however, that the use of these devices—while they may improve sexual performance—tends to obscure or obfuscate any underlying interpersonal distress that may be a causal factor in a couple's difficulties. Tiefer (2001) offers a feminist critique to the medicalization of sex therapy, including the downplaying of the relational aspects of the sexual experience and the denial of the power differential between men and women partners. She notes too that the widespread use of drugs often neglects cultural differences between couples regarding rules concerning sexual initiation, expressiveness, kissing, body contact, and so forth. Since what is considered "healthy sexuality" is not fixed but varies over time and generations, Heiman, Epps, and Ellis (1995) suggest the adoption of a social constructionist view of sexuality, mediated by the current culture (or subculture) of which the partners are a part.

Finally, as Kaplan (1983) points out, although sex therapy may represent a major advance in our understanding and treatment of a couple's sexual difficulties, it is no panacea for a marriage that has already failed. In this regard, David Schnarch (1991, 1995), deviating from the behavioral viewpoint, attempts to integrate couple and sex therapies by focusing on the pair's relational context in conceptualizing their sexual problems. In what he calls the *sexual crucible*, Schnarch teaches couples how to achieve both greater personal autonomy and sexual intimacy by developing emotionally committed relationships rather than attending exclusively to correcting the presenting symptoms of sexual dysfunction.

Basing the therapy primarily on Bowenian theory regarding fusion and self differentiation, he tries to help couples resolve past individual and interpersonal issues by increasing each partner's sense both of self *and* togetherness in the relationship. According to Schnarch, poorly differentiated persons experience an anxiety-driven pressure for togetherness, thus losing autonomy and in turn placing responsibility for adequate functioning in the hands of the other person in the relationship. By contrast, developing a clearly defined sense of oneself allows greater involvement with a partner without the risk of "losing oneself in the process of requiring distancing maneuvers" (Schnarch, 1995, p. 240). For Schnarch, to achieve intimate sex is to celebrate autonomy.

A CONSTRUCTIVIST LINK

Just as cognitive-behavioral techniques have supplemented purely behavioral approaches, so there is movement today among some cognitive therapists to incorporate a constructivist perspective in their work (Mahoney, 1995). Particularly noteworthy are the efforts of Donald Meichenbaum at the University of Waterloo in Canada. Meichenbaum, one of the founders of the "cognitive revolution," is extremely influential, especially through his work on stress inoculation and self-instructional training aimed at helping clients teach themselves to overcome previously stressful situations.

In recent years, his cognitive orientation in treating victims of violence and abuse has led Meichenbaum to adopt some narrative constructive ideas (see Chapter 15) after hearing people describe the "stories" of their traumatizing experiences, constructing their personal realities and creating their own representational models of the world. In effect, as we shall discuss more fully in Part IV, constructivists argue that reality is invented, and that it is a product of the personal meanings each individual creates. From a narrative perspective, the traumatized person constructs stories to explain his or her situations (Meichenbaum, 1995).

To help clients achieve "narrative repair"—change their assumptions and schemas about the world and their ability to manage stress—Meichenbaum and his colleagues conduct collaborative sessions in which distressed persons learn to develop and accept a reconceptualization of the distress they previously helped co-create (Hoyt, 2001a). Put simply, it is not that people become anxious or depressed, since these are natural emotions; rather, it is what they say to themselves about their situation or condition that is critical. In coaching sessions, these cognitive-behavioral therapists help clients talk to themselves differently—unfreezing their beliefs, creating new narratives—in order, ultimately, to behave differently.

SUMMARY

Behavioral models of family therapy attempt to bring the scientific method to bear upon the therapeutic process by developing regularly monitored, data-based intervention procedures. Initially drawing on established principles of human learning, these approaches emphasize the environmental, situational, and social determinants of behavior. Increasingly, in recent years, most behaviorists have also recognized the influence of cognitive factors as events mediating family interactions. Personal functioning is viewed as the result of continuous, reciprocal interaction between behavior and its controlling social conditions. Cognitive-behavioral therapists attempt to increase positive interaction between family members, emphasizing the importance of self-regulation and self-direction in altering behavior. Cognitive restructuring aims at modifying thoughts, perceptions, and attributions about an event.

Currently, cognitive and behavioral approaches are having a significant impact in four distinct areas: behavioral couples therapy, behavioral parent training, functional family therapy, and the conjoint treatment of sexual dysfunction. Proper assessment plays a key role in all of these endeavors, which require identifying the problem, measuring progress, and validating change. Behavioral

couples therapy blends principles of social learning theory and social exchange theory, teaching couples how to achieve positive reciprocity so that their relationship will have more pleasing consequences for both partners. Cognitive interventions view stress in a troubled relationship as influenced by the interaction of cognitive, behavioral, and affective factors; cognitive restructuring is directed at changing dysfunctional interactive patterns and distorted belief systems (schemas), as couples acquire skills in problem solving. Partner acceptance is a key factor in integrative couples therapy.

While research indicates that stable marriages may take several forms, unstable marriages are characterized by a high ratio of negative to positive exchanges. Behavioral parent training, largely based on social learning theory, represents an effort to train parents in behavioral principles of child management. Intervention typically attempts to help families develop a new set of reinforcement contingencies in order to begin learning new behaviors. Skills acquisition, contingency contracting, and the learning of behavioral principles play important roles in parent training.

Functional family therapy attempts to integrate systems, behavioral, and cognitive theories in working with families. Viewing all behavior as serving the interpersonal function of creating specific outcomes in behavior sequences, functional family therapists do not try to change these functions but rather try to change the behaviors used to maintain the functions. The technique has been successfully applied to families with adolescents at-risk for delinquency, violence, or drug abuse.

Conjoint sex therapy involves both partners in an effort to alleviate problems of sexual dysfunction. First developed by Masters and Johnson and elaborated by Kaplan, the treatment of sexual dysfunction typically uses a variety of explicitly cognitive and behavioral techniques (sensate focus, systematic desensitization, communication training) aimed

specifically at remediation of the sexual problem. In recent years, medical interventions have become increasingly popular. While some therapists focus exclusively on the presenting sexual problem, attempting to improve sexual performance, others attempt to integrate marital and sexual therapy by calling attention to the relational context in treating the couple's sexual problems.

An expansion of cognitive therapy has led some clinicians to incorporate a constructivist perspective in their work. Clients who have experienced trauma or abuse are coached to construct new "stories" to explain their conditions or situations, unfreezing hampering beliefs and thereby creating more options in their behavior.

RECOMMENDED READINGS

Dattilio, F. M. (1998). *Case studies in couple and family therapy: Systemic and cognitive perspectives.* New York: Guilford Press.

Jacobson, N. S., & Christensen, A. (1996). *Integrative couple therapy: Promoting acceptance.* New York: Brunner/Mazel.

Kaplan, H. S. (1979). *The new sex therapy: Active treatment of sexual dysfunction.* New York: Brunner/Mazel.

Sanders, M. R., & Dadds, M. R. (1993). *Behavioral family intervention.* Boston: Allyn & Bacon.

Sexton, T. L., & Alexander, J. F. (1999). *Functional family therapy: Principles of clinical intervention, assessment, and implementation.* Henderson, NV: RCH Enterprises.

SOCIAL CONSTRUCTION MODELS I: SOLUTION-FOCUSED THERAPY AND COLLABORATIVE THERAPY

The postmodern social construction therapies we are about to consider reject the idea that there is an objective truth observable to all, and instead focus their attention on the subjective perceptions of the truth or reality that each client presents. Skeptical of the modern scientific assumption that truth is discoverable and waiting to be uncovered by careful, objective observations and measurements, postmodernists, beginning in the 1980s, contended that multiple views of reality exist and that absolute truth can never be known. This challenge to taken-for-granted assumptions—in religion, the arts, and politics, in addition to the sciences—represented a **deconstruction** of fixed ways of thinking, leading to exploration of new assumptions and development of new constructions. It is important here to note the cultural context in which these postmodern trends emerged, reflecting rapidly changing social and political awareness of multiple lifestyles and perceptions that began to gain prominence at the close of the twentieth century. From a postmodern perspective, everything is open to challenge, including postmodernism itself.

The postmodern movement, along with its **constructivist** epistemology—the view that each person involved constructs his or her personalized views and interpretations of what they might be experiencing together—has had a particularly significant impact on the field of family therapy, and is at the cutting edge of today's practice.

The postmodern social construction outlook offers a direct challenge to systems thinking, especially of the first-order cybernetic type, by focusing on examining the assumptions clients make about their problems rather than conceptualizing their difficulties in terms of interactional behavior and feedback loops. Collaboratively helping clients seek new meaning through mutual inquiry replaces the therapist as outside expert. In this new view, the therapist walks alongside the clients toward a previously unknown destination of new meaning and action (Anderson, 2003) rather than directing the couple or family toward the therapist's predetermined notions of what constitutes happiness for them. In this cognitively oriented approach, language (or more precisely, linguistic constructions) is the vehicle through which clients make sense of their world, gain knowledge, attribute meaning to their experiences, and create a sense of their reality.

In what Kenneth Gergen (1993)—a social psychologist and longtime advocate of social constructionism teaching at Swarthmore College—calls a formidable sea

BOX 14.1   THERAPEUTIC ENCOUNTER

CONSTRUCTIVISM AND SOCIAL CONSTRUCTIONISM

Constructivism and social constructionism are related but not identical concepts. Both address the nature of knowing and reject the idea of describing an objective reality. Constructivism, however, is rooted in the biology of cognition—more specifically, in the neurobiology of Humberto Maturana (1978), who emphasized the limitations of our perceptions in ever really knowing what is "out there" because nothing is perceived directly and each person's perceptions are filtered through individual nervous systems. Each of us thus brings different assumptions to the same situation—we construe reality differently—as a result of our own mental and symbolic processes and meaning-making structure.

Social constructionism agrees that none of us sees an objective reality, but it expands on this view by asserting that what we do construct from what we observe arises from the language system, relationships, and culture we share with others. Our attitudes, beliefs, memories, and emotional reactions arise out of relational experiences. It is through language that we inculcate the prepackaged thoughts of our society, and in the process of socialization we learn to speak in acceptable ways and share the values and ideology of our language system (Becvar, 2000).

Hoffman (2002) illustrates the differences between a traditional objective modernist position, a constructivist view, and a social constructionist view in the following Three Umpire joke: First Umpire (Modernist): "I call 'em as they are"; Second Umpire (Constructivist): "I call 'em as I see 'em"; Third Umpire (Social Constructionist): "There ain't nothing till I (or we) call 'em."

Therapeutically, the clinician with the modernist (sometimes called essentialist) outlook, as an outside observer, might search for an objectively knowable condition—the cause of the problem—and try to fix it. By contrast, in applying either of the other two concepts, clinicians are more collaborative in working with family members; their interest is in helping families examine and reassess the assumptions their members make about their lives rather than focusing on family interactive patterns. The constructivist, believing the problem to be in the eyes of the beholder, might try to help the family change the way its members perceive the problem. The social constructionist becomes a part of the system; as a collaborator, he or she engages in conversation with family members to discover new possibilities that reconstruct the meaning they give to their lives and that may help them dissolve their problems.

change, therapists with a postmodern outlook show a remarkable lack of interest in most of those features we traditionally have considered as central to a modernist, problem-focused, objective orientation to human problems—whether they be blocked impulses or unconscious conflicts, flawed family structures, emotional incapacities, distorted cognitions, or dysfunctional personality traits. Nor are they interested in maintaining the conventional barrier between therapist and client—in Gergen's view, "that sacred distance between objectivity, neutrality, and reason on one side, and subjectivity, bias, and passion on the other" (p. ix).

By contrast, therapists with a postmodern, constructivist or social constructionist outlook (see Box 14.1) value diversity and thus argue that preconceived views of what constitutes a functional (or dysfunctional) family are "correct" only in the eyes of the beholder. Rather than imposing a single standard for determining a family's functional level, consideration of ethnicity, culture, gender, sexual orientation, type of family organization, race, and so on, must also be factored into the assessment. The personal experiences and viewpoints of individual family members need to be attended to, and the family's interaction with larger systems (schools, social agencies) addressed. All views of events and relationships are valued equally, irrespective of the person's gender, social class, cultural background, or sexual orientation.

A therapist's prejudgments, then, despite his or her expertise, cannot be considered objective or unbiased. Any subsequent interventions to change the way a family operates may run the risk of imposing a conventional or socially sanctioned view of what constitutes a normal or stable or happy family, or how a family judged to be dysfunctional must change its behavior. The postmodern view rejects the dogmatic notion that the therapist sees the world as it really is, while clients distort their picture of reality. Instead, therapists influenced by social constructionist thinking are apt to take a "not knowing" stance (Anderson & Goolishian, 1988), replacing the predetermined view of how a family should change with a collaborative posture in which all participants— family members and therapist equally as co-investigators—examine the belief systems by which the different family members view "reality." After each family member has considered his or her own assumptions about the world that form the basis for the *meanings* he or she gives to events, the family and therapist are in a position, together, to generate or co-construct new views of the family's "reality" and new options its members might pursue. Instead of concentrating on the origins of problems, the therapist turns, together with family members, to finding workable solutions—searching for possibilities rather than pathology. In the process, the family may be helped to clarify and revise some of the central themes of its personal narratives or stories about its members.

THE IMPACT OF THE POSTMODERN REVOLUTION

For a modernist, the world is simply out there, available for observation (Gergen, 2001). Postmodernists, on the other hand, argue that what we call reality is not an exact replica of what is out there, but rather is socially or communally constructed. As Freedman and Combs (1996) observe:

> A central tenet of the postmodern worldview in which we base our approach to therapy is that beliefs, laws, social customs, habits of dress and diet—all the things that make up the psychological fabric of "reality"—arise through social interaction over time. In other words, people, together, construct their realities as they live them. (p. 23)

Postmodern thinkers emphasize that our beliefs about the world—what constitutes reality—are social inventions, not a reflection or map of the world; they evolve from conversations with other people. It is through the interactive process of language (not merely words, but gestures, facial expressions, vocal inflections, silences) that people connect and construct their shared views of reality. The development of knowledge, then, is a social and cultural phenomenon, mediated through language, and not an objective representation of reality. The concept of adolescence, for example, was not considered a specific period of human development until recently. Did that period suddenly appear, or did people begin within the last century to sort out their perceptions into types or classes based on chronological ages? Obviously the latter explanation makes more sense.

Gergen (1985, 1999) calls attention to such modern concepts as "romantic love" or "maternal love" as *invented* social constructions. In our times, "codependent" or "adult child of alcoholics" or "gay" or "bipolar" or "borderline" are invented terms—social constructions—that we personify, as though they existed. In the postmodern view, each is simply a contrived or invented label that clients and therapists alike may bring to therapy. This can be a useful and handy way of communicating. But it also can have a dangerous consequence, de Shazer (1991) maintains, because as therapists we run the risk of reifying concepts borrowed from first-order cybernetics (such as homeostasis) and describing families as though families really possess those concepts—and those concepts explain their problems.

Postmodern thinkers employ the construct of constructivism to emphasize the subjective construction of reality. Our knowledge of the world derives from our own creating, ordering, constructing, and giving meaning to what we experience, not a world as it objectively exists. That is, each of us constructs a sense of the world out there based on our own previously held dominant beliefs, which in turn reflect the dominant beliefs of society. Those beliefs are kept alive and passed along through stories or narratives we share in conversations with one another. Moreover, these narratives play a key role in organizing and maintaining a view of ourselves and our life situations. People organize their experiences and even their memories primarily in the form of self-narratives—personal and family stories, myths about family characteristics or circumstances, reasons for doing or not doing something—to gain some sense of order, continuity, and meaning in their lives. Each of us unavoidably views the world, as Parry and Doan (1994, p. 24) put it, "through the lens of a succession of stories—not only a personal story, but gender, community, class, and cultural stories."

A Postmodern Therapeutic Outlook

Rather than adopt a systems view—which, according to Lynn Hoffman (1990), runs the risk of seeing family members as objects the therapist can program from the outside—postmodern-oriented therapists attempt to collaborate with family members as self-creating, independent participants. There is an assumption of a shared expertise among all participants. The therapist is no longer a detached, powerful outside observer or sole expert but rather a partaker, with his or her own set of prior beliefs, ready to play a role with family members in constructing the reality being observed. No longer needed to give directives as sole expert, the therapist works with the clients to retell and relive stories and to co-construct possible alternative stories or new outcomes. The therapist engages in a dialogue with family members, helping them shake loose from a set or fixed account of their lives (a story from which they often see no escape) so that they might consider alternatives offering greater promise.

Moving away from exerting power and control over the sessions or establishing authority over clients, these therapists are interested in the shared set of premises of reality a family attaches to a problem that perpetuates its behavior. Together, as part of a unitary therapist-family observer system, therapy becomes a cooperative undertaking in which new meaning and understanding are jointly constructed rather than imposed by the therapist. With new outlooks, family members develop more empowering stories about themselves and as a result find new ways of coping with their difficulties.

Instead of presenting the familiar detached and presumed "objective" assessments by an expert, social constructionists take the position that what is called for is a collaborative dialogue between therapist and family, who respectfully and nonjudgmentally hold "conversations" in which together they examine the meanings each participant has given to the family's problems. For example, Harlene Anderson's (1997) *not-knowing stance* (which we describe in more detail shortly) allows the therapist to follow leads as openings develop rather than imposing some predetermined scheme or framework for uncovering patterns. Several implications follow from this outlook (Goldenberg & Goldenberg, 1999):

> *The therapist has permission not to be an expert.* He or she does not bring to sessions preconceived ideas of what the family should or should not change. Put another way, the therapist learns to do something *with* the family rather than *to* the family.
>
> *There is greater acceptance of eclecticism.* Moving beyond employing specific intervention techniques, the therapist can more readily combine techniques (cognitive, systemic, constructivist) or modalities (individual, couple, family).
>
> *There is increased likelihood to attend to diversity issues.* By avoiding being boxed in by conventional views of normal family life, and not looking for the "truth" of the situation, the therapist can learn about differing views offered by different family members, rather than falling into the trap of promoting his or her own socially acquired prejudices.
>
> *Clients and therapists alike are empowered by believing their situation is changeable.* If accounts of misery or personal failure that troubled families bring to therapy are redefined not as "truths" but rather as social constructions, the prospect of developing alternate accounts of their lives becomes more attainable.

THE POST-MILAN LINK TO THE POSTMODERN VIEW

One of the unique developments of the post-Milan approach, as espoused by Boscolo and Cecchin, was its move toward a second-order cybernetic viewpoint. In practice, that includes a joint, nonhierarchical relationship with families in order to encourage self-examination and provide an opportunity for change without adhering to any prior agenda set by the therapists as to specific therapeutic goals. More inquisitive (Cecchin, 1987) than strategically manipulative, Boscolo and Cecchin took the position that therapists should invite family members to examine their meaning system, and to explore their options, instead of intervening with therapist-formulated directives. Together, therapists and family members can co-construct new ways of considering their choices, creating the possibility of discovering previously unexplored ways of looking at their situation and its remediation. Circular questioning ("Which one of your parents would you turn to in an emergency?" "Who in the family shows the most upset when your parents quarrel?") is especially facilitative here, orienting all the participants to seeing themselves within a relationship context while learning of each other's perspective on what is taking place within the family.

This collaborative post-Milan position provided an influential link to postmodernism. Through the use of a neutral stance and the technique of circular questioning, the post-Milan therapist allows the family to give meaning to how its members have organized or defined their lives. The initial systemicist efforts to take a neutral stance and employ circular questioning led its creators to understand that the questioning process itself is an intervention, defusing the family's emotional intensity and allowing its members to hear other views of the problem. Thus, the therapist's task came to center on this questioning process and its effectiveness based on the types of questions posed in the course of therapy.

Clinically, the therapist is interested in helping the family to reconsider the meaning of its predicament and, if its members choose to do so, encouraging them to make changes on their own. The therapist does not directly try to change the system or determine how it should change. This effort to help families explore their choices—and by implication the consequences of those choices—contrasts sharply with more traditional family therapy approaches, in which the therapist more directly tries to undo rigid family structures or what he or she perceives to be faulty family interactive behavior patterns. This post-Milan theoretical perspective, along with its second-order cybernetic therapeutic implications of the therapist being part of the system he or she is observing, is a precursor to the social constructionist approaches in family therapy.

REALITY IS INVENTED, NOT DISCOVERED

Postmodern thinking draws attention to the ways people make assumptions and draw inferences about—give meaning to—their problems. It contends that truth is relative and dependent on context, and that our belief systems merely reflect social constructions we make about our world—points of view, not "true" reality (Gergen, 1999). If each of us invents our own reality, we also have the option of creating it differently (Watzlawick, 1984).

To offer some historical context, modern psychology places great emphasis on the development of logical and empirical methods for discovering objective truths. Verifiable through replicated research, valid and generalizable laws regarding human behavior are assumed to emerge that correspond to observable reality. From this perspective, we live in a knowable world in which there are universal truths, expressed in cause-and-effect terms, that can be discovered by a detached observer. That observer, as far as possible, attempts to exclude his or her value biases from the research inquiry. Working from hypotheses stated in propositional form and subject to empirical verification, the researcher strives to control as many variables as possible, narrowing the experimental inquiry to the single independent variable under scrutiny, stripped of any context of which it may be a part.

From a clinical perspective the modernist outlook, elaborated in previous chapters, would define the therapist's task as helping families (by providing insight, or promoting differentiation, or clarifying boundaries, or prescribing tasks) to deal more effectively with their situations. From this framework, the therapist is viewed as a skilled observer who looks for, diagnoses, and disrupts the family's pathological cycles, enabling the family to move on (Slovik & Griffith, 1992). However, as Doherty (1991) points out, an increasing number of family therapists have become skeptical of modernist preconceptions, claiming that the prevailing theories of family systems are merely a by-product of mid-twentieth-century modernist culture and reflect its biases and underlying assumptions regarding what constitutes truth or reality.

In particular, Doherty argues that a family therapy based on modernism by and large fails to deal adequately with issues such as gender, ethnicity, and the impact of forces within the larger social system such as political and economic factors. Moreover, defining precisely what constitutes normal families becomes harder and harder to do when we live in an era of single-parent-led families, stepfamilies, gay and lesbian couples, dual-career households, and so on. By narrowly focusing on family interaction as the source of family disharmony, the modernist view, as exemplified by the cybernetic outlook in family therapy, fails to consider the underlying assumptions of the broader social context (for example, ingrained, society-reinforced, patriarchal patterns) on therapists' prevailing attitudes.

Similarly, by ignoring multicultural influences, modernist therapists run the risk of judging ethnically unfamiliar families by their own standards of what "objectively" constitutes a functional family life. The postmodern view rejects such so-called objective knowledge, questioning its certainty and universality. Truth, rather than being immutable or absolute, is simply the best-informed understanding for which there exists a high degree of consensus among people. The postmodern researcher, inevitably subjective with the topic under inquiry, considers his or her findings to be a creation of the inquiry process rather than some extruded fact regarding how things really are or how they really work. As Guba (1990) puts it, reality exists only in the context of each person's set of constructs for thinking about it.

From a deconstructionist viewpoint of skepticism about all so-called absolute truths, challenging the modernist perspective and assumptions, the world is anything but simple, nor can it be known with certainty. Each of us has a personally and culturally based "knowledge" of the world—and makes choices based on such knowledge. However, these life choices are not the only possibilities, but merely reflect our biases regarding how things are and what constitutes our options. In a sense, as Parry (1993) observes, the therapist's job is to assist clients to become agents of their own choices; he urges therapists to first encourage people to tell their stories and then to help them deconstruct and later reconstruct these stories in a way that empowers them. Shunning the traditional barriers often erected between therapist and clients, Doherty (1991) encourages therapists to engage in a subjective but liberating dialogue with family members. As he describes the outlook of postmodern therapists:

> Their goal is to enable clients to find new meanings in their life situations and to "restory" their problems in ways that free them from the mesmerizing power of the dominant culture. (p. 38)

SOCIAL CONSTRUCTIONIST THERAPIES

Social constructionist therapists concern themselves with the assumptions or premises different family members hold about a problem. These therapists reject the customary therapist-client hierarchy by refusing to place their knowledge regarding clients on a higher plane than clients' knowledge about themselves. More egalitarian, they focus their efforts instead on engaging families in conversations to solicit everyone's views, and not on imposing "truth," "objectivity," or "the essential insight" based on "established knowledge." By examining the "stories" about themselves that people live by, therapist and clients search together for new, empowering ways of viewing and resolving client problems.

As we have noted, social constructionists (Gergen, 1985) subscribe to the notion that the assumptions about reality that each of us makes are not objective mirrors of reality, but arise through communication—language and conversation with others— so that any knowledge we have develops out of a social context. More than the mere outward expression of inner thoughts and feelings, language shapes and is shaped by human relationships. If there is no "reality" out there as such, then each of us creates reality by observing, making distinctions about these observations, and sharing our perceptions with others through language. As Campbell, Draper, and Crutchley (1991) contend, "language is a process of consensual agreement between people and is, therefore, the basis of one's view of reality" (p. 336).

In this chapter we offer four social constructionist therapeutic approaches in which the language and meaning given events take precedence for the therapist over attending to behavioral sequences or family interactive patterns. These therapists are intent on engaging families in conversations calculated to facilitate changes in family members' perceptions of their problems, and ultimately in empowering them to restory and actively redirect their lives.

Challenging entrenched and perhaps prematurely sanctified beliefs in the field, these family therapists have urged a shift in attention away from an inspection of the origin or the exact nature of a family's presenting problems to an examination of the stories (interpretations, explanations, theories about relationships) family members have told themselves that account for how they have lived their lives. People often become convinced that their stories are the truth, the way things really are; in effect, they have confused their personal map of the world with the territory the map is intended to represent.[1] Their fixed belief system, then, influences not only what they see but also how they analyze, interpret, and give meaning to those perceptions.

Social constructionist therapists are particularly interested in expanding clients' rigid and inflexible views of the world, since such dogmatic convictions, usually negative, make alternative explanations of events or relationships difficult if not impossible for clients to consider. Client views are mirrored in the language they use in constructing their takes on reality. Language—conversation—in turn becomes the therapeutic vehicle for altering old behaviors by considering new explanations leading to new solutions.

Solution-Focused Brief Therapy (SFBT)

Among today's most popular and influential family therapies, solution-focused brief therapy (SFBT) is concerned with change, rather than with assessing just *why* the family has developed the problems it has. Solution-focused therapists insist that families, right

---

[1]This notion that "the map is not the territory" was first proposed by philosopher and semanticist Alfred Korzybski (1942) and was a favorite point made by Bateson (1972), who credited Korzybski for its original proposal. What this notion points out, and why it has been resurrected by the social constructionists, is that the conceptual frame we bring to the analysis or interpretation of a situation is just that—a personal point of reference—not to be confused with the way the situation really is. The interpretation of reality is only an interpretation and not reality itself. Many—perhaps infinitely many—possible explanations or interpretations could be assigned to the identical experience.

from the start of therapy, join them in *therapeutic conversation* as they attempt to examine their troublesome situation. Discouraging families from speculating about why a particular dilemma or predicament arose, or looking for underlying family pathology, solution-focused therapists listen to the language used as families describe their situations and the conflict resolution they hope to achieve. Led by the therapist, but directed by client goals, family members construct possible solutions together to reach those goals. As Berg and de Shazer (1993) put it:

> As the client and therapist talk more and more about the solution they want to construct together, they come to believe in the truth or reality of what they are talking about. This is the way language works, naturally. (p. 9)

Instead of "problem talk" (searching for explanations of client problems by piling "facts" upon "facts" about their troubled lives) these pragmatic, minimalist therapists urge "solution talk" (in which therapist and clients discuss solutions they want to construct together). For example, instead of saying to a family in the initial session, "Tell me what problems brought you to see me," the solution-focused therapist might ask, "How can we work together to help you change your situation?" Operating from a social constructionist orientation (de Shazer, 1991), the therapist thereby sets the stage for dialogue, brings forward the expectation that change will take place, and solicits the client's active and collaborative participation in achieving change.

The solution-based therapist's emphasis on the language people use in attributing meanings to their behavior, on therapist-client conversations rather than outside analysis to track down "truth" from an expert, on multiple perspectives of reality—these are all consistent with the epistemology of constructionism. If numerous realities exist, with each reality being arbitrarily and subjectively based on personal constructions or stories of what's out there, then what we agree to call reality is nothing more than consensus about our perspectives shared through language. As we noted earlier, the solution-based therapist helps families, by means of solution-talk, to come to believe in the truth or reality of what they are talking about together with the therapist, and to construct solutions consistent with those consensually validated perceptions. Workable solutions result from re-descriptions of themselves—in effect the family creates new, empowering stories about themselves. If successful, clients achieve a cognitive change, reconstructing their sense of their own ability to resolve, control, or contain the presenting problem (Shoham, Rohrbaugh, & Patterson, 1995).

Leading Figures

This internationally recognized short-term approach, which takes a nonpathological view of clients and strives to help them find solutions to current, specified problems, comes primarily from the work of social worker Steve de Shazer (1988, 1991, 1994) and his associates [including at one time or another, Insoo Berg (1994); Eve Lipchik (2002); Scott Miller (1994), and Michele Weiner-Davis (1993) at the Brief Family Therapy Center in Milwaukee (founded in 1978)]. The center was co-founded by de Shazer and his wife, Insoo Berg, a native of Korea; he died in 2005 and she remains the executive director of the Center. Lipchik continues to practice in Milwaukee, as does Miller in Chicago. Weiner-Davis, after leaving the Center, moved to Woodstock, Illinois, where she converted a small clinic into an agency with a solution-focused point of view.

De Shazer had spent time at the Mental Research Institute in Palo Alto and worked closely with John Weakland, one of the founders of brief strategic family therapy. Not surprisingly, SFBT shares with the MRI[2] the notion that dysfunction essentially arises from faulty attempts at problem solution; the family perceives itself as simply stuck, having run out of ways to deal with the problem (Duncan, Miller, & Sparks, 2003). However, de Shazer and associates part company with strategists by emphasizing that the family has developed a faulty or negative set of constructions; as a result, family members experience their options as nonexistent or extremely limited and continue to think of the problem using the same language as before (Lipchik, 1993).

Rather than focus on why or how the particular presenting problem initially arose, solution-focused therapists attempt to aid the family in discovering its own creative solutions for becoming "unstuck." In short, while the MRIers try to get clients to change the behavior that hasn't worked, the SFBTers try to get them to change their cognitions in order to open up the possibility of finding new ways to deal with the troublesome problem. The MRI model is problem-focused, the Milwaukee model solution-focused. The former urges clients to *do* things differently, while the latter urges them to *view* things differently (Shoham, Rohrbaugh, & Patterson, 1995).

The assumption here is that clients already know what they need to do to solve their complaints; the therapist's task is to help them construct a new use for knowledge they already have. The overall aim of this approach, then, is to help clients start the solution process. *The solution does not need to be matched to the specific problem to be effective.* Actually, solution-focused therapists believe that the *solution process* is more similar from one case to another than the problems each intervention is meant to solve. In describing his approach, de Shazer uses a simple metaphor: The complaints clients bring to the therapist are like locks on doors that could open to a more satisfactory life, if only they could find the key. Often, time is wasted and frustration heightened in trying to discover why the lock is in the way or why the door won't open, when the family should be looking for the key.

Steve de Shazer, M.S.W.

De Shazer's (1985, 1988) overall contribution is to provide the family with "skeleton keys"—interventions that work for a variety of locks. Such keys do not necessarily fit a complex lock perfectly; they only need to fit sufficiently well so that a solution evolves. That is, in constructing a solution, the therapist does not need to know about the history of the problem or what maintains the complaint. Nor is the therapist particularly interested in the details of the complaint, preferring to attend instead to developing with the family expectations of change and solution. By limiting the number of sessions (typically five to ten), the therapist

---

[2]Early solution-focused theory was closely identified with the strategic approach to family therapy, incorporating many indirect therapeutic techniques of Milton Erickson. De Shazer (1991, 1994) later turned to the ideas of linguistic philosopher Ludwig Wittgenstein—especially his notions concerning "language games," which are essentially conversations people engage in with one another to determine reality. Wittgenstein (1968) argued for focusing on descriptions in place of hypotheses or explanations. Today solution-focused therapy is clearly in the social constructionist camp, emphasizing the central role of language in how clients view themselves and their problems. Hence, change comes about as clients learn to shift from "problem-talk" to "solution-talk."

BOX 14.3   THERAPEUTIC ENCOUNTER

A THERAPIST INITIATES A SOLUTION PROCESS

Observe how the therapist sets up an expectation of change in the following situation of a woman trying to be a perfect mother (de Shazer, 1985). In the process, he helps create in her a corresponding sense of what to expect after the problem or presenting complaint is gone.

> Mrs. Baker came to therapy complaining about her approach to her children. She thought she should *completely* stop yelling at them because the yelling did not achieve its aim and just left them frustrated. Trying to find a minimal goal, the therapist asked her, "What sort of thing do you think will happen when you start to take a more calm and reasonable approach to your children?" (p. 35)

Several key features are noteworthy in this therapeutic intervention, which resembles an Ericksonian directive in hypnosis. The phrasing recasts the goal (a calmer and more reasonable approach) as small and thus more reachable than stopping yelling completely. The implied therapist suggestion is not only that Mrs. Baker should take a calmer and more reasonable approach but also that she will (the use of *when* rather than *if*). Moreover, there exists the further expectation that taking a calmer and more rea-

sonable approach will make a difference, and that the difference will be sufficient for Mrs. Baker to notice (things will happen).

By turning the goal into a small start, the therapist is encouraging the client to proceed with changes she is likely to view as self-generating, minimizing further therapeutic interference. In fact, due to Mrs. Baker's randomizing her approach and permitting herself the solutions of yelling or being calm, depending on the circumstances, the children no longer found her behavior so predictable (and thus able to be ignored); the "causes" of her yelling therefore diminished in both frequency and intensity. Soon her occasional yelling took on a new meaning, signaling to the children when she meant business. Mrs. Baker did not have to stop yelling completely in order to be a perfect mother, as she had believed at the start of therapy, since she now had a solution—she could choose to yell or not to yell, according to the situation and the response of others. De Shazer's technique fully accepts Mrs. Baker (as a yeller), and does not scold her for yelling nor tell her to change by eliminating the yelling. Any continued yelling, when appropriate, is not seen as a sign of resistance but rather as cooperation with the therapy.

helps create the expectation of change, making the achievement of goals appear more attainable. (It also endears SFBT to managed care organizations that continue to pressure therapists to reduce the length of therapy.)

One theoretical view that particularly sets de Shazer and his colleagues at the Brief Family Therapy Center in Milwaukee apart from the MRI Brief Therapy Center is the rejection of the idea that clients who come asking for change are at the same time resisting change. Solution-focused therapists contend that clients really do want to be cooperative and to change; they resist interpretations or other interventions from the therapist only if these do not seem to them to fit. To promote cooperation, the therapist *compliments* clients ("You seem to be really trying to be a good mother under difficult circumstances"), focusing on client strengths or past successes. Once family members become convinced the therapist is on their side, he or she is in a position to make suggestions that they try something new that might also make them feel better. Typically, therapists offer suggestions for initiating *small changes* that, once achieved, lead to further changes in the system generated by the clients ("Marie seemed to like

BOX 14.4   THERAPEUTIC ENCOUNTER

EITHER/OR OR BOTH/AND CHOICES

Solution-focused therapists believe people who focus on problems often give themselves "either/or choices" (in the example just cited, to continue yelling out of control or stop yelling completely). Instead, solution-focused therapists usually offer constructions of a "both/and choice" (expecting Mrs. Baker to continue yelling when appropriate and to contain her yelling when she deems it unnecessary). Couples therapists often see clients, each of whom takes an "either/or" position ("I'm right and you're wrong"). Without declaring one the winner, the solution-focused therapist is likely to offer a "both/and" substitute (both have valid positions, and each partner's unwillingness to listen to the other leads to a standoff that is nonfunctional) in order to reexamine the couple's viewpoints (de Shazer, 1985).

it when you sat and talked to her on Wednesday. Do you think you could try to do the same thing two nights next week?")

SFBT therapists take the position with clients that change is inevitable; the only issue is when it will occur. In this way they create expectations that change will take place as soon as the "key" is found. As just seen in our example, the therapist might wonder aloud what the client expects to be different after the presenting complaint is gone. As this new framework becomes established, the therapist and client are then likely to set to work finding a solution to resolve the problem. According to de Shazer, just expecting to get somewhere different, somewhere more satisfactory, creates the expectation of beneficial change in the client, and makes it easier to get there.

Solution-focused therapists have devised various therapeutic questions to disrupt problem-maintaining behavioral patterns, change outmoded family beliefs, and amplify **exceptions** to behavior previously thought of by clients as unchangeable. Three kinds of questions, often asked during the initial session, are increasingly central to the solution-focused approach: (a) "miracle questions"; (b) exception-finding questions; and (c) scaling questions (Berg & Miller, 1992).

The *miracle question* (de Shazer, 1991) states:

> Suppose that one night there is a miracle and while you were sleeping the problem that brought you to therapy is solved. How would you know? What would be different? What would you notice the next morning that will tell you that there has been a miracle? What will your spouse notice? (p. 113)

The question is designed to allow clients to describe what they want out of therapy (de Shazer, 1994). Future-oriented and designed to illuminate a hypothetical solution, this therapeutic gambit offers each family member an opportunity to speculate on what their lives will be like when the problem the family brought to therapy (say, marital conflict or struggles between parents and adolescents) is solved. Each family member is also encouraged to reveal differences in his or her behavior that the others will notice. Goals are identified in this way, and potential solutions revealed. Not only does consideration of a brighter future in which all members change increase its likelihood to occur, but the solution calls for a consideration of how to reach the stated goal offered by the family members themselves. The idea here is for the client to gradually construct an image of a fulfilling, productive, rewarding future when the problem

BOX 14.5   THERAPEUTIC ENCOUNTER

ASKING THE MIRACLE QUESTION

In the following excerpt of an interview, Cheryl, a therapist, asks her client, Rosie, what she would notice was different if she woke up the next morning and a miracle had occurred, solving her problems. Rosie is a 23-year-old pregnant high school dropout, with two preschool girls, 2 and 3 years of age, and two older boys at school. She has been a prostitute to supplement welfare payments, and believes she may have gotten pregnant this time from unprotected intercourse with a client.

ROSIE (smiling): That's easy; I would have won the lottery—$3 million.

CHERYL: That would be great, wouldn't it? What else would you notice?

ROSIE: Some nice man would come along who has lots of money and lots of patience with kids, and we'd get married. Or I wouldn't have so many kids and I would finish high school and I would have a good job.

CHERYL: OK, that sounds like a *big* miracle. What do you imagine would be the first thing that you would notice which would tell you that this day is different, it's better, a miracle must have happened?

ROSIE: Well, I would get up in the morning before my kids do, make them breakfast, and sit down with them while we all eat together.

CHERYL: If you were to decide to do that—get up before them and make them breakfast—what would they do?

ROSIE: I think maybe they would come and sit down at the table instead of going and turning on the TV.

CHERYL: And how would that be for you?

ROSIE: I'd be happier because we could talk about nice things, not argue over TV. And my babies won't start crying over all the fighting about the TV.

CHERYL: What else? What else will be different when the miracle happens?

Exception-finding questions, used as soon as possible in therapy (Shoham, Rohrbaugh, & Patterson, 1995), deconstruct a problem by focusing on exceptions to the rules—times when the adolescent was cooperative, the child did not wet his bed, the dinner did not end in a family free-for-all. In the example above, the therapist later asks Rosie if there have been times during the previous two weeks when the miracle she just described happened, to which the client reports that actually things were different four days ago. The therapist is on the way to helping the client see that she has the skills, and if she managed things differently, changes could occur.

ROSIE: Well, I went to bed about ten the night before and had a good night's sleep. I had food in the house, because I had gone to the store and to the food pantry on Saturday. I had even set the alarm for 6:30 and got up when it rang. I made breakfast and called the kids. The boys ate and got ready for school and left on time. (remembering) One even got some homework out of his backpack and did it—real quick—before he went to school.

CHERYL: (impressed) Rosie, that sounds like a big part of the miracle right there. I'm amazed. How did it happen?

Here the solution-focused therapist is encouraging the client to build on times she was able to control the problem. A client who complains of *always* being depressed might be directed to pay attention to an "up day" and later to describe what he or she did differently that day. Later, when a depressing day is expected, the therapist directs the client to do something normally done on an up day, in order to find a solution. Clients who report vague complaints might be told to observe and report back the next time something happens in their lives that they want to continue to have happen. In the following session, they might be asked what they think they need to do to get those satisfying experiences to continue to happen. As in most solution-focused techniques, the therapist does not teach the client what to do differently or teach her or him new tactics for accomplishing behavioral change. The therapist's interventions tend to be simple and minimal, and in most cases are effective in opening doors.

Source: DeJong & Berg, 1998

recedes. It is the movement toward a newly constructed life that constitutes a "solution" (Fish, 1995).

Scaling questions—asking clients to quantify their own perception of a situation—are intended to build a positive outlook and to encourage its achievement. First utilized by behavioral therapists, the technique allows the therapist to assess each client's viewpoint and to motivate partners to expand their goals. Consider the following question asked of a client in the first session (Berg & de Shazer, 1993, p. 10):

> How confident are you that you can stick with this? Let's say 10 means you're confident that you're going to carry this out, that a year from now you'll be back and say, "I did what I set out to do." Okay? And 1 means you're going to back down from this. How confident are you, between 10 and 1?

Here the therapist is getting the client to commit to change, and once having done so, publicly, to stick to or even improve the forecast. Used at various times during therapy, scaling questions may help couples gauge each other's perceptions of an event (She to therapist: "I thought the way we dealt with the money issue last night was a 7." He: "Well, at least we didn't end up fighting, but I think we have a long way to go and I would rate it a 4"). The therapist then uses these numbers to motivate or encourage: "What might the two of you do to make a small change, say move it up one point?" Or perhaps the therapist points out that previously they rated themselves at 2 or 3, so what exception occurred to bring about the improvement? In this way, change is conveyed as continuous and expected.

Solution-focused therapy is complaint based; its interviews are largely organized around two activities: creating well-defined goals and developing solutions based on exceptions (DeJong & Berg, 1998). Feedback is offered to families at the end of each solution-building conversational session, and client efforts toward reaching satisfactory solutions are periodically reviewed. Therapy is concluded, usually in a few sessions of solution-talk, when the presenting complaint is alleviated and the client, feeling empowered, reconstructs his or her view of the world.

Before commencing solution-focused conversation, however, therapists attempt to assess the nature of the therapist-client relationship, categorizing clients as *visitors, complainants,* or *customers* (de Shazer, 1988). Visitors may be there at someone else's suggestion or demand, do not describe a clear complaint, do not expect change, and do not really want to engage in therapy. (The therapist may respond politely but offer no task or seek no change.) Complainants are willing to describe the perceived basis for their unhappiness, but are not currently willing to work on constructing solutions, perhaps waiting for their partner to change first. (Here the therapist is accepting, sometimes suggesting tasks directed at noticing exceptions to the pattern complained about in the partner.) Customers describe their complaints and are prepared to take action to construct a solution. (The therapist here may be more direct in guiding such clients toward solutions.)

While therapists are complimentary and may attempt to engage in solution-focused conversations with all three types of clients, they are more active in helping a client look for exceptions, for example, if he or she is a customer, not just visiting to pacify someone else or complaining without being ready to do something to change an unhappy situation. However, a change in the therapist-client relationship may occur over time, as a complainant, for example, responds to an early assignment or set of questions and becomes a customer, willing to participate more fully in seeking solutions.

Solution-focused therapists aim at initiating new behavior patterns without focusing on the details of the presenting complaint. They offer generic *formula tasks* ("Do something different"; "Pay attention to what you do when you overcome the temptation or urge to overeat"), implying that the client can change while simultaneously focusing attention on the future triumphant moment when success is achieved. Rather than argue with the overeater who complains of *never* being able to control herself, the therapist might simply instruct her to watch for the exception—noticing times when she does control her urge to eat, thus learning for herself that *never* was a gross overstatement.

The Milwaukee group uses one-way mirrors and intercom systems; it is common for the therapist to take a consultation break for ten minutes or so before the end of the session so the team can develop an intervention message. The first part of that message is likely to compliment what the client(s) is doing already that is useful. Subsequent parts might offer clues about possible solutions, give behavioral homework assignments, or issue team-constructed directives that will lead to solutions.

While Fish (1995) applauds the "minimalist elegance" of this approach, critics such as Wylie (1990a) have cautioned that it is too simple, too brief, relies too much on suggestibility, and thus is unlikely to produce the long-term gains claimed. To date there is little evidence, one way or the other, regarding its effectiveness. Efran and Schenker (1993) find the approach too formulaic and wonder if clients haven't simply learned to go along with their therapist and keep their complaints to themselves. Indeed, there are signs that solution-focused therapists themselves have become less doctrinaire in their insistence on upbeat cognitive discourse, at times allowing client feelings and relationship needs to become a part of the treatment. Lipchik (1993, 2002) has been especially influential in integrating emotional issues into the sessions, emphasizing the importance of the client-therapist relationship over reliance on technique alone and using the interpersonal aspects of the therapeutic alliance in "unstuck" cases to reach successful solutions.

Solution-Oriented Brief Family Therapy

An offshoot of the approach just considered, solution-oriented therapy stresses the importance of keeping open for clients the opportunities for change as they search for solutions that work for them. Therapy is viewed as a brief, joint undertaking to which both clients and therapist bring expertise. The former are experts on their own feelings and perceptions and provide the data from which the therapist can construct a workable problem definition, cast in a solution framework. Clients, and not therapists, identify the goals they wish to reach in therapy. The therapist, careful not to impose any single "correct" way for a family to live, is the expert at creating a collaborative solution-oriented dialogue. That conversation is guided by two main principles (O'Hanlon, 1993)—*acknowledgment* (that clients are being heard, validated, and respected) and *possibility* (keeping alive the prospect for change and solution).

According to O'Hanlon (Hoyt, 2001c), one feature that distinguishes SFBT and O'Hanlon's version (which he now refers to as *possibility therapy*) is the latter's validation of the client's emotions (reflecting the early influence of Carl Rogers on O'Hanlon's thinking). In addition, he contends that political, historical, and gender influences on the presenting problem are more likely to be explored in his approach.

Leading Figures

The solution-oriented approach developed by O'Hanlon and Weiner-Davis (1989) derives its therapeutic rationale primarily from three sources: the ideas advanced earlier by Milton Erickson, the earlier solution-focused brief therapy of de Shazer and his colleagues, and the strategic intervention techniques developed at the MRI Brief Therapy Center. Bill O'Hanlon had been a student of Milton Erickson's, and was later a translator and elaborator of his mentor's ideas. Michele Weiner-Davis had been affiliated with de Shazer at the Milwaukee Brief Therapy Center. O'Hanlon currently is associated with Possibilities in Santa Fe, New Mexico, a base from which he conducts numerous workshops around the United States. He is the author of several books emphasizing the application of solution-oriented techniques (Cade & O'Hanlon, 1993; O'Hanlon & Beadle, 1999), as well as a popular book based upon these same principles (Hudson & O'Hanlon, 1992). A collection of his papers, *Evolving Possibilities* (O'Hanlon & Bertolino, 1999), along with accompanying computer programs, is currently available.

Michele Weiner-Davis, a social worker, practices in Woodstock, Illinois. She has written several books for the general reader offering solution-oriented prescriptions (exceptions, miracle questions) and recommendations for marital problems. Especially noteworthy are *Divorce-Busting* (Weiner-Davis, 1992) and *Divorce Remedy* (Weiner-Davis, 2001). Both she and O'Hanlon take the postmodern position of multiple realities presented by their clients, and make use of conversation to collaborate with families, helping them evoke resources and strengths to bring to a previously perceived problematic situation (O'Hanlon & Weiner-Davis, 1989).

Some Theoretical Assumptions

Solution-oriented therapists concur with the constructivist view that there is no single correct view of reality—not the family members' view, not the therapist's view. Therapists therefore rely on the clients to define the goals they wish to reach in treatment. This tactic is based on the assumption that clients have the skills and resources to solve their own problems, but somehow have become so focused on the problem and their more-of-the-same unsuccessful solutions that they have lost sight of alternative ways of problem resolution. (The influence of the MRI brief problem-focused approach is clear here.) The therapist's role is to help clients use their inherent skills to find solutions[3] not previously considered, or in other cases to remind them of what they have done in the past that worked under similar circumstances. Emphasizing hope, encouragement, client strengths, and possibilities, solution-oriented therapists believe they empower clients to improve their lives, and in the process help create self-fulfilling prophesies of success (O'Hanlon & Weiner-Davis, 1989).

---

[3]A frequently told story about Milton Erickson concerns his reported experience of finding a horse without a rider in the meadow. Not knowing whose horse it was, but confident that the horse would know how to get home, Erickson decided all he had to do was follow the horse's lead and keep it on track in order to resolve the problem. Doing so, Erickson rode the horse back to its farm. Durrant and Kowalski (1993) see the therapist's job in the same light: helping clients use their resources while keeping them on track. If therapists follow that strategy, these authors believe clients have the skills that will enable them to find their own way.

Matthew Selekman (1993) outlines the following seven theoretical assumptions followed by solution-oriented therapists:

1. *Resistance is not a useful concept.* Agreeing with de Shazer, they believe clients do want to change and that the therapist should approach the family from a position of cooperation rather than figuring out how to control them to overcome their resistance to help.
2. *Change is inevitable.* The therapist emphasizes that it is only a matter of time before change occurs, employing language that underscores possible solutions.
3. *Only a small change is necessary.* Once clients are able to value minimal changes, they are more likely to expect and look forward to even greater changes.
4. *Clients have the strengths and resources to change.* The therapist achieves more positive results by supporting family strengths than by focusing on problems or pathology.
5. *Problems are unsuccessful attempts to resolve difficulties.* It is the family's repeated attempts at solutions that maintains the problem. Families need help to get "unstuck" from more-of-the-same attempts at seeking solutions.
6. *You don't need to know a great deal about the problem in order to solve it.* Exceptions when the problem did not occur can be used by the therapist as building blocks for co-constructing solutions with families without determining precisely why the problem surfaced in the first place.
7. *Multiple perspectives.* There is no final or "correct" way of viewing reality, and thus there are many ways to look at a situation, and more than one way to find a solution.

Selekman, a social worker who deals especially with aggressive, violent children and adolescents, has recently offered a text for assessing such situations and working collaboratively with these children and their families (Selekman, 2002). Hudson and O'Hanlon (1992) illustrate their technique of brief marital therapy by helping couples in conflict "rewrite their love stories." When couples struggle, they develop stories about one another that poison their relationship ("You just want to control me"; "You're exactly like your father"; "You care more about the children than you do about me"). Convincing themselves that their view is the "truth," they mistake their map for the territory and continue to argue over whose view of reality is the correct one. They typically expect the therapist to be the judge of who is right and who is wrong.

Without imposing their own stories as explanations for the couple's problems, Hudson and O'Hanlon try to help couples co-construct new interpretations of each other's behavior that allow new options in behavior to follow. They believe the couple has been looking in the wrong place (their partner's troubling behavior) for the lost key to love and understanding. Instead, these solution-oriented therapists advocate bypassing blame, replacing destructive stories with action language asking the partner to do something new or different in the future. Focusing on specific actions each person requests in the future, rather than on what they did not want that occurred in the past, provides hope for change. "Catching your partner doing something right" is another useful exception-seeking therapeutic stratagem in the service of finding new perspectives leading to new solutions. The technique incorporates both solution-focused and MRI problem-focused procedures.

A Collaborative Language Systems Approach

The collaborative language systems approach (recently simplified as the collaborative approach) is another popular social construction therapeutic model, based on a post-modern philosophy and emphasizing language and communication. With roots dating back to the Mental Research Institute in Palo Alto, this client-therapist dialogue approach reflects the ideas of psychologists Harlene Anderson and the late Harry Goolishian. Anderson, who has written extensively about the underlying rationale for this collaborative, conversational partners therapy (Anderson, 1997, 2003; Anderson, Burney, & Levin, 1999), contends that meaning is created and experienced in dialogue with others and with oneself. She observes:

> This assumes that human action takes place in a reality of understanding that is created through social construction and dialogue and that we live and understand our lives through socially constructed narrative realities, that is, that we give meaning and organization to our experiences and to our self-identity in the course of these transactions. (1993, p. 324)

To advocates of this view, human systems are essentially language- and meaning-generating systems. Therapy systems are no exceptions; therapist and client together create meaning with one another as they discuss a "problem."[4] Thus, linguistically oriented therapists do not offer a specific set of intervention procedures, nor do they consider themselves objective experts regarding family problems. On the contrary, they actually downplay technique or therapist control, and do not claim detached objectivity.

Instead they adopt a constructivist framework, following social theorists such as Kenneth Gergen (1985). They collaborate with family members in having empathic conversations, out of which are generated new meanings, new outlooks, and the dissolution of the problem. If the solution-focused therapies discussed earlier in this chapter propose various intervention techniques (miracle questions, exception-finding questions, scaling questions), the model we are about to examine is more about attitude than technique or clinical methodology. That attitude is reflected in having egalitarian, purposeful conversations with family members as together they explore their problems and search for understanding and new options. Whatever newness is created is co-constructed from within the conversation (Anderson, 2003).

For these therapists, the essence of the therapy process is dialogic conversation in which a client and therapist are *conversational partners who together engage in a shared inquiry* unique to each relationship and each conversation. While the client is the expert on his or her own life, the therapist has expertise in and responsibility for facilitating a conversational process, out of which comes the opportunities for change. Conversation, tailored to each family rather than based on any preplanned intervention methodology, involves active, respectful, and responsive listening; immersing oneself in client concerns; and asking conversational questions, all intended to encourage the full telling of the client's current story and what gives it shape. The therapist, who may share opinions or offer tentative ideas, takes care not to operate on preconceived ideas of what the story should be, and is always in need of learning

---

[4]Anderson (1995) typically places "problem" in quotation marks to underscore her belief that there is no such thing as one problem. Rather, there are as many descriptions and explanations of the problem as there are members of the system. Similarly, she does not believe "problems" are solved, but rather that they dissolve.

more about the client's views (Anderson, 1993). Together, they engage in a mutual search for altered or new meanings, attitudes, narratives, and behavior. Both must be willing to change as a result of the joint experience.

Leading Figures

A pioneer in family therapy because of his participation in the innovative Multiple Impact Therapy project in the 1960s, in which collaborative collegial efforts were introduced into this brief therapy form, Goolishian became a strategic therapist in the 1970s. Later, stimulated by the work of the Milan group, he began to challenge the applicability of early cybernetic theory to human systems. During the 1980s and early 1990s his outlook evolved with social constructionism and postmodern thinking into what he called language systems. That is, Goolishian maintained that problems are not fixed entities but rather are created through language; if so, he reasoned, they also can be deconstructed through language.

Together with his colleague Anderson, Goolishian began to view therapy as a linguistic process of "dissolving" problems in conversation by co-creating stories that open up new possibilities for clients as well as for the thinking of professionals. Goolishian founded the Galveston Family Institute in 1977, an internationally acclaimed training center for family therapy; since his death in 1991, the renamed Houston-Galveston Family Institute has been under the direction of his close associate, Harlene Anderson. The institute's primary orientation is the "language systems approach"—collaborative in nature and disregarding therapist-client hierarchies, and largely based on the philosophy of social constructionism.

Anderson's 1997 text, *Conversation, Language, and Possibilities,* represents a major effort to tie postmodern thinking to family therapy. In addition, she is active in conducting workshops around the world on her collaborative, linguistically oriented ideas. Lynn Hoffman (1990, 2002) has followed a course similar to Goolishian's, beginning as a strategic therapist (having worked with Jay Haley), moving on to a Milan viewpoint (while at the Ackerman Institute), and finally adopting the collaborative, problem-dissolving conversational outlook espoused by Goolishian and Anderson.

A Linguistic Philosophy

Courtesy of Harlene Anderson

Harlene Anderson, Ph.D.

As Hoffman (1990) puts it, *problems are stories that people have agreed to tell themselves.* This is consistent with the postmodern view, holding that the various accounts of misery or personal failure and so forth that people bring to therapy are not so much approximations of the truth as they are life constructions, made up of narratives, metaphors, and the like (Gergen, 1993). The degree of validity of a person's claims is less important than the social utility the stories play in explaining his or her life. Therapy, then, becomes reconstructive, intended to free the client from a particular self-account in order to open the way for adopting alternative accounts—new linguistic spaces—that offer new options for action.

Building upon Boscolo and Cecchin's idea that the problem creates a system of meanings, psychologists Anderson and Goolishian focused on the conversation or meaning system a family organizes around a problem. To these authors' way of thinking, the problem determines the system (which family members are touched by the problem) more than the system determines the problem (the more traditional family therapy

---

BOX 14.6 THERAPEUTIC ENCOUNTER

HERMENEUTICS AND COLLABORATIVE THERAPY

Hermeneutics, derived from the Greek word for *interpretation,* comes from Bible studies and represents an approach to knowledge. It is a process that is influenced by the beliefs and assumptions of the interpreter. In relationship terms, no one can ever truly understand an event or exchange between people, because each attempt to do so is influenced by what the interpreter brings to the situation (a particular way of looking at people or the world in general). All each of us can see is one version of the truth of another person's meaning or intention.

Understanding, then, calls for a continuing open dialogue as people in a relationship try to understand each other's reality. Collaboration is essential in this back-and-forth activity, and there is no one correct interpretation of, say, the client's symptoms or stated problems. In this uncertain realm, the therapist, who

may understand the process, is not any more of an expert than the client. The client is actually the expert in his or her own life. The therapy session is of necessity an egalitarian one, and the therapist must put previous assumptions aside and attempt to listen to views he or she may not share, while remaining open to any newness in meaning that may emerge.

Language allows us to construct and make sense of what we are experiencing, to help organize and attribute meaning to our stories. But it does not mirror what is—instead, it reveals the meaning the speaker has attributed to the event. As Anderson (2003) observes, the reality we attribute to events, experiences, and people in our lives does not exist in the thing itself, but is a socially constructed attribution created within a particular culture and shaped and reshaped by language.

---

view). Deliberately avoiding the expert's interventionist, change-oriented stance of designing therapeutic outcomes in the modernist tradition, therapists in this postmodern collaborative approach view themselves as "learners" (the clients are the "knowers"), conducting therapy from a position of "not knowing." This is not to say that the therapist lacks knowledge or is without therapeutic skills, but rather that he or she maintains respectful listening, stays in sync with the unfolding story, and tries not to begin with any set ideas about what should or should not change (Anderson, 1997). Ideally, the family and therapist together co-create a new story—that is, come up with understandings or ideas for actions different from those previously held. As Anderson and Goolishian (1988) put it, "the therapy then takes its shape according to the emergent qualities of the conversation that inspires it" (p. 236).

Believing that people exist in relation to each other, and that language helps negotiate and shape our values, choices, and behavior, this collaborative approach urges therapists to engage family members in "therapeutic conversation" as together they seek understanding and co-constructed meaning, leading to the consideration of new options and new behavioral possibilities. As Anderson and Goolishian (1990) described their outlook:

> We see therapy as a linguistic event that takes place in what we call a therapeutic conversation. The therapeutic conversation involves a mutual search and exploration through dialogue (a two-way exchange, a crisscrossing of ideas) in which new meanings are continually evolving toward the "dis-solving" of the problems and, thus, the dissolving of the therapy system and what we have called the problem-organizing and problem-dis-solving system. Change is the evolution of new meaning through the narratives and stories created in the therapeutic conversation and dialogue. (p. 161)

The collaborative approach is rooted in the notion that all of our knowledge is based on inventions that arise from social dialogue. Anderson (1993) maintains that language and conversation help us create meaning with each other. Similarly in therapy, all participants are engaged in a language system coalesced around a "problem"—"something or somebody that someone is worried about and wants to change" (p. 324). That system is made up of those people who wish to "talk" about the problem, and may include teachers, members of social agencies, and so forth. Membership in the therapy system is fluid, is determined on a session-to-session basis, and may change as the conversation changes and new units become the focus of therapy (Anderson, Burney, & Levin, 1999).

Family therapy from this linguistic perspective involves conversation, dialogue often in minute detail, in which all participants explore the problem together and co-develop new perspectives, leading to new self-narratives, new meanings, new takes on reality aimed at "dis-solving" (rather than solving) the problem. The problem, having been created through language, is dissolved (becomes a non-problem) by the same process, as alternate meanings (new co-created stories) of the troublesome thoughts or feelings emerge. Greater self-capability occurs as altered understanding leads to no longer viewing or experiencing the previously distressing matter as a problem. Thus change, whether in understanding or in behavioral action, follows naturally from the "therapeutic conversation" as new solutions arise, dissolving the problem. The therapeutic goal is reached when a conversation takes place in which the complaint is no longer a part (Hoffman, 2002).

The Reflecting Team

One final postmodern approach, again reflecting the constructivist notion of multiple realities, comes from Tom Andersen (1991, 1993) and also relies heavily on therapy as a conversational and collaborative enterprise. In this simple but highly original technique, a "two-way mirror" has replaced the more traditional "one-way mirror," so that in the course of a therapeutic session professionals and families have an opportunity to reverse roles and observe one another openly offering perspectives on the family's issues. This opening up of the therapeutic process between team members and family lowers professional-client barriers, democratizes the undertaking, increases intimacy all around, and lets the client feel all participants are working together to help (not just sitting behind a one-way mirror and judging the client's behavior).

Leading Figure

Tom Andersen, a Norwegian psychiatrist originally working from a Milan orientation, eventually rejected what he considered its distancing therapist-client hierarchical system, especially the stance of the therapist as expert. Instead he proposed a leveling of the playing field—instead of team members observing a session and then talking about the family in private, they invited the families to watch team discussions as they occurred. At certain points during the therapeutic session, team and family switched places. The family heard the team's tentative but nonblaming reflections ("I wondered what it meant when . . ."; "I thought about the exchange between . . ."), and then returned to therapy to themselves reflect on the reflections that had just transpired.

The Listening-to-Each-Other Process

Whereas the earlier Milan interviews called for the therapist to halt a session with a family in order to consult with a team of professionals observing through a one-way mirror, Andersen expands on this tactic, breaking boundaries and opening up family-therapist-consultant team dialogues. He contends that his approach of sharing hypotheses about the family directly with them helps demystify therapy. Sharing team thinking about the family leads to the use of a common "public language" rather than the hidden "private language" professionals often use when discussing cases (Andersen, 1992). The result is often greater common understanding between all participants, from which new conversations and new perspectives might emerge. By discovering a different perspective on their problem, clients could, if they choose to do so, gain a new meaning of what is troubling them; out of this new meaning may come new actions and the creation of a new reality for them.

The Democratization of Therapy

Consistent with social constructionist thinking, this approach is more egalitarian, calls for less of a subject-object dichotomy between therapist and family, and thus is less hierarchical than most therapies. Andersen (1995) makes the following observation from his experiences using **reflecting teams:**

> When we finally began to use this mode we were surprised at how easy it was to talk without using nasty or hurtful words. Later it became evident that how we talk depends on the context in which we talk. If we choose to speak about the family without them present, we easily speak "professionally," in a detached manner. If we choose to speak about them in their presence, we naturally use everyday language and speak in a friendly manner. (p. 16)

In Andersen's original use of reflecting teams, at one or more times during the session, especially during an impasse, the therapist will solicit comments from the professionals behind the mirror, the lights and sound systems are reversed, and the family and therapist become the observers as team members have a conversation about the family conversation they have just observed. Without prior knowledge of the family or preplanning strategies, and unencumbered by hypotheses in order to understand the family's own construction of reality, the team members spontaneously present their views based on what they observed during that particular session. Typically, these views are offered as tentative, non-pejorative speculations regarding the problematic issues—with the team members careful not to make pronouncements, or offer interpretations, or instruct family members regarding what they should talk about. After the team has finished its reflections, family members have an opportunity to talk about the reflecting team's conversations about the family's earlier conversations. Shifting between inner and outer dialogue offers two differing perspectives on the same events and stimulates the search for new outlooks and understanding. In the process, the family feels heard, uncriticized, and important to the process.

Language, as we have stressed, plays a key role in providing a vocabulary that sets our realities and provides stories that we construct to understand our experiences. Andersen (1991) is more interested in listening to what people say than in inferring what they mean. He (Andersen, 1992) has likened the reflecting team approach to a walk into the future. Many roads are possible; some routes lead to dead ends. What did the family expect by taking the road they chose? Might there be other routes to take now? Have they considered those? How can they talk to themselves about which routes were taken and which future routes might be best? Stimulated by reflecting team ideas in an egalitarian and collaborative fashion, and free to select those that are deemed useful, family members are encouraged to develop a new dialogue among themselves from which new perceptions emerge that lead to new meanings and ultimately new solutions.

In true postmodern fashion, therapists practicing differing approaches have offered differing ways of using the reflecting process (Hoffman, 2002). Narrative therapists (see next chapter) in particular see reflecting teams as offering an opportunity to join with the family, support the development of new narratives about themselves, and facilitate the deconstruction of problem-saturated descriptions (Freedman & Combs, 1996). By observing and listening to therapy sessions, and attending to events that do not fit the dominant narrative, team members are in a position to notice unique outcomes. Addressing all family members, without leading or in any way making evaluative statements, the members of the team hold a genuine conversation in which each has an opportunity to personally comment on what he or she observed ("I noticed that Sam said . . ."). Team members speak as individuals, not knowledge experts, so that the "eavesdropping" family can adapt the team members' ideas to fit its own experiences. Later, after the therapy session, Freedman and Combs (1996) gather together everyone involved—therapist, supervisor, team members, and family members if they choose—to reflect on the entire process.

SUMMARY

The postmodern revolution in family therapy challenges systems thinking, especially of the first-order cybernetic type. In the postmodern view, there is no objectively knowable universe—instead, what we call "reality" is socially constructed; people, together, construct their realities as they live them. Therapists with this view value diversity and contend that what constitutes a functional family is inevitably in the eyes of the beholder. Ethnicity, culture, gender, sexual orientation, type of family organization, and so forth, must be addressed in determining a family's functioning level.

Both constructivism and social constructionism figure prominently in the therapies influenced by the postmodern revolution. The former, rooted in neurobiology, points to the limitations of our perceptions, based on the assumptions we make about people, while the latter notes that what we call reality is mediated through language and is socially and culturally determined from our experiences.

Therapists with a social constructionist view focus on the meaning or shared set of premises or assumptions a family holds regarding a problem. These therapists reject the customary therapist-client hierarchy, engaging families on a more collaborative level without seeking "truth" or "objectivity" or "insight." Clients are encouraged to examine the "stories" they have lived by, and to search together with the therapist for new, empowering ways of viewing and resolving their problems.

Reality exists only in the context of each person's set of constructs for thinking about it. The postmodern-influenced therapist is interested in engaging families in collaborative dialogues in which language and meaning assigned to events take precedence over behavioral sequences or family interactive patterns. Therapists help clients to find their own new meanings in their lives and to restory their problems and find more workable solutions.

Four examples of social constructionist family therapy are solution-focused brief therapy (de Shazer), solution-oriented therapy (O'Hanlon and Weiner-Davis), the collaborative approach (Goolishian and Anderson), and the reflecting team (Andersen). Solution-focused therapy emphasizes aiding clients in seeking solutions rather than searching for explanations about their miseries. Miracle questions, exception-finding questions, and scaling questions are commonly employed techniques. A related set of procedures, solution-oriented therapy, helps clients use their inherent skills to explore possibilities and develop solutions without imposing therapist explanations or solutions on the problem.

The collaborative approach pays particular attention to meanings generated between people. Therapists and clients become conversational partners engaged in a shared inquiry aimed at dissolving problems by co-creating stories that open up new possibilities. This approach offers no special techniques, but rather offers a viewpoint or egalitarian attitude in the search for new options.

The reflecting team technique employs two-way mirrors, so that professionals and families can reverse roles and observe one another offering differing perspectives or tentative speculations on family issues. This opening up of the therapeutic process breaks down professional-client barriers and helps all participants communicate with one another using a shared "public language."

RECOMMENDED READINGS

Anderson, H. D. (1997). *Conversations, language, and possibilities: A postmodern approach to therapy.* New York: HarperCollins.

de Shazer, S. (1991). *Putting differences to work.* New York: Norton.

Gergen, K. J. (1999). *An invitation to social construction.* Thousand Oaks, CA: Sage.

Lipchik, E. (2002). *Beyond technique in solution-focused therapy: Working with emotions and the therapeutic relationship.* New York: Guilford Press.

SOCIAL CONSTRUCTION MODELS II: NARRATIVE THERAPY

At the forefront of today's thinking about, and practice of, family therapy is a model that centers on the *narrative metaphor*—the idea that our sense of reality is organized and maintained through the stories by which we circulate knowledge about ourselves and the world we inhabit. These stories emerge from the way people interpret or explain their lives, linking certain life events together in a particular sequence to make sense of how and why they are living their lives as they do. This ongoing process of weaving together events to form a coherent whole forms a variety of stories about ourselves, our abilities, our competencies, our actions, our relationships, our achievements, and our failures (Morgan, 2000). Certain dominant stories explain our current actions and impact our future lives.

Stories, thus, shape our experiences; the stories we enact with one another are not about our lives, but rather *are* our lives (Freedman & Combs, 2000). For many family therapists, influenced by this powerful, original, and optimistic approach regarding change, the long-standing metaphor of systems (feedback loops, interactive behavior patterns) has been replaced by the metaphors of language, stories, and the way people organize, interpret, and assign meanings to their experiences. Narrative therapists believe clients can be helped to liberate themselves from destructive or limiting or problem-saturated stories and to construct alternative stories that offer new options and possibilities for the future.

According to narrative therapists, families frequently construct negative, self-defeating, dead-ended narratives about their lives (myths, excuses, negative self-labeling, reasons for feeling overwhelmed or inadequate or defeated, explanations and justifications for why they are unable to do things differently). To achieve change, they need to gain access to other stories, to learn to consider alternate ways of examining the values, assumptions, and meanings of their life experiences that dominate their views of themselves and their problems. Ultimately, according to this view, families need to create and internalize new stories, make new assumptions, open themselves to new views about future possibilities; in short, they need to rewrite their future story lines and actively change or reshape their lives.

In general, the narrative therapist's task is to join with families in an exploration of more rewarding options or alternative plots for living their lives. Therapy involves respectful, non-blaming narrative conversations, in which clients are the experts in

BOX 15.1 CLINICAL NOTE

A Dominant Story: "I'm a Good Student"

Let's say you feel good about yourself as a student. You look back at your scholastic record, remember the praise your kindergarten teacher gave you for your ability to share and clean up after yourself, and how your fifth-grade teacher told you how proud she was of you when you turned in that original project. You remember that your high school English teacher went out of his way to talk to your parents during the school's Open House, praising you for your diligence in doing the reading assignments on time, neatly typing your paper, participating in class discussion. You recall how your parents bragged to friends about your grades, and one year your mother attached a bumper sticker to her car announcing that her son was an honor student at the local middle school.

In other words, you have selected and strung together a series of events over time, some perhaps even exaggerated, that form a plot, a dominant story about yourself that is privileged over other stories of your academic history. The plot thickens as you continue to add new examples: the time you won the spelling contest, how quick you are at Jeopardy on TV, how you aced the SATs, how you had a choice of colleges.

In telling about your school success to friends, you emphasize these events, but somehow neglect to mention that chemistry baffled you, and you still have trouble balancing your checkbook. When you think about these things, they are insignificant in the light of

your dominant story—scholastic success. When a new intellectual challenge at work or at home occurs, you believe that of course you can handle it; after all, you are a good student, an overall competent human being. If anyone doubts it, you tell them to ask your mother.

Your brother, two years younger, lives by a different dominant story. He remembers his early school years with discomfort, recalling especially how teachers, remembering you, always seemed disappointed in him by comparison. He thought of himself as slow and plodding, rarely experiencing school success. He was diagnosed as dyslexic in second grade and has had difficulty reading all his life. When reminded that as a young child he was a whiz at putting Lego tiles into complex patterns without reading the instructions, he brushes that off as a minor accomplishment. He does the same regarding his hobby of furniture building, even as others praise his ability to work with his hands.

He did graduate from a junior college, but hated applying for jobs, especially filling out the applications. After several months of searching, he went to work at a sports club, where his main job was distributing towels and other accessories to patrons. When the boss offered him a promotion—a job at the front desk, meeting new customers and persuading them to sign up—your brother became agitated and, not feeling confident enough to explain his apprehension, quit. He was still living by his dominant story of incompetence.

their own lives and are assumed to have the skills and competencies needed to construct more positive stories about themselves. New outlooks, in turn, lead to new ways of assigning meaning to what they are experiencing and ultimately, if the process is successful, to new ways of behaving.

Our lives are multistoried, with many ambiguous events occurring simultaneously, and different meanings can be drawn about the same event. What we notice about a new event typically fits into a previously established dominant story. A deconstruction or changed interpretation of an event ("My boss assigned me this task, so he must think I can do it") replaces an old self-negating view ("My boss probably couldn't find anyone else to do it at the last minute"). Once the new interpretation is privileged over other stories ("I know I can handle the assignment"), the client over time may begin to link this new self-confidence to other situations

("I'm going to apply for that more advanced job opening up" or perhaps "I'm going to say yes to the next invitation by my fellow workers to go out together Friday after work" instead of "They ask me to join them but they don't really want me around." The new dominant story has begun to reshape the person's outlook, set of attitudes, and future behavior.

POSTSTRUCTURALISM AND DECONSTRUCTIONISM

If the models we examined in the last chapter emerged from the postmodern intellectual movement, with social construction theory as its operational guide, then it is fair to characterize narrative therapy as having emerged from poststructuralism and deconstruction (Hoffman, 2002). *Poststructural* thought rejects the notions that there is a deep structure to all phenomena and that its complexity can be broken down to its elements. To structuralists, behavior is simply the surface manifestation of deeper elements buried within the individual, these elements can be classified and retrieved, and only by an objective outside expert exploring and interpreting those deeper layers can the "truths" about the meanings of the behavior be revealed. Therapy, then, must look for underlying (deep) causes, proceed by repairing the flaw, and not be satisfied with simply reducing or eliminating symptoms. Such structural ideas (from Freud's intrapsychic structures to family therapy's traditional focus on family structures) characterize much of twentieth-century thought in the social sciences.

Drawing upon the poststructural ideas of cognitive psychologist Jerome Bruner (1986), anthropologist Barbara Meyerhoff (1986), and French political and social philosopher Michel Foucault (1980), narrative therapists such as Michael White (1995) question the static surface/depth dichotomy. They argue that to search for underlying traits or needs or personality attributes is to rely on artificially imposed "thin" descriptions (e.g., superficial, insubstantial descriptors of internal states such as normal/abnormal or functional/dysfunctional) when we should be looking for "thick" (enriched, intentioned, multistoried) descriptions, shaped in part by personal, historical, political, and cultural forces. Beyond helping clients re-author alternative stories, narrative therapists thus look for ways to enhance or endow or make more complex the client's descriptions of his or her life and relationships.

Thin and Thick Descriptions

Early in therapy, narrative therapists often hear stories clients tell about themselves that are problem-filled and based on *thin descriptions*—an anthropological concept (Geertz, 1973)—often imposed on them by others with definitional power (teachers, doctors, parents, clergy) and incorporated in their self-definitions as established, if oppressive, "truths." Thin descriptions of people typically are made by politically powerful or influential outside observers studying the lives of other people, and are rarely informed by interpretations of those engaged in the actions being studied (White, 1997). Consequently, the observers are apt to miss dealing with the complexities of life and the personal meaning given those actions by the protagonist. The resulting thin descriptions are likely to lead to thin conclusions (labeling a person as bad, greedy, selfish, lazy) that are superficial and disempowering to the person being observed. To make matters worse, people who are labeled in such ways often begin to adopt these outside designations ("Yes, I am a selfish person") as true and real, accepting them as unchangeable, problem-saturated stories about themselves, without examining how they themselves attribute meaning to their own behavior (e.g., a frightened or insecure person who doesn't know how to help). Thin conclusions ("There I go putting myself first again; I'm really a bad person") often lead to failing to remember times when one was generous and helpful to others. Positive characteristics are obscured or hidden by the thin description–inspired story.

Thick descriptions, on the other hand, are elaborately presented and multistoried, not simply labeled by others. They involve the views of the person or people whose lives are being discussed, and are usually interwoven with the lives of others. Comprehensive understanding of a person, according to narrative therapists, requires a rich, thick description that comes about through the telling and retelling of the preferred stories about one's history and identity. That is, it is the exploration of subjective experiences—hopes, desires, passions, purposes, fantasies, aspirations, commitments—that contributes to thick descriptions of why people behave as they do. Inevitably the stories are linked to the shared values and beliefs of others (White, 1997).

Freedman and Combs (1996) describe the narrative therapist's efforts to thicken descriptions in the following way:

> Narrative therapists are interested in working with people to bring forth and thicken stories that do not support or sustain problems. As people begin to inhabit and live out alternative stories, the results are beyond solving problems. Within the new stories, people live out their new self images, new possibilities for relationships, and new futures. (p. 16)

In addition to helping clients develop alternate stories and free themselves of problematic stories, narrative therapists support their efforts, through re-authoring conversation, to thicken or enrich the description of their lives and relationships. Here it is important to note that narrative therapists do not help clients replace one story with another, but rather help them begin to view life as multistoried, with options and numerous possibilities available. In place of the one-dimensional view of their lives that a troubled family presents—problem-saturated and deficit-centered, frozen in time and without a sense of the future—narrative therapists aim to help family members expand their lives by changing their limiting and unsatisfying stories about themselves, each other, and the world. In doing so, narrative therapists challenge the structural privileging that implies therapists are more knowledgeable than the people who seek their help. Narrative therapists reject the expert role, that of believing they understand clients better than clients do themselves. They prefer to be collaborating partners with clients, honoring the stories and cultural background each client brings to the therapy.

Deconstruction (disassembling and examining taken-for-granted assumptions), a term introduced by French theorist Jacques Derrida (1978) in examining literary works to indicate they have no single meaning, emphasizes the meaning imposed by the reader as much as by the author. Narrative therapists use the concept to remind clients that the dominance of one meaning or one set of assumptions is an illusion, and that it is possible to apply a multitude of meanings or assumptions in understanding the same event or experience. Thus narrative therapists help clients reexamine so-called truths about themselves—imposed by others or by the culture and internalized as simply given and unchangeable—and construct new narratives. Deconstructing the power of a dominating, problem-saturated narrative helps empower clients to deal more competently with new views of reality and lead more satisfying lives, with hope regarding a better future.

Leading Figures

Michael White at the Dulwich Centre in Adelaide, Australia, is the leading figure in narrative therapy, having described in great detail a philosophy and set of techniques consistent with helping clients re-author their lives. A prolific writer (White, 1989, 1991, 1995, 1997, 2000), White, trained as a social worker, offers workshops throughout the world. Originally drawn to the work of Gregory Bateson—especially Bateson's observations on how people construe and give meaning to the world about them—White later rejected Bateson's cybernetic thinking in favor of a narrative metaphor. Here he was influenced by the feminist thinking of Cheryl White, his wife, and some ideas from anthropology offered by colleague David Epston at the Family Therapy Centre in Auckland, New Zealand (White & Epston, 1990). White is a caring, dedicated, persistent clinician with a social and political agenda: liberating people from oppressive culturally dominated, problem-saturated stories and helping empower them to re-author their lives and develop more rewarding and dominant stories and lead more fulfilling lives.

Michael White, B.A.S.W.

David Epston (1994; Epston & White, 1992), a social worker/family therapist with an interest in anthropology and storytelling, introduced narrative metaphor thinking to White. Epston is particularly known for his innovative *therapeutic letters* to families, which are extensions of conversation aimed at re-authoring lives (we return to these letters later in this chapter). He and two colleagues have provided a useful set of narrative techniques for working with children and their families (Freeman, Epston, & Lebovits, 1997).

Cheryl White is a social activist, primarily responsible for overseeing the publications at the Dulwich Center in Adelaide (C. White & Hales, 1997). She edits the *International Journal of Narrative Therapy and Community Work* (formerly the *Dulwich Centre Newsletter*), an influential journal devoted to interviews, cases, and recent contributions to narrative theory and practice. In the United States, Jill Freedman and Gene Combs (1996, 2000) in Evanston, Illinois; Jeffrey Zimmerman and Victoria Dickerson (1996) in the San Francisco Bay area; Kathe Weingarten (1995) in Boston; and Jennifer Andrews and David Clark (Andrews, Clark, & Baird, 1998) in Los Angeles are noteworthy advocates of the narrative viewpoint and intervention procedures. In Canada, Lorraine Grieves and Stephan Madigan (Madigan, 1994) run the Vancouver Anti-Anorexia/Anti-Bulimia League, an activist organization devoted to helping members shift their thinking about themselves—from being patients to becoming community activists—patterned after similar leagues developed by Epston in New Zealand.

Self-Narratives and Cultural Narratives

Advocates of narrative therapy propose that people, in attempting to make sense of their lives, arrange their experiences of events over time to arrive at a coherent account of themselves and their surroundings. Such self-narratives give each person a sense of continuity and meaning, and in turn become the basis for interpreting subsequent experiences.

Each person's own story or self-narrative (how my parents' divorce turned me against marriage; how my mother's alcoholism frightened me about drinking; how my grandmother inspired me by coming to this country penniless and succeeding in business; how my illness as a child made me feel inferior to others) provides the principal framework for structuring those experiences. Put succinctly, it is the stories we develop about our lives that actually shape or constitute our lives. Helping clients become aware of those previously unrecognized but powerful internalized narratives that limit their lives represents a big step toward allowing them to engage in re-authoring therapeutic conversations that seek to develop alternative life stories (White, 1995). Bear in mind that clients re-author their lives, aided by therapists, but that narrative therapists do not re-author people's lives.

Cultural stories help influence and shape these personal narratives (White, 1991), providing *dominant narratives* specifying the customary or preferred ways of behaving within that culture. For example, if a society applauds women who strive for thinness, judges success by body shape and size, and promotes self-surveillance and individualism, then anorexia or bulimia are likely to be common problems. Similarly, wife battering or other forms of male violence and abuse against women can only thrive in a society that endorses male dominance and patriarchy (Morgan, 2000). Beliefs that form the basis for racism, sexism, ageism, class bias, and so forth, represent other common toxic cultural narratives. Narrative therapists attempt to engage families in conversations that discover, acknowledge, and deconstruct those cultural beliefs and practices (from customs, laws, institutions, language, and so on) that help perpetuate the problem story.

White in particular has been influenced by Michel Foucault (1965, 1980), a French intellectual and social critic who wrote extensively about the politics of power. Foucault saw language as an instrument of power; he insisted that certain "stories" about life, perpetuated as objective "truths" by the dominant culture, help maintain a society's power structure and eliminate alternate accounts of the same events (for example, regarding what constitutes normal sexuality, or what behavior should be classified as pathological, or how to react to members of a minority community, or what it takes to be a "real" man). Those with dominant or expert knowledge (politicians, clergymen, scientists, doctors, therapists), according to Foucault, hold the most power and determine what knowledge is held to be true, right, or proper in society (Freedman & Combs, 1996).

Because oppression is frequently based upon these arbitrary labels, Foucault advocated helping people to throw off the yoke of the culture's dominant discourses.[1] He urged that certain dominant cultural or institutional narratives be challenged, because following them unquestioningly eliminates the consideration of alternative knowledge or viewpoints and thus may be anathema to free choice or to the best interests of a particular individual or family.

Issues of power, privilege, oppression, control, ethics, and social justice remain high priorities for White in his therapeutic work. The role of the therapist, the process of therapy, and its goals all show Foucault's influence, and its commitment to social justice and questioning power have drawn many family therapists to the narrative therapy camp.

---

[1]Cultural or institutional discourses often not only constrain or oppress people, but lead to attitudes of entitlement—that whites are superior to nonwhites, men have the right to dominate women, heterosexuality is normal while homosexuality is not, and so forth. Narrative therapy is at the forefront in challenging such attitudes (Hoffman, 2002).

Therapists with a narrative orientation typically view client stories through a political lens—particularly those stories that oppress people's lives (racism, sexism, gender or class bias, gay bashing). Here they are extending Foucault's analysis of society to the personal or family levels, arguing further that certain internalized narratives (for example, what it means in our society to be successful or worthwhile in life) often become oppressively self-policing and lead to a self-subjugating narrative of failure for falling short of the arbitrary achievement mark. Moreover, internalizing these narrow, culturally based, dominant discourses leads to a self-defeating outlook about the future and restricts alternative ways of thinking about and being in life.

A THERAPEUTIC PHILOSOPHY

A narrative therapist's efforts are respectfully directed at liberating the client from the forces of hopelessness, helping that person render more visible the previously subjugated plots and subplots of his or her life. Instead of attempting to play the role of expert and objectively diagnosing someone's motives, needs, drives, ego strengths, or personality characteristics, the narrative therapist is interested in collaborating or consulting with people, giving what they have to say equal privilege, and helping them substitute alternative dreams for true dreams, visions, values, beliefs, spirituality, and commitments. For example, consistent with his poststructural outlook, White wants to explore with a client what a particular belief or act reflects about the client's visions or outlook or dreams (and not the structuralist outlook of what it reflects about the person's need or strength or personality type).

Such a poststructuralist approach is intended to open up conversation about client values, beliefs, and purposes, giving them the opportunity to consider a wide range of choices while freed from personal or cultural oppressive demands. To White, any interpretations the therapist gives to the client's thoughts or visions is not "privileged" or honored over the meaning the client gives about his or her own views. The narrative therapist is thus *decentered*—still influential, without being at the center of what transpires therapeutically.

For example, the narrative therapist might ask such questions as "What was that experience like for you?" followed by "What effect did it have on your life?" or "Why was this so important to you?" In asking such questions, the therapist is focusing on the person's expressions of his or her experiences of life, and the preferred interpretative acts he or she engages in that give meaning to those experiences. An important therapeutic twin goal here is the deconstruction of domineering self-narratives and the reestablishment of freedom, individually and as a family, from the dominant discourses of the culture. Re-authoring conversations are intended to invigorate clients in understanding what has happened in their lives, how it happened, and what it means, leading to a consideration of more positive options to lead their lives more fully.

THERAPEUTIC CONVERSATIONS

Externalizing the Problem

Because many clients are apt to internalize problems ("I always manage to get things wrong. I'm hopeless."), White developed *externalizing conversations* to help them place the problem outside of themselves and thus attach new meanings to their experiences. The aim here is to help clients recognize that they and the problem are not the same.

CLINICAL NOTE

Externalizing doesn't usually come easily to therapists, who must overcome early training where they often learn to make "objective" judgments of clients ("He's bipolar;" "She's anorexic;" "Depressives act that way") that suggest the problem is within the person.

By de-centering the problem or personal characteristic in people's lives, narrative therapists hope to expose the noxious influence the old story has had on client lives as they begin to consider new outlooks and alternative stories. As light is shed on the problem, it begins to be understood as socially constructed (likely a product of a predominant self or cultural narrative) and changeable.

Externalizations, then, are designed to help separate the person's identity from the problem for which help is sought, while helping the client revise his or her relationship with the problem and its restraining influence over his or her life. This therapeutic stratagem is based on the premise that the client is not the problem, and the family is not the problem; the problem is the problem. Consequently, no time is devoted to discovering family patterns or exploring family dynamics, nor to searching for critical events in the past that led to the current situation. Narrative therapists are not concerned with how family interactional patterns affected the presenting problem; on the contrary, they are interested in how the problem affected the family.

Narrative therapists helps families "externalize" a restraining problem—in effect, by deconstructing the problem as an internal deficiency or pathological condition in the individual and redefining it as an objectified external and unwelcome narrative with a will of its own to dominate their lives. The therapist then encourages the family to unite against that problem. Starting with the family's set of beliefs and use of language in describing the problem (an adolescent daughter's anorexia, a mother's depression, a young boy's tendency to soil his underpants), the family is encouraged by the therapist's questioning to view the problem as existing outside the family. To effect this viewpoint, it sometimes helps to personify the problem, making it a separate entity (sometimes giving it an agreed-upon name based on the family's description of the problem) rather than an internal characteristic or attribute of the symptomatic person. Instead of finding fault with that person for giving the family problems through the appearance of symptoms, the family now looks at the problem as an external entity and is better able to collaborate in altering their way of thinking about developing new options for their lives.

When the adolescent identifies herself by saying, "I am anorexic," the therapist might ask, "What do you believe Anorexia's purpose might have been in deceiving you by promising you happiness but bringing you despair?" Or perhaps the mother will be challenged to look at her depression not as some internalized, objective truth about herself, but rather as an external burden: "How long has it been now that Depression has been controlling your life?" The encopretic young boy might be assisted in externalizing the problem by giving it a name ("How did Mr. Mischief manage to trick you all this time"?); it was Mr. Mischief who caused the boy to soil his underclothes. Although the child has told himself previously that he is helpless to do anything about the encopresis, now he can begin to construct more hopeful ways of viewing and dealing with Mr. Mischief. Guiding clients to separate themselves from the problem can be a useful first step in helping them to notice other possible choices for their own behavior or for their expectations of others (Zimmerman & Dickerson, 1996).

Externalizing conversations, then, are poststructural procedures that emphasize language and meaning attached to an experience. They are intended to pave the way for reducing self-blame and generating thickly described alternative stories not previously considered when the problem was located within the individual. It is these elaborated alternative stories that provide people with expanded options for new actions, allowing for significant life change.

Externalizing is apt to hold great appeal for families who see their inability to rid the symptomatic person of the problem as a reflection of themselves as failures. Or perhaps they have blamed the symptomatic person ("It's Harry's nature to be depressed" or "His constant depression is destroying the family"). Now they are presented with a nonpathological, externalized view of the problem ("Sadness sometimes overtakes Harry"), one in which no one is to blame. Perhaps they begin to realize that the symptomatic person doesn't like the effects of his feelings any more than any other family member does.

Next, they are offered an empowering opportunity to co-construct with the therapist a new narrative that provides an alternate account of their lives. Two related processes are operating here: deconstructing or unraveling the history of the problem that has shaped their lives, and reconstructing or re-authoring an alternate (but previously subjugated) story that has been obscured by the dominant story. Holding externalizing conversations with all family members present enables them to separate from the stories they have told themselves about themselves; they can then begin working as a team on the now-externalized problem they hope to defeat (Payne, 2000).

Employing Therapeutic Questions

The judicious use of questions that open up new avenues for thought—rather than therapist observations or interpretations—characterizes narrative therapy. White's gentle, respectful, but nevertheless persistent questioning typically is directed at *what* the person is experiencing ("What is Self-Consciousness trying to talk you into about yourself?") and *how* the problem is being experienced ("How does Self-Consciousness affect you socially? With women? When you want to ask the boss for a raise?"). To achieve a "rich" or "thick" description, the therapist might ask the client to describe the problematic story—and later, the alternative story—in various ways and in varying situations, often interweaving questions regarding the new story, for example, with the stories of others. Cultural discourses might be questioned in the same way: "How do you think society views aggressive and unaggressive men, and what does that say to you about your self-consciousness?"

White employs directed questions (unlike Anderson and Goolishian's more unstructured, conversational tone) that encourage families to view the problem as some entity or thing situated outside the family, separate from their sense of identity. Stated another way, his intent is to counter the family's previously unworkable and self-defeating assumption that the person who has the problem *is* the problem. Parents with a symptomatic adolescent (say, a teenager who is refusing to attend school) might be asked: How has the problem affected Johnny's life? Your life? Your

---

BOX 15.2   THERAPEUTIC ENCOUNTER

OVERCOMING DOMINANT PROBLEM-SATURATED STORIES

Narrative therapists are interested in joining families in exploring the stories—and the meanings they attach to a series of events—that have led them to feel defeated. Families typically offer thin description ("Our son, Harry has been diagnosed with depression") in explaining the cause of their despair, allowing little room for noting exceptions to his behavior, and likely reflecting a health professional's explanation for the family's troubles. The effect is to isolate and disempower Harry, who may feel weak and ashamed for causing problems for the family. The thin description disconnects him from other family members and rules out alternative ways of viewing the situation. Once family members have established that Harry is the problem, is unchangeable, and is the cause of everyone's misery, they continue gathering further evidence ("He wouldn't get out of bed all day" or "We hate to take Harry places, because there's no telling when he'll become silent and even start crying") to support the problem-saturated stories about him.

To combat these attitudes, the narrative therapist might initiate conversations about alternative stories to help the family break away from the influence of past stories and create preferred possibilities. Externalizing the problem and labeling it as Sadness, the therapist might ask the following questions:

"Harry, when was the last time you were able to turn Sadness away?"

"How did you get to that point?"

"What did you tell yourself that was different?"

"What exactly did you do?"

"What does it say about you, Harry, that you could do this?"

"What else was Harry able to do in the past that helps explain how he's standing up to Sadness now?"

"What does it show the rest of the family about living with Harry when Sadness no longer runs his life?"

All these interventions are in the service of gaining an alternate view of the family's life history, rediscovering neglected aspects of its members, starving the problem rather than feeding it, and re-authoring their stories to now include a new sense of empowerment. Thickly described alternate stories (stretching their imagination by depicting enhanced ways of how they might live together and engage other people in their lives) help in these co-constructed conversations between therapist and family members. In effect, problem-saturated stories start to be replaced by stories rooted in history and richly described in detail concerning the future. Later, families no longer blaming themselves or one another are encouraged to engage in behavior consistent with these alternative stories.

---

relationships? How has the problem affected you as parents? Affected your view of yourselves? How does your view of yourself as a failure affect your behavior with Johnny? Your behavior with one another? With your friends? The technique allows the family to gain distance from the problem, detach from the story line that has shaped their self-view and dominated their lives, and begin to create an alternative account of themselves.

Narrative therapists are less interested in the cause of a problem than in its negative effect on family life over time—sometimes to the point of dominating all aspects of family relationships. They believe that families with problems typically offer *problem-saturated stories*, pessimistic and self-defeating narratives about themselves, likely to reflect their sense of frustration, despair, and powerlessness ("We never know from day to day what mood Harry will be in"). Narrative therapists attempt to help families identify previously obscured *subjugated stories* involving success or alternative views by locating "facts" about themselves (times when Harry overcame his sadness and was fun to be around) that they were not able to perceive when they held problem-saturated accounts of their family life. Seen in a new light, these "facts" commonly contradict earlier self-descriptions of their failures or feelings of impotence in dealing with the problem.

Seeking Unique Outcomes

Following externalization of the problem, the narrative therapist listens for a description of events or experiences that do not fit the problematic story, when the problem's influence was less apparent or nonexistent. These are possible entryways to engaging in re-authoring conversations leading to developing alternative story lines (Freedman & Combs, 2000). Alternatively, the therapist might ask the family to search for **unique outcomes**—perhaps exceptional events, actions, or thoughts contradicting their dominant problem-saturated story,[2] when the problem did not defeat them.

> "Can you think of a time when you refused to go along with Sadness's commands?"
> "How were you able to trust your own thoughts or desires?"
> "What did this tell you about yourself?"

Unique outcomes open doors to exploring alternative narratives—the beginning of a new family story line. They involve any instances or events that do not fit with the dominant story. They may be a plan, action, feeling, statement, quality, desire, dream, thought, belief, ability, or commitment (see Box 15.3). As noted, they may pertain to the past, present, or future. In the following example, a couple caught up in the limiting stories about the possibility of change in their lives seeks help with marital problems. In the first session, the narrative therapist begins looking for ways that unique outcomes deviate from the dominant discourse about the hopelessness of the couple's situation:

HUSBAND: I've carried your phone number with me for over a year and just now got up the courage to call.

THERAPIST: What does it say about you that you did it this time?

WIFE: I actually started to dial you several times last year, but when you answered I hung up. It was frightening. But this time, I forced myself to stick with the task until I completed the call.

THERAPIST: What does this new step tell me about the two of you? Can you think of any other times when you were scared but went ahead and did what you knew you needed to do?

HUSBAND: One thing that comes to mind is how I hated my job but stayed in it because I couldn't get up the courage to leave and try something new. Finally I'd had it, and scared or not, I quit, and within a week I found this job I really like.

WIFE: I remember being frightened too, but encouraged him because we were both miserable and both knew something had to be done.

---

[2]The reader will detect a resemblance between this deconstruction tactic and that employed by solution-focused therapists such as Steve de Shazer. Both approaches direct clients to move away from talk about problems that have a central place in their thinking and to search for exceptions—experiences that contradict a problem-dominated story. Both also attempt to help clients restory their lives and find more empowering alternative stories.

BOX 15.3 CLINICAL NOTE

Unique Outcomes

A plan: Mel planning to go out for a cup of coffee when Anorexia tries to tell her she will get fat and shouldn't go. (past)

An action: Ari ringing a friend when the voice of Depression has tried to isolate him from his friends. (past)

A feeling: Marcy feeling pleased with her exam results when Self-Perfection tried to tell her they weren't good enough. (present)

A statement: Paula giving her opinions in a meeting when Self-Doubt tried to silence her. (past)

A quality: Erin maintaining her care for others in the face of abusive practices in her work environment. (present)

A desire/dream: Dave hoping to share a holiday with his family when his life is free of the influence of alcohol and drugs. (future)

A thought: Xiang thinking "It's not my fault" when Mother Blaming tried to talk her into feeling responsible for her daughter being subject to abuse. (present and past)

A belief: Luz saying "I believe I will get better from this" when Depression tries to tell him that this is impossible. (present)

An ability: Chris and Leanne laughing together about something their daughter had said to them. "Expectations" had on many occasions got between them and made it difficult for them to experience joy with parenting. (present)

A commitment: Roberto and Laurie being committed to nonviolent forms of parenting when their own experience had been one of abuse. (past and present)

Source: Morgan, 2000, p. 53

Co-constructing Alternative Stories

As clients gain a sense of the history of the problem-saturated stories that have dominated their lives, and as the discourses that support their problems are examined, they may begin to gain a sense of other feasible, more open-ended, preferred stories. (Some stories, of course, have greater staying power than others, especially if supported by strong cultural beliefs, and they are not easily deconstructed.) In a sense the therapist has helped build some scaffolding, helping people trapped in the basement of a multistory building gain access to the upper floors, with greater likelihood of enlarging their views and seeing the horizon that was denied to them in their previous location. They no longer feel trapped by their problematic stories and have been helped to make other vistas more visible.

Reporting unique outcomes may further strengthen the alternative story. Narrative therapists encourage clients to tell and retell the preferred stories, thickening them by going into fine detail, interweaving them with the lives and stories of other people. The thickening process is important in keeping clients connected to the new preferred story line and in beginning to live out the preferred story in place of the problematic one. In some cases, reflecting teams (see Chapter 14) or *outside witness groups* (discussed later) help to reinforce the alternative narratives. In the following section, we consider other ways of thickening the preferred story.

Therapeutic Ceremonies, Letters, and Leagues

Creating a richer description of the alternative story—as an aid in staying connected to this preferred narrative—calls for a number of supplementary practices employed by narrative therapists. The goal is for life to become more multistoried.

Definitional Ceremonies

Adapting some of the definitional ceremony metaphors of anthropologist Barbara Meyerhoff (1986) for therapeutic purposes, narrative therapists may provide clients with the opportunity to tell (or perform) the stories of their lives before an audience of outside witnesses, drawing attention to how they attribute meaning to their experiences. Then they may call upon observers from the nonjudgmental audience (reflecting team members if the observers are professionals, outside witness group members if they are not) to respond to the stories they have just heard, in a sense retelling by them of the tellings they have just heard. Through this telling and retelling process, many of the plots and alternative stories of people's lives are thickened and linked to their ongoing values and commitments. Options for future action are sometimes introduced, as clients hear what about their lives or identities captured the attention and imagination of the audience members. The definitional ceremony (White, 1997) helps authenticate clients' preferred claims about themselves.

Definitional ceremonies, then, are multilayered and usually consist of tellings (by the person who is at the center of the ceremony), retellings of tellings (by the reflecting team or outside witnesses who have observed the tellings), retellings of retellings (again by the person who responds to what was told by the outsiders), retellings of retellings of retellings (by the first set of outside witnesses or a secondary group of witnesses), and so forth. The point is to thicken alternative stories, authenticating the persons' preferred claims about their lives, and to promote the idea of options for actions that the person at the center of the ceremony might not otherwise have considered.

Outside witness groups of at least two members may be friends, family members, other therapists, or community members—anyone able to observe the re-authoring conversation between therapist and clients and later offer relevant retelling experiences. Morgan (2000) offers the example of a child, subjected to teasing and harassment, who is willing to meet with a team of children who have experienced similar oppression and may be able to offer their experiences in coping with the tormenting. Observing the narrative interview with the child and family from behind a one-way mirror—so as not to intrude on what is taking place—the outside witness group later changes places with the family, which then observes as each outside witness retells what he or she has just observed and experienced.

In some cases, witnesses may comment on how the conversation between therapist and family affected their thinking about their own lives. Called "decentered sharing" (White, 1997), this technique acknowledges the link between all participants, but does so in a way that respects the client family as the center of the retelling. The focus of discussion for the witnesses—typically in the form of questioning each other about what they heard—is likely to concern the alternative stories and unique outcomes they identified in observing the therapist-family interaction, and to indicate how what they witnessed resonated with their own life experiences. The aim of such dialogue between witnesses is to build upon each other's stories and to further enrich

CLINICAL NOTE

It is not unusual for clients to carry in their purse or wallet significant letters (or newspaper clippings) pertinent to their personal narrative. Therapists sometimes have the experience of a client pulling out an old, much handled personal letter to help tell their story.

the possibly emerging alternative stories that caught their attention, possibly because it reflected their own experiences. In typical narrative fashion, witnesses do not presume to know what is right or best for this particular family, nor is it their place to offer opinions about how the telling person should lead his or her life. Neither do they hold up their own lives and actions as models or examples.

Once again swapping places, the clients comment on the retelling by the outside witness group (retellings of the retellings). Finally, everyone involved—therapist, family, witnesses—meets to further reflect on what transpired. The entire process, if successful, helps separate the clients from the problem-saturated stories and helps rebuild their lives around preferred stories of their identity (Morgan, 2000). The telling–retelling process contributes new options for action not previously available to the person or family whose lives are the center of the ceremony.

Therapeutic Letters

Narrative therapists often use letters sent to clients in a variety of therapeutic ways, especially in supplementing and extending therapeutic sessions and keeping clients connected to the emerging alternative story. With the clients' consent, Epston in particular (White & Epston, 1990; Epston & White, 1992) routinely employs therapeutic letters in summarizing sessions, inviting reluctant members to attend future sessions, addressing the future, and so on.

Doing so enables the therapist to extend conversations while encouraging family members to record or map out their own individualized view of the sequences of events in their lives over a period of time. Letters, because they can be read and reread days, months, or even years later, have great continuity value; they "thicken" or enrich an alternative story line and help clients stay immersed in the re-authoring process. Epston and White (1992) estimate that a single letter can be as useful as at least four or five sessions of therapy.

Letters in narrative therapy[3] typically help therapy endure over time and space. Epston (1994) writes a *summary letter* to the client following each session, based on careful note taking and attuned to discussion (and in the client's own words) during the session that opened up the possibilities for alternatives to the client's problem-saturated stories. A reminder of some unique outcomes discussed during the session might also be included.

---

[3]The reader might be interested in comparing narrative letters with those sent by the Milan systemic therapists. The latter, as we illustrated in Chapter 12, are paradoxical in nature, intended to provoke a response and typically given directly to the client or mailed after verbal paradoxical tactics have failed.

In other cases, Epston sends *letters of invitation* to family members reluctant to attend sessions; most are surprised and pleased about his caring about them and their place in the family, and they may begin to attend. *Redundancy letters* note that certain members have taken on duplicate roles in the family (being a father to one's brother) and wish to change them. In a related *discharge letter,* written with a client, another family member is thanked *but* informed that he or she is no longer needed to play that role. *Letters of prediction,* written at the conclusion of therapy, generally predict continued success in the search for new possibilities.

For Epston letters are not separate interventions, but rather organically intertwined with what took place in the consultation room. Whatever their form, letters render lived experiences into narrative form. Consistent with his or her egalitarian relationship with clients, the narrative therapist's thoughts are not kept secret but are out in the open, to be confirmed, amended, or challenged by the family. Taken together, the letters create an ongoing picture of therapist-client collaboration as they seek to co-construct alternative life stories.

Forming Supportive Leagues

Separating one's identity from an external problem is part of the underlying philosophy of narrative therapy. Typical of this outlook is the development of Anti-Anorexia/Anti-Bulimia Leagues, begun by Epston in New Zealand, that now exist in the United States, Canada, and Australia. They are based on the idea that people who have experienced certain problems, such as anorexia and bulimia, have the experience and knowledge about the problem to help one another by sharing experiences with others—and by building upon each other's skills, to defeat the problem. Offering mutual support, participants can team up and begin changing their relationship to the problem, perhaps re-authoring their lives to cope successfully with food and body image. Members get to speak of personally painful issues they might otherwise keep to themselves, and then get to take some social action to bring about greater public awareness. Audiotapes, artwork, letters to one another, periodic meetings, handbooks, public speeches, a newsletter, monitoring of magazine and newspaper ads—all represent politically inspired efforts to develop a supportive subculture, a logical extension of narrative therapy's goals of achieving liberation from destructive cultural narratives. The therapist plays an influential but decentered role here; in this community effort all voices are privileged, not just those of professional therapists.

One particularly noteworthy effort is the Anti-Anorexia/Anti-Bulimia League of Vancouver, Canada, organized by Lorraine Grieves and Stephan Madigan (Madigan & Epston, 1995; Madigan & Goldner, 1998) to help people with these problems come together and support one another, in the process changing from patient to consultant and community activist. Consistent with narrative theory and practice, this grassroots, politically active group has both an educational purpose—informing the public about issues surrounding societal pressures and body image—and a lobbying purpose—changing the media's portrayal of the emaciated female as the ideal that women, especially adolescent girls, should strive to emulate. As Madigan (1994) puts it, the league represents the joining together of citizens to fight the institutional conditions that keep people with anorexia and bulimia trapped inside their problem stories, seeking help from health care systems that keep them in the patient role. The effort is a reminder of the narrative therapist's insistence that the problem (not the person) is the problem, and that the problem is rooted in the dominant discourses of a society.

SUMMARY

Narrative therapists focus attention on helping clients gain access to preferred story lines about their lives and identities, in place of previous negative, self-defeating, dead-ended narratives about themselves. With the therapist influential but decentered, the clients are helped to create and internalize new dominant stories, draw new assumptions about themselves, and open themselves up to future possibilities by re-authoring their stories.

The model, fast gaining major prominence in the field, is based on poststructural thinking that challenges the need for a deep search for underlying "truths" and the need to repair underlying structures. Deconstructing old notions and replacing them with multistoried possibilities helps reduce the power of dominating, problem-saturated stories. The therapeutic process calls for attending to and overcoming restrictive self-narratives as well as institutionalized cultural narratives.

To narrative therapists, the client is not the problem; the problem is the problem. Thus therapeutic conversations typically begin by externalizing the problem. In some cases the problem is given a name, further identifying it as an outside force. Helping families reclaim their lives from the problem, narrative therapy takes the form of questions, often of a deconstructing kind, as the therapist helps clients achieve "thick" descriptions of an alternate story line about their future. Unique outcomes are searched for as possible entryways to developing alternate stories. As clients gain a history of the problem-saturated stories that have dominated their lives, they begin to develop a sense of other options involving more open-ended and feasible stories. Change calls for creating alternative narratives; the process is facilitated by various means for "thickening" or enriching the new story line and connecting to it in future options.

Definitional ceremonies, using reflecting teams or outside witness groups, help tell and retell the story, helping clients authenticate preferred stories. Therapeutic letters help extend the therapeutic sessions and keep clients connected to the emerging alternative stories. Community-based leagues, such as the Anti-Anorexia/Anti-Bulimia League, represent citizens who band together to offer mutual support, build upon each other's skills, and attempt to act as a political action group to change destructive media portrayals of their problems.

RECOMMENDED READINGS

Freedman, J., & Combs, G. (1996). *Narrative therapy: The social construction of preferred realities.* New York: Norton.

Gilligan, S., & Price, R. (1993). *Therapeutic conversations.* New York: Norton.

White, M., & Epston, D. (1990). *Narrative means to therapeutic ends.* New York: Norton.

Zimmerman, J., & Dickerson, V. (1996). *If problems talked: Adventures in narrative therapy.* New York: Guilford Press.

CHAPTER 16

PSYCHOEDUCATIONAL MODELS: TEACHING SKILLS TO SPECIFIC POPULATIONS

Psychoeducation offers an empirically based form of intervention that seeks to impart information to distressed families, educating them so that they might develop skills for understanding and coping with their disturbed family member or troubled family relationships. Whether directed at supporting and empowering families with schizophrenic members (McFarlane, 2002), or violent families (Henggeler, Mihalic, Rone, Thomas, & Timmons-Mitchell, 1998), or those where alcohol or substance abuse is uncontrolled (Ozechowski, Turner, & Waldron, 2003), or families struggling with chronic illness (Rolland, 2003), or perhaps those simply wishing to improve their relationship skills (Guerney, Brock, & Coufal, 1986), the advent of psychoeducational programs represents a significant development in the field over the last two decades. Unlike the postmodern and poststructural approaches we have been considering that have taken center stage in the contemporary practice of family therapy, psychoeducational efforts unabashedly rely on traditional, modernist experimental methods to develop verifiable intervention procedures.

Psychoeducational approaches, like the newer techniques gaining prominence, make an effort to build and maintain a supportive, collaborative therapist-family partnership. These stress management, skills-building techniques help families gain a sense of control and harness their strengths and resiliency to deal with chronic problems that affect all family members, not simply the symptomatic person. Practitioners typically offer educational/informational programs, supportive in nature and directed at the entire burdened and often despairing family. In other cases, dealing with less severe problems, programs might offer skills training in enhancing family relationships, improving couples communications, or perhaps helping couples become more effective parents or stepparents. Although psychoeducational programs do not, strictly speaking, follow customary family therapy procedures, practitioners do utilize many of the techniques of more traditional family therapy (joining the family, establishing an alliance with its members, maintaining neutrality, assessing how best to foster positive outcomes) in their interventions. Interventions are intended to be *manual-based*, reproducible techniques that follow a how-to-do-it format that can be copied by all mental health workers without requiring high levels of training.

Psychoeducational practices are not derived from any specific theory of family functioning, nor do they adhere to any one set of family therapy techniques. Arising from a need to include the family in the solution to an ongoing stressful situation, psychoeducation offers an eclectic approach, empirically derived, typically involving (in some combination depending upon the family or its circumstances) the application of family systems theory, cognitive behavior therapy, educational psychology, and aspects of structural therapy; in certain cases, such as schizophrenia, these are wedded to a psychopharmacological treatment program. Overall, psychoeducational efforts are directed at educating families in how best to maximize their effectiveness as they attempt to cope with mentally or physically disabled family members or deteriorating family relationships, or perhaps as they simply learn new problem-solving techniques for increasing the likelihood of future successful marital or parent-child relationships.

FAMILIES AND MENTAL DISORDERS

Mental illness in a family can be a "ravaging, devastating disease" that disrupts a family and permits little opportunity for respite (Marsh & Johnson, 1997). In addition to the social stigma and the ostracism of people with mental illness by the larger system, household disarray, financial difficulties, employment problems, strained marital and family relationships, impaired physical health, and a diminished social life are just the most obvious consequences.

Grief, chronic sorrow, the loss of dreams and hopes for the affected person, the emotional roller coaster punctuated by periods of relapse and remission, the potentially harmful or self-destructive behavior, the unpreparedness of families to deal with the challenges—these are the common experiences of family members (Marsh & Johnson, 1997). Marsh (1992) offers the following poignant account from the mother of a mentally ill daughter:

> The problems with my daughter were like a black hole inside of me into which everything else had been drawn. My grief and pain were so intense sometimes that I barely got through the day. It felt like a mourning process, as if I were dealing with the loss of the daughter I had loved for 18 years, for whom there was so much potential. (p. 10)

No family with a mentally ill member can avoid the consequences of the disorder, which include some degree of family disruption. Teaching anguished family members how and from whom in the community[1] to obtain mental health, welfare, and medical services (or in some cases, legal services) is often of great benefit, especially since most families feel helpless and confused when such new roles are thrust upon them (Lefley, 1996).

Problem-solving training to manage day-to-day stressful events, thus guarding against relapses, and crisis management to handle extreme stress involving one or more family members—or when signs of recurrence are evident—are often a part of

---

[1]The National Alliance for the Mentally Ill (NAMI), with over 1000 local affiliates in 50 states, is a particularly important source of information, education, and support. Its membership includes professionals, family members of mentally ill persons, and members of the general public interested in problems of the mentally ill. The organization also serves as an advocacy group for expanding research and obtaining improved services.

psychoeducational undertakings. Simultaneously, therapeutic efforts are intended to ensure that to the extent possible, family members preserve the integrity of their own lives. One major therapeutic task is to bring the family's competencies and resiliency into play, as together the members learn to the extent possible those techniques for prevailing over adversity and changing in constructive ways.

Educating, Supporting, and Empowering Families of Schizophrenics

Interest in the family treatment of severe mental disorders has waxed and waned over the last 40 or more years. Heralded in the late 1950s and 1960s as a breakthrough in understanding family factors contributing to the etiology or maintenance of the schizophrenia, such concepts as the schizophrenogenic mother, double-binding communications, pseudomutuality, and maritally schismed and maritally skewed families initially were greeted with excitement by many in the professional family therapy community as offering new paradigms for understanding this complex disorder (see Chapter 5). By the mid-1970s and early 1980s, largely because of research (such as twin and adoption studies) into a possible genetic link in schizophrenia, as well as an increased recognition that families were being unfairly blamed for "causing" the disorder in the affected member, family therapists appeared to be making a hasty retreat from working with the major psychoses.

Skeptics wondered whether family-related treatments for schizophrenia alone could be effective. By the 1990s, however, now viewing schizophrenia as a thought disorder in a biologically vulnerable person, many therapists were once again working with previously hospitalized schizophrenics and their families. No longer viewing family dysfunction as a cause of schizophrenia in one of its members, and no longer thinking of therapeutic interventions as providing a "cure," therapists now focused on developing methods for treating and preventing acute psychotic episodes in the former patient and the subsequent need to return to the hospital. As Steinglass (1996, p. 1) notes,

> psychoeducational family therapy is now seen as a mandatory component (along with psychopharmacology) of the state-of-the-art treatment of the major psychoses.

One noteworthy example of such educationally based interventions, developed by psychologist Carol Anderson and her colleagues at the Western Psychiatric Institute in Pittsburgh (Anderson, Reiss, & Hogarty, 1986), offers a collaborative undertaking between therapist and family, directed at reducing not only some of the anguish associated with living together as a family with a schizophrenic member but also the high frequency of relapse in previously hospitalized schizophrenic patients after returning home to their families. As these authors eloquently observe in the preface of their influential book:

> We have blamed each other, the patients themselves, their parents and grandparents, public authorities, and society for the cause and for the terrible course of these disorders. When hope and money become exhausted, we frequently tear schizophrenic patients from their families, consigning them to the existential terror of human warehouses, single room occupancy hotels, and more recently to the streets and alleys of American cities. (p. vii)

Among the experiences of Anderson, Reiss, and Hogarty (1986), ultimately leading to their adoption of the psychoeducational approach, was the initial observation that recovering hospitalized schizophrenics frequently relapsed when released to the custody of their families. Was the family at fault? Did the patient stop taking prescribed medication? Did they all need family therapy exploring underlying toxic family dynamics? These researchers discovered that existing interventions intended to head off relapse, including traditional forms of family therapy, failed to stave off rehospitalization in most cases. More to the point, they found that the customary therapeutic search for causes within family life only aroused guilt and defensiveness, and sometimes resulted in failure—or worse, relapse—as the therapist tried to change family dynamics. Moreover, they contended that the encouragement of highly charged emotional exchanges sometimes sought by family therapists may actually be anti-therapeutic in the case of schizophrenia. Instead of the customary focus on the family's effect on the schizophrenic, they proposed a turnaround—attending to the impact of the schizophrenic on family life.

Without blaming the family—or in general looking for a culprit somewhere in society who must surely be at fault—these therapists went about the practical business of helping all family members, including the schizophrenic, overcome obstacles to family functioning. Thus, instead of searching for the source of the symptoms and the disability by ferreting out causal transactional patterns within the family, they favored a more matter-of-fact approach, teaching coping skills to families who must attend daily to "the devastating impact of watching one's child deteriorate into someone who is all but a stranger, and a most incapacitated one" (McFarlane, 1991, p. 364). Instead of being held accountable for the illness, families were recognized as having experienced severe stress that left them feeling depleted and susceptible to dysfunctional behavior patterns. Instead of exploring and uncovering damaging family interactive patterns (which in many cases may indeed exist), families were now given support as they learned new empowering techniques to mitigate stress and strain and to reduce the likelihood of relapse.

Research results (Anderson, Reiss, & Hogarty, 1986) indicated that treatment combining family therapy and social skills training was far more effective in staving off a psychotic relapse in the year following hospital discharge (0% relapse) than were family therapy alone (19% relapse), individual behavior therapy (20% relapse), or treatment involving chemotherapy and social support. Families, no longer held responsible for the schizophrenia, were nevertheless expected to be full partners with the patient in learning effective coping skills for dealing day in and day out with chronic mental illness.

The work done by the Pittsburgh team—Carol Anderson, Douglas Reiss, and Gerald Hogarty—along with similar efforts by other like-minded clinicians/researchers such as Michael Goldstein (1981) at UCLA, Ian Falloon (Falloon et al., 1985) at the University of Southern California, and David Miklowitz (Miklowitz & Goldstein, 1997) at the University of Colorado, are examples of family-focused programs that have emerged in response to briefer mental hospitalization in recent years for patients experiencing a major psychosis (schizophrenia or **bipolar disorder**). Because patients are often discharged while only in partial remission from their psychotic symptoms, they and their families must cope with problems connected with reentry into the community. The psychoeducational focus, then, is on the schizophrenic's impact on family functioning, not the other way around.

Psychoeducational programs, typically highly structured, were designed to fit the bill—to be a part of community-based care, to educate patients and their families regarding the disorder, its typical course, its prognosis, and its psychobiology. "Survival skills workshops" directly addressed everyday family concerns—how to set limits on the schizophrenic when other members are affected, assigning chores the schizophrenic member is able to perform, reducing unrealistic expectations—and were coordinated with maintenance medication, all aimed at forestalling relapse. One consequence of such cost-effective, community-based treatment was to place partially remitted patients in closer contact with their family members (Goldstein & Miklowitz, 1995). When successful, increased treatment compliance and decreased relapse rates were the results of the intervention.

Most therapists today believe family dysfunction is not the cause of schizophrenia. Instead, schizophrenia—which they view as a genetic and/or biological disease whose symptoms are best dealt with by using antipsychotic medication—may arise in well-functioning families as well as those that show a high degree of dysfunction. However, environmental factors within family life do play a role in schizophrenic *relapse rates*. Psychoeducation advocates maintain that helping family members gain knowledge of the disorder and learn specific coping skills is essential in supplementing medication. By combining antipsychotic drugs and psychoeducational interventions, they provide a therapeutic package aimed at reducing family stress and preventing symptomatic relapse in the schizophrenic member.

Families, relieved at not being blamed or shamed for the development of the disorder in one of their members, are apt to be more receptive to such integrated treatment programs, thus increasing the likelihood of improved treatment compliance.[2] Their willingness to collaborate with supportive therapists is increased if they become persuaded that these efforts will help them reduce the family's level of emotional intensity so that relapse in the schizophrenic might be delayed or reduced in severity.

Expressed Emotion and Schizophrenia

While the *causes* of schizophrenia remain incompletely understood, researchers have begun to make headway in linking family interaction to the *course* of the disorder. One promising area of research involves the investigation of stress in the schizophrenic's family environment, particularly the manner in which members express criticism and hostility and become emotionally overinvolved with one another. Studies of schizophrenics following release from the hospital, initially carried out by George Brown and his colleagues (Brown, Monck, Carstairs, & Wing, 1962; Brown, Birley, & Wing, 1972) at the Institute for Social Psychiatry in London, England, attended especially to the relationship between the degree to which intense emotion was expressed in the family and the likelihood of relapse. This contrasted with the then-prevalent view that relapse was due specifically to patients, unmonitored, discontinuing their medication once released from the hospital.

The emerging theory of **expressed emotion** (EE) suggested that schizophrenia is a thought disorder in which the individual is especially vulnerable to, as well as highly

---

[2]Not all families are so receptive, of course. Some reject these therapeutic efforts out of denial, or because they continue to believe any intervention publicly calls attention to the family as pathological. Some families do not wish to be together with other families with schizophrenic members, because they fear the social stigma it might bring to them.

responsive to, stress caused by the expression of intense, negative emotions. Researchers thus reasoned that perhaps affective factors might account for a patient's relapse as he or she tried, unsuccessfully, to process incoming communication. That is, when former patients returned home to a stressful family environment where EE was high—intrusive, emotionally intense exchanges, especially expressed in negative and hypercritical comments about the patient's overtly disturbed behavior—arousal in schizophrenics was more likely to occur, and symptoms soon followed as relapse took place. On the other hand, for patients returning to households manifesting low EE, while family members also tended to be concerned about the disturbed (and disturbing) behavior of the schizophrenic, these relatives were not overly anxious in their response to the patient's condition, allowing the individual more psychological space (Leff & Vaughn, 1985).

Expressed emotion is perhaps the most well-validated indicator for relapses of schizophrenia (Miklowitz, 1995). The value of reducing EE in helping families cope with schizophrenia has now been well documented by subsequent research (Atkinson & Coia, 1995). Lowering EE has also been linked to reduced relapse rates for various forms of depression and bipolar disorder (Mueser & Glynn, 1995). As Miklowitz (1995) observes:

> The family, then, is seen as a risk or protective factor that may augment or diminish the likelihood that underlying genetic and/or biological vulnerabilities in a family member will be expressed as symptoms of a mental disorder. (p. 194)

This line of investigation regarding family stress and patient biological vulnerability has stimulated much research aimed at developing operational aftercare programs to decrease relapse rates. Goldstein, Rodnick, Evans, May, and Steinberg (1978) combined a brief, structured, conflict-reducing, home-based aftercare program with efforts to ensure patient compliance in continuing medication. Falloon and associates (1985) devised an aftercare family management plan following behavioral principles, along with medication, and aimed not at cure but at decreasing negative affect; the plan correspondingly decreased the probability of relapse by increasing patient social functioning. Anderson, Reiss, and Hogarty (1986) experimented with a program in which a psychoeducational effort directed at the family supplements (but does not replace) drug therapy for the schizophrenic family member.

Unlike earlier family therapists who worked with schizophrenics, Anderson and her colleagues were not so much interested in "fixing" a dysfunctional system, probing ever deeper into family dynamics, as they were in creating a nonjudgmental learning environment in which families could improve their skills in understanding and coping with a disturbed family member.

The Therapeutic Process

Family psychoeducation efforts follow one of two formats—working with individual families (Anderson, Reiss, & Hogarty, 1986), or with multiple families simultaneously (McFarlane, 1991, 2002). In the former, Anderson and her colleagues describe a set of phased interventions (often resembling structural family therapy), beginning with engaging the family, typically when an acute schizophrenic decompensation has occurred. Gaining the family's cooperation, the team sets up psychoeducational programs—typically a day-long Survival Skills Workshop—during which they teach family members about the prevalence and course of mental illness, its biological etiology, current modes of pharmacological and psychosocial treatment, common medications, and prognosis. Patient and family needs are discussed, and family coping skills strategized. EE findings are likely to be aired here, and efforts made to provide basic behavioral guidelines for keeping EE in check, taking pressure off the patient to hurry up and behave in a normal manner. Because schizophrenics are usually sensitive to overstimulation, families are urged to respect boundaries, allowing schizophrenics to withdraw whenever necessary. This respect for individual boundaries is supplemented later by the reinforcing of generational boundaries, as parents are urged to form a stronger bond with one another and together remain in charge rather than letting all family decisions be controlled by the patient's needs.

During the subsequent reentry period into the social environment, regularly scheduled outpatient sessions (usually weekly), which may go on for a year or more, are aimed at achieving stability outside of the hospital. Patients may be assigned small tasks and their progress monitored. The therapy team typically uses this period to shift attention to the family structure, which may have changed because of accommodating to the patient's return from the hospital. The team uses the final rehabilitation phase to consolidate gains and raise the patient's level of functioning. As noted earlier, the emphasis by Anderson and her associates on boundaries, hierarchy, and maintaining the integrity of subsystems reflects the influences of structural family therapy.

McFarlane's (1991) multifamily version owes its heritage to multiple family therapy, an early effort (Laqueur, 1976) to treat several families of hospitalized schizophrenic patients together. Originally designed to bring families together in order to solve ward management problems, multiple family therapy also provided social support for families with similar problems who otherwise would have felt isolated. In its psychoeducational reincarnation, informal multiple family therapy lecture-and-discussion educational workshops are held with relatives; typically, groups of five or six families attend. The families meet again with patients and therapist in subsequent sessions for at least 12 months. The multiple-family setting is believed by McFarlane to offer increased social support. Box 16.1 presents a typical set of guidelines offered by psychoeducators for managing rehabilitation following a schizophrenic episode. (It also represents good advice for any family following a period of trauma.)

Psychoeducational interventions set limited goals; symptoms are reduced rather than cured. They nevertheless provide a quiet, sound, stabilizing milieu in which family members do not feel criticized or blamed, and where they can begin to learn coping techniques for the difficult and probably long-term task of living with a schizophrenic person and preventing (or delaying) his or her relapse and rehospitalization.

Overall, Goldstein and Miklowitz's (1995) careful review of the effectiveness of psychoeducational interventions with schizophrenics found it superior to routine care involving medication and crisis intervention as needed. Such intervention at the family level was more effective than individual supportive or skills-oriented therapies, as measured by delayed relapses (over two years in some studies cited), and improved social functioning.

BOX 16.1 CLINICAL NOTE

Psychoeducational Guidelines for Families and Friends of Schizophrenics

Here is a list of things everyone can do to make things run more smoothly:

1. *Go slow.* Recovery takes time. Rest is important. Things will get better in their own time.
2. *Keep it cool.* Enthusiasm is normal. Tone it down. Disagreement is normal. Tone it down, too.
3. *Give 'em space.* Time out is important for everyone. It's okay to offer. It's okay to refuse.
4. *Set limits.* Everyone needs to know what the rules are. A few good rules keep things calmer.
5. *Ignore what you can't change.* Let some things slide. Don't ignore violence or use of street drugs.
6. *Keep it simple.* Say what you have to say clearly, calmly, and positively.
7. *Follow doctor's orders.* Take medications as they are prescribed. Take only medications that are prescribed.
8. *Carry on business as usual.* Reestablish family routines as quickly as possible. Stay in touch with family and friends.
9. *No street drugs or alcohol.* They make symptoms worse.
10. *Pick up on early signs.* Note changes. Consult with your family clinician.
11. *Solve problems step by step.* Make changes gradually. Work on one thing at a time.
12. *Lower expectations, temporarily.* Use a personal yardstick. Compare this month with last month rather than last year with next year.

Source: McFarlane, 1991, p. 375

MEDICAL FAMILY THERAPY

The most effective way to prevent relapse in schizophrenics, as we have just pointed out, appears to be implementing a combined regimen of antipsychotic medication and psychoeducation. If we consider schizophrenia as a chronic disorder, then this medical/psychological set of interventions qualifies as medical family therapy, defined as a coordinated effort by an interdisciplinary team to treat a chronic medical illness, trauma, or disability. In general, the aim here is not so much to achieve a "cure" as to help families to cope better with a chronic illness, engage in less conflict over managing medication, communicate better with medical providers, accept a medical problem that cannot be cured, or perhaps make constructive lifestyle changes (McDaniel, Hepworth, & Doherty, 1995).

This model for family therapy tries to deal with the complex interface between family relationships and family health. It replaces the traditional medical model that focuses exclusively on a sick individual receiving care to one in which the family becomes the cornerstone of the caregiving system, and its ability to cope and adapt are based on family system strengths. From this fresh perspective, psychosocial factors in addition to biological interventions play an important role in healing (Rolland, 2003). A journal devoted to medical family therapy has existed since 1983, first called *Family Systems Medicine*, and more recently renamed *Families, Systems, and Health* to reflect a broader healthcare outlook.

Common Family Adaptations to Chronic Illness

1. *A change in family roles.* Ill person can no longer fulfill old roles (child care, domestic tasks), and family caregivers must increase time devoted to sick person.

2. *Caregivers stressed and overburdened.* Assistance may not be available, and caregivers may feel guilty about their feelings.

3. *Financial hardship.* Ill person's decrease or loss of earning power, particularly if main breadwinner at height of earning potential.

4. *Accommodations to treatment regimen.* From simple dietary changes to time-consuming trips to doctor and hospital, engaged in willingly or resentfully.

5. *Communication regarding illness.* Differing ideas about what and how much to reveal to patient or others, shame if illness the possible result of AIDS or chronic mental illness.

6. *Coping with multiple losses.* Loss of functioning, loss of intimacy with ill person, anticipated death of loved one.

Source: Adapted from Ruddy & McDaniel (2003)

Advocates of this view believe that the family serves as the primary social context for healthcare and, correspondingly, what goes on within the family inevitably influences a family member's medical condition. Simultaneously, medical family therapy has begun to be enthusiastically embraced by the broader field of family therapy. A review of research into the effectiveness of family interventions in the treatment of physical illness offers support for the role of medical family therapy in today's healthcare system (Campbell & Patterson, 1995).

Leading Figures

Medical family therapy attempts to treat illness first by recognizing that it occurs simultaneously at several systemic levels—biological, psychological, social, and interpersonal—and then by planning interventions targeting these levels. George Engel (1977), an internist at the University of Rochester School of Medicine, is usually credited with having been the first to call for an integrated approach to medical problems that he designated the "biopsychosocial approach." Engel argued that the patient and the disease must be understood in context, that families must be involved in medical care, and that all systems must be considered equally. McDaniel, Harkness, and Epstein (2001) suggest that the emergence of this broad biopsychosocial view may be best understood as a reaction to the then-prevalent reductionistic, exclusively biological medical model for understanding medical problems and their alleviation.

In an effort to promote family-centered medical care, further linking family therapy and family medicine, William Doherty and MacAran Baird (Doherty & Baird, 1983, 1987), a psychologist and family physician, early on delineated five levels of physician engagement with families: (a) little if any involvement, (b) keeping family members informed of patient treatment, (c) offering support, (d) planning interventions, and (e) providing family therapy.

In 1992, psychologists Susan McDaniel in New York, Jeri Hepworth in Connecticut, and William Doherty in Minnesota, all having worked in primary care medical settings, coined the term *medical family therapy* to refer to the "biopsychosocial treatment of individuals and families who are dealing with medical problems" (McDaniel, Hepworth, & Doherty, 1992, p. 2). In particular, these authors called attention to the inevitable impact of medical illness not only on the personal life of the patient but also on the interpersonal life of the family. Combining the biopsychosocial and systems perspectives, their book was the first to describe new roles for family therapists in a variety of medical or other healthcare settings.

Other leading figures in this fast-growing area of family therapy include two psychiatrists who specialize in family medicine: John Rolland (1994), a founder of the Chicago Center for Family Health and developer of a Family Systems Health Model relating chronic and life-threatening disorders to couple and family functioning; and Thomas Campbell, in Rochester, New York, a former student of Engel's interested in collaborative work involving general systems theory and family healthcare (Campbell, 1986; Campbell & Patterson, 1995).

Psychosocial Factors and Individual Health

No biomedical event occurs without psychosocial consequences. Endorsing a psychosocial perspective for understanding a wide array of chronic disorders affecting individuals and families across their life spans, Rolland (1994) offers a useful model based on the systemic interaction of a family and illness that evolves over time. He contends that the goodness of "fit" between the psychosocial demands of the disorder (cancer, diabetes, heart disease, AIDS) and the family's customary style of functioning and their resources become the major determinants of how successfully they cope and adapt as a family. He highlights the significance of family belief systems (including those associated with gender, culture, and ethnicity) about illness. If the family's belief system is discrepant with the belief system of the health providers, they may reject treatment or not comply with medical/psychological recommendations and prescriptions.

Rolland's psychoeducational framework highlights the importance of examining the interaction between the illness or disability (its sudden or gradual onset, its severity, its unpredictable or steadily deteriorating course, its outcome) and the characteristics or qualities of the family (its life cycle stage, its resources or resiliencies, the role of the ill person in the family, the family's belief system about illness, and so on). All must be factored in if the therapist is to help the family gain understanding, reorganize, make decisions, and mobilize its resources to deal with the changes in the system that the illness has brought. Family support groups for chronically ill patients and their families are often valuable psychoeducational interventions tailored to a particular type of condition (e.g., leukemia), its course (e.g., progressive or relapsing), or perhaps timed to a critical phase of the disease's manifestations (Steinglass, 1998).

Collaborative Family Healthcare Coalition

Consistent with the work of Rolland and others, such as Cole and Reiss (1993), to understand the impact of illness on a specific family, family therapists, physicians, nurses, and other healthcare workers, primarily working in healthcare facilities, joined together in 1993 to discuss the rapidly changing healthcare delivery system, and together formed the Collaborative Family Healthcare Coalition (Bloch, 1994).

BOX 16.3 CLINICAL NOTE

Psychosocial Types of Illness

Moving beyond the standard disease classification based strictly on biological criteria, Rolland (1994, 2003) adds a psychosocial dimension, broadening the relationship between chronic illness and family functioning. In his "psychosocial typology of illness" he offers the following categories for considering how an illness impacts individuals and families across the life cycle.

Onset: Sudden and Acute (a stroke) or Gradual and Chronic (Alzheimer's Disease). The former calls for family mobilization of crisis management skills, the latter for long-term planning and role adjustments.

Course: Chronic illnesses may challenge the family in different ways: (1) by getting *progressively worse* (lung cancer), entailing continuing role changes, adaptations to new losses, and increased strain on family caregiving; (2) by *remaining constant* (heart attack) so that after initial recovery there are ongoing limitations in functioning and the family needs to make long-term adaptations to change; and (3) by *relapsing* or manifesting *episodic* illnesses (asthma) with alternating periods of freedom from symptoms and flare-ups, so that the family lives with uncertainty and transitions between crisis and non-crisis states.

Outcome: Fatal (metastasized cancer), non-fatal (flu), life-shortening (heart attack), imminent (inoperable brain tumor), or sudden death (hemophilia) are possible, and the family must learn to live with how disease will affect the individual's lifespan. Different family reactions represent different degrees of anticipatory grieving and loss to the family.

Incapacitation: Disability may involve impairment of cognition (Alzheimer's), of sensation (blindness), of movement (paralysis), disfigurement (mastectomy), or social stigma (AIDS) (Olkin, 1999). Family must adapt to loss of breadwinner income, role shifts, output of funds for assistance, social isolation from previous reference group.

Rolland's typology assembles onset, course, outcome, and incapacitation into a grid format (e.g., Emphysema—gradual onset, progressive course, incapacitating, fatal; Spinal Cord Injury—acute onset, remains constant, incapacitating, nonfatal). The course of some diseases is predictable (Alzheimer's) while others progress unevenly and have unpredictable courses (early Multiple Sclerosis). For the latter, future planning is likely to be hindered by anticipatory anxiety and ambiguity about the eventual outcome. Each phase of an illness poses its own psychosocial demands and developmental tasks, calling for significantly different strengths, attitudes, or changes from the family (Rolland, 2003).

Researchers, educators, administrators, healthcare policymakers, social workers, and consumer group representatives are also represented in this family-oriented effort, which now has regional chapters throughout the United States and Europe. The Coalition serves as a communication network, a clearinghouse disseminating information with the purpose of promoting a more coordinated, family-centered model of healthcare delivery integrating traditional medical/nursing care, psychosocial services, and the services of related healthcare providers. Patients, family, community, and providers of healthcare services are seen as parts of one ecosystem and as equal participants in the healthcare process. In contrast to conventional, compartmentalized, and often wasteful treatment methods that involve repeated diagnostic procedures and expensive referrals to specialists, the coalition seeks to help establish a collaborative, team-based family healthcare paradigm aimed at providing cost-effective, humane, and integrated patient and family services.

Courtesy of Susan McDaniel

Susan McDaniel, Ph.D.

Clinical collaboration between medical providers, family therapists, and other related health professionals is the cornerstone of this comprehensive approach for dealing with a variety of medical problems (McDaniel, 1995). Family therapists may serve as consultants, referral resources, or co-therapists with fellow healthcare professionals. Ideally, when family therapists, primary care physicians, nurses and nurse practitioners, rehabilitation specialists, and related professionals can work as a team, adopting a broad biopsychosocial systems perspective, they can benefit families attempting to cope with the impact on overall family life of chronic illness (diabetes, leukemia, cardiovascular disease), life-threatening conditions (AIDS, anorexia nervosa, infants born prematurely), or impairment and disability (spinal cord injury, blindness or deafness, dementia in the elderly) of one of their members. Family-level interventions for lifestyle changes (quitting smoking, losing weight, eating healthier diets) represent a relatively new area for such psychoeducational efforts to improve health and longevity.

Family Therapist–Physician Partnerships

Partnerships between therapist and physician, nurse, or rehabilitation specialist to achieve more comprehensive care call for accepting each other's language, therapeutic assumptions, and working styles,[3] which often are in conflict. Physicians are able to educate the therapist about the causes, likely course, and prognosis of a disease, while the therapist, acting as a consultant or co-therapist, can enlighten the physician and other caregivers about the patient's experience of illness, perhaps exploring how to minimize patient or family anxiety, help them accept the disease, and enable them to participate in their own healing (McDaniel, 1995). Family therapists might also help families examine their belief systems, including possible reasons for noncompliance with a prescribed medical regime. In other cases, overutilization of healthcare services by a family might be examined. An additional positive outcome from this collaboration is that therapists who are nonphysicians will not overlook some important biological aspect of a complex presenting problem. By the same token, in working with therapists or social workers, physicians are less apt to overlook the psychosocial levels of a problem or illness. The task of tending to a family's emotional needs, say after major surgery, often falls on the mental health person and leaves the surgeon free to care for the patient's biomedical needs.

Medical family therapists need a working knowledge of the major chronic illnesses and disabilities, as well as their emotional sequelae, along with familiarity with the healthcare system. Physicians need to understand and accept the help offered by the family therapist without feeling a loss of sovereignty over patient care. While battles over turf and professional competition often exist, working partnerships offering a holistic, ecosystemic approach to healthcare are increasing in frequency.

---

[3]The traditional medical style is to be action oriented, advice giving, and physician dominant, while mental healthcare is more process oriented, facilitative, and patient centered. Another obvious difference is the amount of time spent with a patient or family: most therapists spend 50–60 minutes, while physicians are likely to spend 10–20 minutes (McDaniel, 1995).

CLINICAL NOTE

Dealing with serious illnesses on a daily basis is often a lonely and stressful task for a therapist. Sharing the responsibility (and its satisfactions) with other professionals and with the family is often crucial in avoiding burnout.

Family Therapist–Family Partnerships

One goal of a successful therapist-physician collaboration is to strengthen the shaken family system, allowing its members to regain a sense of choice and power about impending medical decisions. Another is to reduce the emotional consequences to the family of an ongoing medical condition, in the process perhaps reducing the clinical course of the illness. Some serious disorders, such as AIDS, call for special therapeutic sensitivities. Individuals with this diagnosis may appropriately fear disclosure will stigmatize them and expose them to discrimination in employment, housing, insurance coverage, and even medical care by healthcare workers afraid of close contact with the disease. Working closely with physicians, therapists need to help patients deal with loss of independence, physical incapacity, rejection by a lover, and disclosure to family and others. The medical family therapist can be helpful to all concerned—the patient, the patient's partner, his family of origin—in coming to terms with this devastating disease (Macklin, 1989; Landau-Stanton, 1993).

SHORT-TERM EDUCATIONAL PROGRAMS

The psychoeducational approach has also been extended to couples or families without a symptomatic member who wish to acquire better skills or learn specific strategies for coping more effectively with their everyday relationship problems (marital conflicts, parent-adolescent conflicts). In other cases, some may wish to learn how best to prevent the occurrence of problems before they develop, say before an impending marriage, or perhaps upon remarriage where stepchildren are involved. Here the therapist, taking the contemporary view, is less the expert who diagnoses a problem and offers treatment, and more the facilitator who educates people in the skills they need to manage their current difficulties and head off future distress. Brief, practical, positive in tone and outlook, and cost-effective, this form of intervention, when successful, helps empower people to function more effectively within marriage, family, or work situations. The Coalition of Marriage, Couple, and Family Education was formed in 1996, testifying to the coming of age of this subspecialty within the field of marriage counseling. A number of practitioners are from the clergy, bringing with them a clearly articulated set of moral and spiritual beliefs.

Programs involving relationship enhancement, preparation for marriage or childbirth, marriage enrichment, and parent effectiveness training are all examples of these psychoeducational efforts, as are the behavioral parent skills training procedures we described in Chapter 13. Their objectives, depending upon the needs of client families, range from ameliorating an identified problem to enhancing existing skills in

One or both clients may come to premarital counseling with a vague sense of unease about their future together. While such apprehension is common, in some cases it opens for discussion previously overlooked or denied potential sources of conflict (in-laws, money, career conflicts, children) that, if not explored and resolved, can lead to distress later in their marriage.

order to further improve the quality of family life (Levant, 1986). Here the therapist joins the family and identifies client strengths and growth potential along with potential problem areas. Unlike family therapy, however, the therapist's goal in this situation is to deliver educational training and not psychotherapy. Moreover, both the therapist and family share a vision of the educational goals and specific objectives of skills to be acquired in advance of their engagement, and termination usually occurs when the content has been delivered or when a previously agreed-upon time frame has been completed (Fournier & Rae, 1999).

In the following sections, we group and offer a sampling of the many psychoeducational programs of interest to marriage and family therapists. Many are packaged as seminars, video or audio programs, or books written for the public. Among the most popular books are the behavioral-research-based *Marriage Survival Kit* (Gottman & Gottman, 1999), or solution-oriented therapist Michelle Weiner-Davis's 1992 *Divorce-Busting*. Videotaped training programs are also available, supplemented by phone coaching and supervision, making it feasible for non-professionals to provide psychoeducational services.

Relationship Enhancement Programs

Probably the best-known family skills training approach is the highly developed and researched Relationship Enhancement (RE) program created by Bernard Guerney, Jr. (1977) at Penn State (Calvedo & Guerney, 1999). Guerney, who had earlier been one of the authors of the breakthrough *Families of the Slums* (Minuchin, Montalvo, Guerney, Rosman, & Schumer, 1967), had also worked with Carl Rogers, and his client-centered orientation to therapy is evident in his interventions with families. Thus empathy, genuineness, positive regard for clients, and other Rogerian principles are recognizable in Guerney's work, as is his interest, seen in his work with Minuchin, in developing techniques for helping troubled family relationships. Barry Ginsberg, a student of both Bernard and Louise Guerney, husband and wife colleagues, has recently described the contemporary practices of the RE approach as combining psychodynamic, behavioral, communication, and experiential systems perspectives (Ginsberg, 1997, 2000).

The Guerneys' early psychoeducational endeavors go back to the *filial therapy* program they developed during the 1960s (Guerney, 1964; Guerney, Guerney, & Andronico, 1966) to help parents deal better with their young, emotionally disturbed children. In this therapeutic undertaking, usually conducted in groups of six to eight parents, the Guerneys explained how Rogerian principles applied to parent-child relationships and instructed parents in the use of the technique to develop structuring, acknowledging, and limit-setting skills. Weekly play therapy sessions at home augmented the process. In general, the technique was devised to help children with emotional, behavioral, or developmental problems to better understand and communicate their feelings and gain a sense of mastery over their actions. At the same time, if the approach was successful, parents developed more realistic expectations, became more receptive to the children's feelings and experiences, and learned to communicate their new understanding and acceptance. This RE approach later was supplemented by the Parent-Adolescent Relationship Development (PARD) program (Ginsberg, 1977; Guerney, Coufal, & Vogelsang, 1981) to foster trust, empathy, genuineness, intimacy, openness, and satisfaction in parent and adolescent relationships.

RE empathy-building programs provide couples with training in three sets of core skills, which together help couples or families become more emotionally engaged (Ginsberg, 2000):

- The *Expressive (Owning) Skill:* gaining awareness of one's own feelings, and taking responsibility for them without projecting them onto others, and asserting them
- The *Empathic Responding (Receptive) Skill:* learning to listen and gain an understanding of the other person's feelings and motives
- *The Conversive (Discussion-Negotiation/Engagement) Skill:* learning to listen and give back a sense of understanding the meaning of what was heard; partners may "switch" positions between "listener" and "speaker"

Two additional RE skills are *Generalization* and *Maintenance* (learning to practice and extend the aforementioned skills at home and in their everyday lives).

RE is an intensive, time-limited program usually involving ten sessions that may extend over several months. It is based on an educational model; therapists teach clients to recognize their problems more clearly and to understand how learning specific skills (how to improve their self-concept, how to recognize and express—or "own"—what they are feeling, how to accept each other's feelings, how to engage one another and negotiate and work through problems, how to achieve interpersonal satisfaction and become emotional partners) helps them deal with their ongoing lives and also with problems they may encounter in the future (Ginsberg, 2000). Attention to communication cues in themselves and in their partners helps enhance empathic communication abilities between participants. Both didactic presentations and skills practice take place in each session, and homework assignments (practicing, generalizing, and maintaining learned skills) are given to emphasize the client's responsibility for therapeutic success. The program requires people dedicated enough to work at mastering these skills during these sessions and to continue outside to carry out homework assignments.

The intent, according to Ginsberg (1997), is less to help people change than to help them create a context in which constructive change[4] is more likely to occur.

---

[4]Learning constructive relationship skills is consistent with Gottman's (1994) research-based view of the role of positive and negative emotional exchanges between couples and their effect, respectively, on marital happiness or unhappiness. As we described Gottman's results in Chapter 13, spouses who react with negative emotions—criticism, contempt, defensiveness, stonewalling—run a high risk of divorce.

TABLE 16.1   Educational Model Versus Medical Model

Educational Model	Medical Model
Emphasizes developmental processes, psychological needs, and life stresses.	Emphasizes sickness (maladaptation/pathology).
De-emphasizes insight and etiology.	Emphasizes insight and etiology.
Problem lies within individual's control.	Problem lies outside the individual's control.
Client agrees to learn from the practitioner (teacher).	Client depends on the expertise of the practitioner for change.
Best healing and change come from the client's own efforts.	Healing is dependent on the practitioner's skill.
Clients are encouraged to seek the knowledge and resources they need.	Generally, clients under the exclusive care of the provider.
Methods include setting goal(s), understanding rationale and methods of skill, skill practice and learning, generalizing the problems of everyday life, and maintaining skills.	Methods include diagnosis, treatment, and cure.
No distinction between prevention and amelioration.	Methods are skewed more toward treatment than prevention.

Source: Ginsberg, 1997, p. 3

Once the context is established, RE practitioners believe clients become more autonomous and ultimately able to become more intimate with other significant persons in their lives. With greater trust in their own ability to solve problems, they are in a better position to deal with possible future crises should they arise. Table 16.1 demonstrates the major differences between the educational model and that based on medical practice.

In addition to experiential elements (especially client-centered and emotionally focused therapies), RE offers cognitive instruction—critically examining one's thoughts, attitudes, and values—along with behavioral instruction—building skills for handling emotions or engaging in interpersonal relationships. The practitioner's values are explicitly stated, and the client-therapist relationship is one of shared planning and decision making. Regardless of the specific population RE addresses, its signature techniques involve not only empathy, nonjudgmental acceptance, and fostering genuine conversations between clients but also teaching clients to recognize and acknowledge feelings and to express them openly and honestly.

RE programs operate around the country and are extremely popular, especially for premarital couples, both distressed and non-distressed married couples, and parents and their adolescent children. Research demonstrating their effectiveness in skills-building with a variety of clinical populations (enhanced communication reported by participants; greater ability to resolve conflict together; a general improvement in the relationship, especially a greater sense of trust and intimacy) has been encouraging (Giblin, Sprenkle, & Sheehan, 1985; Accordino & Guerney, 2001). Still needed, however, are more long-term follow-ups extending over several years.

Marriage Preparation Programs

In an effort to produce a useful and empirically supported method for evaluating a couple's preparation for marriage, David Olson and his colleagues (Olson, Fournier, & Druckman, 1986) developed and refined the aptly titled PREPARE (PREmarital Personal And Relationship Evaluation) Inventory. This well-researched and reliable 165-item premarital program (including 30 background and demographic questions), filled out separately by each person, is designed to aid premarital couples to better understand and discuss their families of origin with one another and to begin to identify areas where they experience differences in outlook. All of this represents an effort to initiate the process of reconciling such differences if they are to develop a harmonious relationship.

Computer scored and standardized on national norms, results are presented in graphic profile form on a Couple and Family Map, supplying information to the couple regarding their "relationship strengths" and "growth areas" where further work is necessary. Eleven content areas are explored by the couple together with the premarital counselor:

Marriage expectations (what each expects regarding love, commitment, how to deal with conflict),

Communication (the degree of comfort each feels about sharing emotions, listening, and being listened to),

Sexual relationship (feelings and concerns regarding affection, sexual behavior, family planning),

Personality differences,

Financial management,

Attitudes regarding *conflict resolution* and *child rearing,*

Preferences for how to spend *leisure* time,

Expectations about the amount of time spent with *family and friends,*

Attitudes regarding *marital roles,*

Spiritual beliefs.

PREPARE is especially useful for its early identification of potential conflict areas and for promoting couple dialogue likely to be beneficial in their future together (Stahmann & Hiebert, 1997). Psychoeducational efforts to help premarital couples begin to work at resolving key differences frequently are carried out using a companion Ten Steps for Conflict Resolution program (Olson, 1987). According to Olson (1997), over one million couples have taken the PREPARE Inventory (or its companion ENRICH Inventory for married couples) and there now are over 50,000 PREPARE/ENRICH counselors worldwide.

CLINICAL NOTE

Therapists need to pay special attention to the referral source in premarital cases. Does the couple's church require it? Did the rabbi suggest it? Were they referred by a friend who had gone through the experience prior to marriage? Or did one or the other member of the couple suggest it out of doubts about some aspects of their forthcoming marriage?

Marital Enrichment Programs

The Preventive Intervention and Relationship Enhancement Program (PREP), developed by Floyd, Markman, Kelly, Blumberg, and Stanley (1995), represents a carefully designed attempt to help married couples improve their relationship before problems possibly set in and lead to relational deterioration and ultimately heightened conflict and the risk of divorce. Originally developed in the early 1980s to help young couples planning marriage, this *social learning approach,* melding behavior therapy, relationship enhancement, and communication skills instruction, is based on the premise that

> marital satisfaction results from the exchange of rewarding behaviors between spouses, paired with the ability to resolve conflicts in a mutually satisfying way, without resorting either to escalation of negative affect and aggression, or withdrawal and avoidance. (p. 213)

Couples are taught constructive communication and conflict resolution skills, along with realistic attitudes and expectations about marriage. In particular, they learn to develop behavioral interactive patterns that satisfy the emotional and psychological needs of each partner. Overall, the thrust is future-oriented; couples learn to resolve disputes effectively and in a timely manner so that avoidant patterns do not build up, making conflict resolution that much more difficult in the future.

PREP sessions come in two formats (Floyd, Markman, Kelly, Blumberg, & Stanley, 1995): (a) an extended version, in which groups of 4 to 10 couples attend a series of weekly lectures on skills or relationship issues, followed by exercises to learn the discussed skills; and (b) a marathon version, in which 20 to 60 couples at a time hear the lectures in a group setting over the course of a weekend. In the first version, each couple is assigned a communication consultant, who acts as a coach as the couple practices skills acquisition, providing them with feedback to facilitate the learning process. Homework assignments and readings are part of the therapeutic package. In the second version, often held at a hotel, couples practice skills on their own in their rooms. PREP also supplies videotapes and audiotapes for further study. Positive steps to preserve a marriage, based on ongoing research, have been described by Markman, Stanley, and Blumberg (1994). Typical topics of focus include conflict management, communication enhancement, and forgiveness, as well as considerations of religious beliefs and practices, fun and friendship desires, and how best to enhance and maintain commitment (Silliman, Stanley, Coffin, Markman, & Jordan, 2002).

Howard Markman, at the Center for Marital and Family Studies at the University of Denver, is a particularly well-known behavioral researcher who studies marital distress and its prevention (Markman, Renick, Floyd, Stanley, & Clements, 1993). Outcome results of the PREP program developed by Markman and his group have been extensively researched and are encouraging (Stanley, Blumberg, & Markman, 1999). Not surprisingly, short-term gains in relationship satisfaction (measured immediately after the intervention) involving improved communication, sexual satisfaction, and lower problem intensity are especially promising. Long-term follow-ups, up to four years after intervention, generally show sustained benefits as couples undergoing the program continued to rate the impact of their communication behaviors positively. Compared to both a matched control group and a group that declined participation, these couples showed significantly clear group differences in avoiding negative communication patterns (withdrawal, denial, dominance, negative affect), according to Silliman, Stanley, Coffin, Markman, and Jordan (2002).

Marriage Encounter

Less carefully researched, but popular and widespread, is *marriage encounter*—a worldwide weekend retreat enrichment program for couples, frequently sponsored by church groups—directed at raising couple awareness of communication, problem solving, sexual intimacy, and spiritual issues in an effort to prevent marriage complacency or, worse, deterioration. In some cases, such programs appeal to couples who have a satisfactory relationship but wish to make improvements, or those who wish to examine and reaffirm their relationship.

Marriage encounter programs first appeared in Barcelona, Spain, in the early 1960s; they were developed by a Jesuit priest, Father Gabriel Calvo. He originally conceived of arranging weekend retreats to provide support and enrichment for Catholic married couples (Chartier, 1986). Introduced into the United States in 1966, similar religiously oriented programs have been adopted by Protestant and Jewish groups to meet the needs of their members. In addition to couples in long-standing marriages, premarital and remarried couples have also found the experience enlightening and beneficial (Stahmann & Hiebert, 1997). Some denominations require engaged couples to participate in such a program before they can be married in church.

In addition to these religiously based efforts, certain nonreligious, skills training programs, such as Couples Communication (CC) program—originally Minnesota Couple Communication Program—have become popular skills-training programs. The well-researched, skills-focused CC program, intended to appeal to married and premarried couples, is educationally focused rather than remedial, helping participants with satisfactory communication skills (self-awareness, self-disclosure, effective listening, and so on) enhance these skills still further. As in the case with the PREP program described earlier, emphasis is on the couple or dyad, although the group context is believed to facilitate learning. A well-established program (Wampler, 1990), CC usually involves 8 to 12 hours of structured skills training. Results measured by improved communication have been promising, although there is a reported diminution in the quality of communication over time.

Educational programs sponsored by the Association for Couples in Marital Enrichment, an international nonsectarian organization headquartered in Winston-Salem, North Carolina, offer marriage encounter discussions generally led by lay married couples who have successfully been through the program and received some additional leadership training (Doherty, Lester, & Leigh, 1986). Didactic material is kept to a minimum; the major emphasis is on skills building through partner dialogue. Leaders share their personal experiences rather than lecture or advise. Outcome studies, especially of a long-term nature, are inconclusive at this point.

By the end of the 1980s, according to Lasswell and Lasswell (1991), as many as a million people had participated in weekend encounter workshops for married couples and those engaged to be married. (That figure undoubtedly increased greatly in the following decade.) These authors suggest that based on limited studies, marriage encounter can be a valuable experience for couples in good marriages who want to make them better, but it is not designed for couples who have serious problems; such marriages run the risk of further deterioration.

Stepfamily Preparation Programs

Stepfamilies are an increasingly widespread phenomenon; close to half of all new marriages today involve a remarriage of one partner, and one in four a remarriage for both

(Saxton, 1996). Of the more than 11 million remarried households in the United States (Bray, 1995b), most include minor children living in a stepfamily household (Ganong & Coleman, 1999). Inevitably, living through a series of disruptive transitions—from intact family to single parenthood to remarried family—generates a series of structural and relationship shifts and role changes requiring in some cases major adaptations and reorganizations for parents and children alike (Goldenberg & Goldenberg, 2002).

Successful adaptation to stepfamily life calls for the ability to recognize and cope with a variety of problems: stepparents assuming a parental role, rule changes, jealousy and competition between stepsiblings as well as between birth parents and stepparents, loyalty conflicts in children between the absent parent and the stepparent, and financial obligations for child support while entering into a new marriage, to name but a few. Remarriage itself may resurrect old, unresolved feelings, such as anger and hurt left over from a previous marriage.

Children and adults alike come with expectations from previous families, and a major task for most stepfamilies is coming to terms with these differences. Stepfamilies must deal with losses and changes, must negotiate different developmental needs of their members, must create a parental coalition, and must establish new traditions of their own (Visher & Visher, 1988, 1996). Parenting and stepparenting are particularly stressful aspects in most stepfamilies, both during the early years of remarriage and in stepfamilies of longer duration (Bray, 1995b).

Despite the frequency and magnitude of these problems, with few exceptions (Visher & Visher, 1996) there is typically little guidance available from mental health professionals to help families become a more cohesive system and achieve stepfamily integration. For all families, "instant intimacy" is impossible; time is needed for negotiating values and beliefs, for distributing and trying out new roles, and for strengthening the parental bond.

Psychoeducational programs designed to help family members understand common stepfamily relationship patterns, and especially their differences from life in intact families, are frequently effective ways to cement a compatible and united stepfamily life. Knowing that other families are dealing with the same issues is often comforting. For example, Michaels (2000) has described a pilot stepfamily enrichment program aimed at early intervention for recently formed stepfamilies. Working with groups of such families, she uses didactic presentations, group discussions, and experiential exercises to familiarize them with stepfamily life. Her goal is to normalize the stepfamily experience, strengthen the marital bond, and help nurture both the step- and biological parent-child relationship, making certain that the newly formed family makes a place for the noncustodial biological parent.

One important resource to which stepfamilies can turn is the Stepfamily Association of America (headquartered in Lincoln, Nebraska), founded by stepparents Emily Visher and John Visher—a psychologist and a psychiatrist. The Vishers have been at the forefront of psychoeducational efforts to offer informational programs in stepfamily living.

Visher and Visher (1986) developed a stepfamily workbook manual (an excerpt of which appears in Box 16.4) as an aid in group discussions aimed at accomplishing those tasks that lead to restructured stepfamily systems. The Stepfamily Foundation provides a variety of educational programs (training for professionals, referral to

BOX 16.4 CLINICAL NOTE

Tasks That Must Be Completed to Develop a Stepfamily Identity

1. Dealing with losses and changes
2. Negotiating different developmental needs
3. Establishing new traditions
4. Developing a solid couple bond
5. Forming new relationships
6. Creating a "parenting coalition"
7. Accepting continual shifts in household composition
8. Risking involvement despite little societal support

1. Dealing with losses and changes
— Identify/recognize losses for all individuals
— Support expressions of sadness
— Help children talk and not act out feelings
— Read stepfamily books
— Make changes gradually
— See that everyone gets a turn
— Inform children of plans involving them
— Accept the insecurity of change

2. Negotiating different developmental needs
— Take a child development and/or parenting class
— Accept validity of the different life-cycle phases
— Communicate individual needs clearly
— Negotiate incompatible needs
— Develop tolerance and flexibility

3. Establishing new traditions
— Recognize ways are different, not right or wrong
— Concentrate on important situations only
— Stepparents take on discipline enforcement slowly
— Use family meetings for problem solving and giving appreciation
— Shift "givens" slowly whenever possible
— Retain/combine appropriate rituals
— Enrich with new creative traditions

4. Developing a solid couple bond
— Accept couple as primary long-term relationship
— Nourish couple relationship
— Plan for couple "alone time"
— Decide general household rules as a couple
— Support one another with the children

— Expect and accept different parent-child and stepparent-stepchild feelings
— Work out money matters together

5. Forming new relationships
— Fill in past histories
— Make stepparent-stepchild one-to-one time
— Make parent-child one-to-one time
— Parents make space for stepparent-stepchild relationship
— Do not expect instant love and adjustment
— Be fair to stepchildren even when caring not developed
— Follow children's lead in what to call stepparent
— Do fun things together

6. Creating a "parenting coalition"
— Deal directly with parenting adults in other household
— Keep children out of the middle of parental disagreements
— Do not talk negatively about adults in other household
— Control what you can and accept limitations
— Avoid power struggles between households
— Respect parenting skills of former spouse
— Contribute own "specialness" to children
— Communicate between households in most effective manner

7. Accepting continual shifts in household composition
— Allow children to enjoy their households
— Give children time to adjust to household transitions
— Avoid asking children to be messengers or spies
— Consider teenager's serious desire to change residence
— Respect privacy (boundaries) of all households
— Set consequences that affect own household only
— Provide personal place for nonresident children
— Plan special times for various household constellations

(continued)

8. **Risking involvement despite little societal support**
   — Include stepparents in school, religious, sports activities
   — Give legal permission for stepparent to act when necessary
   — Continue stepparent-stepchild relationships

after death or divorce of parent when caring has developed
   — Stepparent includes self in stepchild's activities
   — Find groups supportive of stepfamilies
   — Remember that all relationships involve risk

Source: Visher & Visher, 1986

therapists who work with families) and offers a network of mutual help services (survival courses in stepfamily living). In addition, as an advocacy group, it seeks to change attitudes toward stepfamilies through media coverage of pertinent stepfamily issues.

SUMMARY

Psychoeducational therapy approaches have directed their efforts primarily at reducing the stress on families by educating them so that they might develop better coping skills for dealing with a disturbed family member or a troubled family relationship. In some cases, information and education are offered to prevent conflict or to teach specific skills for managing everyday, nonclinical situations. Typically, psychoeducational programs involve a combination of systems theory, cognitive behavior therapy, and educational psychology.

Psychoeducational efforts are most prominent in working with families where there is a member with a severe mental disorder, such as schizophrenia or bipolar disorder. Viewing such problems as occurring in a biologically vulnerable person, therapists with a psychoeducational viewpoint adopt a nonblaming stance and do not presuppose a dysfunctional family responsible for the disorder. Instead, they direct their therapeutic efforts at offering support and teaching empowering coping skills. Typically they offer guidelines aimed at reducing obstacles to harmonious family living and decreasing the likelihood of symptomatic relapse. Schizophrenia is viewed as a biological disease best treated with medication in combination with educational workshops in which families learn to reduce the level of expressed emotion in their households.

Medical family therapy utilizes the collaboration of an interdisciplinary team in dealing with patients with various illnesses, traumas, or disabilities. Their biopsychosocial undertakings are designed to help families better cope with problems associated with the illness, have less conflict over managing medication, communicate better with medical providers, and in some cases make constructive lifestyle changes to prevent disease and prolong health. Family therapists may serve in a psychoeducational capacity, as consultants, referral resources, or co-therapists with fellow healthcare providers. The Collaborative Family Healthcare Coalition represents a cooperative effort by healthcare providers from various disciplines to promote a coordinated, family-centered approach to offering comprehensive medical/psychological services.

Short-term educational programs are psychoeducational endeavors designed to help families who wish to acquire better coping skills for managing everyday relationships more effectively, or preventing the occurrence of problems before they develop. Brief, practical, and cost-effective, these programs may involve a wide variety of potential educational areas, including relationship enhancement, marriage preparation, marriage enrichment, parent effectiveness training, and stepparenting preparation.

RECOMMENDED READINGS

Anderson, C. M., Reiss, D., & Hogarty, B. (1986). *Schizophrenia and the family: A practitioner's guide to psychoeducation and management.* New York: Guilford Press.

Markman, H. J., Stanley, S. M., & Blumberg, S. L. (1994). *Fighting for your marriage: Positive steps for preventing divorce and preserving a lasting love.* San Francisco: Jossey-Bass.

McDaniel, S. H., Hepworth, J., & Doherty, W. J. (1992). *Medical family therapy: A biopsychosocial approach to families with health problems.* New York: Basic Books.

McFarlane, W. R. (2002). *Multifamily groups in the treatment of severe psychiatric disorders.* New York: Guilford Press.

Rolland, J. S. (1994). *Families, illness, and disability: An integrated treatment model.* New York: Basic Books.

CHAPTER

RESEARCH ON FAMILY ASSESSMENT AND THERAPEUTIC OUTCOMES

While research in couple and family therapy has provided the fertile soil for the blossoming of the field in the last five decades, it is only within the last twenty years that serious efforts have been directed at identifying and delineating assessment techniques and therapeutic interventions that can be empirically validated by outcome studies. Early clinician/researchers such as Lyman Wynne (1983) recall that working with families in the 1950s was regarded primarily as a research idea; the notion of seeing family members together for therapeutic purposes came later and followed from research discoveries and subsequent theorizing. Wynne recollects that the therapy offered to families in those early years was distinctly intended to facilitate the maintenance of contact with research families. Haley (1978), too, looks back on that decade as a time when it "was taken for granted that a therapist and a researcher were of the same species (although the therapist had a more second-class status)" (p. 73). As the field evolved, however, practice took center stage, and many practitioners viewed research studies, often seen as dealing with obscure research issues, as having little if any relevance to their therapeutic efforts.

That situation has now begun to change, as researchers have developed practice-relevant, innovative procedures and diverse methodologies for measuring family functioning and the effectiveness of clinical interventions (Sprenkle & Piercy, 2005). Although there has been no shortage of measurement tools for couples and families—they are said to number well over 1000—researchers today are paying closer attention to issues of reliability and validity and are utilizing a variety of self-report and observational techniques tailored to family interaction (Snyder, Cozzi, & Mangrum, 2002). In addition, they are broadening their outlook beyond the family system itself, paying attention to larger systems of social influence: peers, schools, community and neighborhood influences (Liddle, Bray, Levant, & Santisteban, 2002). Science, in the form of an empirically based set of research investigations, has begun to be better integrated with the delivery of clinical services by many practitioners.

The pioneer family therapists, based on their experiences in working therapeutically with families, generated a multitude of new and exciting clinical techniques, in most cases without benefit of research support. In a rush to create new therapeutic procedures with families, many of their early followers, interested in furthering their clinical skills, tended to dismiss most published research papers as irrelevant to their

real-world needs and interests. For their part, most researchers believed family therapists too readily adopted newly minted therapeutic techniques despite lack of backup
support from randomized, controlled clinical trials testing their effectiveness.

In part a response to pressure from managed care insurance third-party payors to
provide validated treatments, in part the result of increased funding by government
agencies (such as the National Institute of Mental Health and the National Institute of
Drug Abuse), family-focused research expanded in the 1990s. Such efforts brought a dramatic increase in real-world (rather than university laboratory) studies of couples and
families—meaningful to practitioners—particularly in developing empirically based
intervention techniques for treating marital and family problems (Liddle, Bray, Levant, &

© Wadsworth/Thomson Learning

Lyman Wynne, M.D., Ph.D.

Santisteban, 2002). Innovative clinical research strategies and conceptual
frameworks were suggested (Kazdin, 1998), introducing sophisticated
methodologies and valid measures to study complex family interaction—
long an impediment to undertaking meaningful research with families.
Such a breakthrough is especially important when dealing with systems
theories that are inherently nonlinear and circular, emphasize the continuous nature of relationships, and stress the mutual influence of various
aspects of the system (Bray, 1995a).

Twenty-first-century family researchers direct their efforts at a variety of content areas (marital problems, alcohol and drug abuse, physical and mental illness, to name a few) and diverse family structures
(single-parent families, stepfamilies, gay and lesbian families). Today's
approach is to look at the multiple systems of which each family is a
part, and the social, cultural, and community influences that affect our
everyday functioning. To be meaningful, these projects need to include
a more varied population base than the White middle-class subjects of
earlier research efforts. While quantitative methodologies are more
likely to be funded and to find their way into professional journals, there
nevertheless is an important place for qualitative research that is apt to
be more an exploration and less an attempt to test already formulated hypotheses.
Closing the gap between family therapy practice and research can be accomplished to
the extent that quantitative methodologies and qualitative research coalesce (Pinsof
& Wynne, 2000).

QUALITATIVE AND QUANTITATIVE RESEARCH METHODOLOGIES

One encouraging development has been the growing interest in developing research
techniques dedicated to the unique methodological issues of family therapy research
(Sprenkle & Piercy, 2005). Particularly significant has been a greater willingness by
researchers to engage in *qualitative research* in addition to the more customary *quantitative research* methodology, reflecting a greater overall interest in applying qualitative research methods to the social sciences in recent years (Kopala & Suzuki, 1998;
Denzin & Lincoln, 2000). In drawing the distinction, Silverstein and Auerbach (2005)
suggest that qualitative research is *hypothesis-generating,* while quantitative research is
likely to be *hypothesis-testing.* Both are now seen as complementary forms of inquiry
rather than competing paradigms or methodologies.

Most scientific disciplines rely on quantification—observing phenomena, formulating a theory to account for what is being observed, generating hypotheses or predictions

to test that theory experimentally, controlling variables, recording and statistically analyzing resulting data; if the predicted observation is verified, the hypothesis is strengthened because the results were correctly deduced, and support is obtained for the theory from which the hypothesis was derived. Quantitative research, then, calls for the careful integration of experimental design, reliable and valid measurement, and relevant statistical analyses in order to isolate what is being studied (Black, 1999).

Despite the well-established place of modernist quantitative research in psychology, however, critics contend that it may be premature to rely exclusively on this method in the area of family therapy, especially when such a multitude of interacting variables are involved in understanding family processes. Rather than polarize the field into quantitative versus qualitative methodologies, researchers today increasingly are adopting the viewpoint that the two can coexist and meet the current need for greater methodological diversification.[1] Qualitative research methods (Willig, 2001) can expand upon, enrich, and thus complement traditional quantitative methods, providing results usable to researcher and therapist alike. Gilgun (2005) points out that qualitative approaches are useful for theory building, concept development, descriptions of lived experiences and the meaning people attribute to events, as well as the creation of items for surveys, assessment instruments, and other evaluation tools.

Quantitative research emphasizes experimentation, large samples whenever feasible, data collection and statistical analysis, objectivity, and verification. Consistent with a modernist and structural outlook, the researcher is an outside observer who manipulates variables and measures resulting changes. Qualitative research, on the other hand, is more consistent with postmodern, poststructural viewpoints. A frequent tool for educational research, this methodology tends to be exploratory, open-ended, and non-numerical in general, directed more at discovery than at evaluating or justifying a set of hypotheses. Its methods are intended to expand and enhance quantitative research techniques, and to provide a context for better understanding the meaning of the quantitative data collected (Moon, Dillon, & Sprenkle, 1990). Qualitative research methodologies are especially well suited for describing complex phenomena, defining new constructs, discovering new relationships among variables, and trying to answer "why" questions (Sprenkle, 1994).

Although such qualitative investigations of complex phenomena may begin modestly, with small samples, their results may lead to the discovery of new relationships among variables, leading further to theory development. As illustration, Alexander and Barton (1995) cite the early field-defining paper by Minuchin et al. (1975) on their preliminary work with diabetic children, which ultimately led to the breakthrough treatment of psychosomatic families, including children with anorexia nervosa (Minuchin, Rosman, & Baker, 1978).

While both quantitative and qualitative methods generate knowledge, the latter is apt to have far greater appeal to clinicians, since it is consistent with their everyday clinical procedures and is thus more likely to capture the essence and the richness of the therapeutic family-therapist encounter. Moreover, the qualitative method is compatible

---

[1]John Gottman's intervention research with couples (Gottman, Ryan, Carrere, & Erley, 2002) offers a good example of combining quantitative and qualitative methods and of intertwining research and practice. A theory is presented, along with experimentally based longitudinal studies, for predicting divorce as well as marital stability and marital satisfaction.

BOX 17.1   RESEARCH REPORT

QUANTITATIVE-QUALITATIVE COLLABORATION IN FAMILY RESEARCH

Innovative research methodologies are now available for studying the complex relationships found in couples and families that make such undertakings directly applicable to clinical practice (Bray, 2005). Both experimental designs (quantitative) and non-experimental designs (qualitative) are useful; they employ a multitude of measurement techniques and statistical analyses. The thrust of recent outcome research has been directed at understanding the processes that are critical for bringing about therapeutic change.

Qualitative approaches are especially useful in shedding light on specific issues that large-scale quantitative surveys cannot. These methods (in-depth interviewing, case studies, observations by teams through one-way mirrors, audio- and videotapes, focus groups, analysis of personal journals or other documents, content analysis of narratives, oral histories, explorations of belief systems) usually search for universal principles by examining a small number of cases intensively; the researcher is often a participant (rather than the objective, outside observer) who deals with any resulting subjectivity by making the researcher role explicit (Moon, Dillon, & Sprenkle, 1990).

with systems theory in emphasizing context, multiple perspectives, and client perspectives. Postmodernists such as the social constructionists are especially inclined to reject the notion that scientific observation can be objective and unbiased—a fundamental axiom of quantification research methodology. Instead, as we have noted, these clinicians look for the personal, subjective meaning each of us gives to the same event. Thus, they favor the discovery aspect of qualification research, shunning any quantitative undertaking that begins with the assumption that we can know, let alone measure, someone's world in any real or absolute sense.

Many clinicians have been slow in embracing clinical research and using its findings to inform their practices, believing such investigations to be irrelevant to their daily work (Williams, Patterson, & Miller, 2006). Clinicians in general are likely to be more interested in data revealing *clinical significance* (say, the extent to which a specific previously dysfunctional family, following treatment, develops sufficient skills to become functional) rather than *statistical significance* (group differences in improvement between families receiving treatment and those who receive no treatment). In some cases, differences between the groups may be statistically significant, but those who improved statistically may not have become functional as a result of treatment; clinical significance provides such information (Sprenkle & Bischoff, 1995).

Interestingly, early theory-generating research in the field, such as the work of Bowen or Wynne at the National Institute of Mental Health (NIMH), had a markedly qualitative or discovery-oriented flavor. It was only later, as researchers sought greater scientific control and ways of testing the effectiveness of their therapeutic procedures, that more rigorous research designs as well as more formal data collection and more precise statistical analysis occurred. The multiple use of qualitative, quantitative, and mixed research methodologies seems to characterize the field today, as researchers recognize that traditional experimental designs are not readily applicable to family therapy settings in which a multitude of circular systemic processes are occurring. As

Liddle, Bray, Levant, and Santisteban (2002) observe, today's intervention researchers, partly because of funding-related issues involved in large projects, are becoming more integrative, combining different kinds of research designs, methodologies, and different genres of research questions into a single proposal. Increasingly, funding agencies such as the National Institute of Mental Health are encouraging researchers to conduct studies involving both quantitative and qualitative inquiry methodologies.

More and more family therapists have begun to endorse current efforts to strengthen the research base of the field as healthcare professionals increasingly are asked to justify the treatment they offer by providing valid and reliable scientific data about its costs and effectiveness. As Pinsof and Wynne (1995) observe:

> Now, for the first time, family clinicians, training directors, clinic administrators, and family organizations have anxiously begun to clamor for "hard evidence" about the effectiveness of marital and family therapy that they can present to students, third-party payers, legislative bodies, and fellow professionals. (p. 341)

COUPLE AND FAMILY ASSESSMENT RESEARCH

An ongoing debate among family therapists is the extent to which they utilize formal research-based procedures for assessing couple and family processes. Proponents argue that accurately measuring relevant phenomena lies at the heart of any scientific discipline (Snyder, Cozzi, & Mangrum, 2002). Measurement instruments for tracking a wide range of relational variables (marital, parent-child, entire family) have advanced considerably in the past two decades, and advocates point to the recently improved reliable and valid test instruments for appraising the cognitive, affective, communication, and interpersonal patterns within families, taking care to include multiple levels—individuals, dyads, nuclear family, extended family and related social systems, and community and cultural systems. Care too has been taken to avoid measurement errors due to possible cultural bias.

All therapists make evaluations based on their previous experiences with families. All engage in clinical assessments, likely using a combination of interviews and behavioral observations, or perhaps relying on structured test inventories or presenting clients with interactive tasks they must complete together. Few regularly engage in formal assessment procedures using standardized test instruments (Boughner, Hayes, Bubenzer, & West, 1994). Many, however, do so informally, forming impressions of individual family members as well as global impressions of whole families without the aid of formal test instruments. Such assessments are likely to continue throughout the sessions, revised and brought up to date as new impressions are formed. Behaviorally oriented family therapists in particular place importance on administering their own specific standardized tests to couples or families.

Theoretical orientation determines to a large extent what therapists look for—structuralists focus on boundaries and overall transactional patterns; strategists observe triads, hierarchies, and patterns that maintain symptoms; Bowenians evaluate levels of differentiation; and so forth. Social constructionists in particular are interested in how clients view their world, rather than attempting to score how well client responses fit a tester's preconceived categories; for them, emphasis is on the primacy of personal meaning, part of the process of clients creating new realities for their lives (Neimeyer & Neimeyer, 1993).

All therapists, then, carry out some form of ongoing assessments with families, although most do so without following some predetermined evaluation procedure. Striving to keep their inquiries as naturalistic as possible, most are apt to utilize the therapist-family interactive process to learn about family behavioral patterns or belief systems. They are likely to believe that a formal testing setting prior to therapy, especially where the subsequent therapist is also the family evaluator, gets family therapy off on the wrong foot. Moving from this outside, detached, and ascendant testing position to one that calls for democratically interacting with family members is frequently resisted by the family and may make joining the family system that much more difficult. By interacting in a more genuine way with families from the start, many believe they do not need to undo any artificial relationship created as a result of a formal test inquiry.

Family assessment serves two major purposes: as guidance for what the clients need and how best to intervene, and later, in evaluating clinical progress and therapeutic outcome. Bagarozzi (1985) urges the selection of test instruments tailored to the situation under study; the results can be used to form a multidimensional "family profile" and thus act as an aid in outlining treatment goals with clients and together evaluating therapeutic efforts. L'Abate (1994) challenges those who shun formal testing, contending that an overall impressionistic view of the family system may obscure differences in individual contributions to the problem, and thus both a systems (family) and psychological (individual) assessment are needed. As he puts it:

> A traditional systems perspective stresses the subjective nature of the therapist's understanding of the family, whereas a psychological perspective finds an additional need for the objective understanding of the family and therefore uses both subjective (interview) and objective observations (questionnaires, rating sheets, tests). (p. 4)

Families, of course, are complicated systems, difficult to assess and quantify. Parenting styles differ widely, the family's life cycle stage is a factor, subsystems within the family influence each other, and the pressure of larger systems and cultural factors further complicate valid measurements. Acknowledging the complexity of measuring systems concepts, some researchers nevertheless have persisted in developing instruments for assessing family functioning. We present a sampling of the most prominent and carefully researched family assessment instruments.

Self-Report Measures

Typically designed in the form of questionnaires, self-report measures, eliciting family members' attitudes, values, roles, self-perceptions, and satisfactions with family relationships, are the most widely used method for assessing family relations and processes (Bray, 2002). Easy to gather and inexpensive to use, self-report measures expose each family member's privately held thoughts and viewpoints, which are ordinarily covered by behavior and thus not directly open to therapist observation. Having each person in the family give his or her separate, subjective perspective on family relationships grants the therapist an "inside" picture that then can be related to better comprehending behavioral interactions within the family (Grotevant & Carlson, 1989). Self-report measures can also be administered at various stages of family treatment, measuring both change and the effectiveness of the previous interventions (Touliatos, Perlmutter, Strauss, & Holden, 2001).

Some critics contend, however, that such measures are nonobjective, and thus run the risk of providing inaccurate information by clients about themselves. Bias in presenting oneself or others in a favorable or unfavorable light and the possibility of faulty recollections of events can be additional problems. Note too that results reflect individual perceptions and do not yield relational data (Bray, 2002).

The Circumplex Model

A carefully researched and validated, and thus appealing, example of such an "insider" or family member's view of two central properties of family life—flexibility and cohesion—may be obtained from the technique developed and refined by David Olson and his colleagues (Olson, Russell, & Sprenkle, 1989; Olson & Gorall, 2003). Their painstaking investigation, which has extended for more than 25 years and studied over 1000 families (100 or more in each of seven life cycle stages), has been directed at understanding how families cope with various situational stresses and demands throughout the life cycle. Because diagnosis by family pattern, using *DSM-IV* categories,[2] is not very satisfactory, a more applicable classification system for family relational patterns may emerge from this and related research undertakings. While the assessment instrument originally was developed primarily with intact Caucasian two-parent families, it now has been studied with multiform families (single-parent-led families, stepfamilies, same-sex couples) as well as racially and ethnically diverse groups (Gorall & Olson, 1995).

Olson, at the University of Minnesota, and his associates have produced a family map (Figure 17.1) depicting 25 types of couple or family relationships. Grounded in systems theory, the model is based on a family's degree of *flexibility* (its ability to permit changes in its role relationships, family leadership, and relationship rules) and *cohesion* (the emotional bonding of the family members to one another). A third dimension, *communication*, involves the family's skill level in listening to each other, and facilitates or impedes family movement on the two primary dimensions. Flexible family functioning calls for a balance between stability and change, and cohesion requires a balance between enmeshment and disengagement.

As seen in Figure 17.1, there are five levels of family cohesion (closeness), ranging from disconnected (disengaged) to overly connected (enmeshed). Flexibility, designed to measure how families balance stability and change, also has five levels, from inflexible or rigid to overly flexible or chaotic. With too much cohesion, the family is enmeshed and its members overly entwined in each other's lives; with too little, the members remain distant, isolated, and disengaged. Excessive flexibility leads to too much change, unpredictability, and possible chaos; too little may cause rigidity and stagnation. The three balanced levels on each dimension represent various degrees of optimal family functioning; the extremes are indicative of relationship problems for the family over time.

---

[2]One stumbling block here is that the *DSM-IV,* like its predecessors, is individually focused and does not include family diagnosis except to note briefly in its V-Code that certain relational problems (parent-child; marital partners) may be associated with impaired functioning in one or both participants. Kaslow (1996) has led a Coalition on Family Diagnosis attempting to include "relational diagnoses" in the latest *DSM* revision, but has not succeeded in persuading members of the *DSM* task force of its utility. More research is needed on relational problems so that degrees of severity—a key parameter for classifications—can be obtained. One proposed solution involves adoption of the *Global Assessment for Relational Functioning* (GARF), a brief unidimensional rating scale found in the appendix of *DSM-IV,* in which trained observers rate the degree to which the family meets the affective, problem-solving, and organizational needs of its members (Yingling, Miller, McDonald, & Galewaler, 1998). Validity studies of GARF have been encouraging (Ross & Doherty, 2001).

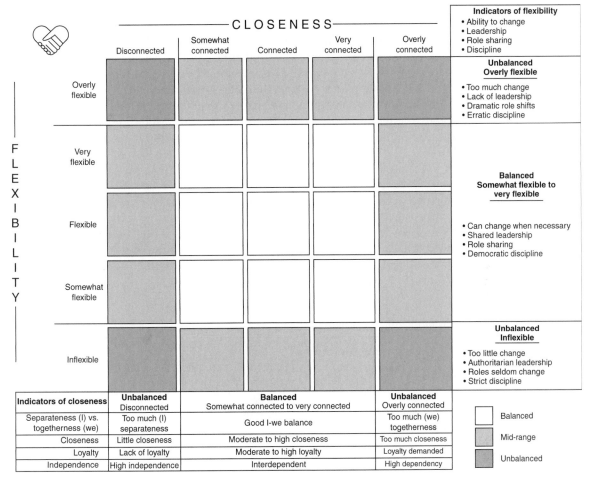

FIGURE 17.1 Couple and family map

Source: Olson & Gorall (2003)

A family's placement on this grid is determined by its members' responses to a 20-item self-report research instrument called the Family Adaptability and Cohesion Evaluation Scale (FACES; see Olson, 2000). Each family member completes the test twice; responses indicate how he or she currently views the family as well as his or her description of ideal family functioning. The discrepancy provides a measure of satisfaction: the greater the discrepancy, the less satisfaction.

Continuing research on the Circumplex Model has been of two types: refining test items and improving test validity of FACES (Kouneski, 2001). As noted in Chapter 16, Olson and his colleagues (Olson & Olson, 1999) also have developed and continue to improve a related assessment device evaluating a couple's preparation for marriage—PREPARE—PREmarital Personal And Relationship Evaluation, a 165-item self-report test intended to identify and measure the future marital partners' relationship strengths and weaknesses. A 15-page computer printout summarizing the findings is available for couples taking one of the PREPARE/ENRICH inventories.

Family Environment Scale

A second self-report questionnaire, the Family Environment Scale (FES), widely used in family research since its introduction by Rudolph Moos (1974), attempts to assess the impact of the family environment on individual and family functioning. Moos began his research with the assumption that all social climates have characteristics that can be portrayed (and thus measured) accurately. For example, some are more supportive than others, some more rigid, controlling, and autocratic; in others, order, clarity, and structure are given high priority. Moos argued that to a large extent, the family environment regulates and directs the behavior of the people within it.

The Family Environment Scale (Moos & Moos, 1994), now translated into 11 languages, has proven to be a reliable and valid test instrument (Boyd, Gullone, Needleman, & Burt, 1997; Sanford, Bingham, & Zucker, 1999). It provides a valuable clinical research tool for evaluating key aspects of a family's functioning. Easy to administer, the scale contains 90 statements to be labeled "true" or "false" by each family member ("Family members really help and support one another"; "Family members often keep their feelings to themselves"; "We fight a lot in our family").

TABLE 17.1 Subscales of the Family Environment Scale

	Relationship Dimensions
1. Cohesion	The extent to which family members are concerned and committed to the family and the degree to which family members are helpful and supportive of each other.
2. Expressiveness	The extent to which family members are allowed and encouraged to act openly and to express their feelings directly.
3. Conflict	The extent to which the open expression of anger and aggression and generally conflictual interactions are characteristic of the family.
	Personal Growth Dimensions
4. Independence	The extent to which family members are encouraged to be assertive, self-sufficient, to make their own decisions, and to think things out for themselves.
5. Achievement orientation	The extent to which different types of activities (for example, school and work) are cast into an achievement-oriented or competitive framework.
6. Intellectual-cultural orientation	The extent to which the family is concerned about political, social, intellectual, and cultural activities.
7. Active recreational orientation	The extent to which the family participates actively in various kinds of recreational and sports activities.
8. Moral-religious emphasis	The extent to which the family actively discusses and emphasizes ethical and religious issues and values.
	System Maintenance Dimensions
9. Organization	How important order and organization are in the family in terms of structuring the family activities, financial planning, and explicitness and clarity in regard to family rules and responsibilities.
10. Control	The extent to which the family is organized in a hierarchical manner, the rigidity of family rules and procedures, and the extent to which family members order each other around.

Source: Moos, 1974

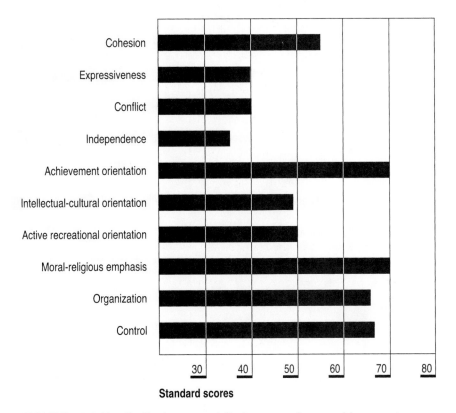

FIGURE 17.2 Family Environmental Scale scores for an achievement-oriented family
Source: Adapted from Moos, 1974

Respondents are asked to rate their families as they see them, and then as how they would ideally like their families to be. (Once again, the discrepancy provides a measure of satisfaction.)

Ten subscales make up the Family Environment Scale. A score is obtained for each, and average scores for the family are placed on a family profile. The family whose profile is shown in Figure 17.2, made up of parents and two children in their early twenties, is strongly upwardly mobile, emphasizing personal development (especially achievement and moral-religious emphasis) above other aspects of family life. These same two factors are de-emphasized by the young couple (no children) whose profile is depicted in Figure 17.3. They agree that for them, relationships are far more important than achievement, conflict is minimal, and control is low. This couple feels very positive about the social environment they have created.

Observational Methods

Observations in real time of interacting couples and families are especially appealing to those who prefer objective "outsider" measures of family functioning to what they consider the less reliable self-reports of family members. These observational measures are likely to take the form of *interactive coding schemes* (diagramming family interactive

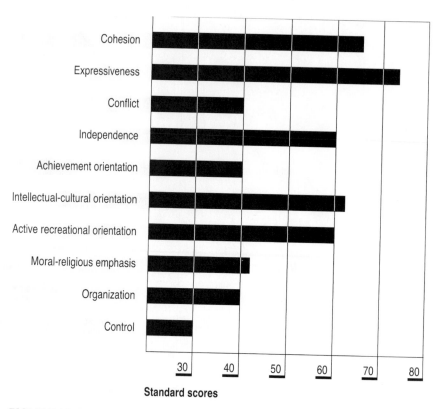

FIGURE 17.3 Family Environmental Scale scores for a high-relationship, low-control family

Source: Adapted from Moos, 1974

patterns along a series of cognitive, affective, and interpersonal dimensions) or *rating scales* (judging and scoring those overt, observable patterns along previously determined dimensions); see Grotevant and Carlson (1989).[3] The former are designed to capture the moment-to-moment contingencies of the behavior of family members toward one another, while the latter seek a more global, objective summary judgment of family interdependent relationship patterns. Carefully constructed test manuals often help ensure objectivity and enhance the reliability and validity of judgments made about family relationships. Observations can take place in the therapist's office, a university laboratory or clinic, or in the client's home.

The McMaster Model of Family Functioning

One long-term, empirically based research project—begun in the late 1950s at McGill University in Montreal and later shifted to McMaster University in Hamilton, Ontario,

---

[3]Minuchin's use of mapping to chart a family's ongoing transactional patterns is an example of the use of an interactive coding system, while Bowen's judgment of a family member's degree of self-differentiation makes use of a rating scale.

BOX 17.2   THERAPEUTIC ENCOUNTER

HOME-BASED SERVICES

Home-based services, long a part of social work and case management activity, have now begun to be practiced by others for family assessment and clinical intervention (Thomas, McCollum, & Snyder, 1999). The practice provides the observer with an opportunity to watch people in their natural surroundings, dealing with parent-children interaction regarding homework, television viewing, bedtime rules and their enforcement, etc. Discord, conflict, coalitions and alliances may all surface. The display of religious artifacts, photographs, trophies, mementos, and such round out the picture of family life. A common observational technique calls for the therapist to give the family the task of identifying a problem and then to watch how they go about discussing it, negotiating differences in view, and arriving at a solution. One potential challenge is maintaining professional boundaries so as not to be caught up in the family triangles, alliances, or coalitions or induced into playing the role of a missing family member.

Canada, in the 1960s and 1970s—attends especially to family structure and organization as well as family transactional patterns. Continued during the 1980s at Brown University in Providence, Rhode Island, this carefully crafted measurement technique pays particular heed to how the family develops and maintains itself through developing coping skills for dealing with certain necessary tasks.

The McMaster Model (Epstein, Bishop, & Baldwin, 1982; Epstein, Bishop, Ryan, Miller, & Keitner, 1993; Epstein, Ryan, Bishop, Miller, & Keitner, 2003) focuses on those dimensions of family functioning selected, based on research, as having the most impact on the emotional and physical well-being of family members. In particular, attention is focused on current functioning in three areas:

1. *Basic task area* (how the family deals with problems of providing food, money, transportation, shelter)
2. *Developmental task area* (how they deal with problems arising as a result of changes over time, such as first pregnancies or last child leaving home)
3. *Hazardous task area* (how they handle crises that arise as a result of illness, accident, loss of income, job change, and such)

A family's difficulty in coping with these three task areas is especially indicative of a propensity to develop clinically significant problems.

The McMaster Clinical Rating Scale (Epstein, Baldwin, & Bishop, 1983) probes family functioning in six crucial areas:

A. *Family problem solving* (the ability to resolve problems sufficiently well to maintain effective family functioning)
B. *Family communication* (how, and how well, a family exchanges information and affect; also whether communication is clear or masked, direct or indirect)
C. *Family roles* (how clearly and appropriately roles are defined, how responsibilities are allocated and accountability is monitored in order to sustain the family and support the personal development of its members)

D. *Affective responsiveness* (the family's ability to respond to a given situation with the appropriate quality and quantity of feelings)
E. *Affective involvement* (the extent to which the family shows interest in and values the particular activities and interests of its members)
F. *Behavior control* (the pattern the family adopts for handling dangerous situations, situations involving social interactions within and outside the family, and for satisfying members' psychobiological needs such as eating, sleeping, sex, handling of aggression, and so on)

The scale attempts to assess how well the family performs its primary mission of providing an environment in which social and biological development can flourish. Ratings are made on a seven-point scale (from 1, *severely disturbed*, to 7, *superior functioning*); a rating lower than 4 suggests the need for therapeutic intervention. Based on how each family member responds, the family's collective health-pathology score is obtained.

The Beavers Systems Model

This well-established measurement instrument provides a means for ordering families along a progressive continuum with respect to their competence—how well they perform the necessary and nurturing tasks of organizing and managing themselves (Beavers & Hampson, 2003). Robert Beavers and associates (Beavers, 1982, Beavers & Hampson, 1993) developed and fine-tuned a 14-item rating scale to be used in assessing and classifying family functioning. At the low end are leaderless, chaotic, invasive families, with diffused boundaries between its members. At the high end, families are described as composed of autonomous individuals who share intimacy and closeness but at the same time respect separateness. The observational assessment, based on the Beavers Interactional Competence Scale, is intended to measure family functioning at a particular moment in the family's life; thus repeated measures chart the family's progress, say after a specific period of therapy. By viewing functional/dysfunctional patterns as a continuum, the scale endorses the idea that growth and adaptation in families is possible.

Families are rated along two axes: their interactive style and their degree of competent family functioning (see Figure 17.4). Such items as the family's response to the needs of the children, overt adult conflict, degree of expression of angry or hostile feelings, the ratio of positive to negative feelings expressed, all go into making up the style rating. Families with **centripetal** styles tend to be inner oriented and to view relationship satisfactions as emanating from within the family; those in extreme **centrifugal** families, outwardly directed and more openly expressive of anger, seek satisfaction outside the family (Hampson & Beavers, 1996).

The competence dimension is judged by observing the expressions of power, the presence of parental coalitions, how clearly family members communicate, and so forth, as indicated on the horizontal axis. The arrow shape of the diagram is intended to convey that extremes in style—whether profoundly centripetal or centrifugal—are associated with poor family functioning. Taken together, family style and family competence judgments provide a useful snapshot of current family functioning and offer a guide to how and how best to begin to intervene in helping to improve family functioning.

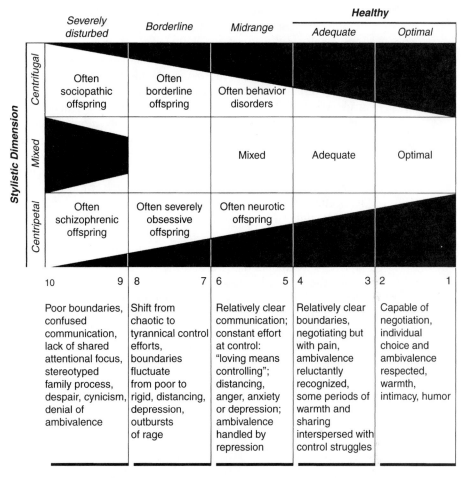

FIGURE 17.4 The Beavers Systems Model, in the form of a sideways A, with one leg representing centripetal families and the other leg representing centrifugal families
Source: Beavers & Voeller, 1983, p. 90

FAMILY THERAPY PROCESS AND OUTCOME RESEARCH

What constitutes therapeutic change? What are the conditions or in-therapy processes that facilitate or impede such changes? How are those changes best measured? How effective is family therapy in general, and are some intervention procedures or therapeutic models more efficacious than others for dealing with specific clinical problems or clients from a specific community or culture? Do certain specific therapist characteristics and family characteristics influence outcomes? Is family therapy the most cost-effective way to proceed in a specific case, say in comparison with alternate interventions such as individual therapy or drug therapy, or perhaps a combined set of therapeutic undertakings? How do race, ethnicity, gender, age, and sexual orientation factor into potential results? These are some of the questions that researchers in family therapy continue to grapple with in an effort to understand and improve the complex psychotherapeutic process.

For the last 40 years, psychotherapy research has concerned itself with investigating the *therapeutic process* (the mechanisms of client change) to develop more effective methods of psychotherapy. While the earlier years were devoted largely to *outcome* research studies in order to confirm the overall legitimacy of the therapeutic endeavor, "by about 1980 a consensus of sorts was reached that psychotherapy, as a generic treatment process, was demonstrably more effective than no treatment" (VandenBos, 1986, p. 111). A recent review of the research literature has found that 75 percent of those clients who enter psychotherapy show some benefit, with little difference between treatments (Lambert & Ogles, 2004). As for couple and family therapy, there now exists considerable research-informed evidence that this modality is effective for virtually every type of disorder and for a variety of relational problems in children, adolescents, and adults (Pinsof & Wynne, 2000; Friedlander & Tuason, 2000).

Now able to move beyond answering the simple outcome question "Does it work?", researchers have turned their attention to comparative outcome studies in which the relative advantages and disadvantages of alternate treatment strategies for clients with different sets of problems are being probed. The research lens has now broadened to examine the application of couple and family therapy to specific clinical problems in specific settings (Sexton, Robbins, Hollimon, Mease, & Mayorga, 2003).

At the same time, explorations of process variables are taking place (Alexander, Newell, Robbins, & Turner, 1995), examining the nature of change mechanisms, so that differential outcomes from various therapeutic techniques can be tentatively linked to

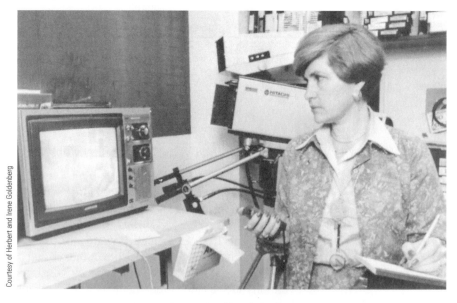

Courtesy of Herbert and Irene Goldenberg

This researcher is in the process of viewing a series of videotapes of therapy sessions with the same family, rating certain interactive patterns along previously determined empirical categories in an effort to measure changes as a result of family therapy.

the presence or absence of specific therapeutic processes. Such investigations of what really goes on inside the therapy room have the potential for identifying specific strategies or interventions that can lead to more effective treatment (Hogue, Liddle, Singer, & Leckrone, 2005).

Process Research

How do couples or families change as a result of going through a successful therapeutic experience? What actually occurs, within and outside the family therapy sessions, that leads to a desired therapeutic outcome? Is there evidence for a set of constructs common to all effective therapies? Do specific therapies make use of these concepts in different ways that are effective? Despite a growing interest in ferreting out precisely what change processes lead to what results (Heatherington, Friedlander, & Greenberg, 2005; Diamond & Diamond, 2002; Alexander, Holtzworth-Munroe, & Jameson, 1994) and a search for why certain therapies are more effective than others for specific problems, it remains true that relatively little is yet known about how personal change, as well as interpersonal change within a family, occurs in this context (Friedlander, Wildman, Heatherington, & Skowron, 1994). That is, in contrast to the growing empirically based data on the efficacy or effectiveness of family therapy, there is still a comparative paucity of major research undertakings on change process mechanisms in couple and family therapy. However, this situation is beginning to improve as new measuring instruments are developed and qualitative, discovery-oriented methodologies employed, producing in many cases some clinically meaningful if less methodologically rigorous research. Successful process research could have the effect of identifying those therapist interventions or therapist-client interactions or changes in client behaviors that lead to increasingly effective treatment. Such information is particularly relevant to practitioners and as such may help bridge the gap between researcher and practitioner (Sprenkle, 2003).

Process research attempts to discover and operationally describe what actually takes place during the course of therapy. What are the day-to-day features of the therapist-client relationship, the actual events or interactions that transpire during sessions that together make up the successful therapeutic experience? Can these be catalogued and measured? What specific clinical interventions lead to therapeutic breakthroughs? How can these best be broken down into smaller units that can be replicated by others, perhaps manualized when possible, and thus taught to trainees learning to become family therapists? Are there specific ways of intervening with families with specific types of problems that are more effective than other ways? What role does therapist gender play in how therapy proceeds? What about therapeutic style (proactive or reactive, interpretive or collaborative, and so on)? What factors determine who remains in treatment and who drops out early on? How do cultural variables influence the therapeutic process?

Answers to such therapeutic process-related questions need to be found in order to demonstrate the efficacy of a particular treatment approach—especially critical at this time to the survival of family therapy in the healthcare marketplace (Alexander, Newell, Robbins, & Turner, 1995). From a practical economic viewpoint, family therapy research must demonstrate to insurance companies, managed care organizations, government agencies, and mental health policymakers that its product is an effective treatment that should be included in any package of mental health services (Pinsof & Hambright, 2002).

BOX 17.3   THERAPEUTIC ENCOUNTER

WHAT WITHIN-SESSION MECHANISMS STIMULATE CHANGE?

Alliance between the family and a caring, competent therapist attuned to the family's presenting problem, especially if established early in therapy; this alliance builds confidence, hope, and a feeling of safety

Cognitive changes in clients: greater awareness and understanding and a shared sense of purpose

Behavioral changes in clients: sustaining engagement with one another

An emotional experience leading to having one's feelings validated by other family members

Maintenance of the therapeutic focus on strengthening family relations rather than blaming the identified patient

Promotion of constructive dialogue and the therapist's effort to block the exchange of negative affect and interactional impasses

Greater self-disclosure, which makes participants feel vulnerable but listened to and protected

Sustained engagement, which leads to the feeling all members are working together for the overall family good

Sources: Sexton, Robbins, Hollimon, Mease, & Mayorga, 2003: Heatherington, Friedlander, & Greenberg, 2005; Christensen, Russell, Miller & Peterson, 1998; Helmeke & Sprenkle, 2000

Greenberg and Pinsof (1986) offer the following definition of process research:

> Process research is the study of the interaction between the patient and therapist systems. The goal of process research is to identify the change processes in the interaction between these systems. Process research covers all the behaviors and experiences of these systems, within and outside the treatment sessions, which pertain to the process of change. (p. 18)

Note that in this definition the terms are used broadly. The patient (or client) system, for example, consists of more than the identified patient; other nuclear and extended family members are included, as well as members of other social systems that interact with the client and the family. Similarly, the therapist system might include other therapeutic team members in addition to the therapist who meets with the family.

Data from measuring the therapist-family interaction are also relevant here. Note too that process research does not simply concern itself with what transpires within the session, but also with out-of-session events occurring during the course of family therapy. Finally, the experiences, thoughts, and feelings of the participants are given as much credence as their observable actions. Thus, certain of the self-report methods we described earlier in this chapter may provide valuable input in the process analysis.

Process research attempts to reveal how therapy works, and what factors (in therapist behaviors, patient behaviors, and their interactive behaviors) are associated with improvement or deterioration. For example, a researcher might investigate a specific process variable concerning family interaction—who speaks first, who talks to whom, who interrupts whom, and so forth. Or perhaps, attending to therapist-family interaction, the researcher might ask if joining an anorectic family in an active and directive way results in a stronger therapeutic alliance than joining the family in a different way, such as being more passive or more reflective. Or perhaps the process researcher wants to find out what special ways of treating families with alcoholic members elicit willing family participation as opposed to those that lead to resistance or dropouts from treatment. Are there certain intervention techniques that work best at an early treatment stage and others that are more effective during either the middle stage or terminating stage of family therapy?

By attempting to link process issues with outcome results, the family therapist would be proceeding using an empirically validated map, which unfortunately is not yet available for most models of family therapy (Pinsof & Hambright, 2002). There do exist some exceptions—what Heatherington, Friedlander, and Greenberg (2005) refer to as well-articulated theories about systemic change processes. *Emotionally focused couple therapy* (see Chapter 9) is based on considerable research on the role of emotion in therapy, integrates such research with attachment theory, and offers a step-by-step manualized therapeutic plan to help clients access and process their emotional experiences. *Functional family therapy* (Chapter 11) represents another successful effort to apply behavioral and systems theories to treat at-risk adolescents. Techniques for building therapeutic alliances and reframing the meaning of problematic behavior have been integrated into successful process studies (Robbins, Alexander, Newell, & Turner, 1996).

Empirically supported process studies thus far have been carried out primarily by the behavioral and cognitive-behavioral approaches. These brief, manualized treatment methods, with specific goals, are not necessarily the most effective, but are easier to test using traditional research methodology than other treatment methods. Least well defined, for research purposes, are the social constructionist therapies. By and large they have not yet developed testable propositions (e.g., how does the miracle question in solution-focused therapy affect client outcomes beyond a shift in "language games"?) (Heatherington, Friedlander, & Greenberg, 2005). Similarly, while narrative therapists purport to "re-author" people's lives, how precisely can that be measured, and how do we know when re-authoring has been successful? For most models discussed in this text, greater evidence for the specifications of change mechanisms is still called for to meet the criteria of empirical researchers into how best to tap into the therapeutic change process.

Outcome Research

Ultimately, all forms of psychotherapy must provide some answer to this key question: Is this procedure more efficient, more cost-effective, less dangerous, with more long-lasting results than other therapeutic procedures (or no treatment at all)? Outcome research in family therapy must address the same problems that hinder such research in individual psychotherapy, in addition to the further complications of gauging and measuring the various interactions and changes taking place within a family group and between various family members.

To be meaningful, such research must do more than investigate general therapeutic efficacy; it must also determine the conditions under which family therapy is effective—the types of families, their ethnic or social class backgrounds, the category of problems or situations, the level of family functioning, the therapeutic techniques, the treatment objectives or goals, and so on. Effective research needs to provide evidence for what models work best for what specific problems, and what specific problems are especially responsive to family-level interventions.

Overall, according to the **meta-analysis** of the findings of 163 published and unpublished outcome studies on the efficacy and effectiveness of marital and family

---

BOX 17.4 RESEARCH REPORT

EFFICACY STUDIES VERSUS EFFECTIVENESS STUDIES

Published outcome research studies today appear in one of two forms: *efficacy studies,* conducted under controlled ("laboratory") conditions, and *effectiveness studies,* as in the everyday practice ("in the field") of providing family therapy services (Pinsof & Wynne, 1995). Efficacy studies seek to discover whether a particular treatment works under ideal "research therapy" situations, while effectiveness studies seek to determine whether the treatment works under normal real-life ("clinic therapy") circumstances. Historically, most outcome studies have focused on efficacy, in effect asking whether a specific treatment approach works under ideal, controlled research conditions. Unfortunately, as Pinsof and Wynne (2000) have more recently pointed out, such laboratory studies, while more readily funded and publishable than are effectiveness studies, nevertheless often bear so slight a likeness to what practitioners do in their everyday practice that they are likely to have little, if any, impact on the practices of most marriage and family therapists.

Outcome research projects carrying out efficacy studies are able to approximate ideal experimental requirements: patients are randomly assigned to treatment or no treatment groups, treatment manuals define the main procedures to be followed, therapists receive training and supervision to ensure standardization of interventions, multiple outcome criteria are designed, and independent evaluators (rather than the therapist or clients) measure outcomes. Such a "dream" setup, under such controlled conditions, often lends itself to a clarification of what components of the therapy specifically affect certain outcomes, and as such may be illuminating. However, the conclusions from such studies, usually carried out in university clinics or hospital settings, are often difficult to translate into specific recommendations for therapy under more real-world, consultation room conditions. Recent efforts to develop empirically supported family therapy represent a concerted effort to bring the mounting research to bear on problems that practicing clinicians deal with in their work.

---

therapy, Shadish, Ragsdale, Glaser, and Montgomery (1995) conclude that, based mainly on efficacy studies, these modalities work; marital/family therapy (MFT) clients did significantly better than untreated control group clients. As they put it in more concrete terms:

> It means that if you randomly chose a client who received MFT, the odds are roughly two out of three that the treatment client will be doing better than a randomly chosen control client at posttest. . . . An effect this big is also considerably larger than one typically finds in medical, surgical, and pharmaceutical outcome trials. (p. 347)

While different marital and family therapy approaches all were found to be superior to no treatment, these reviewers found no single model's efforts stood out over others. (It should be noted, however, that one approach or another may "fit" certain families better than do others, or work best for certain kinds of presenting problems. In addition, certain therapists may be especially skilled or especially experienced in helping families with certain specific sets of problems.) In some cases, a combination of therapeutic efforts (psychoeducational, medication, individual therapy, group therapy) may be the treatment of choice (Pinsof, Wynne, & Hambright, 1996).

A variety of outcome studies, some more carefully designed than others, have lent general support to the effectiveness of specific therapies. Minuchin, Rosman, and

Baker's (1978) *structural family therapy* resulted in a 90 percent improvement rate for 43 anorectic children; that improvement still held in a follow-up several years later. Murdock and Gore (2004) confirmed *Bowenian* theory that self-differentiation influences how family members perceive stress in their lives. In an early, non-rigorous evaluation of *strategic therapy*, Watzlawick, Weakland, and Fisch (1974) checked on families three months after concluding treatment and found that 40 percent reported full symptom relief, 32 percent reported a considerable amount of relief, and 28 percent reported no change. Carr's (1991) review of 10 studies of Milan therapy found a reported rate of 66 percent to 75 percent in symptom reduction in clients. While these results hint at effectiveness of the models espoused, they lack sufficient rigor in methodological design to offer any definitive conclusions regarding general empirically supported effectiveness for any one model.

In recent years, however, research methodology has improved, new statistical methods have become available, and funding has allowed for major research undertakings, particularly studies regarding which models work for specific populations. Evidence supporting family-level interventions have been especially strong for adolescent conduct or behavioral problems, and these approaches are gaining acceptance by practitioners as well as county and state healthcare administrators. Especially noteworthy here are *functional family therapy*, engaging high-risk, acting-out youth and their families by helping change those intra-family cognitive, emotional, and behavioral processes that support the problem (Alexander & Sexton, 2002); *multisystemic therapy*, a manualized, integrated family approach treating chronic juvenile behavioral and emotional problems by addressing the multiple determinants of antisocial behavior and intervening at the family, peer, school, and community levels (Henggeler, Mihalic, Rone, Thomas, & Timmons-Mitchell (1998); and *parent management training*, a brief skills training program based on social learning principles, designed to assist parents at home in changing the behavior of severely oppositional or antisocial children and adolescents (Webster-Stratton & Hammond, 1997).

Family-based treatments for substance-abusing adults and adolescents have received empirical support (Stanton & Shadish, 1997). One long-term approach carried out by Jose Szapocznik and associates (Szapocznik et al., 2002), called *brief strategic family therapy*, utilizes strategic and structural principles to treat behavior problems and substance abuse in Hispanic youth, within a family setting at home. In a similar vein, Malgady and Costantino (2003) report the empirically supported use of narrative therapy in which a group therapy format, sometimes including parents, was used to relate cultural narratives relevant to Puerto Rican and Mexican children and adolescents with conduct disorders, phobias, and anxiety.

Family-level interventions with schizophrenia and bipolar disorders, augmented by pharmaceutical treatment, have largely been of a psychoeducational nature (see Chapter 16), teaching families about the disorder and how best to help avoid relapse. Families are taught that they have a significant influence on their relative's recovery. A significant number of well-designed, empirically supported studies have demonstrated a markedly decreased relapse and rehospitalization rate for schizophrenic patients whose families received psychoeducation compared with those who received standard individual service (McFarlane, Dixon, Lukens, & Luckstead, 2003). Miklowitz et al. (2000) have reported similar findings for bipolar disorders in the clinical trials he and his group conducted.

Finally, marital and couple discord shows evidence of abatement as a result of therapy (Baucom et al., 1998). Dunn and Schwebel (1995) examined 15 methodologically rigorous, published outcome studies and found that behavioral, cognitive-behavioral, and insight-oriented marital therapy were all more effective than no treatment in bringing about changes in spouses' behavior and in the general assessment of the marital relationship. Psychoeducational work with couples, such as the Prevention and Relationship Enhancement Program (PREP), described in Chapter 16, have been shown to be effective in increasing relationship satisfaction (Markman, Renick, Floyd, Stanley, & Clements, 1993) and to remain so in four- to five-year follow-ups. Similarly, emotionally focused couple therapy (Johnson & Greenberg, 1995) aimed at restructuring a couple's negative interactional patterns, has been supported by research results. A significant proportion of couples do not respond to couples therapy, however, and among those that do respond a significant portion's relationship will deteriorate upon later follow-up (Christensen, Baucom, Vu, & Stanton, 2005).

EVIDENCE-BASED FAMILY THERAPY: SOME CLOSING COMMENTS

The recent rush to achieve accountability can be seen in medicine and education as well as in psychology, where professionals are being pressured to base their practices on evidence whenever feasible. Within the psychotherapy realm, there is increasing momentum to establish an empirically validated basis for delivering healthcare services (Goodheart, Kazdin, & Sternberg, 2006; Kazdin & Weisz, 2003; Nathan & Gorman, 2002), based on the assumption that clinical interventions backed up by research will make the effort more efficient, thereby improving the quality of healthcare and reducing healthcare costs (Reed & Eisman, 2006).

Both researchers and practitioners are interested in making therapy more effective. Academically based clinical researchers have been especially supportive of this idea, and have attempted to apply the methodology of scientific research to the therapeutic endeavor, often developing efficacy treatment programs under rigorous and controlled conditions that they believe generalize to real-world problems dealt with by practitioners. Practicing clinicians, who also would like to base their interventions on evidence, nevertheless complain that these narrow treatments based on randomized controlled clinical trials[4] for specific diagnostic categories are of limited use with the varied populations and types of problems they see in their practice (Goodheart, 2006). Many also contend that while the efforts to improve the quality and cost-effectiveness of psychotherapy, as well as enhancing accountability, are clearly laudable, to date evidence that empirically validated techniques improve healthcare services or reduce costs in everyday practice is still limited.

The widely accepted definition of evidence-based practice (APA, 2005) is as follows:

> Evidence-based practice in psychology is the integration of the best available research with clinical expertise in the context of patient characteristics, culture, and patient values.

---

[4]Randomized controlled trials (RCTs) are considered by proponents to be the "gold standard" in drawing causal inferences about the effects of an intervention. Much as in the investigation of the effectiveness of a new drug in medical research, clients are matched and randomly assigned to a treatment group or to a placebo group or perhaps to a no-treatment group. Differences in results are attributed to the treatment, thus providing evidence for its effectiveness with that population.

BOX 17.5   RESEARCH REPORT

ASSUMPTIONS UNDERLYING EVIDENCE-BASED THERAPY RESEARCH

A homogeneous client population is studied.

Clients are randomly assigned to treatment or no treatment.

Therapists are carefully selected, trained, and monitored.

Specific interventions are prescribed.

Treatment is designed for a specific disorder or diagnosis.

Treatment is brief and of a fixed duration.

Treatment manuals are employed to ensure all receive same interventions.

Process change mechanisms are articulated.

Clear goals are delineated.

Multiple outcome measures are specified.

Follow-up procedures over extended periods are employed.

The definition affirms the contributions of:

- research evidence (quantitative and qualitative methodologies, clinical observations, single-case studies, process and outcome research)
- clinical expertise (therapist skill, judgment and experience in assessment, case formulation, treatment planning, techniques of intervention)
- patient characteristics (personality, specific problem, cultural background, gender, sexual orientation, social and environmental context, race)

One difficulty in reconciling the views of practitioners and researchers is that they operate in different worlds—the former focused on service to clients, the latter on expanding understanding of a clinical phenomenon or testing the effects of new procedures (Weisz & Addis, 2006). Experienced clinicians are apt to be integrationists, taking what's most appropriate from a variety of theories or techniques to help their specific client or family, and are not likely to be content to follow fixed rules from manualized guidelines in treating clients who seek their help. Westen, Novotny, and Thompson-Brenner (2004) suggest that researchers might do better by focusing on what works in real-world practice than spend their efforts on developing new treatments or manuals from the laboratory. There also continues to be debate on what constitutes research evidence, and on the extent to which psychotherapy is a human encounter in which *common factors* (attention from a caring therapist, the expectation of improvement, catharsis, hope, feedback, safety in a confidential relationship) help produce successful outcomes, regardless of therapeutic model.

Nevertheless, there is a growing acceptance of the place of evidence-based studies in clinical practice, and practitioners may experience increased pressure from third-party payors to base their interventions on established evidence-based treatments. In some cases, managed care and insurance companies have begun to provide reimbursements only to practitioners using evidence-based treatments. Some local, state, and federally funded programs already are based on evidence-validated programs, and this trend is likely to continue. Clinicians in the future will be held increasingly accountable for providing outcome assessments for their clinical interventions.

SUMMARY

Research in family therapy preceded the development of therapeutic intervention techniques, but beginning in the 1960s priorities changed, and the proliferation of techniques outdistanced research. That situation has now begun to even out, and a renewed family research-therapy connection is beginning to be reestablished. Some practitioners, likely in the past to dismiss research findings as not relevant to their everyday needs and experiences, have found qualitative research methodologies more appealing and germane than the more formal, traditional experimental methodologies based on quantitative methods.

Various research attempts to classify and assess families exist, employing either a self-report or an observational format. Most noteworthy among the former are the attempts by Olson and his associates to construct their Circumplex Model of family functioning based on the family properties of flexibility and cohesion, and work by Moos to construct his Family Environment Scale. Observational measures, usually in the form of rating scales by outside observers, have been designed by Beavers to depict degrees of family competence and by Epstein, Bishop, and Baldwin to classify family coping skills according to the McMaster Model.

Both the process and outcome of family therapy interventions have been studied with increased interest in recent years. The former, involved with what mechanisms in the therapist-client(s) encounter produce client changes, requires the higher priority because identifying the processes that facilitate change helps ensure greater therapeutic effectiveness. Outcome research, including both efficacy and effectiveness studies, having established that marital and family therapy are beneficial, has turned its attention to evidence-based practices—what specific interventions work most effectively with what client populations. Of particular interest today is the search for the relative advantages and disadvantages of alternative therapeutic approaches for individuals and families with different sets of relational difficulties. Evidence-based family therapy is likely to become increasingly prevalent as efforts are underway to make healthcare delivery more effective and cost-efficient.

RECOMMENDED READINGS

Goodheart, C. D., Kazdin, A. E., & Sternberg, R. J. (Eds.) (2006). *Evidence-based psychotherapy: Where practice and research meet.* Washington, DC: American Psychological Association.

Liddle, H. A., Santisteban, D. A., Levant, R. F., & Bray, J. H. (Eds.). (2001). *Family psychology: Science-based interventions.* Washington, DC: American Psychological Association.

Nathan, P. E., & Gorman, J. M. (2002). *A guide to treatment that works.* London: Oxford University Press.

Sprenkle, D. H., & Piercy, F. P. (2005). *Research methods in family therapy* (2nd ed.). New York: Guilford Press.

Touliatos, J., Perlmutter, B. F., Strauss, M. A., & Holden, G. W. (2001). *Handbook of family measurement techniques.* Newbury Park, CA: Sage.

CHAPTER 18

A COMPARATIVE VIEW OF FAMILY THEORIES AND THERAPIES

In this, the final chapter, we present an overview of the various models we have considered, reviewing some of the similarities and differences that exist. It is important to note at the outset that originators of theories by necessity focus on a relatively narrow set of concepts, staking out positions that attempt to make their contribution unique. Little effort is directed toward seeking similarities with other theories; indeed, the opposite is usually the case. However, on closer examination, we find that overlaps in theory and technique, as well as notable differences, exist. It is those differences that bring adherents to a particular model.

Purists in theory are easy to come by; purists in practice, less so. Ideally, it is important to know a variety of theories, fitting specific techniques, regardless of theoretical origin, to appropriate client populations. A well-trained family therapist needs to understand various theories and the populations with which each works best. Most family therapists start out following one theoretical framework and its corresponding set of clinical procedures, but soon learn to supplement and adapt where the theory—inevitably with some shortcomings—is inadequate for certain clients. In practice, then, most therapists become eclectic, ultimately adopting (and adapting) techniques that their experience tells them work best with specific sets of problems.

Many therapists believe that it is harder to stick with a single theory or set of techniques in working with families than when treating individuals. Systems are complex, and each family member has specific needs that may conflict with those of fellow family members. By definition, members of a family are at different stages of life cycle development and may require different intervention procedures. The therapist needs to evaluate and respond to each member, to the entire family system, and further, the larger system of which all are a part—extended families, the community, cultural, racial, social class, and ethnic inputs and considerations. Social constructionists as well as advocates of gender-sensitive family therapy have been especially influential in drawing attention to the social and political climate in which today's families function.

In the end, skilled clinicians are more alike in what they do with families than their different theories would suggest. Intangibles—personal experience, involvement, focused interest, energy, sensitivity, empathy, warmth, humor, and so forth—as well as theoretical knowledge and therapeutic know-how may be the key variables that in some combination, along with an awareness of evidence-based research findings, make for clinical effectiveness.

FAMILY THEORIES: A COMPARATIVE OVERVIEW

For the remainder of this chapter, we have separated family theories from clinical procedures, and developed a set of categories that we believe best highlight the similarities and differences between models.

Units of Study: Monads, Dyads, and Triads

Many of the early family therapy pioneers (Bowen, Jackson, Wynne, Boszormenyi-Nagy), themselves largely schooled in classical psychoanalysis, did what most revolutionaries do—they rejected out of hand the then-mainstream theory of psychoanalysis. They especially rejected the psychoanalytic focus on intrapersonal dynamics—the *monadic* view that problems reside within the individual. Instead, they insisted on the then radical position that people can be understood more accurately—and correspondingly can be more easily helped—if viewed systemically, in the context of their relationships. How people interact with one another, how they define themselves within that relationship, the coalitions and alliances they form—these all require the broader *dyadic* (two-person) and *triadic* (three-person) viewpoints. Thus, boundaries, enmeshments, disengagements, subsystems (Minuchin) or triangles, symbiosis, fusion (Bowen), or relational ethics and family loyalty (Boszormenyi-Nagy) all look beyond the individual to his or her recursive patterns of behavior within a system.

Today there exists less polarity—intrapsychic or interpersonal—between models, than a difference in emphasis. All family therapists attend to monadic, dyadic, or triadic factors in family functioning; the differences lie in the weight and focus they give to each. Many psychoanalytically oriented therapists have themselves moved beyond classical positions and are less insistent on paying exclusive attention to conflicting forces within each family member. In general, modern psychoanalysis has morphed into object relations theory, and the new look is more relationship based. Object relations family therapists, still interested in intrapsychic conflict, now attempt to understand family relationships by studying the imprints from the past that each partner brings to the marriage. The husband-wife dyad may contain examples of projective identification, as the partners project unwanted parts of themselves onto the other.

Behavior therapists are likely to see the symptomatic person (say, an adolescent runaway) as the problem, accepting the parents' view, and teaching the latter parenting skills to cope with the family crisis. Experiential family therapy, along with psychoeducational therapy, also attends to the individual, but within a family context. The former, viewing problems as arising from flawed interactions and communication lapses between family members, might focus on helping the individual express feelings (Satir), but always within the context of ongoing family transactions (emotionally focused family therapies). Psychoeducational therapists, usually directing their efforts at individuals with serious mental disorders, tend to accept the definition of individual pathology; but they recognize the malignant effect of that person's chronic problematic behavior on family functioning. Consequently, they direct their therapeutic efforts at helping the entire family reduce the level of emotionally intense exchanges between its members, reducing family tensions and helping avoid relapse in their symptomatic member.

By definition, family therapists conceptualize from a dyadic or triadic position, recognizing that people define one another (and themselves) through their interactions.

Early communication/strategist therapists emphasized both the dyadic and triadic nature of symptom formation as interpersonal messages, and Haley in particular searched for the three persons involved in any human behavioral exchange. Bowen's theory is clearly triadic, particularly his concept of triangles as the basic building block of a family's emotional system. Similarly, structuralists are triadic—boundary diffusion between two people inevitably involves reciprocal relationships (enmeshments, disengagements) with a third participant. Triadic explanations, such as coalitions and alliances, broaden the lens, providing a larger context for understanding behavior.

What about the newer therapies, influenced by postmodern and poststructural thought? Solution-focused, collaborative, and narrative therapists frequently direct attention to solving the individual's problems, leading some critics to contend that the focus on the family is lost. On the other hand, Michael White, for example, and his narrative colleagues never lose sight of the family; indeed, they try to change the direction of the family's energy in order to help the family detach from a restraining story line. Similarly, de Shazer tries to help family members exchange their "problem" focus for a "solution" focus arrived at together, and Harlene Anderson attempts to help each member "dissolve" his or her version of the "problem." Although they may not directly address the pattern of family conflict, all three persist in getting the family as a whole to abandon seemingly intractable, self-restricting stories about themselves in favor of new self-descriptions with more satisfying options.

Time Frame: Past, Present, Future

Another dimension by which we might compare models involves the prominence given to the past, present, or future. Here again, early family therapy pioneers broke with the psychoanalytic search of the past for explanations of current difficulties, preferring to focus on here-and-now family interactions. Without denying the influence of past experiences on present functioning, most looked to ongoing transactions, turning to past experiences only if necessary to enhance understanding of what is currently transpiring within the family system. Today, among many family therapists, there remains disagreement on which time frame to emphasize in dealing most effectively with the family's presenting problem.[1]

Long-term, classical psychodynamic therapy does focus attention on conflicts developed in each client's early formative years; but the length of treatment and high cost are out of favor today, particularly since the effectiveness of this type of therapy in symptom control has been challenged. In their contemporary form, such as in object relations therapy, they do more than search for past trauma (although they are interested in ferreting out introjects from the past). They are briefer, and they aim more directly at helping clients discover how past unresolved conflicts and attachment loss help explain their current personal and interpersonal difficulties.

The transgenerational models are most apt to attend to unfinished and recurring business from families of origin. Bowen is interested in the client's degree of family fusion, Boszormenyi-Nagy in his or her sense of family loyalty and obligation. Both Bowen and Boszormenyi-Nagy helped families understand the impact from past generations on their values, their typical behavior patterns, attachments, ways of examining and resolving problems, power issues, and so forth. (Framo and Whitaker also adopted a multigenerational outlook, the former by inviting clients to bring in families for family-of-origin sessions,

---

[1] One practical note: In the age of managed care, undue efforts to uncover and reconstruct early memories are apt to meet with rejection by case managers doing utilization reviews.

the latter by bringing in grandparents as consultants to ongoing family sessions.) Bowen's efforts to develop genograms with his client families helped explicate for them a transgenerational basis for their current behavior. Boszormenyi-Nagy's insistence that family debts and obligations may be rooted in the past serves a similar function.

Most family therapies today, on the other hand, tend to be ahistorical, encouraging families to deal with issues they face in the present, without unduly looking for answers from the past as to why the problems currently exist. Experiential (Satir, Kempler), communication/strategic/Milan (the Palo Alto group, Haley, Madanes, Selvini-Palazzoli), and structural (Minuchin) family therapists all may be considered to emphasize the present. Behavioral/cognitive family therapists are not interested in speculating on the exact origin of any maladaptive or problematic behavior; they want to know what circumstances currently help maintain the present problem or symptom, in order to direct interventions at extinguishing the undesirable thoughts and behavior.

Social constructionists, such as de Shazer, deal with problems in the present, looking from the start at future solutions. They do not look at the past for clues to the origin of the problem, nor do they dwell in the present. Beginning with their initial contact with the family, they are looking for signs of change, working toward future solutions. If the past is questioned, it is likely to be in order to help the client recall when an earlier solution helped solve a problem and thus might be employed again in the current situation.

Narrative therapists also help clients search for unique outcomes—times when they overcame a problem-saturated story—in the service of "thickening" stories of success as an aid to overcoming future hurdles. For them, the past is a repository of successful resilient efforts at overcoming problems that can be applied to current difficulties.

Psychoeducationally oriented therapists, working with post-hospitalized schizophrenics and their families, offer practical hints for making day-to-day life together more harmonious and less stressful. They are not interested in how the symptoms emerged, who is to blame, or what in the past caused the present family difficulties. Rather, they would like to teach families how best to stop perpetuating the problem. Similarly, those offering short-term educational programs, teaching ways of coping with marital or parent-child conflict, emphasize the learning of skills and do not search for explanations of the possible origins of the presenting difficulties.

Functional and Dysfunctional Families

All theories have at least an implicit—if in some cases, unstated—viewpoint regarding normal functioning. Bowen essentially bypasses the issue of normality by his concentration on optimal functioning and the related issues of differentiation and the separation of emotional and intellectual functioning. If we assume that most people lead lives they can manage (and proceed hesitantly if at all beyond those limits), then many may appear to have their lives in balance by remaining at relatively low levels of differentiation from the nuclear family emotional system. (The daughter who involves her mother as a partner in rearing her child is an example here.) How well that person functions, then, is dependent on the level of stress they encounter (or are able to avoid). According to Bowen, a well-differentiated person can become dysfunctional, but is likely to recover rapidly and with minimal impairment by calling upon a variety of coping mechanisms at his or her disposal; a poorly differentiated person gets caught up in family turmoil and recovers less well or quickly. The ideal situation in a marriage, according to Bowen, is for two highly differentiated partners to achieve emotional and intellectual intimacy without a loss of autonomy.

Modern psychoanalytic theories, including object relations viewpoints, have a great deal to say about functional and/or dysfunctional families. They stress, as starters, the importance of the infant's attachment to the mother or other caregiving figure as crucial to the development of a strong, cohesive self in an adult. Internalized images and introjects from the past shape future relationships, including marital choices. Splitting, projective identification, and object hunger all play a role in marriage, which is influenced by infantile experiences. In dysfunctional relationships, participants relate to one another as internalized objects, looking to reestablish missing or repudiated parts of themselves. To object relations theorists, dysfunctional family relationships result from unresolved infantile problems with parents, carried over from the individual's parents and, if unresolved, passed along to future generations.

Other models tend to take a broader, less specifically defined view regarding what constitutes normal family development and functional and/or dysfunctional relationships. Experiential family therapists adopt a humanistic, egalitarian stance, and view functional families as naturally self-actualizing; they have free choice, self-determination, and tend to operate as open systems. Individual development through the seeking of new experiences is encouraged and supported by the family. From the perspective of these models, dysfunction arises from societal pressures to deny and suppress natural impulses, consequently inhibiting spontaneity and growth.

Minuchin and the structuralists see normal family life as ever changing and thus continuously in need of making accommodations to changing conditions. What distinguishes such families from dysfunctional ones is the functional family's flexibility in changing or modifying its structure to fit new situations such as changing life cycle stages or adjusting to role changes or situational crises. The clarity of boundaries between subsystems within the family, and an effectively functioning spousal subsystem, help ensure stability despite changing conditions.

Interactional family therapists at the Mental Research Institute believe dysfunction arises from persistent faulty solutions to common difficulties. They contend that mishandled, self-defeating, more-of-the-same solutions imposed by the family are not a symptom of some underlying problem, but rather that those flawed solutions represent the problem itself. Behavioral/cognitive family therapists, supported by the most comprehensive research investigations into marital conflict, stress the importance of a positive communication exchange of rewarding behavior between partners in maintaining a happy relationship. Dysfunctional marriages, according to Gottman, are filled with negativity—criticism, contempt, stonewalling, and defensiveness.

Solution-focused therapists downplay interest in formulating a theory of functionality and/or dysfunctionality, since they contend that whatever preconceived label we use to explain another's behavior is in the eyes of the beholder and therefore an inadequate, arbitrary criterion of normality or abnormality. They add that ethnicity, race, type of family organization, sexual orientation, and so forth, must be factored into any appraisal of the ways a family lives. Collaborative therapists such as Harlene Anderson, also working from a social constructionist framework, are not interested in labels, but rather in "dissolving" problems and co-creating new stories in their place. Narrative therapists, departing from the "therapist as expert" position, honor each family's unique heritage, and avoid pathologizing labels, which they are likely to view as thin descriptions unfairly imposed on families by doctors or others with definitional powers in society.

Table 18.1 compares some of the differences in theoretical viewpoints between the various models of family therapy.

TABLE 18.1 A Comparison of Theoretical Viewpoints in Family Therapy

Model	Primary Theme	Unit of Study	Time Frame	Title or Derivation	Leading Figures	Major Concepts
Psychodynamic	Unresolved conflicts from past continue to attach themselves to current objects and situations.	Monadic; individual intrapsychic conflict brought to current family relations.	Past; early internalized family conflicts lead to interpersonal conflicts within present-day family.	Psychoanalytic	Ackerman	Interlocking pathology; scapegoating; role complementarity
				Object Relations Theory	Scharff & Scharff Framo	Introjects; attachments; projective identification; splitting
				Self Psychology	Kohut	Narcissism; self objects
Experiential	Free choice; self-determination; growth of the self; maturity achieved by overcoming impasses in process of gaining personal fulfillment.	Dyadic; problems arise from flawed interactions and communication lapses between family members (e.g., husband and wife).	Present; here-and-now data from immediate, ongoing interactions.	Symbolic–Experiential	Whitaker	Symbolic factors represent family's internal world and determine meaning given external reality.
						Self-awareness of the moment
				Gestalt	Kempler	
				Human Validation	Satir	Self-esteem; clarity of communication
				Emotionally Focused	Greenberg; Johnson	Explore inner experiences and relationships
Transgenerational	Emotional attachments to one's family of origin need to be resolved.	Triadic; problems arise and are maintained by relational binds with others.	Past and present; current marital relations assumed to result from partner's fusions to their families of origin or to unpaid "debts" and obligations.	Family Systems Theory	Bowen; Kerr; Friedman; Papero	Differentiation of self vs. fusion; triangles; multigenerational transmission process
				Contextual	Boszormenyi-Nagy	Family ledger; ethics; family legacies; entitlements
Structural	Symptoms in an individual are rooted in the context of family transaction patterns, and family restructuring must occur before symptoms are relieved.	Triadic; family enmeshment and disengagement involve family subsystems and family system as a whole.	Present; ongoing interactions maintained by unadaptive family organization, typically unable to deal with transitions in the family life cycle.	Structural Family Theory	Minuchin; Montalvo; Aponte; Fishman	Boundaries; subsystems; coalitions; enmeshment and disengagement

Approach	Description	Focus	Time/Problem	Theory Base	Key Figures	Key Concepts
Strategic	Redundant communication patterns offer clues to family rules and possible dysfunction; a symptom represents a strategy for controlling a relationship while claiming it to be involuntary.	Dyadic and triadic; symptoms are interpersonal communications between at least two, and probably three participants in reciprocal relationships.	Present; current problems or symptoms are maintained by ongoing, repetitive sequences between family members.	Communication Theory; Strategic Family Theory	Haley; Madanes; Weakland; Watzlawick; Jackson; Keim	Symmetrical and complementary communication patterns; paradox; family hierarchy
Milan	Dysfunctional families are caught up in destructive "games" and are guided by belief systems that do not fit the realities of their lives.	Triadic; problems express connecting relationship patterns between family members.	Present; recognition of circular nature of current problems helps family abandon previous limited linear perspectives.	Systemic Family Theory	Selvini-Palazzoli; Boscolo; Cecchin; Prata; Tomm	Paradox and counter-paradox; invariant prescriptions; circular questioning; second-order cybernetics
Behavioral/ Cognitive	Personal functioning is determined by the reciprocal interaction of behavior and its controlling social conditions.	Monadic; symptomatic person is the problem; linear view of causality.	Present; maladaptive behavior in an individual is maintained by current reinforcements from others.	Learning Theory; Social Learning Theory	Patterson; Stuart; Liberman; Alexander; Falloon; Ellis; Beck; Meichenbaum; Gottman	Conditioning; reinforcement; shaping; modeling; schemas
Social Constructionist	People use language to subjectively construct their views of reality and provide the basis for how they create "stories" about themselves.	Triadic; family problems are stories its members have agreed to tell about themselves.	Present and future; current problems based on past "stories" that influence current choices and behavior.	Social Construction Theory	de Shazer; O'Hanlon; Goolishian; Hoffman; Andersen; Anderson	No fixed truths, only multiple perspectives of reality; constructions of meaning
Narrative	Problem-saturated stories people tell themselves organize their experiences and shape their subsequent behavior.	Triadic; family unites to revise self-defeating stories.	Past as repository of successful efforts to overcome problems; future for re-authoring stories and developing options.	Narrative Theory	White; Epston	Poststructural; thin and thick descriptions
Psychoeducational	Educational information reduces stress on families and improves their coping skills.	Dyadic and triadic; range covers nonclinical premarital and marital couples to entire families with physical and mental disorders.	Present and future; enhancing existing skills to improve future quality of life.	Educational Psychology; Cognitive Behavior Therapy; Family Systems Theory	Anderson; Falloon; Goldstein; McFarlane; McDaniel; Guerney; Markman; Vishner	Use of empirically based procedures to manage schizophrenia; expressed emotion; collaborative family health care; marriage preparation and relationship enhancement

FAMILY THERAPIES: A COMPARATIVE OVERVIEW

In a further comparison of therapeutic models, we look at six dimensions of the therapeutic process: the therapist's role, the model's use of formal or informal assessment procedures, the issue of insight versus action intervention mode, key methods of intervention for each model, the duration of therapy (crisis, brief, long-term), and the goals of treatment.

The Role of the Therapist

Object relations therapists are interested in creating a safe, nurturing atmosphere in which to examine and attempt to resolve the client's unconscious conflicts that interfere with current family relationships. To do so these therapists adopt a safe, holding environment; they are empathetic, attentive, and interested in exploration; and they listen without rushing to advise or reassure. In providing clarification or insight into intrapsychic or interpersonal conflicts, they offer interpretations to each participant separately (rather than focusing on the family system), and then examine transference and countertransference reactions.

In contrast to such neutrality and keeping of therapeutic distance, experiential family therapists strive for active, spontaneous, honest, and open encounters. Satir, with her warm and personal manner, tried to provide a role model for straight talk and clear communication, all directed at increasing client self-esteem. She often relied on touch to make contact—unlike Kempler, whose confrontational verbal style, insistent and often uncomfortably open and direct, provoked clients into engaging in honest emotional exchanges with him and with each other. Whitaker—spontaneous, without a plan of engagement prior to a session with clients, and eschewing a neutral stance—shared his feelings and fantasies in order to allow his clients to feel free and safe enough to do the same.

Bowenians are coaches, attempting to minimize their emotional impact on the family (and, in turn, avoiding being caught up in any family emotional turmoil). Therapists using this approach attempt to be calm and low-key, behaving as experienced experts outside of the family who use questioning to help define and clarify the family's emotional system. They try to remain in non-anxious emotional contact with family members, careful not to be triangled into the family's entangling conflicts and toning down family emotional expression, but at the same time directing efforts to help members gain greater self-differentiation (take "I" positions). Helping clients return to their families of origin after coaching them to continue their differentiating efforts is part of the therapist's role.

Structuralists, strategists, and Milan therapists all move in and out of the therapeutic process at key points. Structuralists join the family system in a leadership role, accommodate to the family style, map out the structure the family has developed, and go about helping them change that structure to adapt to changing conditions. As active stage directors, they carefully plan how to adjust to each family, reframe messages, and help families create flexible boundaries and harmonious, integrated subsystems. Strategists are also active and manipulative, issuing directives, relabeling behavior, sometimes prescribing symptom maintenance and employing other paradoxical techniques. Using a wide variety of techniques, they tailor interventions to specific symptoms and custom-design problem-resolving strategies to eliminate the presenting problem. The Milan group employs many strategic techniques, but adds the unique contributions of positive connotations, rituals, and circular questioning (an especially provocative and effective intervention that may allow the system to heal itself). Milan therapists make frequent therapeutic use of an active and intervening observing team behind the one-way mirror.

Solution-focused therapists get right to work helping clients define the changes they are looking for; they do not spend time speculating on the origins of presenting problems. Assuming clients know what it is they wish to change, these therapists collaboratively engage in therapeutic conversations ("miracle questions,""exception questions"), helping clients construct solutions. Therapists who adopt the linguistic approach of Goolishian and Anderson also use collaborative procedures, viewing clients as conversational partners; therapist and clients engage in a joint search for altered or new meanings, attitudes, and narratives. Narrative therapists, as coauthors, also help clients develop new meanings, using questioning to aid clients as they revisit and rewrite old, self-defeating stories, replacing them with preferred empowering stories about actively directing their futures.

Feminist family therapists typically are active in helping both men and women overcome stereotypic thinking about gender roles; they, like the narrative therapists, help family members identify those damaging, culturally influenced, sexist practices that stifle individuality. Psychoeducational family therapists are active teachers or coaches, interested in inculcating skills to aid in reducing family conflict.

Assessment Procedures

All family therapists engage in some form of evaluation with families, beginning with the initial session and continuing throughout treatment, as the therapist gathers data and formulates (and reformulates) hypotheses. As therapy proceeds, some of the original speculations may be confirmed and built upon, others negated by new information and rejected, still others changed as the therapist modifies his or her assumptions and shifts therapeutic strategies. While some family therapists consider a formal assessment procedure to be central to their therapeutic planning, there are those who consider it peripheral to their therapeutic interventions, in some cases believing one should not sit in judgment of others (the client knows best what he or she needs), even for therapeutic purposes. Nevertheless, systematically or not, all therapists make some sort of appraisal of new client families, inevitably comparing them to other families worked with previously who presented similar complaints and who profited from a specific set of interventions.

Behavioral family therapists are particularly interested in defining and, if possible, measuring the extent of the maladaptive problem, using standardized interview procedures and formal test instruments. How frequently does the undesirable behavior occur? What events preceded the appearance of the behavior? What are its consequences? What reinforcements are operating to maintain the problem? The more commonly encountered cognitive-behavioral therapists are likely to employ questionnaires and inventories for each family member, to get a sense of different perspectives about the family problem. In particular, they want to assess not just the frequency but also the reciprocal patterns between members that perpetuate the behavior, all in preparation for introducing a cognitive restructuring program.

Bowenians begin by gathering historical data in the form of genograms, allowing the therapist and family members together to ferret out family patterns extending over several generations. In the process, the therapist and the family obtain an inside picture of unresolved issues and family patterns from the past, and the family also gains a perspective regarding issues that have hampered family functioning over generations. Other family therapists interested in longitudinal history also look for patterns from the past that impose themselves on current family functioning. Boszormenyi-Nagy might assess intergenerational indebtedness; object relations therapists focus on possible unconscious conflicts from the past, within each partner in a relationship, that have led to a stalemate in their attempt to develop intimacy. In gender-sensitive approaches, the feminist therapist working with a couple might review with them a history of exposure to sexist attitudes or current gender discrimination that negatively affects optimal marital functioning.

Another group of family therapists, interested in assessment, prefers a cross-sectional view of family functioning instead of adopting a longitudinal framework. What led the couple or family to seek help *now*? A Mental Research Institute (MRI) strategic therapist might wonder aloud if the family has gotten stuck, trying the same solution and meeting the same frustrating barriers again and again, thus perpetuating the problem.

Structuralists rely on observation of the family in action, mapping transactional patterns, provoking enactments to detect boundary problems such as enmeshment and disengagement. They might perceive the family as being at a transition point, needing a restructuring but unable to move beyond the impasse without therapeutic intervention. Affiliating with the family, they are in a position to understand its organizational structure and ongoing transactional patterns, its subsystems and hierarchical design. Experientialists, especially cross-sectional ("here-and-now"), help families search for suppressed feelings and impulses that need to be unblocked in order to gain greater growth and fulfillment.

Beyond longitudinal and cross-sectional emphases in assessment, there is a third viewpoint—minimal to no interest in the family's history and current system of functioning. The social constructionists believe they are in no position to evaluate others, since their view is just one of many perceptions of the situation, and the clients' knowledge about themselves takes priority. Believing that they are not objective observers with a truthful interpretation of reality, social constructionists adopt the egalitarian viewpoint that they need to engage families in conversation, not evaluation. Such a collaboration results in the therapist and family members examining the family's stories about themselves (and especially the meaning families give to those stories) that families can re-author for greater empowerment.

Solution-focused therapists are a good example of unencumbered elegance, focusing from the start on simply finding the skeleton keys (general guides) to move clients toward solutions. In this brief approach, problems are not uncovered and assessed; rather, the thrust is toward solution development and client empowerment. The collaborative approach of Harlene Anderson also adopts a "not knowing" attitude by the therapist, meaning she does not determine or have set ideas about what is wrong with the family and what needs to change. That shared determination emerges from the conversation together. Narrative therapists, too, do not feel they have special privileges over their clients, nor are they interested in playing expert diagnostician of another person's motives or personality characteristics. What they are interested in doing is liberating people from a sense of helplessness and despair; their persistent questioning is directed at exploring and expanding beliefs and visions about the future, not in gathering data for assessment or diagnostic purposes.

Insight and Action Modes

All therapies are about change; but what is the best, quickest, and most lasting way to achieve such change? Is it by clients gaining insight or new understanding of their situation, perhaps the origins of their problems, in preparation for making changes in their lives? Or is it by taking actions—trying out new ways of thinking or behaving—that lead to new experiences and, subsequently, changes in their lives? Or is some combination of insight and action most effective? If so, does one need to precede the other?

The early family therapists, especially those with classical psychoanalytic training, believed insight produced understanding and clarification, perhaps helping clients better comprehend the underlying conflicts from the past that continued to undermine their current functioning. These therapists contended that by gaining greater self-awareness of such things as interlocking pathology or role complementarity or the function of the symptom in the family system, these families would then take actions on their own behalf.

Ackerman, for example, used psychodynamic techniques such as confrontation and interpretation to expose both intrapsychic and interpersonal conflict when working with troubled families. Bowen also helped clients gain insight into their role in family triangles and other interpersonal aspects of the nuclear family emotional system, encouraging them to use that understanding to attempt new relational patterns—new actions—based on these insights. Stressing the importance of action—they were often breaking away from individual ("talk") psychoanalysis—these therapists nevertheless saw insight as a necessary prerequisite for change through action.

Do action and change necessarily follow from gaining insight? Obviously not, since most of us know we should lose weight, exercise more, drink in moderation, have regular physical checkups, stop smoking, get sufficient sleep, and so on; but we fail to do so on a regular basis, even as we admit such behavior would be in our own best interest. Is insight into hidden and unresolved conflicts always necessary for behavioral change to occur? Strategists insist this is not the case. They argue that believing a family needs to gain insight into causes before change occurs is to erroneously believe in a linear, unidirectional causality from past to present. Behavioral/cognitive family therapists are also emphatically unconcerned with insight or inferred underlying motives, pragmatically focusing on observable behavior and what needs repair. For them, the search for underlying causes calls for high levels of inference, and often ends up producing useless explanations at the cost of needed action.

Structuralists provide a good example of combining action and insight—new actions lead to new experiences that in turn lead to new insights and understanding. Enactments, for example, may demonstrate successful actions that make insight possible and later can be added to the family repertoire. Restructuring helps families view the world differently, and these new views inevitably lead to members flexibly trying out new roles and new experiences. Gestalt therapist Kempler also tries for dramatic emotional breakthroughs in the session, believing these will later be carried forward into greater spontaneity and self-expression.

The Milan group, especially Cecchin and Boscolo, looking beyond insight-versus-action interventions, invites families to examine their *meaning system* and break through old games by building family consensus about reality, in an effort to discover new possibilities not previously considered. Their later formulations have led to the current cognitive emphasis prevalent in the social constructionist therapies. Cognitive change, as opposed to insight, opens avenues for fresh ways of thinking, not necessarily for gaining new understanding.

Narrative therapy bypasses any insight-action dichotomy, focuses instead on cognitive change (finding new meanings) and the collaborative search for more optimistic, productive solutions that are within the client. Rather than offer insights—which would presume they understand the client better than he or she does himself—narrative therapists provide a climate in which client and therapist can co-construct alternative stories in place of those that have left family members or kinship groups feeling defeated and hopeless. In this technique, narrative therapists are joined by advocates of reflecting teams and the linguistic, conversational techniques in giving priority to new meanings over action per se.

Key Methods of Intervention

All family therapists use a variety of techniques selectively borrowed from different models—clarifying feelings being expressed, modeling communication, asking relationship-directed questions, defining options, encouraging desirable behavior, eliciting intimacy between partners, calling upon family strengths, etc. However, advocates of one or the other model rely on certain specific and defining therapeutic moves, and it is those unique efforts to which we now turn.

Psychodynamic family therapists make use of *interpretation* in order to help clients understand the unconscious meaning of their thoughts, verbalizations, and behavior. They may clarify or challenge client statements, or make comments that link one event with another ("You're afraid to commit to your relationship with Sally, here, because you suspect your mother was unfaithful to your father and covered it up"). These therapists rarely ask questions or take the lead in what gets discussed, sometimes deliberately becoming silent to provoke greater family exchange.

Experiential family therapists are often *confrontational,* in an effort to provoke self-discovery or self-examination. ("You always seem to change the subject or make a joke whenever we discuss your sex life together. What's making you so uncomfortable that you need to cover it up?") They may introduce verbal or physical *exercises* (sculpting, role playing, reconstruction) to encourage the expression of feelings, and often use *self-disclosure* to stimulate similar open behavior in clients.

Bowenians question, coach, encourage individual efforts at *self-differentiation* by teaching clients to take "I positions" expressing how they truly feel. Contextual therapists appeal to fairness, promoting the *balancing of the family ledger*. Structuralists work on clarifying *boundary diffusion*, and often turn to *enactments* to introduce changes in the family structure. They join and accommodate to the family's interactive style, and often use *reframing* to relabel a family's perception of an event and make it more conducive to therapeutic change. Strategists also utilize the reframing technique and in addition use *directives* and *paradoxical interventions* to bring about change. Milan therapists use *positive connotations* and *circular questioning* to aid family members in learning about the perceptions of other members.

Behaviorists and cognitive behaviorists attend to the *contingencies of reinforcement,* first observing and analyzing how families reinforce undesirable or problematic behavior. After such a functional analysis, they rely on *skills training* and *cognitive restructuring* to teach families to alter or modify thoughts about the meaning of an event. Psychoeducational family therapists make use of similar techniques to teach skills to specific populations.

Solution-focused therapists address efforts to arrive at successful solutions by utilizing a variety of techniques—*miracle questions, exception-finding questions, scaling.* The narrative therapist's trademark is *externalization,* by which the problem is recast as outside the symptom-bearer and the family is united to deal with the oppressive agent. By a series of persistent questions, clients are encouraged to adopt previously subjugated stories that replace negative and self-defeating dominant stories.

Crisis, Brief, and Long-Term Family Therapy

All family therapists must be prepared to help families in crisis. Whether dealing with a new referral or a family currently in treatment to whom a crisis occurs, the family therapist must respond without delay, in some cases seeing the family daily (for varying lengths of time) during the crucial period, usually lasting several weeks or less. The discovery of a spouse having an affair, a sudden job loss by the major breadwinner, a suicide attempt by an adolescent, the accidental death of a child—these are crises requiring a quick therapeutic response. In severe situations, such as those involving danger to oneself or others, psychiatric hospitalization may be called for. In all cases, therapists are likely to try to help the family call forth its restitutive or resilient forces to reestablish stability, at the same time helping them, whenever possible, to develop new and effective coping mechanisms.

Brief family therapy is usually defined as less urgent, and it has an agreed-upon termination point. The duration of most family therapy has become shorter than in the past (and frequently dramatically shorter than individual therapy), particularly in the age of managed care and long waiting lists at clinics. Brief or time-limited therapy, say with a marital couple in distress, tends to be highly focused on the presenting problem. In most cases its aims are limited to achieving a specific goal, which may range from establishing more effective ways to resolve differences between spouses to decisions about divorce and child custody arrangements.

Strategic therapists, particularly those at the Brief Therapy Project at the Palo Alto Mental Research Institute, limit their treatment to 10 sessions. They announce this policy to clients at the start as a motivator. Solution-focused therapists at the Milwaukee Brief Therapy Center offer still fewer sessions, but do not announce a time limit in advance. They immediately start to work with clients on solutions with the expectations of change and of utilizing client resources, and they often require a handful of sessions to reach the agreed-upon achievable goals. Haley preplans strategies by stages, and the Milan group also sets limits on the number of sessions.

Social constructionists and narrative therapists are also oriented to provide help that is brief and problem-driven, although the length of treatment is not their main concern. Unlike the strategists, who were influenced by Milton Erickson and Gregory Bateson, their focus is on language shaping a person's experiences and sense of reality. Correspondingly, they aim their interventions at cognitive changes as clients reconstruct their experiences through developing new stories.

While there are few long-term family therapies—psychoanalytic couples therapy efforts may be the exception—some approaches contend that change takes time, and thus they require several weeks or even months before therapy termination. Experiential models with vague goals of "growth" or "self-fulfillment" tend to have arbitrary endpoints, letting the family members decide when they wish to stop. Structuralists wait to see how well the family has restructured its dysfunctional sets, and how flexible it has become to accommodating change, before terminating the sessions. Bowenian therapy too—with goals of changing a large, extended family system—may be of considerable duration.

In some cases, families with severe and/or multiple problems require long-term help, or perhaps help from time to time extending over years, as new and difficult situations arise for them. Long-lasting unresolved problems (persistent bickering, gambling episodes, disputes with in-laws, bouts of alcoholism, violence, periodic infidelities, cycling in and out of serious depression) may prolong treatment. In some situations, family therapy may begin as brief but extend to long-term treatment as more underlying conflicts are uncovered. Clients may return to their family therapist, who has become familiar with their problems, for brief visits at different key decision-making phases of their lives if that person has been helpful in the past.

Goals of Treatment

All family therapy models provide an opportunity for change based upon client perceptions of new choices. Differences arise between models in how they go about achieving this goal. Some (psychodynamic) do so by providing insight, some (experiential) by encouraging open communication and emotional expression, some (behavioral/cognitive) by building skills and cognitive restructuring, some by expanding the family system through the use of reflecting teams or outside witness groups. Regardless of procedures, all attempt to create a therapeutic environment conducive to self-examination in order to reduce discomfort and conflict, to mobilize family resilience and empowerment, and to help the family members improve their overall functioning.

Some models seek extensive changes. Object relations therapists, for example, identify and help clients gain awareness of introjects from the past that negatively intrude on current ways of dealing with others. More focused in their aspirations, some (solution-focused or strategic) therapists help families solve the immediate problem they came to therapy to resolve; they are content with symptom reduction. Therapists using psychoeducational approaches are satisfied if they can help a family cope with serious disorders and keep its diagnosed member from returning to the hospital (or at least reducing the necessary number of such returns). Narrative therapists cognitively focus on problem resolution, but go beyond that, challenging the family to revise its relationship with the problem and encouraging members to re-author their lives in more hopeful ways.

Different theorists have different priorities regarding what requires change. Satir was insistent that family members learn to communicate with greater clarity, asking for what they want and expressing how they feel in a direct and undisguised manner. Whitaker wanted to make certain that what clients said was congruent with what they were experiencing internally, in an effort to increase authenticity. Both believed clients enhance their ability to live more fulfilled lives as individuals and as a family as they grow and work at self-discovery.

Bowen, in contrast, argued that individuation or self-differentiation was the key to staving off anxiety and avoiding being swept up in the family's emotional system. Structuralists such as Minuchin very specifically set out to change those parts of the family system that call for reorganizing—its boundaries, its hierarchy, perhaps its parental subsystem.

TABLE 18.2 A Comparison of Therapeutic Techniques and Goals in Family Therapy

Model	Role of Therapist	Assessment Procedures	Key Methods of Intervention	Insight vs. Action	Title or Derivation	Goals of Treatment
Psychodynamic	Neutral; blank screen upon whom each family member projects fantasies	Unstructured; ongoing effort to uncover hidden conflict within and between family members	Interpretations regarding the unconscious meaning of individual verbalizations and behavior and their impact on family functioning	Insight leads to understanding, conflict reduction, and ultimately individual intrapsychic and system change	Psychoanalytic	Individual intrapsychic change; resolution of family pathogenic conflict
					Object Relations	Detriangulation; removal of projections; individuation
Experiential	Egalitarian; active facilitator providing family with new experiences through the therapeutic encounter	Unstructured; search for suppressed feelings and impulses that block growth and fulfillment	Confrontation to provoke self-discovery; self-disclosure by therapist models desired behavior; exercises (e.g., sculpting, family reconstruction) to uncover previously unexpressed inner conflicts	Self-awareness of one's immediate existence leads to choice, responsibility, and change	Symbolic-Experiential	Simultaneous sense of togetherness and healthy separation and autonomy
					Gestalt	Genuineness; learning to express one's sense of being
					Human Validation	Building self-esteem; relieving family pain; overcoming blockages to personal growth
					Emotionally Focused	Overcoming negative interactive patterns
Transgenerational	Coach; direct but nonconfrontational; detriangulated from family fusion	Family evaluation interviews with any combination of family members; genograms	Teaching differentiation; individuation; taking "I" stands; reopening cutoff relations with extended family	Rational processes used to gain insight into current relationships and intergenerational experiences; leads to action with family of origin	Family Systems Theory	Anxiety reduction, symptom relief, and increased self-differentiation of individuals leads to family system change
	Aids family in developing relational fairness	Attention to intergenerational indebtedness	Balancing family ledgers		Contextual	Restoration of trust, fairness, ethical responsibility
Structural	Active; stage director manipulates family structure to change dysfunctional sets	Observation of family transactional patterns for clues to family structure; family mapping; enactments; tracking	Joining; accommodating; reframing; helping families create flexible boundaries and integrated subsystems	Action precedes understanding; change in transactional patterns leads to new experiences and corresponding insights	Structural Family Theory	Restructured family organization; change in dysfunctional transactional patterns; symptom reduction in individual members

(continued)

TABLE 18.2 A Comparison of Therapeutic Techniques and Goals in Family Therapy (continued)

Model	Role of Therapist	Assessment Procedures	Key Methods of Intervention	Insight vs. Action	Title or Derivation	Goals of Treatment
Strategic	Active; manipulative; problem-focused; prescriptive; paradoxical	Unstructured; search for family's repetitive, destructive behavior patterns and flawed solutions that perpetuate the presenting problem	Paradoxical interventions; prescribing the symptom; therapeutic double binds; directives; pretend techniques; relabeling	Action-oriented; symptom reduction and behavior change brought about through directives rather than insight and understanding	Communication Theory; Strategic Family Theory	Symptom relief; resolution of presenting problem
Milan	Neutral; active therapeutic partner; offers hypotheses as new information for family belief system; use of reflecting team behind one-way mirror	Unstructured; non-manipulative; collaborates with family in developing systemic hypotheses regarding their problems	Positive connotations; circular questioning; reframing; paradox; invariant prescription; rituals	Emphasis on family gaining new meaning rather than insight or action based on therapist choice of therapeutic outcome	Systemic Family Theory	System change chosen by family because of new meaning given to their life patterns; interruption of destructive family "games"
Behavioral/Cognitive	Teacher; trainer; model of desired behavior; contract negotiator	Structured; reliance on formal standardized tests and questionnaires; behavioral analysis before commencing treatment	Reinforcement of desired behaviors; skills training; contingency contracting; positive reciprocity between marital partners as well as parents and children; self-regulated modification of thoughts and activities	Actions taught to reward desired outcomes and ignore or punish undesired behavior; unconcerned with insight	Learning Theory; Social Learning Theory; Behavioral/Cognitive Theory	Modification of behavioral consequences between persons in order to eliminate maladaptive behavior and/or alleviate presenting symptoms; cognitive restructuring
Social Constructionist	Collaborative; engages in therapeutic conversation; non-expert co-constructing meaning and understanding	Unstructured; examination of explanations and interpretations families have used to account for their views of "truth"	Solution focus rather than focus on problems; miracle questions; exception-finding questions; use of reflecting teams; conversational partners in "dissolving" problem	Emphasis on gaining new meaning through narrative reconstructions of stories families have told about themselves	Social Construction Theory	Learning and creating new viewpoints by giving new meanings or constructions to old sets of problems

Narrative	Collaborative; help clients rewrite old self-defeating stories, replacing them with empowering stories with multiple options	Unstructured; no privileged position over client's views; do not believe in expert position or correct view of objective reality	Externalization of restraining problem, redefining it as outside the family and unwelcome; search for new options and unique outcomes; use of definitional ceremonies, letters, and supportive leagues	Attempt to achieve cognitive change and give new meaning to co-constructed alternative stories	Narrative Theory	Separate person from problem; liberation reenvision past and rewrite future
Psycho-educational	Builds and maintains supportive, collaborative partnership with family; facilitates family learning management skills	Assessment of family stress level, expressed emotion in order to tailor problem-solving training to each family; identifies problem areas to aid in skills acquisition	Education; social support; skills training; relationship building	Action: developing techniques to reduce rehospitalization for mental disorders; partnership with physicians in health care; short-term educational programs	Psychoeducational Family Therapy; Medical Family Therapy	Harness family strengths and resiliencies to improve their communication patterns and learn more effective coping skills

Competing family models try to facilitate new ways of perceiving, feeling, and behaving in different ways. Some do so formally, in some cases following step-by-step procedures. Structuralists, for example, join the family, accommodate to its style, assess the family structure, and so forth, before making therapeutic moves directed at restructuring flawed parts of the system. Cognitively oriented family therapists also follow prescribed therapeutic formats. Some approaches (solution-focused), however, are less structured and pragmatic, aiming their interventions at finding new solutions to presenting complaints, and not particularly concerned about any underlying set of problems. If some models (experiential) have imposing goals (self-actualization), others (strategic) are content with more modest specific aspirations (resolving the presenting problem and concluding treatment).

Table 18.2 (starting on page 441) compares the different models along several key therapeutic dimensions.

SUMMARY

Overlaps in both theory and technique, as well as notable differences, characterize today's models of family therapy. Regardless of model, families need to be looked upon as systems; beyond that, the family must be viewed in the context of its extended family and the community, as well as its cultural, racial, social class, and ethnic attributes.

Family theories differ in their emphasis on units of study (monad, dyad, and triad), depending upon their primary focus on the individual family member or the family context. All operate from a dyadic or triadic position, based on the view that people define themselves through their interactions with others. The time frame emphasized might be primarily past, present, or future. All theories draw distinctions between functional and dysfunctional families. Some operate with distinctive ideas of what constitutes normal behavior, based upon the past, while others take a here-and-now position in conceptualizing the basis for current difficulties.

Family therapy techniques of intervention can be differentiated by the role of the therapist (ranging from neutral to collaborative) and by the assessment procedures the technique utilizes (ranging from formal to informal appraisals and from longitudinal to cross-sectional emphases). All models attempt to achieve change in the most efficient way; some favor action preceding insight and some favor the reverse. Although therapists regularly borrow from other theories, each follows a distinctive set of specific markers that are outlined.

Family therapy may be crisis oriented, brief, or long-term, depending on such factors as urgency, clinic policy, managed care restrictions, degree of chronicity, or type of intervention. The goals of treatment may be alike for many models, but differ in the extensiveness of change they seek and the priorities they give to what requires change. While some approaches are formal and follow set procedures, others are informal, pragmatic, and limited to resolving the presenting complaint.

RECOMMENDED READINGS

Dattilio, F. M. (1998). *Case studies in couple and family therapy: Systemic and cognitive perspectives.* New York: Guilford Press.

Hoffman, L. (2002). *Family therapy: An intimate history.* New York: Norton.

Kerr, M. E., & Bowen, M. (1988). *Family evaluation: An approach based on Bowen theory.* New York: Norton.

Minuchin, S. (1974). *Families and family therapy.* Cambridge, MA: Harvard University Press.

White, M., & Epston, D. (1990). *Narrative means to therapeutic ends.* New York: Norton.

AAMFT Code of Ethics

Effective July 1, 2001

Preamble

The Board of Directors of the American Association for Marriage and Family Therapy (AAMFT) hereby promulgates, pursuant to Article 2, Section 2.013 of the Association's Bylaws, the Revised AAMFT Code of Ethics, effective July 1, 2001.

The AAMFT strives to honor the public trust in marriage and family therapists by setting standards for ethical practice as described in this Code. The ethical standards define professional expectations and are enforced by the AAMFT Ethics Committee. The absence of an explicit reference to a specific behavior or situation in the Code does not mean that the behavior is ethical or unethical. The standards are not exhaustive. Marriage and family therapists who are uncertain about the ethics of a particular course of action are encouraged to seek counsel from consultants, attorneys, supervisors, colleagues, or other appropriate authorities.

Both law and ethics govern the practice of marriage and family therapy. When making decisions regarding professional behavior, marriage and family therapists must consider the AAMFT Code of Ethics and applicable laws and regulations. If the AAMFT Code of Ethics prescribes a standard higher than that required by law, marriage and family therapists must meet the higher standard of the AAMFT Code of Ethics. Marriage and family therapists comply with the mandates of law, but make known their commitment to the AAMFT Code of Ethics and take steps to resolve the conflict in a responsible manner. The AAMFT supports legal mandates for reporting of alleged unethical conduct.

The AAMFT Code of Ethics is binding on Members of AAMFT in all membership categories, AAMFT-Approved Supervisors, and applicants for membership and the Approved Supervisor designation (hereafter, AAMFT Member). AAMFT members have an obligation to be familiar with the AAMFT Code of Ethics and its application to their professional services. Lack of awareness or misunderstanding of an ethical standard is not a defense to a charge of unethical conduct.

The process for filing, investigating, and resolving complaints of unethical conduct is described in the current Procedures for Handling Ethical Matters of the AAMFT Ethics Committee. Persons accused are considered innocent by the Ethics Committee until proven guilty, except as otherwise provided, and are entitled to due process. If an AAMFT Member resigns in anticipation of, or during the course of, an ethics investigation, the Ethics Committee will complete its investigation. Any publication of action taken by the Association will include the fact that the Member attempted to resign during the investigation.

Contents

1. Responsibility to clients
2. Confidentiality
3. Professional competence and integrity
4. Responsibility to students and supervisees
5. Responsibility to research participants
6. Responsibility to the profession
7. Financial arrangements
8. Advertising

Principle I
Responsibility to Clients

Marriage and family therapists advance the welfare of families and individuals. They respect the rights of those persons seeking their assistance, and make reasonable efforts to ensure that their services are used appropriately.

1.1 Marriage and family therapists provide professional assistance to persons without discrimination on the basis of race, age, ethnicity, socioeconomic status, disability, gender, health status, religion, national origin, or sexual orientation.

1.2 Marriage and family therapists obtain appropriate informed consent to therapy or related procedures as early as feasible in the therapeutic relationship, and use language that is reasonably understandable to clients. The content of informed consent may vary depending upon the client and treatment plan; however, informed consent generally necessitates that the client: (a) has the capacity to consent; (b) has been adequately informed of significant information concerning treatment processes and procedures; (c) has been adequately informed of potential risks and benefits of treatments for which generally recognized standards do not yet exist; (d) has freely and without undue influence expressed consent; and (e) has provided consent that is appropriately documented. When persons, due to age or mental status, are legally incapable of giving informed consent, marriage and family therapists obtain informed permission from a legally authorized person, if such substitute consent is legally permissible.

1.3 Marriage and family therapists are aware of their influential positions with respect to clients, and they avoid exploiting the trust and dependency of such persons. Therapists, therefore, make every effort to avoid conditions and multiple relationships with clients that could impair professional judgment or increase the risk of exploitation. Such relationships include, but are not limited to, business or close personal relationships with a client or the client's immediate family. When the risk of impairment or exploitation exists due to conditions or multiple roles, therapists take appropriate precautions.

1.4 Sexual intimacy with clients is prohibited.

1.5 Sexual intimacy with former clients is likely to be harmful and is therefore prohibited for two years following the termination of therapy or last professional contact. In an effort to avoid exploiting the trust and dependency of clients, marriage and family therapists should not engage in sexual intimacy with former clients after the two years following termination or last professional contact. Should therapists engage in sexual intimacy with former clients following two years after termination or last professional contact, the burden shifts to the therapist to demonstrate that there has been no exploitation or injury to the former client or to the client's immediate family.

1.6 Marriage and family therapists comply with applicable laws regarding the reporting of alleged unethical conduct.

1.7 Marriage and family therapists do not use their professional relationships with clients to further their own interests.

1.8 Marriage and family therapists respect the rights of clients to make decisions and help them to understand the consequences of these decisions. Therapists clearly advise the clients that they have the responsibility to make decisions regarding relationships such as cohabitation, marriage, divorce, separation, reconciliation, custody, and visitation.

1.9 Marriage and family therapists continue therapeutic relationships only so long as it is reasonably clear that clients are benefiting from the relationship.

1.10 Marriage and family therapists assist persons in obtaining other therapeutic services if the therapist is unable or unwilling, for appropriate reasons, to provide professional help.

1.11 Marriage and family therapists do not abandon or neglect clients in treatment without making reasonable arrangements for the continuation of such treatment.

1.12 Marriage and family therapists obtain written informed consent from clients before videotaping, audio recording, or permitting third-party observation.

1.13 Marriage and family therapists, upon agreeing to provide services to a person or entity at the request of a third party, clarify, to the extent feasible and at the outset of the service, the nature of the relationship with each party and the limits of confidentiality.

Principle II
Confidentiality

Marriage and family therapists have unique confidentiality concerns because the client in a therapeutic relationship may be more than one person. Therapists respect and guard the confidences of each individual client.

2.1 Marriage and family therapists disclose to clients and other interested parties, as early as feasible in their professional contacts, the nature of confidentiality and possible limitations of the clients' right to confidentiality. Therapists review with clients the circumstances where confidential information may be requested and where disclosure of confidential information may be legally required. Circumstances may necessitate repeated disclosures.

2.2 Marriage and family therapists do not disclose client confidences except by written authorization or waiver, or where mandated or permitted by law. Verbal authorization will not be sufficient except in emergency situations, unless prohibited by law. When providing couple, family or group treatment, the therapist does not disclose information outside the treatment context without a written authorization from each individual competent to execute a waiver. In the context of couple, family or group treatment, the therapist may not reveal any individual's confidences to others in the client unit without the prior written permission of that individual.

2.3 Marriage and family therapists use client and/or clinical materials in teaching, writing, consulting, research, and public presentations only if a written waiver has been obtained in accordance with Subprinciple 2.2, or when appropriate steps have been taken to protect client identity and confidentiality.

2.4 Marriage and family therapists store, safeguard, and dispose of client records in ways that maintain confidentiality and in accord with applicable laws and professional standards.

2.5 Subsequent to the therapist moving from the area, closing the practice, or upon the death of the therapist, a marriage and family therapist arranges for the storage, transfer, or disposal of client records in ways that maintain confidentiality and safeguard the welfare of clients.

2.6 Marriage and family therapists, when consulting with colleagues or referral sources, do not share confidential information that could reasonably lead to the identification of a client, research participant, supervisee, or other person with whom they have a confidential relationship unless they have obtained the prior written consent of the client, research participant, supervisee, or other person with whom they have a confidential relationship. Information may be shared only to the extent necessary to achieve the purposes of the consultation.

Principle III
Professional Competence and Integrity

Marriage and family therapists maintain high standards of professional competence and integrity.

3.1 Marriage and family therapists pursue knowledge of new developments and maintain competence in marriage and family therapy through education, training, or supervised experience.

3.2 Marriage and family therapists maintain adequate knowledge of and adhere to applicable laws, ethics, and professional standards.

3.3 Marriage and family therapists seek appropriate professional assistance for their personal problems or conflicts that may impair work performance or clinical judgment.

3.4 Marriage and family therapists do not provide services that create a conflict of interest that may impair work performance or clinical judgment.

3.5 Marriage and family therapists, as presenters, teachers, supervisors, consultants and researchers, are dedicated to high standards of scholarship, present accurate information, and disclose potential conflicts of interest.

3.6 Marriage and family therapists maintain accurate and adequate clinical and financial records.

3.7 While developing new skills in specialty areas, marriage and family therapists take steps to ensure the competence of their work and to protect clients from possible harm. Marriage and family therapists practice in specialty areas new to them only after appropriate education, training, or supervised experience.

3.8 Marriage and family therapists do not engage in sexual or other forms of harassment of clients, students, trainees, supervisees, employees, colleagues, or research subjects.

3.9 Marriage and family therapists do not engage in the exploitation of clients, students, trainees, supervisees, employees, colleagues, or research subjects.

3.10 Marriage and family therapists do not give to or receive from clients (a) gifts of substantial value or (b) gifts that impair the integrity or efficacy of the therapeutic relationship.

3.11 Marriage and family therapists do not diagnose, treat, or advise on problems outside the recognized boundaries of their competencies.

3.12 Marriage and family therapists make efforts to prevent the distortion or misuse of their clinical and research findings.

3.13 Marriage and family therapists, because of their ability to influence and alter the lives of others, exercise special care when making public their professional recommendations and opinions through testimony or other public statements.

3.14 To avoid a conflict of interests, marriage and family therapists who treat minors or adults involved in custody or visitation actions may not also perform forensic evaluations for custody, residence, or visitation of the minor. The marriage and family therapist who treats the minor may provide the court or mental health professional performing the evaluation with information about the minor from the marriage and family therapist's perspective as a treating marriage and family therapist, so long as the marriage and family therapist does not violate confidentiality.

3.15 Marriage and family therapists are in violation of this Code and subject to termination of membership or other appropriate action if they: (a) are convicted of any felony; (b) are convicted of a misdemeanor related to their qualifications or functions; (c) engage in conduct which could lead to conviction of a felony, or a misdemeanor related to their qualifications or functions; (d) are expelled from or disciplined by other professional organizations; (e) have their licenses or certificates suspended or revoked or are otherwise disciplined by regulatory bodies; (f) continue to practice marriage and family therapy while no longer competent to do so because they are impaired by physical or mental causes or the abuse of alcohol or other substances; or (g) fail to cooperate with the Association at any point from the inception of an ethical complaint through the completion of all proceedings regarding that complaint.

Principle IV
Responsibility to Students and Supervisees

Marriage and family therapists do not exploit the trust and dependency of students and supervisees.

4.1 Marriage and family therapists are aware of their influential positions with respect to students and supervisees, and they avoid exploiting the trust and dependency of such persons. Therapists, therefore, make every effort to avoid conditions and multiple relationships that could impair professional objectivity or increase the risk of exploitation. When the risk of impairment or exploitation exists due to conditions or multiple roles, therapists take appropriate precautions.

4.2 Marriage and family therapists do not provide therapy to current students or supervisees.

4.3 Marriage and family therapists do not engage in sexual intimacy with students or supervisees during the evaluative or training relationship between the therapist and student or supervisee. Should a supervisor engage in sexual activity with a former supervisee, the burden of proof shifts to the supervisor to demonstrate that there has been no exploitation or injury to the supervisee.

4.4 Marriage and family therapists do not permit students or supervisees to perform or to hold themselves out as competent to perform professional services beyond their training, level of experience, and competence.

4.5 Marriage and family therapists take reasonable measures to ensure that services provided by supervisees are professional.

4.6 Marriage and family therapists avoid accepting as supervisees or students those individuals with whom a prior or existing relationship could compromise the therapist's objectivity. When such situations cannot be avoided, therapists take appropriate precautions to maintain objectivity. Examples of such relationships include, but are not limited to, those individuals with whom the therapist has a current or prior sexual, close personal, immediate familial, or therapeutic relationship.

4.7 Marriage and family therapists do not disclose supervisee confidences except by written authorization or waiver, or when mandated or permitted by law. In educational or training settings where there are multiple supervisors, disclosures are permitted only to other professional colleagues, administrators, or employers who share responsibility for training of the supervisee. Verbal authorization will not be sufficient except in emergency situations, unless prohibited by law.

Principle V
Responsibility to Research Participants

Investigators respect the dignity and protect the welfare of research participants, and are aware of applicable laws and regulations and professional standards governing the conduct of research.

5.1 Investigators are responsible for making careful examinations of ethical acceptability in planning studies. To the extent that services to research participants may be compromised by participation in research, investigators seek the ethical advice of qualified professionals not directly involved in the investigation and observe safeguards to protect the rights of research participants.

5.2 Investigators requesting participant involvement in research inform participants of the aspects of the research that might reasonably be expected to influence willingness to participate. Investigators are especially sensitive to the possibility of diminished consent when participants are also receiving clinical services, or have impairments which limit understanding and/or communication, or when participants are children.

5.3 Investigators respect each participant's freedom to decline participation in or to withdraw from a research study at any time. This obligation requires special thought and consideration when investigators or other members of the research team are in positions of authority or influence over participants. Marriage and family therapists, therefore, make every effort to avoid multiple relationships with research participants that could impair professional judgment or increase the risk of exploitation.

5.4 Information obtained about a research participant during the course of an investigation is confidential unless there is a waiver previously obtained in writing. When the possibility exists that others, including family members, may obtain access to such information, this possibility, together with the plan for protecting confidentiality, is explained as part of the procedure for obtaining informed consent.

Principle VI
Responsibility to the Profession

Marriage and family therapists respect the rights and responsibilities of professional colleagues and participate in activities that advance the goals of the profession.

6.1 Marriage and family therapists remain accountable to the standards of the profession when acting as members or employees of organizations. If the mandates of an organization with which a marriage and family therapist is affiliated, through employment, contract or otherwise, conflict with the AAMFT Code of Ethics, marriage and family therapists make known to the organization their commitment to the AAMFT Code of Ethics and attempt to resolve the conflict in a way that allows the fullest adherence to the Code of Ethics.

6.2 Marriage and family therapists assign publication credit to those who have contributed to a publication in proportion to their contributions and in accordance with customary professional publication practices.

6.3 Marriage and family therapists do not accept or require authorship credit for a publication based on research from a student's program, unless the therapist made a substantial contribution beyond being a faculty advisor or research committee member. Coauthorship on a student thesis, dissertation, or project should be determined in accordance with principles of fairness and justice.

6.4 Marriage and family therapists who are the authors of books or other materials that are published or distributed do not plagiarize or fail to cite persons to whom credit for original ideas or work is due.

6.5 Marriage and family therapists who are the authors of books or other materials published or distributed by an organization take reasonable precautions to ensure that the organization promotes and advertises the materials accurately and factually.

6.6 Marriage and family therapists participate in activities that contribute to a better community and society, including devoting a portion of their professional activity to services for which there is little or no financial return.

6.7 Marriage and family therapists are concerned with developing laws and regulations pertaining to marriage and family therapy that serve the public interest, and with altering such laws and regulations that are not in the public interest.

6.8 Marriage and family therapists encourage public participation in the design and delivery of professional services and in the regulation of practitioners.

Principle VII
Financial Arrangements

Marriage and family therapists make financial arrangements with clients, third-party payors, and supervisees that are reasonably understandable and conform to accepted professional practices.

7.1 Marriage and family therapists do not offer or accept kickbacks, rebates, bonuses, or other remuneration for referrals; fee-for-service arrangements are not prohibited.

7.2 Prior to entering into the therapeutic or supervisory relationship, marriage and family therapists clearly disclose and explain to clients and supervisees: (a) all financial arrangements and fees related to professional services, including charges for canceled or missed appointments; (b) the use of collection agencies or legal measures for non-payment; and (c) the procedure for obtaining payment from the client, to the extent allowed by law, if payment is denied by the third-party payor. Once services have begun, therapists provide reasonable notice of any changes in fees or other charges.

7.3 Marriage and family therapists give reasonable notice to clients with unpaid balances of their intent to seek collection by agency or legal recourse. When such action is taken, therapists will not disclose clinical information.

7.4 Marriage and family therapists represent facts truthfully to clients, third-party payors, and supervisees regarding services rendered.

7.5 Marriage and family therapists ordinarily refrain from accepting goods and services from clients in return for services rendered. Bartering for professional services may be conducted only if: (a) the supervisee or client requests it, (b) the relationship is not exploitative, (c) the professional relationship is not distorted, and (d) a clear written contract is established.

7.6 Marriage and family therapists may not withhold records under their immediate control that are requested and needed for a client's treatment solely because payment has not been received for past services, except as otherwise provided by law.

Principle VIII
Advertising

Marriage and family therapists engage in appropriate informational activities, including those that enable the public, referral sources, or others to choose professional services on an informed basis.

8.1 Marriage and family therapists accurately represent their competencies, education, training, and experience relevant to their practice of marriage and family therapy.

8.2 Marriage and family therapists ensure that advertisements and publications in any media (such as directories, announcements, business cards, newspapers, radio, television, Internet, and facsimiles) convey information that is necessary for the public to make an appropriate selection of professional services. Information could include: (a) office information, such as name, address, telephone number, credit card acceptability, fees, languages spoken, and office hours; (b) qualifying clinical degree (see subprinciple 8.5); (c) other earned degrees (see subprinciple 8.5) and state or provincial licensures and/or certifications; (d) AAMFT clinical member status; and (e) description of practice.

8.3 Marriage and family therapists do not use names that could mislead the public concerning the identity, responsibility, source, and status of those practicing under that name, and do not hold themselves out as being partners or associates of a firm if they are not.

8.4 Marriage and family therapists do not use any professional identification (such as a business card, office sign, letterhead, Internet, or telephone or association directory listing) if it includes a statement or claim that is false, fraudulent, misleading, or deceptive.

8.5 In representing their educational qualifications, marriage and family therapists list and claim as evidence only those earned degrees: (a) from institutions accredited by regional accreditation sources recognized by the United States Department of Education, (b) from institutions recognized by states or provinces that license or certify marriage and family therapists, or (c) from equivalent foreign institutions.

8.6 Marriage and family therapists correct, wherever possible, false, misleading, or inaccurate information and representations made by others concerning the therapist's qualifications, services, or products.

8.7 Marriage and family therapists make certain that the qualifications of their employees or supervisees are represented in a manner that is not false, misleading, or deceptive.

8.8 Marriage and family therapists do not represent themselves as providing specialized services unless they have the appropriate education, training, or supervised experience.

This Code is published by:

American Association for Marriage and Family Therapy
112 South Alfred Street, Alexandria, VA 22314
Phone: (703) 838-9808—Fax: (703) 838-9805
www.aamft.org

© Copyright 2001 by the AAMFT. All rights reserved. Printed in the United States of America. No part of this publication may be reproduced, stored in a retrieval system, or transmitted, in any form or by any means, electronic, mechanical, photocopying, recording, or otherwise, without the prior written permission of the publisher. Violations of this Code should be brought in writing to the attention of:

AAMFT Ethics Committee
112 South Alfred Street, Alexandria, VA 22314
Phone: (703) 838-9808—Fax: (703) 838-9805
email: ethics@aamft.org

© 2002 American Association for Marriage and Family Therapy

112 South Alfred Street, Alexandria, VA 22314
Phone: (703) 838-9808—Fax: (703) 838-9805

Becoming a Competent Family Therapist: Training and Supervision

This appendix is intended to present, in outline and chart form, the basic information needed by readers interested in pursuing a career in the science and practice of family therapy. Systemic training should provide an opportunity to work professionally in a wide variety of settings: universities; independent practice; mental health clinics and other hospital, rehabilitative, or health-related facilities; schools; legal settings; public service domains; and many others.

The following areas will be addressed:

Obtaining Academic Credentials

Obtaining Clinical Training

Using Training Aids—journals, books, videos, conferences

Obtaining Supervision—live supervision, co-therapy teams

Maintaining Core Competencies

Obtaining Academic Credentials

One of the strengths of the family therapy movement is that its members come from a variety of academic backgrounds: clinical psychology, social work, marriage and family therapy, counseling (including pastoral counseling), nursing, and psychiatry. All participate in specialized programs but also engage in common course work. Some settings require doctoral degrees (psychiatry, clinical psychology), others master's level (e.g., MSW in social work), still others training specifically in marriage and family therapy. In general, training requires not merely learning a set of therapeutic tools (paradoxical interventions, reframing, contingency contracting, circular questioning, externalizing problems, and so on) but also acquiring the theoretical understanding of how, and under what circumstances, and with which sets of families to use them.

Therapists with a family psychology orientation conceptualize problems in systems terms. The current trend is to adopt an integrated view that understands psychological theories within a broad systemic framework. Individual development, family processes, and diversity factors (culture, socioeconomic status, ethnicity, race, religion, language, sexual orientation, etc.) represent interlocking parts to consider in this ecological systems outlook. All are related and exert reciprocal influences on one another. Ethical issues play an important part in the practice of family therapy, and, because of the complexities involved in dealing with several members simultaneously, the ethics involved in family therapy calls for care beyond that required in individual therapy.

Which program to pursue depends on career aspirations. Researchers and/or those wanting to teach at a college or university would do well to obtain a doctorate, as would solo practitioners who want a career with a variety of options—working with clients, consulting, coaching, supervising, writing, and so forth. MFTs and licensed social workers with master's-level training may also practice within their specialty in private practice settings or formal private or public agencies.

OBTAINING CLINICAL TRAINING

Training Programs

Growth in graduate programs during the last three decades has been primarily at the master's level. Considering the master's degree to represent the entry-level education for independent clinical practice for those beginning a practice in the profession, the American Association for Marriage and Family Therapy (AAMFT) Commission on Accreditation for Marriage and Family Therapy Education (COAMFTE) also accredits doctoral-level programs (for those interested in academic careers, research, advanced clinical practice, and supervision work) and postgraduate programs (for those with master's or doctoral degrees who wish further specialized training in a particular modality or treatment population).

Table A.1 lists approximately 100 accredited MFT training programs at the master's, doctoral, and postgraduate levels in the United States and Canada as of 2006.

At present, training in family therapy occurs in three kinds of settings—degree-granting programs in family therapy, freestanding family therapy training institutes, and university-affiliated programs. Degree-granting programs view family therapy as a profession, an orientation for conceptualizing problems people encounter, and a field or body of knowledge in itself; consequently, they offer the most in-depth training.

Similarly, freestanding family therapy institutes (see Table A.2) generally define family therapy as a profession, a separate and distinct field of knowledge, and an orientation to human problems. Freestanding programs also offer intensive family therapy training, but compared with degree-granting programs, the training is less comprehensive since it tends to be shorter and is offered to trainees on a part-time basis. Such programs are likely to appeal most to professionals who already hold advanced degrees but seek intensive training in marital and family therapy free of the usual constraints of a formal degree program. These family therapy institutes operate primarily outside of academia.

University-affiliated programs focus on family therapy as one study among many—perhaps another therapeutic modality or a field with a body of knowledge, or a set of clinical skills and research opportunities—that are interesting but not central to their training mission.

TABLE A.1   AAMFT Accredited Graduate and Postgraduate MFT Training Programs in the United States and Canada—2006

State or Province	School	Degree Program
UNITED STATES		
Alabama	Auburn University	MS
California	San Diego State University	MS
	Southern California Counseling Center	Postgrad
	Alliant International University (San Diego)	MA, Doctoral
	Alliant International University (Sacramento)	MA
	Alliant International University (Irvine)	MA, MA
	University of San Diego	MA
	Loma Linda University	MS, Doctoral
Colorado	Denver Family Institute	Postgrad
	Colorado State University	MS
	Colorado School for Family Therapy (Aurora)	Postgrad
Connecticut	Fairfield University	MA
	University of Connecticut	MA, Doctoral
	Southern Connecticut State University	MS
	Central Connecticut State University	MS
	Saint Joseph College	MA
Florida	Nova Southeastern University	MA, Doctoral
	Florida State University	Doctoral
Georgia	Valdosta State University	MS
	University of Georgia	Doctoral
	Mercer University	MFT
Illinois	Northern Illinois University	MS
	Family Institute (Northwestern)	MS
Indiana	Purdue (West Lafayette)	Doctoral
	Purdue—Calumet (Hammond)	MS
	Christian Theological Seminary	MA
Iowa	Iowa State University	Doctoral
Kansas	Friends University (Lenexa)	MS
	Friends University (Wichita)	MS
	Kansas State University	MS, Doctoral
Kentucky	University of Kentucky	MS
	University of Louisville	MSSW, Postgrad
	Louisville Presbyterian Theological Seminary	MA
Louisiana	University of Louisiana (Monroe)	MA, Doctoral
Maryland	University of Maryland	MS
Massachusetts	University of Massachusetts (Boston)	MS
Michigan	Michigan State University	MA, Doctoral
Minnesota	University of Minnesota	Doctoral
Mississippi	Reformed Theological Seminary	MA
	Southern Mississippi University	MS
Missouri	Forest Institute of Psychology (Springfield)	Doctoral
Nebraska	University of Nebraska (Lincoln)	MS

State or Province	School	Degree Program
New Hampshire	Antioch University (New England)	MA
	University of New Hampshire	MS
New Jersey	Seton Hall University	Ed.S
New York	Syracuse University	MA, Doctoral
	University of Rochester	MS, Postgrad
	Iona College	MA
	Blanton-Peale Institute (New York)	Postgrad
North Carolina	East Carolina University	MS
	Appalachian State University	MA
North Dakota	North Dakota State University	MS
Ohio	Ohio State University	Doctoral
	University of Akron	MS, Doctoral
Oklahoma	Oklahoma State University	MS
Oregon	University of Oregon	M.Ed.
Pennsylvania	Drexel (Philadelphia)	MA, Postgrad
	Council for Relationships (Philadelphia)	Postgrad
	Philadelphia Child-Family Therapy Training	Postgrad
	Center Seton Hall (Greensburg)	MS
Rhode Island	University of Rhode Island	MS
South Carolina	WestGate Training and Consulting Network	Postgrad
	Converse College	Ed.S.
Texas	St. Mary's University (San Antonio)	MA, Doctoral
	Abilene Christian University	MFT
	Texas Tech University	Doctoral
	University of Houston (Clear Lake)	MA
Utah	Utah State University	MS
	Brigham Young University	MS, Doctoral
Virginia	Virginia Tech University (Falls Church)	MS
	Virginia Tech University (Blacksburg)	Doctoral
Washington	Pacific Lutheran University (Tacoma)	MA
	Seattle Pacific University	MS
Wisconsin	University of Wisconsin (Menomonie)	MS
	Family Therapy Training Institute (Milwaukee)	Postgrad
CANADA		
Alberta	Calgary Health Region	Postgrad
Manitoba	University of Winnipeg	MMFT
Ontario	Interfaith Pastoral Counseling Center	Postgrad
	University of Guelph	MS
Quebec	Jewish General Hospital	Postgrad
	Argyle Institute of Human Relations	Postgrad

TABLE A.2 A Sample of Freestanding Family Therapy Training Institutes in the United States

Name	Location
Mental Research Institute	Palo Alto, CA
The Georgetown Family Center	Washington, DC
The Family Institute at Northwestern	Evanston, IL
The Chicago Center for Family Health	Chicago, IL
The Family Institute of Cambridge	Watertown, MA
The Kantor Family Institute	Somerville, MA
Multicultural Family Institute	Highland Park, NJ
Ackerman Institute for Family Therapy	New York, NY
Minuchin Center for the Family	New York, NY
The Center for Family Learning	Rye Brook, NY
The Family Institute of Westchester	White Plains, NY
The Family Therapy Training Program at the University of Rochester	Rochester, NY
The Institute for Contextual Growth	Ambler, PA
The Family Therapy Practice Center	Washington, DC
The Philadelphia Child and Family Guidance Center	Philadelphia, PA
The Houston-Galveston Institute	Houston, TX
The Brief Family Therapy Center	Milwaukee, WI

USING TRAINING AIDS

Family therapy programs use three primary methods for training:

(a) didactic presentations, in course work or seminar form, in which trainees learn family therapy's body of knowledge;
(b) direct clinical experiences with families; and
(c) supervision, on a regular, ongoing basis, by an experienced family supervisor who, together with trainees, may observe ongoing sessions by a fellow trainee through a one-way mirror and/or through videotaped sessions.

Reading about families and family theory, observing trainers as they demonstrate work with families, seeing videotapes of master family therapists at work, critiquing (and being critiqued by) fellow trainees reviewing taped sessions, even studying examples of family therapy failures, all add to conceptual and clinical knowledge. But in the last analysis, the trainee learns experientially—by treating families under supervision.

Didactic Course Work

In an effort to provide some uniform structure for evaluating the relevance and completeness of family therapy training, the AAMFT has established educational and

BOX A.1 CLINICAL NOTE

AAMFT Classes of Membership

The AAMFT recognizes four sets of members: clinical, associate, student, and affiliate. Clinical members must possess a graduate degree in marriage and family therapy or a related mental health discipline from a regionally accredited institution, have completed 11 courses in theory, practice, human development, research and ethics, and have had a minimum of 300 hours of supervision during their graduate training, as well as 1000 hours of direct client contact and 200 hours of postgraduate supervision. Associate membership calls for the completion of a qualifying graduate degree, 8 of the 11 courses in theory, practice, human development, research, and ethics, and a minimum of 300 hours of supervised clinical practicum during their graduate program. To become a student member, the applicant must be currently enrolled in an accredited program leading to a graduate degree or postgraduate certificate in marriage and family therapy or related mental health discipline. Affiliate membership is for those mental health workers who are not pursuing a marriage and family therapy license, but who want to develop their clinical skills in working with couples and families. All classes of membership must agree to abide by the AAMFT Code of Ethics (see Appendix A).

training guidelines involving preparation in theory (systems theory, personality theory, gender and cultural issues), practice (assessment, treatment, and intervention methods), human development (individual and family life cycle changes, human sexuality), research (methodology, quantitative and qualitative approaches), and ethics (legal responsibilities and liabilities). Understanding larger systems, and especially the relationships between intrapsychic factors (within the individual), interpersonal factors (between family members) and the community adds to the family therapist's professional competencies.

The didactic component of family therapy training, typically offering a systemic perspective, includes lectures (family life cycle development, diversity, ethics, legal issues, sex therapy, research methodology), demonstrations of assessment as well as therapeutic and psychoeducational intervention techniques and strategies, instructional videotapes, assigned readings, role playing, and observations through the use of one-way mirrors (allowing multiple therapists or therapists-in-training to observe the family in action).

Readings in the field constitute a significant part of the learning experience. Gurman and Kniskern's (1991) edited *Handbook of Family Therapy*, Wolman and Stricker's (1983) edited *Handbook of Family and Marital Therapy*, L'Abate's (1985) edited *The Handbook of Family Psychology and Therapy*, and Falloon's (1988) edited *Handbook of Behavioral Family Therapy* all offer large collections of theoretical as well as clinical papers, usually by experts in their respective areas. More recent updates can be found in Mikesell, Lusterman, and McDaniel's (1995) *Integrating Family Therapy*, Piercy, Sprenkle, Wetchler, and Associates' (1996) *Family Therapy Sourcebook*, Nichols, Pace-Nichols, Becvar, and Napier's (2000) edited *Handbook of Family Development and Intervention*, and Sexton, Weeks, and Robbins's (2003) edited *Handbook of Family Therapy*.

A proliferation of journals helps keep students and professionals abreast of developments in family therapy. *Family Process*, begun in 1961, and the AAMFT

Journal of Marital and Family Therapy remain the most influential. Others, addressing a variety of contemporary issues in the field, include the following sample:

The American Journal of Family Therapy
American Journal of Orthopsychiatry
Australian and New Zealand Journal of Family Therapy
Contemporary Family Therapy
Family Coordinator
Families in Society
Family Relations
Family Therapy
Family Therapy Case Studies
Family Therapy Collections
Human Systems
International Journal of Family Therapy
Journal of Couple and Relationship Therapy
Journal of Family Psychology (APA)
Journal of Family Psychotherapy
Journal of Family Therapy (England)
Journal of Marriage and the Family
Journal of Psychotherapy and the Family
Journal of Social Casework
Marriage and Family Review
The Family Journal
Topics in Family Psychology and Counseling

More specialized journals include:

Adoption Quarterly
Alternative Lifestyles
Child and Family Behavior Therapy
Family Systems (Bowen)
Families, Systems, and Health (coordinating family medicine and family therapy)
International Journal of Narrative Therapy and Community Work (Australia)
Journal of Child Custody
Journal of Couples Therapy
Journal of Divorce and Remarriage
Journal of Feminist Family Therapy
Journal of Gay and Lesbian Psychotherapy
Journal of Immigrant and Refugee Services
Journal of Sex and Marital Therapy
Journal of Systemic Therapies

In addition, influential periodicals help keep practitioners alerted to current developments in the field:

AFTA Newsletter (American Family Therapy Academy)

Brown University Family Therapy Newsletter

Family Therapy News (AAMFT newsletter)

The Family Psychologist (Newsletter of APA Division of Family Psychology)

The Family Therapy Networker (recently renamed *Psychotherapy Newsletter*)

Most of the field's leaders have published their theoretical and conceptual ideas in book form: Ackerman (Bloch & Simon, 1982), Boscolo and Cecchin (Boscolo, Cecchin, Hoffman, & Penn, 1987), Boszormenyi-Nagy (Boszormenyi-Nagy & Krasner, 1986), Bowen (1978), de Shazer (1988, 1991), Framo (1982, 1992), Haley (1976, 1984, 1996), Kempler (1981), Madanes (1990), Minuchin (1974, 1984), Satir (1967, 1972), Selvini-Palazzoli (Selvini-Palazzoli, Cirillo, Selvini, & Sorrentino, 1989), Watzlawick (1978, 1984), Whitaker (Whitaker & Bumberry, 1988), White (White & Epston, 1990; White, 1995). Finally, it is a worthwhile and at times exciting experience to read verbatim accounts of family therapy sessions (for example, Haley & Hoffman, 1967; Napier & Whitaker, 1978; Satir & Baldwin, 1983), following step by step what takes place as a master therapist puts theory into practice. More recently, Dattilio (1998) as well as Lawson and Prevatt (1999) have edited case study books in which contributors expert in various approaches to couple and family therapy describe their theoretical orientation, followed by examples of their interventions with clients.

Videotapes and DVDs

Videotaping therapeutic sessions has provided an indispensable tool for teaching family therapy. Students early in their training have an opportunity to watch tapes of master therapists at work with real families; they also can record their own sessions with families for later playback during supervisory meetings. Taping of ongoing therapy sessions now plays a significant part in training because videotapes convey an immediate sense of awareness of the processes by which therapists and families communicate.

Videotapes of master therapists demonstrating their techniques in actual sessions with families are readily available from the following organizations: Philadelphia Child and Family Guidance Center; Ackerman Institute for Family Therapy; Georgetown University Family Center; the Center for Family Learning in New Rochelle, New York; the Institute of Contextual Growth in Ambler, Pennsylvania; the Eastern Pennsylvania Psychiatric Institute; the Minuchin Center for the Family in New York; the Kempler Institute in Laguna Niguel, California; and the Mental Research Institute in Palo Alto. Beyond these training centers, teaching tapes are available for purchase from Master's Work Productions in Los Angeles; Golden Triad Films in Kansas City, Missouri; as well as from the AAMFT, through its "Master Series" of tapes—live demonstrations by noted family therapists carried out at that organization's annual conference. Videos and DVDs of many master therapists can be ordered online from psychotherapy net.

According to Whiffen (1982), videotaping has three unique properties that make it especially valuable in supervision: (a) It freezes time so that every aspect and angle of a crucial sequence is available for post-therapy play and replay by the therapist, impossible to achieve during the session; (b) it enables the therapist to see himself or herself more objectively as a contributor to the whole system, a different perspective from the one available in the midst of the often-bewildering multiple stimuli occurring during the session; and (c) it allows the effect of a therapeutic intervention to be studied and its success evaluated.

A trainee's verbal report of a family therapy session to a supervisor and/or class is subject to the inherent risks of unreliable recall, defensiveness, distortion, and subjective description. The instant replay of the session on tape overcomes many of these obstacles. Subtle idiosyncratic patterns of interviewing style (for example, avoiding certain topics or retreating from certain emotional expressions) may become more obvious to the trainee after supervisor comments or self-observation following the viewing of a taped family session. The interplay of verbal and especially nonverbal messages and interactions may become clearer. Not only does the trainee confront his or her own behavior with a family, but the other viewers also provide additional corrective feedback.

Trainees learn from each other's errors as well as successes. The tape can be played and replayed, preserved, and retrieved for further study and analysis. By observing trainees with families over closed-circuit television, the supervisor and others retain all the benefits of a one-way mirror along with a permanent videotaped record of precisely what took place. In some cases, the supervisory sessions themselves are videotaped for later playback as the trainee plans further therapeutic strategies with the family.

Conferences

Local, regional, national, and international workshops and conferences are excellent ways of keeping up with new ideas and new directions, while at the same time allowing the attendee to network with other family therapists. The AAMFT annual meeting is the largest, with thousands attending over a period of several days, followed in size by the yearly meeting sponsored by the *Family Therapy Newsletter* (now broadened and renamed the *Psychotherapy Newsletter*). Top-level speakers are invited and the latest topics discussed, all in an atmosphere of collegiality and enthusiasm.

The American Family Therapy Academy (AFTA) is more modest by comparison, deliberately kept small and open only to screened members. Informal in setting, and organized around interest groups so that members can choose specific topics they wish to discuss, the conference is known for heated exchanges, ongoing debates, and great loyalty to the organization. Division 43 of the American Psychological Association meets semi-annually, at the national conference and at a midwinter retreat, where devotees present clinical and research papers relevant to family therapy. The American Board of Family Psychology (ABFamP) offers an opportunity to achieve a diplomate level of expertise for advanced members in the field.

The American Orthopsychiatric Association, a well-established, multidisciplinary group, attracts both family therapists and other mental health professionals to its annual meeting. The organization has a long history of focusing on social concerns such as poverty, racism, and similar larger system issues. Social workers are prominent in its hierarchy, and psychologists and psychiatrists are also well represented.

The International Family Therapy Association, organized in 1987, provides a vehicle for family therapists to meet, each year in a different country, to share new developments.

OBTAINING SUPERVISION

An effective teaching program in family therapy must meld relevant theory with profitable practical experience. However, clinical contact with families is of limited value without regularly scheduled, attentive supervision, which is especially crucial during

BOX A.2 CLINICAL NOTE

Common Supervisory Procedures

Reviewing audiotapes of trainee sessions
Reviewing videotapes of trainee sessions
Reviewing trainee's written process notes
Observing ongoing sessions through a one-way
　mirror
Co-therapy with trainees

Conducting continuous case conferences during
　which a trainee presents an outline of his or her
　work with a client family for several class sessions
Live, on-the-spot supervision in which the supervisor
　stays in direct communication with the trainee
　during a session

the early stages of training. The AAMFT has a roster of approved clinical supervisors. Such supervision, when provided by highly competent and experienced family therapists who also have teaching as well as supervisory skills, may take a number of forms, as outlined in Box A.2.

Probably the two procedures most commonly used by family therapy supervisors are live supervision and working as members of co-therapy teams.

Live Supervision

Live supervision, in which a supervisor or observing team watches an ongoing session through a one-way mirror or on a video monitor, introduces a sense of immediacy to the supervisory process. It calls for the supervisor (or more frequently today, an observing or reflecting team) to actively guide the trainee's work by providing feedback on what the trainee is doing while he or she is working with the family. In live supervision, then, the supervisor or team behind the one-way mirror is an active and integral part of the session itself.

The supervisor can intervene in several ways:

1. By calling the therapist out of the room midway through a session for consultation, after which the therapist returns to the session with directives to be given to the family
2. By calling the therapist by telephone with suggestions during the treatment process
3. By entering the consultation room during a session with comments and suggestions
4. By using a "bug in the ear" wireless transmitter to communicate directly, and relatively unobtrusively, to the therapist

According to Byng-Hall (1982), live supervisory interventions are likely to take the form of instructions ("Ask . . ." or "Say to the mother . . ."); suggestions for strategies ("Get father and son to negotiate on that"); efforts to direct the therapist's attention ("Notice how . . ." or "See how they repeat . . ."); moves to increase or decrease intensity ("Encourage mother and father to confront . . ." or "Tell them to stop and listen to one another, instead of . . ."); or perhaps encouragement ("That was well done"). As we have noted, trainees nowadays may be observed through one-way mirrors by supervisory teams (including fellow trainees), who offer reflections and suggestions for intervention while therapy is taking place. The objective is to help the trainee get disentangled from recurring, nonproductive interactional sequences with the family in order to regain control and direction of the session. Looking at one's own tape after a session can often be instructive.

Co-therapy Teams

Co-therapy—the simultaneous involvement of two therapists in the treatment setting—gives trainees the opportunity to work hand in glove with a supervisor. Today, the technique is employed largely by family therapists who contend that two-person co-therapy teams (when possible, a man and a woman) provide families with mutual complementarity and support, continuity of care, autonomy, models of intimacy, division of roles during the session, and an opportunity for increased creativity on the part of both therapists. The technique also may be employed in managed care situations in which the payors do not accept trainee billing unless the attending supervisor is available during the entire session.

Co-therapy has some obvious training advantages. The trainee has an opportunity to learn a distinctive approach at close range and to see an expert in action without taking full or even major responsibility for treating the family. The trainee has the added benefit of seeing his or her mentor as a real person who makes mistakes at times, does not always understand all that is happening, and is not always positive in outlook—all very reassuring to a beginning family therapist, who at times has felt exactly the same way about himself or herself. The supervisor as co-therapist can give the supervisee an opportunity to try creative interventions with the family while being assured of skillful support and rescue when trouble arises, as it inevitably does.

MAINTAINING CORE COMPETENCIES

In Box 6.1 in Chapter 6 we outlined efforts to build core competencies in family therapy. Specifically, we followed the AAMFT suggestion that therapists need to develop and maintain professional skills in six domains:

Admission to treatment

Clinical assessment

Treatment planning and case management

Therapeutic interventions

Legal issues, ethics, and standards

Research and program evaluation

After a professional has been licensed, continuing education requirements for relicensing, peer reviews, workshops, conferences, case presentations, readings, preparations for further certification (e.g., American Board of Family Psychologists for family therapists) all require attention if competencies are to be maintained.

accommodating A therapeutic tactic, used primarily by structural family therapists, whereby the therapist attempts to make personal adjustments in adapting to the family style, in an effort to build a therapeutic alliance with the family.

alignments Clusters of alliances between family members within the overall family group; affiliations and splits from one another, temporary or permanent, occur in pursuit of homeostasis.

anorexia nervosa Prolonged, severe diminution of appetite, particularly although not exclusively in adolescent girls, to the point of becoming life-threatening.

baseline A stable, reliable performance level, against which changes, particularly of a behavioral nature, can be compared.

behavioral The viewpoint that objective and experimentally verified procedures should be the basis for modifying maladaptive, undesired, or problematic behaviors.

behavioral analysis An assessment procedure in which a therapist identifies the targeted behavior to be changed, determines the factors currently maintaining the behavior, and formulates a treatment plan that includes specific criteria for measuring the success of the change effort.

behavioral couples therapy Training couples in communication skills, the exchange of positive reinforcements, cognitive restructuring, and problem-solving skills in order to facilitate marital satisfaction.

behavioral parent training Training parents in behavioral principles and the use of contingency management procedures in altering or modifying undesirable behavior in their children.

bipolar disorder An affective disorder in which the patient experiences alternating periods of depression and mania.

binuclear family A postdivorced family structure in which the former spouses reside in separate households and function as two separate units; their nuclear family is thus restructured but remains intact.

blank screen In psychoanalytic therapy, the passive, neutral, unrevealing behavior of the analyst, onto which the patient may project his or her fantasies.

boundary An abstract delineation between parts of a system or between systems, typically defined by implicit or explicit rules regarding who may participate and in what manner.

boundary making A technique of structural family therapists aimed at realigning boundaries within a family by changing the psychological proximity (closer or further apart) between family subsystems.

centrifugal Tending to move outward or away from the center; within a family, forces that push the members apart, especially when the family organization lacks cohesiveness, so that they seek gratification outside of, rather than within, the family.

centripetal Tending to move toward the center; within a family, forces that bind or otherwise keep the members together so that they seek fulfillment from intrafamilial rather than outside relationships.

certification A statutory process established by a government agency, usually a state or province, allowing persons who have met predetermined qualifications to call themselves by a particular title, and prohibiting the use of that title without a certificate.

circular causality The view that causality is nonlinear, occurring instead within a relationship context and through a network of interacting loops; any cause is thus seen as an effect of a prior cause, as in the interactions within families.

circular questioning An interviewing technique, first formulated by Milan systemic therapists, aimed at eliciting differences in perception about events or relationships from different family members, particularly regarding points in the family life cycle when significant coalition shifts and adaptations occurred.

classical conditioning A form of learning in which a previously neutral stimulus, through repeated pairing with a stimulus that ordinarily elicits a response, eventually elicits the response by itself.

closed system A self-contained system with impermeable boundaries, operating without interactions outside the system, resistant to change and thus prone to increasing disorder

coalitions Covert alliances or affiliations, temporary or long-term, between certain family members against others in the family.

cognitive Pertaining to mental processes, such as thinking, remembering, perceiving, expecting, and planning.

cognitive behavior therapy A set of therapeutic procedures, derived from behavior therapy, that attempts to change behavior by modifying or altering faulty thought patterns or destructive self-verbalizations.

cognitive restructuring An intervention procedure whereby the therapist attempts to modify client thoughts, perceptions, and attributions about an event.

complementarity The degree of harmony in the meshing of family roles, as between husband and wife; to the extent that the roles dovetail satisfactorily, the partners both are able, together, to provide and receive satisfaction from the relationship.

complementary A type of dyadic transaction or communication pattern in which inequality and the maximization of differences exist (for example, dominant/submissive) and in which each participant's response provokes or enhances a counter-response in the other in a continuing loop.

conductor A type of family therapist who is active, aggressive, and charismatic, openly and directly confronting the family's dysfunctional interactive patterns.

confidentiality An ethical standard aimed at protecting client privacy by ensuring that information received in a therapeutic relationship will not be disclosed without prior client consent.

conjoint Involving two or more family members seen together in a therapy session.

conjoint sex therapy Therapeutic intervention with a couple in an effort to treat their sexual dysfunction.

constructivism The belief that an individual's knowledge of reality results from his or her subjective perceiving and subsequent constructing or inventing of the world, rather than resulting from how the world objectively exists.

contextual Pertaining to circumstances or situations in which an event took place; as a therapeutic approach, an emphasis on the relational determinants, entitlements, and indebtedness across generations that bind families together.

contingency contract An agreement, usually in written form, made by two or more family members specifying the circumstances under which each is to do something for the other, so that they may exchange rewarding behavior.

continuing education Voluntary or, increasingly, mandated postgraduate training, typically in the form of workshops and in-service training programs.

co-therapy The simultaneous involvement of two therapists, often for training purposes, in working with an individual, couple, or family.

counterparadox In systemic family therapy, placing the family in a therapeutic double bind in order to counter the members' paradoxical interactions.

countertransference According to psychoanalytic theory, the analyst's unconscious emotional responses to a patient that are reminiscent of feelings he or she experienced with a person in the past.

culture Shared behaviors, meanings, symbols, and values transmitted from one generation to the next.

cybernetics The study of methods of feedback control within a system, especially the flow of information through feedback loops.

deconstruction A postmodern procedure for gaining meaning by reexamining assumptions previously taken for granted, in the service of constructing new and unencumbered meanings.

defense mechanism According to psychoanalytic theory, the process, usually unconscious, whereby the ego protects the individual from conscious awareness of threatening and therefore anxiety-producing thoughts, feelings, and impulses.

detriangulate The process of withdrawing from a family role of buffer or go-between with one's parents, so as to not be drawn into alliances with one against the other.

developmental tasks Problems to be overcome and conflicts to be mastered at various stages of the life cycle, enabling movement to the next developmental stage.

differentiation of self According to Bowen, the separation of one's intellectual and emotional functioning; the greater the distinction, the better one is able to resist being overwhelmed by the emotional reactivity of his or her family, thus making one less prone to dysfunction.

disengagement A family organization with overly rigid boundaries, in which members are isolated and feel unconnected to each other, with each functioning separately and autonomously and without involvement in the day-to-day transactions within the family.

double-bind concept The view that an individual who receives important contradictory injunctions at different levels of abstraction—about which he or she is unable to comment or escape—is in a no-win, conflict-producing situation.

drive theory The psychoanalytic theory that instinctual forces such as sex or aggression create tension states that motivate the individual to take action to lessen the tension.

dyad A liaison, temporary or permanent, between two persons.

ecomap An appraisal tool designed to graphically depict a family's connections with outside agencies and institutions, enabling the therapist to examine pictorially those relationship bonds that connect the family to these systems.

ecosystemic approach A perspective that goes beyond intrafamilial relationships to attend to the family's relationships with larger systems (schools, courts, healthcare).

ego According to psychoanalytic theory, the mediator between the demands of the instinctual drives (id) and the social prohibitions (superego); thus, the rational, problem-solving aspect of personality.

emotional cutoff The flight from unresolved emotional ties to one's family of origin, typically manifested by withdrawing or running away from the parental family, or denying its current importance in one's life.

emotionally focused couples therapy (EFCT) An experiential approach, based on humanistic, systemic foundations and attachment theory, that attempts to change a couple's negative interactions while helping them to cement their emotional bond.

enactment In structural family therapy, a facilitating intervention in which the family is induced by the therapist to enact or play out its relationship patterns spontaneously during a therapeutic session, allowing the therapist to observe and ultimately to develop a plan or new set of rules for restructuring future transactions.

encounter group A kind of therapeutic group in which intense interpersonal experiences are promoted in order to produce insight, personal growth, and sensitivity to the feelings and experiences of others.

enmeshment A family organization in which boundaries between members are blurred and members are overconcerned and overinvolved in each other's lives, limiting individual autonomy.

entropy The tendency of a system to go into disorder, and if unimpeded, to reach a disorganized and undifferentiated state.

epistemology The study of the origin, nature, and methods, as well as the limits, of knowledge; thus, a framework for describing and conceptualizing what is being observed and experienced.

ethnicity The defining characteristics of a social grouping sharing cultural traditions, transmitted over generations and reinforced by the expectations of the subgroup in which the individual or family maintains membership.

exceptions In solution-focused therapy, attention to the times when the problem did not occur, intended to help build problem-solving skills.

expressed emotion The degree of affect expressed within a family, especially noteworthy in families with schizophrenic members, where emotionally intense and negative interactions are considered a factor in the schizophrenic's relapse.

externalization In the narrative approach, helping families view the problem or symptom as occurring outside of themselves, in an effort to mobilize them to fight to overcome it.

family crisis therapy A crisis-oriented therapeutic approach in which the family as a system is helped to restore its previous level of functioning; in some cases, as with schizophrenia, rehospitalization can be avoided.

family group therapy The intervention technique developed by Bell based on social-psychological principles of small-group behavior.

family life cycle The series of longitudinal stages or events that mark a family's life, offering an organizing schema for viewing the family as a system proceeding through time.

family life fact chronology An experiential technique of Satir's in which clients retrace their family history, particularly the family's relationship patterns, to better understand current family functioning.

family mapping An assessment technique used by structural family therapists to graphically describe a family's overall organizational structure and determine which subsystem is involved in dysfunctional transactions.

family projection process The mechanism by which parental conflicts and immaturities are transmitted, through the process of projection, to one or more of the children.

family reconstruction An auxiliary therapeutic approach developed by Satir, whereby family members are guided back through stages of their lives in order to discover and unlock dysfunctional patterns from the past.

family sculpting A physical arrangement of the members of a family in space, with the placement of each person determined by an individual family member acting as "director"; the resulting tableau represents that person's symbolic view of family relationships.

family systems theory The theory advanced by Bowen that emphasizes the family as an emotional unit or network of interlocking relationships best understood from a historical or transgenerational perspective.

feedback The reinsertion into a system of the results of its past performance, as a method of controlling the system.

feedback loops Those circular mechanisms by which information about a system's output is continuously reintroduced back into the system, initiating a chain of subsequent events.

feminist family therapy A form of collaborative, egalitarian, nonsexist intervention, applicable to both men and women, addressing family gender roles, patriarchal attitudes, and social and economic inequalities in male-female relationships.

first-order changes Temporary or superficial changes within a system that do not alter the basic organization of the system itself.

first-order cybernetics A view from outside the system of the feedback loops and homeostatic mechanisms that transpire within a system.

functional analysis A behavioral assessment of a problem in order to determine what interpersonal or environmental contingencies elicit the problematic behavior and how to extinguish or reduce its occurrence.

functional family therapy A therapeutic approach based on systems theory, cognitive theory, and behavioral principles in which clients are helped to understand the function or interpersonal payoff of certain of their behaviors as a prelude to substituting more effective ways to achieve the same results.

fusion The merging of the intellectual and emotional aspects of a family member, paralleling the degree to which that person is caught up in, and loses a separate sense of self in, family relationships.

gender A learned set of culturally prescribed attitudes and behaviors presumed to be masculine or feminine, associated with but distinct from the biological status of being male or female.

gender schema A feminist term depicting a person's ingrained set of associations that sees others from the viewpoint of gender rather than any other set of characteristics.

gender-sensitive family therapy A therapeutic perspective, regardless of theoretical persuasion, that examines the impact of gender socialization on the outlooks, attitudes, behaviors, and interpersonal relationships of men and women; its aim is to empower clients to make sexist-free role choices rather than be limited by roles determined by their biological status as male or female.

general system theory As proposed by biologist Ludwig von Bertalanffy in regard to living systems, the study of the relationship of interactional parts in context, emphasizing their unity and organizational hierarchy.

genogram A schematic diagram of a family's relationship system, in the form of a genetic tree and usually including at least three generations; used in particular by Bowen and his followers to trace recurring behavior patterns within the family.

Gestalt family therapy A form of experiential family therapy, loosely based on the principles of Gestalt psychology, that focuses on here-and-now experiences in an effort to heighten self-awareness and increase self-direction.

homeostasis A dynamic state of balance or equilibrium in a system, or a tendency toward achieving and maintaining such a state in an effort to ensure a stable environment.

humanistic The life-affirming view that emphasizes each person's uniqueness and worth, as well as potential for continued personal growth and fulfillment.

hypothesizing As used by systemic therapists, the process by which a team of therapists forms suppositions, open to revision, regarding how and why a family's problems have developed and persisted; to facilitate asking relevant questions and organizing incoming information, it occurs before meeting the family.

identified patient (IP) The family member with the presenting symptom; thus, the person who initially seeks treatment or for whom treatment is sought.

information processing The gathering, distilling, organizing, storing, and retrieving of information through a system or between that system and larger systems.

informed consent The legal rights of patients or research subjects to be told of the purposes and risks involved before agreeing to participate.

integrative couples therapy A behaviorally based technique emphasizing the emotional acceptance of behavior in a partner that is not open to change.

interpersonal Interactional, as between persons.

intrapsychic Within the mind or psyche; used especially in regard to conflicting forces.

introjects Imprints or memories from the past, usually based on unresolved relationships with one's parents, that continue to impose themselves on current relationships, particularly with one's spouse or children.

invariant prescription As developed by Selvini-Palazzoli, a single, unchanging verbal directive issued to all parents with symptomatic children, intended to help the parents and children break out of collusive and destructive "games" and establish clearer and more stable intergenerational boundaries.

invisible loyalty In contextual family therapy, a child's unconscious commitment to help the parents, as in becoming the family scapegoat.

joining The therapeutic tactic of entering a family system by engaging its separate members and subsystems, gaining access in order to explore and ultimately to help modify dysfunctional aspects of that system.

joint legal custody A term used in the law to denote the rights of divorced parents to share in certain major decisions (e.g., religious upbringing or choice of schools) regarding their children.

licensing A statutory process established by a government agency, usually a state or province, granting permission to persons having met predetermined qualifications to practice a specific profession.

linear causality The view that a nonreciprocal relationship exists between events in a sequence, so that one event causes the next event, but not vice versa.

malpractice A legal concept addressing the failure to provide a level of professional skill or render a level of professional services ordinarily expected of professionals in a similar situation.

managed care A system in which third-party payors regulate and control the cost, quality, and terms of treatment of medical (including mental health) services.

marital quid pro quo An initial rule arrangement or bargain between husband and wife regarding the ways in which they intend to define themselves vis-à-vis one another in the marital relationship.

marital schism A disturbed marital situation characterized by family disharmony, self-preoccupation, the undermining of the spouse, and frequent threats of divorce by one or both partners.

marital skew A disturbed marital situation in which one partner dominates the family to an extreme degree, and in which the marriage is maintained at the expense of the distortion of reality.

medical family therapy A form of psychoeducational family therapy involving collaboration with physicians and other health care professionals in the treatment of persons or families with health problems.

meta-analysis A statistical technique for reviewing, analyzing, and summarizing the results of a discrete group of studies, as in investigating the differences between treatment and no-treatment groups in outcome research.

metacommunication A message about a message, typically nonverbal (a smile, a shrug, a nod, a wink), offered simultaneously with a verbal message, structuring, qualifying, or adding meaning to that message.

metarules A family's unstated rules regarding how to interpret or, if necessary, to change its rules.

mimesis A tactic used particularly by structural family therapists, who attempt to copy or mimic a family's communication and behavioral patterns in order to gain acceptance by the family members.

monad Properties or characteristics of a single individual.

multigenerational transmission process The process, occurring over several generations, in which poorly differentiated persons marry similarly differentiated mates, ultimately resulting in offspring suffering from schizophrenia or other severe mental disorders.

multiple family therapy A form of therapy in which members of several families meet together as a group to work on individual as well as family problems.

multiple impact therapy A crisis-focused form of intervention in which members of a single family are seen all together, or in various combinations, for intensive interaction with a team of professionals over a two-day period.

narcissistic personality disorder A pattern of outlandish self-investment and exhibitionistic recognition seeking in which the individual attempts to evoke attention and admiration from others, but is himself or herself unable or unwilling to empathize with their needs or desires.

narrative therapy A postmodern therapeutic approach in which the therapist and family members co-construct new stories about their lives that encourage the possibility of new experiences.

negative feedback The flow of corrective information from the output of a system back into the system in order to attenuate deviation and keep the system functioning within prescribed limits.

negentropy The tendency of a system to remain flexible and open to new input, necessary for change and survival of the system.

network therapy A form of therapy, typically carried out in the home of a patient (for example, a schizophrenic recently discharged from a hospital), in which family members, friends, neighbors, and other involved persons participate in treatment and rehabilitation.

neutrality As used by systemic family therapists, a nonjudgmental and impartial position, eliciting all viewpoints, intended to enable the therapist to avoid being caught up in family "games" through coalitions or alliances.

nuclear family A family composed of a husband, wife, and their offspring, living together as a family unit.

nuclear family emotional system An unstable, fused family's way of coping with stress, typically resulting in marital conflict, dysfunction in a spouse, or psychological impairment of a child; their pattern is likely to mimic the patterns of past generations and to be repeated in future generations.

object relations theory The theory that the basic human motive is the search for satisfying object (human) relationships, and that parent-child patterns, especially if frustrating or unfulfilling, are internalized as introjects and unconsciously imposed on current family relationships.

open system A system with more or less permeable boundaries that permits interaction between the system's component parts or subsystems and outside influences.

operant conditioning A form of learning in which correct or desired responses are rewarded or reinforced, thus increasing the probability that these responses will recur.

operant interpersonal therapy A marital therapy approach based on operant conditioning theory, particularly the exchange between partners of positive rewards.

organization The notion that the components of a system relate to each other in some consistent fashion, and that the system is structured by those relationships.

paradigm A set of assumptions delimiting an area to be investigated scientifically and specifying the methods to be used to collect and interpret the forthcoming data.

paradoxical injunction A communication to obey a command that is internally inconsistent and contradictory, as in a double-bind message, forcing the receiver to disobey in order to obey.

paradoxical intervention A therapeutic technique whereby a therapist gives a client or family a directive he or she wants resisted; as a result of defying the directive, a change takes place.

peer review A process of assessing another therapist's professional procedures or intended procedures; under managed care contracts, such evaluations in a case-by-case procedure are performed by a case management coordinator representing a third-party payor.

permeability The ease or flexibility with which members can cross subsystem boundaries within the family.

phenomenological The view that to fully understand the causes of another person's behavior requires an understanding not of the physical or objective reality of the person's world, but of how he or she subjectively experiences that world.

positive connotation A reframing technique used primarily by systemic family therapists whereby positive motives are ascribed to family behavior patterns because these patterns help maintain family balance and cohesion; as a result, the family is helped to view each other's motives more positively.

positive feedback The flow of information from the output of a system back into the system in order to amplify deviation from the state of equilibrium, thus leading to instability and change.

postmodernism A philosophical outlook rejecting the notion that there exists an objectively knowable universe discoverable by impartial science, and instead arguing that there are multiple views of reality ungoverned by universal laws.

power Influence, authority, and control over an outcome.

prescribing the symptom A paradoxical technique in which the client is directed to voluntarily engage in the symptomatic behavior; as a result, the client is put in the position of rebelling and abandoning the symptom or obeying, thereby admitting it is under voluntary control.

pretend techniques Paradoxical interventions based on play and fantasy, in which clients are directed to "pretend" to have a symptom; the paradox is that if they are pretending, the symptom may be reclassified as voluntary and unreal, and thus able to be altered.

privileged communication A legal concept protecting a client's disclosure to a therapist from being revealed in court; if the client waives the right, the therapist has no legal grounds for withholding the information.

problem analysis An investigation of a presenting problem, typically carried out by behaviorists, in order to determine as precisely as possible what behavioral deficiencies require targeting.

projective identification An unconscious defense mechanism whereby certain unwanted aspects of oneself are attributed to another person (e.g., a spouse), who is then induced or incited to behave according to the first person's projected but split-off feelings.

pseudohostility A process by which families employ bickering and turmoil to maintain their relationship, avoiding tenderness and covering up deeper feelings, often of greater underlying hostility.

pseudomutuality A homeostasis-seeking relationship between and among family members that gives the surface appearance of being open, mutually understanding, and satisfying, when in fact it is not.

psychoanalysis A comprehensive theory of personality development and set of therapeutic techniques developed by Sigmund Freud in the early 1900s.

psychodrama A form of group therapy in which participants role-play themselves or significant others in their lives to achieve catharsis or to resolve conflicts and gain greater spontaneity.

psychodynamics The interplay of opposing forces within an individual as the basis for understanding that person's motivation.

psychopathology A disease concept derived from medicine, referring to the origins of abnormal behavior.

punctuation The communication concept that each participant in a transaction believes whatever he or she says is caused by what the other says, in effect holding the other responsible for his or her reactions.

radical behaviorism The outlook offered by B. F. Skinner that overt or observable behavior is the only acceptable subject of scientific investigation.

reactor Therapist whose style is subtle and indirect, and who prefers to observe and clarify the family process rather than serve as an active, aggressive, or colorful group leader.

redundancy principle Repetitive behavioral sequences within a family.

reflecting teams A process involving two-way mirrors in which team members observe a family and then discuss their thoughts and observations in front of the family and therapist. Later, the therapist and family discuss the team's conversations about them.

reframing Relabeling behavior by putting it into a new, more positive perspective ("Mother is trying to help" rather than "She's intrusive"), thus altering the context in which it is perceived and inviting new responses to the same behavior.

reinforcement A response, in the form of a reward or punishment, intended to change the probability of the occurrence of a previous response.

relabeling Verbal redefinition of an event in order to make dysfunctional behavior seem more reasonable and understandable, intended to provoke in others a more positive reaction to that behavior.

relational ethics In contextual family therapy, the overall, long-term preservation of fairness within a family, ensuring that each member's basic interests are taken into account by other family members.

resilience The ability to maintain stability and rebound in response to loss or trauma.

rituals Symbolic ceremonial prescriptions offered by a therapist, intended to address family conflict over its covert rules, to be enacted by the family in order to provide clarity or insight into their roles and relationships.

rubber fence As proposed by Wynne, a shifting boundary around a family, intended to protect them from outside contact, arbitrarily permitting certain acceptable bits of information to penetrate, but not others.

schemas Relatively stable cognitive structures involving underlying core beliefs a person develops about the world.

schizoid The inability to form social relationships or to concern oneself with the desires, needs, or feelings of others.

schizophrenia A group of severe mental disorders characterized by withdrawal from reality, blunted or inappropriate emotion, delusions, hallucinations, incoherent thought and speech, and an overall breakdown in personal and social functioning.

schizophrenogenic mother According to Fromm-Reichmann, a cold, domineering, possessive but rejecting mother (usually married to an inadequate, passive husband) whose behavior toward her son is thought to be a determining factor in his schizophrenic behavior.

second-order changes Fundamental changes in a system's organization, function, and frame of reference, leading to permanent change in its interactive patterns.

second-order cybernetics A view of an observing system in which the therapist, rather than attempting to describe the system by being an outside observer, is part of what is being observed and treated.

self objects According to Kohut, unconscious images or representations of another person or object viewed by infants as extension of themselves while they are in the process of gaining self-esteem.

self psychology An object-relations-based theory, advanced by Kohut, that emphasizes the role of narcissism in forming an authentic and coherent sense of self.

shaping A form of behavioral therapy, based on operant conditioning principles, in which successive approximations of desired behavior are reinforced until the desired behavior is achieved.

sibling position The birth order of children in a family, which influences their personalities as well as their interactions with future spouses.

social learning theory The theory that a person's behavior is best understood when the conditions under which the behavior is learned are taken into account.

societal regression Bowen's notion that society responds emotionally in periods of stress and anxiety, offering short-term "Band-Aid" solutions, rather than seeking more rational solutions that lead to greater individuation.

splitting According to object relations theory, a primitive process by which an infant makes contradictory aspects of a mother or other nurturing figure less threatening by dividing the external person into a good object and a bad object and internalizing the split perception.

stepfamily A linked family system created by the marriage of two persons, one or both of whom has been previously married, in which one or more children from the earlier marriage(s) live with the remarried couple.

strategic approach A therapeutic approach in which the therapist develops a specific plan or strategy and designs interventions aimed at solving the presenting problem.

structural A therapeutic approach directed at changing or realigning the family organization or structure in order to alter dysfunctional transactions and clarify subsystem boundaries.

subsystem An organized, coexisting component within an overall system, having its own autonomous functions as well as a specified role in the operation of the larger system; within families, a member can belong to a number of such units.

suprasystem A higher-level system in which other systems represent component parts and play subsystem roles.

symbiosis An intense attachment between two or more individuals, such as a mother and child, to the extent that the boundaries between them become blurred, and they respond as one.

symmetrical A type of dyadic transaction or communication pattern characterized by equality and the minimization of differences; each participant's response provokes a similar response in the other, sometimes in a competitive fashion.

symmetrical escalation A spiraling competitive effect in the communication between two people whose relationship is based on equality, so that vindictiveness leads to greater vindictiveness in return, viciousness to greater viciousness, and so forth.

system A set of interacting units or component parts that together make up a whole arrangement or organization.

systemic family therapy A Milan-model therapeutic approach in which the family, as an evolving system, is viewed as continuing to use an old epistemology that no longer fits its current behavior patterns; the therapist indirectly introduces new information into the family system and encourages alternative epistemologies to develop.

systems theory A generic term in common use, encompassing general systems theory and cybernetics, referring to the view of interacting units or elements making up the organized whole.

therapeutic contracts As used by behavioral family therapists, written negotiated agreements between family members to make specific behavior changes in the future.

time out A behavioral technique for extinguishing undesirable or inappropriate behavior by removing the reinforcing consequences of that behavior; the procedure is used primarily with children.

token economy A program in which tokens (points, gold stars) are dispensed contingent upon the successful completion of previously designated desired behaviors; the accumulated tokens can be redeemed later for money or special privileges.

tracking A therapeutic tactic associated with structural family therapy, in which the therapist deliberately attends to the symbols, style, language, and values of the family, using them to influence the family's transactional patterns.

transference In psychoanalytic treatment, the unconscious shifting onto the analyst of a patient's feelings, drives, attitudes, and fantasies, displaced from unresolved reactions to significant persons in the patient's past.

triad A three-person set of relationships.

triangle A three-person system, the smallest stable emotional system; according to Bowen, a two-person emotional system, under stress, will recruit a third person into the system to lower the intensity and anxiety and gain stability.

triangulation A process in which each parent demands that a child ally with him or her against the other parent during parental conflict.

unbalancing In structural family therapy, a technique for altering the hierarchical relationship between members of a system or subsystem by supporting one member and thus upsetting family homeostasis.

undifferentiated family ego mass Bowen's term for an intense, symbiotic nuclear family relationship; an individual sense of self fails to develop in members because of the existing fusion or emotional "stuck-togetherness."

unique outcomes In narrative therapy, those instances when the client did not experience the problem; such outcomes are intended to help contradict a client's problem-saturated outlook.

wholeness The systems view that combining units, components, or elements produces an entity greater than the sum of its parts.

Accordino, M. P., & Guerney, B. G., Jr. (2001). The empirical validation of Relationship Enhancement couple and family therapy. In D. J. Cain & J. Seeman (Eds.), *Humanistic psychotherapies: Handbook of research and practice*. Washington, DC: American Psychological Association.

Ackerman, N. W. (1937). The family as a social and emotional unit. *Bulletin of the Kansas Mental Hygiene Society, 12*(2).

Ackerman, N. W. (1956). Interlocking pathology in family relationships. In S. Rado & G. Daniels (Eds.), *Changing conceptions of psychoanalytic medicine*. New York: Grune & Stratton.

Ackerman, N. W. (1958). *The psychodynamics of family life.* New York: Basic Books.

Ackerman, N. W. (1966). *Treating the troubled family.* New York: Basic Books.

Ackerman, N. W. (1970). *Family therapy in transition.* Boston: Little, Brown.

Ackerman, N. W. (1972). The growing edge of family therapy. In C. Sager & H. Kaplan (Eds.), *Progress in group and family therapy.* New York: Brunner/Mazel.

Acuff, C., Bennett, B. E., Bricklin, P. M., Canter, M. B., Knapp, S. J., Moldawsky, S. J., & Phelps, R. (1999). Considerations for ethical practice of managed care. *Professional Psychology: Research and Practice, 30,* 563–575.

Adams, A., & Benson, K. (2005). Considerations for gay and lesbian families. *Family Therapy, Nov–Dec.,* 20–23.

Ahia, C. E., & Martin, D. (1993). *The danger-to-self-or-others exception to confidentiality.* Alexandria, VA: American Counseling Association.

Ahrons, C. R., & Rodgers, R. H. (1987). *Divorced families: A multidisciplinary approach.* New York: Norton.

Ainsworth, M. D. S., Blehar, M. C., Waters, E., & Wall, S. (1978). *Patterns of attachment: A psychological study of the strange situation.* Hillsdale, NJ: Erlbaum.

Alexander, J. F., & Barton, C. (1995). Family therapy research. In R. H. Mikesell, D. D. Lusterman, & S. H. McDaniel (Eds*.), Integrating family therapy: Handbook of family psychology and systems theory.* Washington, DC: American Psychological Association.

Alexander, J. F., Holtzworth-Munroe, A., & Jameson, P. (1994). The process and outcome of marital and family therapy: Research review and evaluation. In A. Bergin & S. Garfield (Eds.), *Handbook of psychotherapy and behavior change* (4th ed.). New York: Wiley.

Alexander, J. F., Newell, R. M., Robbins, M. S., & Turner, C. W. (1995). Observational coding in family therapy process research. *Journal of Family Psychology, 9,* 355–365.

Alexander, J., & Parsons, B. (1973). Short-term behavioral interventions with delinquent families: Impact on family process and recidivism. *Journal of abnormal psychology, 81,* 219–225.

Alexander, J. F., & Parsons, B. V. (1982). *Functional family therapy.* Pacific Grove, CA: Brooks/Cole.

Alexander, J. F., & Sexton, T. L. (2002). Functional family therapy: A model for treating high-risk, acting-out youth. In J. Lebow (Ed.), *Comprehensive handbook of psychotherapy* (Vol. IV). New York: Wiley.

Alexander, J. F., Sexton, T. L., & Robbins, M. S. (2000). The developmental status of family therapy in family psychology intervention science. In H. A. Liddle, D. A. Santisteban, R. F. Levant, & J. H. Bray (Eds.), *Family psychology: Science-based interventions.* Washington, DC: American Psychological Association.

Alexander, J., Waldon, H. B., Newberry, A. M., & Liddle, N. (1990). The functional family therapy model. In A. S. Friedman & S. Granick (Eds.), *Family therapy for adolescent drug abuse.* Lexington, MA: Lexington Books/D. C. Health.

Alger, I. (1976). Integrating immediate video playback in family therapy. In P. J. Guerin, Jr. (Ed.), *Family therapy: Theory and practice.* New York: Gardner Press.

Allman, L. R. (1982). The aesthetic preference: Overcoming the pragmatic error. *Family Process, 21,* 43–56.

Almeida, R., Woods, R., Messineo, T., & Font, R. (1998). The context model. In M. McGoldrick (Ed.), *Re-visioning family therapy: Race, gender, and culture in clinical practice.* New York: Guilford Press.

American Association for Marriage and Family Therapy. (2001). *AAMFT code of ethics.* Washington, DC: AAMFT.

American Association for Marriage and Family Therapy. (2004). *Marriage and family therapy core competencies.* Washington, DC: AAMFT.

American Psychological Association. (2002). Ethical principles of psychology and code of conduct. *American Psychologist, 57,* 1060–1073.

American Psychological Association. (2005). *Report of the 2005 task force on evidence-based practice.* Washington, DC: American Psychological Association.

Andersen, T. (1987). The reflecting team: Dialogue and metadialogue in clinical work. *Family Process, 26,* 415–426.

Andersen, T. (1991). *The reflecting team: Dialogues and dialogues about dialogues.* New York: Norton.

Andersen, T. (1992). Personal communication.

Andersen, T. (1993). See and hear, and be seen and heard. In S. Friedman (Ed.), *The new language of change: Constructive collaboration in psychotherapy.* New York: Guilford Press.

Andersen, T. (1995). Reflecting processes: Acts of informing and forming: You can borrow my eyes, but you must not take them away from me! In S. Friedman (Ed.), *The reflecting team in action: Collaborative practices in psychotherapy.* New York: Guilford Press.

Anderson, C. (2003). The diversity, strength, and challenges of single-parent households. In F. Walsh (Ed.), *Normal family process: Growing diversity and complexity.* New York: Guilford Press.

Anderson, C. M., Reiss, D., & Hogarty, B. (1986). *Schizophrenia and the family: A practitioner's guide to psychoeducation and management.* New York: Guilford Press.

Anderson, H. D. (1993). On a roller coaster: A collaborative language systems approach to therapy. In S. Friedman (Ed.), *The new language of change: Constructive collaboration in psychotherapy.* New York: Guilford Press.

Anderson, H. D. (1995). Collaborative language systems: Toward postmodern therapy. In R. H. Mikesell, D-D. Lusterman, & S. H. McDaniel (Eds.), *Integrating family therapy: Handbook of family psychology and systems theory.* Washington, DC: American Psychological Association.

Anderson, H. D. (1997). *Conversation, language, and possibilities: A postmodern approach to therapy.* New York: HarperCollins.

Anderson, H. D. (2003). Postmodern social construction therapies. In T. L. Sexton, G. R. Weeks, & M. S. Robbins (Eds.), *Handbook of family therapy: The science and practice of working with families and couples.* New York: Brunner-Routledge.

Anderson, H. D., Burney, J. P., & Levin, S. B. (1999). A postmodern collaborative approach to therapy. In D. M. Lawson & F. F. Prevatt (Eds.), *Casebook in family therapy.* Pacific Grove, CA: Brooks/Cole.

Anderson, H. D., & Goolishian, H. A. (1988). Human systems as linguistic systems: Preliminary and evolving ideas about the implications for clinical theory. *Family Process, 27,* 371–393.

Anderson, H. D., & Goolishian, H. A. (1990). Beyond cybernetics: Comments on Atkinson and Heath's "Further thoughts on second-order family therapy." *Family Process, 29,* 157–163.

Andolfi, M. (1979). *Family therapy: An interactional approach.* New York: Plenum.

Andreas, S. (1991). *Virginia Satir: The patterns of her magic.* Palo Alto: Science and Behavior Books.

Andrews, J., Clark, D., & Baird, F. (1998). Therapeutic letter-writing: Creating relational case notes. *The Family Journal: Counseling and Therapy for Couples and Families, 5,* 149–158.

Aponte, H. J. (1987). The treatment of society's poor: An ecological perspective on the underorganized family. *Family Therapy Today, 2,* 1–7.

Aponte, H. J. (1994). *Bread and spirit: Therapy with the new poor.* New York: Norton.

Aponte, H. J. (1999). The stresses of poverty and the comfort of spirituality. In F. Walsh (Ed.), *Spiritual resources in family therapy.* New York: Guilford Press.

Aponte, H. J., & DiCesare, E. J. (2000). Structural theory. In F. M. Dattilio & L. J. Bevilacqua (Eds.), *Comparative treatments for relationship dysfunction.* New York: Springer.

Aponte, H. J., & Van Deusin, J. M. (1981). Structural family therapy. In A. S. Gorman & D. P. Kniskern (Eds.), *Handbook of family therapy.* New York: Brunner/Mazel.

Aponte, J. F., & Wohl, J. (2000). *Psychological intervention and cultural diversity* (2nd ed.). New York: Allyn & Bacon.

Ariel, J., & McPherson, D. W. (2000). Therapy with lesbian and gay parents and their children. *Journal of Marital and Family Therapy, 26,* 421–432.

Atkins, D. C., Dimidjian, S., & Christensen, A. (2003). Behavioral couple therapy: Past, present, future. In T. L. Sexton, G. R. Weeks, & M. S. Robbins (Eds.), *Handbook of family therapy: The science and practice of working with families and couples.* New York: Brunner-Routledge.

Atkinson, J. M., & Coia, D. A. (1995). *Families coping with schizophrenia: A practitioner's guide to family groups.* New York: Wiley.

Atwood, J. D. (1997). *Challenging family therapy situations: Perspectives in social constructions.* New York: Springer.

Avis, J. M. (1985). The politics of functional family therapy: A feminist critique. *Journal of Marital and Family Therapy, 11,* 127–138.

Avis, J. M. (1996). Deconstructing gender in family therapy. In F. P. Piercy, D. H. Sprenkle, J. Wetchler, & Associates (Eds.), *Family therapy sourcebook* (2nd ed.). New York: Guilford Press.

Axelson, J. A. (1999). *Counseling and development in a multicultural society* (3rd ed.). Pacific Grove, CA: Brooks/Cole.

Aylmer, R. C. (1986). Bowen family systems marital therapy. In N. S. Jacobson & A. S. Gurman (Eds.), *Clinical handbook of marital therapy.* New York: Guilford Press.

Back, K. W. (1974). Intervention techniques: Small groups. In M. R. Rosenzweig & L. W. Porter (Eds.), *Annual review of psychology, 39,* 367–387.

Baerger, D. R. (2001). Risk management with the suicidal patient: Lessons from case law. *Professional Psychology: Research and practice, 32,* 359–366.

Bagarozzi, D. A. (1985). Dimensions of family evaluation. In L. L'Abate (Ed.), *The handbook of family psychology and therapy* (Vol. II). Homewood, IL: Dorsey Press.

Bandler, R., Grinder, J., & Satir, V. M. (1976). *Changing with families.* Palo Alto, CA: Science and Behavior Books.

Barnett, R. C., & Hyde, J. S. (2001). Women, men, work, and family. *American Psychologist, 56,* 781–796.

Barnhill, L. H., & Longo, D. (1978). Fixation and regression in the family life cycle. *Family Process, 17,* 469–478.

Bates, C. M., & Brodsky, A. M. (1989). *Sex in the therapy hour: A case of professional incest.* New York: Guilford Press.

Bateson, G. (1972). *Steps to an ecology of mind.* New York: Dutton.

Bateson, G., Jackson, D. D., Haley, J., & Weakland, J. (1956). Towards a theory of schizophrenia. *Behavioral Science, 1,* 251–264.

Bateson, M. C. (2001). *Full circle, overlapping lives: Culture and generation in transition.* New York: Ballantine Books.

Baucom, D., Shoham, V., Mueser, K., Daiuto, A., & Stickle, T. (1998). Empirically supported couple and family intervention for marital distress and adult mental health problems. *Journal of Consulting and Clinical Psychology, 66,* 53–88.

Beavers, W. R. (1982). Healthy, midrange, and severely dysfunctional families. In F. Walsh (Ed.), *Normal family processes.* New York: Guilford Press.

Beavers, W. R., & Hampson, R. B. (1993). Measuring family competence: The Beavers Systems Model. In F. Walsh (Ed.), *Normal family processes* (2nd ed.). New York: Guilford Press.

Beavers, W. R., & Hampson, R. B. (2003). Measuring family competence: The Beavers Systems Model. In F. Walsh (Ed.), *Normal family processes* (3rd ed.), New York: Guilford Press.

Beavers, W. R., & Voeller, M. N. (1983). Family models: Comparing and contrasting the Olson circumplex with the Beavers model. *Family Process, 22,* 85–98.

Becvar, D. S. (2000). Human development as a process of meaning making and reality construction. In W. C. Nichols, M. A. Pace-Nichols, D. S. Becvar, & A. Y. Napier (Eds.), *Handbook of family development and intervention.* New York: Wiley.

Becvar, D. S. (2003). Eras of epistemology: A survey of family therapy thinking and theorizing, In T. S. Sexton, G. R. Weeks, & M. S. Robbins (Eds.), *Handbook of family therapy: The science and practice of working with families and couples.* New York: Brunner-Routledge.

Beck, A. T. (1976). *Cognitive therapy and emotional disorders.* New York: International Universities Press.

Beck, A. T. (1995). Cognitive therapy. In R. J. Corsini & D. Wedding (Eds.), *Current psychotherapies* (5th ed). Itasca, IL: Peacock.

Beels, C., & Ferber, A. (1969). Family therapy: A view. *Family Process, 8,* 280–332.

Bell, J. E. (1961). *Family group therapy* (Public Health Monograph No. 64). Washington, DC: U.S. Government Printing Office.

Bell, J. E. (1975). *Family therapy.* New York: Aronson.

Bem, S. L. (1981). Gender schema theory: A cognitive account of sex typing. *Psychological Review, 88,* 354–364.

Bem, S. L. (1983). Gender schema theory and its implications for child development: Raising gender-aschematic children in a gender-schematic society. *Signs, 8,* 598–616.

Bem, S. L. (1998). *An unconventional family.* New Haven, CT: Yale University Press.

Bennett, B. E., Bryant, B. K., VandenBos, G. R., & Greenwood, A. (1990). *Professional liability and risk management.* Washington, DC: American Psychological Association.

Bentovim, A., & Kinston, W. (1991). Focal family therapy: Joining systems theory with psychodynamic understanding. In A. S. Gurman & D. P. Kniskern (Eds.), *Handbook of family therapy* (Vol. 2). New York: Brunner/Mazel.

Berg, I. K. (1994). *Family-based services: A solution-focused approach.* New York: Norton.

Berg, I. K., & de Shazer, S. (1993). Making numbers talk: Language in therapy. In S. Friedman (Ed.), *The new language of change: Constructive collaboration in psychotherapy.* New York: Guilford Press.

Berg, I. K., & Miller, S. D. (1992). *Working with the problem drinker: A solution-focused approach.* New York: Norton.

Berger, R. (2000). Stepfamilies in cultural context. *Journal of Divorce and Remarriage, 33,* 111–130.

Bergman, J. (1985). *Fishing for barracuda: Pragmatics of brief therapy.* New York: Norton.

Bernstein, A. C. (1999). Reconstructing the Brothers Grimm: New tales for stepfamilies. *Family Process, 38,* 415–429.

Berry, J. W. (1997). Immigration, acculturation, and adaptation. *Applied Psychology: An International Review, 46,* 5–68.

Bevilacqua, L. J., & Dattilio, F. M. (2001). *Brief family therapy homework planner.* New York: Wiley.

Bianchi, S. M. (1995). The changing demographic and socioeconomic characteristics of single-parent families. *Marriage and Family Review, 20,* 71–97.

Bion, W. R. (1961). *Experiences in groups.* New York: Basic Books.

Black, T. R. (1999). *Doing quantitative research in the social sciences: An integrated approach to research design, measurement, and statistics.* London: Sage.

Bloch, D. A. (1994). Staying alive while staying alive. *Family Systems Medicine, 12,* 103–105.

Bloch, D. A., & Simon, R. (Eds.). (1982). *The strength of family therapy: Selected papers of Nathan W. Ackerman.* New York: Brunner/Mazel.

Bodin, A. M. (1981). The interactional view: Family therapy approaches of the Mental Research Institute. In A. S. Gurman & D. P. Kniskern (Eds.), *Handbook of family therapy.* New York: Brunner/Mazel.

Bodin, A. M. (1983). *Family therapy.* Unpublished manuscript.

Bonanno, G. A. (2004). Loss, trauma, and human resilience: Have we underestimated the human capacity to thrive after extreme aversive events? *American Psychologist, 59,* 20–28.

Bond, J. T., Galinsky, E., & Swanberg, J. E. (1998). *The 1997 national study of the changing workforce.* New York: Families and Work Institute.

Booth, A., Crouter, A. C., & Landale, N. (Eds.). (1997). *Immigration and the family.* Mahwah, NJ: Lawrence Erlbaum.

Booth, A., & Dunn, J. (Eds.). (1994). *Stepfamilies: Who benefits? Who does not?* Hillsdale, NJ: Erlbaum.

Borders, L. D. (1991). A systematic approach to peer group supervision. *Journal of Counseling and Development, 69*(3), 248–252.

Boscolo, L., Cecchin, G., Hoffman, L., & Penn, P. (1987). *Milan systemic family therapy: Conversations in theory and practice.* New York: Basic Books.

Boszormenyi-Nagy, I. (1987). *Foundations of contextual therapy: Collected papers of Ivan Boszormenyi-Nagy.* New York: Brunner/Mazel.

Boszormenyi-Nagy, I., & Framo, J. L. (Eds.). (1965). *Intensive family therapy: Theoretical and practical aspects.* New York: Harper & Row.

Boszormenyi-Nagy, I., Grunebaum, J., & Ulrich, D. (1991). Contextual therapy. In A. S. Gurman & D. P. Kniskern (Eds.), *Handbook of family therapy* (Vol. II). New York: Brunner/Mazel.

Boszormenyi-Nagy, I., & Krasner, B. R. (1986). *Between give and take: A clinical guide to contextual therapy.* New York: Brunner/Mazel.

Boszormenyi-Nagy, I., & Spark, G. M. (1973). *Invisible loyalties: Reciprocity in intergenerational family therapy.* New York: Harper & Row.

Boszormenyi-Nagy, I., & Ulrich, D. (1981). Contextual family therapy. In A. S. Gurman & D. P. Kniskern (Eds.), *Handbook of family therapy.* New York: Brunner/Mazel.

Boughner, S. R., Hayes, S. F., Bubenzer, D. L., & West, J. D. (1994). Use of standardized assessment instruments by marital and family therapists: A survey. *Journal of Marital and Family Therapy, 20,* 69–75.

Bowen, M. (1960). A family concept of schizophrenia. In D. D. Jackson (Ed.), *The etiology of schizophrenia.* New York: Basic Books.

Bowen, M. (1966). The use of family theory in clinical practice. *Comprehensive Psychiatry, 7,* 345–374.

Bowen, M. (1975). Family therapy after twenty years. In S. Arieti, D. X. Freedman, & J. E. Dyrud (Eds.), *American handbook of psychiatry V: Treatment* (2nd ed.). New York: Basic Books.

Bowen, M. (1976). Theory in the practice of psychotherapy. In P. J. Guerin, Jr. (Ed.), *Family therapy: Theory and practice.* New York: Gardner Press.

Bowen, M. (1978). *Family therapy in clinical practice.* New York: Aronson.

Bowlby, J. (1969). *Attachment and loss* (Vol. 1). *Attachment.* New York: Basic Books.

Boyd, C. P., Gullone, E., Needleman, G. L., & Burt, T. (1997). The Family Environment Scale: Reliability and normative data for an adolescent sample. *Family Process, 36,* 369–373.

Boyd-Franklin, N. (1989). *Black families in therapy: A multisystems approach.* New York: Guilford Press.

Boyd-Franklin, N. (Fall 2002). Training psychologists to work with African American families. *The Family Psychologist, 17,* 1–3.

Boyd-Franklin, N. (2003a). *Black families in therapy: Understanding the African American experience.* New York: Guilford Press.

Boyd-Franklin, N. (2003b). Race, class, and poverty. In F. Walsh (Ed.), *Normal family processes: Growing diversity and complexity* (3rd ed.). New York: Guilford Press.

Boyd-Franklin, N., Franklin, A. J., & Toussaint, P. (2000). *Boys into men: Raising our African American teenage sons.* New York: Dutton.

Braverman, S. (1986). Heinz Kohut and Virginia Satir: Strange bedfellows. *Contemporary Family Therapy, 8*(2), 101–110.

Bray, J. H. (1995a). Methodological advances in family psychology research: Introduction to the special section. *Journal of Family Psychology, 9,* 107–109.

Bray, J. H. (1995b). Systems-oriented therapy with stepfamilies. In R. H. Mikesell, D-D. Lusterman, & S. H. McDaniel (Eds.), *Integrating family therapy: Handbook of family psychology and systems theory.* Washington, DC: American Psychological Association.

Bray, J. H. (2002). Methodological issues and innovations in family psychology intervention research. In H. A. Liddle, D. A. Santisteban, R. F. Levant, & J. H. Bray (Eds.), *Family psychology: Science-based interventions.* Washington, DC: American Psychological Association.

Bray, J. H. (2005). Quantitative approaches to family psychology research. *The Family Psychologist, 21*(4), 7–9.

Bray, J. H., & Kelly, J. (1998). *Stepfamilies: Love, marriage, and parenting in the first decade.* New York: Broadway Books.

Breunlin, D. C. (1988). Oscillation theory and family development. In C. J. Falicov (Ed.), *Family transitions: Continuity and change over the life cycle.* New York: Guilford Press.

Broderick, C. B., & Schrader, S. S. (1991). The history of professional marriage and family counseling. In A. S. Gurman & D. P. Kniskern (Eds.), *Handbook of family therapy* (Vol. II). New York: Brunner/Mazel.

Bronfenbrenner, U. (1986). Ecology of the family as a context for human development. *American Psychologist, 32,* 513–531.

Brooks, G. R. (1992). Gender-sensitive family therapy in a violent culture. *Topics in Family Psychology and Counseling, 1*(4), 24–36.

Brothers, B. J. (Ed.) (1991). *Virginia Satir: Foundational ideas.* Binghampton, NY: Haworth Press.

Brown, G. W., Birley, J. L., & Wing, J. K. (1972). The influence of family life on the course of schizophrenic disorders: A replication. *British Journal of Psychiatry, 121,* 241–258.

Brown, G. W., Monck, E. M., Carstairs, G. M., & Wing, J. K. (1962). Influence on family life in the course of schizophrenic illness. *British Journal of Psychiatry, 16,* 55–68.

Brubaker, L. (2006). Integrating emotion-focused therapy with the Satir model. *Journal of Marital and Family Therapy, 32,* 141–153.

Bruner, J. (1986). Experience and its expression. In E. Bruner & V. W. Turner (Eds.), *The anthropology of experience.* Chicago: University of Illinois Press.

Burbatti, G. L., & Formenti, L. (1988). *The Milan approach to family therapy.* Northvale, NJ: Aronson.

Burg, J. E., & Sprenkle, D. H. (1996). Sex therapy. In F. P. Piercy, D. H. Sprenkle, J. Wetchler, & Associates (Eds.), *Family therapy sourcebook* (2nd ed.). New York: Guilford Press.

Cade, B., & O'Hanlon, W. (1993). *A brief guide to brief therapy.* New York: Norton.

Calvedo, C., & Guerney, B. G. (1999). Relationship Enhancement enrichment and problem-prevention programs: Therapy-derived, powerful, versatile. In R. Berger & M. T. Hannah (Eds.), *Preventive approaches in couples therapy.* Philadelphia: Brunner/Mazel.

Campbell, D., & Draper, R. (Eds.) (1985). *Applications of systemic family therapy: The Milan approach.* London: Grune & Stratton.

Campbell, D., Draper, R., & Crutchley, E. (1991). The Milan systemic approach to family therapy. In A. S. Gurman & D. P. Kniskern (Eds.), *Handbook of family therapy* (Vol. II). New York: Brunner/Mazel.

Campbell, T. L. (1986). Family's impact on health: A critical review and annotated bibliography. *Family Systems Medicine, 18,* 129–142.

Campbell, T. L., & Patterson, J. M. (1995). The effectiveness of family interventions in the treatment of physical illness. *Journal of Marital and Family Therapy, 21,* 545–583.

Carlson, J., Sperry, L., & Lewis, J. A. (1997). *Family therapy: Ensuring treatment efficacy.* Pacific Grove, CA: Brooks/Cole.

Carlson, K. (1996). Gay and lesbian families. In M. Harway (Ed.), *Treating the changing family: Handling normative and unusual events.* New York: Wiley.

Carr, A. (1991). Milan systemic family therapy: A review of ten empirical investigations. *Journal of Family Therapy, 13,* 237–263.

Carter, B., & McGoldrick, M. (1999). Overview: The expanded family life cycle: Individual, family, and social perspectives. In B. Carter & M. McGoldrick (Eds.), *The expanded family life cycle: Individual, family, and social perspectives* (3rd ed.). Boston: Allyn & Bacon.

Cecchin, G. (1987). Hypothesizing, circularity, and neutrality revisited: An invitation to curiosity. *Family Process, 26,* 405–413.

Cecchin, G., Lane, G., & Ray, W. (1992). *Irreverence: A strategy for therapist survival.* London: Karnac.

Chambless, D. L., Baker, M. J., Baucom, D. H., Beutler, L. E., Calhoun, K. S., Crits-Cristoph, P. (1998). Update on empirically validated therapies, II. *The Clinical Psychologist, 51,* 3–16.

Chambless, D. L., Sanderson, W. C., Shoham, V., Bennett Johnson, S., Pope, K. S., Crits-Cristoph, P. (1996). An update on empirically validated therapies. *The Clinical Psychologist, 49,* 5–18.

Chandler, K. (1997). *Passages of pride: True stories of lesbian and gay teenagers.* Los Angeles: Alyson.

Chartier, M. R. (1986). Marriage enrichment. In R. F. Levant (Ed.), *Psychoeducational approaches to family therapy and counseling.* New York: Springer.

Cheung, M. (1997). Social construction theory and the Satir model: Toward a synthesis. *American Journal of Family Therapy, 25,* 331–343.

Christensen, A., Baucom, D. H., Vu, C. T. A., & Stanton, S. (2005). Methodologically sound, cost-effective research on the outcome of couple therapy. *Journal of Consulting and Clinical Psychology, 72,* 176–191.

Christensen, A., & Jacobson, N. S. (1999). *Reconcilable differences.* New York: Guilford Press.

Christensen, A., Jacobson, N. S., & Babcock, J. C. (1995). Integrative behavioral couples therapy. In N. S. Jacobson & A. S. Gurman (Eds.), *Clinical handbook of couple therapy.* New York: Guilford Press.

Christensen, L. L., Russell, C. S., Miller, R. B., & Peterson, C. M. (1998). The process of change in couple therapy: A qualitative investigation. *Journal of Marital and Family Therapy, 24,* 177–188.

Cicirelli, V. G. (1995). *Sibling relationships across the life span.* New York: Plenum Press.

Colapinto, J. (1982). Structural family therapy. In A. M. Horne & M. M. Ohlsen (Eds.), *Family counseling and therapy.* Itasca, IL: Peacock.

Colapinto, J. (1991). Structural family therapy. In A. S. Gurman & D. P. Kniskern (Eds.), *Handbook of family therapy* (Vol. II). New York: Brunner/Mazel.

Colapinto, J. (2000). Structural family therapy. In A. M. Horne (Ed.), *Family counseling and therapy* (3rd ed.). Itasca, IL: Peacock.

Cole, R. E., & Reiss, D. (1993). *How do families cope with chronic illness?* Hillsdale, NJ: Erlbaum.

Coley, R. L., & Chase-Lansdale, P. L. (1998). Adolescent pregnancy and parenthood: Recent evidence and future directions. *American Psychologist, 53,* 152–166.

Coltrane, S. (1998). *Gender and families.* Thousand Oaks, CA: Pine Forge Press.

Combrinck-Graham, L. (1988). Adolescent sexuality in the family life cycle. In C. Falicov (Ed.), *Family transitions.* New York: Guilford Press.

Compton, B. R., & Galaway, B. (1999). *Social work processes* (6th ed.). Pacific Grove, CA: Brooks/Cole.

Constantine, L. L. (1986). *Family paradigms: The practice of theory in family therapy.* New York: Guilford Press.

Coontz, S. (1992). *The way we never were: American families and the nostalgia trap.* New York: HarperCollins.

Coontz, S. (2005). *Marriage, a history: From obedience to intimacy or how love conquered marriage.* New York: Viking.

Corey, G., Corey, M. S., & Callanan, P. (2007). *Issues and ethics in the helping profession*s (7th ed.). Pacific Grove, CA: Brooks/Cole.

Cox, F. D. (1996). *Human intimacy: Marriage, the family, and its meaning.* Minneapolis: West.

Cox, W. M., & Alm, R. (2005, February 28). Scientists are made, not born. *New York Times,* p. A25.

Cuellar, I., & Glazer, M. (1996). The impact of culture on the family. In M. Harway (Ed.), *Treating the changing family: Handling normative and unusual events.* New York: Wiley.

Cummings, N. A. (1995). Impact of managed care on employment and training: A primer for survival. *Professional Psychology: Research and Practice, 26,* 10–15.

Cummings, N. A. (1996). Does managed mental health care offset costs related to medical treatment? In A. Lazarus (Ed.), *Controversies in managed mental health care.* Washington, DC: American Psychiatric Press.

Dangel, R. F., Yu, M., Slot, N. W., & Fashimpar, G. (1994). Behavioral parent training. In D. K. Granvold (Ed.), *Cognitive and behavioral treatment: Methods and applications.* Pacific Grove, CA: Brooks/Cole.

Dattilio, F. M. (Ed.). (1998). *Case studies in couple and family therapy: Systemic and cognitive perspectives.* New York: Guilford Press.

Dattilio, F. M. (2001). Cognitive-behavior family therapy: Contemporary myths and misconceptions. *Contemporary Family Therapy, 23,* 3–17.

Dattilio, F. M. (2005). The restructuring of family schemas: A cognitive-behavior perspective. *Journal of marital and family therapy, 31,* 15–30.

Dattillio, F. M., & Bevilacqua, L. J. (Eds.). (2000). *Comparative treatments for relationship dysfunction.* New York: Springer.

Dattilio, F. M., & Epstein, N. B. (2003). Cognitive-behavior couple and family therapy. In T. L. Sexton, G. R. Weeks, & M. S. Robbins (Eds.), *Handbook of family therapy: The science and practice of working with families and couples.* New York: Brunner-Routledge.

Dattilio, F. M., & Epstein, N. B. (2005). Introduction to the special section: The role of cognitive-behavioral interventions in couple and family therapy. *Journal of Marital and Family Therapy, 31,* 7–13.

Dattilio, F. M., Epstein, N. B., & Baucom, D. H. (1998). An introduction to cognitive-behavioral therapy with couples and families. In F. M. Dattilio (Ed.), *Case studies in couple and family therapy: Systemic and cognitive perspectives.* New York: Guilford Press.

Dattilio, F. M., & Padesky, C. A. (1990). *Cognitive therapy with couples.* Sarasota, FL: Professional Resource Exchange.

Davis, S. R., & Meier, S. T. (2001). *The elements of managed care: A guide for helping professionals.* Pacific Grove, CA: Brooks/Cole.

Deegear, J., & Lawson, D. M. (2003). The utility of empirically supported treatments. *Professional Psychology: Research and Practice, 34*(3), 271–277.

DeHay, T. L. (2006). The rewards of training in school-based family practice. *The Family Psychologist, 22,* 15–16.

DeJong, P., & Berg, I. K. (1998). *Interviewing for solutions.* Pacific Grove, CA: Brooks/Cole.

del Carmen, R. (1990). Assessment of Asian-American families for family therapy. In F. C. Serafica, A. I. Schwebel, R. K. Russell, P. D. Isaac, & L. B. Myers (Eds.), *Mental health of ethnic minorities.* New York: Praeger.

Dell, P. F. (1982). Beyond homeostasis: Toward a concept of coherence. *Family Process, 21,* 21–42.

Denzin, N. K., & Lincoln, Y. S. (Eds.). (2000). *Handbook of qualitative research.* Thousand Oaks, CA: Sage.

Derrida, J. (1978). *Writing and difference.* Chicago: University of Chicago Press.

de Shazer, S. (1985). *Keys to solution in brief therapy.* New York: Norton.

de Shazer, S. (1988). Clues: Investigating solutions in brief therapy. New York: Norton.

de Shazer, S. (1991). *Putting differences to work.* New York: Norton.

de Shazer, S. (1994). *Words were originally magic.* New York: Norton.

Diamond, G. S., & Diamond, G. M. (2002). Studying a matrix of change mechanisms: An agenda for family-based process research. In H. A. Liddle, D. A. Santisteban, R. F. Levant, & J. H. Bray (Eds.), *Family psychology: Science-based interventions.* Washington, DC: American Psychological Association.

Dicks, H. V. (1967). *Marital tensions.* New York: Basic Books.

Diller, J. V. (1999). *Cultural diversity: A primer for the human services.* Belmont, CA: Brooks/Cole-Wadsworth.

Dinkmeyer, D., McKay, G., Dinkmeyer, Jr., D., & McKay, J. (1997). *STEP: The parent handbook.* Circle Pines, MN: American Guidance Service.

Doherty, W. J. (1991). Family therapy goes postmodern. *Family Networker, 15*(5), 36–42.

Doherty, W. J., & Baird, M. A. (1983). *Family therapy and family medicine: Toward the primary care of patients.* New York: Guilford Press.

Doherty, W. J., & Baird, M. A. (Eds.). (1987). *Family-centered medical care: A clinical casebook.* New York: Guilford Press.

Doherty, W. J., & Boss, P. G. (1991). Values and ethics in family therapy. In A. S. Gurman & D. P. Kniskern (Eds.), *Handbook of family therapy* (Vol. II). New York: Brunner/Mazel.

Doherty, W. J., Lester, M. E., & Leigh, G. (1986). Marriage Encounter weekends: Couples who win and couples who lose. *Journal of Marital and Family Therapy, 12,* 49–61.

Donahey, K. M., & Miller, S. D. (2001). "What works" in sex therapy: A common factors perspective. In P. L. Kleinplatz (Ed.), *New directions in sex therapy: Innovations and alternatives.* New York: Brunner-Routledge.

Doyle, J. A. (1994). *The male experience* (3rd ed.). Dubuque, IA: W. C. Brown.

Ducommun-Nagy, C. (1999). Contextual therapy. In D. M. Lawson & F. F. Prevatt (Eds.), *Casebook in family therapy.* Pacific Grove, CA: Brooks/Cole.

Duhl, F. J., Kantor, D., & Duhl, B. S. (1973). Learning, space, and action in family therapy: A primer of sculpture. In D. A. Bloch (Ed.), *Techniques of family psychotherapy: A primer.* New York: Grune & Stratton.

Duncan, B. L., Miller, S. D., & Sparks, J. A. (2003). Interactional and solution-focused brief therapies: Evolving concepts of change. In T. L. Sexton, G. R.

Weeks, & M. S. Robbins (Eds.), *Handbook of family therapy: The science and practice of working with families and couples.* New York: Brunner-Routledge.

Dunn, R. L., & Schwebel, A. I. (1995). Meta-analysis of marital therapy outcome research. *Journal of Family Psychology, 9,* 58–68.

Durrant, M., & Kowalski, K. (1993). Enhancing views of competence. In S. Friedman (Ed.), *The new language of change: Constructive collaboration in psychotherapy.* New York: Guilford Press.

Duvall, E. M. (1977). *Marriage and family development* (5th ed.). New York: Lippincott.

Duvall, E. M., & Hill, R. (1948). *Report to the committee on the dynamics of family interaction.* Washington, DC: National Conference on Family Life.

Edelman, M. W. (1987). *Families in peril: An agenda for social change.* Cambridge, MA: Harvard University Press.

Efran, J., & Schenker, M. (1993). A potpourri of solutions: How new and different is solution-focused therapy? *The Family Therapy Networker, 17*(3), 71–74.

Eidelson, R. J., & Epstein, N. (1982). Cognitive and relationship maladjustment: Development of a measure of dysfunctional relationship beliefs. *Journal of Consulting and Clinical Psychology, 50,* 715–720.

Eldridge, K., Christensen, A., & Jacobson, N. S. (1999). Integrative couple therapy. In D. M. Lawson & F. F. Prevatt (Eds.), *Casebook in family therapy.* Pacific Grove, CA: Brooks/Cole.

Ellis, A. (1979). Rational-emotive therapy. In R. J. Corsini (Ed.), *Current psychotherapies* (2nd ed.). Itasca, IL: Peacock.

Ellis, A. (1995). Rational emotive behavior therapy. In R. J. Corsini & D. Wedding (Eds.), *Current psychotherapies* (5th ed.). Itasca, IL: Peacock.

Elizur, J., & Minuchin, S. (1989). *Institutionalizing madness: Families, therapy, and society.* New York: Basic Books.

Engel, G. L. (1977). The need for a new medical model: A challenge for biomedicine. *Science, 196,* 129–136.

Enns, C. Z. (1997). *Feminist theories and feminist psychotherapies: Origins, themes, and variations.* New York: Haworth.

Epstein, N. B. (1992). Marital therapy. In A. Freeman & F. M. Dattilio (Eds.), *Comprehensive casebook of cognitive therapy.* New York: Plenum Press.

Epstein, N. B., Baldwin, L. M., & Bishop, D. S. (1983). The McMaster family assessment device. *Journal of Marital and Family Therapy, 9,* 171–186.

Epstein, N. B., & Baucom, D. H. (1989). Cognitive-behavioral marital therapy. In A. Freeman, K. M. Simon, L. E. Butler, & H. Arkowitz (Eds.), *Comprehensive handbook of cognitive therapy.* New York: Plenum.

Epstein, N. B., & Baucom, D. H. (2002). *Enhanced cognitive-behavioral therapy for couples: A contextual approach.* Washington, DC: American Psychological Association.

Epstein, N. B., Bishop, D. S., & Baldwin, L. M. (1982). McMaster Model of family functioning: A view of the normal family. In F. Walsh (Ed.), *Normal family processes.* New York: Guilford Press.

Epstein, N. B., Bishop, D. S., Ryan, C., Miller, I., & Keitner, G. (1993). The McMaster Model: View of healthy family functioning. In F. Walsh (Ed.), *Normal family processes* (2nd ed.). New York: Guilford Press.

Epstein, N. B., Ryan, C. E., Bishop, D. S., Miller, I. W., & Keitner, G. I. (2003). The McMaster model: A view of healthy family functioning. In F. Walsh (Ed.), *Normal family processes* (3rd ed.), New York: Guilford Press.

Epstein, N. B., Schlesinger, S. E., & Dryden, W. (Eds.). (1988). Concepts and methods of cognitive-behavioral family treatment. In N. Epstein, S. E. Schlesinger, & W. Dryden (Eds.), *Cognitive-behavioral therapy with families.* New York: Brunner/Mazel.

Epston, D. (1994). Extending the conversation. *The Family Networker, 18*(6), 30–37, 62–63.

Epston, D., & White, M. (1992). *Experience, contradiction, narrative, and imagination: Selected papers of David Epston and Michael White.* Adelaide, Australia: Dulwich Centre Publications.

Everett, C. A., & Volgy Everett, S. S. (2000). Single-parent families: Dynamics and treatment issues. In W. C. Nichols, M. A. Pace-Nichols, D. S. Becvar, & A. Y. Napier (Eds.), *Handbook of family development and intervention.* New York: Wiley.

Fairbairn, W. R. (1952). *An object-relations theory of personality.* New York: Basic Books.

Falicov, C. J. (1983). *Cultural perspectives in family therapy.* Rockville, MD: Aspen.

Falicov, C. J. (1988). Learning to think culturally. In H. A. Liddle, D. C. Breunlin, & R. C. Schwartz (Eds.), *Handbook of family therapy training and supervision.* New York: Guilford Press.

Falicov, C. J. (1995a). Cross-cultural marriages. In N. Jacobson & A. S. Gurman (Eds.), *Clinical handbook of couple therapy.* New York: Guilford Press.

Falicov, C. J. (1995b). Training to think culturally: A multidimensional comparative framework. *Family Process, 34,* 373–388.

Falicov, C. J. (1998). *Latino families in therapy: A guide to multicultural practice.* New York: Guilford Press.

Falicon, C. J. (1999). The Latino family life cycle. In B. Carter & M. McGoldrick (Eds.), *The expanded family life cycle: Individual, family, and social perspectives* (3rd ed.). Boston: Allyn & Bacon.

Falicov, C. J. (2003). Immigrant family processes. In F. Walsh (Ed.), *Normal family processes* (3rd ed.). New York: Guilford Press.

Falloon, I. R. H. (1991). Behavioral family therapy. In A. S. Gurman & D. P. Kniskern (Eds.), *Handbook of family therapy* (Vol. II). New York: Brunner/Mazel.

Falloon, I. R. H., Boyd, J. L., McGill, C. W., Williamson, M., Razani, J., Moss, H. B., Gilderman, A. M., & Simpson, G. M. (1985). Family management in the prevention of morbidity of schizophrenia: Clinical outcome of a two-year longitudinal study. *Archives of General Psychiatry, 42,* 887–896.

Falloon, I. R. H., & Liberman, R. D. (1983). Behavior therapy for families with child management problems. In M. R. Textor (Ed.), *Helping families with special problems.* New York: Aronson.

Falloon, I. R. H., & Lillie, F. J. (1988). Behavioral family therapy: An overview. In I. R. H. Falloon (Ed.), *Handbook of behavioral family therapy.* New York: Guilford Press.

Falvey, J. E. (2002). *Managing clinical supervision: Ethical practices and legal risk management.* Pacific Grove, CA: Brooks/Cole.

Fincham, F. D., & Bradbury, T. N. (1992). Assessing attributions in marriage: The Relationship Attribution Measure. *Journal of Personality and Social Psychology, 62,* 457–468.

Fine, M. J. (1995). Family-school intervention. In R. H. Mikesell, D-D. Lusterman, & S. H. McDaniel (Eds.),*Integrating family therapy: Handbook of family psychology and systems theory.* Washington, DC: American Psychological Association.

Fine, M. J., & Carlson, C. (Ed.). (1992). *The handbook of family-school intervention: A systems perspective.* Needham Heights, MA: Allyn & Bacon.

Fine, M. J., McKenrey, P. C., & Chung, H. (1992). Postdivorce adjustment of black and white single parents. *Journal of Divorce and Remarriage, 17,* 121–134.

Fisch, R., Weakland, J., & Segal, L. (1982). *The tactics of change: Doing therapy briefly.* San Francisco: Jossey-Bass.

Fish, J. M. (1995). Solution focused therapy in global perspective. *World Psychology, 1,* 43–67.

Fisher, C. (2003). *Decoding the ethics code.* Thousand Oaks, CA: Sage.

Fishman, H. C. (1993). *Intensive family therapy: Treating families in their social context.* New York: Basic Books.

Floyd, F. J., Markman, H. J., Kelly, S., Blumberg, S. L., & Stanley, S. M. (1995). Preventive intervention and relationship enhancement. In N. S. Jacobson & A. S. Gurman (Eds.), *Clinical handbook of couple therapy.* New York: Guilford Press.

Fontes, L. A., & Thomas, V. (1996). Cultural issues in family therapy. In F. P. Piercy, D. H. Sprenkle, J. L. Wetchler, & Associates (Eds.), *Family therapy sourcebook* (2nd ed.). New York: Guilford Press.

Forgatch, M. S., & Patterson, G. R. (1998). Behavioral family therapy. In F. M. Dattilio (Ed.), *Case studies in couple and family therapy: Systemic and cognitive perspectives.* New York: Guilford Press.

Foucault, M. (1965). *Madness and civilization: A history of insanity in the age of reason.* New York: Random House.

Foucault, M. (1980). *Power/knowledge: Selected interviews and other writings, 1972–1977.* New York: Pantheon Books.

Fournier, C. J., & Rae, W. A. (1999). Psychoeducational family therapy. In D. M. Lawson & F. F. Prevatt (Eds.), *Casebook in family therapy.* Pacific Grove, CA: Brooks/Cole.

Fraenkel, P. (2003). Contemporary two-parent families: Navigating work and family challenges. In F. Walsh (Ed.), *Normal family processes* (3rd ed.). New York: Guilford Press.

Fraenkel, P. (2005). Whatever happened to family therapy? *Psychotherapy Networker,* 29(3).

Framo, J. L. (1972). *Family interaction: A dialogue between family researchers and family therapists.* New York: Springer.

Framo, J. L. (1976). Family of origin as a therapeutic resource for adults in marital and family therapy: You can and should go home again. *Family Process, 15,* 193–210.

Framo, J. L. (1981). The integration of marital therapy with sessions with family of origin. In A. S. Gurman & D. P. Kniskern (Eds.), *Handbook of family therapy.* New York: Brunner/Mazel.

Framo, J. L. (1982). *Explorations in marital and family therapy: Selected papers of James L. Framo.* New York: Springer.

Framo, J. L. (1992). *Family-of-origin therapy: An intergenerational approach.* New York: Brunner/Mazel.

Freedman, J., & Combs, G. (1996). *Narrative therapy: The social construction of preferred realities.* New York: Norton.

Freedman, J., & Combs, G. (2000). Narrative therapy with couples. In F. M. Dattilio & L. J. Bevilacqua (Eds.), *Comparative treatments for relationship dysfunction.* New York: Springer.

Freeman, J., Epston, D., & Lebovits, D. (1997). *Playful approaches to serious problems.* New York: Norton.

Freud, S. (1955). Analysis of a phobia in a five-year-old boy (1909). *The standard edition of the complete psychological works of Sigmund Freud* (Vol. 10). London: Hogarth.

Freud, S. (1959). Fragments of an analysis of a case of hysteria (1905). *Collected papers* (Vol. 3). New York: Basic Books.

Friedlander, M. L., & Tuason, M. T. (2000). Processes and outcomes in couples and family therapy. In S. D. Brown & R. W. Lent (Eds.), *Handbook of counseling therapy* (3rd ed.). New York: Guilford Press.

Friedlander, M. L., Wildman, J., Heatherington, L., & Skowron, E. A. (1994). What we do and don't know about the process of family therapy. *Journal of Family Therapy, 8,* 390–416.

Friedman, E. (1991). Bowen theory and therapy. In A. S. Gurman & D. P. Kniskern (Eds.), *Handbook of family therapy* (Vol. II). New York: Brunner/Mazel.

Friedman, S. (Ed.). (1993). *The new language of change: Constructive collaboration in psychotherapy.* New York: Guilford Press.

Fromm-Reichmann, F. (1948). Notes on the development of treatment of schizophrenics by psychoanalytic psychotherapy. *Psychiatry, 11,* 253–273.

Fulmer, R. (1988). Lower-income and professional families: A comparison of structure and life cycle process. In B. Carter & M. McGoldrick (Eds.), *The changing family life cycle: A framework for family therapy* (2nd ed.). New York: Gardner Press.

Fulmer, R. (1999). Becoming an adult: Leaving home and staying connected. In B. Carter & M. McGoldrick (Eds.), *The expanded life cycle: Individual, family, and social perspectives* (3rd ed.). Boston: Allyn & Bacon.

Galinsky, E. (1999). *Ask the children: What America's children really think about working parents.* New York: Morrow.

Gambrill, E. D. (1994). Concepts and methods of behavioral treatment. In D. K. Granvold (Ed.), *Cognitive and behavioral treatment: Methods and applications.* Pacific Grove, CA: Brooks/Cole.

Ganong, L., & Coleman, M. (1994). *Remarried family relationships.* Thousand Oaks, CA: Sage.

Ganong, L., & Coleman, M. (1999). *Changing families, changing responsibilities: Family obligations following divorce and remarriage.* Mahway, NJ: Erlbaum.

Gartrell, N., Deck, A., Rodas, C., Peyser, H., & Banks, A. (2005). The national lesbian family study: 4. Interviews with the 10-year-old children. *American Journal of Orthopsychiatry, 75,* 518–524.

Gartrell, N., Hamilton, M. D., Banks, A., Mosbacher, D., Reed, N., Sparks, C. H., & Bishop, H. (1996). The national lesbian family study: 1. Interviews with prospective mothers. *American Journal of Orthpsychiatry, 66,* 272–281.

Geertz, C. (1973). Thick descriptions: Toward an interpretive theory of culture. In C. Geertz (Ed.), *The interpretations of cultures.* New York: Basic Books.

Gelcer, E., McCabe, A. E., & Smith-Resnick, C. (1990). *Milan family therapy: Variant and invariant methods.* Northvale, NJ: Aronson.

Gergen, K. J. (1985). The social construction movement in modern psychology. *American Psychologist, 40,* 266–275.

Gergen, K. J. (1993). Foreword. In S. Friedman (Ed.), *The new language of change: Constructive collaboration in psychotherapy.* New York: Guilford Press.

Gergen, K. J. (1996). Technology and the self: From the essential to the sublime. In D. Grodin & T. R. Lindlof (Eds.), *Constructing the self in a mediated world.* Thousand Oaks, CA: Sage Publications.

Gergen, K. J. (1999). *An invitation to social construction.* Thousand Oaks, CA: Sage.

Gergen, K. J. (2001). Psychological science in a postmodern context. *American Psychologist, 56,* 803–813.

Gergen, K. J. (2002). Psychological science: To conserve or create? *American Psychologist, 57,* 463–464.

Gerson, R. (1995). The family life cycle: Phases, stages, and crises. In R. H. Mikesell, D-D. Lusterman, & S. H. McDaniel (Eds.), *Integrating family therapy: Handbook of family psychology and systems theory.* Washington, DC: American Psychological Association.

Giblin, P., Sprenkle, D. H., & Sheehan, R. (1985). Enrichment-outcome research: A meta-analysis of premarital, marital, and family interventions. *Journal of Marital and Family Therapy, 11,* 257–271.

Gilgun, J. F. (1999). An ecosystemic approach to assessment. In B. R. Compton & B. Galaway (Eds.), *Social work processes* (6th ed.). Pacific Grove, CA: Brooks/Cole.

Gilgun, J. F. (2005). Qualitative research and family therapy. *Journal of Family Psychology, 19*(1), 40–50.

Gilligan, C. (1982). *In a different voice: Psychological theory and women's development.* Cambridge, MA: Harvard University Press.

Ginsberg, B. G. (1977). Parent-adolescent relationship development program. In B. G. Guerney, Jr. (Ed.) *Relationship enhancement: Skills training for therapy problem prevention and enrichment.* San Francisco: Jossey-Bass.

Ginsberg, B. G. (1997). *Relationship enhancement family therapy.* New York: Wiley.

Ginsberg, B. G. (2000). Relationship enhancement couples therapy. In F. M. Dattilio & L. J. Bevilacqua (Eds.), *Comparative treatments of relationship disorders.* New York: Springer.

Giordano, J., & Carini-Giordano, M. A. (1995). Ethnic dimensions in family treatment. In R. H. Mikesell, D-D. Lusterman, & S. H. McDaniel (Eds.), *Integrating family therapy: Handbook of family psychology and systems theory.* Washington, DC: American Psychological Association.

Gladding, S. T., Remley, T. P., & Huber, C. H. (2001). *Ethical, legal, and professional issues in the practice of marriage and family therapy* (3rd ed.). Upper Saddle River, NJ: Merrill/Prentice-Hall.

Glantz, M. D., & Johnson, J. L. (1999). *Resilience and development: Positive life adaptations.* New York: Plenum.

Glosoff, H. L., Herlihy, S. B., Herlihy, B., & Spence, E. B. (1997). Privileged communication in the psychologist-client relationship. *Professional Psychology: Research and Practice, 28,* 573–581.

Goldenberg, H. (1983). *Contemporary clinical psychology* (2nd ed.). Pacific Grove, CA: Brooks/Cole.

Goldenberg, H., & Goldenberg, I. (1993). Multiculturalism and family systems. *Progress: Family Systems Research and Therapy, 2,* 7–12.

Goldenberg, H., & Goldenberg, I. (1999). Current issues and trends in family therapy. In D. M. Lawson & F. F. Prevatt (Eds.), *Casebook in family therapy.* Pacific Grove, CA: Brooks/Cole.

Goldenberg, H., & Goldenberg, I. (2002). *Counseling today's families* (4th ed.). Pacific Grove, CA: Brooks/ Cole.

Goldenberg, I., & Goldenberg, H. (1983). Historical roots of contemporary family therapy. In B. B. Wolman & G. Stricker (Eds.), *Handbook of family and marital therapy.* New York: Plenum.

Goldenberg, I., & Goldenberg, H. (2005). Family therapy. In R. J. Corsini & D. Wedding (Eds.), *Current psychotherapies* (7th ed.). Itasca, IL: Peacock.

Goldner, V. (1985). Feminism and family therapy. *Family Process, 24,* 13–47.

Goldner, V. (1998). The treatment of violence and victimization in intimate relationships. *Family Process, 37,* 263–286.

Goldner, V., Penn, P., Sheinberg, M., & Walker, G. (1990). Love and violence: Gender paradoxes in volatile attachments. *Family Process, 29,* 343–364.

Goldstein, M. J. (Ed.). (1981). *New developments in interventions with families of schizophrenics.* San Francisco: Jossey-Bass.

Goldstein, M. J. (1988). The family and psychopathology. In M. R. Rosenzweig & L. W. Porter (Eds.), *Annual Review of Psychology, 39,* 283–299.

Goldstein, M. J., & Miklowitz, D. J. (1995). The effectiveness of psychoeducational family therapy in the treatment of schizophrenic disorders. *Journal of Marital and Family Therapy, 21,* 361–376.

Goldstein, M. J., Rodnick, E. H., Evans, J. R., May, P. R., & Steinberg, M. (1978). Drug and family therapy in the aftercare treatment of acute schizophrenia. *Archives of General Psychiatry, 35,* 1169–1177.

Good, G., Gilbert, L., & Scher, M. (1990). Gender aware therapy: A synthesis of feminist therapy and knowledge about gender. *Journal of Counseling and Development, 68,* 376–380.

Goodheart, C. D. (2006). Evidence, endeavor, and expertise in psychology practice. In C. D. Goodheart, A. E. Kazdin, & R. J. Sternberg (Eds.), *Evidence-based psychotherapy: Where practice and research meet.* Washington, DC: American Psychological Association.

Goodheart, C. D., Kazdin, A. E., & Sternberg, R. J. (Eds.) (2006). *Evidence-based psychotherapy: Where practice and research meet.* Washington, DC: American Psychological Association.

Goodrich, T. J., Rampage, C., Ellman, B., & Halstead, K. (1988). *Feminist family therapy: A casebook.* New York: Norton.

Gorall, D. M., & Olson, D. H. (1995). Circumplex model of family systems: Integrating ethnic diversity and other social systems. In R. H. Mikesell, D-D. Lusterman, & S. H. McDaniel (Eds.), *Integrating family therapy: Handbook of family psychology and systems theory.* Washington, DC: American Psychological Association.

Gordon, S. B., & Davidson, N. (1981). Behavioral parent training. In A. S. Gurman & D. P. Kniskern (Eds.), *Handbook of family therapy.* New York: Brunner/Mazel.

Gottman, J. M. (1994). *Why marriages succeed or fail.* New York: Simon and Schuster.

Gottman, J. M. (Ed.). (1996). *What predicts divorce?* Hillsdale, NJ: Erlbaum.

Gottman, J. M., Coan, J., Carrere, S., & Swanson, C. (1998). Predicting marital happiness and stability from newlywed interactions. *Journal of Marriage and the Family, 60,* 5–22.

Gottman, J. M., & Gottman, J. S. (1999). The marriage survival kit: A research-based marital therapy. In R. Berger & M. T. Hannah (Eds.), *Preventive approaches in couple therapy.* Philadelphia, PA: Brunner/Mazel.

Gottman, J. M., & Krokoff, I. (1989). Marital interaction and satisfaction: A longitudinal view. *Journal of Consulting and Clinical Psychology, 57,* 47–52.

Gottman, J. M., Ryan, K. D., Carrere, S., & Erley, A. M. (2002). Toward a scientifically based marital therapy. In H. A. Liddle, D. A. Santisteban, R. F. Levant, & J. H. Bray (Eds.), *Family psychology: Science-based interventions.* Washington, DC: American Psychological Association.

Green, R. J. (1998). Race and the field of family therapy. In M. McGoldrick (Ed.), *Re-Visioning family therapy: Race, culture, and gender in clinical practice.* New York: Guilford Press.

Green, R. J., & Framo, J. L. (Eds.). (1981). *Family therapy: Major contributions.* New York: International Universities Press.

Greenberg, L. S. (1999). (Ed.). *Handbook of experiential psychotherapy.* New York: Guilford Press.

Greenberg, L. S. (2002). *Emotion-focused therapy: Coaching clients to work through their feelings.* Washington, DC: American Psychological Association.

Greenberg, L. S., & Johnson, S. M. (1986). Emotionally focused couples therapy. In N. S. Jacobson & A. S. Gurman (Eds.), *Clinical handbook of marital therapy.* New York: Guilford Press.

Greenberg, L. S., & Johnson, S. M. (1988). *Emotionally focused therapy for couples.* New York: Guilford Press.

Greenberg, L. S., & Pinsof, W. M. (Eds.). (1986). *The psychotherapeutic process: A research handbook.* New York: Guilford Press.

Greenberg, L. S., Rice, L. N., & Elliott, R. (1996). *Facilitating emotional change: The moment-by-moment process.* New York: Guilford Press.

Greenburg, S. L., Lewis, G. J., & Johnson, J. (1985). Peer consultation groups for private practitioners. *Professional Psychology: Research and Practice, 16*(3), 437–447.

Grotevant, H. D., & Carlson, C. I. (1989). *Family assessment: A guide to methods and measurements.* New York: Guilford Press.

Grotstein, J. J., & Rinsley, D. B. (Eds.). (1994). *Fairbairn and the origins of object relations.* New York: Guilford.

Group for the Advancement of Psychiatry. (1970). *The field of family therapy* (Report No. 78). New York: Group for the Advancement of Psychiatry.

Grunebaum, H. (1997). Commentary: Why integration may be a misguided goal for family therapy. *Family Process, 36,* 19–21.

Guba, E. (Ed.). (1990). *The paradigm dialogue.* Newbury Park, CA: Sage.

Guerin, P. J., Jr. (1976). Family therapy: The first twenty-five years. In P. J. Guerin, Jr. (Ed.), *Family therapy: Theory and practice.* New York: Gardner Press.

Guerin, P. J., Jr., Fay, L. E., Burden, S., & Kautto, J. G. (1987). *The evaluation and treatment of marital conflict: A four-stage approach.* New York: Basic Books.

Guerin, P. J., Jr., Fogarty, T. F., Fay, L. E., & Kautto, J. G. (1996). *Working with relationship triangles: The one-two-three of psychotherapy.* New York: Guilford Press.

Guerney, B. G., Jr. (1964). Filial therapy: Description and rationale. *Journal of Consulting Psychology, 28,* 304–310.

Guerney, B. G., Jr. (Ed.). (1977). *Relationship enhancement: Skills training for therapy problem prevention and enrichment.* San Francisco: Jossey-Bass.

Guerney, B. G., Jr., Brock, G., & Coufal, J. (1986). Integrating marital therapy and enrichment: The relationship enhancement approach. In N. D. Jacobson & A. S. Gurman (Eds.), *Clinical handbook of marital therapy.* New York: Guilford Press.

Guerney, B. G., Jr., Coufal, J., & Vogelsang, E. (1981). Relationship enhancement versus a traditional approach to therapeutic/preventive/enrichment parent-adolescent program. *Journal of Consulting and Clinical Psychology, 49,* 927–939.

Guerney, B. G., Jr., Guerney, L., & Andronico, M. (1966). Filial therapy: Description and rationale. *Yale Scientific Magazine, 40,* 6–14.

Gurman, A. S., & Kniskern, D. P. (1981). Family therapy outcome research: Knowns and unknowns. In A. S. Gurman & D. P. Kniskern (Eds.), *Handbook of family therapy.* New York: Brunner/Mazel.

Gurman, A. S., & Knudson, R. M. (1978). Behavior marriage therapy: I. A psychodynamic-systems analysis and critique. *Family Process, 17,* 121–138.

Guttman, H. A. (1991). Systems theory, cybernetics, and epistemology. In A. S. Gurman & D. P. Kniskern (Eds.), *Handbook of family therapy* (Vol. II). New York: Brunner/Mazel.

Haas, L. J., & Malouf, J. L. (1995). *Keeping up the good work: A practitioner's guide to mental health ethics* (2nd ed.). Sarasota, FL: Professional Resource Exchange.

Haddock, S. A., Zimmerman , T. S., & Lyness, K. P. (2003). Changing gender roles: Transitional dilemmas. In F. Walsh (Ed.), *Normal family processes* (3rd ed.). New York: Guilford Press.

Haley, J. (1963). *Strategies of psychotherapy.* New York: Grune & Stratton.

Haley, J. (1973). *Uncommon therapy: The psychiatric techniques of Milton H. Erickson, M. D.* New York: Norton.

Haley, J. (Ed.). (1976). *Problem-solving therapy.* San Francisco: Jossey-Bass.

Haley, J. (1978). Ideas which handicap therapists. In M. M. Berger (Ed.), *Beyond the double-bind: Communication and family systems, theories, and techniques with schizophrenics.* New York: Brunner/Mazel.

Haley, J. (1979). *Leaving home: Therapy with disturbed young people.* New York: McGraw-Hill.

Haley, J. (1984). *Ordeal therapy: Unusual ways to change behavior.* San Francisco: Jossey-Bass.

Haley, J. (1988). Personal communication.

Haley, J. (1996). *Learning and teaching family therapy.* New York: Guilford Press.

Haley, J. & Hoffman, L. (1967). *Techniques of family therapy.* New York: Basic Books.

Hampson, R. B., & Beavers, W. R. (1996). Measuring family therapy outcome in a clinical setting: Families that do better or do worse in therapy. *Family process, 35*(3), 347–361.

Hardy, K. V., & Laszloffy, T. A. (1995). The cultural genograms: Key to training culturally competent family therapists. *Journal of Marital and Family Therapy, 21,* 221–237.

Hare-Mustin, R. T. (1978). A feminist approach to family therapy. *Family Process, 17,* 181–194.

Hare-Mustin, R. T. (1980). Family therapy may be dangerous to your health. *Professional Psychology, 11,* 935–938.

Hare-Mustin, R. T. (1987). The problem of gender in family therapy theory. *Family Process, 26,* 15–27.

Hare-Mustin, R. T., & Maracek, J. (Eds.). (1990). *Making a difference: Psychology and the construction of gender.* New Haven, CT: Yale University Press.

Harway, M., & Wexler, K. (1996). Setting the stage for understanding and treating the changing family. In M. Harway (Ed.), *Treating the changing family: Handling normative and unusual events.* New York: Wiley.

Hawkins, A. J., Marshall, C. M., & Allen, S. M. (1998). The orientation toward domestic labor questionnaire: Exploring dual-earner wives' sense of fairness about family work. *Journal of Family Psychology, 12,* 244–258.

Hawley, D. R., & DeHaan, L. (1996). Toward a definition of family resilience: Integrating life-span and family perspectives. *Family Process, 35,* 283–298.

Hayden, T. (2001). *Irish on the inside: In search of the soul of Irish Americans.* New York: Verso.

Hazan, C. & Shaver, P. (1987). Romantic love conceptualized as an attachment process: *Journal of Personality and Social Psychology, 52,* 511–524.

Healy, M. (1998, March 13). Study says poverty persists for kids of working poor. *Los Angeles Times.*

Heatherington, L., Friedlander, M. L., & Greenberg, L. (2005). Change process research in couple and family therapy: Methodological challenges and opportunities. *Journal of Family Psychology, 19,* 18–27.

Heiman, J. R., Epps, P. H., & Ellis, B. (1995). Treating sexual desire disorders in couples. In N. S. Jacobson & A. S. Gurman (Eds.), *Clinical handbook of couple therapy.* New York: Guilford Press.

Heiman, J. R., LoPiccolo, L., & LoPiccolo, J. (1981). The treatment of sexual dysfunction. In A. S. Gurman & D. P. Kniskern (Eds.), *Handbook of family therapy.* New York: Brunner/Mazel.

Heiman, J. R., & Verhulst, J. (1990). Sexual dysfunction and marriage. In F. D. Fincham & T. N. Bradbury (Eds.), *The psychology of marriage: Basic issues and applications.* New York: Guilford Press.

Helmeke, K. B., & Srenkle, D. H. (2000). Clients' perceptions of pivotal moments in couples therapy: A qualitative study of change in therapy. *Journal of marital & family therapy, 26,* 469–483.

Henggeler, S. W., & Borduin, C. M. (1990). *Family therapy and beyond: A multisystemic approach to treating the behavioral problems of children and adolescents.* Pacific Grove, CA: Brooks/Cole.

Henggeler, S. W., & Cunningham, P. B. (2006). School-related interventions and outcomes for multisystemic therapy (MST). *The Family Psychologist, 22*(1), 4–5, 28–29.

Henggeler, S. W., Mihalic, S. F., Rone, L., Thomas, C., & Timmons-Mitchell, J. (1998). *Blueprints for violence prevention, book six: Multisystemic therapy.* Boulder, CO: Center for the Study and Prevention of Violence.

Hernandez, M., & McGoldrick, M. (1999). Migration and the family life cycle. In B. Carter & M. McGoldrick (Eds.), *The expanded family life cycle: Individual, family, and social perspectives.* Boston: Allyn & Bacon.

Hersch, L. (1995). Adapting to health care reform and managed care: Three strategies for survival and growth. *Professional Psychology: Research and Practice, 26,* 16–26.

Hetherington, E. M. (Ed.). (1999). *Coping with divorce, single parenting, and remarriage: A risk and resiliency perspective.* Mahwah, NJ: Erlbaum.

Hetherington, E. M., Bridges, M., & Insabella, G. M. (1998) What matters? What does not? Five perspectives on the association between marital transitions and children's adjustments. *American Psychologist, 53,* 167–184.

Hines, P. M. (1999). The family life cycle of African American families living in poverty. In B. Carter & M. McGoldrick (Eds.), *The expanded life cycle: Individual, family, and social perspectives* (3rd ed.). Boston: Allyn & Bacon.

Hines, P. M., Garcia-Preto, N., McGoldrick, M., Almeida, R., & Weltman, S. (1999). Culture and the family cycle. In B. Carter & M. McGoldrick (Eds.), *The expanded family life cycle: Individual, family, and social perspectives* (3rd ed.). Boston: Allyn & Bacon.

Ho, M. K. (1987). *Family therapy with ethnic minorities.* Newbury Park, CA: Sage.

Hochschild, A. (1997). *The second shift.* New York: Avon.

Hodge, D. R. (2005). Spiritual assessment in marital and family therapy: A methodological framework for selecting from among six qualitative assessment tools. *Journal of Marital and Family Therapy, 31,* 341–356.

Hoffman, L. (1981). *Foundations of family therapy.* New York: Basic Books.

Hoffman, L. (1988). The family life cycle and discontinuous change. In B. Carter & M. McGoldrick (Eds.), *The changing family life cycle* (2nd ed.). New York: Gardner Press.

Hoffman, L. (1990). Constructing realities: An art of lenses. *Family Process, 29,* 1–12.

Hoffman, L. (2002). *Family therapy: An intimate history.* New York: Norton.

Hogue, A., Liddle, H. A., Singer, A., & Leckrone, J. (2005). Intervention fidelity in family-based prevention counseling for adolescent problem behaviors. *Journal of Community Psychology, 33,* 191–211.

Holtzworth-Munroe, A., & Jacobson, N. S. (1991). Behavioral marital therapy. In A. S. Gurman & D. P. Kniskern (Eds.), *Handbook of family therapy* (Vol. II). New York: Brunner/Mazel.

Homma-True, R., Greene, B., Lopez, S. R., & Trimble, J. E. (1993). Ethnocultural diversity in clinical psychology. *Clinical Psychologist, 46,* 50–63.

Hong, G. K. (2006). School-based family services: A promising service model for ethnic minorities. *The Family Psychologist, 22,* 16–17.

Howells, J. G. (1975). *Principles of family psychiatry.* New York: Brunner/Mazel.

Hoyt, M. F. (2001a). Cognitive-behavioral treatment of posttraumatic stress disorder with a narrative constructivist perspective: A conversation with Donald Meichenbaum. In M. F. Hoyt (Ed.), *Interviews with brief therapy experts.* New York: Brunner-Routledge.

Hoyt, M. F. (2001b). Honoring our internalized others and the ethics of caring: A conversation with Karl Tomm and Stephen Madigan. In M. Hoyt (Ed.), *Interviews with brief therapy experts.* New York: Brunner-Routledge.

Hoyt, M. F. (2001c). Welcome to possibilityland: A conversation with Bill O'Hanlon. In M. Hoyt (Ed.), *Interviews with brief therapy experts.* New York: Brunner-Routledge.

Huber, C. H. (1994). *Ethical, legal, and professional issues in the practice of marriage and family therapy* (2nd ed.). New York: Macmillan.

Hudson, P., & O'Hanlon, W. H. (1992). *Rewriting love stories: Brief marital therapy.* New York: Norton.

Hyde, J. S. (1996). *Half the human experience: The psychology of women* (5th ed.). Lexington, MA: Heath.

Imber-Black, E. (1988). *Families and larger systems: A family therapist's guide through the labyrinth.* New York: Guilford Press.

Imber-Black, E. (1999). Creating meaningful rituals for new life cycle transitions. In B. Carter & M. McGoldrick (Eds.), *The expanded family life cycle: Individual, family, and social perspectives* (3rd ed.). Boston: Allyn & Bacon.

Imber-Black, E., Roberts, J., & Whiting, R. (Eds.). (1989). *Rituals in families and family therapy.* New York: Guilford Press.

Incan, J., & Ferran, E. (1990). Poverty, politics, and family therapy: A role for systems theory. In M. P. Mirkin (Ed.), *The social and political contexts of family therapy.* Boston: Allyn & Bacon.

Jackson, D. D. (1965a). Family rules: Marital quid pro quo. *Archives of General Psychiatry, 12,* 589–594.

Jackson, D. D. (1965b). The study of the family. *Family Process, 4*(1), 1–20.

Jacobson, N. S. (1991). To be or not to be behavioral when working with couples. *Journal of Family Psychology, 4,* 436–445.

Jacobson, N. S., & Christensen, A. (1996). *Integrative couple therapy: Promoting acceptance.* New York: Norton.

Jacobson, N. S., & Margolin, G. (1979). *Marital therapy: Strategies based on social learning and behavior exchange principles.* New York: Brunner/Mazel.

Jacobson, N. S., & Martin, B. (1976). Behavioral marital therapy. *Psychological Bulletin, 83,* 540–556.

Johnson, S. M. (2002). *Emotionally focused couples therapy for trauma survivors: Strengthening attachment bonds.* New York: Guilford Press.

Johnson, S. M. (2003). Emotionally focused couples therapy: Empiricism and art. In T. L. Sexton, G. R. Weeks, & M. S. Robbins (Eds.), *Handbook of family therapy: The science and practice of working with families and couples.* New York: Brunner/Mazel.

Johnson, S. M. (2004). *The practice of emotionally focused marital therapy: Creating connections* (2nd ed.). New York: Brunner/Mazel.

Johnson, S. M., & Greenberg, L. S. (1995). The emotionally focused approach to problems in adult attachment. In N. S. Jacobson & A. S. Gurman (Eds.), *Clinical handbook of couple therapy.* New York: Guilford Press.

Johnson, S. M., Hunsley, J., Greenberg, L., & Schindler, D. (1999). Emotionally focused couples therapy: Status and challenges. *Clinical psychology: Science and Practice, 6,* 67–79.

Johnson, S. M., Makinen, J. A., & Millikin, J. W. (2001). Attachment injuries in couple relationships: A new perspective on impasses in couple therapy. *Journal of Marital and Family Therapy, 27,* 145–155.

Johnson, T. W., & Colucci, P. (1999). Lesbians, gay men, and the family life cycle. In B. Carter & M. McGoldrick (Eds.), *The expanded family life cycle: Individual, family, and social perspectives* (3rd ed.). Boston: Allyn & Bacon.

Jones, E. (1993). *Family systems therapy: Developments in the Milan-Systemic therapies.* New York: Wiley.

Jones, J. T., Christensen, A., & Jacobson, N. (2000). Integrative behavioral couple therapy. In F. M. Dattilio & L. J. Bevilacqua (Eds.), *Comparative treatments for relationship dysfunction.* New York: Springer.

Kalichman, S. C., & Craig, M. E. (1991). Professional psychologists' decisions to report suspected child abuse: Clinical and situational influences. *Professional Psychology: Research and Practice, 26,* 5–9.

Kantor, D., & Lehr, W. (1975). *Inside the family.* San Francisco: Jossey-Bass.

Kaplan, H. S. (1974). *The new sex therapy: Active treatment of sexual dysfunction.* New York: Brunner/Mazel.

Kaplan, H. S. (1979). *Disorders of sexual desire and other new concepts and techniques in sex therapy.* New York: Brunner/Mazel.

Kaplan, H. S. (1983). *The evaluation of sexual disorders: Psychological and medical aspects.* New York: Brunner/Mazel.

Kaplan, H. S. (1995). *The sexual desire disorders: Dysfunctional regulation of sexual motivation.* New York: Brunner/Mazel.

Kaplan, M. L., & Kaplan, N. R. (1978). Individual and family growth: A Gestalt approach. *Family Process, 17,* 195–206.

Karpel, M. A. (Ed.). (1986). *Family resources: The hidden partner in family therapy.* New York: Guilford Press.

Karpel, M. A., & Strauss, E. S. (1983). *Family evaluation.* New York: Gardner Press.

Kaslow, F. W. (1996). (Ed.). *Handbook of relational diagnosis and dysfunctional family patterns.* New York: Wiley.

Kaslow, N. J., Smith, G. G., & Croft, S. S. (2000). Families with young children: A developmental–family systems perspective. In W. C. Nichols, M. A. Pace-Nichols, D. S. Becvar, & A. Y. Napier (Eds.), *Handbook of family development and intervention.* New York: Wiley.

Kaye, K. (1985). Toward a developmental psychology of the family. In L. L'Abate (Ed.), *The handbook of family psychology and therapy* (Vol. 1). Homewood, IL: Dorsey Press.

Kazdin, A. E. (1984). *Behavior modification in applied settings* (3rd ed.). Homewood, IL: Dorsey Press.

Kazdin, A. E. (1998). *Methodological issues and strategies in clinical research* (2nd ed.). Washington, DC: American Psychological Association.

Kazdin, A. E., & Weisz, J. R. (Eds.). (2003). *Evidence-based psychotherapies for children and adolescents.* New York: Guilford Press.

Keeney, B. P., & Sprenkle, D. H. (1982). Ecosystemic epistemology: Critical implications for the aesthetics and pragmatics of family therapy. *Family Process, 21,* 1–19.

Keim, J. (1998). Strategic family therapy. In F. M. Dattilio (Ed.), *Case studies in couple and family therapy: Systemic and cognitive perspectives.* New York: Guilford Press.

Keim, J. (1999). Strategic therapy. In D. M. Lawson & F. F. Prevatt (Eds.), *Casebook in family therapy.* Pacific Grove, CA: Brooks/Cole.

Keim, J. (2000). Strategic family therapy: The Washington school. In A. M. Horne (Ed.), *Family counseling and therapy.* Itasca, IL: Peacock.

Keith, D. V. (1998). Symbolic-experiential family therapy for chemical imbalance. In F. M. Dattilio (Ed.), *Case studies in couple and family therapy: Systemic and cognitive perspectives.* New York: Guilford Press.

Keith, D. V. (2000). Symbolic experiential family therapy. In A. M. Horne (Ed.), *Family counseling and therapy* (3rd ed.). Itasca, IL: Peacock.

Keith, D. V., & Whitaker, C. A. (1982). Experiential-symbolic family therapy. In A. M. Horne & M. M. Ohlsen (Eds.), *Family counseling and therapy.* Itasca, IL: Peacock.

Kempler, W. (1981). *Experiential psychotherapy with families.* New York: Brunner/Mazel.

Kempler, W. (1982). Gestalt family therapy. In A. M. Horne & M. M. Ohlsen (Eds.), *Family counseling and therapy.* Itasca, IL: Peacock.

Kerr, M. E. (1981). Family systems theory and therapy. In A. S. Gurman & D. P. Kniskern (Eds.), *Handbook of family therapy.* New York: Brunner/Mazel.

Kerr, M. E., & Bowen, M. (1988). *Family evaluation: An approach based on Bowen theory.* New York: Norton.

Kleinplatz, P. J. (Ed.). (2001). *New directions in sex therapy: Innovations and alternatives.* New York: Brunner-Routledge.

Kliman, J. (1994). The interweaving of gender, class, and race in family therapy. In M. P. Mirkin (Ed.), *Women in context: Toward a feminist reconstruction of psychotherapy.* New York: Guilford Press.

Kliman, J., & Madsen, W. (1999). Social class and the family life cycle. In B. Carter & M. McGoldrick (Eds.), *The expanded family life cycle: Individual, family, and social perspectives* (3rd ed.). Boston: Allyn & Bacon.

Knoff, H. (Ed.). (1986). *The assessment of child and adolescent personality.* New York: Guilford.

Kohut, H. (1971). *The analysis of self.* New York: International Universities Press.

Kohut, H. (1977). *The restoration of the self.* New York: International Universities Press.

Kopala, M., & Suzuki, L. A. (1998). *Using qualitative methods in psychology.* Thousand Oaks, CA: Sage.

Korzybski, A. (1942). *Science and sanity: An introduction to non-Aristotelian systems and general semantics* (2nd ed.). Lancaster, PA: Science Books.

Kouneski, E. (2001). Circumplex Model and FACES: Review of the literature. Available online at http://www.lifeinnovations.com/familyinventoriesdatabase.html.

Kressel, K. (1985). *The process of divorce: How professionals and couples negotiate settlements.* New York: Basic Books.

Kuhn, T. (1970). *The structure of scientific revolutions.* Chicago: University of Chicago Press.

L'Abate, L. (1994). *Family evaluation: A psychological approach.* Thousand Oaks, CA: Sage.

Laird, J. (2003). Lesbian and gay families. In F. Walsh (Ed.), *Normal family processes: Diversity and complexity* (3rd ed.). New York: Guilford Press.

Lambert, M. J., & Ogles, B. M. (2004). The efficacy and effectiveness of psychotherapy. In M. J. Lambert (Ed.), *Bergin and Garfield's handbook of psychotherapy and behavior change* (5th ed.). New York: Wiley.

Landau-Stanton, J. (1993). *AIDS, health, and mental health: A primary sourcebook.* New York: Brunner/Mazel.

Langsley, D. G., Pittman, F. S., Machotka, P., & Flomenhaft, K. (1968). Family crisis therapy: Results and implications. *Family Process, 7,* 145–158.

Laqueur, H. P. (1976). Multiple family therapy. In P. J. Guerin, Jr. (Ed.), *Family therapy: Theory and practice.* New York: Gardner Press.

Lasswell, M., & Lasswell, T. (1991). *Marriage and the family* (3rd ed.). Belmont, CA: Wadsworth.

Laszloffy, T. A. (2002). Rethinking family development theory: Teaching with the systemic family development (SFD) model. *Family Relations, 51,* 206–214.

Lawrence, E. C. (1999). The humanistic approach of Virginia Satir. In D. M. Lawson & F. F. Prevatt (Eds.), *Casebook in family therapy.* Pacific Grove, CA: Brooks/Cole.

Lawson, D. M., & Prevatt, F. F. (Eds.) (1999). *Casebook in family therapy.* Pacific Grove, CA: Brooks/Cole.

Lazarus, A. A. (1977). Has behavior therapy outlived its usefulness? *American Psychologist, 32,* 550–554.

Lebow, J. (1997). The integrative revolution in couple and family therapy. *Family Process, 36,* 1–17.

Lebow, J. L. (2003). Integrative approaches to couple and family therapy. In T. L. Sexton, G. R. Weeks, & M. S. Robbins (Eds.), *Handbook of family therapy: The science and practice of working with families and couples.* New York: Brunner-Routledge.

Leff, J., & Vaughn, C. (1985). *Expressed emotions in families.* Thousand Oaks, CA: Sage.

Lefley, H. P. (1996). *Family caregiving in mental illness.* Thousand Oaks, CA: Sage.

Lennon, M. C., & Rosenfeld, S. (1994). Relative fairness and the division of housework: The importance of options. *American Journal of Sociology, 100,* 506–531.

Lerner, Q. (1986). *The creation of patriarchy.* New York: Oxford University Press.

Leslie, L. A. (1988). Cognitive-behavioral and systems models of family therapy: How compatible are they? In N. Epstein, S. E. Schlesinger, & W. Dryden (Eds.), *Cognitive-behavioral therapy with families.* New York: Brunner/Mazel.

Levant, R. F. (Ed.). (1986). *Psychoeducational approaches to family therapy and counseling.* New York: Springer.

Levant, R. F., & Philpot, C. L. (2002). Conceptualizing gender in marital and family therapy research: The gender role strain paradigm. In H. A. Liddle, D. A. Santisteban, R. F. Levant, & J. H. Bray (Eds.), *Family psychology: Science-based interventions.* Washington, DC: American Psychological Association.

Lewis, J. A. (1992). Gender sensitivity and family empowerment. *Topics in Family Psychology and Counseling, 1*(4), 1–7.

Liberman, R. P. (1970). Behavioral approaches to family and couple therapy. *American Journal of Orthopsychiatry, 40,* 106–118.

Liddle, H. A. (1982). On the problem of eclecticism: A call for epistemological clarification and human-scale theories. *Family Process, 21,* 243–250.

Liddle, H. A., Bray, J. H., Levant, R. F., & Santisteban, D. A. (2002). Family psychology intervention science: An emerging area of science and practice. In H. A. Liddle, D. A. Santisteban, R. F. Levant, & J. H. Bray (Eds.), *Family psychology: Science-based interventions.* Washington, DC: American Psychological Association.

Lidz, T., Cornelison, A., Fleck, S., & Terry, D. (1957a). The intrafamilial environment of schizophrenic patients: I. The father. *Psychiatry, 20,* 329–342.

Lidz, T., Cornelison, A., Fleck, S., & Terry, D. (1957b). The intrafamilial environment of schizophrenic patients: II. Marital schism and marital skew. *American Journal of Psychiatry, 114,* 241–248.

Lindahl, K. M., Clements, M., & Markman, H. (1997). Predicting marital and parent functioning in dyads and triads: A longitudinal investigation of marital processes. *Journal of Family Psychology, 11,* 139–151.

Lindblad-Goldberg, M. (1989). Successful minority single-parent families. In L. Combrinck-Graham (Ed.), *Children in family context: Perspectives on treatment.* New York: Guilford Press.

Lindblad-Goldberg, M., Dore, M. M., & Stern, L. (1998). *Creating competence from chaos: A comprehensive guide for home-based services.* New York: Guilford Press.

Lipchik, E. (1993). "Both/and" solutions. In S. Friedman (Ed.), *The new language of change: Constructive collaboration in psychotherapy.* New York: Guilford Press.

Lipchik, E. (2002). *Beyond technique in solution-focused therapy: Working with emotions and the therapeutic relationship.* New York: Guilford.

Litwin, H. (1996). *The social network of older people: A cross-national analysis.* Greenwood, CT: Praeger.

Lott, B., & Bullock, H. E. (2001). Who are the poor? *Journal of Social Issues, 57,* 189–206.

Lowe, R. N. (1982). Adlerian/Dreikursian family counseling. In A. M. Horne & M. M. Ohlsen (Eds.), *Family counseling and therapy.* Itasca, IL: Peacock.

Ludtke, M. (1997). *On our own: Unmarried motherhood.* New York: Random House.

Luepnitz, D. A. (1988). *The family interpreted: Feminist theory in clinical practice.* New York: Basic Books.

Lusterman, D-D. (1988). Family therapy and schools: An ecosystemic approach. *Family Therapy Today, 3*(7), 1–3.

MacCluskie, K. C., & Ingersoll, R. E. (2001). *Becoming a 21st-century agency counselor: Personal and professional explorations.* Pacific Grove, CA: Brooks/Cole.

MacCormack, T., & Tomm, K. (1998). Social constructionist/ narrative therapy. In F. M. Dattilio (Ed.), *Case studies in couple and family therapy: Systemic and cognitive perspectives.* New York: Guilford Press.

MacGregor, R., Ritchie, A. N., Serrano, A. C., & Schuster, F. P. (1964). *Multiple impact therapy with families.* New York: McGraw-Hill.

MacKinnon, L. K. (1983). Contrasting strategic and Milan therapies. *Family Process, 22,* 425–440.

Macklin, E. (Ed.). (1989). *AIDS and the family.* New York: Haworth.

Madanes, C. (1981). *Strategic family therapy.* San Francisco: Jossey-Bass.

Madanes, C. (1984). *Behind the one-way mirror: Advances in the practice of strategic therapy.* San Francisco: Jossey-Bass.

Madanes, C. (1990). *Sex, love, and violence.* New York: Norton.

Madanes, C. (1991). Strategic family therapy. In A. S. Gurman & D. P. Kniskern (Eds.), *Handbook of family therapy* (Vol. II). New York: Brunner/Mazel.

Madigan, S. (1994). Body politics. *The Family Therapy Networker, 18*(6), 18.

Madigan, S., & Epston, D. (1995). From "spy-chiatric gaze" to communities of concern: From professional monologue to dialogue. In S. Friedman (Ed.), *The reflecting team in action: Collaborative practice in family therapy.* New York: Guilford Press.

Madigan, S., & Goldner, E. (1998). A narrative approach to anorexia: Discourse, reflexivity, and questions. In M. Hoyt (Ed.), *The handbook of constructive therapies.* San Francisco: Jossey-Bass.

Mahoney, M. J. (Ed.). (1995). *Cognitive and constructive psychotherapies: Theory, research, and practice.* New York: Springer.

Malcolm, J. (1978, May 15). A reporter at large: The one-way mirror. *New Yorker,* 39–114.

Malgady, R. G., & Constantino, G. (2003). Narrative therapy for Hispanic children and adolescents. In A. E. Kazdin & J. R. Weisz (Eds.), *Evidence-based psychotherapies for children and adolescents.* New York: Guilford Press.

Malley, P. B., & Reilly, E. P. (1999). *Legal and ethical dimensions for mental health professionals.* Philadelphia: Accelerated Development.

Manus, G. (1966). Marriage counseling: A technique in search of a theory. *Journal of Marriage and the Family, 28,* 449–453.

Margolin, G. (1982). Ethical and legal considerations in marital and family therapy. *American Psychologist, 37,* 788–801.

Markman, H. J. (1992). Marital and family psychology: Burning issues. *Journal of Family Psychology, 5,* 264–275.

Markman, H. J., Renick, M. J., Floyd, F. J., Stanley, S. M., & Clements, M. (1993). Preventing marital distress through communication and conflict management training: A 4- and 5-year follow-up. *Journal of Consulting and Clinical Psychology, 61,* 70–77.

Markman, H. J., Stanley, S. M., & Blumberg, S. L. (1994). *Fighting for your marriage: Positive steps for preventing divorce and preserving a lasting love.* San Francisco: Jossey-Bass.

Marrelli, A. F. (1998). An introduction to competency analysis and modeling. *Performance Improvement, 37*(5), 8–17.

Marsh, D. T. (1992). *Families and mental illness: New directions in professional practice.* New York: Praeger.

Marsh, D. T., & Johnson, D. L. (1997). The family experience of mental illness: Implications for intervention. *Professional Psychology: Research and Practice, 28,* 229–237.

Mason, M. J. (1991). Family therapy as the emerging context for sex therapy. In A. S. Gurman & D. P. Kniskern (Eds.), *Handbook of family therapy* (Vol. II). New York: Brunner/Mazel.

Masten, A. S. (2001). Ordinary magic: Resilience processes in development. *American Psychologist, 56,* 227–238.

Masten, A. S., & Coatsworth, J. D. (1998). The development of competence in favorable and unfavorable environments: Lessons from research on successful children. *American Psychologist, 53,* 205–220.

Masters, W. H., & Johnson, V. E. (1970). *Human sexual inadequacy.* Boston: Little, Brown.

Maturana, H. R. (1978). Biology of language: The epistemology of reality. In G. A. Miller & E. Lennenberg (Eds.), *Psychology and biology of language and thought.* New York: Academic Press.

McDaniel, S. H. (1995). Collaboration between psychologists and family physicians: Implementing the biopsychosocial model. *Professional Psychology, 26,* 117–122.

McDaniel, S. H., Harkness, J. I., & Epstein, R. M. (2001). Medical family therapy for a woman with endstage Crohn's disease and her son. *The American Journal of Family Therapy, 29,* 375–395.

McDaniel, S. H., Hepworth, J., & Doherty, W. J. (1992). *Medical family therapy: A biopsychosocial approach to families with health problems.* New York: Basic Books.

McDaniel, S. H., Hepworth, J., & Doherty, W. J. (1995). Medical family therapy with somatizing patients: The co-creation of therapeutic stories. In R. H. Mikesell, D-D. Lusterman, & S. H. McDaniel (Eds.), *Integrating family therapy: Handbook of family psychology and systems theory.* Washington, DC: American Psychological Association.

McDaniel, S. H., Lusterman, D-D., & Philpot, C. L. (2001). Introduction to integrative ecosystemic family therapy. In S. H. McDaniel, D-D. Lusterman, & C. L. Philpot (Eds.), *Casebook for integrating family therapy: An ecosystemic approach.* Washington, DC: American Psychological Association.

McFarlane, W. R. (1991). Family psychoeducational treatment. In A. S. Gurman & D. P. Kniskern (Eds.), *Handbook of family therapy* (Vol. II). New York: Brunner/Mazel.

McFarlane, W. R. (2002). *Multifamily groups in the treatment of severe psychiatric disorders.* New York: Guilford Press.

McFarlane, W. R., Dixon, L., Lukens, E., & Luckstead, A. (2003). Family psychoeducation and schizophrenia: A review of the literature. *Journal of Marital and Family Therapy, 29*(2), 223–245.

McGoldrick, M. (Ed.). (1998). *Re-Visioning family therapy: Race, culture, and gender in clinical practice.* New York: Guilford Press.

McGoldrick, M. (1999). Becoming a couple. In B. Carter & M. McGoldrick (Eds.), *The expanded life cycle: Individual, family, and social perspectives.* Boston: Allyn & Bacon.

McGoldrick, M. (2003). Culture: A challenge to concepts of normality. In F. Walsh (Ed.), *Normal family processes* (3rd ed.). New York: Guilford Press.

McGoldrick, M., Anderson, C. M., & Walsh, F. (1989). Women in families and in family therapy. In M. McGoldrick, C. M. Anderson, & F. Walsh (Eds.), *Women in families: A framework for family therapy.* New York: Norton.

McGoldrick, M., & Carter, B. (1999). Remarried families. In Carter, B., & McGoldrick, M. (Eds.), *The expanded family life cycle: Individual, family, and social perspectives* (3rd ed.).

McGoldrick, M., & Carter, B. (2001). Advances in coaching: Family therapy with one person. *Journal of Marital and Family Therapy, 27,* 281–300.

McGoldrick, M., & Carter, B. (2003). The family life cycle. In F. Walsh (Ed.), *Normal family processes* (3rd ed.). New York: Guilford Press.

McGoldrick, M., Garcia-Preto, N., Hines, P. M., & Lee, E. (1991). Ethnicity and family therapy. In A. S. Gurman & D. P. Kniskern (Eds.), *Handbook of family therapy* (2nd ed.). New York: Brunner/Mazel.

McGoldrick, M., & Gerson, R. (1985). *Genograms in family assessment.* New York: Norton.

McGoldrick, M., Gerson, R., & Shellenberger, S. (1999). *Genograms: Assessment and intervention.* New York: Norton.

McGoldrick, M., Giordano, J., & Pearce, J. K. (2005). *Ethnicity and family therapy* (3rd ed.). New York: Guilford Press.

McGoldrick, M., Pearce, J. K., & Giordano, J. (1982). *Ethnicity and family therapy.* New York: Guilford Press.

Meichenbaum, D. (1995). Changing conceptions of cognitive behavior modification: Retrospect and prospect. In M. J. Mahoney (Ed.), *Cognitive and constructive psychotherapies: Theory, research, and practice.* New York: Springer.

Meissner, W. W. (1978). The conceptualization of marriage and family dynamics from a psychoanalytic perspective. In T. J. Paolino & B. S. McCrady (Eds.), *Marriage and marital therapy: Psychoanalytic, behavioral, and systems perspectives.* New York: Brunner/Mazel.

Meyerhoff, B. (1986). "Life, not death in Venice": Its second life. In V. W. Turner & E. M. Bruner (Eds.), *The anthropology of experience.* Chicago: University of Illinois Press.

Michaels, M. L. (2000). The stepfamily enrichment program: A preliminary evaluation using focus groups. *The American Journal of Family Therapy, 28,* 61–73.

Midelfort, C. F. (1957). *The family in psychotherapy.* New York: Viking Press.

Mikesell, R. H., Lusterman, D-D., & McDaniel, S. H. (Eds.). (1995). *Integrating family therapy: Handbook of family psychology and systems theory.* Washington, DC: American Psychological Association.

Miklowitz, D. J. (1995). The evolution of family-based psychopathology. In R. H. Mikesell, D-D. Lusterman, & S. H. McDaniel (Eds.), *Integrating family therapy: Handbook of family psychology and systems theory.* Washington, DC: American Psychological Association.

Miklowitz, D. J., & Goldstein, M. J. (1997). *Bipolar disorder: A family-focused treatment approach.* New York: Guilford Press.

Miklowitz, D. J., Simoneau, T. L., George, E. L., Richards, J. A., Kalbag, A., Sachs-Ericsson, et al. (2000). Family-focused treatment of bipolar disorder: One-year effects of a psychoeducational program in conjunction with pharmacotherapy. *Biological Psychiatry, 48,* 582–592.

Miller, I. J. (1996). Managed care is harmful to outpatient mental health services: A call for accountability. *Professional Psychology: Research and Practice, 27,* 349–363.

Miller, J. B. (1976). *Toward a new psychology of women.* Boston: Beacon.

Miller, J. B., Jordan, J. V., Kaplan, A. G., Stiver, F. P., & Surrey, J. L. (1997). Some misconceptions and reconceptions of a relational approach. In J. V. Jordan (Ed.), *Women's growth in diversity.* New York: Guilford.

Miller, J. B., & Stiver, I. P. (1991). A relational reframing of therapy. *Work in Progress,* No. 52. Wellesley, MA: Stone Center Working Papers Series.

Miller, N. (1992). *Single parents by choice: A growing trend in family life.* New York: Insight Books.

Miller, S. (1994). The solution-conspiracy: A mystery in three installments. *Journal of Systemic Therapies, 13,* 18–37.

Minuchin, P., Colapinto, J., & Minuchin, S. (1998). *Working with families of the poor.* New York: Guilford Press.

Minuchin, S. (1974). *Families and family therapy.* Cambridge, MA: Harvard University Press.

Minuchin, S. (1984). *Family kaleidoscope.* Cambridge, MA: Harvard University Press.

Minuchin, S. (1991). The seductions of constructivism. *The Family Networker, 15*(5), 47–50.

Minuchin, S., Baker, L., Rosman, B., Liebman, R., Milman, L., & Todd, T. (1975). A conceptual model of psychosomatic illness in children: Family organization and family therapy. *Archives of General Psychiatry, 32,* 1031–1038.

Minuchin, S., & Fishman, H. C. (1981). *Family therapy techniques.* Cambridge, MA: Harvard University Press.

Minuchin, S., Lee, W-Y., & Simon, G. M. (1996). *Mastering family therapy: Journeys of growth and transformation.* New York: Wiley.

Minuchin, S., Montalvo, B., Guerney, B. G., Jr., Rosman, B. L., & Schumer, F. (1967). *Families of the slums: An exploration of their structure and treatment.* New York: Basic Books.

Minuchin S., & Nichols, M. P. (1993). *Family healing: Tales of hope and renewal from family therapy.* New York: Free Press.

Minuchin, S., & Nichols, M. P. (1998). Structural family therapy. In F. M. Dattilio (Ed.), *Case studies in couple and family therapy: Systemic and cognitive perspectives.* New York: Guilford Press.

Minuchin, S., Rosman, B. L., & Baker, L. (1978). *Psychosomatic families: Anorexia nervosa in context.* Cambridge, MA: Harvard University Press.

Mitrani, V. B., & Perez, B. A. (2003). Structural-strategic approaches to couple and family therapy. In T. L. Sexton, G. R. Weeks, & M. S. Robbins (Eds.), *Handbook of family therapy: The science and practice of working with families and couples.* New York: Brunner-Routledge.

Monahan, J. (1993). Limiting therapist exposure to *Tarasoff* liability: Guidelines for risk containment. *American Psychologist, 48,* 242–250.

Moon, S. M., Dillon, D. R., & Sprenkle, D. H. (1990). Family therapy and qualitative research. *Journal of Marital and Family Therapy, 16,* 357–373.

Moos, R. H. (1974). *Combined preliminary manual: Family, work, and group environment scales.* Palo Alto, CA: Consulting Psychologists Press.

Moos, R. H., & Moos, B. S. (1994). *Family environmental scale manual* (3rd ed.) Palo Alto, CA: Consulting Psychologists Press.

Morgan, A. (2000). *What is narrative therapy? An easy-to-read introduction.* Adelaide, Australia: Dulwich Centre Publications.

Morris, S. B., Alexander, J. F., & Waldron, H. (1988). Functional family therapy. In I. R. H. Falloon (Ed.), *Handbook of behavioral family therapy.* New York: Guilford Press.

Moultrop, D. J. (1986). Integration: A coming of age. *Contemporary Family Therapy, 8,* 157–167, 189.

Mudd, E. H. (1951). *The practice of marriage counseling.* New York: Association Press.

Mueser, K. T., & Glynn, S. M. (1995). *Behavioral family therapy for psychiatric disorders.* Boston: Allyn & Bacon.

Murdock, N. L., & Gore, P. A. J. (2004). Stress, coping, and differentiation of self: A test of Bowen theory. *Contemporary Family Therapy, An International Journal, 26,* 319–335.

Nagy, T. F. (2005). *Ethics in plain English: An illustrative casebook for psychologists.* (2nd ed.). Washington, DC: American Psychological Association.

Napier, A.Y. (2000). Making a marriage. In W. C. Nichols, M. A. Pace-Nichols, D. S. Becvar, & A. Y. Napier (Eds.), *Handbook of family development and intervention.* New York: Wiley.

Napier, A.Y., & Whitaker, C. A. (1978). *The family crucible.* New York: Harper & Row.

Nathan, P. E., & Gorman, J. M. (2002). *A guide to treatment that works.* London: Oxford University Press.

National Association of Social Workers. (1999). *Code of ethics.* Washington, DC: NASW.

Neill, J. R., & Kniskern, D. P. (Eds.). (1982). *From psyche to system: The evolving therapy of Carl Whitaker.* New York: Guilford Press.

Neimeyer, R. A., & Neimeyer, G. J. (1993). Constructivist assessment: What and when. In G. J. Neimeyer (Ed.), *Constructivist assessment: A casebook.* Thousand Oaks, CA: Sage.

Nerin, W. F. (1986). *Family reconstruction: Long day's journey into light.* New York: Norton.

Nerin, W. F. (1989). You can go home again. *The Family Networker, 13*(1), 54–55.

Neugarten, B. (1976). Adaptation and the life cycle. *Counseling Psychologist, 6,* 16–20.

Nichols, M. P. (1987). *The self in the system: Expanding the limits of family therapy.* New York: Brunner/Mazel.

Nichols, W. C., & Everett, C. A. (1986). *Systemic family therapy: An integrative approach.* New York: Guilford Press.

Nichols, W. C., & Pace-Nichols, M. A. (2000). Family development and family therapy. In W. C. Nichols, M. A. Pace-Nichols, D. S. Becvar, & A. Y. Napier (Eds.), *Handbook of family development and intervention.* New York: Wiley.

Nicolai, K. M., & Scott, N. A. (1994). Provisions of confidentiality information and its relation to child abuse reporting. *Professional Psychology, Research and Practice, 25,* 154–160.

Norcross, J. C. (Ed.). (2002). *Psychotherapy relationships that work: Therapist contributions and responsiveness to patient needs.* New York: Oxford University Press.

Northey, Jr., W. F. (2005, July-August). Are you competent to practice marriage and family therapy? *Family Therapy Magazine,* 10–13.

O'Hanlon, W. H. (1993). Take two people and call them in the morning: Brief solution-oriented therapy with depression. In S. Friedman (Ed.), *The new language of change: Constructive collaboration in psychotherapy.* New York: Guilford Press.

O'Hanlon, W. H., & Beadle, S. (1999). *A guide to possibility land: Fifty-one methods of doing brief, respectful therapy.* New York: Norton.

O'Hanlon, W. H., & Bertolino, B. (Eds.). (1999). *Evolving possibilities: Selected papers of Bill O'Hanlon.* Philadelphia: Brunner/Mazel.

O'Hanlon, W. H., & Weiner-Davis, M. (1989). *In search of solutions: A new direction in psychotherapy.* New York: Norton.

Olkin, R. (1999). *What psychotherapists should know about disability.* New York: Guilford Press.

Olson, D. H. (1970). Marital and family therapy: Integrative reviews and critique. *Journal of Marriage and Family Counseling, 4,* 77–98.

Olson, D. H. (1987). *Building a strong marriage.* Minneapolis, MN: Prepare/Enrich, Inc.

Olson, D. H. (1997). *PREPARE/ENRICH counselor's manual.* Minneapolis, MN: Life Innovations.

Olson, D. H. (2000). Circumplex model of marital and family systems. *Journal of Family Therapy, 22,* 144–167.

Olson, D. H., Fournier, D. G., & Druckman, J. M. (1986). *PREPARE/ENRICH counselor's manual.* Minneapolis, MN: Prepare/Enrich, Inc.

Olson, D. H., & Gorall, D. M. (2003). Circumplex model of marital and family systems. In F. Walsh (Ed.), *Normal family processes: Growing diversity and complexity* (3rd ed.). New York: Guilford Press.

Olson, D. H., & Olson, A. K. (1999). PREPARE/ENRICH Program: Version 2000. In R. Berger & M. T. Hannah (Eds.), *Preventive approaches in couple therapy.* Philadelphia: Brunner/Mazel.

Olson, D. H., Russell, C. S., & Sprenkle, D. H. (Eds.). (1989). *Circumplex model: Systemic assessment and treatment of families.* New York: Haworth Press.

O'Neil, J. M. (1982). Gender-role conflict and strains in men's lives. In K. Solomon & N. Levy (Eds.), *Men in transition: Theory and therapy.* New York: Plenum.

Ozechowski, T. J., Turner, C. W., & Waldron, H. B. (2003). The treatment of adolescent conduct disorders and drug abuse. In T. L. Sexton, G. R. Weeks, & M. S. Robbins (Eds.), *Handbook of family therapy: The science and practice of working with families and couples.* New York: Brunner-Routledge.

Papero, D. V. (1990). *Bowen family system theory.* Boston: Allyn & Bacon.

Papero, D. V. (1995). Bowen's family systems and marriage. In N. S. Jacobson & A. S. Gurman (Eds.), *Clinical handbook of couple therapy.* New York: Guilford Press.

Papero, D. V. (2000). The Bowen theory. In A. M. Horne (Ed.), *Family counseling and therapy* (3rd ed.). Itasca, IL: Peacock.

Papp, P. (1983). *The process of change.* New York: Guilford Press.

Parry, A., & Doan, R. E. (1994). *Story re-visions: Narrative therapy in the postmodern world.* New York: Guilford Press.

Parry, T. A. (1993). Without a net: Preparations for postmodern living. In S. Friedman (Ed.), *The new language of change: Constructive collaboration in psychotherapy.* New York: Guilford Press.

Parsons, T., & Bales, R. F. (1955). *Family, socialization, and interaction process.* Glencoe, IL: Free Press.

Patten, C., Barnett, T., & Houlihan, D. (1991). Ethics in marital and family therapy: A review of the literature. *Professional Psychology: Research and Practice, 22*(2), 171–175.

Patterson, C. J. (1995). *Lesbian and gay parenting: A resource for psychologists.* Washington, DC: American Psychological Association.

Patterson, G. R. (1971). *Families: Application of social learning to family life.* Champaign, IL: Research Press.

Patterson, G. R. (1985). Beyond technology: The next stage in developing an empirical base for parent training. In L. L'Abate (Ed.), *Handbook of family psychology and therapy* (Vol. II). Homewood, IL: Dorsey Press.

Patterson, G. R., & Brodsky, M. (1966). Behavior modification for a child with multiple problem behaviors. *Journal of Child Psychology and Psychiatry, 7,* 277–295.

Patterson, G. R., & Reid, J. (1970). Reciprocity and coercion: Two facets of social systems. In C. Neuringer & J. Michael (Eds.), *Behavior modification in clinical psychology.* New York: Appleton-Century-Crofts.

Patterson, G. R., Reid, R. B., Jones, R. R., & Conger, R. E. (1975). *A social learning approach to family intervention, Vol. I: Families with aggressive children.* Eugene, OR: Castalia.

Patterson, T. (1997). Theoretical unity and technical eclecticism: Pathways to coherence in family therapy. *American Journal of Family Therapy, 25,* 97–109.

Paul, N. L. (1974). The use of empathy in the resolution of grief. In J. Ellard, V. Volkan, & N. L. Paul (Eds.), *Normal and pathological responses to bereavement.* New York: MSS Information Corporation.

Payne, M. (2000). *Narrative therapy: An introduction to counsellors.* London: Sage Publications.

Peake, T. H., Borduin, C. M., & Archer, R. P. (1988). *Brief psychotherapies: Changing frames of mind.* Newbury Park, CA: Sage.

Pedersen, P. (2000). *A handbook of developing multicultural awareness* (3rd ed.). Alexandria, VA: American Counseling Association.

Penn, P. (1982). Circular questioning. *Family Process, 21,* 267–280.

Perlin, M. L. (1997). The "duty to protect" others from violence. In *The Hatherleigh guide to ethics in therapy.* New York: Hatherleigh Press.

Perls, F. S. (1969). *Gestalt therapy verbatim.* Lafayette, CA: Free People Press.

Perry, H. S. (1982). *Psychiatrist of America: The life of Harry Stack Sullivan.* Cambridge, MA: Harvard University Press.

Philpot, C. L. (2000). Socialization of gender roles. In W. C. Nichols, M. A. Pace-Nichols, D. S. Becvar, & A.Y. Napier (Eds.), *Handbook of family development and intervention.* New York: Wiley.

Philpot, C. L., & Brooks, G. R. (1995). Intergender communication and gender-sensitive family therapy. In R. H. Mikesell, D-D. Lusterman, & S. H. McDaniel (Eds.), *Integrating family therapy: Handbook of family psychology and systems theory.* Washington, DC: American Psychological Association.

Philpot, C. L., Brooks, G. R., Lusterman, D-D., & Nutt, R. L. (1997). *Bridging separate gender worlds: Why men and women clash and how therapists can bring them together.* Washington, DC: American Psychological Association.

Piercy, F. P., & Sprenkle, D. H. (1990). Marriage and family therapy: A decade review. *Journal of Marriage and the Family, 52,* 1116–1126.

Pigott, S., & Monaco, L. (2004). Enabling children to succeed: Community-based supports for families. Presented at the Making Children Matter Conference, Toronto, Canada, 2004.

Pinsof, W. M. (1995). *Integrative problem-centered therapy: A synthesis of family, individual, and biological therapies.* New York: Basic Books.

Pinsof, W. M., & Hambright, A. B. (2002). Toward prevention and clinical relevance: A preventive intervention model for family therapy research and practice. In H. A. Liddle, D. A. Santisteban, R. F. Levant, & J. H. Bray (Eds.), *Family psychology: Science-based interventions.* Washington, DC: American Psychological Association.

Pinsof, W. M., & Wynne, L. C. (1995). The effectiveness and efficacy of marital and family therapy: Introduction to the special issue. *Journal of Marital and Family Therapy, 21,* 341–343.

Pinsof, W. M., & Wynne, L. C. (2000). Toward progress research: Closing the gap between family therapy practice and research. *Journal of Marital and Family Therapy, 26,* 1–8.

Pinsof, W. M., Wynne, L. C., & Hambright, A. B. (1996). The outcomes of couple and family therapy: Findings, conclusions, and recommendations. *Psychotherapy, 33,* 321–331.

Pipher, M. (1994). *Reviving Ophelia: Saving the selves of adolescent girls.* New York: Ballantine.

Pirrotta, S. (1984). Milan revisited: A comparison of the two Milan schools. *Journal of Strategic and Systemic Therapies, 3,* 3–15.

Pittman, F. (1989). Remembering Virginia. *The Family Therapy Networker, 13*(1), 34–35.

Plaut, S. M., & Donahey, K. M. (2003). Evaluation and treatment of sexual dysfunction. In T. L. Sexton,

G. R. Weeks, & M. S. Robbins (Eds.), *Handbook of family therapy: The science and practice of working with families and couples.* New York: Brunner-Routledge.

Pope, K. S. (1994). *Sexual involvement with therapists: Patient assessment, subsequent therapy, forensics.* Washington, DC: American Psychological Association.

Pope, K. S., & Vasquez, M. J. T. (1998). *Ethics in psychotherapy and counseling: A practical guide for psychologists* (2nd ed.). San Francisco: Jossey-Bass.

Prata, G. (1990). *A systemic harpoon into family games: Preventive interventions in therapy.* New York: Brunner/Mazel.

Preto, N. G. (1999). Transformation of the family system during adolescence. In B. Carter & M. McGodrick (Eds.), *The expanded life cycle: Individual, family, and social perspectives.* Boston: Allyn & Bacon.

Prevatt, F. F. (1999). Milan systemic therapy. In D. M. Lawson & F. F. Prevatt (Eds.), *Casebook in family therapy.* Pacific Grove, CA: Brooks/Cole.

Price, J. (1996). *Power and compassion: Working with difficult adolescents and abused parents.* New York: Guilford Press.

Prochaska, J. O., & Norcross, J. C. (1999). *Systems of psychotherapy: A transtheoretical analysis* (4th ed.). Pacific Grove, CA: Brooks/Cole.

Rank, M. R. (2000). Socialization of socioeconomic status. In W. C. Nichols, M. A. Pace-Nichols, D. S. Becvar, & A. Y. Napier (Eds.), *Handbook of family development and intervention.* New York: Wiley.

Real, T. (1990). The therapeutic use of self in constructionist systematic therapy. *Family Process, 29,* 255–272.

Reaves, R. P., & Ogloff, J. R. P. (1996). Liability for professional misconduct. In L. J. Bass et al. (Eds.), *Professional conduct and discipline in psychology.* Washington, DC: American Psychological Association.

Reed, G. M., & Eisman, E. J. (2006). Uses and misuses of evidence: Managed care, treatment guidelines, and outcome measurements in professional practice. In C. D. Goodheart, A. E. Kazdin, & R. J. Sternberg (Eds.), *Evidence-based psychotherapy: Where practice and research meet.* Washington, DC: American Psychological Association.

Rice, E. P. (1993). *Intimate relationships, marriages, and families.* Mountain View, CA: Mayfield.

Risman, B. J. (1998). *Gender vertigo: American families in transition.* New Haven, CT: Yale University Press.

Robbins, M. S., Alexander, J. F., Newell, R. M., & Turner, C. W. (1996). The immediate effect of reframing on client attitude in family therapy. *Journal of Family Psychology, 10,* 28–34.

Robbins, M. S., Mayorga, B. A., & Szapocznik, J. (2003). The ecosystemic "lens" for understanding family functioning. In T. L. Sexton, G. R. Weeks, & M. S. Robbins (Eds.), *Handbook of family therapy: The science and practice of working with families and couples.* New York: Brunner-Routledge.

Roberto, L. G. (1991). Symbolic-experiential family therapy. In A. S. Gurman & D. P. Kniskern (Eds.), *Handbook of family therapy* (Vol. II). New York: Brunner/Mazel.

Roberto, L. G. (1992). *Transgenerational family therapies.* New York: Guilford Press.

Rolland, J. S. (1994). *Families, illness, and disability: An integrative treatment model.* New York: Basic Books.

Rolland, J. S. (2003). Mastering family challenges in illness and disability. In F. Walsh (Ed.), *Normal family processes: Growing diversity and complexity* (3rd ed.). New York: Guilford Press.

Rosen, R. C., & Leiblum, S. R. (Eds.). (1995). *Case studies in sex therapy.* New York: Guilford Press.

Rosenberg, J. B. (1983). Structural family therapy. In B. B. Wolman & G. Stricker (Eds.), *Handbook of family and marital therapy.* New York: Plenum.

Ross, N. M., & Doherty, W. J. (2001). Validity of the global assessment of relational functioning (GARF) when used by community-based therapists. *The American Journal of Family Therapy, 29,* 293–253.

Roth, A., & Fonagy, P. (2004). *What works for whom? A critical review of psychotherapy research* (2nd ed.). New York: Guilford Press.

Rotheram, M. J. (1989). The family and the school. In L. Combrinck-Graham (Ed.), *Children in family context: Perspectives on treatment.* New York: Guilford Press.

Ruddy, N. B., & McDaniel, S. H. (2003). Medical family therapy. In T. L. Sexton, G. R. Weeks, & M. S. Robbins (Eds.), *Handbook of family therapy: The science and practice of working with families and couples.* New York: Brunner-Routledge.

Rupert, P. A., & Baird, K. A. (2004). Managed care and the independent practice of psychology. *Professional Psychology: Research and Practice, 35,* 185–193.

Sampson, J. P., Kolodinsky, R. W., & Greeno, B. P. (1997). Counseling on the information highway: Future possibilities and potential problems. *Journal of Counseling and Development, 75,* 203–212.

Sander, F. M. (1998). Psychoanalytic couple therapy. In F. M. Dattilio (Ed.), *Case studies in couple and family therapy: Systemic and cognitive perspectives.* New York: Guilford Press.

Sanders, M. R., & Dadds, M. R. (1993). *Behavioral family intervention.* Needham Heights, MA: Allyn & Bacon.

Sanford, K., Bingham, C. R., & Zucker, R. A. (1999). Validity issues with the Family Environment Scale: Psychometric resolution and research application with alcoholic families. *Psychological Assessment, 11,* 315–325.

Santisteban, D. A., Muir-Malcolm, J. A., Mitrani, V. B., & Szapocznik, J. (2002). Integrating the study of ethnic culture and family psychology intervention science. In H. A. Liddle, D. A. Santisteban, R. F. Levant, & J. H. Bray (Eds.), *Family psychology: Science-based interventions.* Washington, DC: American Psychological Association.

Satir, V. M. (1964). *Conjoint family therapy.* Palo Alto, CA: Science and Behavior Books.

Satir, V. M. (1967). *Conjoint family therapy* (rev. ed.). Palo Alto, CA: Science and Behavior Books.

Satir, V. M. (1972). *Peoplemaking.* Palo Alto, CA: Science and Behavior Books.

Satir, V. M. (1982). The therapist and family therapy: Process model. In A. M. Horne & M. M. Ohlsen (Eds.), *Family counseling and therapy.* Itasca, IL: Peacock.

Satir, V. M. (1986). A partial portrait of a family therapist in process. In H. C. Fishman & B. L. Rosman (Eds.), *Evolving models for family change: A volume in honor of Salvador Minuchin.* New York: Guilford Press.

Satir, V. M., & Baldwin, M. (1983). *Satir step by step: A guide to creating change in families.* Palo Alto, CA: Science and Behavior Books.

Satir, V. M., Banmen, J., Gerber, J., & Gomori, M. (1991). *The Satir model: Family therapy and beyond.* Palo Alto, CA: Science and Behavior Books.

Satir, V. M., & Bitter, J. R. (2000). The therapist and family therapy: Satir's human validation model. In A. M. Horne & J. L. Passmore (Eds.), *Family counseling and therapy* (3rd ed.). Itasca, IL: Peacock.

Saxton, L. (1996). *The individual, marriage, and the family* (9th ed.). Belmont, CA: Wadsworth.

Scharf, R. S. (2000). *Theories of psychotherapy and counseling: Concepts and cases* (3rd ed.). Pacific Grove, CA: Wadsworth-Brooks/Cole.

Scharff, D. E. (1989). An object relations approach to sexuality in family life. In J. S. Scharff (Ed.), *Foundations of object relations family therapy.* Northvale, NJ: Aronson.

Scharff, D. E., & Scharff, J. S. (1987). *Object relations family therapy.* Northvale, NJ: Aronson.

Scharff, J. S. (1989). The development of object relations family therapy. In J. S. Scharff (Ed.), *Foundations of object relations family therapy.* Northvale, NJ: Aronson.

Scharff, J. S. (1995). Psychoanalytic marital therapy. In N. S. Jacobson & A. S. Gurman (Eds.), *Clinical handbook of couple therapy.* New York: Guilford Press.

Scharff, J. S., & Scharff, D. E. (1992). *Scharff notes: A primer of object relations therapy.* Northvale, NJ: Aronson.

Scharff, J. S., & Scharff, D. E. (1997). Object relations couple therapy. *American Journal of Psychotherapy, 51,* 141–173.

Scharff, J. S., & Scharff, D. E. (2003). Object-relations and psychodynamic approaches to couple and family therapy. In T. L. Sexton, G. R. Weeks, & M. S. Robbins (Eds.), *Handbook of family therapy: The science and practice of working with families and couples.* New York: Brunner-Routledge.

Schlanger, K., & Anger-Diaz, B. (1999). The brief therapy approach of the Palo Alto group. In D. M. Lawson & F. F. Prevatt (Eds.), *Casebook in family therapy.* Pacific Grove, CA: Brooks/Cole.

Schnarch, D. M. (1991). *Constructing the sexual crucible: An integration of sexual and marital therapy.* New York: Norton.

Schnarch, D. M. (1995). A family systems approach to sex therapy and intimacy. In R. H. Mikesell, D-D. Lusterman, & S. H. McDaniel (Eds.), *Integrating family therapy: Handbook of family psychology and systems theory.* Washington, DC: American Psychological Association.

Schultheis, G. M., O'Hanlon, W., & O'Hanlon, S. (1999). *Brief couples therapy homework planner.* New York: Wiley.

Schwebel, A. I., & Fine, M. A. (1994). *Understanding and helping families: A cognitive-behavioral approach.* Hillsdale, NJ: Erlbaum.

Segal, L. (1982). Brief family therapy. In A. M. Horne & M. M. Ohlsen (Eds.), *Family counseling and therapy.* Itasca, IL: Peacock.

Segal, L. (1987). What is a problem? A brief family therapist's view. *Family Therapy Today, 2*(7), 1–7.

Segal, L. (1991). Brief therapy: The MRI approach. In A. S. Gurman & D. P. Kniskern (Eds.), *Handbook of family therapy* (Vol. II). New York: Brunner/Mazel.

Segal, L., & Bavelas, J. B. (1983). Human systems and communication theory. In B. B. Wolman & G. Stricker (Eds.), *Handbook of family and marital therapy.* New York: Plenum.

Seibt, T. H. (1996). Nontraditional families. In M. Harway (Ed.), *Treating the changing family: Handling normative and unusual events.* New York: Wiley.

Selekman, M. D. (1993). Solution-oriented brief therapy with difficult adolescents. In S. Friedman (Ed.), *The new language of change: Constructive collaboration in psychotherapy.* New York: Guilford Press.

Selekman, M. D. (2002). *Living on the razor's edge: Solution-oriented brief family therapy with self-harming adolescents.* New York: Norton.

Seligman, M. E. P., & Csikszentmihalyi, M. (Eds.). (2000). Positive psychology (Special issue). *American Psychologist, 55.*

Seligman, M. E. P., & Levant, R. F. (1998). Managed care policies rely on inadequate research. *Professional Psychology: Research and Practice, 29,* 211–212.

Seltzer, L. F. (1986). *Paradoxical strategies in psychotherapy: A comprehensive overview and guidebook.* New York: Wiley.

Selvini-Palazzoli, M. (1978). *Self-starvation.* New York: Aronson.

Selvini-Palazzoli, M. (1980). Why a long interval between sessions? The therapeutic control of the family-therapist suprasystem. In M. Andolfi & I. Zwerling (Eds.), *Dimensions of family therapy.* New York: Guilford Press.

Selvini-Palazzoli, M. (1986). Towards a general model of psychotic family games. *Journal of Marital and Family Therapy, 12,* 339–349.

Selvini-Palazzoli, M., Boscolo, L., Cecchin, G., & Prata, G. (1974). The treatment of children through brief therapy of their parents. *Family Process, 13,* 429–442.

Selvini-Palazzoli, M., Boscolo, L., Cecchin, G. F., & Prata, G. (1978). *Paradox and counterparadox: A new model in the therapy of the family in schizophrenic transaction.* New York: Aronson.

Selvini-Palazzoli, M., Boscolo, L., Cecchin, G. F., & Prata, G. (1980). Hypothesizing-circularity-neutrality: Three guidelines for the conductor of the session. *Family Process, 19,* 3–12.

Selvini-Palazzoli, M., Cirillo, S., Selvini, M., & Sorrentino, A. M. (1989). *Family games: General models of psychotic processes in the family.* New York: Norton.

Sexton, T. L., & Alexander, J. F. (1999). *Functional family therapy: Principles of clinical intervention, assessment, and implementation.* Henderson, NV: RCH Enterprises.

Sexton, T. L., & Alexander, J. F. (2003). Functional family therapy: A mature clinical model for working with at-risk adolescents and their families. In T. L. Sexton, G. R. Weeks, & M. S. Robbins (Eds.), *Handbook of family therapy: The science and practice of working with families and couples.* New York: Brunner-Routledge.

Sexton, T. L., Robbins, M. S., Holliman, A. S., Mease, A. L., & Mayorga, C. C. (2003). Efficacy, effectiveness, and change mechanisms in couple and family therapy. In T. L. Sexton, G. R. Weeks, & M. S. Robbins (Eds.), *Handbook of family therapy: The science and practice of working with families and couples.* New York: Brunner-Routledge.

Sexton, T. L., Weeks, G. R., & Robbins, M. S. (2003). The future of couple and family therapy. In T. L. Sexton, G. R. Weeks, & M. S. Robbins (Eds.), *Handbook of family therapy: The science and practice of working with families and couples.* New York: Brunner-Routledge.

Shadish, W. R., Ragsdale, K., Glaser, R. R., & Montgomery, L. M. (1995). The efficacy and effectiveness of marital and family therapy: A perspective from meta-analysis. *Journal of Marital and Family Therapy, 21,* 345–360.

Shapiro, P. G. (1996). *My turn: Women's search for self after the children leave.* Princeton, NJ: Peterson.

Sheldon, K. M., & King, L. (2001). Why positive psychology? *American Psychologist, 56,* 216–217.

Shellenberger, S., & Hoffman, S. S. (1995). The changing work-family system. In R. H. Mikesell, D.-D. Lusterman, & S. H. McDaniel (Eds.), *Integrating family therapy: Handbook of family psychology and systems theory.* Washington, DC: American Psychological Association.

Sherman, J. R., & Dinkmeyer, D. (1987). Systems of family therapy: An Adlerian integration. New York: Brunnel/Mazel.

Shoham, V., Rohrbaugh, M., & Patterson, J. (1995). Problem- and solution-focused couples therapies: The MRI and Milwaukee models. In N. S. Jacobson & A. S. Gurman (Eds.), *Clinical handbook of couple therapy.* New York: Guilford Press.

Shueman, S. A., Troy, W. G., & Mayhugh, S. L. (1994). Principles and issues in managed behavioral health care. In S. A. Shueman, W. G. Troy, & S. L. Mayhugh (Eds.), *Managed behavioral health care: An industry perspective.* Springfield, IL: Thomas.

Silliman, B., Stanley, S. M., Coffin, W., Markman, H. J., & Jordan, P. L. (2002). Preventive intervention for couples. In H. A. Liddle, D. A. Santisteban, R. F. Levant, & J. H. Bray (Eds.), *Family psychology: Science-based interventions.* Washington, DC: American Psychological Association.

Silverstein, L., & Auerbach, C. F. (2005). What does qualitative research have to offer family psychologists? *The Family Psychologist, 21*(4), 10, 24.

Silverstein, L., & Quartironi, B. (1996, Winter). Gay fathers. *Family Psychologist, 12,* 23–24.

Simon, R. (1984). Stranger in a strange land: An interview with Salvador Minuchin. *Family Therapy Networker, 6*(6), 22–31.

Simon, R. (1987). Goodbye paradox, hello invariant prescription: An interview with Mara Selvini-Palazzoli. *Family Therapy Networker, 11*(5), 16–33.

Simon, R. (1997). Fearsome foursome: An interview with the Women's Project. *Family Therapy Networker, 21*(6), 58–68.

Simons, R. L. (1996). The effect of divorce on adult and child adjustment. In R. L. Simons & Associates (Eds.), *Understanding differences between divorced and intact families: Stress, interaction, and child outcome.* Thousand Oaks, CA: Sage.

Singleton, G. (1982). Bowen family systems theory. In A. M. Horne & M. M. Ohlsen (Eds.), *Family counseling and therapy.* Itasca, IL: Peacock.

Skowron, E. A., & Friedlander, M. L. (1998). The Differentiation of Self Inventory development and initial validation. *Journal of Counseling Psychology, 45,* 235–246.

Skynner, A. C. R. (1981). An open-systems, group analytic approach to family therapy. In A. S. Gurman & D. P. Kniskern (Eds.), *Handbook of family therapy.* New York: Brunner/Mazel.

Slavson, S. R. (1964). *A textbook in analytic group psychotherapy.*

Slipp, S. (1984). *Object relations: A dynamic bridge between individual and family treatment.* New York: Jason Aronson.

Slipp, S. (1988). *The technique and practice of object relations family therapy.* Northvale, NJ: Aronson.

Slipp, S. (1991). *Object relations: A dynamic bridge between individual and family treatment.* Northvale, NJ: Aronson.

Slovik, L. S., & Griffith, J. L. (1992). The current face of family therapy. In J. S. Rutan (Ed.), *Psychotherapy for the 1990s.* New York: Guilford Press.

Sluzki, C. E. (1978). Marital therapy from a systems theory perspective. In T. J. Paolino & B. S. McCrady (Eds.), *Marriage and marital therapy: Psychoanalytic, behavioral, and systems theory perspectives.* New York: Brunner/Mazel.

Sluzki, C. E. (1979). Migration and family conflict. *Family Process, 18,* 379–390.

Smith, R. L. (1999) Client confidentiality in marriage and family counseling. In P. Stevens (Ed.), *Ethical casebook for the practice of marriage and family counseling.* Alexandria, VA: American Counseling Association.

Snow, J. E. (2004). *How it feels to have a gay or lesbian parent.* New York: Harrington Park Press.

Snyder, D. K., Cozzi, J. J., & Mangrum, L. F. (2002). Conceptual issues in assessing couples and families. In H. A. Liddle, D. A. Santisteban, R. F. Levant, & J. H. Bray (Eds.), *Family psychology: Science-based interventions.* Washington, DC: American Psychological Association.

Speck, R. V., & Attneave, C. L. (1973). *Family networks.* New York: Pantheon Books.

Sprenkle, D. H. (1994). Editorial: The role of qualitative research and a few suggestions for aspiring authors. *Journal of Marital and Family Therapy, 20,* 227–229.

Sprenkle, D. H. (2003). Effectiveness research in marriage and family therapy: Introduction. *Journal of Marital and Family Therapy, 29*(1), 85–96.

Sprenkle, D. H., & Bischoff, R. (1995). Research in family therapy: Trends, issues, and recommendations. In M. Nichols & R. Schwartz (Eds.), *Family therapy: Concepts and methods* (3rd ed.). Needham Heights, MA: Allyn & Bacon.

Sprenkle, D. H., & Piercy, F. P. (2005). *Research methods in family therapy* (2nd ed.). New York: Guilford.

St. Clair, M. (2000). *Object relations and self psychology: An introduction* (3rd ed.). Pacific Grove, CA: Brooks/Cole-Wadsworth.

Stahmann, R. F., & Hiebert, W. J. (1997). *Premarital and remarital counseling: The professional's handbook.* San Francisco: Jossey-Bass.

Stanley, S. M., Blumberg, S. L., & Markman, H. J. (1999). Helping couples fight for their marriages: The PREP approach. In R. Berger & M. T. Hannah (Eds.), *Preventive approaches to couples therapy.* Philadelphia, PA: Brunner/Mazel.

Stanton, M. D., & Shadish, W. R. (1997). Outcome, attrition, and family-couples treatment for drug abuse: A meta-analysis and review of the controlled, comparative studies. *Psychological Bulletin, 122,* 170–191.

Stanton, M. D., Todd, T., & Associates. (1982). *The family therapy of drug abuse and addiction.* New York: Guilford Press.

Steinglass, P. (1996). Editorial: Family Process at 35. *Family Process, 35,* 1–2.

Steinglass, P. (1998). Multiple family discussion groups for patients with chronic medical illness. *Families, Systems, and Health, 16,* 55–71.

Stierlin, H. (1972). *Separating parents and adolescents.* New York: Quadrangle.

Stierlin, H. Simon, F. B., & Schmidt, G. (Eds.) (1987) *Family realities: The Heidelberg Conference.* New York: Brunner/Mazel.

Stromberg, C., & Dellinger, A. (1993). *Malpractice and other professional liability.* Washington, DC: National Register of Health Service Providers in Psychology.

Stromberg, C., Schneider, J., & Joondeph, B. (1993). Dealing with potentially dangerous patients. *The Psychologist's Legal Update.* Washington, DC: National Register of Health Service Providers in Psychology.

Stuart, R. B. (1969). Operant-interpersonal treatment of marital discord. *Journal of Consulting and Clinical Psychology, 33,* 675–682.

Stuart, R. B. (1976). An operant-interpersonal program for couples. In D. H. L. Olson (Ed.), *Treating relationships.* Lake Mills, IA: Graphic.

Stuart, R. B. (1980). *Helping couples change: A social learning approach to marital therapy.* Champaign, IL: Research Press.

Suarez-Orozco, C., & Suarez-Orozco, M. (2001). *Children of immigrants.* Cambridge, MA: Harvard University Press.

Sue, D. (1994). Incorporating cultural diversity in family therapy. *Family Psychologist, 10,* 19–21.

Sue, D. W., Carter, R. T., Casa, J. M., Fouard, N. A., Ivey, A. E., Jensen, M., LaFromboise, T., Manese, J. E., Ponterotto, J. G., & Vasquez-Nuttall, E. (1998). *Multicultural counseling competencies: Individual and organizational development.* Thousand Oaks, CA: Sage.

Sue, D. W., & Sue, D. (1999). *Counseling the culturally different: Theory and practice* (3rd ed.). New York: Wiley.

Sullivan, H. S. (1940). *Conceptions of modern psychiatry.* New York: Norton.

Sullivan, H. S. (1953). *The interpersonal theory of psychiatry.* New York: Norton.

Sutherland, J. (1980). The British object relations theorists: Balint, Winnicott, Fairbairn, Guntrip. *British Journal of Medical Psychology, 28,* 829–860.

Sweeney, T. J. (1995). Accreditation, credentialing, and professionalism: The role of specialties. *Journal of Counseling and Development, 74,* 117–125.

Swenson, L. C. (1997). *Psychology and law for the helping professions.* Pacific Grove, CA: Brooks/Cole.

Szapocznik, J., Kurtines, W., & Contributors. (1989). *Breakthroughs in family therapy with drug-abusing and problem youth.* New York: Springer.

Szapocznik, J., Robbins, M., Mitrani, V. B., Santisteban, D., Hervis, O., & Williams, R. A. (2002). Brief strategic family therapy with behavior problem Hispanic youth. In J. Lebow (Ed.), *Integrative and eclectic psychotherapies* (Vol. IV). In F. Kaslow (Ed.), *Comprehensive handbook of psychotherapy.* New York: Wiley.

Thibaut, J. W., & Kelley, H. H. (1959). *The social psychology of groups.* New York: Wiley.

Thomas, A., & Sillen, S. (1974). *Racism and psychiatry.* Secaucus, NJ: Citadel.

Thomas, V., McCollum, E. E., & Snyder, W. (1999). Beyond the clinic: In-home therapy with Head Start families. *Journal of marital and family therapy, 25,* 177–189.

Tiefer, L. (2001). Feminist critique of sex therapy: Foregrounding the politics of sex. In P. L. Kleinplatz (Ed.), *New directions in sex therapy: Innovations and alternatives.* New York: Brunner-Routledge.

Titelman, P. (1987). *The therapist's own family: Toward a differentiation of self.* Northvale, NJ: Aronson.

Titelman, P. (1998). *Clinical applications of Bowen family systems theory.* New York: Haworth Press.

Todd, T. C. (1988). Behavioral and systemic family therapy. In I. R. H. Falloon (Ed.), *Handbook of behavioral family therapy.* New York: Guilford Press.

Toman, W. (1961). *Family constellation: Its effects on personality and social behavior.* New York: Springer.

Tomm, K. M. (1984a). One perspective on the Milan approach: Part I. Overview of development, theory, and practice. *Journal of Marital and Family Therapy, 10,* 113–125.

Tomm, K. M. (1984b). One perspective on the Milan approach: Part II. Description of session format, interviewing style, and interventions. *Journal of Marital and Family Therapy, 10,* 253–271.

Tomm, K. (1987a). Interventive interviewing: Part I. Strategizing as a fourth guideline for the therapist. *Family Process, 26,* 3–13.

Tomm, K. (1987b). Interventive interviewing: Part II. Reflexive questioning as a means to enable self-healing. *Family Process, 26,* 167–183.

Tomm, K. (1988). Interventive interviewing: Part III. Intending to ask lineal, circular, strategic, or reflexive questions? *Family Process, 27,* 1–15.

Touliatos, J., Perlmutter, B. F., Strauss, M. A., & Holden, G. W. (2001). *Handbook of family measurement techniques.* Newbury Park, CA: Sage.

Toward a differentiation of self in one's family. (1972). In J. L. Framo (Ed.), *Family interaction: A dialogue between family researchers and family therapists.* New York: Springer.

Ulrich, D. N. (1983). Contextual and marital therapy. In B. B. Wolman & G. Stricker (Eds.), *Handbook of family and marital therapy.* New York: Plenum.

Ulrich, D. N. (1998). Contextual family therapy. In F. M. Dattilio (Ed.), *Case studies in couple and family therapy: Systemic and cognitive perspectives.* New York: Guilford Press.

Umbarger, C. C. (1983). *Structural family therapy.* New York: Grune & Stratton.

U.S. Census Bureau. (2000). Poverty in the United States: 1999. *Current Population Reports,* Series, P60-210. Washington, DC: U.S. Government Printing Office.

U.S. Census Bureau. (2003). Married couple and unmarried partner households: 2000. Washington, DC: Government Printing Office.

VandenBos, G. R. (1986). Psychotherapy research: A special issue. *American Psychologist, 41,* 111–112.

Varela, F. J. (1979). *Principles of biological autonomy.* New York: Elsevier North Holland.

Vesper, J. H., & Brock, G. W. (1991). *Ethics, legalities, and professional practice issues in marriage and family therapy.* Boston: Allyn & Bacon.

Visher, E. B., & Visher, J. S. (1986). *Stepfamily workbook manual.* Baltimore: Stepfamily Association of America.

Visher, E. B., & Visher, J. S. (1988). *Old loyalties, new ties: Therapeutic strategies with stepfamilies.* New York: Brunner/Mazel.

Visher, E. B., & Visher, J. S. (1993). Remarriage families and stepparenting. In F. Walsh (Ed.), *Normal family processes* (2nd ed.). New York: Guilford Press.

Visher, E. B., & Visher, J. S. (1996). *Therapy with stepfamilies.* New York: Brunner/Mazel.

Visher, E. B., Visher, J. S., & Pasley, K. (2003). Remarriage families and stepparenting. In F. Walsh (Ed.), *Normal family processes: Diversity and complexity.* (3rd ed.). New York: Guilford Press.

von Foerster, H. (1981). *Observing systems.* Seaside, CA: Intersystems.

von Glaserfeld, E. (1987). *The construction of knowledge.* Salinas, CA: Intersystems.

Wachtel, E. F., & Wachtel, P. L. (1986). *Family dynamics in individual psychotherapy: A guide to clinical strategies.* New York: Guilford Press.

Wachtel, P. L. (1997). *Psychoanalysis, behavior therapy, and the relational world.* Washington, DC: American Psychological Association.

Walen, S. R., & Perlmutter, R. (1988). Cognitive-behavioral treatment of adult sexual dysfunctions from a family perspective. In N. Epstein, S. E. Schlesinger, & W. Dryden (Eds.), *Cognitive-behavioral therapy with families.* New York: Brunner/Mazel.

Walker, G., & Goldner, V. (1995). The wounded prince and the women who love him. In C. Burke & B. Speed (Eds.), *Gender and power in relationships.* London: Routledge, Chapman, & Hall.

Walrond-Skinner, S. (1976). *Family therapy: The treatment of natural systems.* London: Routledge.

Walsh, F. (1998). *Strengthening family resilience.* New York: Guilford Press.

Walsh, F. (1999a). Families in later life: Challenges and opportunities. In B. Carter & M. McGoldrick (Eds.), *The expanded family life cycle: Individual, family, and social perspectives* (3rd ed.). Boston: Allyn & Bacon.

Walsh, F. (Ed.). (1999b). *Spiritual resources in family therapy.* New York: Guilford Press.

Walsh, F. (2003a). Changing families in a changing world: Reconstructing family normality. In F. Walsh (Ed.), *Normal family processes: Growing diversity and complexity* (3rd ed.). New York: Guilford Press.

Walsh, F. (2003b). Family resilience: Strengths forged through adversity. In F. Walsh (Ed.), *Normal family processes: Growing diversity and complexity* (3rd ed.). New York: Guilford Press.

Walsh, F., & Pryce, J. (2003). The spiritual dimension of family life. In F. Walsh (Ed.), *Normal family processes: Growing diversity and complexity.* New York: Guilford Press.

Walters, M., Carter, B., Papp, P., & Silverstein, O. (1989). *The invisible web: Gender patterns in family relationships.* New York: Guilford Press.

Wampler, K. S. (1990). An update of research on the Couples Communication Program. *Family Science Review, 3,* 21–40.

Waters, D., & Lawrence, E. C. (1993). *Competence, courage and change: An approach to family therapy.* New York: Norton.

Watzlawick, P. (1978). *The language of change.* New York: Basic Books.

Watzlawick, P. (Ed.) (1984). *The invented reality: How do we know what we believe we know?* New York: Norton.

Watzlawick, P., Beavin, J. H., & Jackson, D. D. (1967). *Pragmatics of human communication.* New York: Norton.

Watzlawick, P., Weakland, J. H., & Fisch, R. (1974). *Change: Principles of problem formation and problem resolution.* New York: Norton.

Weakland, J. H. (1976). Communication theory and clinical change. In P. J. Guerin, Jr. (Ed.), *Family therapy: Theory and practice.* New York: Gardner Press.

Weathers, L., & Liberman, R. P. (1975). The family contracting exercise. *Journal of Behavior Therapy and Experimental Psychiatry, 6,* 208–214.

Webster-Stratton, C., & Hammond, M. (1997). Treating children with early-onset conduct problems: A comparison of child and parent training interventions. *Journal of Consulting and Clinical Psychology, 65*(1), 93–109.

Weeks, G. R., & Gambescia, N. (2002). *Hypoactive sexual desire: Integrating couple therapy and sex therapy.* New York: Norton.

Weeks, G. R., & L'Abate, L. (1982). *Paradoxical psychotherapy: Theory and technique.* New York: Brunner/Mazel.

Weiner-Davis, M. (1992). *Divorce-busting.* New York: Summit Books.

Weiner-Davis, M. (1993). Pro-constructed realities. In S. Gilligan & R. Price (Eds.), *Therapeutic conversations.* New York: Norton.

Weiner-Davis, M. (2001). *Divorce remedy: The proven 7-step program for saving your marriage.* New York: Simon and Schuster.

Weingarten, K. (1995). Radical listening: Challenging cultural beliefs for and about mothers. *Journal of Feminist Family Therapy, 7,* 7–22.

Weisz, J. R., & Addis, M. E. (2006). The research-practice tango and other choreographic challenges: Using and testing evidence-based psychotherapies in clinical care settings. In C. D. Goodheart, A. E. Kazdin, & R. J. Sternberg (Eds.), *Evidence-based psychotherapy: Where practice and research meet.* Washington, DC: American Psychological Association.

Welfel, E. R. (2006). *Ethics in counseling and psychotherapy: Standards, research, and emerging issues* (3rd ed.). Belmont, CA: Thomson Brooks/Cole.

Wells, R. A., & Dezen, A. E. (1978). The results of family therapy revisited: The nonbehavioral methods. *Family Process, 17,* 251–274.

Westen, D., Novotny, C. M., & Thompson-Brenner, H. (2004). Empirical status of empirically supported psychotherapies: Assumptions, findings, and reporting in controlled clinical trials. *Psychological Bulletin, 130*, 631–663.

Wetchler, J. L., & Piercy, F. P. (1996). Experiential family therapies. In F. P. Piercy, D. H. Sprenkle, J. L. Wetchler, & Associates. (Eds.), *Family therapy sourcebook* (2nd ed.). New York: Guilford Press.

Whitaker, C. A. (Ed.). (1958). *Psychotherapy of chronic schizophrenic patients.* Boston: Little, Brown.

Whitaker, C. A. (1976). Comment: Live supervision in psychotherapy. *Voices, 12*, 24–25.

Whitaker, C. A. (1977). Process techniques of family therapy. *Interaction, 1*, 4–19.

Whitaker, C. A., & Bumberry, W. M. (1988). *Dancing with the family: A symbolic-experiential approach.* New York: Brunner/Mazel.

Whitaker, C. A., & Keith, D.V. (1981). Symbolic-experiential family therapy. In A. S. Gurman & D. P. Kniskern (Eds.), *Handbook of family therapy.* New York: Brunner/Mazel.

Whitaker, C. A., & Malone, T. P. (1953). *The roots of psychotherapy.* New York: Blakiston.

Whitaker, C. A., & Ryan, M. O. (1989). *Midnight musings of a family therapist.* New York: Brunner/Mazel.

White, C., & Hales, J. (Eds.). (1997). *The personal is the professional: Therapists reflect on their families, life, and work.* Adelaide, Australia: Dulwich Centre Publications.

White, M. (1989). *Selected papers.* Adelaide, Australia: Dulwich Centre Publications.

White, M. (1991). Deconstruction and therapy. *Dulwich Centre Newsletter, 3*, 21–40.

White, M. (1995). *Re-authoring lives: Interviews and essays.* Adelaide, Australia: Dulwich Centre Publications.

White, M. (1997). *Narratives of therapists' lives.* Adelaide, Australia: Dulwich Centre Publications.

White, M. (2000). *Reflections on narrative practice: Essays and interviews.* Adelaide, Australia: Dulwich Centre Publications.

White, M., & Epston, D. (1990). *Narrative means to therapeutic ends.* New York: Norton.

Whiteside, M. F., & Becker, B. J. (2000). Parental factors and the young child's postdivorce adjustment: A meta-analysis with implications for parenting arrangements. *Journal of Family Psychology, 14*, 5–26.

Wiener, N. (1948). Cybernetics. *Scientific American, 179*(5), 14–18.

Williams, L. M., Patterson, J. E., & Miller, R. B. (2006). Panning for gold: A clinician's guide to using research. *Journal of Marital and Family Therapy, 32*, 17–32.

Williamson, D. (1991). *The intimate paradox: Personal authority in the family system.* New York: Guilford Press.

Willig, C. (2001). *Introducing qualitative research in psychology: Adventures in theory and method.* London: Taylor-Routledge.

Wilson, W. J. (1996). *When work disappears: The world of the new urban poor.* New York: Knopf.

Winnicott, D. W. (1965). *The maturational processes and the facilitating environment.* New York: International Universities Press.

Wittgenstein, L. (1968). *Philosophical investigations* (3rd ed.). New York: Macmillan.

Wolpe, J. (1958). *Psychotherapy by reciprocal inhibition.* Stanford, CA: Stanford University Press.

Wong, L., & Mock, M. (1997). Developmental and life cycle issues of Asian American young adults. In E. Lee (Ed.), *Working with Asian Americans: A guide for clinicians.* New York: Guilford Press.

Woods, M. D., & Martin, D. (1984). The work of Virginia Satir: Understanding her theory and technique. *American Journal of Family Therapy, 11*(1), 35–46.

Woody, R. H., & Woody, J. D. (2001). *Ethics in marriage and family therapy.* Washington, DC: AAMFT.

Worell, J., & Remer, P. (1992). *Feminist perspectives in therapy: An empowerment model for women.* New York: Wiley.

Wylie, M. S. (1990a). Brief therapy on the couch. *Family Therapy Networker, 14*, 26–34, 66.

Wylie, M. S. (1990b). Family therapy's neglected prophet. *Family Networker, 15*(2), 25–37.

Wynne, L. C. (1983). Family research and family therapy: A reunion? *Journal of Marital and Family Therapy, 9*, 113–117.

Wynne, L. C., McDaniel, S. H., & Weber, T. T. (1986). *Systems consultation: A new perspective for family therapy.* New York: Guilford Press.

Wynne, L. C., Ryckoff, I. M., Day, J., & Hirsch, S. I. (1958). Pseudomutuality in the family relationships of schizophrenics. *Psychiatry, 21*, 205–220.

Wynne, L. C., Shields, C., & Sirkin, M. (1992). Illness, family theory and family therapy: I. Conceptual issues. *Family Process, 31*, 3–18.

Wynne, L. C., & Singer, M. T. (1963). Thought disorder and family relations of schizophrenics, I and II. *Archives of General Psychiatry, 9*, 191–206.

Yalom, I. D. (1995). *The theory and practice of group psychotherapy* (4th ed.). New York: Basic Books.

Yingling, L. C., Miller, W. E., McDonald, A. L., & Galewaler, S. T. (Eds.). (1998). *GARF assessment sourcebook: Using the DSM-IV Global Assessment of Relational Functioning.* Washington, DC: Taylor and Francis.

Yorgason, J. B., McWey, L. M., & Felts, L. (2005). In-home family therapy: Indicators of success. *Journal of Marital and Family Therapy, 32,* 301–312.

Zastrow, C. H. (1999). *The practice of social work* (6th ed.). Pacific Grove, CA: Brooks/Cole.

Zeig, J. K. (Ed.). (1980). *A teaching seminar with Milton H. Erickson.* New York: Brunner/Mazel.

Zilbach, J. J. (1989). The family life cycle: A framework for understanding children in family therapy. In L. Combrinck-Graham (Ed.), *Children in family contexts: Perspectives on treatment.* New York: Guilford Press.

Zimmerman, J., & Dickerson, V. (1996). *If problems talked: Adventures in narrative therapy.* New York: Guilford Press.

Zuk, G. H., & Boszormenyi-Nagy, I. (Eds.). (1967). *Family therapy and disturbed families.* Palo Alto, CA: Science and Behavior Books.

This page constitutes an extension of the copyright page. We have made every effort to trace the ownership of all copyrighted material and to secure permission from copyright holders. In the event of any question arising as to the use of any material, we will be pleased to make the necessary corrections in future printings. Thanks are due to the following authors, publishers, and agents for permission to use the material indicated.

Chapter 2. 27: From A. S. Masten and J. D. Coatsworth, "The Development of Competence in Favorable and Unfavorable Environments," *American Psychologist, 53,* 1998, p. 207, Table 1. Copyright © 1998 by the American Psychological Association, Washington, DC. Reprinted with permission. **29:** From Betty Carter & Monica McGoldrick, *The Expanded Family Life Cycle: Individual, Family and Social Perspectives,* 3rd ed. Published by Allyn & Bacon, Boston, MA. Copyright © 1999 by Pearson Education. Reprinted by permission of the publisher. **33:** Based on Duvall, 1977, and Barnhill and Longo, 1978. **34:** Figure from *The Changing Family Life Cycle: A Framework for Family Therapy,* p. 9. Edited by Betty Carter, Monica McGoldrick. Boston: Allyn & Bacon, 1989. Copyright © 1989 by Allyn & Bacon. **46:** From Betty Carter & Monica McGoldrick, *The Expanded Family Life Cycle: Individual, Family and Social Perspectives,* 3rd ed. Published by Allyn & Bacon, Boston, MA. Copyright © 1999 by Pearson Education. Reprinted by permission of the publisher. **49:** From "Overview: The Expanded Family Life Cycle: Individual, Family, and Social Perspectives," by B. Carter and M. McGoldrick. In B. Carter and

M. McGoldrick (Eds.), *The Expanded Family Life Cycle: Individual, Family, and Social Perspectives,* 3rd Ed., 1999, p. 377. Copyright © 1999 Allyn & Bacon, Inc. Reprinted by permission.

Chapter 3. 63: Zastrow, 1999, pp. 188–189 **65:** Reprinted with permission from J. A. Lewis, "Gender Sensitivity and Family Empowerment," *Topics in Family Psychology and Counseling, 1*(4), p. 3, © 1992, Aspen Publishers, Inc. **71:** From *Counseling Today's Families,* Fourth Edition, by H. Goldenberg and I. Goldenberg, pp. 331–333. Copyright © 2002 Brooks/Cole Thomson Learning. Reprinted with permission.

Chapter 4. 92: Goldenberg & Goldenberg, 2002, pp. 20–21. **93:** Imber-Black, Evan. From *Families and Larger Systems: A Family Therapist's Guide through the Labyrinth,* p. 117. NY: Guilford Press, 1988. Copyright © 1988 by Guilford Press. All rights reserved. Reproduced by permission. **97:** From *Families and Larger Systems: A Family Therapist's Guide Through the Labyrinth,* by E. Imber-Black, 1988, p. 117. Copyright © 1988 Guilford Press. Reprinted by permission.

Chapter 5. 112: Goldenberg, 1983.

Chapter 6. 141: Falvey, 2002, p. 93.

Chapter 7. 157: Ackerman, Nathan W. From *Treating the Troubled Family,* pp. 3–4. New York: Basic Books, 1966. Reprinted by permission. **163:** St. Clair, 2000. **169:** Scharff, Jill. From *Handbook of Family Therapy: The Science and Practice of Working with Families and Couples,* pp. 68–69. Edited by Thomas L. Sexton, Gerald R. Weeks, Michael S. Robbins. NY: Brunner-Routledge, 2003. All rights

reserved. Reproduced by permission. **173:** St. Clair, 2000.

Chapter 8. 183: From *Family Evaluation: An Approach Based on Bowen Theory,* by M. E. Kerr and M. Bowen, 1988, p. 71. Copyright © 1988 W. W. Norton and Co. Reprinted by permission. **193:** Based on McGoldrick & Gerson, 1985. **194:** From *Counseling Today's Families,* Fourth Edition, by H. Goldenberg and I. Goldenberg, p. 61. Copyright © 2002 Brooks/Cole Thomson Learning. Reprinted with permission. **196:** Sylvia Shellenberger and Sandra S. Hoffman. From *Integrating Family Therapy: Handbook of Family Psychology and Systems Theory,* pp. 464–465. Edited by Richard H. Mikesell, Don-David Lusterman, and Susan H. McDaniel. Washington, DC: American Psychological Association, 1995. Copyright © 1995 by APA. All rights reserved. Reproduced by permission of the publisher. **199:** Monica McGoldrick and Betty Carter. "Advances in coaching: Family therapy with one person" in *Journal of Marital and Family Therapy,* July 2001, p. 289. American Association for Marriage and Family Therapy, 2001. All rights reserved. Reproduced by permission. **203:** Ivan Boszormenyi-Nagy and B. R. Krasner. From *Between Give and Take: A Clinical Guide to Contextual Therapy,* pp. 45–46. New York: Brunner/Mazel, 1986. Copyright © 1986 Brunner/Mazel. Reprinted with permission.

Chapter 9. 214: Carl A. Whitaker and William M. Bumberry. From *Dancing With The Family: A Symbolic-Experiential Approach.* New York: Brunner/Mazel, 1988. Copyright © 1988 by Carl A. Whitaker and William M. Bumberry.